The Essence of Anthropology

THIRD EDITION

WILLIAM A. HAVILAND

Professor Emeritus, University of Vermont

HARALD E.L. PRINS

Kansas State University

DANA WALRATH

University of Vermont

BUNNY McBRIDE

Kansas State University

 **WADSWORTH**
CENGAGE Learning·

Australia • Brazil • Japan • Korea • Mexico • Singapore • Spain • United Kingdom • United States

The Essence of Anthropology, Third Edition

**William A. Haviland, Harald E.L. Prins,
Dana Walrath, Bunny McBride**

Anthropology Editor: Erin Mitchell

Developmental Editor: Lin Gaylord

Assistant Editor: Linda Stewart

Editorial Assistant: Mallory Ortberg

Media Editor: John Chell

Marketing Program Manager: Tami Strang

Sr. Content Project Manager: Tanya Nigh

Design Director: Rob Hugel

Art Director: Caryl Gorska

Print Buyer: Judy Inouye

Rights Acquisitions Specialist: Don Schlotman

Production Service: Joan Keyes, Dovetail
Publishing Services

Text Designer: Caryl Gorska

Illustrator: Graphic World

Photo Researcher: Sarah Evertson

Text Researcher: Isabel Saraiva

Copy Editor: Jennifer Gordon

Cover Designer: Larry Didona

Cover image: Larry Didona

Cover images (clockwise, from upper right):
Chinese fisherman with cormorant, Prisma/
Superstock; Excavation in Egypt, Marc Deville/
akg-images/The Image Works; Capuchin with
rock, Pete Oxford/Minden Pictures/Getty Images; bionic arm, Mark Thiessen/National Geographic Society/Corbis; girls with laptop, Scott
Stulberg/Corbis; detail from Assyrian relief
sculpture, Peter Aprahamian/Corbis.

Compositor: PreMediaGlobal

For product information and technology assistance, contact us at
Cengage Learning Customer & Sales Support, 1-800-354-9706
For permission to use material from this text or product,
submit all requests online at **www.cengage.com/permissions**
Further permissions questions can be e-mailed to
permissionrequest@cengage.com

Library of Congress Control Number: 2011941007

Student Edition:

ISBN-13: 978-1-111-83344-2

ISBN-10: 1-111-83344-3

Loose-leaf Edition:

ISBN-13: 978-1-111-83508-8

ISBN-10: 1-111-83508-X

Wadsworth
20 Davis Drive
Belmont, CA 94002-3098
USA

Cengage Learning is a leading provider of customized learning solutions with
office locations around the globe, including Singapore, the United Kingdom,
Australia, Mexico, Brazil, and Japan. Locate your local office at
www.cengage.com/global.

Cengage Learning products are represented in Canada by Nelson Education, Ltd.

To learn more about Wadsworth, visit **www.cengage.com/wadsworth**

Purchase any of our products at your local college store or at our preferred
online store **www.cengagebrain.com**.

Printed in the United States of America
1 2 3 4 5 6 7 16 15 14 13 12

Anthropology needs the power of language, harnessed to humanistic ends by those who possess the scientific mind and the literary touch. —EDMUND S. CARPENTER

We are honored to dedicate this book to the memory of anthropologist Edmund ("Ted") Carpenter (1922–2011), a free spirit who creatively crossed traditional boundaries between disciplines.

About the Authors

While each has a distinct voice, all four members of this author team share overlapping research interests and a similar vision of what anthropology is (and should be) about. For example, all are "true believers" in the four-field approach to anthropology, and all have some involvement in applied work.

Dr. William A. Haviland is professor emeritus at the University of Vermont, where he has taught since 1965. He holds a Ph.D. in anthropology from the University of Pennsylvania and has published widely on archaeological, ethnological, and physical anthropological research carried out in Guatemala, Maine, and Vermont. Dr. Haviland is a member of many professional societies, including the American Anthropological Association and the American Association for the Advancement of Science. Throughout his distinguished career, he has participated in many projects, including "Gender and the Anthropological Curriculum," sponsored by the American Anthropological Association in 1988. Dr. Haviland has always loved teaching and writing for anthropology students, and he has a passionate interest in indigenous rights, having worked with the Maya for years. He continues to work with Native Americans in the northeastern United States.

Dr. Harald E.L. Prins is a University Distinguished professor of cultural anthropology at Kansas State University. Academically trained at half a dozen Dutch and U.S. universities, he previously taught at Radboud University (Netherlands), Bowdoin College and Colby College in Maine, and was a visiting professor at the University of Lund, Sweden. Also ranked a distinguished university teaching scholar, he received numerous honors for his outstanding academic teaching, including the Presiden-

tial Award in 1999, Carnegie Professor of the Year for Kansas in 2006, and most recently the AAA/Oxford University Press Award for Excellence in Undergraduate Teaching of Anthropology in 2010. His fieldwork focuses on indigenous peoples in the western hemisphere, and he has long served as an advocacy anthropologist on land claims and other native rights. In that capacity, Dr. Prins has been a key expert witness in both the U.S. Senate and Canadian courts. His numerous academic publications appear in seven languages, and his books include *The Mi'kmaq: Resistance, Accommodation, and Cultural Survival*. Also trained in filmmaking, he was president of the Society for Visual Anthropology, and co-produced award-winning documentaries. He has been the visual anthropology editor of the *American Anthropologist*, principal investigator for the U.S. National Park Service, international observer in Paraguay's presidential elections, and a research associate at the National Museum of Natural History, Smithsonian Institution.

Dr. Dana Walrath is assistant professor of family medicine at the University of Vermont and an affiliated faculty member for women's and gender studies. After earning her Ph.D. from the University of Pennsylvania, she taught at the University of Pennsylvania and Temple University. Dr. Walrath broke new ground in medical and biological anthropology through her work on biocultural aspects of childbirth. She has also written on a wide range of topics related to gender in paleoanthropology, the social production of sickness and health, sex differences, genetics, and evolutionary medicine. Her work has appeared in edited volumes and in journals such as *Current Anthropology, American Anthropologist, American Journal of Physical Anthropology,* and *Anthropology Now*. She developed a novel curriculum in medical education at the University of Vermont's College of Medicine that brings humanism, anthropological theory and practice, narrative medicine, and professionalism skills to first-year medical students. Dr. Walrath also has a master of fine arts in creative writing from Vermont College of Fine Arts and has shown her art work in galleries throughout the country. Her recent work on Alzheimer's disease combines anthropology with memoir and visual art. Spanning a variety of disciplines, her work has been supported by diverse sources such as the National Science Foundation, the Templeton Foundation, the New York Foundation for the Arts, the Centers for Disease Control, the Health Resources and Services Administration, the Vermont Studio Center, the Vermont Arts Council, and the National Endowment for the Arts.

Bunny McBride (M.A., Columbia University, 1980) is an award-winning author specializing in cultural anthropology, indigenous peoples, international tourism, and nature conservation issues. Published in dozens of national and international print media, she has reported from Africa, Europe, China, and the Indian Ocean. Highly rated as a teacher, she served as visiting anthropology faculty at Principia College, the Salt Institute for Documentary Field Studies, and since 1996 as adjunct lecturer of anthropology at Kansas State University. McBride's many publications include *Molly Spotted Elk: A Penobscot in Paris; Women of the Dawn; Indians in Eden* (with Dr. Prins); and *The Audubon Field Guide to African Wildlife* (co-author). Honors include a special commendation from the Maine State legislature for significant contributions to Native women's history. A community activist and researcher for the Aroostook Band of Micmacs (1981–91), she assisted this Maine Indian community in its successful efforts to reclaim lands, gain tribal status, and revitalize cultural traditions. In recent years, she served as co-principal investigator for a National Park Service ethnography project and curated several museum exhibits, including "Journeys West: The David and Peggy Rockefeller American Indian Art Collection." Her latest exhibit, "Indians & Rusticators," profiles 19th-century tourism and Indian art. Currently, she serves as vice president of the Women's World Summit Foundation, based in Geneva, Switzerland, and is completing a collection of essays. ∎

Brief Contents

Preface *xv*

Detailed Contents

CHAPTER 12
Sex, Marriage, and Family 244

CHAPTER 13
Kinship and Other Forms of Grouping 268

CHAPTER 14
Politics, Power, and Violence 290

CHAPTER 15

Spirituality and Religion 314

CHAPTER 16

Global Changes and the Role of Anthropology 336

Features Contents

Preface

the number three has significance in many situations in numerous cultures. In fairy tales, it is commonly the number of wishes granted. In religious teachings, it often stands for that which is substantial, sound, and complete. And then there is the old adage, "third time's the charm." So, with the third edition of *Essence*, it is our wish that readers experience this text as a seasoned one that has come of age through repeated honing—a book that is substantial but not burdensome, sound but not stodgy, and complete but not "done."

The truth is that our textbooks are never really done. They are part of an ongoing dialogue, fueled by vital feedback from our students and from anthropology professors who have reviewed and used previous editions. Their input—along with our own ongoing research and the surprisingly delightful task of rethinking familiar concepts that appear self-evident—has helped us bring fresh insight into classical themes.

With each edition, we look anew at the archetypal examples of our discipline and weigh them against the latest innovative research methodologies, archaeological discoveries, genetic and other biological findings, linguistic insights, and ethnographic descriptions, theoretical revelations, and significant examples of applied anthropology. We combine these considerations with attention to compelling issues in our global theater to fashion a thought-provoking textbook that presents both classical and fresh material in ways that stimulate student interest, stir critical reflection, and prompt "ah-ha" moments.

The word *essence* has served as our guiding principle—alerting us to reach for content that covers anthropology's established foundations and modern ramifications without getting distracted by too many details or examples. With each revision, one thing has remained constant: the goal of presenting four-field anthropology to undergraduates in a concise text that does justice to the breadth and depth of the discipline—a book that is light in weight, but not "lightweight." We remain committed to creating a stimulating, quick-moving narrative that gives anthropology majors a solid basis for more advanced coursework while sowing seeds of awareness in all students concerning cultural and biological diversity.

For those unfamiliar with the Haviland et al. textbook series, it is important to note that like the earlier editions of *Essence*, this one stands on the substantial shoulders of our *Anthropology: The Human Challenge*—now in its 13th edition and the discipline's leading introductory textbook for many years.

Our Mission

Most students enter an introductory anthropology class intrigued by the general subject but with little more than a vague sense of what it is all about. Thus the first and most obvious task of our text is to provide a thorough introduction to the discipline—its foundations as a domain of knowledge and its major insights into the rich diversity of humans as a culture-making species. Recognizing the wide spectrum of students enrolled in entry-level anthropology courses, we cover the fundamentals of the discipline in an engaging, illustrative fashion—creating a textbook that establishes a broad platform on which teachers can expand the exploration of concepts and topics in ways that are particularly meaningful to them and their students.

In doing this, we draw from the research and ideas of a number of traditions of anthropological thought, exposing students to a mix of theoretical perspectives and methodologies. Such inclusiveness reflects our conviction that different approaches offer distinctly important insights about human biology, behavior, and beliefs.

If most students start out with only a vague sense of what anthropology is, they often have less clearly defined but potentially more problematic views of the superiority of their own species and culture. A second task for this text, then, is to encourage students to appreciate the richness and complexity of human diversity. Along with this goal is the aim of helping them understand why there are so many differences and similarities in the human condition, past and present.

Debates regarding globalization and notions of progress, the "naturalness" of the mother, father, child(ren) nuclear family, new genetic technologies, and how gender roles relate to biological variation all benefit greatly from the fresh and often fascinating insights gained through anthropology. This probing aspect of the discipline is perhaps the most valuable gift we can pass on to those who take our classes. If we, as teachers (and textbook authors), do our jobs well, students will gain a wider and more open-minded outlook on the world and a critical but constructive perspective on human origins and on their own biology and culture today. To borrow a favorite line from the famous poet T. S. Eliot, "the end of all our exploring will be to arrive where we started and know the place for the first time" (*Four Quartets*).

There has never been as great a need for students to acquire the anthropological tools to allow them to transcend culture-bound ways of thinking and acting and to gain tolerance and respect for other ways of life. We have written this text, in large part, to help students make sense of our increasingly complex world and to navigate through its interrelated biological and cultural networks with knowledge and skill, whatever professional path they take. We see the book as a guide for people entering the often bewildering maze of global crossroads in the 21st century.

A Distinctive Approach

Two key factors distinguish *The Essence of Anthropology* from other introductory anthropology texts: our integrative presentation of the discipline's four fields and a trio of unifying themes that tie the book together.

Integration of the Four Fields

Unlike traditional texts that present anthropology's four fields—physical anthropology, archaeology, linguistics, and cultural or social anthropology—as if they were separate or independent, our book takes an integrative approach. This reflects the holistic character of our discipline, a domain of knowledge where members of our species are studied in their totality—as social creatures biologically evolved with the inherent capacity for learning and sharing culture by means of symbolic communication. This approach also reflects our collective experience as practicing anthropologists who recognize that we cannot fully understand humanity in all its fascinating complexity unless we see the systemic interplay among environmental, physiological, material, social, ideological, psychological, and symbolic factors, both past and present.

For analytical purposes, however, we discuss physical anthropology as distinct from archaeology, linguistics, and sociocultural anthropology. Accordingly, there are separate chapters that focus primarily on each field, but the links among them are shown repeatedly. Among many examples of this integrative approach, "Modern Human Diversity—Race and Racism" (Chapter 7) discusses the social context of race and recent cultural practices that have impacted the human genome. Similarly, material concerning linguistics appears not only in the chapter on language (Chapter 9), but in "Living Primates" (Chapter 3), "Human Evolution" (Chapter 4), and "The Emergence of Cities and States" (Chapter 6). These chapters include material on the linguistic capabilities of apes, the emergence of human language, and the origin of writing. In addition, every chapter includes a Biocultural Connection feature to further illustrate the interplay of biological and cultural processes in shaping the human experience.

Unifying Themes

In our own teaching, we recognize the value of marking out unifying themes that help students see the big picture as they grapple with the vast array of material involved with the study of human beings. In *Essence* we employ three such themes:

1. *Systemic adaptation:* We emphasize that every culture, past and present, is an integrated and dynamic system of adaptation that responds to a combination of internal and external factors, including influences of the environment.

2. *Biocultural connection:* We highlight the integration of human culture and biology in the steps humans take to meet the challenges of survival. The biocultural connection theme is interwoven throughout the text—as a thread in the main narrative and in boxed features that highlight this connection with a topical example for each chapter.

3. *Globalization:* We track the emergence of globalization and its disparate impact on various peoples and cultures around the world. European colonization was a global force for centuries, leaving a significant and often devastating footprint on the affected peoples in Asia, Africa, and the Americas. Decolonization began about 200 years ago and became a worldwide wave in the mid-1900s. However, since the 1960s, political and economic hegemony has taken a new and fast-paced form—namely, globalization (in many ways a concept that expands or builds on imperialism). Attention to both forms of global domination—colonialism and globalization—runs through *Essence*, culminating in the final chapter where we apply the concept of structural power to globalization, discussing it in terms of hard and soft power and linking it to structural violence.

Pedagogy

The Essence of Anthropology features a range of learning aids, in addition to the three unifying themes described above. Each pedagogical piece plays an important role in the learning process—from clarifying and enlivening the material to revealing relevancy and aiding recall.

Accessible Language and a Cross-Cultural Voice

In the writing of this text, we consciously cut through unnecessary jargon to speak directly to students. Manuscript reviewers have recognized this, noting that even the most difficult concepts are presented in prose that is straightforward and understandable for today's first- and second-year college students. Where technical terms are necessary, they appear in bold type, are carefully defined in the narrative, and are defined again in the running glossary in simple, clear language. These terms also appear in a glossary at the end of the book.

To make the narrative more accessible to students, we have broken it up into smaller bites, shortening the length of the paragraphs. We have also inserted additional subheads to provide visual cues to help students track what has been read and what is coming next.

Accessibility involves not only clear writing enhanced by visual cues, but also an engaging voice or style. The voice of *Essence* is distinct among introductory texts in the discipline, for it has been written from a cross-cultural perspective. We avoid the typical Western "we/they" voice in favor of a more inclusive one that will resonate with both Western and non-Western students and professors. Also, we highlight the theories and work of anthropologists from all over the world. Finally, we have drawn the text's cultural examples from industrial and postindustrial societies as well as nonindustrial ones.

Compelling Visuals

Haviland texts repeatedly garner high praise from students and faculty for having a rich array of visuals, including maps, photographs, and figures. This is important because humans—like all primates—are visually oriented, and a well-chosen image may serve to "fix" key information in a student's mind. Unlike some competing texts, all of our visuals are in color, enhancing their appeal and impact. This edition of *Essence* features about nine photographs per chapter, many presented in large format to increase their impact. Notably, all maps and figures have been created with a colorblind-sensitive palette.

PHOTOGRAPHS

As authors with strong backgrounds in the visual arts and communication, we are keenly aware of the pull and power of images—especially for this generation of students who are so enculturated in visual media. Our pages feature a hard-sought collection of meaningful photographs, many new to this edition. Large in size, numerous photos are accompanied by substantial captions that help students do a "deep read" of the image.

Each chapter begins with the Visual Essence feature—an especially compelling photograph accompanied by a paragraph that prompts students to study the image and think about the essence of that particular chapter. Some chapters also contain one of our popular Visual Counterpoints—side-by-side photos that effectively compare and contrast biological or cultural features.

MAPS

Throughout the book are geographic aids, including locator maps, as well as distribution maps that provide overviews of key issues such as pollution, energy consumption, migration, and religion.

Student Learning Objectives and Knowledge Skills

New to this edition is the set of learning objectives at the start of every chapter. These objectives focus students on the main goals, identifying the knowledge skills they are expected to have mastered after reading each chapter. The main goals are incorporated in a closing Chapter Checklist, which is also new to this edition. The Chapter Checklist summarizes the chapter's content in an easy-to-follow format.

Thought-Provoking Questions

Each chapter closes with five Questions for Reflection designed to stimulate and deepen thought, trigger class discussion, and link the material to the student's own life. Questions for Reflection follow the Chapter Checklist and ask students to apply the concepts they have learned by analyzing and evaluating situations.

In addition, the Biocultural Connection essay featured in every chapter ends with a thought-provoking question aimed toward helping students grapple with and firmly grasp that connection.

The Barrel Model of Culture

Past and present, every culture is an integrated and dynamic system of adaptation that responds to a combination of internal and external factors. This is illustrated by a pedagogical device we refer to as the "barrel model" of culture. Depicted in a simple but telling drawing (Figure 8.2), the barrel model shows the interrelatedness of social, ideological, and economic factors within a cultural system along with outside influences of environment, climate, and other societies. Throughout the book examples are linked to this point and this image.

Integrated Gender Coverage

In contrast to many introductory texts, *The Essence of Anthropology* integrates coverage of gender throughout the book. Thus material on gender-related issues is included in *every* chapter. As a result of this approach, gender-related material in *Essence* far exceeds the single chapter that most books devote to the subject.

We have chosen to integrate this material because concepts and issues surrounding gender are almost always too complicated to remove from their context. Spreading this material through all of the chapters has a pedagogical purpose, for it emphasizes how considerations of gender enter into virtually everything people do. Further, integration of gender into the book's "biological" chapters allows students to grasp the analytic distinction between *sex* and *gender*, illustrating the subtle influence of gender norms on biological theories about sex difference. Gender-related material ranges from discussions of gender roles in evolutionary discourse and studies of nonhuman primates, to intersexuality, homosexual identity, same-sex marriage, and female genital mutilation. Through a steady drumbeat of such coverage, this edition avoids ghettoizing gender to a single chapter that is preceded and followed by resounding silence.

Glossary as You Go

The running glossary is designed to catch the student's eye, reinforcing the meaning of each newly introduced term. It is also useful for chapter review, as the student may readily isolate the new terms from those introduced in earlier chapters. A complete glossary is also included at the back of the book. In the glossaries, each term is defined in clear, understandable language. As a result, less class time is required for going over terms, leaving instructors free to pursue other matters of interest.

Special Boxed Features

Essence includes three types of special boxed features. Every chapter contains a Biocultural Connection, along with either an Original Study or an Anthropology Applied profile. These features are carefully placed and introduced within the main narrative to alert students to their importance and relevance.

BIOCULTURAL CONNECTION FEATURES

Appearing in every chapter, this signature feature of the Haviland textbooks illustrates how cultural and biological processes interact to shape human biology, beliefs, and behavior. It reflects the integrated biocultural approach central to the field of anthropology today. New to this edition is a critical thinking question to accompany each topic explored. The sixteen Biocultural Connection titles hint at the intriguing array of topics covered in *Essence,* from Meredith F. Small's "Why Red Is Such a Potent Color" (Chapter 3), to Charles C. Mann's "Perilous Pigs: The Introduction of Swine-Borne Disease to the Americas" (Chapter 6), "Paleolithic Prescriptions for the Neolithic and Beyond" (Chapter 5), and "Toxic Breast Milk Threatens Arctic Culture" (Chapter 16).

ORIGINAL STUDY FEATURES

Written expressly for this text or selected from ethnographies and other original works by anthropologists, Original Study features present concrete examples that bring specific concepts to life and convey the passion of the authors. Each study sheds additional light on an important anthropological concept or subject area found in the chapter where it appears. Notably, each Original Study is integrated within the flow of the chapter narrative, signaling students that the content is not extraneous or supplemental. Appearing in nine chapters, Original Study features cover a wide range of topics, such as "The Real Dirt on Rainforest Fertility" by Charles C. Mann (Chapter 5), "Arranging Marriage in India" by Serena Nanda (Chapter 12), and "African Burial Ground Project" by Michael Blakey (Chapter 13).

ANTHROPOLOGY APPLIED FEATURES

These succinct and compelling profiles illustrate anthropology's wide-ranging relevance in today's world and give students a glimpse into a variety of the careers anthropologists enjoy. Featured in eight of the chapters, they include "Forensic Anthropology: Voices for the Dead" (Chapter 1), "Tell It to the Marines: Teaching Troops about Cultural Heritage" by Jane C. Waldbaum (Chapter 6), "Anthropologist S. Ann Dunham: Mother to a U.S. President" by Nancy I. Cooper (Chapter 11), and "Paul Farmer: Anthropology and Local Health Care Worldwide" (Chapter 16).

Changes and Highlights in the Third Edition

The pedagogical features described above strengthen each of the sixteen chapters in *The Essence of Anthropology*, serving as threads that tie the text together and help students feel the holistic nature of the discipline. In addition, the engagingly presented concepts themselves provide students with a solid foundation in the principles and practices of anthropology today.

The book in hand is distinct from the first two editions. Throughout, data and examples have been updated, less relevant material has been trimmed or cut, and the writing has been further chiseled to make it all the more clear and engaging. Each chapter opens with a new Visual Essence photograph and caption, and many new compelling pictures will be found in the book from start to finish.

Completely new in this edition is the list of student learning objectives at the start of every chapter, tied to the new Chapter Checklists at the end of every chapter. (Both are described in the pedagogy inventory above.) Presented under the heading "In this chapter you will learn to," this feature gives students a tangible grip on the critical goals of the chapter and the knowledge skills they are expected to develop while reading and studying the material. Other changes with this edition include new Questions for Reflection in many of the chapters and a new discussion question in every chapter's Biocultural Connection feature.

Beyond these changes, each chapter has undergone specific modifications and additions. The inventory that follows provides brief previews of the chapter contents and changes in this edition.

CHAPTER 1: THE ESSENCE OF ANTHROPOLOGY

This chapter's introduction to the four anthropological fields has been entirely reworked and reordered. We have placed cultural anthropology first to show its role as a defining and unifying aspect of the field; we then present enhanced sections on archaeology and linguistics, and we close with biological anthropology. Our expanded archaeology and linguistics sections include distinct sub-headings that correspond to the treatment given only to cultural and physical anthropology in previous editions. The archaeology section now includes a discussion of the broader issues such as settlement or migration patterns that archaeologists study as well as an enlarged section on historical archaeology. We have updated the chapter's ta-ble on dating methods to show how each method is used.

The chapter opens with a new Visual Essence photo featuring a program of health and education promotion for girls in South Sudan, the world's newest state. In re-sponse to reviewers' suggestions, we reduced the section on infant sleeping to a caption-rich Visual Counterpoint feature. The organ transplant discussion that appeared as a Biocultural Connection in previous editions has been moved into the body of the text and updated with a brief discussion of illegal global trafficking and the role of medical anthropologist Nancy Scheper-Hughes in founding the watchdog organization Organs Watch. This change made room for a new Biocultural Connection, "Picturing Pesticides," about the effects of pesticide use on the cognitive development of Yaqui children.

Chapter 1 also includes a new Original Study, "Whis-pers from the Ice," featuring successful collaboration between archaeologists and the community in Barrow, Alaska. Coverage of applied anthropology is expanded and integrated into the chapter. The updated Anthro-pology Applied box on forensic anthropology contains new information and a new photo about this important cross-disciplinary applied specialty. Applied anthropology is also addressed individually in each of the four fields in the chapter. A new Question for Reflection on applied anthropology supports the chapter's new material.

CHAPTER 2: BIOLOGY AND EVOLUTION

A new Visual Essence chapter opener features evolution as the force responsible for human biological diversity while contrasting short-term and evolutionary adapta-tion through the example of Kenyan runners. The chap-ter's discussion of creation stories and evolution has been expanded to include subjects as varied as Hinduism and intelligent design.

The biological details of the chapter are supported by several new images to aid student learning. These include a new photo of a bat wing to help explain analo-gies versus homologies; a new figure featuring the hu-man karyotype with select loci to show some of what has been learned through the Human Genome Project

and to illustrate the concept of alleles; a new figure of Punnett squares; and a new figure of sickling red blood cells. By streamlining and tightening the sections on heredity and genetic drift, we made room in this chapter for the material on macroevolution and speciation that appeared in Chapter 4 of previous editions. This allows us to present the concepts of micro- and macroevolu-tion side-by-side in the same chapter. A new Question for Reflection on macroevolution and time scales further integrates evolutionary theory for students.

CHAPTER 3: LIVING PRIMATES

The new Visual Essence feature opens the chapter with a compelling discussion of the ethical issues raised by the use of chimps in biomedical research. Our updated chapter introduction hooks student interest through a discussion of Jane Goodall's earliest discoveries of tool use by chimps when she was a very young researcher on her first trip into the field.

A contemporary focus on primate conservation appears throughout the chapter including a new figure showing the global distribution of primates, featuring the endangered species. A streamlined section on primate anatomy emphasizes a comparative approach among pri-mate species and their importance in understanding our-selves. The new Biocultural Connection on color vision in primates highlights this human–nonhuman primate connection. Finally, new Questions for Reflection on cultural aspects of the human life cycle and on the use of nonhuman primates in biomedical research drive home the chapter's themes.

CHAPTER 4: HUMAN EVOLUTION

By moving the section on macroevolution to Chapter 2, we are able to include more thematic material on the relevance of paleoanthropology in this revised chapter. Now that paleoanthropology has captured the public's imagination, we discuss the controversial U.S. tour of the ancient Lucy fossils in the new Visual Essence chapter opener, showing students the global flows of informa-tion, money, and even the fossils themselves. Similarly, the chapter also introduces students to the unprec-edented impact that human actions have on the planet and on our collective survival during this new geological period defined as the "Anthropocene."

We have devoted some of the chapter to the spec-tacular recent news on the Ardi specimens, emphasizing how paleoanthropologists do their research. Rich new figures help to explain the details of human evolution such as a new photo illustrating slow, gradual brain expansion along with an accompanying thought ques-tion; an updated figure on Australopithecine sites; new information on aging and sexing the Nariokotome *Homo erectus* specimen; a new figure comparing Mousterian to Upper Paleolithic tools; and a new thought question and discussion associated with the image from Grotte de Chauvet. We have updated the chapter with recent studies of Neandertal genetics showing their continuity with living humans, and we have included a discussion of the impact of these new data on the modern human origins debate.

CHAPTER 5: THE NEOLITHIC REVOLUTION

This streamlined and updated chapter emphasizes the contemporary relevance of the Neolithic revolution. A new Visual Essence feature shows the competition for resources, set into motion during the Neolithic and playing out today in the context of globalization as farmers from a village in India battle with a Coca-Cola bottling plant for water rights. This theme of competition for resources weaves throughout the chapter.

The section on primary and secondary innovation features recent discoveries of the earliest figurines and pottery from Yuchanyan Cave in China. New chapter visuals include a figure on the domestication of corn as well as an updated figure on global centers of domestication showing which crops appeared where and the diffusion of the crops today. By incorporating into the text relevant sections of the box feature from previous editions on breastfeeding, fertility, and beliefs, we are able to include the Biocultural Connection feature on Paleolithic prescriptions for today. This feature was also expanded to add tobacco and alcohol abuse to the list of human health challenges that started in the Neolithic. A new thought question on today's genetically modified crops drives home the point that today we are still facing challenges introduced during the Neolithic.

CHAPTER 6: THE EMERGENCE OF CITIES AND STATES

War, power, and monumental structures thematically thread through this updated chapter. This begins with the new Visual Essence feature about the relationship between centralized authority and war using the Temple at Angkor Wat and the Khmer Rouge as an example. An updated introductory section on the interdependence of cities includes Hurricane Katrina, the 2011 Japanese earthquake and tsunami, as well as the role of social media in revolutions in the Middle East in the spring of 2011.

The section on cultural change now implicitly links to the discussion of the barrel model in Chapter 8. Incorporating key points into the body of the text from the previous edition's Biocultural Connection (on social stratification and disease) allows us to include a fascinating new box feature by Charles Mann on the introduction of infectious disease through the pigs the conquistadores brought with them to the Americas. Rich new visuals include new locator maps indicating Mesopotamian sites and the Inca empire; a new figure showing the origins of cuneiform writing; and a new

figure showing the independent global origin of writing. The chapter's new Anthropology Applied feature, "Tell It to the Marines," details the U.S. military's practice of employing archaeologists to train soldiers about how to preserve archaeological remains in war zones.

CHAPTER 7: MODERN HUMAN DIVERSITY— RACE AND RACISM

Enlivened writing throughout this chapter improves the pedagogy and makes the challenging concepts of race and racism more interesting and accessible for today's students. The new Visual Essence features Yao Ming at the Chinese Special Olympics celebration to illustrate the variation present in one so-called racial group. We explain our use of the terms *black, white,* and *race* as purely social and cultural constructs.

The chapter now includes the seminal work of Audrey Smedley on the roots of racism in North America, drawn from the English treatment of the Irish along with reference to Bacon's Rebellion (1676). The updated section on the cultural construct of race includes the 2010 U.S. Census Bureau categories, and a new footnote to the Tiger Wood story updates the history of African Americans in golf. Race and behavior is discussed with an example of structural violence, detailing differences in prison sentences for users of crack versus powdered cocaine, a difference that preferentially privileges the predominantly white users of the more expensive powdered form of the drug. Links to Mendel's work on heredity in Chapter 2 strengthen this chapter's discussion of the faults inherent in theories about race and intelligence.

The chapter's closing section on legitimate study of true biological adaptation across populations includes the work of Gary Nabhan and Laurie Monti on "slow release" foods and activity instead of the thrifty genotype. A new Biocultural Connection called "Beans, Enzymes, and Adaptation to Malaria" illustrates how distinct cultural and biological adaptations can inadvertently work at cross-purposes.

CHAPTER 8: THE CHARACTERISTICS OF CULTURE

This chapter addresses anthropology's core concept of culture, exploring the term and its significance for individuals and societies. We begin with a new Visual Essence photo and caption highlighting one of China's ethnic minorities—the Uyghur—easily recognized by their distinctive dress. Elaborating on culture as the medium through which humans handle the problems of existence, we mark out its characteristics: Culture is learned, shared, based on symbols, integrated, and dynamic. The chapter includes discussions on culture and adaptation; the functions of culture; culture, society and the individual; ethnocentrism; and cultural change in the age of globalization. Special features include Marvin Harris's Biocultural Connection, "Pig Lovers and Pig Haters," and the Anthropology Applied feature "New Houses for Apache Indians" by George Esber, who describes his role in designing culturally appropriate homes for a Native American community. Also in this chapter is our original illustration of the barrel model of culture, which conveys the integrative and dynamic nature of culture. This model also introduces the concepts of infrastructure, social structure, and superstructure.

There are several new photographs, including one added to illustrate nonsustainable agriculture within a new discussion of maladaptation. A new image of Russian Nationalists, placed within the "Ethnocentrism and the Evaluation of Culture" section, illustrates notions of cultural superiority. In the "Pluralism" section we offer a new map showing ethnolinguistic groups in China. Other notable changes are additional details and examples woven into the "Culture Is Integrated" section and a revamped conclusion in the "Culture Is Dynamic" section to clarify the distinction between dynamism and change.

CHAPTER 9: LANGUAGE AND COMMUNICATION

This chapter on our species' most distinctive characteristic—language—begins with a new Visual Essence picture of a Tuareg nomad talking on his satellite phone while astride a camel. The caption speculates on the language he is speaking based on clues in the photo. Continuing, we investigate the nature of language and the three branches of linguistic anthropology—descriptive linguistics, historical linguistics, and the study of language in its social and cultural settings (ethnolinguistics and sociolinguistics). A completely revised ethnolinguistics section, specifically concerning linguistic relativity and the Sapir-Whorf hypothesis, enhances the third branch of linguistic anthropology. Also found here are updated sections on paralanguage and tonal languages and a fascinating new exploration of talking drums and whistled speech. We have retooled the section on language and gender, and we have revised and retitled the body language section to "Nonverbal Communication" to make it a more fitting header for discussions on proxemics and kinesics.

A revised and expanded discussion of language loss and revival features an intriguing look at new technology used by linguistic anthropologists collaborating on field research with speakers of endangered Khoisan "click" languages in southern Africa. That section also includes the latest data on the digital divide and its impact on ethnic minority languages—plus an updated chart showing Internet language populations.

This chapter includes two boxed features: an illustrated Biocultural Connection on the biology of human speech and S. Neyooxet Greymorning's new Anthropology Applied essay, "When Bambi Spoke Arapaho: Preserving Indigenous Languages." Also new

is the concluding section, "Literacy and Modern Telecommunication in Our Globalizing World." It recounts the prevalence of illiteracy in many parts of the globe, discusses literacy as a human right, and relays how the telecommunication revolution—mobile phones in particular—are transforming the social and economic lives of nearly everyone, even those in the most remote corners of the world.

CHAPTER 10: SOCIAL IDENTITY, PERSONALITY, AND GENDER

Looking at individual identity within a sociocultural context, this chapter surveys the concept of self, enculturation and the behavioral environment, social identity through personal naming, the development of personality, the concepts of group and modal personality, and the idea of national character. It opens with a stunning Visual Essence image of a Kazakh herder in the Altai Mountains of Mongolia teaching his son how to hunt on horseback with a trained golden eagle.

The personality development section has been streamlined, while incorporating two new ethnographic examples: one about childrearing and gender among the Ju/'hoansi and another about interdependence training among the Beng of West Africa. A substantial section of the chapter provides a thought-provoking historical overview of intersexuality, transsexuality, and transgendering, including current statistics on the incidence of intersexuality worldwide. It includes a revised and shortened version of "The Blessed Curse," an Original Study on intersexuality. In conjunction with the latter is a recent photograph and caption update of the intersexed South African track star Caster Semenya, whose 2009 international championship was marred by accusations that she was not "fully female."

The revised discussion on normal and abnormal personality in a social context includes sobering statistics from a global report on state-sponsored homophobia. We have substantially rewritten the discussion of culture-bound syndromes to shed light on the unfamiliar (Windingo psychosis) through a link to the familiar (bulimia nervosa and anorexia nervosa). The Biocultural Connection by Katherine Dettwyler about Down syndrome provides an example of cross-cultural variation in the experience and interpretation of this biological condition. Finally, a new concluding section, "Personal Identity and Mental Health in Globalizing Society," drives home the need for medical pluralism with a variety of modalities fit for humanity in the worldwide dynamics of the 21st century.

CHAPTER 11: SUBSISTENCE AND EXCHANGE

Here we investigate the various ways humans meet their basic needs and how societies adapt through culture to the environment, beginning with a dramatic new Visual

Essence photo of peasant farmers practicing wet-rice cultivation on the steep slopes of China's Guangxi Province. This connects to the subject matter of economic systems—the production, distribution, and consumption of goods—also covered in the chapter. We begin with a discussion of adaptation, followed by profiles on modes of subsistence in which we look at food-foraging and food-producing societies—pastoralism, crop cultivation, and industrialization. We introduce several new sections, including one about mixed farming that revises and clarifies the process of transhumance. Another new section discusses intensive agriculture, urbanization, and peasantry. And a third zeros in on industrial food production with an overview of the poultry industry.

Under the heading "Subsistence and Economics," we delve into the control of resources (natural, technological, labor) and types of labor division (gender, age, cooperative, craft specialization). A section on distribution and exchange defines various forms of reciprocity (with a detailed, illustrated description of the Kula ring), along with redistribution (including a potlatch account) and market exchange. We also touch on leveling mechanisms.

This chapter features a fascinating Biocultural Connection, "Surviving in the Andes: Aymara Adaptation to High Altitude." In the section "Local Economies and Global Capitalism," we present a new Anthropology Applied feature profiling the rural development work of Ann Dunham (President Obama's mother) in Asia, particularly as a pioneer in the field of microfinance. Finally, a much-revised concluding section looks at the informal economy that exists in the shadows of state bureaucracies and global corporations—an economy that in some countries may involve over half of the labor force and up to 40 percent of the gross national product.

CHAPTER 12: SEX, MARRIAGE, AND FAMILY

This chapter explores the inseparable connections among sexual reproductive practices, marriage, family, and household. We discuss the household as the basic building block in a culture's social structure, at the core of which is some form of family—people who are married to each other and/or a group of relatives stemming from the parent–child bond and the interdependence of men and women. The chapter opens with a compelling new Visual Essence feature revealing the symbolism in a traditional Japanese Shinto wedding at Meiji shrine in Tokyo.

Particulars addressed in this chapter include the incest taboo, endogamy and exogamy, dowry and bridewealth, cousin marriage, same-sex marriage, divorce, residence patterns, and nonfamily households. The chapter also includes a discussion contrasting past and present Christian and Muslim Shariah laws concerning the regulation of sexual relations. Two popular boxed features

remain in this chapter: Serena Nanda's Original Study, "Arranging Marriage in India" and Martin Ottenheimer's Biocultural Connection on marriage prohibitions in the United States.

We have reworked and reorganized this chapter's opening paragraphs on marriage and the regulation of sexual relations so they are more logically constructed and easier to follow. We provide a new, recent example of Shariah law as it relates to women and adultery and include nuanced commentary about the relationship between such restrictive rules and the incidence of HIV/ AIDS. A short, timely piece on the breakaway Mormon group, the Fundamentalist Church of Jesus of the Latter-Day Saints (FLDS), has been added to the discussion of polygamy in the United States, along with new data on the decline of polygyny in sub-Saharan Africa. New visuals include a striking photo of a polyandrous family in Nepal and a vibrant picture of a joyous gay wedding in Connecticut.

In the section on residence patterns, we have added brief explanations of *ambilocal* and *avunculocal*, and we have fleshed out the section on divorce to clarify its broad impact and the most common reasons for divorce across cultures. Finally, we have revised the chapter's closing section with a new introductory paragraph sketching the impact of global capitalism, electronic communication, and transnationalism on love relations. We have also included new subheads marking the discussions of diversity in families (adoption and new reproductive technologies) and changes in households (migrant workforces).

CHAPTER 13: KINSHIP AND OTHER FORMS OF GROUPING

This chapter deals with the fact that in most cultural systems, solutions to many organizational challenges (such as defense, resource allocation, and labor) are beyond the scope of family and household and require broader cooperative efforts based on kinship and other forms of grouping that help ensure material and emotional security. The new Visual Essence chapter opener highlights clans with a lively photo of the Clan Grant highland games in Scotland. A substantial section on grouping beyond kinship includes discussions of grouping by gender, age, and common interest. Included in the latter is a new and vivid overview of the impact that social networking platforms and digital entertainment options have on human relations. Also of note, our expanded discussion of women's organizations includes a profile of India's far-reaching Self-Employed Women's Association, which is having an enormously positive influence on women's economic opportunities and contributions.

Our revised section about grouping based on social hierarchy includes three historical case studies: one on caste and its role in India's Hindu culture (accompanied by a new figure illustrating the traditional Hindu caste system) and two concerning racial segregation in South Africa and the United States. The section on social mobility features a new discussion of the civil rights movement among India's Untouchables and the lowest Sudra castes (collectively called Dalits), in particular a brief profile and dramatic photograph of a group of women activists known as the "pink vigilantes." The chapter ends with a brief commentary on the role globalization plays in both increasing and decreasing social stratification. Special features include archaeologist Michael Blakey's Original Study on the African Burial Ground Project, illustrated with a new photograph, and the Biocultural Connection, "Maori Origins: Ancestral Genes and Mythical Canoes."

CHAPTER 14: POLITICS, POWER, AND VIOLENCE

Looking at a range of uncentralized and centralized political systems—from kin-ordered bands and tribes to chiefdoms and states—this chapter explores the question of power, the intersection of politics and religion, and issues of political leadership and gender. It opens with a new Visual Essence photograph of a crowd of tribal elders at a Loya Jirga (Grand Assembly) in Afghanistan. Discussing the maintenance of order, we look at internalized and externalized controls, along with social control through witchcraft and through law.

We mark the functions of law and the ways different societies deal with crime and settle disputes—including sentencing laws in Canada based on traditional Native American restorative justice techniques such as the Talking Circle. Next, we shift our focus from maintaining order within a society to external affairs, including a discussion of violent conflict and warfare, with a 5,000-year historical overview of armed conflicts among humans, including a section on domination and repression with a new global map showing the relationship between violent conflict and pluralistic societies with two or more ethnic groups or nationalities—often thrown together as a result of colonial domination.

The chapter concludes by exploring both violent and nonviolent resistance. Two new photos highlight nonviolent resistance: one of Gandhi and Nehru, shortly before India gained independence from British colonial rule, and one of Zapatista revolutionaries in Mexico, who shifted from armed rebellion to nonviolent resistance after a strong Internet presence helped them build an international network of political support. Special features in this chapter include a Biocultural Connection, "Gender, Sex, and Human Violence," and an Anthropology Applied box about the work of William Ury on dispute resolution.

CHAPTER 15: SPIRITUALITY AND RELIGION

This chapter's new Visual Essence feature shows hundreds of Bugis sailors from the island of Sulawesi praying in front of the elegantly upturned hulls of their traditional cargo ships. The main narrative begins with a description of the anthropological approach to religion and the current distinctions between religion and spirituality, followed by an overview of the status of religion and spirituality today. The latter includes a new world map depicting the global distribution of major religions. We then discuss beliefs concerning supernatural beings and spiritual forces (gods and goddesses, ancestral spirits, animism, animatism, and sacred spaces), and religious specialists (priests and priestesses, as well as shamans). The section on shamanism explores the origins of the term and presents our shamanic complex model of how these healings take place.

Under the heading "Sacred Performances: Rituals and Ceremonies," we present a much-revised discussion of rites of passage with two coming of age examples: male initiation rites among Aborigines and female initiation rites among the Mende in West Africa. A new subsection on rites of intensification features a discussion of death and a dramatic new photo of a Balinese cremation ceremony. Another new discussion about Roman Catholic nuns segues to Buddhist nuns and Hillary Crane's arresting new Biocultural Connection, "Change Your Karma and Change Your Sex?" based on her research in Thailand. The other special boxed feature in this chapter is Marjorie Shostak's Original Study about Ju/'hoansi healers and the trance dance.

A substantial section on religion, magic, and witchcraft highlights Ibibio witchcraft. Exploring religion and cultural change, this chapter introduces revitalization movements with a new ethnographic example—revitalization of the ancient tradition of Druidry in Great Britain, illustrated with a new photo of a modern-day Druid ceremony at Stonehenge. We conclude the chapter with a very brief new section titled "Persistence of Spirituality and Religion."

CHAPTER 16: GLOBAL CHANGES AND THE ROLE OF ANTHROPOLOGY

This final chapter—rich with global maps depicting pollution, migrations, and energy consumption—zeroes in on numerous global challenges confronting the human species today. It prompts students to use anthropological tools to think critically about these issues and to help bring about a future in which humans live in harmony with one another and with the nature that sustains us all.

Following a new Visual Essence featuring an Internet bar in China, we begin the main narrative with a discussion of modernization and a succinct historical tracing of human movement and interaction across the globe from 500 years ago through today's era of globalization. Next we explore the forces pressing toward and against the emergence of a global culture, taking a look at Westernization and its counterforce of growing nationalism and the breakup of multi-ethnic states. We present examples of resistance to globalization and discuss pluralism and multiculturalism—and revisit the issue of ethnocentrism.

We also recount the ever-widening gap between those who have wealth and power and those who do not. We define and illustrate the term *structural power* and its two branches—hard power (military and economic might) and soft power (media might that gains control through ideological influence). The section on hard power includes a new figure showing the global distribution of military expenditure, as well as a detailed discussion of the rise of global corporations, accompanied by a revised graph comparing corporate revenues to country GDPs.

We next look at problems of structural violence—from pollution and global warming to epidemics of hunger and obesity. We also discuss the roles structural power and violence play in internal and external migrations, touching on the lives of refugees, migrant workers, and diasporic communities. Extensive revisions to the section on global migrations better convey the "why" of these movements, including a new photo of Somali refugees.

A revised and expanded concluding section offers a positive note about anthropology's potential for helping to resolve some of the negative aspects of globalization covered in the chapter. It features a new, heartening Anthropology Applied essay about the work of world-renowned medical doctor, anthropologist, and human rights activist Paul Farmer.

SUPPLEMENTS

The Essence of Anthropology, third edition, comes with a comprehensive supplements program to help instructors efficiently create an effective learning environment both inside and outside the classroom and to aid students in mastering the material.

Supplements for Instructors

ONLINE INSTRUCTOR'S MANUAL WITH TEST BANK FOR *THE ESSENCE OF ANTHROPOLOGY,* THIRD EDITION

The Instructor's Manual offers detailed chapter outlines, learning objectives, key terms and concepts, lecture suggestions, and student Internet activities. New to this edition is a sample syllabus to guide instructors in scheduling their course. The fully revised test bank contains at least 120 test questions per chapter, including multiple choice, true/false, completion, short answer, and essay. (ISBN: 9781111826413).

POWERLECTURE WITH EXAMVIEW® FOR *THE ESSENCE OF ANTHROPOLOGY,* THIRD EDITION

This easy-to-use tool includes two components: (1) pre-assembled, customizable Microsoft PowerPoint presentations using charts, graphs, line art, and images from the text; and (2) ExamView® testing software that allows you to create, deliver, and customize tests and study guides (both print and online) in minutes. ExamView offers both a Quick Test Wizard and an Online Test Wizard that guide you step-by-step through the process of creating tests; moreover, it allows you to see the test you are creating on screen exactly as it will print or display online. You can build tests of up to 250 questions using up to 12 question types. Using ExamView's complete word processing capabilities, you can enter an unlimited number of new questions or edit existing questions. Available upon adoption of the text. (ISBN: 9781111834586)

WEBTUTOR™ ON BLACKBOARD AND WEBCT FOR *THE ESSENCE OF ANTHROPOLOGY,* THIRD EDITION

Use WebTutor and WebCT to create the course you want: Jumpstart your course with content that is customizable, rich, and text-specific, within your own course management system.

- *Jumpstart:* Simply load a WebTutor cartridge into your course management system.
- *Customize:* Easily blend, add, edit, reorganize, or delete content.
- *Access:* Give students access to a full array of study tools, including learning objectives, chapter-specific quizzing material, flashcards, and videos.

With WebTutor, instructors can provide virtual office hours, post syllabi, track student progress with the quiz material, and even customize the content to suit their needs. Whether you want to web-enable your class or put an entire course online, WebTutor delivers. Visit **webtutor.cengage.com** to learn more.

VISUAL ANTHROPOLOGY VIDEO

Bring engaging anthropology concepts to life with this dynamic 60-minute video from Documentary Educational Resources and Wadsworth. Video clips highlight key scenes from more than 30 new and classical anthropology films that serve as effective lecture launchers. (ISBN: 9780534566517)

AIDS IN AFRICA DVD

Expand your students' global perspective of HIV/AIDS with this award-winning documentary series focused on controlling HIV/AIDS in southern Africa. The films focus on caregivers in the faith community; young people sharing messages of hope through song and dance; the relationship of HIV/AIDS to gender, poverty, stigma, education, and justice; and the story of two HIV-positive women helping others. (ISBN: 9780495171836)

ALTERNATE FORMAT: LOOSE LEAF FOR *THE ESSENCE OF ANTHROPOLOGY,* THIRD EDITION

We offer a value-priced loose-leaf version of this text, presented in a three-hole-punched format. Students can purchase this version at www.cengagebrain.com. Instructors can also specify this format when placing your textbook order at the bookstore. (ISBN: 9781111835088)

Supplements for Students

COURSEMATE FOR *THE ESSENCE OF ANTHROPOLOGY,* THIRD EDITION

The more you study, the better the results. Make the most of your study time by accessing everything you need to succeed in one place with chapter-specific learning tools including glossaries, flashcards, quizzes, videos, and more—online with CourseMate. Go to www.cengagebrain.com and search for your book.

Acknowledgments

In this day and age, no textbook comes to fruition without extensive collaboration. Beyond the shared endeavors of our author team, this book owes its completion to a wide range of individuals, from colleagues in the discipline to those involved in the development and production processes. We are particularly grateful for the exceptional group of manuscript reviewers listed below. They provided detailed and thoughtful feedback that helped us to hone and re-hone our narrative.

Virginia Anderson-Stojanovic, *Wilson College*
Christine Hippert, *University of Wisconsin–La Crosse*
Eric Joost, *Hillsborough Community College*
Doug Reeser, *University of South Florida*
Peter Sinelli, *University of Central Florida*
Tim Sullivan, *Cedar Valley College*

We carefully considered and made use of the wide range of comments provided by these individuals. Our decisions on how to utilize their suggestions were influenced by our own perspectives on anthropology and teaching, combined with the priorities and page limits of this text. Thus, neither our reviewers nor any of the other anthropologists mentioned here should be held responsible for any shortcomings in this book. They should, however, be credited as contributors to many of the book's strengths.

Thanks, too, go to colleagues who provided material for some of the Anthropology Applied, Biocultural Connection, and Original Study features in this text: Michael Blakey, Nancy I. Cooper, Hillary Crane, Katherine A. Dettwyler, George S. Esber, S. Neyooxet Greymorning, Marvin Harris, Charles C. Mann, Jonathan Marks, Serena Nanda, Martin Ottenheimer, Marjorie Shostak, Sherry Simpson, Meredith F. Small, Frans B. M. de Waal, Jane C. Waldbaum, and R. K. Williamson.

We have debts of gratitude to office workers in our departments for their cheerful help in clerical matters: Karen Rundquist, Emira Smailagic, and Melissa Fisher, along with research librarian extraordinaire Nancy Bianchi.

And to colleagues Yvette Pigeon, Jessica Falcone, and Michael Wesch for lively discussions on anthropological and pedagogical approaches. Also worthy of note here are the introductory anthropology teaching assistants at Kansas State University who, through the years, have shed light for us on effective ways to reach new generations of students. And, finally, the students themselves, who are at the heart of this educational endeavor and who continually provide feedback in formal and informal ways.

Our thanksgiving inventory would be incomplete without mentioning individuals at Wadsworth / Cengage Learning who helped conceive this text and bring it to fruition. Special gratitude goes to sponsoring acquisitions editor Erin Mitchell, our go-to person on countless fronts. After many years of working with senior development editor Lin Marshall Gaylord, our thanks for her vision and anthropological knowledge continues to grow and deepen. Our thanks also go out to Wadsworth's editorial, marketing, design, and production team: Sean Foy (marketing manager), Mary Noel (media editor), Mallory Ortberg (editorial assistant), Linda Stewart (assistant editor), as well as Tanya Nigh (content project manager) and Caryl Gorska (art director). In addition to all of the above, we have had the invaluable aid of several most proficient freelancers, including our able photo researcher Sarah Everston and our skilled graphic designer Caryl Gorska. We are especially thankful to have had the opportunity to work once again with copy editor Jennifer Gordon and production coordinator Joan Keyes of Dovetail Publishing Services. Consummate professionals and generous souls, both of them keep track of countless details and bring calm efficiency and grace to the demands of meeting difficult deadlines. Their efforts and skills play a major role in making our work doable and pleasurable.

And finally, all of us are indebted to family members who have not only put up with our textbook preoccupation but cheered us on in the endeavor.

The Essence
of Anthropology

VISUAL ESSENCE

Part of being human is our fascination with ourselves. Where did we come from? Why do we act in certain ways? What makes us tick? While some answer these questions with biological mechanisms and others with social or spiritual explanations, anthropologists address them through a holistic, integrated approach. Anthropology considers human culture and biology, in all times and places, as inextricably intertwined, each affecting the other in important ways. For example, consider these smiling schoolgirls in Yei, South Sudan, the world's newest country. Celebrating independence on July 9, 2011, South Sudan became Africa's 54th state through peaceful elections in a region ravaged by five decades of war that took the lives of 2 million people. In a country where "a 15-year-old girl has a higher chance of dying in childbirth than she does of finishing primary school . . . and more than ten percent of children do not make it to their first birthday,"[1] these girls have good reason to smile. Through the support of Africa ELI—an organization dedicated to improving economic conditions by advancing educational opportunities for young women in South Sudan—these girls will soon graduate from secondary school. Africa ELI (Education and Leadership Initiative) was founded in 2006 by members of the Sudanese diaspora with help from a U.S. anthropologist and other American friends. Today, local Sudanese leaders have assumed more of the program's direction. Anthropology provides insight into every part of this story—the relation between gender and social change, the cultures of the ethnic groups who call this region home, the effects of colonialism, the complex lives of refugees in new lands, the forces that enabled democratic elections, and the social determinants of health. Just as education serves these young women, a holistic anthropological perspective will equip you to negotiate today's globalized world.

1 The Essence of Anthropology

The Anthropological Perspective

anthropology is the study of humankind in all times and places. Of course many other disciplines focus on humans in one way or another. For example, anatomy and physiology concentrate on our species as biological organisms. The social sciences examine human relationships, leaving artistic and philosophical aspects of human cultures to the humanities. Anthropology focuses on the interconnections and interdependence of all aspects of the human experience in all places, in the present and deep into the past, well before written history. This unique, broad **holistic perspective** equips anthropologists to address that elusive thing we call human nature.

Anthropologists welcome the contributions of researchers from other disciplines and in return offer their own findings to these other disciplines. An anthropologist might not know as much about the structure of the human eye as an anatomist or as much about the perception of color as a psychologist. As a synthesizer, however, the anthropologist seeks to understand how anatomy and psychology relate to color-naming practices in different societies. Because they look for the broad basis of ideas and practices without limiting themselves to any single social or biological aspect, anthropologists can acquire an especially expansive and inclusive overview of human biology and culture.

Keeping a holistic perspective allows anthropologists to prevent their own cultural ideas and values from distorting their research. As the old saying goes, people often see what they believe, rather than what appears before their eyes. By maintaining a critical awareness of their own assumptions about human nature—checking and rechecking how their beliefs and actions might be shaping their research—anthropologists strive to gain objective knowledge. With this in mind, anthropologists aim to avoid the pitfalls of **ethnocentrism**, a way of viewing other cultures in relation to one's own in the belief that the familiar sets a universal standard of what is proper or correct. Thus anthropologists have expanded our understanding of diversity in human thought, biology, and behavior, as well as to our understanding of the many things humans have in common.

In this chapter you will learn to:

- **Describe the discipline of anthropology and make connections among its four fields.**

- **Compare anthropology to the sciences and the humanities.**

- **Identify the characteristics of anthropological field methods and the ethics of anthropological research.**

- **Explain the usefulness of anthropology in light of globalization.**

---

[1]Gettleman, J. (2011, July 9). South Sudan, the newest nation, is full of hope and problems. *New York Times.* http://www.post-gazette.com/pg/11190/1159402-82-0.stm (retrieved August 22, 2011).

3

VISUAL COUNTERPOINT

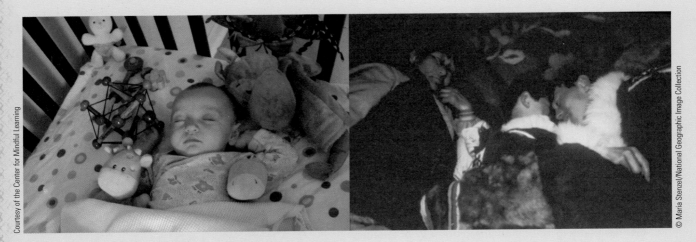

▲▲▲ Although infants in the United States typically sleep apart from their parents, a practice thought to promote independence, cross-cultural research shows that co-sleeping, particularly of mother and baby, is the rule. Unfortunately, without the breathing cues provided by someone sleeping nearby, an infant is more susceptible to sudden infant death syndrome (SIDS), a phenomenon in which a baby, usually between 4 and 6 months old, stops breathing and dies while asleep. The highest rates of SIDS are found among infants in the United States.[2] The photo on the right shows a Nenet family sleeping together in their *chum* (reindeer-skin tent). Nenet people are sub-Arctic reindeer pastoralists living in Siberia.

While other social sciences have predominantly concentrated on contemporary peoples living in North American and European (Western) societies, anthropologists have traditionally focused on non-Western peoples and cultures. Anthropologists work with the understanding that to fully access the complexities of human ideas, behavior, and biology, *all humans*, wherever and whenever, must be studied. A cross-cultural and long-term evolutionary perspective distinguishes anthropology from other social sciences. This approach guards against culture-bound theories—that is, theories based on assumptions about the world and reality that come from the researcher's own particular culture.

Consider the case of organ transplantation, a medical practice that has become widespread since the first kidney transplant between identical twin brothers in Boston in 1954. Today transplants between unrelated individuals are common, so much so that organs are trafficked in the black market, often across continents from the poor to the wealthy. In order to reduce the illegal traffic, several European countries have enacted policies that assume that any individual who is brain dead is automatically an organ donor unless the person has "opted out" ahead of time.

A practice like organ transplantation can only exist if it fits with cultural beliefs about death and the human body. The North American and European view—that the body is a machine that can be repaired much like a car—makes a practice like organ transplant acceptable. But this is not the view shared by all societies. Anthropologist

Margaret Lock has explored differences between Japanese and North American acceptance of the biological state of brain death and how it affects the practice of organ transplants.[3]

Brain death relies upon the absence of measurable electrical currents in the brain and the inability to breathe without technological assistance. The brain-dead individual, though attached to machines, still seems alive with a beating heart and normal skin coloring. Part of the reason why North Americans find brain death acceptable is that personhood and individuality are culturally located in the brain. North American comfort with brain death has allowed for the "gift of life" through organ donation and subsequent transplantation.

By contrast, in Japan the concept of brain death is hotly contested, and organ transplants are rarely performed. The Japanese idea of personhood does not incorporate a mind–body split; instead, the person's identity is located throughout the body rather than solely in the brain. Consequently the Japanese resist accepting a warm body as a corpse from which organs can be harvested. Further, organs cannot be transformed into

---

[2]Barr, R. G. (1997, October). The crying game. *Natural History*, 47. Also, McKenna, J. J., & McDade, T. (2005, June). Why babies should never sleep alone: A review of the co-sleeping controversy in relation to SIDS, bedsharing, and breast feeding. *Pediatric Respiratory Reviews 6*(2), 134–152.

[3]Lock, M. (2001). Twice dead: Organ transplants and the reinvention of death. Berkeley: University of California Press.

"gifts" because anonymous donation is not compatible with Japanese social patterns of reciprocal exchange.

Organ transplantation carries far greater social meaning than the purely biological movement of an organ from one individual to another. And although this practice may fit with the beliefs of some societies, it may be an opportunity for human rights abuses in another.

Anthropology and Its Fields

Individual anthropologists tend to specialize in one of four fields or subdisciplines: cultural anthropology, linguistic anthropology, archaeology, and physical (biological) anthropology (▶ **Figure 1.1**). Some anthropologists consider archaeology and linguistics as part of the broader study of human cultures, but archaeology and linguistics also have close ties to biological anthropology. For example, while linguistic anthropology focuses on the cultural aspects of language, it has deep connections to the evolution of human language and the biological basis of speech and language studied within physical anthropology.

Researchers in each of anthropology's fields gather and analyze data to explore similarities and differences among humans, across time and space. Moreover, individuals within each of the four fields practice **applied anthropology**, which entails the use of anthropological knowledge and methods to solve practical problems. Most applied anthropologists actively collaborate with the communities in which they work—setting goals, solving problems, and conducting research together. In this book, examples of how anthropology contributes to solving a wide range of the challenges humans face appear in the Anthropology Applied features.

One of the earliest contexts in which anthropological knowledge was applied to a practical problem was the international public health movement that began in the 1920s. This marked the beginning of **medical**

Figure 1.1 The Four Fields of Anthropology Note that the divisions between them are not sharp, indicating that their boundaries overlap.

anthropology—a specialization that brings theoretical and applied approaches from cultural and biological anthropology to the study of human health and disease. The work of medical anthropologists sheds light on the connections between human health and political and economic forces, both locally and globally. Examples of this specialization appear in some of the Biocultural Connections featured in this text, including the one presented on the next page, "Picturing Pesticides."

Cultural Anthropology

Cultural anthropology (also called *social* or *sociocultural anthropology*) is the study of patterns of human behavior, thought, and feelings. It focuses on humans as culture-producing and culture-reproducing creatures. To understand the work of the cultural anthropologist, we must clarify the meaning of **culture**—a society's shared and socially transmitted ideas, values, and perceptions, which are used to make sense of experience and which generate behavior and are reflected in that behavior. These are the (often unconscious) standards by which societies—structured groups of people—operate. These standards are socially learned, rather than acquired through biological inheritance. The manifestations of culture may vary considerably from place to place, but no person is "more cultured" in the anthropological sense than any other.

Integral to all the anthropological fields, the concept of culture might be considered anthropology's distinguishing feature. After all, a biological anthropologist is distinct from a biologist *primarily* because he or she takes culture into account. The earliest anthropologists

▲▲▲

anthropology The study of humankind in all times and places.

holistic perspective A fundamental principle of anthropology: The various parts of human culture and biology must be viewed in the broadest possible context in order to understand their interconnections and interdependence.

ethnocentrism The belief that the ways of one's own culture are the only proper ones.

culture-bound Theories about the world and reality based on the assumptions and values of one's own culture.

applied anthropology The use of anthropological knowledge and methods to solve practical problems, often for a specific client.

medical anthropology The specialization in anthropology that brings theoretical and applied approaches from cultural and biological anthropology to the study of human sickness and health.

cultural anthropology The study of customary patterns in human behavior, thought, and feelings. It focuses on humans as culture-producing and culture-reproducing creatures. Also known as *social* or *sociocultural anthropology*.

culture A society's shared and socially transmitted ideas, values, and perceptions, which are used to make sense of experience and which generate behavior and are reflected in that behavior.

▼▼▼

BIOCULTURAL CONNECTION

Picturing Pesticides

The toxic effects of pesticides have long been known. After all, these compounds are designed to kill bugs. However, documenting the toxic effects of pesticides on humans has been more difficult, as they are subtle—sometimes taking years to become apparent.

Anthropologist Elizabeth Guillette, working in a Yaqui Indian community in Mexico, combined ethnographic observation, biological monitoring of pesticide levels in the blood, and neurobehavioral testing to document the impairment of child development by pesticides.[a] Working with colleagues from the Technological Institute of Sonora in Obregón, Mexico, Guillette compared children and families

from two Yaqui communities: one living in farm valleys who were exposed to large doses of pesticides and one living in ranching villages in the foothills nearby.

Guillette documented the frequency of pesticide use among the farming Yaqui to be forty-five times per crop cycle with two crop cycles per year. In the farming valleys she also noted that families tended to use household bug sprays on a daily basis, thus increasing their exposure to toxic pesticides. In the foothill ranches, she found that the only pesticides that the Yaqui were exposed to consisted of DDT sprayed by the government to control malaria. in these communities, indoor bugs were swatted or tolerated.

Pesticide exposure was linked to child health and development through two sets of measures. First, Guillette examined the levels of pesticides in the blood of valley children at birth and throughout their childhood and found these levels to be far higher than in the children from the foothills. She also documented the presence of pesticides in breast milk of nursing mothers from the valley farms.

The second study examined the children's performance on a variety of normal childhood activities, such as jumping, memory games, playing catch, and draw-

ing pictures. The children exposed to high doses of pesticides had significantly less stamina, poorer eye–hand coordination, less large motor coordination, and poorer drawing ability compared to the Yaqui children from the foothills. Although these children exhibited no overt symptoms of pesticide poisoning, they did demonstrate delays and impairment in their neurobehavioral abilities that might be irreversible.

Though Guillette's study was thoroughly embedded in one ethnographic community, she emphasizes that the exposure to pesticides among the Yaqui farmers is typical of agricultural communities globally and thus has significance for changing human practices regarding the use of pesticides everywhere. ■

Biocultural Question

Given the documented developmental damage these pesticides have inflicted on children, should their sale and use be regulated globally? Are potentially damaging toxins in use in your community?

[a]Guillette, E. A., et al. (1998, June). An anthropological approach to the evaluation of preschool children exposed to pesticides in Mexico. *Environmental Health Perspectives 106*, 347.

Foothills   **Valley**

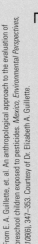

60-month-old female   71-month-old male   71-month-old female   71-month-old male

 ▲▲▲ Compare the drawings typically done by Yaqui children heavily exposed to pesticides (valley) to those made by Yaqui children living in nearby areas who were relatively unexposed (foothills).

stepped outside of their own cultural framework in order to learn how other societies organized themselves. Today a cultural anthropologist might study the legal, medical, economic, political, or religious system of a given society, knowing that all aspects of the culture interrelate as part of a unified whole. A cultural anthropologist will think about social categories in a society, such as gender, age, or class. Indeed these factors will be explored in depth in the second half of this text. But it is also worth noting the importance of these same cultural factors to the archaeologist who studies a society through its material remains, to the linguistic anthropologist who examines ancient and modern languages, and to the biological anthropologist who investigates the physical human body.

Cultural anthropology has two main components: ethnography and ethnology. An **ethnography** is a detailed description of a particular culture primarily based on **fieldwork**, which is the term all anthropologists use for on-location research. Because the hallmark of ethnographic fieldwork is a combination of social participation and personal observation within the community being studied and interviews and discussions with individual members of a group, the ethnographic method is commonly referred to as **participant observation**. Ethnographies provide the information used to make systematic comparisons among cultures all across the world. Known as **ethnology**, such cross-cultural research allows anthropologists to develop theories that help explain why certain important differences or similarities occur among groups.

ETHNOGRAPHY

Through participant observation in another people's culture—eating their food, sleeping under their roof, learning how to speak and behave acceptably, and personally experiencing their habits and customs—the ethnographer seeks to gain the best possible understanding of a particular way of life. Being a participant observer does not mean that the anthropologist must join in battles to study a society in which warfare is prominent; but by living among a warring people, the ethnographer should be able to understand how warfare fits into their overall cultural framework.

The ethnographer must observe carefully to gain an overview without placing too much emphasis on one part at the expense of another. Only by discovering how all aspects of a culture—its social, political, economic, and religious practices and institutions—relate to one another can the ethnographer begin to understand the cultural system. An ethnographer's most essential tools are notebooks, pen/pencil, camera, recording devices, and a laptop computer. Most important of all, he or she needs flexible social skills.

The popular image of ethnographic fieldwork is that it occurs among people who live in far-off, isolated places. To be sure, much ethnographic work has been done in the remote villages of Africa or South America, the islands of the Pacific Ocean, the Indian tribal reservations of North America, the deserts of Australia, and so on. However, as the discipline of anthropology developed, Western industrialized societies also became a legitimate focus of anthropological study. Some of this shift occurred as scholars from non-Western cultures became anthropologists. Ethnographic fieldwork has transformed from expert Western anthropologists studying people in "other" places to a collaborative approach among anthropologists from all parts of the world and the varied communities in which they work. Today, anthropologists from all around the globe employ the same research techniques that were used in the study of non-Western peoples to explore such diverse subjects as religious movements, street gangs, land rights, schools, conflict resolution, homeless encampments, corporate bureaucracies, and health-care systems in Western cultures.

ETHNOLOGY

Largely descriptive in nature, ethnography provides the raw data needed for ethnology—the branch of cultural anthropology that involves cross-cultural comparisons and theories that explain differences or similarities among groups. Intriguing insights into one's own beliefs and practices may come from cross-cultural comparisons. Consider, for example, the amount of time spent on domestic chores by industrialized peoples and traditional food foragers—people who rely on wild plant and animal resources for subsistence.

Anthropological research has shown that food foragers work far less at domestic tasks and other subsistence pursuits compared to people in industrialized societies. Despite access to "labor-saving" appliances such as dishwashers, washing machines, clothes dryers, vacuum cleaners, food processors, and microwave ovens, urban people in the United States who are not working for

▲▲

ethnography A detailed description of a particular culture primarily based on fieldwork.

fieldwork The term anthropologists use for on-location research.

participant observation In ethnography, the technique of learning a people's culture through social participation and personal observation within the community being studied, as well as interviews and discussion with individual members of the group over an extended period of time.

ethnology The study and analysis of different cultures from a comparative or historical point of view, utilizing ethnographic accounts and developing anthropological theories that help explain why certain important differences or similarities occur among groups.

▼▼

◀ Linguistic anthropologist David Anderson has devoted his career to saving indigenous languages. He founded and heads the Living Tongues Institute for Endangered Languages and works throughout the globe to preserve languages that are dying out at a shocking rate of about one every two weeks. Here he is working with Don Francisco Ninacondis and Ariel Ninacondis in Charazani, Bolivia, to help preserve their language, Kallawaya.

wages outside their homes put 55 hours a week into their housework. In contrast, aboriginal women in Australia devote 20 hours a week to their chores.[4] Nevertheless, consumer appliances have become important indicators of a high standard of living all across the world due to the widespread belief that household appliances reduce housework and increase leisure time.

By making systematic comparisons, ethnologists seek to arrive at scientific explanations concerning the function and operation of cultural practices in all times and places.

APPLIED CULTURAL ANTHROPOLOGY

Today cultural anthropologists contribute to applied anthropology in a variety of contexts ranging from business to education to health care to governmental interventions to humanitarian aid. For example, medical anthropologist Nancy Scheper-Hughes has taken her investigative work on the global illegal trafficking of organs and used it to help found Organs Watch, an organization dedicated to solving this human rights issue.

Linguistic Anthropology

Perhaps the most distinctive feature of the human species is language. Although the sounds and gestures made by some other species—especially apes—may serve functions comparable to those of human language, no other animal has developed a system of symbolic communication as complex as that of humans. Language allows people to preserve and transmit countless details of their culture from generation to generation.

The branch of anthropology that studies human languages is called **linguistic anthropology**. Although it shares data and methods with the discipline of linguistics, it differs in that it focuses on anthropological questions, such as, how does language use differ among distinct members of a society? And how does the culture shape the language?

When this field began, it emphasized the documentation of languages in cultures under ethnographic study—particularly those whose future seemed precarious. When the first Europeans began to colonize the world, an estimated 12,000 distinct languages existed. By the late nineteenth and early twentieth century—when anthropological fieldwork, particularly of American Indian groups, began to take off—many languages and peoples were on the brink of extinction. Sadly this trend continues, with predictions that nearly half of the world's remaining 6,000 languages will disappear over the next hundred years.[5]

LANGUAGE AND BELIEFS

In the early twentieth century, mastery of Native American languages—with grammatical structures so different from the Indo-European and Semitic languages to which Euramerican scholars were accustomed—prompted the notion of *linguistic relativity*. This refers to the idea that linguistic diversity reflects not just differences in sounds and grammar but differences in ways of looking at the world. For example, the observation that the language of the Hopi Indians of the American Southwest had no words for the concepts of past, present, and future led the early proponents of linguistic relativity to suggest that the Hopi people had a unique conception of time.[6] Similarly, the observation that English-speaking North Americans use a number of slang words—such as *dough, greenback, dust, loot, bucks,*

---

[4]Bodley, J. H. (1985). *Anthropology and contemporary human problems* (2nd ed., p. 69). Palo Alto, CA: Mayfield.

[5]Crystal, D. (2002). *Language death.* Cambridge, UK: Cambridge University Press; Knight, C., Studdert-Kennedy, M., & Hurford, J. (Eds.). (2000). *The evolutionary emergence of language: Social function and the origins of linguistic form.* Cambridge: Cambridge University Press.

[6]Whorf, B. (1946). The Hopi language, Toreva dialect. In *Linguistic structures of Native America.* New York: Viking Fund.

change, paper, cake, moolah, benjamins, and bread—to refer to money could be a product of linguistic relativity. The profusion of terms helps to identify a thing of special importance to a culture. Similarly, the importance of money within North American culture is also evident in the equation of money with time, in phrases such as "time is money," "a waste of time," and "spend some time."

Complex ideas and practices integral to a culture's survival can also be reflected in language. For example, among the Nuer, a nomadic group that travels with grazing animals throughout South Sudan, a baby born with a visible deformity is not considered a human baby. Instead it is called a baby hippopotamus. This name allows for the safe return of the "hippopotamus" to the river where it belongs. Such infants would not be able to survive in Nuer society, and so linguistic practice is compatible with the compassionate choice the Nuer have had to make.

Some theorists have challenged the notion of linguistic relativity, arguing that the human capacity for language is based on biological universals that underlie all human thought. Cognitive scientist Stephen Pinker has even suggested that, at the universal biological level, thought is nonverbal.[7] Whatever the case, a holistic anthropological approach considers language as dependent both on a biological basis shared by all humans and on specific cultural patterning.

SOCIOLINGUISTICS

In order to examine anthropological questions through linguistic analyses, linguistic anthropologist Dell Hymes developed a framework that focused on specific speech events.[8] Such events form a **discourse** or an extended communication on a particular subject. Within a speech event or series of events, the researcher can focus on features such as the physical and psychological setting, the participants, the purpose, the sequence, and social rules. For example, linguistic anthropologists may deal with the relationship between language and the social roles/identity within a society. How does financial status, age, or gender affect the way individuals use their culture's language? The linguistic anthropologist might examine whether the tendency for females in the United States to end statements with an upward inflection, as though the statement were a question, reflects a pattern of male dominance in this society. Because members of any culture may use a variety of different registers and inflections, the ones they choose to express their thoughts at a specific instance can convey particular meanings.

Linguistic anthropologists also focus on the socialization process through which an individual becomes part of a culture. Children take on this fundamental task as they grow and develop, but it can be seen in adults as well. Adults may need to assimilate because of a geographic move or because they are taking on a professional identity. First-year medical students, for example, amass 6,000 new vocabulary words and a series of linguistic conventions as they begin to take on the role of a physician.

HISTORICAL LINGUISTICS

As with the anthropological perspective on culture, language is similarly regarded as alive, malleable, and changing. Online tools such as Urban Dictionary track the changes in North American slang, and traditional dictionaries include new words and usages each year. These language changes have important implications as linguistic anthropologists track them to increase our understanding of the human past. By working out relationships among languages and examining their spatial distributions, linguistic anthropologists may estimate how long the speakers of those languages have lived where they do. By identifying those words in related languages that have survived from an ancient ancestral tongue, anthropological linguists can also suggest not only where but *how* the speakers of the ancestral language lived. Such work has shown, for example, how the Bantu family of languages spread from its origins in western Africa (in the region of today's Nigeria and Cameroon) to the majority of the continent. Over the course of several millennia, Bantu-speaking peoples came to inhabit most of sub-Saharan Africa, bringing their language, farming technology, and other aspects of their culture with them.

APPLIED LINGUISTIC ANTHROPOLOGY

Linguistic anthropology is practiced in a number of applied settings. For example, linguistic anthropologists have collaborated with ethnic minorities in the revival of languages suppressed or lost during periods of oppression by another ethnic group. Anthropologists have helped to create written forms of languages that previously existed only orally. These examples of applied linguistic anthropology represent the kind of true collaboration that is characteristic of anthropological research today.

▲▲▲

---

[7] Pinker, S. (1994). *The language instinct: How the mind creates language.* New York: William Morrow.

[8] Hymes, D. (1974). *Foundations in sociolinguistics: An ethnographic approach.* Philadelphia: University of Pennsylvania Press.

linguistic anthropology The study of human languages.
discourse An extended communication on a particular subject.

▼▼▼

Archaeology

Archaeology is the branch of anthropology that studies human cultures through the recovery and analysis of material remains and environmental data. Such material products include tools, pottery, hearths, and enclosures that remain as traces of cultural practices in the past, as well as human, plant, and marine remains, some of which date back 2.5 million years. The arrangement of these traces, as much as the traces themselves, reflects specific human ideas and behavior. For example, shallow, restricted concentrations of charcoal that include oxidized earth, bone fragments, and charred plant remains, located near pieces of fire-cracked rock, pottery, and tools suitable for food preparation, indicate cooking and food processing. Such remains can reveal much about a people's diet and subsistence practices.

In addition to asking specific questions about a single group of people at a specific place and time, archaeologists also use material remains to investigate broad questions such as settlement or migration patterns across vast areas, such as the peopling of the Americas or the spread of the earliest humans from Africa. Together with skeletal remains, material remains help archaeologists reconstruct the biocultural context of past human lifeways and patterns. Archaeologists organize this material through time and use it to explain cultural variability and culture change.

Because archaeological research is explicitly tied to unearthing material remains in particular environmental contexts, a variety of innovations in the geographical and geological sciences have been readily incorporated into archaeological research. Innovations such as geographic information systems (GIS), remote sensing, and ground-penetrating radar (GPR) complement traditional explorations of the past through archaeological digs. While archaeologists tend to specialize in particular culture zones or time periods that are connected with particular regions of the world, a number of topical subspecializations also exist.

HISTORICAL ARCHAEOLOGY

Archaeologists can reach back for clues to human behavior far beyond the mere 5,000 years to which historians are confined by their reliance on written records. Calling this time period "prehistoric" does not mean that these societies were less interested in their history or that they did not have ways of recording and transmitting information. It simply means that written records do not exist.

That said, archaeologists are not limited to the study of societies without written records; they may study those for which historic documents are available to supplement the material remains. **Historical archaeology,** the archaeological study of places for which written records exist, often provides data that differ considerably from the historical record. In most literate societies, written records are associated with governing elites rather than with farmers, fishers, laborers, or slaves, and therefore they include the biases of the ruling classes. In fact, according to historical archaeologist James Deetz, in many historical contexts, "material culture may be the most objective source of information we have."[9]

BIOARCHAEOLOGY

A number of archaeological specializations deal with the ways that cultural practices are preserved in the remains of living things. **Bioarchaeology**, for example, is the archaeological study of human remains, emphasizing the preservation of cultural and social processes in the skeleton. For example, mummified skeletal remains from the Andean highlands in South America preserve not only this burial practice but also provide evidence of some of the earliest brain surgery ever documented. In addition, these bioarchaeological remains exhibit skull deformations, which were used to distinguish nobility from other members of society.

Other archaeologists specialize in *ethnobotany*, studying how people of a given culture made use of indigenous plants. Still others specialize in *zooarchaeology*, tracking the animal remains recovered in archaeological excavations.

CONTEMPORARY ARCHAEOLOGY

Although most archaeologists concentrate on the past, some of them study material objects in contemporary settings. One example is the Garbage Project, founded by William Rathje at the University of Arizona in 1973. This anthropological study of household waste of Tucson residents continues to produce thought-provoking information about contemporary social issues. For example, when surveyed by questionnaires, only 15 percent of households report consuming beer, and no household reported drinking more than eight cans a week. Analysis of garbage from the same area showed that some beer was consumed in over 80 percent of the households, and 50 percent of households discarded more than eight cans per week.

In addition to providing actual data on beer consumption, the Garbage Project has tested the validity of research survey techniques, upon which sociologists, economists, and other social scientists and policymakers rely heavily. The tests show a significant difference between what people *say* they do and what the garbage analysis shows they *actually* do. Ideas about human behavior based on simple survey techniques therefore may be seriously in error.

APPLIED ARCHAEOLOGY

The Garbage Project also gives us one of the finest examples of applied archaeology. In 1987, researchers began a program of excavating landfills in different

---

[9]Deetz, J. (1977). *In small things forgotten: The archaeology of early American life* (p. 160). Garden City, NY: Anchor Press/Doubleday.

parts of the United States and Canada. From this work came the first reliable data on what materials go into landfills and what happens to them there. Again, common beliefs turned out to be at odds with the actual situation. For example, biodegradable materials such as newspapers take far longer to decay when buried in deep compost landfills than anyone had suspected. This kind of information is a vital step toward solving waste disposal problems. The data gathered from the Garbage Project's landfill studies on hazardous wastes and rates of decay of various materials play a major role in landfill regulation and management today.[10]

CULTURAL RESOURCE MANAGEMENT

While archaeology may conjure up images of ancient pyramids and the like, much archaeological fieldwork is carried out as cultural resource management. What distinguishes this work from traditional archaeological research is that it is a legally required part of any activity that might threaten important aspects of a country's prehistoric and historic heritage. For example, in the United States, if the transportation department of a state government plans to replace an inadequate highway bridge, the state must first contract with archaeologists to identify and protect any significant resources that might be affected by this new construction.

A series of legislative acts starting with the Historic Preservation Act of 1966 require cultural resource management for any construction project that is partially funded or licensed by the U.S. government. As a result, the specialization of cultural resource management has flourished. Numerous agencies—such as the Army Corps of Engineers, the National Park Service, the U.S. Forest Service, and the U.S. Natural Resource Conservation Service—employ archaeologists to assist in the preservation, restoration, and salvage of archaeological resources. Other countries, such as Canada and the United Kingdom, have programs very similar to those of the United States, and from Chile to China various governments use archaeological expertise to manage their cultural heritage.

In the United States when cultural resource management work or other archaeological investigation unearths Native American cultural items or human remains, federal laws come into the picture again. The Native American Graves Protection and Repatriation Act (NAGPRA), passed in 1990, provides a process for the return of these remains to lineal descendants, culturally affiliated Indian tribes, and Native Hawaiian organizations. NAGPRA has become central to the work of anthropologists who study Paleo-Indian cultures in the United States. The Kennewick Man controversy (see photo on

the previous page) highlights some of the ethics debates surrounding NAGPRA.

In addition to working in all the capacities mentioned, archaeologists also consult for engineering firms to help them prepare environmental impact statements. Some of these archaeologists operate out of universities and colleges, while others are on the staff of independent consulting firms. When state legislation sponsors any kind of archaeological work, it is referred to as *contract archaeology*.

Physical Anthropology

Physical anthropology, also called *biological anthropology*, focuses on humans as biological organisms. Traditionally, biological anthropologists concentrated on human evolution, primatology, growth and development, human adaptation, and forensics. Today, **molecular anthropology**, or the anthropological study of genes and genetic relationships, contributes significantly to our understanding of human evolution, adaptation, and diversity. Comparisons among groups separated by time, geography, or the frequency of a particular gene can reveal how humans have adapted and where they have migrated. As experts in the anatomy of human bones and tissues, physical anthropologists lend their knowledge about the body to applied areas such as gross anatomy laboratories, public health, and criminal investigations.

PALEOANTHROPOLOGY

Dealing with much greater time spans than other branches of anthropology, **paleoanthropology** focuses on biological changes through time (evolution) to understand how, when, and why we became the kind of organisms we are

▲▲▲

archaeology The study of human cultures through the recovery and analysis of material remains and environmental data.

historical archaeology The archaeological study of places for which written records exist.

bioarchaeology The archaeological study of human remains, emphasizing the preservation of cultural and social processes in the skeleton.

cultural resource management A branch of archaeology concerned with survey and/or excavation of archaeological and historical remains that might be threatened by construction or development; also involved with policy surrounding protection of cultural resources.

physical anthropology The systematic study of humans as biological organisms. Also known as *biological anthropology*.

molecular anthropology The anthropological study of genes and genetic relationships, which contributes significantly to our understanding of human evolution, adaptation, and diversity.

paleoanthropology The anthropological study of biological changes through time (evolution) to understand the origins and predecessors of the present human species.

▼▼▼

---

[10]Rathje, W., & Murphy, C. (2001). *Rubbish! The archaeology of garbage.* Tucson: University of Arizona Press.

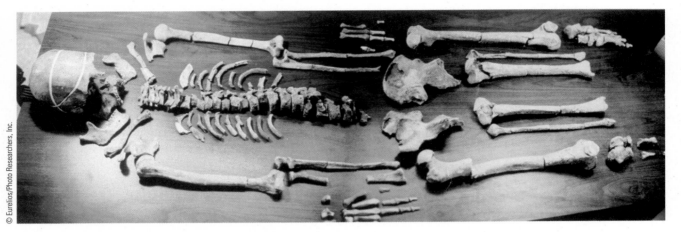

▲▲▲ The "Ancient One" and the "Kennewick Man" both refer to the 9,300-year-old skeletal remains that were found in 1996 near Kennewick, Washington. Surrounded by controversy since its discovery, Kennewick Man is among the oldest human remains ever unearthed in the western hemisphere and has great potential to advance scientific understanding of ancient lifeways and migration patterns in the Americas. Because Kennewick Man was found within their ancestral homelands, a group of Native American tribes claimed the remains under the Native American Graves Protection and Repatriation Act (NAGPRA). Viewing these human bones as belonging to an ancestor, they wish to return them to the earth in a respectful ceremony. Scientists challenged this in federal court, and in 2004 the scientists were granted permission to continue research and analysis of the remains. Doug Owsley, the forensic anthropologist from the Smithsonian Institution who is leading the research team, has said that scientific investigation is yielding even more information than expected. Because conflicting worldviews are at the center of this controversy, it is unlikely that it will be easily resolved.

today. In biological terms, we humans are primates, one of the many kinds of mammals. Because we share a common ancestry with other primates, most specifically apes, paleoanthropologists look back to the earliest primates (65 or so million years ago, abbreviated mya), or even the earliest mammals (225 mya), to reconstruct the complex path of human evolution. Paleoanthropology, unlike other evolutionary studies, takes a **biocultural** approach focusing on the interaction of biology and culture.

Comparing the fossilized skeletons of our ancestors to other fossils and to the bones of living groups, and combining this knowledge with biochemical and genetic evidence, allows paleoanthropologists to reconstruct the course of human evolutionary history. With each new fossil discovery, paleoanthropologists have another piece to add to the puzzle. As we will see in later chapters, genetic evidence establishes the close relationship between humans and the African ape species—chimpanzees, bonobos, and gorillas. Genetic analyses indicate that the distinctive human line split from the apes sometime between 5 and 8 million years ago.

PRIMATOLOGY

Studying the anatomy and behavior of the other primates helps us understand what we share with our closest living relatives and what makes humans unique. Therefore, **primatology,** or the study of living and fossil primates, is a vital part of physical anthropology. Primates include the Asian and African apes, as well as monkeys, lemurs, lorises, and tarsiers.

Biologically, humans are members of the ape family—large-bodied, broad-shouldered primates with no tail. Detailed studies of ape behavior in the wild indicate that the sharing of learned behavior is a significant part of their social life. Increasingly, primatologists designate the shared, learned behavior of nonhuman apes as *culture*. For example, tool use and communication systems indicate the elementary basis of language in some ape societies. Primate studies offer scientifically grounded perspectives on the behavior of our ancestors, as well as greater appreciation and respect for the abilities of our closest living relatives. As human activity encroaches on all parts of the world, many primate species are endangered. Primatologists often advocate for the preservation of primate habitats so that these remarkable animals will be able to continue to inhabit the earth with us.

HUMAN GROWTH, ADAPTATION, AND VARIATION

Some physical anthropologists specialize in the study of human growth and development. They examine biological mechanisms of growth as well as the impact of the environment on the growth process. For example, Franz Boas, a pioneer of American anthropology of the

Though Jane Goodall originally began her studies of chimpanzees to shed light on the behavior of our distant ancestors, the knowledge she has amassed through over forty years in the field has reinforced how similar we are. In turn, this British primatologist has devoted her career to championing the rights of our closest living relatives.

early 20th century, compared the heights of immigrants who spent their childhood in the "old country" to the increased heights obtained by their children who grew up in the United States. Today, physical anthropologists study the impact of disease, pollution, and poverty on growth. Comparisons between human and nonhuman primate growth patterns can provide clues to the evolutionary history of humans. Detailed anthropological studies of the hormonal, genetic, and physiological bases of healthy growth in living humans also contribute significantly to the health of children today.

Studies of human adaptation focus on the capacity of humans to adapt or adjust to their material environment— biologically and culturally. This branch of physical anthropology takes a comparative approach to humans living today in a variety of environments. Humans are the only primate group to inhabit the entire earth. Though cultural adaptations make it possible for humans to live in some environmental extremes, biological adaptations also contribute to survival in extreme cold, heat, and high altitude.

Some of these biological adaptations are built into the genetic makeup of populations. The long period of human growth and development provides ample opportunity for the environment to shape the human body. *Developmental adaptations* are responsible for some features of human variation such as the enlargement of the right ventricle of the heart to help push blood to the lungs among the Quechua Indians of the altiplano, or Andean highlands, that extend along the western rim of South America. *Physiological adaptations* are short-term changes in response to a particular environmental stimulus. For example, if a woman who normally lives at sea level flies to La Paz, Bolivia—a city at an altitude of 3,660 meters (nearly 12,000 feet)—her body will undergo a series of physiological responses, such as increased production of the red blood cells that carry oxygen. All of these kinds of biological adaptations contribute to present-day human variation.

Genetically based human differences include visible traits such as height, body build, and skin color,

as well as biochemical factors such as blood type and susceptibility to certain diseases. Still, we remain members of a single species. Physical anthropology applies all the techniques of modern biology to achieve fuller understanding of human variation and its relationship to the different environments in which people have lived. Physical anthropologists' research on human variation has debunked false notions of biologically defined races, a notion based on widespread misinterpretation of human variation.

FORENSIC ANTHROPOLOGY

One of the many practical applications of physical anthropology is **forensic anthropology**—the identification

▲▲

biocultural An approach that focuses on the interaction of biology and culture.

primatology The study of living and fossil primates.

forensic anthropology The analysis of human skeletal remains for legal purposes.

▼▼

ANTHROPOLOGY APPLIED

Forensic Anthropology: Voices for the Dead

The work of Clyde C. Snow, Karen Burns, Amy Zelson Mundorff, and Michael Blakey

Forensic anthropology is the analysis of skeletal remains for legal purposes. Law enforcement authorities call upon forensic anthropologists to use skeletal remains to identify murder victims, missing persons, or people who have died in disasters, such as plane crashes. Forensic anthropologists have also contributed substantially to the investigation of human rights abuses in all parts of the world by identifying victims and documenting the cause of their death.

Among the best-known forensic anthropologists is Clyde C. Snow. He has been practicing in this field for forty years, first for the Federal Aviation Administration and more recently as a freelance consultant. In addition to the usual police work, Snow has studied the remains of General George Armstrong Custer and his men from the 1876 battlefield at Little Big Horn, and in 1985 he went to Brazil, where he identified the remains of the notorious Nazi war criminal Josef Mengele.

Snow was also instrumental in establishing the first forensic team devoted to documenting cases of human rights abuses around the world. This began in 1984 when he went to Argentina at the request of a newly elected civilian government to help with the identification of remains of the *desaparecidos*, or

"disappeared ones," the 9,000 or more people who were eliminated by government death squads during seven years of military rule. A year later, he returned to give expert testimony at the trial of nine junta members and to teach Argentineans how to recover, clean, repair, preserve, photograph, x-ray, and analyze bones. Besides providing factual accounts of the fate of victims to their surviving kin and refuting the assertions of revisionists that the massacres never happened, the work of Snow and his Argentinean associates was crucial in convicting several military officers of kidnapping, torture, and murder.

Since Snow's pioneering work, forensic anthropologists have become increasingly involved in the investigation of human rights abuses in all parts of the world—from Chile to Guatemala, Haiti, the Philippines, Rwanda, Iraq, Bosnia, and Kosovo. Meanwhile, they continue to do important work for more typical clients. In the United States these clients include the Federal Bureau of Investigation and city, state, and county medical examiners' offices.

Forensic anthropologists specializing in skeletal remains commonly work closely with forensic archaeologists. Their interaction is rather like that between a forensic pathologist, who examines a

corpse to establish time and manner of death, and a crime scene investigator, who searches the site for clues. While the forensic anthropologist deals with the human remains—often only bones and teeth—the forensic archaeologist controls the site, recording the position of all the relevant finds and recovering any clues associated with the remains.

In Rwanda, for example, a team assembled in 1995 to investigate a mass atrocity for the United Nations included archaeologists from the U.S. National Park Service's Midwest Archaeological Center. They performed the standard archaeological procedures of mapping the site, determining its boundaries, photographing and recording all surface finds, and excavating, photographing, and recording buried skeletons and associated materials in mass graves.[a]

In another example, Karen Burns of the University of Georgia was part of a team sent to northern Iraq after the 1991 Gulf War to investigate alleged atrocities. On a military base where there had been many executions, she excavated the remains of a man's body found lying on its side facing Mecca, conforming to Islamic practice. Although there was no intact clothing, two threads of polyester used to sew clothing were found along the sides of both legs. Although the

---

of human skeletal remains for legal purposes. In addition to helping law enforcement authorities identify murder victims, forensic anthropologists investigate human rights abuses such as systematic genocide, terrorism, and war crimes. These specialists use details of skeletal anatomy to establish the age, sex, population affiliation, and stature of the deceased. Forensic anthropologists can also determine whether the person was right- or left-handed,

exhibited any physical abnormalities, or had experienced trauma.

While forensics relies upon differing frequencies of certain skeletal characteristics to establish population affiliation, it is nevertheless false to say that all people from a given population have a particular type of skeleton. See the Anthropology Applied feature above to read about the work of several forensic anthropologists and forensic archaeologists.

AP Images/Rodrigo Abd

▲▲▲ The excavation of mass graves by the Guatemalan Foundation for Forensic Anthropology (Fernando Moscoso Moller, director) documents the human rights abuses committed during Guatemala's bloody civil war, a conflict that left 200,000 people dead and another 40,000 missing. In 2009, in a mass grave in the Quiche region, Diego Lux Tzunux uses his cell phone to photograph the skeletal remains believed to belong to his brother Manuel who disappeared in 1980. Genetic analysis allows forensic anthropologists to confirm the identity of individuals so that family members can know the fate of their loved ones. The analysis of skeletal remains provides evidence of the torture and massacre sustained by these individuals.

supervise and coordinate the management, treatment, and cataloguing of people who lost their lives in the tragedy.

Also in lower Manhattan, in 1991 construction workers discovered an African burial ground dating from the 17th and 18th centuries. Archaeological investigation of the burial ground revealed the horror of slavery in North America; researchers' findings showed that even young children were worked to such an extreme that their spines were fractured. Biological archaeologist Michael Blakey, who led the research team, notes:

> Although bioarchaeology and forensics are often confused, when skeletal biologists use the population as the unit of analysis (rather than the individual), and incorporate cultural and historical context (rather than simply ascribing biological characteristics), and report on the lifeways of a past community (rather than on a crime for the police and courts), it is bioarchaeology rather than forensics.[c]

As we have just seen, forensic anthropologists analyze human remains for a variety of purposes. Their work makes a vital contribution to the documentation and correction of atrocities committed by humans of the past and present. ▪

[a]Conner, M. (1996). The archaeology of contemporary mass graves. *SAA Bulletin 14* (4), 6, 31.
[b]Cornwell, T. (1995, November 10). Skeleton staff. *Times Higher Education*, 20.
[c]Blakey, M. (2003, October 29). Personal communication.

threads survived, the clothing, because it was made of natural fiber, had decayed. "Those two threads at each side of the leg just shouted that his family didn't bury him," says Burns.[b] Proper though his position was, no Islamic family would bury their own in a garment sewn with polyester thread; proper ritual would require a simple shroud.

In recent years two major anthropological analyses of skeletal remains have occurred in New York City dealing with both present and past atrocities. Amy Zelson Mundorff, a forensic anthropologist for the city's Office of the Chief Medical Examiner, was injured in the World Trade Center terrorist attack on September 11, 2001. Two days later she returned to work to

Anthropology, Science, and the Humanities

With its broad scope of subjects and methods, anthropology has sometimes been called the most humane of the sciences and the most scientific of the humanities—a designation that most anthropologists accept with pride.

Given their intense involvement with people of all times and places, anthropologists have amassed considerable information about human failure and success, weakness and greatness—the real stuff of the humanities. While anthropologists steer clear of a "cold" impersonal scientific approach that reduces people and the things they do and think to mere numbers, their quantitative studies have contributed substantially to the scientific study of the human condition. But even the most scientific anthropologists always keep in mind that human societies are made up of individuals with rich assortments of emotions and aspirations that demand respect.

Beyond this, anthropologists remain committed to the proposition that one cannot fully understand another culture by simply observing it; as the term *participant observation* implies, one must *experience* it as well. This same commitment to fieldwork and to the systematic collection of data, whether it is qualitative or quantitative, is also evidence of the scientific side of anthropology. Anthropology is an **empirical** social science based on observations or information about humans taken in through the senses and verified by others, rather than on intuition or faith. But anthropology is distinguished from other sciences by the diverse ways in which scientific research is conducted within this discipline.

Science, a carefully honed way of producing knowledge, aims to reveal and explain the underlying logic, the structural processes that make the world tick. The creative scientific endeavor seeks testable explanations for observed phenomena, ideally in terms of the workings of hidden but unchanging principles or laws. Two basic ingredients are essential for this: imagination and skepticism. Imagination, though having the potential to lead us astray, helps us recognize unexpected ways phenomena might be ordered and to think of old things in new ways. Without it, there can be no science. Skepticism allows us to distinguish fact (an observation independently verified by others) from fancy, to test our speculations, and to prevent our imaginations from running away with us.

In their search for explanations, scientists do not assume that things are always as they appear on the surface. After all, what could be more obvious than the earth staying still while the sun travels around it every day?

Like other scientists, anthropologists often begin their research with a **hypothesis** (a tentative explanation or hunch) about the possible relationships among certain observed facts or events. By gathering various kinds of data that seem to ground such suggested explanations on evidence, anthropologists come up with a **theory**—an explanation supported by a reliable body of data. In their effort to demonstrate connections among *known* facts or events, anthropologists may discover *unexpected* facts, events, or relationships. An important function of theory is that it guides us in our explorations and may result in new knowledge. Equally important, the newly discovered facts may provide evidence that certain explanations, however popular or firmly believed to be true, are unfounded. When the evidence is lacking or fails to support the suggested explanations, promising hypotheses or attractive hunches must be dropped. In other words, anthropology relies on empirical evidence. Moreover,

no scientific theory—no matter how widely accepted by the international community of scholars—is beyond challenge.

It is important to distinguish between scientific theories—which are always open to future challenges born of new evidence or insights—and doctrine. A **doctrine,** or dogma, is an assertion of opinion or belief formally handed down by an authority as true and indisputable. For instance, those who accept a creationist doctrine on the origin of the human species as recounted in sacred texts or myths do so on the basis of religious authority, conceding that such views may be contrary to genetic, geological, biological, or other explanations. Such doctrines cannot be tested or proved one way or another: They are accepted as matters of faith.

Straightforward though the scientific approach may seem, its application is not always easy. For instance, once a hypothesis has been proposed, the person who suggested it is strongly motivated to verify it, and this can cause one to unwittingly overlook negative evidence and unanticipated findings. This is a familiar problem in all science as noted by paleontologist Stephen Jay Gould: "The greatest impediment to scientific innovation is usually a conceptual lock, not a factual lock."[11] Because culture provides humans with their concepts and shapes our very thoughts, it can be challenging to frame hypotheses or develop interpretations that are not culture-bound. The anthropological principle that culture shapes our thoughts created a cascade of keys to previously sealed conceptual locks. By encompassing both humanism and science, the discipline of anthropology can draw on its internal diversity to overcome conceptual locks.

Fieldwork

Anthropologists are keenly aware that their personal and cultural background may shape their research questions or even affect their actual observations. To avoid these pitfalls they rely heavily on a technique that has been successful in other disciplines: They immerse themselves in the data to the fullest extent possible. In the process, anthropologists become so thoroughly familiar with even the smallest details of the culture they study that they can begin to recognize underlying patterns in the data, many of which might have been overlooked. Recognition of such patterns enables anthropologists to frame meaningful hypotheses, which then may be subjected

---

[11]Gould, S. J. (1989). *Wonderful life* (p. 226). New York: Norton.

to further testing or validation in the field. Within anthropology, fieldwork completes total immersion in the data.

Although fieldwork was introduced earlier in the chapter in connection with cultural anthropology, it is characteristic of *all* the anthropological subdisciplines. Archaeologists and paleoanthropologists excavate sites in the field. A biological anthropologist interested in the effects of globalization on nutrition and growth will live in the field among a community of people to study this question. A primatologist might live among a group of chimpanzees or baboons just as a linguist will study the language of a community by living with that group. Such immersion challenges anthropologists to be constantly aware of the ways that cultural factors influence the research questions. Anthropological researchers self-monitor through constantly checking their own biases and assumptions as they work; they present these self-reflections along with their observations, a practice known as *reflexivity*.

Unlike many other social scientists, anthropologists usually do not go into the field armed with prefigured questionnaires. Though they will have completed considerable background research and devised some tentative hypotheses, anthropologists recognize that maintaining an open mind can lead to many of the best discoveries. As fieldwork proceeds, anthropologists sort out their observations, sometimes by formulating and testing limited or low-level hypotheses or by intuition. Anthropologists work closely with the community so that the research process becomes a collaborative effort. The results are constantly checked for consistency, for if the parts fail to fit together in a manner that is consistent, then anthropologists know that a mistake may have been made and that further inquiry is necessary. Validity, or the reliability of the research conclusions, is established through the replication of observations and/or experiments by other researchers. It therefore becomes obvious if one's colleagues have gotten it right.

Traditional validation by others is uniquely challenging in anthropology because observational access is often limited. Contact with a particular research site can be constrained by a number of factors. Difficulties of travel, obtaining permits, insufficient funding, or social, political, and environmental conditions can hamper the process, and what may be observed in a certain context at a certain time may not be at others, and so on. Thus, one researcher cannot easily confirm the reliability or completeness of another's account. For this reason, anthropologists bear a special responsibility for accurate reporting. In the final research report, she or he must be clear about several basic things: Why was a particular location selected as a re-search site? What were the research objectives? What were the local conditions during fieldwork? Which local individuals provided the key information and major insights? How were the data collected and recorded? How did the researcher check his or her own biases? Without such background information, it is difficult for others to judge the validity of the account and the soundness of the researcher's conclusions.

On a personal level, fieldwork requires the researcher to step out of his or her cultural comfort zone into a world that is unfamiliar and sometimes unsettling. Anthropologists in the field are likely to face a host of challenges—physical, social, mental, political, and ethical. They may have to deal with the physical challenge of adjusting to unfamiliar food, climate, and hygiene conditions. Typically, anthropologists in the field struggle with emotional and psychological challenges such as loneliness, feeling like a perpetual outsider, being socially awkward in their new cultural setting, and having to be alert around the clock because anything that is happening or being said may be significant to their research. Political challenges include the possibility of unwittingly letting oneself be used by factions within the community, or being viewed with suspicion by government authorities who may see the anthropologist as a spy. And there are ethical dilemmas: What does one do if faced with a troubling cultural practice such as female circumcision? How does the anthropologist deal with demands for food supplies or medicine? Is it acceptable to use deception to gain vital information?

At the same time, fieldwork often leads to tangible and meaningful personal, professional, and social rewards, ranging from lasting friendships to vital knowledge and insights concerning the human condition. Something of the meaning of anthropological fieldwork—its usefulness and its impact on researcher and subject in a context of mutual cooperation and respect—is conveyed in the following Original Study featuring arctic archaeologist Anne Jensen and the Inupiat Eskimo community of Barrow, Alaska.

▲▲▲

empirical An approach based on observations of the world rather than on intuition or faith.

hypothesis A tentative explanation of the relationships among certain phenomena.

theory In science, an explanation of natural phenomena, supported by a reliable body of data.

doctrine An assertion of opinion or belief formally handed down by an authority as true and indisputable.

▼▼▼

ORIGINAL STUDY

Whispers from the Ice

By Sherry Simpson

People grew excited when a summer rainstorm softened the bluff known as Ukkuqsi, sloughing off huge chunks of earth containing remains of historic and prehistoric houses, part of the old village that predates the modern community of Barrow. Left protruding from the slope was a human head. Archaeologist Anne Jensen happened to be in Barrow buying strapping tape when the body appeared. Her firm, SJS Archaeological Services, Inc., was closing a field season at nearby Point Franklin, and Jensen offered the team's help in a kind of archaeological triage to remove the body before it eroded completely from the earth.

The North Slope Borough hired her and Glenn Sheehan, both associated with Pennsylvania's Bryn Mawr College, to conduct the work. The National Science Foundation, which supported the 3-year Point Franklin project, agreed to fund the autopsy and subsequent analysis of the body and artifacts. The Ukkuqsi excavation quickly became a community event. In remarkably sunny and calm weather, volunteers troweled and picked through the thawing soil, finding trade beads, animal bones, and other items. Teenage boys worked alongside grandmothers. The smell of sea mammal oil, sweet at first then corrupt, mingled with ancient organic odors of decomposed vegetation.

One man searched the beach for artifacts that had eroded from the bluff, discovering such treasures as two feather parkas.

Elder Silas Negovanna, originally of Wainwright, visited several times, "more or less out of curiosity to see what they have in mind," he said. George Leavitt, who lives in a house on the bluff, stopped by one day while carrying home groceries and suggested a way to spray water to thaw the soil without washing away valuable artifacts. Tour groups added the excavation to their rounds.

"This community has a great interest in archaeology up here just because it's so recent to their experience," says oral historian Karen Brewster, a tall young woman who interviews elders as part of her work with the North Slope Borough's division of Inupiat History, Language, and Culture. "The site's right in town, and everybody was really fascinated by it."

Slowly, as the workers scraped and shoveled, the earth surrendered its historical hoard: carved wooden bowls, ladles, and such clothing as a mitten made from polar bear hide, bird-skin parkas, and mukluks. The items spanned prehistoric times, dated in Barrow to before explorers first arrived in 1826.

The work prompted visiting elders to recall when they or their parents lived in traditional sod houses and relied wholly on the land and sea for sustenance. Some remembered sliding down the hill as children, before the sea gnawed away the slope. Others described the site's use as a lookout for whales or ships. For the archaeologists, having elders stand beside them and identify items and historical context is like hearing the past whispering in their ears. Elders often know from experience, or from stories, the answers to the scientists' questions about how items were used or made. "In this instance, usually the only puzzled people are the archaeologists," jokes archaeologist Sheehan.

A modern town of 4,000, Barrow exists in a cultural continuum, where history is not detached or remote but still pulses through contemporary life. People live,

hunt, and fish where their ancestors did, but they can also buy fresh vegetables at the store and jet to other places. Elementary school classes include computer and Inupiaq language studies. Caribou skins, still ruddy with blood, and black brant carcasses hang near late-model cars outside homes equipped with television antennas. A man uses power tools to work on his whaling boat. And those who appear from the earth are not just bodies, but relatives. "We're not a people frozen in time," says Jana Harcharek, an Inupiat Eskimo who teaches Inupiaq and nurtures her culture among young people. "There will always be that connection between us [and our ancestors]. They're not a separate entity."

The past drew still closer as the archaeologists neared the body. After several days of digging through thawed soil, they used water supplied by the local fire station's tanker truck to melt through permafrost until they reached the remains, about 3 feet below the surface. A shell of clear ice encased the body, which rested in what appeared to be a former meat cellar. With the low-pressure play of water from the tanker, the archaeologists teased the icy casket from the frozen earth, exposing a tiny foot. Only then did they realize they had uncovered a child. "That was kind of sad, because she was about my daughter's size," says archaeologist Jensen.

The girl was curled up beneath a baleen toboggan and part of a covering that Inupiat elder Bertha Leavitt identified as a kayak skin by its stitching. The child, who appeared to be 5 or 6, remained remarkably intact after her dark passage through time. Her face was cloaked by a covering that puzzled some onlookers. It didn't look like human hair, or even fur, but something with a feathery residue. Finally they concluded it was a hood from a feather parka made of bird skins. The rest of her body was delineated muscle that had freeze-dried into a dark brick-red color. Her hands rested on her knees, which were drawn up to her chin. Frost particles coated the bends of her arms and legs.

"We decided we needed to go talk to the elders and see what they wanted, to get some kind of feeling as to whether they wanted to bury her right away, or whether they were willing to allow some studies in a respectful manner—studies that would be of some use to residents of the North Slope," Jensen says. Working with community elders is not a radical idea to Jensen or Sheehan, whose previous work in the Arctic has earned them high regard from local officials who appreciate their sensitivity. The researchers feel obligated not only to follow community wishes, but to invite villagers to sites and to share all information through public presentations. In fact, Jensen is reluctant to discuss findings with the press before the townspeople themselves hear it.

"It seems like it's a matter of simple common courtesy," she says. Such consideration can only help researchers, she points out. "If people don't get along with you, they're not going to talk to you, and they're liable to throw you out on your ear." In the past, scientists were not terribly sensitive about such matters, generally regarding human remains—and sometimes living natives—as artifacts themselves. Once, the girl's body would have been hauled off to the catacombs of some university or museum, and relics would have disappeared into exhibit drawers in what Sheehan describes as "hit-and-run archaeology."

"Grave robbers" is how Inupiat Jana Harcharek refers to early Arctic researchers. "They took human remains and their burial goods. It's pretty gruesome. But, of course, at the time they thought they were doing science a big favor. Thank goodness attitudes have changed."

Today, not only scientists but municipal officials confer with the Barrow Elders Council when local people find skeletons from traditional platform burials out on the tundra, or when bodies appear in the house mounds. The elders appreciate such consultations, says Samuel Simmonds, a tall, dignified man known for his carving. A retired Presbyterian minister, he presided at burial ceremonies of the famous "frozen family," ancient Inupiats discovered in Barrow thirteen years ago. "They were part of us, we know that," he says simply, as if the connection between old bones and bodies and living relatives is self-evident. In the case of the newly discovered body, he says, "We were concerned that it was reburied in a respectful manner. They were nice enough to come over and ask us."

The elders also wanted to restrict media attention and prevent photographs of the body except for a few showing her position at the site. They approved a limited autopsy to help answer questions about the body's sex, age, and state of health. She was placed in an orange plastic body bag in a stainless steel morgue with the temperature turned down to below freezing.

With the help of staff at the Indian Health Service Hospital, Jensen sent the girl's still-frozen body to Anchorage's Providence Hospital. There she assisted with an autopsy performed by Dr. Michael Zimmerman of New York City's Mount Sinai Hospital. Zimmerman, an expert on prehistoric frozen bodies, had autopsied Barrow's frozen family in 1982, and was on his way to work on the prehistoric man recently discovered in the Alps.

The findings suggest the girl's life was very hard. She ultimately died of starvation, but also had emphysema caused by a rare congenital disease—the lack of an enzyme that protects the lungs. She probably was sickly and needed extra care all her brief life. The autopsy also found soot in her lungs from the family's sea mammal oil lamps, and she had osteoporosis, which was caused by a diet exclusively of meat from marine mammals. The girl's stomach was empty, but her intestinal tract contained dirt and animal fur. That remains a mystery and raises questions about the condition of the rest of the family. "It's not likely that she would be hungry and everyone else well fed," Jensen says.

That the girl appears to have been placed deliberately in the cellar provokes further questions about precontact burial practices, which the researchers hope Barrow elders can help answer. Historic accounts indicate the dead often were wrapped in skins and laid out on the tundra on wooden platforms, rather than buried in the frozen earth. But perhaps the entire family was starving and too weak to remove the dead girl from the house, Jensen speculates. "We probably won't ever be able to say, 'This is the way it was,'" she adds. "For that you need a time machine."

The scientific team reported to the elders that radiocarbon dating places the girl's death in about AD 1200. If correct—for dating is technically tricky in the Arctic—the date would set the girl's life about 100 years before her people formed settled whaling villages, Sheehan says.

Following the autopsy and the body's return to Barrow in August, one last request by the elders was honored. The little girl, wrapped in her feather parka, was placed in a casket and buried in a small Christian ceremony next to the grave of the other prehistoric bodies. Hundreds of years after her death, an Inupiat daughter was welcomed back into the midst of her community.

The "rescue" of the little girl's body from the raw forces of time and nature means researchers and the Inupiat people will continue to learn still more about the region's culture. Sheehan and Jensen returned to Barrow in winter 1994 to explain their findings to townspeople. "We expect to learn just as much from them," Sheehan said before the trip. A North Slope Cultural Center scheduled for completion in 1996 will store and display artifacts from the dig sites.

Laboratory tests and analysis also will contribute information. The archaeologists hope measurements of heavy metals in the girl's body will allow comparisons with modern-day pollution contaminating the sea mammals that Inupiats eat today. The soot damage in her lungs might offer health implications for Third World people who rely on oil lamps, dung fires, and charcoal for heat and light. Genetic tests could illuminate early population movements of Inupiats. The project also serves as a model for good relations between archaeologists and Native people. "The larger overall message from this work is that scientists and communities don't have to be at odds," Sheehan says. "In fact, there are mutual interests that we all have. Scientists have obligations to communities. And when more scientists realize that, and when more communities hold scientists to those standards, then everybody will be happier." ∎

Adapted from Simpson, S. (1995, April). Whispers from the ice. *Alaska*, 23–28. Reprinted by permission of the author.

Field Methods

While fieldwork and the comparative method cut across all anthropological fields, some particular methods are characteristic only of paleoanthropology and archaeology with their focus on humans and their ancestors in the distant past. Other methods are typical of research focused on the cultures of contemporary societies. Some additional methods particular to primatology and linguistic anthropology will be described in Chapters 3 and 9, respectively.

Archaeological and Paleoanthropological Methods

Archaeologists and paleoanthropologists face a dilemma. The only way to thoroughly investigate our past is to excavate sites where biological and cultural remains are found. Unfortunately, excavation results in the site's destruction. Thus anthropologists precisely record the location and context of everything recovered, no matter how small, as they excavate. Without these records, knowledge that can be derived from physical and cultural remains diminishes dramatically.

Archaeologists work with **artifacts,** any object fashioned or altered by humans—a flint scraper, a basket, an axe, or things such as house ruins or walls. An artifact expresses a facet of human culture. Because it is something that someone made, archaeologists like to say that an artifact is a product or representation of human behavior and beliefs, or, in more technical terms, artifacts are **material culture**. Artifacts are not considered in isolation; rather, they are integrated with biological and ecological remains to provide a context that permits reconstruction of past lifeways in broad environmental contexts. Archaeologists and paleoanthropologists place a series of sites connected through space and time in order to focus on sweeping aspects of human experience ranging from settlement and migration patterns to the broad course of human evolutionary history.

Some of the oldest biological remains have survived through the process of fossilization. Broadly defined, a **fossil** is any trace or impression of an organism that has been preserved in the earth's crust from past geologic time. Fossilization typically involves the hard parts of an organism. Bones, teeth, shells, horns, and the woody tissues of plants are the most successfully fossilized materials. Although the soft parts of an organism are rarely fossilized, the casts or impressions of footprints, brains, and even whole bodies have sometimes been found. Entirely preserved fossil skeletons dating from before the cultural practice of burial about 100,000 years ago are exceedingly rare.

Because dead animals quickly attract meat-eating scavengers and bacteria that cause decomposition, they rarely survive long enough to become fossilized. For an organism to become a fossil, some protective substance must cover it soon after death. The materials surrounding the physical remains gradually harden, forming a protective shell around the skeleton of the organism. The internal cavities of bones or teeth and other parts of the skeleton fill in with mineral deposits from the sediment immediately surrounding the specimen. Then the external walls of the bone decay and are replaced by calcium carbonate or silica.

SITES

Where are artifacts and fossils found? Places containing archaeological remains of previous human activity are known as *sites*. There are many kinds of sites, and sometimes it is difficult to define their boundaries, for remains may be strewn over large areas. Sites are even found underwater. Some examples of sites identified by archaeologists and paleoanthropologists are hunting campsites, from which hunters went out to hunt game; kill sites, in which game was killed and butchered; village sites, in which domestic activities took place; and cemeteries, in which the dead, and sometimes their belongings, were buried.

Locating and mapping archaeological sites are vital aspects of archaeological and paleoanthropological investigation. Many sites, particularly very old ones, frequently are buried underground, covered by layers of sediment deposited since the site was in use. Most sites are revealed by the presence of artifacts. But as we go back in time, the association of skeletal and cultural remains becomes less likely. Physical remains dating to times before 2.5 million years ago are found without any associated cultural remains.

While chance may play a crucial role in a site's discovery, survey techniques in which the archaeologist explores and maps large geographic areas allow researchers to plot the sites available for excavation. A survey can be made from the ground, but more common today is the use of remote sensing techniques. Archaeologists have used aerial photographs to find sites since the 1920s. They are still widely used today along with more recent technological innovations such satellite mapping and ground-penetrating radar (GPR).

Climate and geography can influence the discovery of archaeological and paleoanthropological sites. In open areas, sites are visible from the ground by mounds or **soil marks** or stains showing up on the surface of recently plowed fields. In forested regions changes in vegetation provide evidence of a site. For example, the topsoil of ancient storage and refuse pits is often richer in organic matter than that of the surrounding areas, and so it grows distinctive vegetation. At Tikal,

EXCAVATION AND ANALYSIS

Once an investigator identifies a site likely to contribute to the research agenda, he or she plans out an excavation designed to meet the research goals. To begin the excavation, the team clears the land and plots the area as a **grid system,** dividing the surface of the site into squares of equal size, and numbering each square and marking it with stakes. This way, every object found can be located precisely in the square from which it came. Remember, context is everything!

Each grid system has a starting point, such as a large rock, the edge of a stone wall, or an iron rod sunk into the ground located precisely in three dimensions. This point is the reference or **datum point.** At large sites covering several square miles, the plotting may be done in terms of individual structures, numbered according to the squares that make up a giant grid. With great care, archaeological teams dig each square of the grid separately, using trowels to scrape the soil and screens to sift all the loose soils, to recover even the smallest artifacts such as flint chips or beads.

Successful excavation of fossils requires particular skills in the techniques of geology, or ready access to geologic expertise, because paleoanthropological interpretation of the fossil record relies on the placement of the specimen in the rock sequence. Only with surgical skill and great caution can a fossil be removed from its burial place without damage. The paleoanthropologist's toolkit includes an unusual combination of instruments and materials—pickaxes, enamel coating, burlap for bandages, and sculpting plaster.

Excavation involves removing both the fossil and the earth immediately surrounding it, or the matrix, as a single block. In the laboratory many more painstaking hours of work will separate the fossil from the surrounding matrix. Before leaving the discovery area, the investigator makes a thorough sketch map of the terrain and pinpoints the find on geologic maps to aid future investigators.

▲▲▲ Here a diver recovers antique jugs used for transporting wine, olives, olive oil, grain, and other commodities from the underwater site of a shipwreck in the Mediterranean Sea near the village of Kas, Turkey. The shipwreck dates back to the time of the Trojan War (over 3,000 years ago). Underwater archaeologists—led in this expedition by George Bass from the Institute of Nautical Archaeology of Texas A&M University collaborating with the Bodrum Museum of Underwater Archaeology in Istanbul, Turkey—can reconstruct facets of the past, ranging from ancient trade routes to shipbuilding techniques, through the analysis of such remains.

© Waterframe/Alamy

an ancient Maya site in Guatemala, breadnut trees usually grow near the remains of ancient houses, so that archaeologists can use these trees to help guide their search.

Sometimes natural processes, such as soil erosion or droughts, expose sites or fossils. For example, in eastern North America and other areas where shellfish consumption was common, **middens,** prehistoric refuse mounds filled with shells, have been exposed by erosion along coastlines or river banks. As will be seen below, erosion and other geologic processes have played a key role in fossil discovery.

artifact Any object fashioned or altered by humans.

material culture The durable aspects of culture such as tools, structures, and art.

fossil The preserved remains of past life forms.

soil marks The stains that show up on the surface of recently plowed fields that reveal an archaeological site.

midden A refuse or garbage disposal area in an archaeological site.

grid system A system for recording data from an archaeological excavation into three dimensions.

datum point The starting point or reference for a grid system.

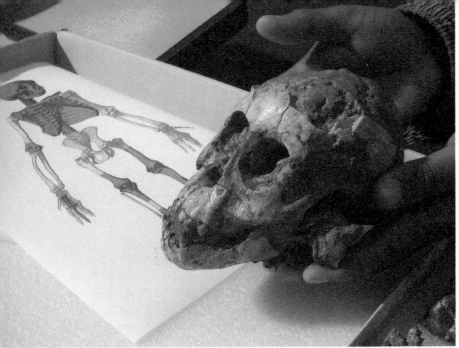

Lealisa Westerhoff/AFP/Getty Images

◄
◄
◄ In September 2006 researchers announced the discovery of a spectacular new fossil—the skeleton of a young child dated to 3.3 million years ago. The fossil was first discovered in the Dikka Area of northern Ethiopia in 2000. Since then, researchers worked on careful recovery and analysis of the fossilized remains so that when the announcement was made in 2006, a great deal was already known about the specimen. Their analyses have determined that this child, a little girl about 3 years old who likely died in a flash flood, was a member of the same species as the famous Lucy specimen (see Chapter 4). Due to the importance of this find, scientists have referred to this child as "Lucy's baby" though the child lived about 150,000 years before Lucy.

For both paleoanthropology and archaeology, at least three hours of laboratory work correspond to a single hour of excavation time. A wide variety of molecular and chemical testing techniques provide evidence about the context and nature of the recovered remains. Establishing the date of remains is particularly vital for the reconstruction of our past.

Remains can be dated by noting their position in the earth, by measuring the amount of chemicals contained in fossil bones and artifacts, or through association with other plant, animal, or cultural remains. These methods, known as **relative dating** techniques, do not establish precise dates for remains. Instead, they establish the relationship among a series of remains by using geologic principles to place remains in chronological order. **Absolute dating** or **chronometric dating** (from the Latin for "measuring time") methods provide actual dates calculated in years "before the present" (BP). Relying upon advances in the disciplines of chemistry and physics, these methods use properties such as rates of decay of radioactive elements. The radioactive elements may be present in the remains themselves or in the surrounding soil. By comparing dates and remains across a variety of sites, anthropologists can scientifically establish actual dates for the major events of geologic and evolutionary history such as human origins, migrations, and technological developments.

Many relative and absolute dating techniques are available, but each has certain weaknesses. Ideally, archaeologists and paleoanthropologists try to utilize as many methods as are appropriate, given the materials available and the funds at their disposal. By doing so, they significantly reduce the risk of error. Several of the most frequently employed dating techniques are presented in Table 1.1.

Ethnographic Methods

For the archaeologist and paleoanthropologist, location of material and physical remains determines where fieldwork must take place. For the ethnographic researcher, the entire world is a potential field site. The research problem or question can drive the choice of field site.

Cultural anthropologists prepare for fieldwork by studying theoretical, historical, ethnographic, and any other literature relevant to the research problem to be investigated, as well as studying all that has previously been documented about the particular culture they wish to study. Having delved into the existing literature, they may then formulate a theoretical framework and research question to guide them in their fieldwork. If possible, ethnographers make a preliminary trip to the field site before moving there for more extended research.

Because anthropologists must be able to communicate with the people they have chosen to study, they will also have to learn the people's language. Many of the 6,000 languages currently spoken in the world have already been recorded and written down, especially during the past hundred years or so. Therefore, anthropologists may learn many different languages prior to their fieldwork.

relative dating In archaeology and paleoanthropology, designating an event, object, or fossil as being older or younger than another by noting the position in the earth, by measuring the amount of chemicals contained in fossil bones and artifacts, or through association with other plant, animal, or cultural remains.

absolute dating (chronometric dating) In archaeology and paleoanthropology, dating archaeological or fossil materials in units of absolute time using scientific properties such as rates of decay of radioactive elements.

Table 1.1 Absolute and Relative Dating Methods Used by Archaeologists and Paleoanthropologists

Dating Method	Time Period	Process and Use	Drawbacks
Stratigraphy	Relative only	Based on the law of superposition, which states that lower layers or strata are older than higher strata; establishing the age of biological and cultural remains based on the layer in which they are found	Site specific; natural forces, such as earthquakes, and human activity, such as burials, disturb stratigraphic relationships
Fluorine analysis	Relative only	Comparing the amount of fluorine from surrounding soil absorbed by specimens after deposition; older remains will have absorbed more fluorine	Site specific
Faunal and floral series	Relative only	Sequencing remains into relative chronological order based on an evolutionary order established in another region with reliable absolute dates; called *palynology* when done with pollen grains	Dependent upon known relationships established elsewhere
Seriation	Relative only	Sequencing cultural remains into relative chronological order based on stylistic features	Dependent on known relationships established elsewhere
Dendrochronology	About 3,000 years before present (BP) maximum	Comparing tree growth rings preserved in a site with a tree of known age	Requires ancient trees of known age
Radiocarbon	Accurate <50,000 BP	Comparing the ratio of radioactive carbon 14 (^{14}C), with a half-life of 5,730 years, to stable carbon (^{12}C) in organic material; after organisms die, only the ^{14}C decays (half of it every 5,730 years), so the ratio between ^{14}C and ^{12}C determines an actual date since death	Increasingly inaccurate when assessing remains from more than 50,000 years ago
Potassium argon (K-Ar)	>200,000 BP	Using volcanic ash, comparing the amount of radioactive potassium (^{40}K), with a half-life of 1.25 billion years, to stable argon (^{40}Ar)	Requires volcanic ash; requires cross-checking due to contamination from atmospheric argon
Amino acid racemization	40,000–180,000 BP	Comparing the ratio of right- and left-sided proteins in a three-dimensional structure; decay after death causes these proteins to change	Variation in leaching of amino acids from soil causes error
Thermoluminescence	Possibly up to 200,000 BP	Measuring the amount of light given off due to radioactivity when the specimen is heated to high temperatures	Technique developed for recent materials such as Greek pottery; not clear how accurate the dates are for older remains
Electron spin resonance	Possibly to about 200,000 BP	Measuring the resonance of trapped electrons in a magnetic field	Works with tooth enamel, not yet developed for bone; problems with accuracy
Fission track	Wide range of times	Measuring the tracks left in crystals by uranium as it decays; good cross-check for K-Ar technique	Useful for dating crystals only
Paleomagnetic reversals	Wide range of times	Measuring the orientation of magnetic particles in stones and linking them to whether the earth's magnetic field pulled toward the north or south during their formation	Large periods of normal or reversed magnetic orientation require dating by some other method; some smaller events are known to interrupt the sequence
Uranium series	40,000–400,000	Measuring the amount of uranium decaying in cave sites	Large error range

© Cengage Learning 2013

IN THE FIELD

When participating in an unfamiliar culture, anthropologists are often helped by one or more generous individuals in the village or neighborhood or a family may take them in. Through participation in the daily routine of a household, they will soon become familiar with the community's basic shared cultural features.

Anthropologists may also formally enlist the assistance of **key consultants**—members of the society being studied who provide information that helps researchers understand the meaning of what they observe. (Early anthropologists referred to such individuals as *informants*.) Just as parents guide a child toward proper behavior, so do these insiders help researchers unravel the mysteries of what at first is a strange and puzzling world. To compensate local individuals for their help in making the anthropologists feel welcome in the community and gain access to the treasure troves of inside information, fieldworkers may thank them for their time and expertise with goods, services, or cash.

Asking questions is fundamental to ethnographic fieldwork and takes place in **informal interviews**—unstructured, open-ended conversations in everyday life—and **formal interviews**—structured question–answer sessions carefully notated as they occur and based on prepared questions. Informal interviews may be carried out anytime and anywhere: on horseback, in a canoe, by a cooking fire, during ritual events, while walking through the community, and so on. Such casual exchanges are essential, for it is often in these conversations that people share most freely. Moreover, questions put forth in formal interviews typically grow out of cultural knowledge and insights gained during informal ones.

Getting people to open up requires dropping all assumptions and cultivating the ability to ask questions and to *really* listen. Questions generally fall into one of two categories: broad, *open-ended questions*, such as, "Can you tell me about your childhood?" and *closed questions* seeking specific pieces of information, such as, "Where and when were you born?"

Researchers employ numerous **eliciting devices**—activities and objects used to draw out individuals and encourage them to recall and share information. For example, an ethnographic researcher may take and share photographs of cultural objects or activities and ask locals to explain what they see in the pictures.

Because many anthropologists still do fieldwork among traditional peoples in all corners of the earth, they may find themselves in distant places about which there is little detailed geographic knowledge. Therefore ethnographers frequently construct maps of the area that document the cultural meaning given to particular geographic features. Satellite geographic information systems (GIS) serve the ethnographer as they do the archaeologist and the paleoanthropologist.

THE ETHNOGRAPHY

After collecting ethnographic information, the next challenge is to piece together all that has been gathered into a coherent whole that accurately describes the culture. Traditionally, ethnographies are detailed written descriptions that document the culture under study

in terms of the research question at hand. Ethnographers may focus on topics such as the circumstances and place of fieldwork itself; historical background; the community or group today; its natural environment, settlement patterns, subsistence practices, networks of kinship relations, and other forms of social organization; marriage and sexuality; economic exchanges; political institutions; myths, sacred beliefs, and ceremonies; and current developments. These may be illustrated with photographs and accompanied by maps, kinship diagrams, and figures showing social and political organization, settlement layout, floor plans of dwellings, seasonal cycles, and so on.

Sometimes ethnographic research is documented not only in writing but also with sound recordings, on film or digital media. Visual records may be used not only for documentation and illustration, but also for analysis or as a means of gathering additional information in interviews. Moreover, motion picture or video footage shot for the sake of documentation and research may also be edited into a documentary film or a digital ethnography, which provides an accurate visual representation of the ethnographic subject.[12]

Anthropology's Comparative Method

The end product of any anthropological research, if properly carried out, is a coherent statement about a people that provides an explanatory framework for understanding the beliefs, behavior, or biology of those who have been studied. And this, in turn, is what permits the anthropologist to frame broader hypotheses about human beliefs, behavior, and biology.

A single instance of any phenomenon is generally insufficient for supporting a plausible hypothesis. Without some basis for comparison, the hypothesis grounded in a single case may be no more than a particular historical coincidence. On the other hand, a single case may be enough to cast doubt on, if not refute, a theory that had previously been held to be valid. For example, the discovery in 1948 that Aborigines living in the tropics of northern Australia put in an average workday of less than 6 hours, while living well above a level of bare sufficiency, was enough to call into question the widely accepted notion that food-foraging peoples are so preoccupied with finding scarce food that they lack time for any of life's more pleasurable activities. The observations

---

[12]See Collier, J., & Collier, M. (1986). *Visual anthropology: Photography as a research method.* Albuquerque: University of New Mexico Press; el Guindi, F. (2004). *Visual anthropology: Essential method and theory.* Walnut Creek, CA: Altamira Press.

made in this anthropological study have since been confirmed many times over in various parts of the world.

Hypothetical explanations of cultural and biological phenomena may be tested through comparison of archaeological, biological, linguistic, historical, and/or ethnographic data for several societies found in a particular region. Carefully controlled comparisons provide a broader basis for drawing general conclusions about humans than does the study of a single culture or population.

A key resource for cross-cultural comparison is the **Human Relations Area Files (HRAF)**, a vast collection of cross-indexed ethnographic and archaeological data catalogued by cultural characteristics and geographic location. Initiated at Yale University in the mid-1900s, this ever-growing data bank classifies more than 700 cultural and biocultural characteristics and includes nearly 400 societies, past and present, from all around the world. Archived in about 300 libraries (on microfiche and/or online) and approaching a million pages of information, the HRAF facilitates comparative research on almost any cultural feature imaginable—warfare, subsistence practices, settlement patterns, birth practices, marriage, rituals, and so on.

Ideally, theories in anthropology are generated from worldwide comparisons or comparisons across species or through time. The cross-cultural researcher examines a global sample of societies in order to discover whether or not hypotheses proposed to explain cultural phenomena or biological variation are universally applicable. The cross-cultural researcher depends upon data gathered by other scholars as well as his or her own. These data can be in various forms: written accounts, artifacts and skeletal collections housed in museums, published descriptions of these collections. Recently, genetic comparisons have become popular as databases have permitted scientists to look at the molecular structure of specific genes or proteins among distinct populations of humans or across species of animals.

Questions of Ethics

The kinds of research carried out by anthropologists, and the settings in which they work, raise a number of important moral questions about the potential uses and abuses of our knowledge. In the early years of the discipline, many anthropologists documented traditional cultures they assumed would disappear due to disease, warfare, or acculturation imposed by colonialism, growing state power, or international market expansion. Some worked as government anthropologists, gathering data used to formulate policies concerning indigenous peoples or even to help predict the behavior of enemies during wartime.

After the colonial era ended half a century ago, anthropologists began to establish a code of ethics to ensure their research does not harm the groups they study.

This code grapples with serious questions: Who will utilize our findings and for what purposes? Who decides what research questions are asked? Who, if anyone, will profit from the research? For example, in the case of research on an ethnic or religious minority whose values may be at odds with dominant mainstream society, will government or corporate interests use anthropological data to suppress that group? And what of traditional communities around the world? Who is to decide what changes should, or should not, be introduced for community "betterment"? And who defines what constitutes betterment—the community, a national government, or an international agency like the World Health Organization? What are the limits of cultural relativism when a traditional practice is considered a human rights abuse globally?

Today, universities require that anthropologists, like other researchers, obtain the **informed consent** of those whom they study. Of course, this requirement is easier to fulfill in some societies or cultures than in others, as most anthropologists recognize. When it is a challenge to obtain informed consent, or even impossible to precisely explain the meaning and purpose of this concept and its actual consequences, anthropologists may protect the identities of individuals, families, or even entire communities by altering their names and locations. For example, when a Dutch anthropologist studied the Sicilian mafia, he did not obtain the informed consent of this violent secret group but opted not to disclose their real identities.[13] Anthropologists deal with matters that are private and sensitive, including things that individuals would prefer not to have generally known about them. How does one write about such important but delicate issues and at the same time protect the privacy of the individuals who have shared their stories?

▲▲

key consultants Members of the society being studied who provide information that helps the researchers understand the meaning of what they observe. Early anthropologists referred to such individuals as *informants*.

informal interview An unstructured, open-ended conversation in everyday life.

formal interview A structured question–answer session, carefully notated as it occurs and based on prepared questions.

eliciting devices Activities and objects used to draw out individuals and encourage them to recall and share information.

Human Relations Area Files (HRAF) A vast collection of cross-indexed ethnographic, biocultural, and archaeological data catalogued by cultural characteristics and geographic location; archived in about 300 libraries (on microfiche or online).

informed consent A formal recorded agreement between the subject and the researcher to participate in the research; federally mandated for all researchers in the United States and Europe.

▼▼

---

[13]Blok, A. (1974). *The mafia of a Sicilian village 1860–1960.* New York: Harper & Row.

The dilemma anthropologists face is also recognized in the preamble of the code of ethics of the American Anthropological Association (AAA). The code, first formalized in 1971, was modified to its current form in 1998. This document outlines the various ethical responsibilities and moral obligations of anthropologists, including this central maxim: "Anthropological researchers must do everything in their power to ensure that their research does not harm the safety, dignity, or privacy of the people with whom they work, conduct research, or perform other professional activities."

The AAA ethics statement is an educational document that lays out the rules and ideals applicable to anthropologists in all the subdisciplines. While the AAA has no legal authority, it does issue policy statements on ethical research questions as they come up. For example, recently the AAA recommended that field notes from medical settings should be protected and not subject to subpoena in malpractice lawsuits. This honors the ethical imperative to protect the privacy of individuals who have shared their stories with anthropologists.

Emerging technologies have ethical implications that impact anthropological inquiry. For example, the ability to sequence and patent particular genes has led to debates about who has the right to hold a patent—the persons from whom the particular genes were obtained or the researcher who studies the genes? Similarly, as seen in the Kennewick Man controversy mentioned on pages 11 and 12, the ethics of ownership when it comes to ancient remains are particularly thorny.

Given the radical changes taking place in the world today, a scientific understanding of the past has never been more important. Do ancient remains belong to the scientist, to the people living in the region under scientific investigation, or to whoever happens to have possession of them? Market forces convert these remains into very expensive collectibles and lead to systematic mining of archaeological and fossil sites. Collaborations between local people and scientists not only preserves the ancient remains from market forces, but also honors the connections of indigenous people to the places and remains under study.

To sort out the answers to all of the above questions, anthropologists recognize that they have special obligations to three sets of people: those whom they study, those who fund the research, and those in the profession who rely on the findings to increase our collective knowledge. Because fieldwork requires a relationship of trust between fieldworkers and the community in which they work, the anthropologist's first responsibility clearly is to the people who have shared their stories and to their greater community. Everything possible must be done to protect their physical, social, and psychological welfare and to honor their dignity and privacy. This task is frequently complex. For example, telling the story of a people gives information both to relief agencies who might help them and to others who might take advantage of them.

Even though anthropologists consider a people's right to maintain their own culture as fundamental, any connections with outsiders can endanger the cultural identity of the community being studied. To surmount this obstacle, anthropologists frequently collaborate with and contribute to the communities in which they work. This allows the people being studied to have some say about how their stories are told.

Anthropology and Globalization

A holistic perspective and a long-term commitment to understanding the human species in all its variety equip anthropologists to grapple with an issue that has overriding importance for all of us today: **globalization**. This term refers to worldwide interconnectedness, evidenced in global movements of natural resources, trade goods, human labor, finance capital, information, and infectious diseases. Although worldwide travel, trade relations, and information flow have existed for several centuries, the pace and magnitude of these long-distance exchanges have picked up enormously in recent decades; the Internet, in particular, has greatly expanded information exchange capacities.

The powerful forces driving globalization are technological innovations, cost differences among countries, faster knowledge transfers, and increased trade and financial integration among countries. Touching almost everybody's life on the planet, globalization is about economics as much as politics, and it changes human relations and ideas as well as our natural environments. Even geographically remote communities are quickly becoming more interdependent through globalization.

Doing research in all corners of the world, anthropologists are confronted with the impact of globalization on human communities wherever they are located. As participant observers, they describe and try to explain how individuals and organizations respond to the massive changes confronting them. Anthropologists may also find out how local responses sometimes change the global forces sweeping through communities.

Dramatically increasing every year, globalization can be a two-edged sword. It may generate economic growth and prosperity, but it also undermines long-established institutions and contributes to the erosion of traditional cultures. Generally, globalization has brought significant gains to those with more education in wealthier countries, while doing little to boost those in developing countries. Upheavals born of globalization are key causes for rising levels of ethnic and religious conflict throughout the world.

Since all of us now live in a global village, we can no longer afford the luxury of ignoring our neighbors, no matter how distant they may seem. In this age of globalization, anthropology equips global citizens to approach one another openly and without ethnocentrism. Anthropology

◄◄
◄ The symbolic burning of opium, part of an antidrug demonstration, outside of the compound of the governor of Farah Province in Afghanistan, belies the ongoing war fueled by opium money. For years, the global opium economy has funded a weapons buildup for warlords and fortunes for those who traffic drugs to Europe and North America. Despite the official Afghan policy and efforts by foreign governments to end the poppy trade, opium-generated capital continues to fund militias and the armed ethnic conflicts that persist in Afghanistan.

may not only provide humanity with useful insights concerning diversity, but it may also assist us in avoiding or overcoming significant problems born of that diversity.

For example, in the United States today discrimination based on notions of race continues to affect economic, political, and social relations. Anthropologists have shown that the concept of race is far from the biological reality it is presumed to be. The classification of human groups into higher and lower racial types emerged in the 18th century as an ideological vehicle for justifying European dominance over Africans and American Indians. In fact, differences of skin color are simply surface adaptations to different climactic zones and have nothing to do with physical or mental capabilities. Indeed, geneticists find far more biological variation *within* any given human population than *among* them. In short, human "races" are divisive categories based on prejudice, false ideas of differences, and erroneous notions of the superiority of one's own group. Given the importance of this issue, race will be discussed further in Chapter 7.

A second example involves the issue of same-sex marriage. In 1989, Denmark became the first country to enact a comprehensive set of legal protections for same-sex couples, known as the Registered Partnership Act. At this writing, ten countries—including Argentina, Belgium, Canada, Iceland, Netherlands, Norway, Portugal, South Africa, Spain, and Sweden—and some individual states within the United States have passed similar laws, variously named,

and numerous countries around the world are considering or have passed legislation providing people in homosexual unions the benefits and protections afforded by marriage.[14] In these societies same-sex marriages are considered socially acceptable and allowed by law, even though opposite-sex marriages are far more common.

As individuals, countries, and states struggle to define the boundaries of legal protections they will grant to same-sex couples, the anthropological perspective on marriage is useful. Anthropologists have documented same-sex marriages in human societies in various parts of the world, where they are regarded as acceptable under appropriate circumstances. Homosexual behavior occurs in the animal world just as it does among humans.[15] The key difference between people and other animals is that human societies possess beliefs regarding homosexual behavior, just as they do for heterosexual behavior. An understanding of global variation in marriage patterns and sexual behavior does not dictate that one pattern is more right than another. It simply illustrates that all human societies define boundaries for social relationships.

A final example relates to the common confusion of *state* with *nation*. Anthropology makes an important distinction between these two: States are politically organized, internationally recognized territories, whereas nations are socially organized bodies of people who share ethnicity—a common origin, language, and cultural heritage. For example, the Kurds constitute a nation, but their homeland is divided among several states: Iran, Iraq, Turkey, and Syria. The international boundaries among these states were drawn up after World War I, with little

[14]Merin, Y. (2002). *Equality for same-sex couples: The legal recognition of gay partnerships in Europe and the United States.* Chicago: University of Chicago Press; Axel-Lute, P. (2002, September). Same-sex marriage: A selective bibliography of the legal literature. http://law-library.rutgers.edu/SSM.html (retrieved August 23, 2011). Up-to-date overviews and breaking news on the global status of same-sex marriage are posted on the Internet by the Partners Task Force for Gay & Lesbian Couples at www.buddybuddy.com.

[15]Kirkpatrick, R. C. (2000). The evolution of human homosexual behavior. *Current Anthropology 41,* 384.

▲▲

globalization Worldwide interconnectedness, evidenced in global movements of natural resources, trade goods, human labor, finance capital, information, and infectious diseases.

▼▼

regard for the region's ethnic groups or nations. Similar processes have taken place throughout the world, especially in Asia and Africa, which have often made the political conditions in these countries inherently unstable. As we will see in later chapters, states and nations rarely coincide—nations being split among different states, and states typically being dominated by members of one nation who commonly use their control to gain access to the land, resources, and labor of other nationalities within the state. Most of the armed conflicts in the world today derive from these arrangements, rather than from acts of tribalism or terrorism as is commonly asserted.

As these examples show, ignorance about other peoples and their ways is a cause of serious problems throughout the world. Anthropology offers a way of looking at and understanding the world's peoples—insights that are nothing less than basic skills for survival in this age of globalization. ✳

Chapter Checklist

What is anthropology?

✔ Anthropology is the objective and systematic study of humankind in all times and places.

✔ Anthropology contains four major fields: cultural anthropology, linguistic anthropology, archaeology, and physical or biological anthropology.

✔ In each of anthropology's fields some individuals practice applied anthropology, which uses anthropological knowledge to solve practical problems.

What do anthropologists do in each of its four fields?

✔ Cultural anthropologists study humans in terms of their cultures, the often-unconscious standards by which social groups operate.

✔ Linguistic anthropologists study human languages and may deal with the description of a language, with the history of languages, or with how languages are used in particular social settings.

✔ Archaeologists study human cultures through the recovery and analysis of material remains and environmental data.

✔ Physical anthropologists focus on humans as biological organisms; they particularly emphasize tracing the evolutionary development of the human animal and studying biological variation within the species today.

How do anthropologists conduct research?

✔ Fieldwork, characteristic of all the anthropological subdisciplines, includes complete immersion in research settings ranging from archaeological and paleo-anthropological survey and excavation, to living with a group of primates in their natural habitat, to biological data gathered while living with a group. Ethnographic participant observation with a particular culture or subculture is the classic field method of cultural anthropology.

✔ After the fieldwork of archaeologists and physical anthropologists, researchers conduct laboratory analyses of excavated remains or biological samples collected in the field.

✔ The comparative method is key to all branches of anthropology. Anthropologists make broad comparisons among peoples and cultures—past and present. They also compare related species and fossil groups. Ethnology, the comparative branch of cultural anthropologists, uses a range of ethnographic accounts to construct theories about cultures from a comparative or historical point of view. Ethnologists often focus on a particular aspect of culture, such as religious or economic practices.

How do anthropologists face the ethical challenges that emerge through conducting anthropological research?

✔ Anthropologists must stay aware of the potential uses and abuses of anthropological knowledge and the ways that it is obtained.

✔ The anthropological code of ethics, first formalized in 1971 and continually revised, outlines the moral and ethical responsibilities of anthropologists to the people whom they study, to those who fund the research, and to the profession as a whole.

What can anthropology contribute to the understanding of globalization?

✔ A long tradition of studying the connections among diverse peoples over time gives anthropology a theoretical framework to study globalization in a world increasingly linked through recent technological advancements.

✔ Anthropology equips global citizens to challenge ethnocentrism and to understand human diversity.

How is anthropology different from other disciplines?

✔ Unique among the sciences and humanities, anthropology has long emphasized the study of non-Western societies and a holistic approach, which aims to formulate theoretically valid explanations and interpretations of human diversity based on detailed studies of all aspects of human biology, behavior, and beliefs in all known societies, past and present.

✔ In anthropology, the humanities, social sciences, and natural sciences come together into a genuinely humanistic science. Anthropology's link with the humanities can be seen in its concern with people's beliefs, values, languages, arts, and literature—oral as well as written—but above all in its attempt to convey the experience of living in different cultures.

✔ As part of both the sciences and the humanities, anthropology has essential insights to offer the modern world, particularly in this era of globalization when understanding our neighbors in the global village has become a matter of survival for all.

# Questions for Reflection

1. Anthropology uses a holistic approach to explain all aspects of human beliefs, behavior, and biology. How might anthropology challenge your personal perspective on the following questions: Where did we come from? Why do we act in certain ways? What makes us tick?

2. From the holistic anthropological perspective, humans have one leg in culture and the other in nature. Are there examples from your life that illustrate the interconnectedness of human biology and culture?

3. Globalization can be described as a two-edged sword. How does it foster growth and destruction simultaneously?

4. The textbook definitions of state and nation are based on scientific distinctions between both organizational types. However, this distinction is commonly lost in everyday language. Consider, for instance, the names United States of America and the United Nations. Can you think of any other examples of confusing terminology distinctions? What are the consequences of this confusion?

5. This chapter contains several examples of applied anthropology. Can you think of a practical problem in the world today that would benefit from anthropological knowledge and methods?

Key Terms

anthropology
holistic perspective
ethnocentrism
culture-bound
applied anthropology
medical anthropology
cultural anthropology
culture
ethnography
fieldwork
participant observation
ethnology
linguistic anthropology
discourse
archaeology
historical archaeology

bioarchaeology
cultural resource management
physical anthropology
molecular anthropology
paleoanthropology
biocultural
primatology
forensic anthropology
empirical
hypothesis
theory
doctrine
artifact
material culture
fossil

soil marks
midden
grid system
datum point
relative dating
absolute dating or
   chronometric dating
key consultants
informal interview
formal interview
eliciting devices
Human Relations Area
   Files (HRAF)
informed consent
globalization

# Online Study Resources

Login to **www.cengagebrain.com** to access the resources your instructor has assigned and to purchase materials. For this book, you can access:

 CourseMate
Access chapter-specific learning tools including flashcards, glossaries, practice quizzes, videos, and more in your Anthropology CourseMate.

© Darren McCollester/Getty Images

VISUAL ESSENCE

The only primate species capable of inhabiting the entire globe, humans are remarkably diverse. We come in all shapes and sizes. Our diets, daily practices, and beliefs all vary. Some of human diversity has been etched into the genetic makeup of human populations as they adapted to fit the specific environments they inhabited. For example, forces in the environment, such as the need to dissipate heat, worked through the process of natural selection over countless generations to bring about the long, lean build characteristic of the inhabitants of the dry East African highlands. This allows Kenyan runners like Rita Jeptoo, pictured here winning the Boston Marathon, to sweep many distance running competitions as they have for the past several decades. In addition to body type, living and training at high altitudes affords Kenyan runners the physiological adaptation of increased oxygen-carrying capacity. Today, runners from all over the world train at high altitudes so that when race day comes, that they too can carry more oxygen. But such short-term changes are distinct from the evolutionary changes, which are alterations in the genetic structure of populations. Evolution underlies far more than human diversity. Ultimately it provides a scientific mechanism that accounts for the diversity of all life on earth today.

2

Biology and Evolution

Evolution and Creation Stories

The mythology of most peoples includes a story explaining the appearance of humans on earth. The accounts of creation recorded in the Bible's Book of Genesis, for example, explain human origins. The Nez Perce, American Indians native to eastern Oregon and Idaho, provide us with a vastly different example that serves the same function. For the Nez Perce, human beings are the creation of Coyote, a trickster-transformer. Coyote chased the giant beaver monster Wishpoosh over the earth, leaving a trail to form the Columbia River. When Coyote caught Wishpoosh, he killed him, dragged his body to the riverbank, and cut it into pieces, each body part transforming into one of the various peoples of this region. The Nez Perce were made from Wishpoosh's head, thus conferring on them great intelligence and horsemanship.[1]

Creation stories depict the relationship between humans and the rest of the natural world, sometimes reflecting a deep connection among people, other animals, and the earth. In the traditional Nez Perce creation story, groups of people derive from specific body parts—each possessing a special talent and relationship with a particular animal. By contrast, the story of creation in Genesis emphasizes human uniqueness and the concept of time. Creation takes place as a series of actions over the course of six days. God's final act of creation is to fashion the first human from the earth in his own image before the seventh day of rest.

This linear creation story from Genesis—shared by Jews, Christians, and Muslims—differs from the cyclical creation stories characteristic of Hinduism, which emphasize reincarnation and the cycle of life, including creation and destruction. For Hindus, the diversity of life on earth comes from three gods—Lord Brahma, the creator; Lord

In this chapter you will learn to:

- **Compare evolution to creation stories.**

- **Identify the place of humans in the classification of all living things.**

- **Explain the molecular basis of evolution and the four evolutionary processes: mutation, gene flow, genetic drift, and adaptation.**

- **Describe how evolutionary processes account for the diversity of life on earth.**

- **Contrast how evolutionary processes work at the individual and population level.**

- **Explain how humans have adapted to their environments.**

- **Identify how new species come into being.**

---

[1]Clark, E. E. (1966). *Indian legends of the Pacific Northwest* (p. 174). Berkeley: University of California Press.

Vishnu, the preserver; and Lord Shiva, the destroyer and re-creator—all of whom are part of the Supreme One. Lord Brahma destroys the world as he sleeps, then he re-creates it again when he awakes. Similarly, intelligent design (ID)—proposed by a conservative think tank called the Discovery Institute in Seattle, Washington—considers creation to be the result of a supreme intelligent being.

Like creation stories, evolution, the major organizing principle of the biological sciences, accounts for the diversity of life on earth. Theories of evolution provide mechanisms for change and explanations for how the variety of organisms, both in the past and today, came into being. However, evolution differs from creation stories in that it explains the diversity of life in consistent scientific language, using testable ideas (hypotheses). Contemporary scientists make comparisons among living organisms to test hypotheses drawn from evolutionary theory. Through their research, scientists have deciphered the molecular basis of evolution and the mechanisms through which evolutionary forces work on populations of organisms. At the same time scientific thought does not come out of a vacuum. As you will see, historical and cultural processes contribute to scientific thought.

The Classification of Living Things

As European explorers exploited foreign lands, their approach to the natural world changed. The discovery of new life forms challenged the previously held notion of fixed unchanging life on earth.

Before this time, Europeans organized living things and inanimate objects alike into a ladder or hierarchy known as the Great Chain of Being—an approach to nature first developed by the philosopher Aristotle in ancient Greece over 2,300 years ago. The categories were based upon visible similarities, and one member of each category was considered its "primate" (from the Latin *primus*), meaning the first or best of the group. For example, the primate of rocks was the diamond, the primate of birds was the eagle, and so forth. Humans stood at the very top of the ladder, just below the angels.

This classificatory system was in place until Carolus Linnaeus (also known as Carl von Linné) developed the *Systema Naturae*, or system of nature, in the 18th century to classify the diversity of living things collected and brought to Europe by ship from throughout the globe. Linnaeus's system reflected a new understanding of life on earth and of the place of humanity among the animals.

Linnaeus noted the similarity among humans, monkeys, and apes, classifying them together as **primates**. Not the first or the best of the animals on earth, primates are just one of several kinds of **mammal**, animals having body hair or fur who suckle or nurse their young. In other

From *Lindauer Bilderbogen* no. 5, edited by Friedrich Boer, Jan Thorbecke Verlag, Sigmaringen, Germany

▲▲▲ Swedish professor of medicine and botany, Carolus Linnaeus created the first comprehensive system of living things: the *Systema Naturae*. As a practicing doctor he also prepared and prescribed medicinal plants for his patients. He arranged for his students to join the major European voyages so they could bring back medicinal plants and other life forms. Famous for his bawdy lectures on plant reproduction, Linnaeus also showed his imaginative flair when he proposed a "flower clock" that could show the time of day according to whether blossoms of particular species were open or shut.

words, Linnaeus classified living things into a series of categories that are progressively more inclusive on the basis of internal and external visual similarities. **Species**, the smallest working units in biological classificatory systems, are reproductively isolated populations or groups of populations capable of interbreeding to produce fertile offspring. Species are subdivisions of larger, more inclusive groups, called **genera** (singular, **genus**). Humans, for example, are classified in the genus *Homo* and the species *sapiens*.

Linnaeus based his classificatory system on the following criteria:

1. *Body structure*: A Guernsey cow and a Holstein cow are the same species because they have identical body structure. A cow and a horse do not.
2. *Body function*: Cows and horses give birth to live young. Although they are different species, they are closer than either cows or horses are to chickens, which lay eggs and have no mammary glands.
3. *Sequence of bodily growth*: At the time of birth—or hatching out of the egg—young cows and chickens possess body plans basically like that of their parents. They are therefore more closely related to each

other than either one is to the frog, whose tadpoles undergo a series of changes before attaining the basic adult form.

Modern **taxonomy**, or the science of classification (from the Greek for "naming divisions"), while retaining the structure of the Linnaean system, takes more than body structure, function, and growth into account. Today's scientists also compare protein structure and genetic material to construct the relationships among living things. Such molecular comparisons can even be aimed at parasites, bacteria, and viruses, allowing scientists to classify or trace the origins of particular diseases, such as swine flu or HIV (human immunodeficiency virus). An emphasis on genetics rather than morphology has led to a reworking of taxonomic designation in the human family, among others, as is described in Table 2.1.

Cross-species comparisons identify anatomical features of similar function as **analogies**, while anatomical features that have evolved from a common ancestral feature are called **homologies**. For example, the arm and

primates The group of mammals that includes lemurs, lorises, tarsiers, monkeys, apes, and humans.

mammals The class of vertebrate animals distinguished by bodies covered with hair or fur who suckle or nurse their young.

species The smallest working units in biological classificatory systems; reproductively isolated populations or groups of populations capable of interbreeding to produce fertile offspring.

genus, genera In the system of plant and animal classification, a group of like species.

taxonomy The science of classification.

analogies In biology, structures possessed by different organisms that are superficially similar due to similar function but that do not share a common developmental pathway or structure.

homologies In biology, structures possessed by two different organisms that arise in similar fashion and pass through similar stages during embryonic development, although they may have different functions.

Table 2.1 The Classification of Humans

Taxonomic Category	Category to Which Humans Belong	Biological Features Used to Define and Place Humans in This Category
Kingdom	Animalia	Humans are animals. We do not make our own food (as plants do) but depend upon intake of living food.
Phylum	Chordata	Humans are chordates. We have a notochord (a rodlike structure of cartilage) and nerve chord running along the back of the body as well as gill slits in the embryonic stage of our life cycle.
Subphylum*	Vertebrata	Humans are vertebrates, possessing an internal backbone with a segmented spinal column.
Class	Mammalia	Humans are mammals: warm-blooded animals covered with hair or fur and possessing mammary glands for nourishing their young after birth.
Order	Primates	Humans are primates: a kind of mammal with a generalized anatomy, a relatively large brain, and grasping hands and feet.
Suborder	Anthropoidea	Humans are anthropoids: social, daylight-active primates.
Superfamily	Hominoid	Humans are hominoids with broad, flexible shoulders and no tail. Chimps, bonobos, gorillas, orangutans, gibbons, and siamangs are also hominoids.
Family Subfamily	Hominid Hominin	Humans are hominids. We are hominoids from Africa, genetically more closely related to chimps, bonobos, and gorillas than to hominoids from Asia. Some scientists use "hominid" to refer only to humans and their ancestors. Others include chimps and gorillas in this category, using the subfamily "hominin" to distinguish humans and their ancestors from chimps and gorillas and their ancestors. The two taxonomies differ according to emphasis on genetic versus morphological similarities. Those who use "hominin" do so to emphasize the genetic relationship among humans, chimps, and gorillas. Those who refer to humans and their ancestor as "hominids" give preference to the similarities in body shape among chimpanzees, gorillas, and orangutans.
Genus Species	*Homo sapiens*	Humans have large brains and rely on cultural adaptations to survive. Ancestral fossils are placed in this genus and species depending upon details of the skull shape and interpretations of their cultural capabilities. Genus and species names are always italicized.

*Most categories can be expanded or narrowed by adding the prefix "sub" or "super." A family could thus be part of a superfamily and in turn contain two or more subfamilies.

hand of a human and the wing of a bat evolved from the front leg of a common ancestor, though they have acquired different functions. The human hand and bat wing are homologous structures. During their early embryonic development, homologous structures arise in a similar fashion and pass through similar stages before differentiating. The wings of bats and butterflies look similar and have a similar function—flying. These are analogous, but not homologous, structures because they do not follow the same developmental sequence. When constructing evolutionary relationships, only homologies matter.

Through careful comparison and analysis of organisms, Linnaeus and his successors have grouped species into genera and into even larger groups such as families, orders, classes, phyla, and kingdoms. Characteristics shared by all the organisms in the group define each taxonomic level.

The Discovery of Evolution

Just as European seafaring and colonial exploration brought about an awareness of the diversity of life across the earth, industrialization in Europe brought about an awareness of change in life forms through time. As workers cut away the earth to lay railway tracks and excavated for limestone, fossils—preserved remains of past life forms—were brought into the light.

At first, the fossilized remains of elephants and giant saber-toothed tigers in Europe were interpreted according to religious doctrine. For example, the early 19th-century theory of *catastrophism,* championed by French paleontologist and anatomist George Cuvier, invoked natural events like the Great Flood described in Genesis to account for the disappearance of these species on European lands. At about the same time, British geologist Charles Lyell proposed a nonreligious theory to account for variations in the earth's surface. His theory, *uniformitarianism,* maintained that just as changes in the earth's surface that are immediately observable are caused by erosion and other natural processes, other changes are caused by gradual processes over extremely long periods of time. Lyell's theory was incompatible with biblical accounts of creation because the length of time required for uniformitarianism far exceeded the religious version that the earth is a mere 6,000 or so years old.

With industrialization, Europeans became more comfortable with the ideas of change and progress. In hindsight, it seems inevitable that someone would hit upon the idea of evolution. So it was that, by the start of the 19th century, many naturalists had come to accept the idea that life had evolved, even though they were not clear about how it happened. It remained for Charles Darwin (1809–1882) to formulate a theory that has withstood the test of time.

© BIOS Hugeut Pierre/Peter Arnold, Inc.

▲▲▲ **The bat wing is homologous to the human hand. Look closely at the bones supporting the wing, and you can see that they are the same bones found in the human arm and hand. Homologous structures have the same embryonic origins but ultimately take on different functions. Bats and butterflies both use their wings to fly. These analogous structures look alike due to similar function, but the course of their development and structure differ.**

Darwin began the study of medicine at the University of Edinburgh, Scotland. Finding himself unfit for this profession, he went to Christ's College, Cambridge, to study theology. He then left Cambridge to take the position of companion to Captain Robert FitzRoy on the *H.M.S. Beagle,* which was about to embark on an expedition to various poorly mapped parts of the world. The voyage lasted for almost five years, taking Darwin along the coasts of South America, to the Galápagos Islands, across the Pacific to Australia, and then across the Indian and Atlantic oceans to South America before returning to England in 1836.

Observing the tremendous diversity of living creatures as well as the astounding fossils of extinct animals, Darwin began to note that species varied according to the environments they inhabited. The observations he made on this voyage, his readings of Lyell's *Principles of Geology* (1830), and the arguments he had with the orthodox and dogmatic FitzRoy all contributed to the ideas culminating in Darwin's most famous book, *On the Origin of Species.* This book, published in 1859, over twenty years after he returned from his voyage, described a theory of evolution accounting for change within species and for the emergence of new species in purely naturalistic terms.

Darwin added observations from English farm life and intellectual thought to the ideas he began to develop on the *Beagle.* He paid particular attention to domesticated animals and farmers' "artificial selection," a practice of breeding their stock to select for specific traits. Darwin's theoretical breakthrough derived from an essay by economist Thomas Malthus (1766–1834), which warned of the potential consequences of increased human population, particularly of the poor. Malthus observed that animal populations, unlike human populations, remained stable, due to an overproduction of young followed by a large proportion of animal offspring not surviving to maturity. Darwin wrote in his autobiography, "It at once struck me that under these circumstances favourable variations would tend to be preserved, and unfavourable ones to be destroyed. The results of this would be the formation of a new species. Here, then I had at last got a theory by which to work."[2]

Darwin combined his observations into the theory of **natural selection** as follows: All species display a range of variation, and all have the ability to expand beyond their means of subsistence. It follows that, in their "struggle for existence," organisms with variations that help them to survive in a particular environment will reproduce with greater success than those without such variations. Thus, as generation succeeds generation, nature selects the most advantageous variations, and species evolve. In retrospect, the idea seemed so obvious that Thomas Henry Huxley, one of the era's most prominent scientists, remarked, "How extremely stupid of me not to have thought of that."[3]

However straightforward the idea of evolution by natural selection may appear, the theory was (and is) a source of considerable controversy. Two problems plagued Darwin's theory throughout his career. First, how did variation arise to begin with? Second, what was the mechanism of heredity by which variable traits could be passed from one generation to the next?

Heredity

Ironically, some of the information Darwin needed was available by 1866. Gregor Mendel (1822–1884), a Roman Catholic monk, developed the basic laws of heredity while working in the monastery gardens in Brno, a city in today's Czech Republic.

Mendel, who was raised on a farm, possessed two particular talents: a flair for mathematics and a passion for gardening. As with all farmers of his time, Mendel had an intuitive understanding of biological inheritance. He went a step farther, though, in that he recognized the need for theoretical explanations. At age 34, he began careful breeding experiments in the monastery garden, starting with pea plants.

Over 8 years, Mendel planted over 30,000 plants, controlling their pollination, observing the results, and

figuring out the mathematics behind it all. This allowed him to unravel the basic laws of heredity. Though his findings were published in 1866 in a respected scientific journal, no one recognized the importance of Mendel's work during his lifetime.

In 1900, cell biology had advanced to the point where rediscovery of Mendel's laws was inevitable, and in that year three European botanists, working independently of one another, rediscovered not only the laws but also Mendel's original paper. With this rediscovery, the science of genetics began. Still, it would be another 53 years before the molecular mechanisms of heredity and the discrete units of inheritance would be discovered. Today, a comprehensive understanding of heredity, molecular genetics, and population genetics supports Darwinian evolutionary theory.

The Transmission of Genes

Although today we define a **gene** as a portion of the DNA molecule containing a sequence of base pairs that encodes a particular protein, the molecular basis of the gene was not known at the turn of the 20th century when biologists coined the term from the Greek word for "birth." Mendel had deduced the presence and activity of genes by experimenting with garden peas to determine how various traits are passed from one generation to the next. Specifically, he discovered that inheritance was *particulate*, rather than *blending*, as Darwin and many others thought. That is, the units controlling the expression of visible traits come in pairs, one from each parent, and retain their separate identities over the generations rather than blending into a combination of parental traits in offspring. This was the basis of Mendel's first **law of segregation**, which states that pairs of genes separate, keep their individuality, and are passed on to the next generation unaltered. Another finding—Mendel's **law of independent assortment**—states that different traits (under the control of distinct genes) are inherited independently of one another.

Mendel based his laws on statistical frequencies of observed characteristics, such as color and texture in

natural selection The evolutionary process through which factors in the environment exert pressure, favoring some individuals over others to produce the next generation.

genes The portions of DNA molecules that direct the synthesis of specific proteins.

law of segregation The Mendelian principle that variants of genes for a particular trait retain their separate identities through the generations.

law of independent assortment The Mendelian principle that genes controlling different traits are inherited independently of one another.

[2]Darwin, C. (1887). *Autobiography*. Reprinted in *The life and letters of Charles Darwin* (1902). F. Darwin (Ed.). London: John Murray.

[3]Quoted in Durant, J. C. (2000, April 23). Everybody into the gene pool. *New York Times Book Review*, 11.

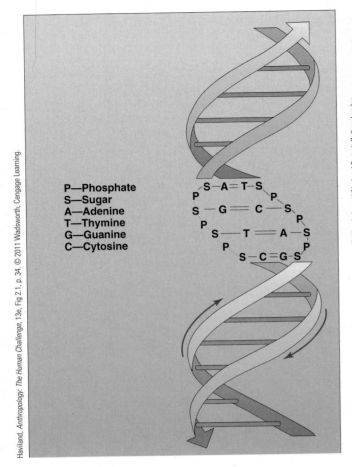

P—Phosphate
S—Sugar
A—Adenine
T—Thymine
G—Guanine
C—Cytosine

Figure 2.1 A Portion of DNA This diagrammatic representation of a portion of DNA (deoxyribonucleic acid) illustrates its twisted ladderlike structure. Alternating sugar and phosphate groups form the structural sides of the ladder. The connecting "rungs" are formed by pairings between complementary bases—adenine with thymine and cytosine with guanine.

▲▲▲ British scientist Rosalind Franklin's pioneering work in x-ray crystal photography played a vital role in unlocking the secret of the genetic code in 1953. Without her permission, Franklin's colleague Maurice Wilkins showed one of her images to James Watson. In his book *The Double Helix,* Watson wrote, "The instant I saw the picture my mouth fell open and my pulse began to race." Franklin's untimely death in 1958 made her ineligible for the Nobel prize that was awarded to Watson, Crick, and Wilkins for the double-helix model of DNA in 1962.

generations of plants. When **chromosomes,** the cellular structures containing the genetic information, were discovered at the start of the 20th century, they provided a visible vehicle for transmission of traits proposed in Mendel's laws.

Then in 1953 James Watson and Francis Crick found that genes are actually portions of molecules of **DNA (deoxyribonucleic acid)**—long strands of which form chromosomes. DNA is a complex molecule with an unusual shape, rather like two strands of a rope twisted around each other with ladderlike steps between the two strands (▶ **Figure 2.1**). Alternating sugar and phosphate molecules form the backbone of these strands connected to each other by four base pairs: adenine, thymine, guanine, and cytosine (usually written as A, T, G, and C). Connections between the strands occur between so-called complementary pairs of bases (A to T, G to C). Sequences of three complementary bases specify the sequence of amino acids in protein synthesis. This arrangement also confers upon genes the unique property of replication—being able to make exact copies of themselves. The term **chromatid** refers to one half of the X

shape of chromosomes visible once replication is complete. Sister chromatids are exact copies of each other.

Genes and Alleles

A sequence of chemical bases on a molecule of DNA (a gene) constitutes a recipe for making proteins. As science writer Matt Ridley puts it, "Proteins . . . do almost every chemical, structural, and regulatory thing that is done in the body: they generate energy, fight infection, digest food, form hair, carry oxygen, and so on and on."[4] Almost everything in the body is made of or by proteins.

There are alternate forms of genes, known as **alleles.** For example, the gene for a human blood type in the A-B-O system refers to a specific portion of a DNA molecule on chromosome 9 and corresponds to alternate forms that determine the specific blood type (the A allele and B allele). Genes, then, are not really separate structures, as had once been imagined, but locations, like dots on a map. (▶ **Figure 2.2** displays a *karyotype,* which is the number and shape of chromosomes inside each cell of a species.) These genes provide the recipe for the many proteins that keep us alive and healthy.

The human **genome**—the complete sequence of human DNA—contains 3 billion chemical bases, with about 20,000 to 25,000 genes, a number similar to that found in most mammals. Of the 3 billion bases, humans and mice

---

[4]Ridley, M. (1999). *Genome: The autobiography of a species in 23 chapters* (p. 40). New York: HarperCollins.

Haviland, Anthropology: The Human Challenge, 13e, Fig 2.1, p. 34. © 2011 Wadsworth, Cengage Learning.

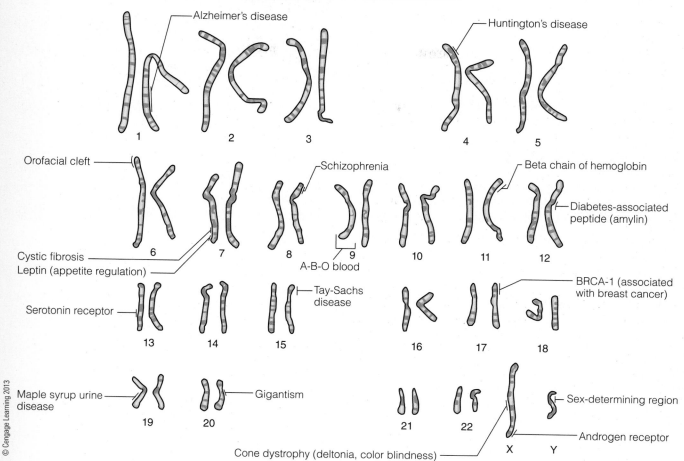

Karyotype with a Few Genetic Loci

Figure 2.2 Karyotype An array of chromosomes from inside the nucleus of one cell of one individual is called a karyotype. The twenty-three pairs of chromosomes humans possess include twenty-two pairs of somatic or body chromosomes, plus one pair of sex chromosomes, for a total of forty-six chromosomes. Here you can see the characteristic shape and relative size of each of the chromosomes. The locations of certain genes associated with various diseases and conditions identified by the Human Genome Project are labeled. Although we would need to sequence the DNA to see what alleles this individual had for various genes, a glance at the overall karyotype indicates a normal number of chromosomes and that this individual is genetically male. The female phenotype is determined by the presence of two X chromosomes. Offspring inherit an X chromosome from their mothers but either an X or a Y from their fathers, resulting in approximately equal numbers of male and female offspring in subsequent generations. Though the Y chromosome is critical for differentiation into a male phenotype, compared to other chromosomes the Y is tiny and carries little genetic information. With only one X chromosome, males are far more likely to express certain X-linked traits such as color blindness.

are about 90 percent identical. Both species have three times as many genes as does the fruit fly, but surprisingly both humans and mice have only half the genes of the rice plant! In other words the number of genes or base pairs does not explain every difference among organisms. At the same time, those 20,000 to 25,000 human genes account for only 1 to 1.5 percent of the entire genome, indicating that scientists still have far more to learn about how genes work. Frequently, genes themselves are split by long stretches of DNA that are not part of the known protein code. For example, five such stretches interrupt the 1,062 bases of the A-B-O blood group gene. In the course of protein production, these stretches of DNA are metaphorically snipped out and left on the cutting-room floor.

chromosomes In the cell nucleus, the structures visible during cellular division containing long strands of DNA combined with a protein.

DNA (deoxyribonucleic acid) The genetic material consisting of a complex molecule whose base structure directs the synthesis of proteins.

chromatid One half of the X shape of chromosomes visible once replication is complete. Sister chromatids are exact copies of each other.

alleles Alternate forms of a single gene.

genome The complete structure sequence of DNA for a species.

Cell Division

In order to grow and maintain good health, the body cells of an organism must divide and produce new cells. Cell division begins when the chromosomes replicate, forming a second pair that duplicates the original pair of chromosomes in the nucleus. To do this, the DNA "unzips" between the base pairs—adenine from thymine and guanine from cytosine—and then each base on each now-single strand attracts its complementary base, reconstituting the second half of the double helix. After they separate, a new cell membrane surrounds each new chromosome pair and becomes the nucleus that directs the activities of a new cell. This kind of cell division is called **mitosis**. Barring errors in this replication process, cells divide mitotically to form daughter cells that are exact genetic copies of the parent cell.

Like most animals, humans reproduce sexually. The "popularity" of sex from an evolutionary perspective derives from the genetic variation that it provides. All animals contain two copies of each chromosome, having inherited one from each parent. In humans this involves twenty-three pairs of chromosomes. Sexual reproduction can bring favorable alleles together, purge the genome of harmful ones, and allow beneficial alleles to spread without being held back by the baggage of disadvantageous variants of other genes. While human societies have always regulated sexual reproduction in some ways, the science of genetics has had a tremendous impact on social aspects of reproduction as seen in this chapter's Biocultural Connection.

Sexual reproduction increases genetic diversity, which in turn has contributed to a multitude of adaptations among sexually reproducing species such as humans. Sexual reproduction involves the merging of two cells, one from each parent, to make a new individual. If two regular body cells, each containing twenty-three pairs of chromosomes, were to merge, the lethal result would be a new individual with forty-six pairs of chromosomes. Instead, sexual reproduction involves joining specialized sex cells (eggs and sperm) produced by a different kind of cell division, called **meiosis**.

Although meiosis begins like mitosis, with the replication and doubling of the original genes in chromosomes through the formation of sister chromatids, it proceeds to divide that number into four new cells rather than two (▶ **Figure 2.3**). Thus each new cell has only half the number of chromosomes compared to the parent cell. Human eggs and sperm have only twenty-three single chromosomes (half of a pair), whereas body cells have twenty-three pairs, or forty-six chromosomes.

The process of meiotic division has important implications for genetics. Because paired chromosomes are separated, the daughter cells will not be identical. Two of the four new cells will have half of each pair of chromosomes, and the other two will have the second half of

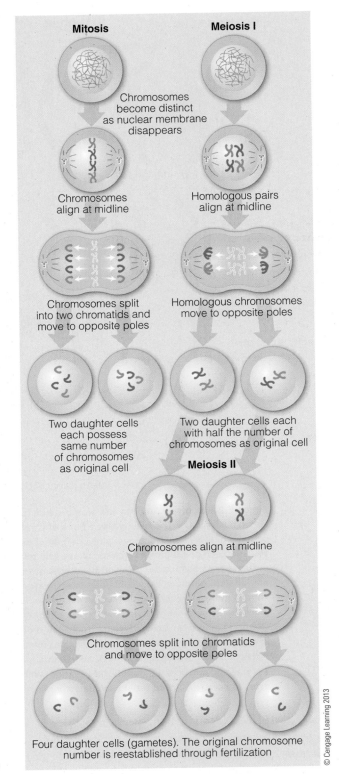

Figure 2.3 Mitosis and Meiosis Each chromosome consists of two sister chromatids, which are exact copies of each other. During mitosis, these sister chromatids separate into two identical daughter cells. In meiosis, the cell division responsible for the formation of gametes, the first division halves the chromosome number. The second meiotic division is essentially like mitosis and involves the separation of sister chromatids. Chromosomes in red came from one parent; those in blue came from the other. Meiosis results in four daughter cells that are not identical.

Within figure:

Mitosis | **Meiosis I**

Chromosomes become distinct as nuclear membrane disappears

Chromosomes align at midline | Homologous pairs align at midline

Chromosomes split into two chromatids and move to opposite poles | Homologous chromosomes move to opposite poles

Two daughter cells each possess same number of chromosomes as original cell | Two daughter cells each with half the number of chromosomes as original cell

Meiosis II

Chromosomes align at midline

Chromosomes split into chromatids and move to opposite poles

Four daughter cells (gametes). The original chromosome number is reestablished through fertilization

© Cengage Learning 2013

The Social Impact of Genetics on Reproduction

While pregnancy and childbirth have been traditional subjects for cultural anthropology, the advances in genetics are raising new questions for the biocultural study of reproduction. At first glance, the genetics revolution has simply expanded biological knowledge. Individuals today, compared to a hundred years ago, can see their own genetic makeup, even down to the base-pair sequence level. But this new biological knowledge also has the capacity to profoundly transform cultures, and in many places new genetic information has dramatically affected the social experience of pregnancy and childbirth.

New reproductive technologies allow for the genetic assessment of fertilized eggs and embryos (the earliest stage of animal development), with far-reaching social consequences. These technologies have also become of interest to cultural anthropologists who are studying the social impact of biological knowledge. For twenty-five years, anthropologist Rayna Rapp has examined the social influence of prenatal genetic testing in North America.[a] Her work illustrates that biological facts pertaining to reproduction do not exist outside of an interpretive framework provided by the culture.

Prenatal genetic testing is conducted most frequently through amniocentesis—a technique developed in the 1960s in which fluid containing cells from the developing embryo is drawn from the womb of a pregnant woman. The chromosomes and specific genes are then analyzed for abnormalities. Rapp has traced the development of amniocentesis from an experimental procedure to one routinely used in pregnancy in North America. For example, today pregnant women over the age of 35 routinely undergo this test because certain genetic conditions are associated with older maternal age. Trisomy 21 or Down syndrome, in which individuals have an extra 21st chromosome, can be easily identified through amniocentesis.

Through ethnographic study, Rapp has shown that a biological fact (such as an extra 21st chromosome) is open to diverse interpretations and reproductive choices by "potential parents." She also illustrates how genetic testing may lead to the labeling of certain people as "undesirable," pitting women's reproductive rights against the rights of the disabled—born or unborn. Generally, until a fetus reaches a "point of viability," women in the United States have a constitutionally protected right to decide whether to terminate or continue a pregnancy for any reason at all, including the diagnosis of a genetic anomaly. Following this window, federal law protects the rights of disabled individuals with these same anomalies.

Individual women must negotiate a terrain in which few rules exist to guide them. Advances in reproductive technology that reveal genetic anomalies have created an utterly novel social situation. Rapp's anthropological investigation of the social impact of amniocentesis illustrates the complex interplay between biological knowledge and cultural practices. ■

Biocultural Question

What do you think about prenatal genetic testing for diseases? Would you like to know if you carry the recessive allele for a harmful condition?

[a]Rapp, R. (1999). *Testing women, testing the fetus: The social impact of amniocentesis in America.* New York: Routledge.

the original chromosome pair. In addition, corresponding portions of one chromosome may "cross over" to the other one, somewhat scrambling the genetic material compared to the original chromosomes.

Sometimes, the original pair is **homozygous**, possessing identical alleles for a specific gene. For example, if in both chromosomes of the original pair the gene for A-B-O blood type is represented by the allele for type A blood, then all new cells will have the A allele. But if the original pair is **heterozygous,** with the A allele on one chromosome and the allele for type B blood on the other, then half of the new cells will contain only the B allele; the offspring have a 50–50 chance of getting either one. It is impossible to predict any single individual's **genotype**, or genetic composition, but, as Mendel originally discovered, statistical probabilities can be established.

What happens when a child inherits the allele for type O blood from one parent and that for type A from the other? Will the child have blood of type A, O, or

▲▲▲

mitosis A kind of cell division that produces new cells having exactly the same number of chromosome pairs, and hence copies of genes, as the parent cell.

meiosis A kind of cell division that produces the sex cells, each of which has half the number of chromosomes found in other cells of the organism.

homozygous A term to describe a chromosome pair that bears identical alleles for a single gene.

heterozygous A term to describe a chromosome pair that bears different alleles for a single gene.

genotype The alleles possessed for a particular trait.

▼▼▼

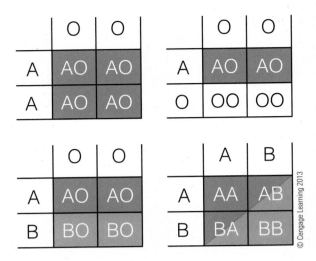

© Cengage Learning 2013

Figure 2.4 Punnett Squares These four Punnett squares (named for British geneticist Reginald Punnett) illustrate some of the possible phenotypes and genotypes of offspring within the A-B-O system. Each individual possesses two alleles within this system, and together these two alleles constitute the individual's genotype. "Phenotype" refers to the physical characteristic expressed by the individual. The alleles of one parent are listed on the left-hand side of the square, while the other parent's alleles are listed across the top. The potential genotypes of offspring are listed in the colored squares by letter. Phenotypes are indicated by color: blue indicates the type A phenotype; orange indicates the B phenotype. Individuals with one A and one B allele have the AB phenotype and make both blood antigens. Individuals with the O phenotype have two O alleles.

some mixture of the two? ▶ **Figure 2.4** illustrates some of the possible outcomes. Many of these questions were answered by Mendel's original experiments.

Mendel discovered that certain alleles are able to mask the presence of others; one allele is **dominant**, whereas the other is **recessive**. Actually, it is the traits that are dominant or recessive rather than the alleles themselves; geneticists merely speak of dominant and recessive alleles for the sake of convenience. Thus one might speak of the allele for type A blood as being dominant to the one for type O. An individual whose blood type genes are heterozygous, with one A and one O allele, will have type A blood. In other words, the heterozygous

condition (AO) will show exactly the same physical characteristic, or **phenotype,** as the homozygous (AA), even though the two have a somewhat different genetic composition, or genotype. Only the homozygous recessive genotype (OO) will show the phenotype of type O blood.

The dominance of one allele does not mean that the recessive one is lost or in some way blended. A type A heterozygous parent (AO) will produce sex cells containing both A and O alleles. (This is an example of Mendel's law of segregation, that alleles retain their separate identities.) Recessive alleles can be handed down for generations before they are matched with another recessive allele in the process of sexual reproduction and show up in the phenotype. The presence of the dominant allele simply masks the expression of the recessive allele.

All of the traits Mendel studied in garden peas showed this dominant–recessive relationship, and so for some years it was believed that this was the only relationship possible. Later studies, however, have indicated that patterns of inheritance are not always so simple. In some cases, neither allele is dominant; they are both co-dominant. An example of co-dominance in human heredity can be seen also in the inheritance of blood types. Type A is produced by one allele; type B by another. A heterozygous individual will have a phenotype of AB because neither allele can dominate the other.

The inheritance of blood types points out another complexity of heredity. Although we each have at most two alleles for any given gene, the number of possible alleles for that gene found in a population is by no means limited to two. Certain traits have three or more allelic forms. For example, over 100 alleles exist for **hemoglobin,** the blood protein that carries oxygen. Only one allele can appear on each of the two homologous chromosomes, so each individual is limited to two genetic alleles.

Polygenetic Inheritance

So far, we have described the traits of organisms as if they are determined by just one gene. However, most physical traits—such as the lean body build described at the start of the chapter, skin color, or susceptibility to disease—are controlled by multiple genes. In such cases, we speak of **polygenetic inheritance,** where the respective alleles of two or more genes influence phenotype. For example, several individuals may have the exact same height, but because there is no single height gene that determines an individual's size, it is impossible to neatly unravel the genetic underpinnings of 5 foot 3 inches or 160 centimeters. Characteristics subject to polygenetic inheritance exhibit a continuous range of variation in their phenotypic expression that does not correspond to simple Mendelian rules. As biological anthropologist Jonathan Marks demonstrates in the following Original Study, the relationship between genetics and continuous traits remains a mystery.

dominant A term to describe the ability of an allele for a trait to mask the presence of another allele.

recessive A term to describe an allele for a trait whose expression is masked by the presence of a dominant allele.

phenotype The observable or testable appearance of an organism that may or may not reflect a particular genotype due to the variable expression of dominant and recessive alleles.

hemoglobin The protein that carries oxygen in the red blood cells.

polygenetic inheritance Two or more genes contributing to the phenotypic expression of a single characteristic.

ORIGINAL STUDY

Ninety-Eight Percent Alike: What Our Similarity to Apes Tells Us about Our Understanding of Genetics

By Jonathan Marks

It's not too hard to tell Jane Goodall from a chimpanzee. Goodall is the one with long legs and short arms, a prominent forehead, and whites in her eyes. She's the one with a significant amount of hair only on her head, not all over her body. She's the one who walks, talks, and wears clothing.

A few decades ago, however, the nascent field of molecular genetics recognized an apparent paradox: However easy it may be to tell Jane Goodall from a chimpanzee on the basis of physical characteristics, it is considerably harder to tell them apart according to their genes.

More recently, geneticists have been able to determine with precision that humans and chimpanzees are over 98 percent identical genetically, and that figure has become one of the most well-known factoids in the popular scientific literature. It has been invoked to argue that we are simply a third kind of chimpanzee, together with the common chimp and the rarer bonobo; to claim human rights for nonhuman apes; and to explain the roots of male aggression.

Using the figure in those ways, however, ignores the context necessary to make sense of it. Actually, our amazing genetic similarity to chimpanzees is a scientific fact constructed from two rather more mundane facts: our familiarity with the apes and our unfamiliarity with genetic comparisons.

To begin with, it is unfair to juxtapose the differences between the bodies of people and apes with the similarities in their genes. After all, we have been comparing the bodies of humans and chimpanzees for 300 years, and we have been comparing DNA sequences for less than 20 years. Now that we are familiar with chimpanzees, we quickly see how different they look from us. But when the chimpanzee was a novelty, in the 18th century, scholars were struck by the overwhelming similarity of human and ape bodies. And why not? Bone for bone, muscle for muscle, organ for organ, the bodies of humans and apes differ only in subtle ways. And yet, it is impossible to say just how physically similar they are. Forty percent? Sixty percent? Ninety-eight percent? Three-dimensional beings that develop over their lifetime don't lend themselves to a simple scale of similarity.

Genetics brings something different to the comparison. A DNA sequence is a one-dimensional entity, a long series of A, G, C, and T subunits. Align two sequences from different species and you can simply tabulate their similarities; if they match 98 out of 100 times, then the species are 98 percent genetically identical.

But is that more or less than their bodies match? We have no easy way to tell, for making sense of the question "How similar are a human and a chimp?" requires a frame of reference. In other words, we should be asking: "How similar are a human and a chimp, compared to what?" Let's try and answer the question. How similar are a human and a chimp, compared to, say, a sea urchin? The human and chimpanzee have limbs, skeletons, bilateral symmetry, a central nervous system; each bone, muscle, and organ matches. For all intents and purposes, the human and chimpanzee aren't 98 percent identical, they're 100 percent identical.

On the other hand, when we compare the DNA of humans and chimps, what does the percentage of similarity mean? We conceptualize it on a linear scale, on which 100 percent is perfectly identical, and 0 percent is totally different. But the structure of DNA gives the scale a statistical idiosyncrasy. Because DNA is a linear array of those four bases—A, G, C, and T—only four possibilities exist at any specific point in a DNA sequence. [see Figure 2.1] The laws of chance tell us that two random sequences from species that have no ancestry in common will match at about one in every four sites.

Thus, even two unrelated DNA sequences will be 25 percent identical, not 0 percent identical. (You can, of course, generate sequences more different than that, but greater differences would not occur randomly.) The most different two DNA sequences can be, then, is 75 percent different. Now consider that all multicellular life on earth is related. A human, a chimpanzee, and the banana the chimpanzee is eating share a remote common ancestry, but a common ancestry nevertheless. Therefore, if we compare any particular DNA sequence in a human and a banana, the sequence would have to be more than 25 percent identical. For the sake of argument, let's say 35 percent. In other words, your DNA is over one-third the same as a banana's. Yet, of course, there are few ways other than genetically in which a human could be shown to be one-third identical to a banana.

That context may help us to assess the 98 percent DNA similarity of humans and chimpanzees. The fact that our DNA is 98 percent identical to that of a chimp is not a transcendent statement about our natures but merely a decontextualized and culturally interpreted datum.

Moreover, the genetic comparison is misleading because it ignores qualitative differences among genomes. Genetic evolution involves much more than simply replacing one base with another. Thus, even among such close relatives as human and chimpanzee, we find that the chimp's genome is estimated to be about 10 percent larger than the human's; that one human chromosome contains a fusion of two small chimpanzee chromosomes; and that the tips of each chimpanzee chromosome contain a DNA sequence that is not present in humans.

In other words, the pattern we encounter genetically is actually quite close to the pattern we encounter anatomically. In spite of the shock the figure of 98 percent may give us, humans are obviously identifiably different from, as well as very similar to, chimpanzees. The apparent paradox is simply a result of how mundane the apes have become, and how exotic DNA still is. ∎

Adapted from Marks, J. (2000). 98% alike (what our similarity to apes tells us about our understanding genetics). *The Chronicle of Higher Education*, May 12, B7. Reprinted by permission of the author.

Evolution, Individuals, and Populations

At the level of the individual, the study of genetics shows how traits are transmitted from parent to off-spring, enabling a prediction about the chances that any given individual will display some phenotypic characteristic. At the level of the group, the study of genetics takes on additional significance, revealing how evolutionary processes account for the diversity of life on earth.

A key concept in genetics is that of the **population**, or a group of individuals within which breeding takes place. **Gene pool** refers to all the genetic variants possessed by members of a population. Natural selection takes place within populations as some members contribute a disproportionate share of the next generation. Over generations, the relative proportions of alleles in a population change (biological evolution) according to the varying reproductive success of individuals within that population. In other words, at the level of population genetics, **evolution** can be defined as changes in allele frequencies in populations. This is also known as *micro-evolution*. Evolution could not occur without variation. Four evolutionary forces—mutation, gene flow, genetic drift, and natural selection—create and pattern biological diversity.

Mutation

Mutation, the ultimate source of evolutionary change, constantly introduces new genetic variation. Mutation occurs randomly. Although some mutations may be harmful or beneficial to individuals, most mutations are neutral. But in an evolutionary sense, random mutation is inherently positive: It provides the variation upon which the other evolutionary forces work. New body plans—such as walking on two legs compared to knuckle-walking like our closest relatives, chimpanzees and gorillas—ultimately depended on a series of genetic mutations. A random mutation might create a new allele that creates a modified protein making a new biological task possible. Without the variation brought in through random mutations, populations cannot change over time in response to changing environments.

Mutations may arise whenever copying mistakes are made during cell division. This may involve a change in a single base of a DNA sequence or, at the other extreme, relocation of large segments of DNA, including entire chromosomes. As you read this page, the DNA in each cell of your body is being damaged.[5] Fortunately, DNA repair enzymes constantly scan DNA for mistakes, slicing out damaged segments and patching up gaps. Moreover,

for sexually reproducing species like humans, the only mutations of any evolutionary consequence are those occurring in sex cells, because these cells form future generations.

New mutations arise continuously because no species has perfect DNA repair; thus all species continue to evolve. Geneticists have calculated the rate at which various types of mutant genes appear. In human populations, they run from a low of about five mutations per million sex cells formed, in the case of a gene abnormality that leads to the absence of an iris in the eye, to a high of about a hundred per million, in the case of a gene involved in a form of muscular dystrophy. The average is about thirty mutants per million. Environmental factors may increase the rate at which mutations occur. These include certain dyes, antibiotics, and chemicals used in the preservation of food. Radiation, whether of industrial or solar origin, represents another important cause of mutations. Even stress can increase mutation rates, augmenting the diversity necessary for selection if successful adaptation is to occur.[6]

In humans, as in all multicellular animals, the very structure of DNA ensures that mutations will occur. The fact that many genes are split by stretches of DNA that are not a part of that gene allows the gene segments themselves to reshuffle, like a deck of cards, which can then put together new proteins with new functions. No fewer than fifty such segments of DNA fragment the gene for collagen—the main structural protein of the skin, bones, and teeth. Although mutations can lead to individual suffering, they confer versatility at the population level, making it possible for an evolving species to adapt more quickly to environmental changes. Bear in mind that mutations occur randomly and thus do not arise out of need for some new adaptation.

Genetic Drift

Genetic drift refers to chance fluctuations of allele frequencies in the gene pool of a population. This evolutionary force produces changes at the population level as a result of random events at the individual level. Over the course of a lifetime, a number of random events affect each individual's survival. For example, an individual squirrel in good health and possessed of a number of advantageous traits may be killed in a chance forest fire; a genetically well-adapted baby

[5]Culotta, E., & Koshland, D. E., Jr. (1994). DNA repair works its way to the top. *Science 266*, 1926.

[6]Chicurel, M. (2001). Can organisms speed their own evolution? *Science 292*, 1824–1827.

◄ In evolutionary terms, mutations serve as the ultimate source of all new genetic variation. A generally positive force, most mutations have minimal effects or are neutral. Nevertheless, human-produced mutagens—such as pollutants, preservatives, cigarette smoke, radiation, and even some medicines—increasingly threaten people in industrial societies. While the negative effects of mutation are evident in the clear link between cigarette smoke and cancer, the positive side of mutation has been fictionalized in the special talents of the X-Men.

cougar may not live longer than a day if its mother gets caught in an avalanche, whereas the weaker offspring of another cougar mother may survive. In a large population, such accidents of nature are unimportant; the accidents that preserve individuals with certain alleles will be balanced out by the accidents that destroy them. However, in small populations, such averaging out may not be possible. Some alleles may become overrepresented in a population due to chance events such as a rockslide or a fire.

A particular kind of genetic drift, known as **founder effects**, may occur when an existing population splits up into two or more new ones, especially if a particularly small number of individuals founds one of the new populations. In such cases, the gene frequencies of the smaller population tend not to contain the full range of variation present in the larger one.

Isolated island populations may have limited variability due to founder effects. An interesting example can be seen on the Pacific Ocean island of Pingelap in Micronesia, where 5 percent of the population is completely colorblind, a condition known as *achromatopsia*. This is not the "normal" red–green colorblindness that affects 8 to 20 percent of males in most populations but rather a complete inability to see color. The high frequency of achromotopsia occurred sometime around 1775 after a typhoon swept through the island, reducing its total population to only twenty individuals. Among the survivors was a single individual who was heterozygous for this condition. After a few generations, this gene became fully embedded in the expanding population. Today a full 30 percent of the island's inhabitants are carriers of this

population In biology, a group of similar individuals that can and do interbreed.

gene pool All the genetic variants possessed by members of a population.

evolution The changes in allele frequencies in populations; also known as *microevolution*.

mutation The chance alteration of genetic material that produces new variation.

genetic drift The chance fluctuations of allele frequencies in the gene pool of a population.

founder effects A particular form of genetic drift deriving from a small founding population not possessing all the alleles present in the original population.

colorblind gene, compared to a mere .003 percent seen in the United States.[7]

Genetic drift likely played a role in human evolution, because until 10,000 years ago, all humans were food foragers generally living in relatively small, self-contained populations. Whenever biological variation is observed, whether it is the distant past or the present, the chance events of genetic drift can account for the presence of this variation.

Gene Flow

Gene flow, or the introduction of new alleles from nearby populations, brings new genetic variation into a population: Interbreeding allows "road-tested" genes to flow into and out of populations. Migration of individuals or groups into the territory occupied by others may lead to gene flow. Geographic factors also affect gene flow. For example, if a river separates two populations of small mammals, preventing interbreeding, these populations will begin to accrue random genetic differences due to their isolation (genetic drift). If the river changes course and the two populations can again interbreed freely, new alleles that may have been present in only one population will now be present in both populations due to gene flow.

Among humans, social factors—such as mating rules, intergroup conflict, and our ability to travel great distances—affect gene flow. For example, the last 500 years have seen the introduction of alleles into American Indian populations from both the European colonists and the Africans they imported as slaves. More recent migrations of people from Asia have added to this mix. Throughout the history of human life on earth, gene flow has prevented populations from developing into separate species.

Natural Selection

Although gene flow and genetic drift may produce changes in the allele frequency of a population, that change would not necessarily make the population better adapted to its biological and social environment.

Natural selection, the evolutionary force described by Darwin, accounts for adaptive change. Adaptation—a series of beneficial adjustments to the environment—is the outcome of natural selection. As we will explore throughout this textbook, humans can adapt to their environment through culture as well as biology. When biological adaptation occurs at a genetic level, natural selection is at work.

Natural selection shapes genetic variation at the population level to fit local environmental conditions. In other words, instead of random individuals passing their traits on to the next generation, selection by the forces of nature favors some individuals over others. In the process, the frequency of genetic variants for harmful or nonadaptive traits within the population reduces while the frequency of genetic variants for adaptive traits increases. Over time, changes in the genetic structure of the population can result in the formation of new species.

Natural selection differs from the concept of design seen in religious theories of creation because it works only with the existing store of genetic variation; it cannot create something entirely new. Variation protects populations from dying out or species from going extinct in changing environments. Evolution is a process of tinkering, rather than design. Often tinkering involves balancing beneficial and harmful effects of a specific allele in a specific environment, as the following case study of sickle-cell anemia illustrates.

The Case of Sickle-Cell Anemia

Sickle-cell anemia, a painful disease in which the oxygen-carrying red blood cells change shape (sickle) and clog the finest parts of the circulatory system, first came to the attention of geneticists in Chicago who observed that the disease disproportionately impacted African Americans. Further investigation found that populations that live in a clearly defined belt across Central Africa had the sickle-cell allele at surprisingly high frequencies. Geneticists were curious to know why such a harmful hereditary disability persisted in these populations. ▶ Figure 2.5 demonstrates the sickle shape of these abnormal red blood cells.

According to the theory of natural selection, any alleles that are harmful will tend to disappear from the group, because the individuals who are homozygous for the abnormality generally die—are "selected out"— before they reproduce. Why then has this seemingly harmful condition persisted in populations from Central Africa?

---

gene flow The introduction of alleles from the gene pool of one population into that of another.

adaptation A series of beneficial adjustments to the environment.

sickle-cell anemia An inherited form of anemia caused by a mutation in the hemoglobin protein that causes the red blood cells to assume a sickle shape.

---

[7] Sacks, O. (1998). *Island of the colorblind*. New York: Knopf.

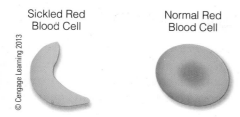

© Cengage Learning 2013

Sickled Red
Blood Cell

Normal Red
Blood Cell

**Figure 2.5 Sickled Red Blood Cell and Normal Red Blood
Cell** Sickle-cell anemia is caused by a genetic mutation in a
single base of the hemoglobin gene, resulting in abnormal
hemoglobin, called hemoglobin S. Those afflicted by the
disease are homozygous for the allele S, and all their red
blood cells "sickle." Co-dominance is observable with the
sickle and normal alleles. Heterozygotes make 50 percent
normal hemoglobin and 50 percent sickle hemoglobin. Shown
here is a sickle hemoglobin red blood cell compared to a
normal red blood cell.

The answer to this mystery began to emerge when
researchers noticed that a particularly deadly form
of malaria (falciparum malaria) was prevalent in the
same areas that had high rates of sickle-cell anemia
(▶ **Figure 2.6**). This severe form of malaria causes many
deaths or, in those who survive, high fever that significantly interferes with people's reproductive abilities.

Moreover, researchers discovered hemoglobin abnormalities among humans living in parts of the Arabian Peninsula, Greece, Algeria, Syria, and India, all regions where
malaria is (or was) common. Further research established
that although individuals with hemoglobin abnormalities
could still contract malaria, the effects of the malarial
parasite were less injurious.

Thus selection favored heterozygous individuals
with normal and sickling hemoglobin. The mutation
that causes hemoglobin to sickle consists of a change
in a single base of DNA, so it can arise readily by
chance. The loss of alleles for abnormal hemoglobin
caused by the death of those homozygous for it (from
sickle-cell anemia) was balanced out by the loss of alleles for normal hemoglobin, as those homozygous
for normal hemoglobin were more likely to die from
malaria.

This example also points out how adaptations tend
to be specific; the abnormal hemoglobin was adaptive
only in environments in which the malarial parasite
flourished. When individuals adapted to malarial regions came to regions relatively free of malaria, the
abnormal hemoglobin became comparatively disadvantageous. Although the rates of sickle-cell trait remain
relatively high among African Americans—about 9

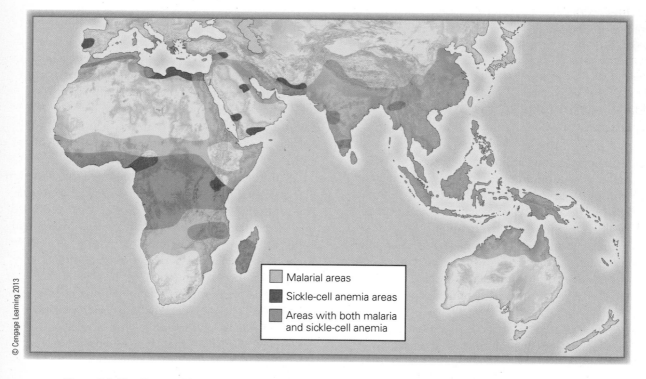

© Cengage Learning 2013

Malarial areas

Sickle-cell anemia areas

Areas with both malaria
and sickle-cell anemia

Figure 2.6 The Geographic Distribution of Malaria and Sickle-Cell Anemia People native to regions with
a high incidence of falciparum malaria have a higher than normal rate of the allele that causes sickle-cell
anemia. Researchers have surmised that natural selection preserved the allele for the sickle-cell trait to
protect individuals from the devastating effects of malaria.

percent have the sickling trait—this has significantly declined from the 22 percent estimated among the first African captives who were shipped across the Atlantic and sold as slaves. A similar decline in the sickle-cell allele would occur over the course of several generations in malarial zones if this deadly disease were brought under control.

This example also illustrates the important role culture plays in biological adaptation. In Africa, the severe form of malaria was not a significant problem until humans abandoned food foraging for farming a few thousand years ago. In order to farm, people had to clear areas of the natural forest cover. In the forest, decaying vegetation on the forest floor gave the ground an absorbent quality so that the heavy rainfall rapidly soaked into the soil. But once stripped of its natural vegetation, the soil lost this quality.

Without the forest canopy to break the force of the rainfall, the heavy rains compacted the soil further. The stagnant puddles that formed after rains provided the perfect breeding environment for the type of mosquito that hosts the malarial parasite. These mosquitoes then began to flourish and transmit the malarial parasite to humans.

Thus humans unwittingly created the kind of environment that made a disadvantageous trait, the abnormal hemoglobin associated with sickle-cell anemia, advantageous. While the biological process of evolution accounts for the frequency of the sickle-cell allele, cultural processes shape the environment to which humans adapt.

Adaptation and Physical Variation

Anthropologists study biological diversity in terms of **clines**, or the continuous gradation over space in the form or frequency of a trait. The spatial distribution or cline for the sickle-cell allele allowed anthropologists to identify the adaptive function of this gene in a malarial environment. Clinal analysis of a continuous trait such as body shape, which is controlled by a series of genes, allows anthropologists to interpret human global variation in body build as an adaptation to climate.

Generally, people long native to regions with cold climates tend to have greater body bulk (not to be equated with fat) relative to their extremities (arms and legs) than do people native to regions with hot climates, who tend to be relatively tall and slender (recall the chapter opener). Interestingly, tall, slender bodies show up in human evolution as early as 2 million years

ago. A person with larger body bulk and relatively short extremities may suffer more from summer heat than someone with a slender body and relatively long extremities. But this person will conserve needed body heat under cold conditions because a bulky body has less surface area relative to volume. In hot, open country, by contrast, people benefit from a long, slender body that can get rid of excess heat quickly. A small, slender body can also promote heat loss due to a high surface area to volume ratio.

In addition to these sorts of very long-term effects that climate may have imposed on human variation, climate can also contribute to human variation through its impact on the process of growth and development (developmental adaptation). For example, some of the biological mechanisms for withstanding cold or dissipating heat have been shown to vary depending upon the climate an individual experiences as a child. Individuals spending their youth in very cold climates develop circulatory system modifications that allow them to remain comfortable at temperatures people from warmer climates cannot tolerate. Similarly, hot climate promotes the development of a higher density of sweat glands, creating a more efficient system for sweating to keep the body cool.

Cultural processes complicate studies of biological adaptation to climate. For example, a poor diet during childhood affects the growth process and ultimately impacts adult body shape and size. Clothing also complicates these studies. In fact, culture rather than biology accounts for much of the way people adapt to cold. For instance, to cope with bitter Arctic climates, the Inuit peoples of northern Canada long ago developed efficient clothing to keep the body warm. The Inuit (and other Eskimos) created artificial tropical environments for themselves inside their clothing. Such cultural adaptations allow humans to inhabit the entire globe.

Some anthropologists have suggested that variation in features such as face and eye shape relate to climate. For example, biological anthropologists once proposed that the flat facial profile and round head—common in populations native to East and Central Asia, as well as Arctic North America—derive from adaptation to very cold environments. Though these features are common in Asian and Native American populations, considerable physical variation exists within each population. Some individuals who spread to North America from Asia have a head shape that is more common among Europeans. Such variation lies at the heart of the Kennewick Man controversy described in Chapter 1. Furthermore, genetic drift could also account for regional variation of traits. Because specific examples of adaptation, particularly of continuous traits, can be difficult to prove at times, scientists sometimes suggest that their colleagues' scenarios about adaptation are "Just So" stories.

Macroevolution and the Process of Speciation

While *microevolution* refers to changes in the allele frequencies of populations, **macroevolution** focuses on **speciation**—the formation of new species—and on the evolutionary relationships between groups of species. The microevolutionary forces of mutation, gene flow, genetic drift, and natural selection can lead to macroevolutionary change as species diverge.

As defined above, *species*—a population or group of populations capable of interbreeding and producing viable, fertile offspring—are reproductively isolated. The bullfrogs in one farmer's pond are the same species as those in a neighboring pond, even though the two populations may never actually interbreed; in theory, they could interbreed if brought together. But isolated populations may be in the process of evolving into different species, and it is hard to tell exactly when they become biologically distinct.

Certain factors, known as *isolating mechanisms*, can separate breeding populations and lead to the appear-ance of new species. Because isolation prevents gene flow, changes that affect the gene pool of one population cannot be introduced into the gene pool of the other. Random mutation may introduce new alleles in one of the isolated populations but not in the other. Genetic drift and natural selection may affect the two populations in different ways. Over time, as the two populations come to differ from each other, speciation occurs in a branching fashion known as **cladogenesis**. Speciation can also happen without branching, as a single population accumulates sufficient new mutations over time to be considered a separate species. This process is known as **anagenesis** (▶ **Figure 2.7**). Speciation is inferred in the fossil record when a group of organisms takes on a different appearance over time.

Because speciation is a process, it can occur at various rates. Scholars generally consider speciation through the process of natural selection as proposed in Darwin's *Origin of Species* (1859) to occur at a slow rate. In this model, speciation happens as organisms become better adapted to their environments. Sometimes, however, speciation can occur quite rapidly. For example, a genetic mutation such as one involving a key regulatory gene can lead to the formation of a new body plan. Such genetic accidents may involve material that is broken off, transposed, or transferred from one chromosome to another.

Genes that regulate the growth and development of an organism may have a major effect on its adult form. Scientists have discovered certain key genes called *homeobox genes* that are responsible for large-scale effects on the growth and development of the organism. If a new body plan happens to be adaptive, natural selection will maintain this new form during long periods of time rather than promoting change.

Paleontologists Stephen Jay Gould and Niles Eldredge proposed that speciation occurs in a pattern

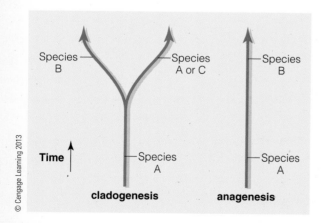

© Cengage Learning 2013

Figure 2.7 Cladogenesis and Anagenesis Cladogenesis occurs as different populations of an ancestral species become reproductively isolated. Through genetic drift and differential selection, the number of descendant species increases. By contrast, anagenesis can occur through a process of variational change that takes place as small differences in traits that (by chance) are advantageous in a particular environment accumulate in a species' gene pool. Over time, this may produce sufficient change to transform an old species into a new one. Genetic drift may also account for anagenesis.

clines The gradual changes in the frequency of an allele or trait over space.

macroevolution Evolution above the species level or leading to the formation of new species.

speciation The process of forming new species.

cladogenesis Speciation through a branching mechanism whereby an ancestral population gives rise to two or more descendant populations.

anagenesis A sustained directional shift in a population's average characteristics.

of **punctuated equilibria,** or the alternation between periods of rapid speciation and times of stability. Often this model of evolutionary change is contrasted with speciation through adaptation sometimes referred to as *Darwinian gradualism*. A close look at the genetics and the fossil record indicates that both models of evolutionary change have shaped the diversity of life on earth.

In biological terms, evolution accounts for all that humans share as well as the broad array of human diversity. Evolution is also responsible for the creation of new species over time. Primatologist Frans de Waal has said, "Evolution is a magnificent idea that has won over essentially everyone in the world willing to listen to scientific arguments."[8] We will return to the topic of human evolution in chapters that follow, but first we will look at the other living primates in order to understand the kinds of animals they are, what they have in common with humans, and what distinguishes the various forms. ✳

© David Scharf/Photo Researchers, Inc.

▲▲▲ Sometimes mutation in a single gene can cause reorganization of an organism's body plan. Here the "bithorax" homeobox gene has caused this fruit fly to have two thoraxes and two sets of wings. Another homeobox gene, "antennepedia," caused legs to develop in the place of antennae on the heads of fruit flies.

punctuated equilibria A model of macroevolutionary change that suggests evolution occurs via long periods of stability or stasis punctuated by periods of rapid change.

[8]de Waal, F. (2001). Sing the song of evolution. *Natural History 110* (8), 77.

Chapter Checklist

How are living things classified and how did this system come about?

✓ The science of taxonomy classifies living organisms into a series of progressively more inclusive categories on the basis of internal and external visual similarities.

✓ In the 18th century, Carolus Linnaeus devised his *System Naturae*, the first system to classify living things then known on the basis of similarities in body structure, body function, and sequence of bodily growth.

✓ Modern taxonomy still uses the basic Linnaean system but now looks at such characteristics as chemical reactions of blood, protein structure, and the makeup of the genetic material itself. These new

kinds of data have led to the revision of some existing taxonomies.

✓ Species, the smallest working units in biological classificatory systems, are reproductively isolated populations or groups of populations capable of interbreeding to produce fertile offspring.

What is evolution, and when was this central biological theory formulated?

✓ Charles Darwin formulated a theory of evolution in 1859. His conception of evolution was descent with modification, which occurred as a population (a group of interbreeding individuals) adapted to its environment through natural selection.

✓ Today evolution is understood in terms of the four evolutionary forces—mutation, genetic drift, gene flow, and natural selection—that affect the genetic structures of populations. Evolution, at the level of population genetics, is change in allele frequencies, which is also known as microevolution.

✓ Different versions or alternate forms of a gene for a given trait are called alleles. The total number of different alleles of genes available to a population is called its gene pool.

✓ Macroevolution focuses on the formation of new species (speciation) and on the evolutionary relationships among groups of species.

What is the molecular basis of evolution?

✔ Genes, the units of heredity, are segments of molecules of DNA (deoxyribonucleic acid), and the entire sequence of DNA is known as the genome.

✔ DNA is a complex molecule resembling two strands of rope twisted around each other with ladderlike rungs connecting the two strands.

✔ The sequence of bases along the DNA molecule directs the production of proteins. Proteins, in turn, constitute specific identifiable traits such as blood type. Just about everything in the human body is made of or by proteins, and human DNA provides the instructions for the thousands of proteins that keep us alive and healthy.

How do cells and organisms reproduce?

✔ DNA molecules have the unique property of being able to produce exact copies of themselves. As long as no errors are made in the process of replication, new daughter cells will be exact genetic copies of the parent cell.

✔ DNA molecules are located on chromosomes, structures found in the nucleus of each cell. Chromosomes consist of two sister chromatids, which are exact copies of each other.

✔ Each kind of organism has a characteristic number of chromosomes, which are usually found in pairs in sexually reproducing organisms. Humans have twenty-three pairs.

✔ Mitosis, one kind of cell division that results in new cells, begins when the chromosomes (hence, the genes) replicate, forming a duplicate of the original pair of chromosomes in the nucleus. Sister chromatids separate during mitosis and form identical daughter cells.

✔ Meiosis is related to sexual reproduction; it begins with the replication of original chromosomes, but these are divided into four cells, in humans each containing twenty-three single chromosomes. Fertilization, the union of an egg and a sperm cell, reestablishes the normal human number of twenty-three pairs of chromosomes.

How do different traits get inherited across generations?

✔ In the late 19th century Gregor Mendel discovered the particulate nature of heredity: Individuals inherit traits independently from each parent.

✔ Dominant alleles are able to mask the presence of recessive alleles. The allele for type A blood in humans, for example, is dominant to the allele for type O blood. Alleles that are both expressed when present are termed co-dominant. For example, an individual with the alleles for type A and type B blood has the AB blood type.

✔ Phenotype refers to the physical characteristics of an organism, whereas genotype refers to its genetic composition. Two organisms may have different genotypes but the same phenotype. An individual with the type A blood phenotype may possess either the AO or the AA genotype, having inherited one allele from each parent.

How do the four evolutionary forces contribute to the diversity of life on earth?

✔ Mutation provides the ultimate source of genetic variation. These changes in DNA may be helpful or harmful to the individual organism though most are neutral. Although mutations are inevitable given the nature of cellular chemistry, environmental factors—such as heat, chemicals, or radiation—can increase the mutation rate.

✔ Genetic drift refers to the effects of random events on the gene pool of a small population. Genetic drift may have been an important factor in human evolution because until 10,000 years ago humans lived in small isolated populations.

✔ Gene flow, the introduction of new variants of genes from nearby populations, distributes new variation to all populations and serves to prevent speciation.

✔ Natural selection, the evolutionary force involved in adaptive change, reduces the frequency of alleles for harmful or maladaptive traits within a population and increases the frequency of alleles for adaptive traits.

What are some examples of human adaptation through natural selection?

✔ A well-studied example of adaptation through natural selection in humans is inheritance of the trait for sickling red blood cells. The sickle-cell trait, caused by the inheritance of an abnormal form of hemoglobin, is an adaptation to life in regions in which malaria is common.

✔ Physical anthropologists have determined that some human physical variation appears related to climatic adaptation. People native to cold climates tend to have greater body bulk relative to their extremities than individuals from hot climates; the latter tend to be relatively tall and slender.

✔ Studies involving body build and climate are complicated by other factors such as the effects on physique of diet and clothing.

How are new species formed?

✔ Speciation can occur in a branching fashion (cladogenesis) or without branching (anagenesis), as a single population accumulates sufficient new mutations over time to be considered a separate species.

✔ Microevolutionary forces of mutation, gene flow, genetic drift, and natural selection can lead to macroevolutionary change, but the tempo of evolutionary change varies.

✔ A mutation in a regulatory gene can bring about rapid change. The punctuated equilibrium model proposes that macroevolution is characterized by long spans of relative stability with interspersed periods of rapid change.

Questions for Reflection

1. Humans can adapt to the environments they inhabit through biological and cultural means. But humans also shape their environments through a variety of cultural practices. What changes do you see occurring in the environment today due to human action? How do you imagine humans will adapt to these changes?

2. Scientific fact and theory can challenge other belief systems. Is it possible for scientific models of human evolution and religious stories of creation to coexist? How do you personally reconcile science and religion?

3. The discovery of the structure and function of the DNA molecule affects individuals and societies in many ways. Has the scientific understanding of the human genetic code challenged your conception of what it means to be human? How much of your life is dictated by the structure of your DNA? What will be the social consequences of depicting humans as entities programmed by their DNA?

4. The frequency of the sickle-cell allele in populations provides a classic example of adaptation on a genetic level. Describe the benefits of this deadly allele. Are mutations good or bad?

5. Are you likely to witness the appearance of a new species in your lifetime? If so, how might this come about? How would you recognize that this is truly a new species?

Key Terms

primates
mammals
species
genus, genera
taxonomy
analogies
homologies
natural selection
genes
law of segregation
law of independent
    assortment
chromosomes
DNA (deoxyribonucleic acid)

chromatid
alleles
genome
mitosis
meiosis
homozygous
heterozygous
genotype
dominant
recessive
phenotype
hemoglobin
polygenetic inheritance
population

gene pool
evolution
mutation
genetic drift
founder effects
gene flow
adaptation
sickle-cell anemia
clines
macroevolution
speciation
cladogenesis
anagenesis
punctuated equilibria

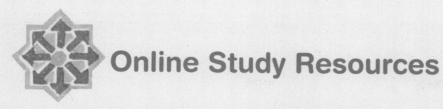

Online Study Resources

Login to **www.cengagebrain.com** to access the resources your instructor has assigned and to purchase materials. For this book, you can access:

CourseMate

Access chapter-specific learning tools including flashcards, glossaries, practice quizzes, videos, and more in your Anthropology CourseMate.

VISUAL ESSENCE

Biological similarities among humans, apes, and Old World monkeys have led to the extensive use of nonhuman primate species in biomedical research aimed at preventing or curing disease in humans. These research animals are subjected to procedures that would be considered morally questionable if done on humans. Mickey, for example, was one of the hundreds of chimps who spent decades of her life alone in a concrete-and-steel windowless cage in a private research facility in New Mexico. After years of testing the effects of various infectious diseases, cosmetics, drugs, and pesticides on chimps like Mickey, the laboratory finally closed in 2002 when government research funding was withdrawn due to repeated violations of the Animal Welfare Act. But after years of abuse and neglect, research chimpanzees lack the skills to participate in chimpanzee social life. Furthermore, research animals have often been infected with deadly diseases such as HIV or hepatitis and cannot be released into the wild. Fortunately, Mickey and the other research chimps were given sanctuary through Save the Chimps, one of several organizations that rescue research animals. As you learn about our closest living relatives in the animal kingdom, you will see how much we have in common. Although many countries now ban or severely limit experiments on the great apes, this research continues in the United States. Humans must direct some of our abundant intelligence and social conscience, traits that nonhuman primates also possess, to protect our cousins in the animal kingdom.

3 Living Primates

n October 1960, the young Jane Goodall sent word back to her mentor, paleoanthropologist Louis Leakey, that she had observed two chimps turning sticks into tools for fishing termites out of their nesting mounds at her research site in the wilds of Tanzania, East Africa. Leakey replied, "Now we must redefine 'tool,' redefine 'man,' or accept chimpanzees as humans."[1]

Field studies of primates by Western scientists have always contained a degree of anthropocentrism and a focus on what nonhuman primates can tell us about ourselves. Indeed, that is the purpose of this chapter. By looking at the biology and behavior of the primates, we gain a firmer understanding of those characteristics we share with other primates, as well as those that distinguish us from them and make us distinctively human. Studying communication and tool use among our primate cousins today, for example, can help anthropologists reconstruct how and why humans developed as they did. Studies of primate behavior might unravel an old nature–nurture question: How much of human behavior is biologically determined and how much of it derives from culture?

Today we are the only primate to inhabit the entire globe. As human population size rises to unsustainable levels, many primate groups are hovering on the brink of extinction. ▶ **Figure 3.1** shows the natural global distribution of living and fossil primates. It also indicates where the twenty-five most endangered species are struggling to survive. In this light, the purpose of this chapter is not just to learn more about ourselves, but to learn how to protect our primate cousins and the planet we share.

In this chapter you will learn to:

- **Identify the key methods of primatologists and the ethics they uphold.**

- **Situate primates in the animal kingdom and compare them to other mammals and reptiles.**

- **Recognize the basic features of primate anatomy and behavior.**

- **Distinguish the characteristics of the five natural groups of primates.**

- **Examine the biological basis of primate behavior, with particular emphasis on our closest relatives—chimpanzees and bonobos.**

- **Define primate culture in the context of human evolution.**

- **Identify critical issues and methods in primate conservation.**

---

[1]Jane Goodall Institute. www.janegoodall.org/janes-story (retrieved August 6, 2011).

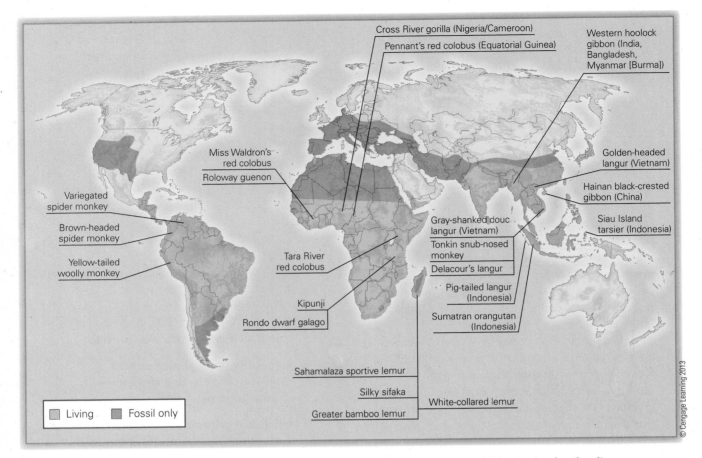

Cross River gorilla (Nigeria/Cameroon)
Pennant's red colobus (Equatorial Guinea)
Western hoolock gibbon (India, Bangladesh, Myanmar [Burma])
Miss Waldron's red colobus
Roloway guenon
Golden-headed langur (Vietnam)
Hainan black-crested gibbon (China)
Variegated spider monkey
Brown-headed spider monkey
Yellow-tailed woolly monkey
Tara River red colobus
Gray-shanked douc langur (Vietnam)
Tonkin snub-nosed monkey
Delacour's langur
Siau Island tarsier (Indonesia)
Pig-tailed langur (Indonesia)
Kipunji
Rondo dwarf galago
Sumatran orangutan (Indonesia)
Sahamalaza sportive lemur
Silky sifaka
White-collared lemur
Greater bamboo lemur

Living   Fossil only

© Cengage Learning 2013

Figure 3.1 The Global Distribution of Living and Fossil Nonhuman Primates In addition to showing the sites of fossil finds, this map shows the location of the twenty-five most endangered primate species today. In the past, when tropical forests covered more of the world, the primates enjoyed a greater range. Today primates face serious challenges, all deriving from human activity, such as war, habitat destruction, and hunting for bushmeat and souvenirs. Nearly 50 percent of the 634 known primate species and subspecies are threatened with extinction in the next decade.

Methods and Ethics in Primatology

Just as anthropologists employ diverse methods to study humans, primatologists today use a variety of methods to study the biology, behavior, and evolutionary history of our closest living relatives. Some primatologists concentrate on the comparative anatomy of ancient skeletons, while others trace evolutionary relationships by studying the comparative physiology and genetics of living species. Primatologists study the biology and behavior of living primates both in their natural habitats and in captivity in zoos, primate research colonies, or learning laboratories.

The classic image of a primatologist is of someone like Jane Goodall, a world-renowned British researcher who has devoted her career to in-depth observation of chimpanzees in their natural habitat. While documenting the range and nuance of chimpanzee behavior, she has also championed primate habitat conservation and humane treatment of primates in captivity. This philosophy of conservation and preservation has led to further

innovations in research methods. For example, primatologists have developed a number of noninvasive methods that allow them to study primate biology and behavior in the field while minimizing physical disruption. Primatologists gather hair, feces, and other body secretions left by the primates in the environment for later analysis in the laboratory. These analyses provide invaluable information about characteristics such as dietary habits or genetic relatedness among a group of individuals.

Work with captive animals provides more than knowledge about the basic biology of primates. It has also allowed primatologists to document the humanity of our primate cousins. Many of the amazing linguistic and conceptual abilities of primates became known through studies of captive animals. Individual primatologists have devoted their careers to working with primates in captivity, teaching them to communicate through pictures on a computer screen or American Sign Language. Of course, even compassionate captivity imposes stress on primates. Still, the knowledge gained through these studies ultimately will contribute to primate conservation and survival.

At first glance it might seem inherently more humane to work with animals in the field compared to captivity. But even field studies raise important ethical issues for primatologists to consider. Primatologists must maintain an awareness of how their presence affects the behavior of the group. For example, does becoming tolerant of human observers make the primates more vulnerable? Primates habituated to humans commonly range beyond established wilderness preserves and come in close contact with other humans who may be more interested in hunting than observing. Contact between primates and humans can also expose endangered primates to infectious diseases carried by humans. Whether working with primates in captivity or in the field, primatologists seriously consider the well-being of the primates they study.

Primates as Mammals

Biologists classify humans within the primate order, a subgroup of the class Mammalia. The other primates include lemurs, lorises, tarsiers, monkeys, and apes. Humans—together with chimpanzees, bonobos, gorillas, orangutans, gibbons, and siamangs—form the hominoids, colloquially known as apes, a superfamily within the primate order. Biologically speaking, as hominoids, humans are apes.

The primates are only one of several different kinds of mammal, such as rodents, carnivores, and ungulates (hoofed mammals). Primates, like other mammals, are intelligent animals, having more in the way of brains than reptiles or other kinds of vertebrates. Increased brainpower and the mammalian growth and development process form the biological basis of the flexible behavior patterns typical of mammals. In most species, the young are born live, the egg being retained within the womb of the female until the embryo achieves an advanced state of growth.

Once born, the young receive milk from their mothers' mammary glands, the physical feature from which the class Mammalia gets its name. During this period of infant dependency, young mammals learn many of the things they will need for survival as adults. Primates in general, and apes in particular, have a very long period of infant and childhood dependency in which the young learn the ways of their social group. Thus primate behavioral patterns derive from mammalian primate biology.

Mammals tend to be more active than other members of the animal kingdom. Their high activity levels depend upon a relatively constant body temperature, an efficient respiratory system featuring a separation between the nasal (nose) and mouth cavities (allowing them to breathe while they eat), a diaphragm to assist in drawing in and letting out breath, and an efficient four-chambered heart that prevents mixing of oxygenated and deoxygenated blood.

Mammals possess a skeleton in which the limbs are positioned beneath the body, rather than out to the sides. This arrangement allows for direct support and easy, flexible movement. The bones of the limbs have joints constructed to permit growth in the young while simultaneously providing strong, hard joint surfaces that will stand up to the stresses of sustained activity. Mammals stop growing when they reach adulthood, whereas reptiles continue to grow through their lives.

© Martin Harvey/Peter Arnold, Inc.

▲▲▲ Nursing their young is an important part of the general mammalian tendency to invest high amounts of energy into rearing relatively few offspring at a time. Reptiles, by contrast, lay many eggs that hatch independently, with the young fending for themselves. Ape mothers, such as this chimpanzee, tend to nurse their young for four to five years. The practice of bottle-feeding infants, common in North America, Europe, and many other parts of the world today, is a dramatic departure from the typical ape pattern. Although the health benefits of breastfeeding for mothers (reduced cancer rate) and infants (strengthened immune system) have been well documented, cultural norms present obstacles to breastfeeding. Across the globe, however, women nurse their children for about three years, on average.

Mammals and reptiles also differ in terms of their teeth. Reptilian teeth are pointed, peglike, and all identical; mammalian teeth are specialized for particular purposes: incisors for nipping, gnawing, and cutting; canines for ripping, tearing, killing, and fighting; premolars for either slicing and tearing or crushing and grinding (depending on the kind of animal); and molars for crushing and grinding (▶ **Figure 3.2**). This enables mammals to eat a wide variety of food—an advantage to them, since they require more food than reptiles to sustain their high activity level.

But mammals pay a price for their dental specialization: Reptiles have unlimited tooth replacement throughout their lives, whereas mammals are limited to two sets. The first set serves the immature animal and is replaced by the "permanent" or adult teeth. The specializations of mammalian teeth allow species and evolutionary relationships to be identified through dental comparisons.

Evidence from ancient skeletons indicates the first mammals appeared over 200 million years ago as small **nocturnal**—active at night— creatures. The earliest primatelike creatures came into being about 65 million years ago when a new mild climate favored the spread of dense tropical and subtropical forests over much of the earth. The change in climate and habitat, combined with the sudden extinction of dinosaurs, favored mammal diversification, including the evolutionary development of **arboreal**—tree-living—mammals from which primates evolved.

The ancestral primates possessed biological characteristics that allowed them to adapt to life in the forests. Their relatively small size enabled them to use tree branches not accessible to larger competitors and predators. Arboreal life opened up an abundant new food supply. The primates could gather leaves, flowers, fruits, insects, birds' eggs, and even nesting birds, rather than having to wait for them to fall to the ground. Natural selection favored those who judged depth correctly and gripped the branches tightly. Those individuals who survived life in the trees passed on their genes to succeeding generations.

Although the earliest primates were nocturnal, today most primate species are **diurnal**—active in the day. The transition to diurnal life in the trees involved important biological adjustments that helped shape the biology and behavior of humans today.

Primate Characteristics

While the living primates are a varied group of animals, they do share a number of features. We humans, for example, can grasp, throw things, and see in three dimensions because of shared primate characteristics.

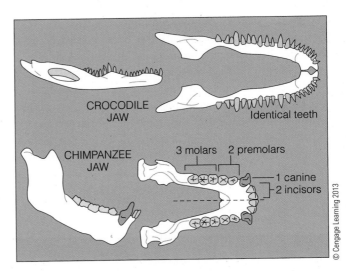

Figure 3.2 Teeth of Reptiles and Mammals Crocodile jaws, like the jaws of all reptiles, contain a series of identical teeth. If a tooth breaks or falls out, a new tooth will emerge in its place. Mammals, by contrast, possess precise numbers of specialized teeth, each with a particular shape characteristic of the group, as indicated on the chimpanzee jaw: Incisors in front are shown in blue, canines behind in red, followed by two premolars and three molars in yellow (the last being the "wisdom teeth" in humans).

© Cengage Learning 2013

Compared to other mammals, primates possess a relatively unspecialized anatomy, whereas their behavioral patterns are diverse and flexible. Many primate characteristics are useful in one way or another to arboreal animals, although (as any squirrel knows) they are not essential to life in the trees. For animals preying upon the many insects living on the fruit and flowers of trees and shrubs, however, primate characteristics such as manipulative hands and keen vision would have been enormously adaptive. Life in the trees along with the visual predation of insects played a role in the evolution of primate biology.

Primate Teeth

The varied primate diet available to arboreal primates—shoots, leaves, insects, and fruits—did not require the specialization of teeth seen in other mammals. Unlike some mammals, they have retained incisors, canines, premolars, and molars—each with a distinct shape and function as described above (recall Figure 3.2). Primates use their large, flaring, fanglike canines for defense and communication as well as for tearing and shredding food. Humans possess relatively small canines, although our oversized roots suggest we had larger canines in our ancestry.

Sensory Organs

The primates' adaptation to arboreal life involved changes in the form and function of their sensory organs. The sense of smell was vital for the earliest ground-dwelling,

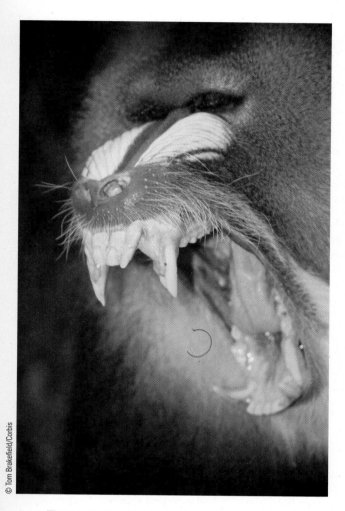

© Tom Brakefield/Corbis

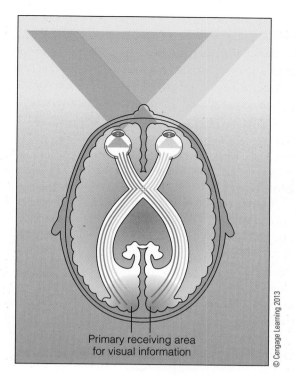

Primary receiving area
for visual information

© Cengage Learning 2013

Figure 3.3 Binocular Stereoscopic Vision Monkeys,
apes, and humans possess binocular stereoscopic
vision. Binocular vision refers to overlapping visual
fields due to forward-facing eyes. Three-dimensional
or stereoscopic vision comes from binocular vision
and the transmission of information from each eye
to both sides of the brain.

▲▲▲ Though the massive canine teeth of some male primates
are serious weapons, they are more often used to communicate rather than to draw blood. Raising his lip to "flash" his
canines, this mandrill will quickly get the young members of his
group in line. Over the course of human evolution, overall canine size decreased, as did differences in canine size between
males and females.

nocturnal mammals. It enabled them to operate in the
dark, to sniff out their food, and to detect hidden predators. However, good vision is more valuable than good
smell for an arboreal animal that is active during daylight,
because it allows for expert judgment in locating the next
branch or tasty morsel. Accordingly, the sense of smell
declined in primates, while vision became highly developed.

Travel through the trees demands judgments concerning depth, direction, distance, and the relationships
of objects hanging in space, such as vines or branches.
Monkeys, apes, and humans achieved this through binocular stereoscopic vision (▶ **Figure 3.3**), the ability to
see the world in the three dimensions of height, width,
and depth. **Binocular vision**—in which two eyes sit next
to each other on the same plane so that their visual fields
overlap—together with nerve connections that run from
each eye to both sides of the brain confer complete depth

perception characteristic of three-dimensional or **stereoscopic vision**. This arrangement allows nerve cells to integrate the images derived from each eye. Increased brain
size in the visual area in primates and a greater complexity
of nerve connections also contribute to stereoscopic vision.

Monkeys, apes, and humans also possess color vision,
which markedly improves the diet of these primates
compared to most other mammals. The ability to distinguish colors allows them to choose ripe fruits or tender
immature leaves due to their red rather than green col-
oration. See this chapter's Biocultural Connection to see
how our primate ancestry affects our response to color.

▲▲

nocturnal Active at night and at rest during the day.

arboreal Living in the trees.

diurnal Active during the day and at rest at night.

binocular vision Vision with increased depth perception from
two eyes set next to each other allowing their visual fields to
overlap.

stereoscopic vision Complete three-dimensional vision, or
depth perception, from binocular vision and nerve connections
that run from each eye to both sides of the brain, allowing nerve
cells to integrate the images derived from each eye.

▼▼▼

BIOCULTURAL CONNECTION

Why Red Is Such a Potent Color

By Meredith F. Small

The Olympic athletes have been parading around like fashionistas in an array of colorful outfits, and we, their adoring public, can't resist commenting on the style and color of their high-end athletic wear. My favorite was the faux silk, faux embroidered, slinky red leotards of the Chinese women's gymnasts.

Apparently, as researchers have recently discovered, the choice of red for those leotards might also have given the Chinese gymnasts an advantage. But why is the color red so impressive?

The answer lies in our tree-living past. In the back of the vertebrate eyeball are two kinds of cells called rods and cones that respond to light. Cones take in a wide range of light, which means they recognize colors, and they are stimulated best during daylight. Rods respond to a narrower range of light (meaning only white light) but notice that light from far away and at night.

Isaac Newton was the first person to hold up a prism and refract white light into a rainbow of colors and realize that there might be variation in what the eye can see. Color comes at us in electromagnetic waves. When the wavelength of light is short we perceive purple or blue. Medium wavelengths of lights tickle the cones in another way and we think green. Long light wavelengths make those cones stand up and dance as bright spots of yellow, orange, and red.

Various animals distinguish only parts of that rainbow because their cones respond in different ways. Butterflies, for example, see into the ultraviolet end of the rainbow, which allows them to see their own complex markings better than we can. Foxes and owls are basically colorblind and it doesn't matter because they are awake at night when the light spectrum is limited anyway.

Humans are lucky enough to be primates, animals with decent color vision, and we can thank monkeys for this special ability.

Long ago, primitive primates that resemble today's lemurs and lorises saw only green and blue, the longer wavelengths of color. But when monkeys evolved, around 34 million years ago, their cones became sensitive to even shorter wavelengths of color and they saw red.

And what a difference. With red, the forest comes alive. Instead of a blanket of bluish-green leaves, the world is suddenly accented with ripe red, yellow, and orange fruits, and even the leaves look different.

For a monkey leaping through the forest canopy, color vision would be an essential advantage. Unripe fruit doesn't have enough carbs to sustain a hungry primate and they taste really sour. Unripe leaves not only taste bad, they are toxic and indigestible.

For the first humans foraging about the forest and savannah around 5 mil-

lion years ago, it would have been much more efficient to spot a ripe fruit or tuber than bite into a zillion just to get the right one. And so humans ended up with color vision even though we no longer live in trees.

But color is more than wavelengths, more than an indicator of ripeness, to us. Color has become symbolic, meaning it has meaning, and that meaning is highly cultural.

Chinese athletes and Chinese brides wear red because red is considered lucky. The U.S. athletes also wear red because that bright color is in the U.S. flag, and because designers of athletic wear, as well as scientists, know that red gets you noticed. ∎

Biocultural Question

While the vast majority of humans see color as described here, 8 to 20 percent of human males have red–green color-blindness. Do you know someone who is colorblind? What could a conversation with a colorblind person reveal about the anthropological perspective? What colors besides red have particular meanings? Do these meanings derive from biology or culture?

Adapted from Small, M. F. (2008, August 15). Why red is such a potent color. *Live Science*. www.livescience.com/5043-red-potent-color.html (retrieved August 8, 2011).

Tree-living primates also possess an acute sense of touch. An effective feeling and grasping mechanism helps keep them from falling and tumbling while speeding through the trees. The early mammals from which primates evolved had tiny touch-sensitive hairs at the tips of their hands and feet. In primates, sensitive pads backed up by nails on the tips of the animals' fingers and toes replaced these hairs.

The Primate Brain

An increase in brain size, particularly in the cerebral hemispheres—the areas supporting conscious thought—occurred in the course of primate evolution. In monkeys, apes, and humans, the cerebral hemispheres completely cover the cerebellum, the part of the brain that coordinates the muscles and maintains body balance. One of

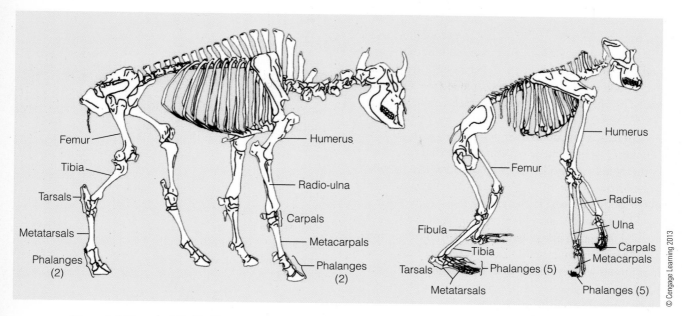

Figure 3.4 Bison and Gorilla Skeletons All primates possess the same ancestral vertebrate limb pattern seen in reptiles and amphibians, consisting of a single upper long bone, two lower long bones, and five radiating digits (fingers and toes), as seen in this gorilla (*right*) skeleton. Other mammals such as bison (*left*) have a modified version of this pattern. In the course of evolution, bison have lost all but two of their digits, which form their hooves. The second long bone in the lower part of the limb is reduced. Note also the joining of the skull and vertebral column in these skeletons. In bison (as in most mammals) the skull projects forward from the vertebral column, but in semi-erect gorillas, the vertebral column is further beneath the skull.

the most significant outcomes of this development is the flexibility seen in primate behavior. Rather than relying on reflexes controlled by the cerebellum, primates constantly react to a variety of features in the environment. Messages from the hands and feet, eyes and ears—as well as from the sensors of balance, movement, heat, touch, and pain—are simultaneously relayed to the cerebral cortex.

Obviously the cortex had to evolve considerably in order to receive, analyze, and coordinate these impressions and transmit the appropriate response back to the motor nerves. The enlarged, responsive cerebral cortex provides the biological basis for flexible behavior patterns found in all primates, including humans.

The emphasis on vision in primates described above corresponded to changes in the primate brain. Reptiles possess nerve cells in the backs of their eyes that process visual information. All mammals, by contrast, process visual messages in the brain, which allows this information to be integrated with other sensory information: sound, touch, taste, position sense, and smell.

It is also likely that primates' insect predation in an arboreal setting played a role in the enlargement of the brain. This behavior pattern would have required great

agility and motor coordination, which would favor development of these areas of the brain. Interestingly, the parts of the brain responsible for higher mental faculties developed in an area alongside the motor centers of the brain.[2]

The Primate Skeleton

The skeleton gives vertebrates—animals with internal backbones—their basic shape or silhouette, supports the soft tissues, and helps protect vital internal organs (▶ **Figure 3.4**). Some evolutionary trends are evident in the primate skeleton. For example, as primates relied increasingly on vision rather than smell, the eyes rotated forward to become enclosed in a protective layer of bone. Simultaneously, the snout reduced in size. The opening at the base of the skull for passage of the spinal cord assumed a more forward position, reflecting some degree of upright posture rather than a constant four-footed stance.

The limbs of the primate skeleton follow the same basic ancestral plan seen in the earliest vertebrates. The upper portion of each arm or leg has a single long bone, the lower portion has two bones, and then hands or feet with five radiating digits. Many other animals possess limbs specialized to optimize a particular behavior, such as running. The generalized limb pattern allows for flexible movements by primates.

[2]Romer, A. S. (1945). *Vertebrate paleontology* (p. 103). Chicago: University of Chicago Press.

In nearly all of the primates, the big toe and thumb are **opposable**, making it possible to grasp and manipulate objects such as sticks and stones with both the hands and feet. Humans and their direct ancestors are the only exceptions, having lost the opposable big toe. Other aspects of primate skeletal variation include the shape of the collarbone (clavicle), which varies among primate groups depending upon their pattern of locomotion. Monkeys move about on all fours and so have narrow bodies with short collarbones. In the apes, a long collarbone orients the arms at the side rather than at the front of the body, allowing for heightened flexibility. With their broad flexible shoulder joints, apes can hang suspended from tree branches and swing from tree to tree.

The retention of the flexible vertebrate limb pattern in primates was a valuable asset to evolving humans. In part, it was having hands capable of grasping that enabled our own ancestors to manufacture and use tools and thus alter the course of their evolution. Today our ape anatomy allows humans to do things as varied as throw a baseball at lightning speed or weave intricate patterns from threads suspended on wide looms.

Living Primates

Except for a few species of monkeys who live in temperate climates and humans who inhabit the entire globe, the living primates inhabit warm areas of the world. We will briefly explore the diverse biology and behavior of five natural groupings of contemporary primates: (1) lemurs and lorises, (2) tarsiers, (3) New World monkeys (native to Central and South America), (4) Old World monkeys (native to Africa and Eurasia), and (5) apes.

Traditionally, primatologists grouped lemurs, lorises, and tarsiers together as **prosimians** (from the Latin for "before monkeys") based on morphological similarities they share with the most ancient primates. They placed monkeys, apes, and humans together as **anthropoids** (from the Greek for "humanlike"). Recent molecular evidence has shown that tarsiers are more closely related to monkeys, apes, and humans than to lemurs and lorises. Thus, a molecular approach divides the primates into two groups called the **strepsirhines** (lemurs and lorises) and the **haplorhines** (tarsiers, monkeys, apes, and humans). For the purposes of this chapter, which emphasizes the entire adaptive package of primate groups, dividing the primates into prosimians and anthropoids makes sense. The anatomy and behavior of the prosimians most closely resemble the nocturnal behavioral pattern of the earliest primates. The anthropoid primates tend to be larger, active in the daytime, and live in large social groups. The anthropoids out-competed diurnal prosimians in regions where both kinds of primate coexist.

Lemurs and Lorises

Lemurs live only on the island of Madagascar (off the east coast of Africa), while lorises range from Africa to southern and eastern Asia. Nocturnal and arboreal, the lorises most resemble the ancestral primates. On Madagascar, without competition from anthropoid primates until humans arrived, lemurs diversified substantially, with many lemur species becoming ground-dwelling and diurnal, or active during the day. The fossil evidence from Madagascar shows that some lemurs even reached very large sizes.

All living prosimian species are small, with none larger than a good-sized dog. In general body outline they resemble rodents and insect-eating animals, with short pointed snouts, large pointed ears, and big eyes. In the anatomy of the upper lip and snout, lemurs and lorises resemble nonprimate mammals, with an upper lip tethered down to the gum and split, moist, naked skin on the nose around the nostrils. They also have long tails. The striped tail of a ring-tailed lemur resembles the tail of a raccoon.

Lemurs and lorises have typical primate "hands," although they use them in pairs, rather than one at a time. Sensitive pads and flattened nails are located at the tips of the fingers and toes, and they retain a claw on their second toe, sometimes called a grooming claw, which they use for scratching and cleaning. Lemurs and lorises possess another unique structure for grooming: a dental comb made up of the lower incisors and canines that projects forward from the jaw. They use the dental comb for grooming by running it through their fur. Though lemurs and lorises have retained a number of ancestral characteristics typical of the earliest fossil primates and the insectivores from which primates evolved, they are not "less evolved"; their unique evolutionary path since their divergence from the other primates includes the retention of some ancestral traits.

Tarsiers

Outwardly and in their nocturnal habit, tarsiers resemble the lemurs and lorises. Genetically, however, they are more closely related to monkeys and apes. In the structure of the nose and lips, and in the part of the brain governing vision, tarsiers resemble monkeys.

© Cengage Learning 2013

◄ Over the course of their evolutionary history, primates came to rely more on their vision than on their sense of smell. Prosimians, who were the earliest group of primates to appear, maintain their primary reliance on smell. On the island of Madagascar, home to many species of diurnal ground-dwelling lemurs, such as the ring-tailed lemurs shown here, the prosimians mark their territory and communicate through "smelly" messages left for others with a squirt from glands located on their wrists. Though prosimians appeared before the anthropoids in primate evolution, and retain many ancestral features such as their dependence on smell, they are no less evolved. Outside of Madagascar, prosimians remained arboreal and nocturnal due to competition from monkeys and apes.

Tarsiers are mainly nocturnal insect eaters. The head, eyes, and ears of these kitten-sized arboreal creatures are huge in proportion to the body, making them well adapted for nocturnal life. Tarsiers have the remarkable ability to turn their heads 180 degrees, so they can see where they have been as well as where they are going.

Tarsiers, like some lemurs and lorises, possess longer hind limbs than their front limbs, allowing them to move from tree to tree by vertical clinging and leaping. First they hang onto the trunk of one tree in an upright position, with their long legs curled up tightly like springs and their heads twisted to look in the direction they are headed. They propel themselves into the air, do a "180," and land facing the trunk on their tree of choice. Tarsiers get their name from the elongated tarsal, or foot bone, that provides these tiny animals leverage for jumps of 6 feet or more.

▲▲▲ With their large eyes, tarsiers are well adapted for nocturnal life. If human faces had eyes with the same proportions as tarsiers, our eyes would be approximately the size of oranges. In their nocturnal habit and outward appearance, tarsiers resemble lemurs and lorises. Genetically, however, they are more closely related to monkeys and apes, causing scientists to rework the suborder divisions in primate taxonomy to reflect this evolutionary relationship.

opposable The ability to bring the thumb or big toe in contact with the tips of the other digits on the same hand or foot in order to grasp objects.

prosimians A subdivision within the primate order based on shared anatomical characteristics; includes lemurs, lorises, and tarsiers.

anthropoids A subdivision within the primate order based on shared anatomical characteristics; includes New World monkeys, Old World monkeys, and apes (including humans).

strepsirhines A subdivision within the primate order based on shared genetic characteristics; includes lemurs and lorises.

haplorhines A subdivision within the primate order based on shared genetic characteristics; includes tarsiers, New World monkeys, Old World monkeys, and apes (including humans).

Anthropoids: Monkeys and Apes

Monkeys, apes, and humans resemble one another more than any of these groups resemble lemurs, lorises, or tarsiers. We humans are remarkably like monkeys but even more like the other apes in our appearance.

New World monkeys live in the tropical forests of South and Central America, and southern Mexico. All are arboreal with long tails. Some groups of New World monkeys possess **prehensile** or grasping tails, which they use as a fifth limb. The naked skin on the undersides of their tails resembles the sensitive skin found at the tips of our fingers and is even covered with whorls like fingerprints. These and other features distinguish the New World monkeys from the Old World monkeys, apes, and humans. Old World monkeys and apes, including humans, share an evolutionary history that spans 40 million years in Africa; this history is distinct from the course taken by anthropoid primates in the tropical Americas.

The Old World monkeys, divided from the apes at the superfamily taxonomic level, possess nonprehensile tails. They may live on the ground or in the trees, using a quadrupedal or four-footed pattern of locomotion on the ground or a palms-down position in the trees. They have narrow bodies with hind limbs and forelimbs of equal length and relatively fixed and sturdy shoulder, elbow, and wrist joints. Old World monkey species range from the tropical regions of Africa and Asia to Gibraltar, a small island off the southern coast of Spain to as far north as Japan.

Baboons, a kind of Old World monkey, have been of particular interest to paleoanthropologists because some baboon species live in environments similar to those in which humans may have originated. These baboons have abandoned trees (except for sleeping and refuge) and have become largely terrestrial, living in the savannahs, deserts, and highlands of Africa. They have long, fierce faces and eat a diet consisting of leaves, seeds, insects, and lizards. They live in large, well-organized troops comprised of related females and adult males that have transferred out of other troops.

Small and Great Apes

The other apes (the hominoid superfamily) are the closest living relatives we humans have in the animal world. They include gibbons, siamangs, orangutans, gorillas, chimpanzees, and bonobos. Apes (including humans) are large, tail-less, wide-bodied primates. All apes possess a shoulder anatomy specialized for hanging suspended below tree branches, although among apes only gibbons and talented gymnasts swing from branch to branch in the pattern known as **brachiation** (Latin for "arm motion"). All apes except humans and their immediate ancestors possess arms that are longer than their legs.

When moving on the ground, the African apes "knuckle-walk" on the backs of their hands, resting their weight on the middle joints of the fingers. They stand erect when reaching for fruit, looking over tall grass, or doing any activity where they find an erect position advantageous. Though apes can walk on two legs (bipedally) for short periods of time, the structure of the ape pelvis is not well suited to support the weight of the torso and limbs for more than several minutes.

Standing about 3 feet high, gibbons and siamangs, small apes native to Southeast Asia, have compact, slim bodies with extraordinarily long arms compared to their short legs. Masters of brachiation, they can also run erect, holding their arms out for balance. Gibbon and siamang males and females are similar in size, living in social groups of two adults and offspring.

Found in the Indonesian islands of Borneo and Sumatra, orangutans, like the other great apes, are considerably

© Ingo Arndt/Minden Pictures

▲▲▲ Grasping hands and three-dimensional vision enable primates like these South American monkeys to lead an active life in the trees. In some New World monkey species, a grasping or prehensile tail makes that life even easier. The naked skin on the undersides of their tails resembles the sensitive skin found at the tips of our fingers and is even covered with whorls like fingerprints. This sensory skin allows New World monkeys to use their tails as a fifth limb.

◄
◄
◄ All apes, including humans, possess widely spaced flexible shoulder joints for hanging suspended below the branches or swinging from branch to branch. Gibbons are the masters of the swinging form of locomotion called brachiation. Large apes, such as this orangutan, move slowly through the lower branches, using their long arms to span great distances.

taller and heavier than gibbons and siamangs. The closeness of the eyes and their facial prominence give orangutans a human look. The people of Indonesia gave orangutans their name, "person of the forest," using the Malay terms *orang,* which means "human" and *hutan,* which means "forest." More arboreal than the African apes, on the ground orangutans walk with their forelimbs in a fist-sideways or a palm-down position. Although sociable by nature, the orangutans of upland Borneo spend most of their time alone (except in the case of females with young), as they have to forage over a wide area to obtain sufficient food. By contrast, abundant fruits and insects in the swamps of Sumatra sustain groups of adults and permit coordinated group travel. Thus gregariousness is a function of the richness of their habitat.[3]

Gorillas, found in tropical Africa, are the largest of the apes; an adult male can weigh over 450 pounds, with females about half that size. A thick coat of glossy black hair covers their bodies, and mature males have a silvery gray upper back. Gorillas possess a strikingly human look about the face, and like humans, they focus on things in their field of vision by directing the eyes rather than moving the head.

Mostly ground-dwellers, gorillas also climb trees, using their hands and feet to grip the trunks and branches. The lighter females and young may sleep in trees in carefully constructed nests. Because of their weight, adult males spend less time in the trees but raise and lower themselves among the tree branches when searching for fruit.

Gorillas knuckle-walk, using all four limbs with the fingers of the hand flexed, placing the knuckles instead of the palm of the hand on the ground. They stand erect to reach for fruit, to see something more easily, or to threaten perceived sources of danger with their famous chest-beating displays. Though known for these displays

to protect the members of their troop, adult male silverback gorillas are the gentle giants of the forest. As vegetarians, gorillas devote a major portion of each day to eating volumes of plant matter to sustain their massive bodies. Although gorillas are gentle and tolerant, bluffing is an important part of their behavioral repertoire.

Chimpanzees and bonobos, two closely related species of the same genus (*Pan*), differ in their distribution and in certain behaviors. The bonobos inhabit only the rainforests of the Democratic Republic of Congo while chimpanzees are widely distributed in the forested portions of sub-Saharan Africa.

Long-time favorites in zoos and circuses, chimpanzees and bonobos have a particular reputation for cleverness. Nevertheless, all four great apes are of equal intelligence, despite some differences in cognitive styles. More arboreal than gorillas, but less so than orangutans, chimpanzees and bonobos forage on the ground much of the day, knuckle-walking like gorillas. At sunset, they return to the trees, where they build their nests. Chimps build their nests over a wide area, whereas bonobos prefer to build their nests close to one another.

Primate Behavior

Primates adapt to their environments through a wide variety of behaviors. As social animals, primates live and travel in groups that vary in size from species to species. In many primate species, including humans, adolescence marks the time when individuals change the relationships

▲▲

prehensile The ability to grasp.
brachiation Moving from branch to branch using the arms, with the body hanging suspended below.

▼▼

[3]Normile, D. (1998). Habitat seen as playing larger role in shaping behavior. *Science* 279, 1454.

they have had with the group they have known since birth. Among primates this change takes the form of migration of either males or females to new social groups.

Young apes spend more time reaching adulthood than do most other mammals. During this lengthy period of growth and development, they learn the behaviors of their social group. Although biological factors play a role in the duration of primate dependency, many of the specific behaviors learned during childhood derive solely from the traditions of the group. The behavior of primates, particularly apes, provides anthropologists with clues about the earliest development of human culture.

Primatologists have carried out many studies of ape behavior in the animals' natural habitats, seeking models to help reconstruct the behavior of evolving humans. As we discussed earlier, Louis Leakey sent Jane Goodall to study the chimpanzees; he also sent U.S. primatologist Dian Fossey to study mountain gorillas and her German colleague Birute Galdikas to study orangutans, all with the purpose of understanding human origins.

While no living primate lives exactly as our ancestors did, these studies have revealed remarkable variation and sophistication in ape behavior. Primatologists increasingly interpret these variations as cultural because they are learned rather than genetically programmed or instinctive. We shall concentrate on the behavior of two closely related African species of chimpanzee: common chimpanzees and bonobos.

Chimpanzee and Bonobo Behavior

Like nearly all primates, chimpanzees and bonobos are highly social. Among chimps, the largest social organizational unit is the **community**, usually composed of fifty or more individuals who collectively inhabit a large geographic area. Rarely, however, do all of these animals congregate. Instead, they range singly or in small subgroups consisting of adult males, or females with their young, or males and females together with their young. In the course of their travels, subgroups may join forces and forage together, but sooner or later these will break up into smaller units. Typically, when some individuals split off, others join, so the composition of subunits shifts frequently.

In the past, primatologists believed that male **dominance hierarchies**, in which some animals outrank and dominate others, formed the basis of primate social structures. They noted that physical strength and size play a role in determining an animal's rank. By this measure, males generally outrank females. However, the male-biased cultures of many early primatologists may have contributed to this theoretical perspective, with their emphasis on domination through superior size and strength. Male dominance hierarchies seemed "natural" to these initial researchers.

With the benefit of detailed field studies over the last forty years, including cutting-edge research by primatolo-gists such as Goodall, the nuances of primate social behavior, the relative harmony of primate social life, and the importance of female primates have been documented. High-ranking female chimpanzees may dominate low-ranking males. And among bonobos, female rank determines the social order of the group far more than male rank. While greater strength and size do contribute to an animal's higher rank, several other factors also come into play in determining its social position. These include the rank of its mother, a factor largely determined through her cooperative social behavior and how effectively each individual animal creates alliances with others.

On the whole, bonobo females form stronger bonds with one another than do chimpanzee females. Moreover, the strength of the bond between mother and son interferes with bonds among males. Bonobo males defer to females in feeding, and alpha (high-ranking) females have been observed chasing alpha males; such males may even yield to low-ranking females, particularly when groups of females form

▲▲▲ Although chimps and bonobos live in large communities of fifty or more individuals, on a daily basis they tend to split up into smaller groups that forage together. A relative harmony characterizes chimp and bonobo life, although among chimps "war" between neighboring communities has been documented. Bonobos, by contrast, remain the consummate peacemakers.

Grooming strengthens bonds among individual members of the group. Some individuals have favorite grooming partners, and some, like the chimps pictured here, lined up in a pattern known as the domino effect for a group grooming experience. Cultural traditions for grooming vary. In some groups, chimps always groom face-to-face, clasping their hands while grooming. Others incorporate leaves into their grooming practices.

alliances.[4] Further, allied females will band together to force an aggressive male out of the community. These bonobo females cooperate even though they are not genetically related to one another.[5]

The emphasis on social ranking, competition, and attack behavior by Western primatologists may have derived in part from the values of Western cultures. By contrast, Japanese primatologist Kinji Imanishi, who initiated field studies of bonobos in the early 20th century, investigated the importance of social cooperation rather than competition. Likewise, Dutch primatologist Frans de Waal's research, highlighted in the following Original Study, shows that

---

[4]de Waal, F., Kano, T., & Parish, A. R. (1998). Comments. *Current Anthropology 39,* 408, 410, 413.

[5]Gierstorfer, C. (2007). Peaceful primates, violent acts. *Nature 447,* 7.

ORIGINAL STUDY

Reconciliation and Its Cultural Modification in Primates

Frans B. M. de Waal

Despite the continuing popularity of the struggle-for-life metaphor, it is increasingly recognized that there are drawbacks to open competition, hence that there are sound evolutionary reasons for curbing it. The dependency of social animals on group life and cooperation makes aggression a socially costly strategy. The basic dilemma facing many animals, including humans, is that they sometimes cannot win a fight without losing a friend.

This photo shows what may happen after a conflict—in this case between two female bonobos. About 10 minutes after their fight, the two females approach each other, with one clinging to the other and both rubbing their clitorises and genital swellings together in a pattern known as genito-genital (or GG) rubbing. This sexual contact, typical of bonobos,

▲▲▲ Two adult female bonobos engage in so-called GG rubbing, a sexual form of reconciliation typical of this species. While some researchers attribute the bonobos use of sex to keep the peace as rooted in their biology, others believe that cultural processes have established these behaviors.

CONTINUED

constitutes a so-called reconciliation. Chimpanzees, which are closely related to bonobos (and to us: bonobos and chimpanzees are our closest animal relatives), usually reconcile in a less sexual fashion, with an embrace and mouth-to-mouth kiss.

There is now evidence for reconciliation in more than twenty-five different primate species, not just in apes but also in many monkeys. The same sorts of studies have been conducted on human children in the schoolyard, and of course children show reconciliation as well. Researchers have even found reconciliation in dolphins, spotted hyenas, and some other nonprimates. Reconciliation seems widespread: a common mechanism found whenever relationships need to be maintained despite occasional conflict.[a, b]

The definition of reconciliation used in animal research is a friendly reunion between former opponents not long after a conflict. This is somewhat different from definitions in the dictionary, primarily because we look for an empirical definition that is useful in observational studies—in our case, the stipulation that the reunion happen not long after the conflict. There is no intrinsic reason that a reconciliation could not occur after hours or days, or, in the case of humans, generations.

Let me describe two interesting elaborations on the mechanism of reconciliation. One is *mediation*. Chimpanzees are the only animals to use mediators in conflict resolution. In order to be able to mediate conflict, one needs to understand relationships outside of oneself, which may be the reason why other animals fail to show this aspect of conflict resolution. For example, if two male chimpanzees have been involved in a fight, even on a very large island as where I did my studies, they can easily avoid each other, but instead they will sit opposite from each other, not too far apart, and avoid eye contact. They can sit like this for a long time. In this situation, a third party, such as an older female, may move in and try to solve the issue. The female will approach one of the males and groom him

for a brief while. She then gets up and walks slowly to the other male, and the first male walks right behind her.

We have seen situations in which, if the first male failed to follow, the female turned around to grab his arm and make him follow. So the process of getting the two males in proximity seems intentional on the part of the female. She then begins grooming the other male, and the first male grooms her. Before long, the female disappears from the scene, and the males continue grooming: She has in effect brought the two parties together.

There exists a limited anthropological literature on the role of conflict resolution, a process absolutely crucial for the maintenance of the human social fabric in the same way that it is crucial for our primate relatives. In human society, mediation is often done by high-ranking or senior members of the community, sometimes culminating in feasts in which the restoration of harmony is celebrated.[c]

The second elaboration on the reconciliation concept is that it is not purely instinctive, not even in our animal relatives. It is a learned social skill subject to what primatologists now increasingly call "culture" (meaning that the behavior is subject to learning from others as opposed to genetic transmission[d]). To test the learnability of reconciliation, I conducted an experiment with young rhesus and stumptail monkeys.

Not nearly as conciliatory as stumptail monkeys, rhesus monkeys have the reputation of being rather aggressive and despotic. Stumptails are considered more laid-back and tolerant. We housed members of the two species together for 5 months. By the end of this period, they were a fully integrated group: They slept, played, and groomed together. After 5 months, we separated them again and measured the effect of their time together on conciliatory behavior. The research controls—rhesus monkeys who had lived with one another, without any stumptails—showed absolutely no change in the tendency to reconcile. Stumptails showed a high rate of reconciliation, which was also expected, because they also do so if

living together. The most interesting group was the experimental rhesus monkeys, those who had lived with stumptails.

These monkeys started out at the same low level of reconciliation as the rhesus controls, but after they had lived with the stumptails, and after we had segregated them again so that they were now housed only with other rhesus monkeys who had gone through the same experience, these rhesus monkeys reconciled as much as stumptails do. This means that we created a "new and improved" rhesus monkey, one that made up with its opponents far more easily than a regular rhesus monkey.[e]

This was in effect an experiment on social culture: We changed the culture of a group of rhesus monkeys and made it more similar to that of stumptail monkeys by exposing them to the practices of this other species. This experiment also shows that there exists a great deal of flexibility in primate behavior. We humans come from a long lineage of primates with great social sophistication and a well-developed potential for behavioral modification and learning from others. ■

By Frans B. M. de Waal, Living Links, Yerkes National Primate Research Center, Emory University.

[a]de Waal, F. B. M. (2000). Primates—A natural heritage of conflict resolution. *Science 28*, 586–590.

[b]Aureli, F., & de Waal, F. B. M. (2000). *Natural conflict resolution*. Berkeley: University of California Press.

[c]Reviewed by Frye, D. P. (2000). Conflict management in cross-cultural perspective. In F. Aureli & F. B. M. de Waal, *Natural conflict resolution* (pp. 334–351). Berkeley: University of California Press.

[d]See de Waal, F. B. M. (2001). *The ape and the sushi master*. New York: Basic Books, for a discussion of the animal culture concept.

[e]de Waal, F. B. M., & Johanowicz, D. L. (1993). Modification of reconciliation behavior through social experience: An experiment with two macaque species. *Child Development 64*, 897–908.

reconciliation after an attack may be even more important from an evolutionary perspective than the actual attack.

Primate behaviors that at first glance might seem wholly practical often contain significant social meaning and sophistication. For example, chimpanzees and bonobos frequently engage in **grooming**, the ritual cleaning of another animal to remove parasites and other matter from its skin or coat. Besides serving hygienic purposes, it can be a gesture of friendliness, closeness, appeasement, reconciliation, or even submission. Bonobos and chimpanzees have favorite grooming partners. Primates also show their group sociability, an important behavioral trait undoubtedly also found among human ancestors, through embracing, touching, and the joyous welcoming of other members of the ape community.

Prior to the 1980s scientists thought most primates were vegetarian while humans alone were considered meat-eating hunters. Pioneering research by Goodall, among others, revealed that the diets of monkeys and apes were extremely varied. Goodall's fieldwork among chimpanzees in their natural habitat at Gombe, a wildlife reserve on the eastern shores of Lake Tanganyika in Tanzania, revealed that these apes supplement their pri-

mary diet of fruits and other plant foods with insects and meat. Even more surprising, she found that in addition to killing small invertebrate animals for food, they also hunted and ate monkeys. Goodall observed chimpanzees grabbing adult red colobus monkeys and flailing them to death.[6] Other primatologists have since documented hunting behavior in baboons and capuchin monkeys, among others.

Chimpanzee females sometimes hunt, but males do so far more frequently. When on the hunt, they may spend up to 2 hours watching, following, and chasing intended prey. Moreover, in contrast to the usual primate practice of each animal finding its own food, hunting frequently involves teamwork to trap and kill prey, particularly when hunting for baboons. Once a potential victim has been isolated from its troop, three or more adult chimps will carefully position themselves so as to block off escape routes while another pursues the prey. Following the kill, those present get a share of the meat, either by grabbing a piece as chance affords or by begging for it.

U.S. anthropologist Craig Stanford, who has been doing fieldwork among the chimpanzees of Gombe since the early 1990s, found that these sizable apes (100-pound males are common) frequently kill animals weighing up to 25 pounds and eat much more meat than previously believed. Their preferred prey is the red colobus monkey that shares their forested habitat. Annually, chimpanzee hunting parties at Gombe kill about 20 percent of these monkeys, many of them babies that are shaken from the tops of 30-foot trees. They may capture and kill as many as seven victims in a raid. These hunts usually take place during the dry season when plant foods are less available and when females display genital swelling, which signals that they are ready to mate. On average, each chimp at Gombe eats about a quarter of a pound of meat per day during the dry season. For female chimps, a supply of protein-rich food helps support the increased nutritional requirements of pregnancy and lactation.

Somewhat different chimpanzee hunting practices have been observed in West Africa. At Tai National Park on the Ivory Coast (Côte d'Ivoire), for instance, chimpanzees engage in highly coordinated team efforts to chase monkeys hiding in very tall trees in the dense tropical forest. Individuals who have especially distinguished themselves in a successful hunt see their contributions rewarded with more

meat. Recent research shows that bonobos in Congo's rainforest also supplement their diet with meat obtained by means of hunting. Although their behavior resembles that of the chimpanzees, there are crucial differences.

Among bonobos, hunting is primarily a female activity. Also, female hunters regularly share carcasses with other females, but less often with males. Even when the most dominant male throws a tantrum nearby, he may still be denied a share of meat.[7] Female bonobos behave in much the same way when it comes to sharing other foods such as fruits.

▲▲

community In primatology, a unit of social organization composed of fifty or more individuals who together inhabit a large geographic area.

dominance hierarchy An observed ranking system in animal groups ordering individuals from high (alpha) to low standing, corresponding to predictable behavioral interactions including domination.

grooming The ritual cleaning of another animal's skin and fur to remove parasites and other matter.

[6]Goodall J. (1986). *The chimpanzees of Gombe: Patterns of behavior.* Cambridge, MA: Belknap Press.

[7]Ingmanson, E. J. (1998). Comment. *Current Anthropology 39,* 409.

▼▼

The sexual practices of chimpanzees and bonobos differ as much as their hunting strategies. For chimps, sexual activity—initiated by either the male or the female—occurs primarily during the periods when females signal their fertility through genital swelling. By most human standards, chimp sexual behavior is promiscuous. A dozen or so males have been observed to have as many as fifty copulations in one day with a single female. Dominant males try to monopolize sexually receptive females, although this requires female cooperation. An individual female and a lower-ranking male sometimes form a temporary bond, leaving the group together for a few private days during the female's fertile period. Thus dominant males do not necessarily father all (or even most) of the offspring in a social group. Social success, achieving alpha male status, does not translate neatly into the evolutionary currency of reproductive success.

Concealed Ovulation

In contrast to chimpanzees, bonobos (like humans) do not limit their sexual behavior to times of female fertility. Whereas the genitals of chimpanzee females are swollen only at times of fertility, female bonobo genitals are perpetually swollen. The constant swelling, in effect, conceals the females' **ovulation**, or moment when an egg released into the womb is receptive for fertilization. The constant absence of genital swelling in humans also conceals ovulation.

Concealed ovulation in humans and bonobos may play a role in separating sexual activity for social reasons and pleasure from the purely biological task of reproduction. In fact, among bonobos, as among humans, sexuality goes far beyond male–female mating for purposes of biological reproduction.

Primatologists have observed virtually every possible combination of ages and sexes engaging in a remarkable array of sexual activities, including oral sex, tongue kissing, and massaging each other's genitals. Male bonobos may mount each other, or one may rub his scrotum against that of the other. They have also been observed "penis fencing"—hanging face-to-face from a branch and rubbing their erect penises together as if crossing swords. Among females, genital rubbing is particularly common. As described in this chapter's Original Study, this hetero- and homosexual behavior functions to reduce tensions and resolve social conflicts. Since the documentation of sexual activities among bonobos, field studies by primatologists working with other species are now recording a variety of sexual behaviors among these species as well.

Reproduction and Care of Young

Most mammals mate only during specified breeding seasons occurring once or twice a year, but many primate species are able to breed at any time during the course of the year. The average adult female monkey or ape spends most of her adult life either pregnant or nursing her young, times at which she is not sexually receptive. Apes generally nurse each of their young for about four years. After weaning her infant, she will become pregnant again. Human societies modify the succession and timing of pregnancy and lactation by a variety of cultural means.

Among most (but not all) primates, females generally give birth to one infant at a time. Natural selection may have favored single births among primate tree-dwellers because the primate infant, which has a highly developed grasping ability (the grasping reflex can also be seen in human infants), must be transported about by its mother, and more than one clinging infant would seriously encumber her as she moved about the trees.

Primates follow a pattern of bearing few young but devoting more time and effort to the care of each individual offspring. Compared to other mammals such as mice, which pass from birth to adulthood in a matter of weeks, primates spend a great deal of time growing up. As a general rule, the more closely related to humans the primate species is, the longer the period of infant and childhood dependency (▶ **Figure 3.5**). For example, a lemur depends upon its mother for only a few months after birth, while

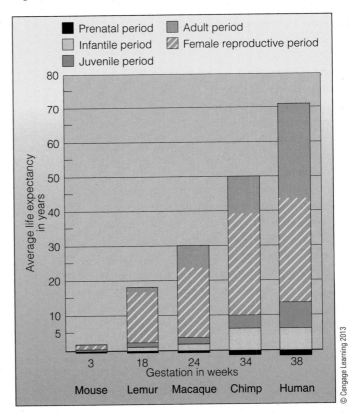

Figure 3.5 A Comparison of Life Cycles: Mouse, Lemur, Macaque, Chimp, Human Primates typically have a long life cycle, including a long period of childhood dependency. In biological terms infancy ends when young mammals are weaned, and adulthood is defined as sexual maturation. In many species such as mice, animals become sexually mature as soon as they are weaned. Among primates a juvenile period for social learning occurs between infancy and adulthood. Humans modify these biological definitions according to cultural norms.

an ape is dependent for four or five years. A chimpanzee infant cannot survive if its mother dies before it reaches the age of 4 at the very least. During the juvenile period, the young primate still depends upon the larger social group rather than on the mother alone, using this period for learning and refining a variety of behaviors. If a juvenile's mother dies, an older member of the social group, either male or female, may adopt the youngster.

The long interval between births, particularly among the apes, results in small population sizes among our closest relatives. A female chimpanzee, for example, does not reach sexual maturity until about the age of 10, and once she produces her first live offspring, on average 5.6, years passes before she will bear another. Thus, assuming that none of her offspring die before adulthood, a female chimpanzee must survive for at least twenty or twenty-one years just to maintain the size of chimpanzee populations at existing levels. In fact, chimpanzee infants and juveniles do die from time to time, and not all females live full reproductive lives. These chance events—combined with the long intervals between births, habitat destruction, and hunting—contribute further to declining ape populations.

A long, slow period of growth and development, particularly among the hominoids, also provides opportunities. Born without built-in responses dictating specific behavior in complex situations, the young chimp or bonobo, like the young human, learns how to strategically interact with others and even manipulate them for his or her own benefit—by trial and error, observation, imitation, and practice. Young primates make mistakes along the way, learning to modify their behavior based on the reactions of other members of the group.

Each member of the community has a unique physical appearance and personality. Youngsters learn to match their interactive behaviors according to each individual's social position and temperament. Anatomical features such as a free upper lip (unlike lemurs or cats, for example) allow monkeys and apes varied facial expression, contributing to greater communication among individuals.

Communication

Primates, like many animals, vocalize. They combine a great range of calls with movements of the face or body to convey messages. Primatologists have identified specific warning calls, threat calls, defense calls, and gathering calls. The behavioral reactions of other animals hearing the call have also been studied. Bonobos and chimpanzees use vocalizations to express emotions. Much of these species' communication takes place by the use of specific gestures and postures. Indeed, humans share a number of these, such as kissing and embracing, with the apes.

Primatologists have classified numerous chimpanzee vocalizations and visual communication signals. Facial expressions convey emotional states such as distress, fear, or excitement. Distinct vocalizations or calls have been associated with a variety of sensations. For example, chimps will smack their lips or clack their teeth to express pleasure with sociable body contact. Chimps use different kinds of calls (known as "pant-hoots") to announce arrival of individuals or to inquire. Together, these facilitate group protection, coordination of group efforts, and social interaction in general.

One form of communication appears to be unique to bonobos: the use of trail markers. When foraging, the community breaks up into smaller groups, rejoining again in the evening to nest together. To keep track of each party's whereabouts, those in the lead will, at the intersections of trails or where downed trees obscure trails, deliberately stomp the vegetation to indicate their direction or rip off large leaves and place them carefully for the same purpose. Thus they all know where to come together at the end of the day.[8]

Experiments with captive apes, carried out over several decades, reveal that their communication abilities exceed what they make use of in the wild. In some of

© Tim Davis/Corbis

▲▲▲ We easily recognize many ape nonverbal communication gestures because we share them. Individuals who have been blind since birth also perform these same body gestures, indicating that they are hardwired into humans and presumably derive from our primate heritage.

▲▲

ovulation The moment when an egg released from an ovary into the womb is receptive for fertilization.

▼▼

[8]Recer, P. (1998, February 16). Apes shown to communicate in the wild. *Burlington Free Press,* 12A.

these experiments, bonobos and chimpanzees have been taught to communicate using symbols, as in the case of Kanzi, a bonobo who uses a keyboard. Other chimpanzees, gorillas, and orangutans have been taught American Sign Language. By documenting that apes understand language quite well, even using rudimentary grammar, this research challenges notions of human uniqueness. Apes are able to generate original utterances, ask questions, distinguish naming something from asking for it, develop original ways to tell lies, coordinate their actions, and even spontaneously teach language to others. Even though they cannot literally *speak*, it is now clear that all of the great ape species can develop *language skills* to the level of a 2- to 3-year-old human child.[9]

Interestingly, a Japanese research team led by primatologist Tetsuro Matsuzawa, demonstrated that chimps can outperform college students at a computer-based memory game that tests relative ability to take a "quick mental snapshot" of the environment. The researchers propose that some of the ape's spatial skill may have been lost to make brain space for human language.[10]

Use of Objects as Tools

Young chimpanzees also learn other functional behaviors from adults, such as how to make and use tools. A **tool** may be defined as an object used to facilitate some task or activity. Beyond deliberately modifying objects to make them suitable for particular purposes, chimps can modify them to some extent to regular patterns and may even prepare objects at one location in anticipation of future use at another place. Recall Jane Goodall's observation from the start of the chapter that chimps select long, slender branches, strip off their leaves, and carrying them on "fishing" expeditions to termite nests. Reaching their destination, they insert the stick into the nest, wait a few minutes, and then pull it out to eat the insects clinging to it.

Examples of tool use by chimpanzees abound: They use leaves as wipes or sponges to get drinking water out of a hollow. Large sticks may serve as clubs or as missiles (as may stones) in aggressive or defensive displays. Recently a chimp group in Senegal has even been observed fashioning sticks into spears and using them to hunt.[11] Stones are used as hammers and anvils to crack open certain kinds of nuts. Twigs are used as toothpicks to clean teeth as well as to extract loose baby teeth. Chimps use these dental tools not just on themselves but on other individuals as well.[12]

Bonobos in the wild have not been observed making and using tools to the extent that chimpanzees do. However, their use of large leaves as trail markers may be considered a form of tool use. Tool-making capabilities have also been demonstrated by a captive bonobo who independently made stone tools remarkably similar to the earliest tools made by our own ancestors.

The Question of Culture

The more we learn of the behavior of our nearest primate relatives, the more we become aware of the importance to apes of learned, socially shared practices and knowledge. This raises the question: Do chimpanzees, bonobos, and the other apes have culture? The answer appears to be yes. The detailed study of ape behavior has revealed variation among groups in use of tools and patterns of social engagement that seem to derive from the traditions of the group rather than a biologically determined script. Humans share with the other apes an ability to learn the complex but flexible patterns of behavior particular to a social group during a long period of childhood dependency.

Primate Behavior and Human Evolution

In Western societies there has been an tendency to erect what paleontologist Stephen Jay Gould referred to as "golden barriers" that set us apart from the rest of the animal kingdom.[13] These unfortunate barriers blind us to the continuum that exists between "us" and "them" (other animals). The differences between humans and apes are largely differences of degree, rather than kind. As primatologist Richard Wrangham once put it,

> Like humans, [chimpanzees] laugh, make up after a quarrel, support each other in times of trouble, medicate themselves with chemical and physical remedies, stop each other from eating poisonous foods, collaborate in the hunt, help each other over physical obstacles, raid neighboring groups, lose their tempers, get excited by dramatic weather, invent ways to show off, have family traditions and group traditions, make tools, devise plans, deceive, play tricks, grieve, and are cruel and are kind.[14]

Obviously, "degree" does make a difference. While the continuities between our primate kin and us reflect a

---

[9]Lestel, D. (1998). How chimpanzees have domesticated humans. *Anthropology Today 12* (3); Miles, H. L. W. (1993). Language and the orangutan: The "old person" of the forest. In P. Cavalieri & P. Singer (Eds.), *The great ape project* (pp. 45–50). New York: St. Martin's Press.

[10]Inoue, S., & Matsuzawa, T. (2007). Working memory of numerals in chimpanzees. *Current Biology 17* (23), 1004–1005; Callaway, E. (2007, December 3). Chimp beats students at computer game. *Nature.* www.nature.com/news/2007/071203/full/news.2007.317.html (retrieved August 8, 2011).

[11]Hopkin, M. (2007, February 22). Chimps make spears to catch dinner. *Nature.* www.nature.com/news/2007/070219/full/news070219-11.html (retrieved August 8, 2011).

[12]McGrew, W. C. (2000). Dental care in chimps. *Science 288,* 1747.

[13]Quoted in de Waal, F. (2001). *The ape and the sushi master* (p. 235). New York: Basic Books.

[14]Quoted in Mydens, S. (2001, August 12). He's not hairy, he's my brother. *New York Times.* www.nytimes.com/2001/08/12/weekinreview/ideas-trends-he-s-not-hairy-he-s-my-brother.html (retrieved August 8, 2011).

common evolutionary heritage, our more recent evolution has taken us in a somewhat different direction. The behaviors displayed by contemporary apes and other primates provide us with clues about the practices and capabilities of our own ancestors as their evolutionary path diverged from those of the other African apes. The human capacity for compassion has roots in our mammalian primate heritage. Now we must focus our extra degrees of compassion and intelligence toward ensuring the survival of our primate cousins.

Primate Conservation

At present, nearly 50 percent of the known primate species and subspecies face extinction in the next decade.[15] In Asia, the statistics are alarming, with more than 70 percent of species threatened and at least 80 percent at risk in Indonesia and Vietnam. All of the great apes, as well as such formerly widespread and adaptable species as rhesus macaques, number among the endangered. Threats to primates include habitat destruction caused by economic development (farming, lumbering, cattle ranching, rubber tapping), as well as hunters and trappers who pursue them for food, trophies, research, or as exotic pets. Primatologists have long known the devastating effects of habitat destruction through slash-and-burn agriculture. Recent studies also document the powerful impact of human hunting of primates for bushmeat or traditional medicines.

Primate habitats are threatened by far more than human subsistence practices, such as the burning and clearing of tropical forests. War also impacts primate habitats significantly, even after a war has ended. Hunters may use the automatic weapons left over from human conflicts in their pursuit of bushmeat. Also, because monkeys and apes are so closely related to humans, they are regarded as essential for biomedical research as discussed at the opening of the chapter. While most primates in laboratories are bred in captivity, an active trade in live primates still threatens their local extinction.

Globalization also exerts a profound impact on local conditions. For example, miners harvest the mineral coltan—a key component of cell phones—primarily from gorilla habitats in the Democratic Republic of Congo. As the world becomes increasingly cell phone dependent, new mining roads destroy more of gorilla habitats. On the positive side, a global emphasis on recycling cell phones will reduce the amount of new coltan needed.

Because of their vulnerability, the conservation of primates has become a matter of urgency. Traditional conservation efforts emphasized habitat preservation above all else. Primatologists are now calling for new efforts that educate local communities to curtail hunting primates for

© Steve Bloom Images/Alamy

▲▲▲ Over a decade of civil war in the Democratic Republic of Congo, the natural habitat of bonobos, and genocide in neighboring Rwanda have drastically threatened the survival of this peace-loving species. These violent times have prompted the hunting of bonobos to feed starving people and the illegal capture of baby bonobos as pets. Primatologists have turned from observational fieldwork to economic development projects aimed at restoring the stability in the region required for the continued survival of bonobos and the mountain gorillas that share their forest habitat.

food and medicine to complement their existing habitat preservation efforts. Primatologists work to maintain some populations in the wild, either by establishing preserves where animals are already living or by moving populations to places where suitable habitat exists. This approach requires constant monitoring and management to ensure that sufficient space and resources remain available.

Primatologists also maintain captive breeding colonies that provide the kind of physical and social environment that encourages psychological and physical well-being, as well as reproductive success. Primates in zoos and laboratories do not successfully reproduce when deprived of such amenities as opportunities for climbing, materials to use for nest building, others with whom to socialize, and places for privacy. While such amenities contribute to the success of breeding colonies in captivity, in the years to come humans must meet the far greater challenge of ensuring the survival of these primates in suitable natural habitats.

The good news is the results of conservation efforts are beginning to show. For example, due to intense conservation programs, the population size of the mountain gorilla (*Gorilla beringei beringei*) is increasing, even with the political chaos of Rwanda, Uganda, and the Democratic

---

[15]Kaplan, M. (2008, August 5). Almost half of primate species face extinction. *Nature*.www.nature.com/news/2008/080805/full/news.2008.1013.html (retrieved August 8, 2011).

▲▲▲▲▲▲▲▲▲▲▲▲▲▲▲▲▲▲▲▲▲▲▲▲▲▲▲▲▲▲▲▲▲▲▲

tool An object used to facilitate some task or activity.

▼▼▼▼▼▼▼▼▼▼▼▼▼▼▼▼▼▼▼▼▼▼▼▼▼▼▼▼▼▼▼▼▼

Republic of Congo. Western lowland gorilla populations are also on the rise. Similarly, tamarin monkey populations in Brazil have stabilized despite being on the brink of extinction thirty years ago, demonstrating the effectiveness of the conservation initiatives put into place. A leading primatologist has said, "The presence alone of scientists has been shown to protect primates, acting as a deterrent to habitat destruction and hunting. The more people we can send, the more we can help to protect endangered primates."[16] ✳

---

[16]Ibid.

Chapter Checklist

What are the key methods of primatologists and the ethics they uphold?

✔ Primatologists study the biology and behavior of living primates in their natural habitats and in captivity in zoos, primate research colonies, or learning laboratories.

✔ Primatologists work to protect our closest living relatives while studying them using methods that are minimally invasive.

Where are primates in the animal kingdom and how do they compare to other mammals and reptiles?

✔ As mammals, primates are intelligent animals whose young are born live and nourished with milk from their mothers.

✔ Like other mammals, they maintain constant body temperature and have respiratory and circulatory systems that will sustain high activity levels.

✔ Among the mammals, primates have relatively unspecialized biology and very flexible behavior patterns.

What are the basic features of primate anatomy and behavior?

✔ A number of primate characteristics developed as adaptations to insect predation and life in the trees, including a generalized set of teeth, suited to eating insects but also a variety of fruits and leaves.

✔ Other adaptations that developed in the course of primate evolution include binocular stereoscopic color vision, or depth perception, and an intensified sense of touch, particularly in the hands.

✔ The primate reproductive pattern can be characterized by fewer offspring born to each female and a longer period of infant dependency compared to most mammals. This period of dependency allows young primates to learn the behaviors of its group.

What are the five natural primate groups and what characteristics distinguish them?

✔ Primates can be divided into five natural groupings: (1) lemurs and lorises, (2) tarsiers, (3) New World monkeys, (4) Old World monkeys, and (5) apes, including humans.

✔ On the basis of shared anatomical characteristics, lemurs, lorises, and tarsiers are sometimes grouped together as prosimians while monkeys, apes, and humans are considered anthropoid or humanlike primates.

✔ Because genetic evidence indicates that tarsiers are more closely related to the monkeys and apes, the primate order can also be divided into strepsirhines (lemurs and lorises) and haplorhines (tarsiers, monkeys, apes, and humans).

What are the main differences between prosimians and anthropoid primates?

✔ Prosimians are more dependent on the sense of smell while anthropoids are more dependent upon vision.

✔ Where competition from anthropoids is present, prosimians are nocturnal arboreal creatures. Nearly all anthropoids are diurnal, exploiting a wide range of habitats and expressing considerable behavioral flexibility and variation.

✔ This combination of developments resulted in the following in anthropoids relative to prosimians: larger size and greater complexity of the brain, a reduction of the snout, an enlargement of the braincase, and numerous adaptations for upright posture and flexibility of limb movement.

Who are the apes?

✔ The apes, humans' closest relatives, include gibbons, siamangs, orangutans, gorillas, bonobos, and chimpanzees. From a biological perspective, humans are apes.

✔ In their outward appearance, the apes resemble one another more than they do humans, but their genetic structure and biochemistry reveal that the African apes, bonobos, chimpanzees, and gorillas are closer to humans than they are to orangutans, gibbons, and siamangs.

What is the biological basis of primate behavior, and how do our closest primate relatives—chimps and bonobos—exhibit this?

✔ Primates are social animals, and most species live and travel in groups.

✔ Frequently individuals transfer to new groups at adolescence.

✔ Learned behavior is especially important for primates.

✔ In many primate species, both males and females can be organized into dominance hierarchies. In the case of females, high rank is associated with enhanced reproductive success. In males, however, high rank does not necessarily confer a reproductive advantage.

✔ A characteristic primate activity is grooming, which is a sign of closeness between individuals.

✔ Among chimpanzees, sexual interaction between adults of opposite sex generally takes place only when a female is in estrus. In bonobos, however, constant swelling of the female's genitals suggests constant estrus, whether or not she is actually fertile.

✔ A consequence of this concealed ovulation in bonobos is a separation of sexual activity from the biological task of reproduction.

✔ Among bonobos, sex between both opposite- and same-sex individuals serves as a means of reducing tensions, as in the genital rubbing that frequently takes place between females.

✔ Primates have elaborate systems of communication based on vocalizations and gestures. In addition, bonobos employ trail signs to communicate their whereabouts to others.

✔ Most primates eat a variety of fruits, leaves, and insects.

How do we define primate culture in the context of human evolution?

✔ From adults, juveniles learn to use a variety of tools and substances for various purposes. Innovations made by one individual may be adopted by other animals, standardized, and passed on to succeeding generations.

✔ Learned, socially shared practices often differ from one group to another. Therefore we may speak of chimpanzee culture.

What are the critical issues and methods in primate conservation?

✔ Nearly 50 percent of all primate species and subspecies are threatened with extinction in the next decade.

✔ Human actions—such as global flows of technology, demand for commodities, and political and social conditions—threaten the other primates.

✔ Intense conservation efforts have been successful; we urgently need to reinforce these efforts to protect our closest living relatives in the animal kingdom.

Questions for Reflection

1. Those who fully support the use of nonhuman primates in biomedical research argue that using a limited number of chimpanzees and rhesus macaques to lessen human suffering and to spare human lives is justified. Do you agree or disagree? What alternatives might be developed to replace nonhuman primates in biomedical research?

2. In the 21st century many primate species are threatened with extinction.

Why is it so important to prevent this from happening? What could you do to contribute to this personally?

3. Considering some of the trends seen among the primates, such as increased brain size or reduced tooth number, why is it incorrect to say that some primates are more evolved than others? Are humans more evolved than chimpanzees?

4. Given the variation seen in the specific behaviors of chimp and bonobo

groups, do you think that these primates possess culture?

5. Biologists break the mammalian life cycle into prenatal, infant, juvenile, and adult periods according to specific biological events. How has your culture defined these same periods? What are the advantages and disadvantages of the way your culture defines infant, juvenile, and adult?

Key Terms

nocturnal
arboreal
diurnal
binocular vision
stereoscopic vision
opposable

prosimians
anthropoids
strepsirhines
haplorhines
prehensile
brachiation

community
dominance hierarchy
grooming
ovulation
tool

Online Study Resources

Login to **www.cengagebrain.com** to access the resources your instructor has assigned and to purchase materials. For this book, you can access:

CourseMate
Access chapter-specific learning tools including flashcards, glossaries, practice quizzes, videos, and more in your Anthropology CourseMate.

VISUAL ESSENCE

The story of our own evolution has captured the public imagination since the scientific theories about human origins were first proposed. Today that imagination is fed through popular writing, television specials about new fossil discoveries, and even traveling museum exhibitions. Often the subject of contentious debate, one of today's public debates surrounds how best to preserve the precious fossil remains uncovered over the course of the past hundred years or so. The debate became particularly heated when a 3.2-million-year-old fossil specimen named "Lucy" was beginning her 6-year tour of the United States as part of a traveling exhibit organized and curated by the Ethiopian government and the Houston Museum of Natural History. Though Lucy, who was named after the Beatles song "Lucy in the Sky with Diamonds," has done much to popularize paleoanthropology and evolutionary studies since her discovery in 1974, some paleoanthropologists argue that placing her fragile ancient skeleton on public display is far too risky. The Smithsonian Institution declined to host the show for this reason. Others—like her discoverer Donald Johanson, pictured here with Lucy in the exhibition space in Times Square, New York—felt that the benefits outweighed the risks. One of those benefits was that Lucy's remains could be examined via CT scans so that future generations of scientists could study them without actually handling the fragile bones. In addition, tour revenues were used to modernize Ethiopia's museums. Overall, increased public awareness of human origins and of the vital role of the African continent in our evolutionary history contribute substantially to our understanding of who we are and may even shed some light on our future.

4 Human Evolution

Paleoanthropologists piecing together the puzzle of human evolution must be imaginative thinkers and patient detectives as well as scholars, because the available evidence is often scant or full of misleading and even contradictory clues. The quest for the origins of humans from more ancient species has elements of a detective story. It involves mysteries concerning the emergence of humanity that have never been completely resolved. Which ancestors were the first to walk on two legs? Which were the first with human-sized brains? Who were the first to use tools? The first to use fire? The first to actually use sounds to produce what we call language?

Because each new discovery contributes to resolving the puzzle of human evolution, the order of discovery is important. Each new fossil, stone tool, painted cave wall, or laboratory result has the potential to reconfigure our understanding of human evolutionary history. Although all discoveries impact evolutionary studies, the role of culture in human evolution makes unraveling our past particularly complex.

Differences in the rates of cultural and biological change account for some of the complications and debates relating to human evolutionary history. Cultural practices and technologies can change rapidly with innovations occurring during the lifetime of individuals. By contrast, because it depends upon genetically inherited traits, biological change requires many generations. Paleoanthropologists try to decipher whether an evident change in culture in the past corresponds to a major biological change, such as the appearance of a new species. The biological evidence for new species often consists of small changes in the shape or size of the skull. However, the cultural variation present today within the species *Homo sapiens* reminds us not to attribute a simple one-to-one relation between skull shape and culture change.

Anthropologist Misia Landau has noted that the story of human evolution follows the narrative form of a heroic epic.[1] The hero, or evolving human, faces a series of natural challenges that the individual cannot overcome from a strictly biological standpoint. Endowed

In this chapter you will learn to:

- **Identify the course of human evolution and its major geologic events.**

- **Recognize the anatomy of bipedalism and how the human line and distinct species are identified in the fossil record.**

- **Compare the earliest bipeds to one another.**

- **Identify the distinct characteristics of the genus *Homo*.**

- **Describe the spread of the genus *Homo* from Africa to the rest of the globe.**

- **Discuss the relationship between cultural change and biological change throughout the course of human evolutionary history.**

- **Compare the various theories to account for modern human origins.**

---

[1]Landau, M. (1991). *Narratives of human evolution* (pp. xii, 202). New Haven and London: Yale University Press.

with the gift of intelligence, the hero can meet these challenges and become fully human. In this story, culture separates humans from other evolving animals and unintentionally implies a false notion of progress.

While the evolution of culture was critical to our becoming the kind of species we are today, it did not "improve" us biologically. Each species has followed its own evolutionary course over millions of years, changing through time in directions that ensured its biological success. We continue to share this planet with some of these species, while others who were biologically successful for a time, surviving for millions of years, have since gone extinct.

Consider also the challenges of identifying species in the past. How can we tell whether two sets of fossilized bones represent species that were capable of interbreeding and producing fertile, viable offspring? To approximate an answer to this question, paleoanthropologists use as many sources of information as possible to check the proposed evolutionary relationships. Paleoanthropologists use genetic and biochemical data, along with observations about the biology and behavior of living groups, to support their theories about speciation. Thus reconstructing evolutionary relationships draws on much more than bones alone.

Even with this rich array of scientific knowledge to draw upon, prevailing beliefs and biases can influence the interpretation of fossil finds. Fortunately, the self-correcting nature of scientific investigation, one of its greatest strengths, allows evolutionary lineages to be redrawn in light of all new discoveries. As technological innovations allow for new experiments, new investigations, and new discoveries that in turn reveal new aspects of the mysteries of life on earth, scientists develop theories and test hypotheses consistent with the complete data available. The reliance of science upon data and testable hypotheses distinguishes it from storytelling.

Mammalian Primate Evolution

Humans have a long evolutionary history as mammals and primates that set the stage for the cultural beings we are today. Evidence from ancient skeletons indicates the first mammals appeared over 200 million years ago as small nocturnal creatures.

In the time since the appearance of the first mammals, the earth itself has changed considerably. During the past 200 million years, the position of the continents has shifted through a process called **continental drift**. This process accounts for the rearrangement of the adjacent landmasses through the theory of plate tectonics (▶ **Figure 4.1**). According to this theory, the continents, embedded in platelike segments of the earth, shift in position as the edges of the underlying plates are created or destroyed. Plate movements also bring about geologic phenomena such as earthquakes, volcanic activity, and mountain formation. Continental drift not only affected the distribution of fossil primate groups, whose history we

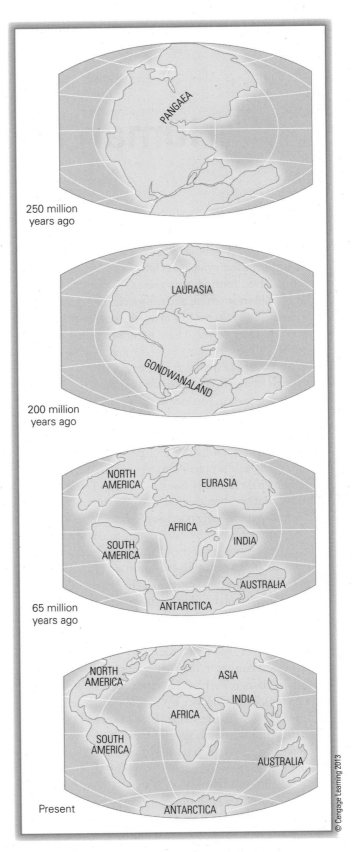

Figure 4.1 Continental Drift Continental drift is illustrated by the position of the continents during different geologic periods. At the time of the extinction of the dinosaurs 65 million years ago, continental drift caused the seas to open up, creating isolating barriers between major landmasses. About 23 million years ago, at the start of the geologic time period known as the Miocene epoch, African and Eurasian landmasses reconnected.

will now explore, but it brought about climatic changes in the environment that impacted the course of their evolution.

The earliest primatelike mammals came into being about 65 million years ago when a new, mild climate favored the spread of dense tropical and subtropical forests over much of the earth. The change in climate and habitat, combined with the sudden extinction of dinosaurs, favored mammal diversification, including the evolutionary development of arboreal mammals from which primates evolved. Fossil evidence indicates that the earliest primates began to develop around 65 million years ago, when the mass extinction of the dinosaurs opened new ecological niches, or ways of life within a complete environmental system, for mammals. By 60 million years ago, primates inhabited North America and Eurasia (Europe and Asia), which were still geographically close from the time that they were joined as the supercontinent Laurasia. At this time they were also near to Africa, which had separated from the other supercontinent Gondwanaland. The earliest primates were small nocturnal insect eaters adapted to life in the trees.

By about 40 million years ago, diurnal anthropoid primates appeared, and fossil evidence indicates that Old World and New World species had separated by about this time. Many of the Old World anthropoid species became ground-dwellers. By about 23 million years ago, at the start of the geologic epoch known as the Miocene (▶ **Figure 4.2**), the first fossil apes or hominoids began to appear in Asia, Africa, and Europe; hominoids are the broad-shouldered tailless primates that include all living and extinct apes and humans. The word *hominoid* comes from the Latin roots *homo* and *homin* (meaning "human being") and the suffix *oïdes* ("resembling"). As a group, hominoids get their name from their resemblance to humans. Although some of these ancient primates were relatively small, others were larger than present-day gorillas.

During the Miocene, the African and Eurasian landmasses made direct contact. For most of the preceding 100 million years, the Tethys Sea—a continuous body of water that joined today's Mediterranean and Black seas to the Indian Ocean—barred migration between Africa and Eurasia. Connection of these landmasses through today's Middle East allowed Old World primate groups such as African apes to expand their ranges into Eurasia. The climatic changes set into motion during the Miocene epoch played a role in the success of the human line once it originated. In particular, the uplifting and drying of the eastern third of Africa (a process known as *rifting*) opened new ecological niches for our ancestors.

Miocene remains of apes from this time period have been found from the caves of China, to the forests of France, to eastern Africa where the earliest fossils of

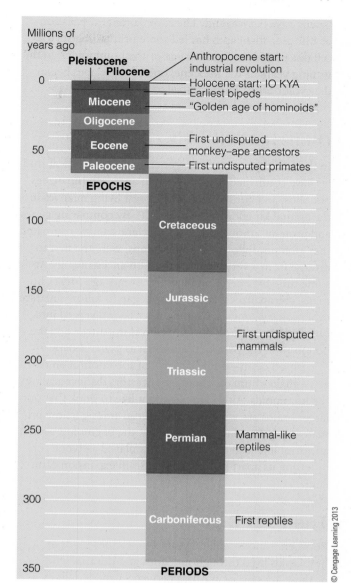

Figure 4.2 Timeline of Mammalian Primate Evolution This timeline highlights the major milestones in the course of mammalian primate evolution that ultimately led to humans and their ancestors. The Paleocene, Eocene, Oligocene, and Miocene epochs are subsets of the Tertiary period. The Quaternary period begins with the Pleistocene and continues today. It includes the Holocene epoch that began at the end of the last Ice Age around 10,000 years ago. In 2000, the Nobel Prize–winning chemist Paul Crutzen coined the term *Anthropocene* to describe the world since the industrial revolution because of the profound geologic changes human activity imposes on the earth. Geologic societies around the globe are currently debating the inclusion of Anthropocene as a formal geologic unit.

continental drift In the theory of plate tectonics, the movement of continents embedded in underlying plates on the earth's surface in relation to one another over the history of life on earth.

bipeds have been found. The abundance and variation of Miocene fossil apes has led some primatologists to call this period the "golden age of the hominoids." In the waning years of the Miocene, one of these apes began the evolutionary line ancestral to humans.

Human Evolution

In the past thirty-five years, genetic and biochemical studies have confirmed that the African apes—chimpanzees, bonobos, and gorillas—are our closest living relatives in the animal kingdom (▶ **Figure 4.3**). By comparing genes and proteins among all the apes, scientists have estimated that gibbons, followed by orangutans, were the first to diverge from a very ancient common ancestral line. At some time between 5 and 8 million years ago (mya), humans, chimpanzees, and gorillas began to follow separate evolutionary courses. Chimpanzees later diverged into two separate species: the common chimpanzee and the bonobo—in the past, better known as *pygmy chimps*.

Bipedalism—a special form of locomotion on two feet—makes humans and their ancestors distinct among the hominoids. Although we might like to think that our larger brains are what make us special among fellow primates, only bipedalism appeared at the beginning of the ancestral line leading to humans. It played a pivotal role in setting us apart from the apes. Brain expansion came later.

The First Bipeds

Between 5 and 15 million years ago, various kinds of hominoids lived throughout Africa and Eurasia. One of these apes living in Africa between 5 and 8 million years ago was a direct ancestor to the human line. Fossil evidence for early African apes from the late Miocene is relatively rare because the forested environments these apes inhabited were not conducive to fossilization. Nevertheless, the fossil evidence, such as the recent discovery of a 10-million-year-old ape thought to be ancestral to gorillas, supports the genetic evidence.[2] This specimen suggests that the human–chimp–gorilla split occurred about 2 million years earlier than previously thought. Other discoveries have begun to fill in the fossil record from this critical time period, such as the 6-million-year-old *Orrorin*—meaning "original man"—fossils discovered in Kenya in 2001.[3] Also, a beautifully preserved 6- to 7-million-year-old skull nicknamed *Toumai*—meaning "hope for life"—was discovered in Chad, Central Africa, in 2002.[4] It too has been suggested as the original human ancestor.

Ardipithecus ramidus

In the fall of 2009, a dramatic paleoanthropological find was announced: a remarkably complete skeleton of a

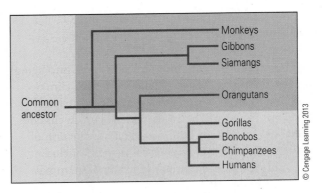

Figure 4.3 Evolutionary Relationships among Primate Species The relationship among monkeys, apes, and humans can be established by comparing molecular similarities and differences. Although chimpanzees, gorillas, and orangutans physically resemble one another more than any of them resemble humans, molecular evidence indicates that humans are most closely related to the African ape species. Using a "molecular clock," scientists date the split between the human and African ape lines to between 5 and 8 million years ago. Recently, researchers have made several important fossil finds dating from between 5 and 7 million years ago that support the molecular evidence.

presumed human ancestor dated to 4.4 million years ago. Only half a dozen partially complete fossil skeletons on the human line older than 1 million years have ever been discovered, and this one is the oldest. Nicknamed "Ardi," short for the new species *Ardipithecus ramidus,* the fossil remains themselves were first discovered between 1992 and 1995. Features such as the small size of Ardi's canine tooth led paleoanthropologists to determine that she is female. For the following fifteen-plus years, an international team of nearly fifty scientists conducted painstaking excavation, reconstruction, and analysis to create a complete picture of the lifeways of this new species; through this process Ardi has become "personified." Their research also placed her definitively on the human line.

The genus *Ardipithecus* is actually divided into two species, the older of which dates to between 5.2 and 5.8 million years ago. The *Ardipithecus* remains show that some of the earliest bipeds inhabited a forested environment much like that of contemporary chimpanzees, bonobos, and gorillas; these remains were found in fossil-rich deposits along Ethiopia's Awash River accompanied by

---

[2]Suwa, G., et al. (2007, August 23). A new species of great ape from the late Miocene epoch in Ethiopia. *Nature 448*, 921–924. www.nature.com/nature/journal/v448/n7156/abs/nature06113.html (retrieved August 9, 2011).

[3]Senut, B., et al. (2001). First hominid from the Miocene (Lukeino formation, Kenya). *C. R. Academy of Science, Paris 332*, 137–144.

[4]Brunet, M., et al. (2002). A new hominid from the Upper Miocene of Chad, Central Africa. *Nature 418*, 145–151.

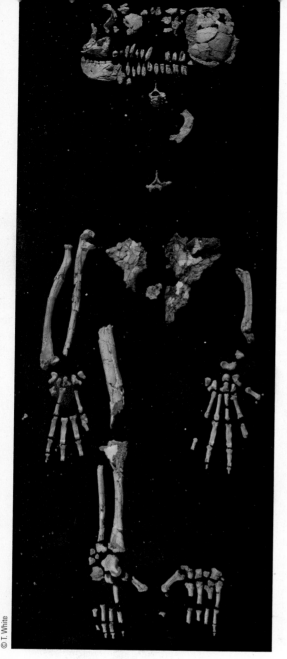

© T. White

▲▲▲ The remarkably complete remains of *Ardipithecus ramidus* have captured our collective imagination. A series of research papers in the prestigious journal *Science,* along with a Discovery Channel documentary, show how the scientists used these bones to reconstruct the lifeways of one of our earliest bipedal ancestors. Sophisticated computer graphics allowed scientists to simulate how regulatory genes might have shaped the development of Ardi's bones that allowed her to move in a more humanlike fashion. Researchers had gymnasts mimic her gait for scientific analysis, and physicists and chemists used their expertise to reconstruct the ancient forested environment she inhabited.

fossils of forest animals. The name *Ardipithecus ramidus* is fitting for an ultimate human ancestor as *ardi* means "floor" and *ramid* means "root" in the local Afar language.

Now that the spectacular Ardi specimen has been sufficiently analyzed by the team who discovered her, paleoanthropologists debate her exact place on the human line. Because the other African apes share a body plan similar to one another, many paleoanthropologists expected the earliest bipeds to resemble something halfway between chimps and humans. Instead, Ardi shows that these forest creatures moved about in a combination of ways: They moved across the tops of branches with the palms of their hands and feet facing downward, and they walked between the trees on the ground in an upright position. The other African apes, as we saw in previous chapters, knuckle-walk on the forest floor and hang suspended below the branches. In other words, Ardi resembles some of the early Miocene apes more than she does the living African apes.

This calls into question what the last common ancestor of humans and the other African apes looked like. Does Ardi represent the more ancestral form, with the other apes evolving independently after they split from the human line but still converging to the typical African ape body plan? Or does Ardi represent a new body plan, characteristic of the earliest bipeds that evolved away from the African ape plan shared by chimps and gorillas? And what of Ardi's relationship to the later bipeds?

In terms of size, the famous Ardi specimen resembles a female chimpanzee, as she does in the size and shape of her brain and the enamel thickness of her teeth. Although she has a grasping big toe, scholars have placed her on the human line because she locomotes bipedally.

The Anatomy of Bipedalism

For a hominoid fossil to be definitively classified as part of the human evolutionary line requires evidence of bipedalism. Anatomical changes literally from head to toe accompany this human form of locomotion. Evidence of walking on two feet is preserved in the skull because balancing the skull above the spinal column in an upright posture requires a skull position relatively centered above the spinal column (▶ **Figure 4.4**). The spinal cord leaves the skull at its base through an opening called the *foramen magnum* (Latin for "big opening"). In a knuckle-walker like a chimp, the foramen magnum sits toward the back of the skull, whereas in a biped it has a more forward position.

Extending down from the skull of a biped, the spinal column makes a series of convex and concave curves that together maintain the body in an upright posture by

▲▲

bipedalism A special form of locomotion on two feet found in humans and their ancestors.

Ardipithecus One of the earliest genera of bipeds that lived in eastern Africa. Ardipithecus is actually divided into two species the older of which dates to between 5.2 and 5.8 million years ago, and the younger, *A. ramidus,* dated to around 4.4 million years ago.

▼▼

positioning the body's center of gravity above the legs rather than forward. The curves correspond to the neck (cervical), chest (thoracic), lower back (lumbar), and pelvic (sacral) regions of the spine, respectively (▶ **Figure 4.5**). In a chimp, the shape of the spine follows a single arching curve. Interestingly, at birth the spine of a human baby has a single arching curve as seen in the adult ape. As it matures, the curves characteristic of bipedalism appear—the cervical curve at about 3 months on average, a time when the baby begins to hold up its own head, and the lumbar curve at around 12 months, when the baby may begin to walk.

The shape of the pelvis also differs considerably between bipeds and other apes. Rather than an elongated shape following the arch of the spine as seen in chimps, the biped pelvis is wider and foreshortened so that it can provide structural support for the upright body. With a wide bipedal pelvis, the lower limbs would be oriented away from the body's center of gravity if the thighbones (femora) did not angle in toward each other from the hip to the knee, a phenomenon described as "kneeing-in." (Notice how your own knees and feet can touch when standing while your hip joints remain widely spaced.) This angling does not continue past the knee to the shinbones (tibia), which are oriented vertically. The resulting asymmetrical knee joint allows the thighbones and shinbones to meet despite their different orientations. Stable arches and the absent opposable big toe characterize the bipedal foot. In general, humans and their ancestors possess shorter toes than the other apes.

These anatomical features allow paleoanthropologists to diagnose bipedal locomotion even in fragmentary remains, such as the top of a shinbone or the base of a skull. In addition, bipedal locomotion can also be established through fossilized footprints, preserving not so much the shape of bones but the characteristic stride used by humans and their ancestors. In fact, bipedal locomotion involves a process of shifting the body's weight from one foot to the other as the nonsupporting foot swings forward.

The most dramatic confirmation of walking ability in early human ancestors comes from Laetoli, Tanzania, in East Africa, where 3.6 million years ago three individuals walked across newly fallen volcanic ash. Because it was damp, their feet made impressions in the ash, and these footprints were sealed beneath subsequent ash falls until discovered in 1978. The shape of the footprints and the linear distance between each step are quite human.

Paleoanthropologists consider bipedalism an important adaptive feature in the more open country known as *savannah*—grasslands with scattered trees and groves.[5] A biped could not run as fast as a quadruped but could keep up a steady pace over long distances in search of food and water without tiring. With free hands, a biped could take food where it could be eaten in relative safety

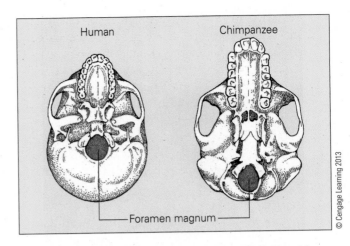

Figure 4.4 Foramen Magnum Bipedalism can be inferred from the position of the foramen magnum, the large opening at the base of the skull. Note its relatively forward position on the human skull (*left*) compared to its position on the chimp skull.

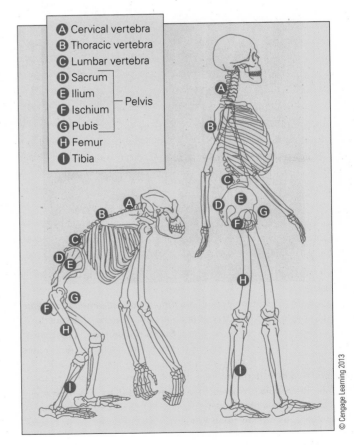

A Cervical vertebra
B Thoracic vertebra
C Lumbar vertebra
D Sacrum
E Ilium ⎤
F Ischium ⎬ Pelvis
G Pubis ⎦
H Femur
I Tibia

Figure 4.5 Chimp and Human Skeletons When viewed side by side, the differences in the backbones of chimps and humans are apparent. Notice the single continuous curve in the chimp backbone and the elongated pelvis. In humans, the four vertebral regions make a series of concave and convex curves to position the skull above the legs. Also, the human pelvis is more basin-shaped. Notice too the differences between chimps and humans in the lengths of the arms and legs and in where the cervical vertebra meet the skull base.

[5]Lewin, R. (1987). Four legs bad, two legs good. *Science 235*, 969.

and could carry infants rather than relying on the babies hanging on for themselves. Bipeds could use their hands to wield sticks or other objects in threat displays and to protect themselves against predators. (Other apes can do this but only for short bursts of time.) Also, erect posture supports endurance running, as it exposes a smaller area of the body to the direct heat of the sun than a quadrupedal position, helping to prevent overheating on the open savannah. Furthermore, a biped, with its head held high, could see farther, spotting food as well as predators from a distance.

Australopithecines

Between 4 and 5 million years ago, the environment of eastern and southern Africa was a mosaic of open country with pockets of closed woodland. While Ardi inhabited some of the woodland pockets, later human ancestors inhabited the savannah, and researchers assign them to one or another species of the genus *Australopithecus* (from Latin *australis,* meaning "southern," and Greek *pithekos,* meaning "ape"). Scholars debate just how many distinct species lived in Africa between about 1.1 and 4.3 million years ago. For our purposes, we refer to them collectively as "australopithecines."

Although adapted fully to bipedalism, the curved bones of the toe and relatively long arms indicate australopithecines had not given up tree climbing altogether. One reason may be that sparsely distributed trees continued to be important places of refuge on the African savannah, a land teeming with dangerous predatory animals. Chimpanzees today build their night nests in trees, suggesting a habit that may have been part of the australopithecine pattern as well. In addition, trees provide rich sources of food such as fruits, seeds, and nuts. A bipedal stance may have also been advantageous for obtaining food in trees, a technique employed by orangutans today.[6]

The earliest definite australopithecine fossils date back 4.2 million years,[7] whereas the most recent ones are only about 1 million years old. Found up and down the length of eastern Africa from Ethiopia to South Africa and westward into Chad (▶ **Figure 4.6**), the australopithecines include Lucy, pictured at the start of the chapter.

Among the later australopithecines, a number of species had particularly large back teeth and correspondingly

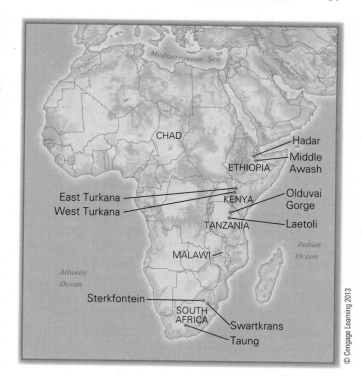

Figure 4.6 Sites of Australopithecine Fossil Finds Australopithecine fossils have been found in South Africa, Malawi, Tanzania, Kenya, Ethiopia, and Chad. In the Miocene the Eurasian and African continents made contact at the eastern and western ends of what now is the Mediterranean Sea. As these landmasses met, rifting also occurred, gradually raising the elevation of the eastern third of Africa. The dryer climates that resulted may have played a role in human evolution in the distant past. In the present, this rifting creates excellent geologic conditions for finding fossils.

large muscles and bones associated with chewing. Collectively, these species are considered **robust australopithecines** because of the rugged nature of their chewing apparatus, which also included modifications on the skull to allow for large chewing muscles. The robust australopithecines inhabited both eastern and southern Africa until about 1 million years ago when they appear to have gone extinct. Based on their teeth and the chemicals preserved in their bones, the robust australopithecines had

---

[6]Thorpe, S. K. S., Holder, R. L., & Crompton, R. H. (2007). Origin of human bipedalism as an adaptation for locomotion on flexible branches. *Science 316,* 1328–1331; Kaplan, M. (2007, May 31). Upright orangutans point way to walking. *Nature.* www.nature.com/news/2007/070531/full/news070528-8.html (retrieved August 9, 2011).

[7]Wolpoff, M. (1996). *Australopithecus:* A new look at an old ancestor. *General Anthropology 3* (1), 2.

▲▲▲

Australopithecus The genus including several species of early bipeds from southern and eastern Africa living between about 1.1 and 4.3 million years ago, one of whom was directly ancestral to humans.

robust australopithecines Several species within the genus *Australopithecus* who lived from 1.1 to 2.5 million years ago in eastern and southern Africa; known for the rugged nature of their chewing apparatus (large back teeth, large chewing muscles, and bony ridge on their skull tops to allow for these large muscles).

▼▼▼

diets that included considerable vegetable matter. They are contrasted with the **gracile australopithecines**, which possessed a more delicate chewing apparatus and were likely to have had a diet that included more meat. The proliferation of bipedal species indicates the success of this new mode of locomotion.

Smaller than most modern humans, the australopithecines had well-developed musculature for their size. Males seem to have been significantly larger than females, with size differences between the sexes less than those found in living apes such as gorillas and orangutans but greater than those among living humans. Taking their relative body size into consideration, australopithecines possessed brains comparable to those of modern African apes. However, the shape of the jaw and some aspects of the teeth resemble those of modern humans more than those of apes.

To survive in their savannah environment, early bipeds may have tried out supplementary sources of food on the ground, as they likely did around the time when the first members of the genus *Homo* appeared about 2.5 million years ago. In addition to plant foods, the major new source was animal protein. But this was not protein from monkey meat obtained as a result of coordinated hunting parties, like those of the chimpanzees and bonobos of today. Instead, our ancestors ate the fatty marrow and leftover edible flesh that remained in and on the bones of dead animals.

Homo habilis

On the dry savannah, a primate with a humanlike digestive system would have difficulty satisfying its protein requirements from the limited available plant resources. Chimpanzees have a similar problem today when out on the savannah. In this environment, they spend more than a third of their time going after insects like ants and termites while also searching for eggs and small vertebrate animals. Not only are such animal foods easily digestible, but they provide high-quality proteins that contain all the essential amino acids, the building blocks of protein, in just the right percentages. No single plant food does this by itself. Only the right combination of plants can supply the balance of amino acids provided by meat alone.

Our ancestors probably solved their dietary problems in much the same way that chimps on the savannah do today but with one key difference: For more efficient utilization of animal protein, our ancestors probably used sharp tools rather than daggerlike teeth for scavenging meat and later for butchering carcasses.

The earliest identifiable tools consist of a number of stone implements made by striking sharp-edged flakes from the surface of a stone core. In the process, cores were transformed into choppers. First discovered

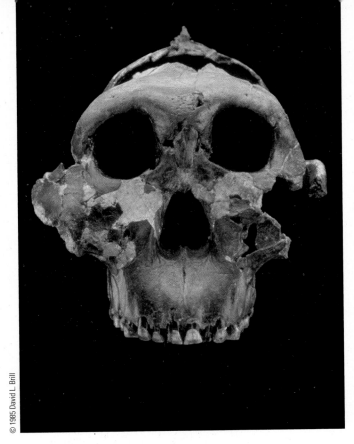

▲▲▲ Robust australopithecines had extremely large cheek teeth (molars) compared to the size of their front teeth. They also had large chewing muscles and a bony ridge on the top of their skulls for the attachment of those large muscles. If you place your own hands on the sides of your skull above your ears while opening and closing your jaw, you can feel where your chewing muscles attach to your skull. By moving your hands toward the top of your skull, you can feel where these muscles end in humans.

in Olduvai Gorge in Tanzania, these flakes and choppers constitute the **Oldowan tool tradition**. They mark the beginning of the **Lower Paleolithic**, or Old Stone Age, a very long time period spanning from approximately 200,000 to 2.6 million years ago. The earliest tools of this sort, which were recently found in Ethiopia, are perhaps as much as 2.6 million years old.

Before this time, australopithecines probably used tools such as heavy sticks to dig up roots or ward off animals, unmodified stones to hurl as weapons or to crack open nuts and bones, and simple carrying devices made of hollow gourds or knotted plant fibers. These kinds of tools disintegrate instead of becoming a part of the archaeological record.

Since the late 1960s, a number of sites in southern and eastern Africa have yielded fossil remains of a lightly built biped with a body all but indistinguishable from that of the earlier australopithecines, except that the teeth are smaller and the brain is significantly larger relative to body size. Furthermore, the pattern from the left cerebral hemisphere imprinted on these ancient skulls

▲▲▲ The oldest stone tools, dated to between 2.5 and 2.6 million years ago, were discovered in Gona, Ethiopia, by Ethiopian paleoanthropologist Sileshi Semaw. These mark the beginning of the Lower Paleolithic or Old Stone Age.

instinct wielding tools on a savannah teeming with meat, while the female members of the species stayed at home tending their young. Flaws with this theoretical reconstruction of ancient human life abound: It reflects a male-centered bias in both the discipline's earlier accounts and in the ethnographic record of still-existing foraging cultures used for comparative purposes, not to mention the absence of evidence to support this view.

Until the 1960s, most anthropologists doing fieldwork among foragers stressed the role of male hunters and underreported the significance of female gatherers in providing food for the community. As anthropologists became aware of their own biases, they began to set the record straight, documenting the vital role of "woman the gatherer" in provisioning the social group in foraging cultures, past and present. (See the Biocultural Connection for another example of gender and paleoanthropological interpretation.) Uncovering biases, like other new discoveries, lead to better interpretations of the fossil record.

Tools, Food, and Brain Expansion

New evidence suggests that early humans depended more on scavenging than on hunting. Indeed, microscopic analysis of cut marks on fossil bones, which commonly overlie marks made by the teeth of carnivores, suggests that the lightly built *Homo habilis* may have been a *tertiary scavenger:* third in line to feed off an animal killed by a predator. Tool-wielding ancestors broke open the shafts of long bones to get at the fat and protein-rich marrow inside. Recently, scholars have suggested that predators hunting early humans prompted our ancestors' brain expansion, rather than the other way around.[9]

Many scenarios proposed for the adaptation of early *Homo*—such as the relationship among tools, food, and

indicates changes associated with language. Although this does not conclusively indicate language use, it suggests a marked advance in information-processing capacity over that of australopithecines.

Because major brain-size increase and tooth-size reduction are important trends in the evolution of the genus *Homo,* paleoanthropologists have designated these fossils as a new species: **Homo habilis** ("handy human").[8] Significantly, the earliest fossils to exhibit these trends appeared around 2.5 million years ago, coincident with the earliest evidence of stone tool making.

Interpreting the Fossil Record

When paleoanthropologists from the 1960s and 1970s depicted the lifeways of early *Homo,* they concentrated on "man the hunter," a tough guy with a killer

▲▲▲

gracile australopithecines One member of the genus *Australopithecus* possessing a more lightly built chewing apparatus; likely had a diet that included more meat than that of the robust australopithecines.

Oldowan tool tradition The first stone tool industry beginning between 2.5 and 2.6 million years ago.

Lower Paleolithic A period of time beginning with the earliest Oldowan tools, spanning from about 200,000 to 2.6 million years ago; also known as *Old Stone Age.*

Homo habilis "Handy human." The first fossil members of the genus *Homo* appearing 2.5 million years ago, with larger brains and smaller faces than australopithecines.

[8]Leakey, L. S. B., Tobias, P. B., & Napier, J. R. (1964). A new species of the genus *Homo* from Olduvai Gorge. *Nature 202,* 7–9. (Some have argued that *H. habilis* was too varied to be considered a single species.)

[9]Hart, D., & Sussman, R. W. (2005). *Man the hunted: Primates, predators, and human evolution.* Boulder, CO: Westview Press.

▼ ▼

BIOCULTURAL CONNECTION

Evolution and Human Birth

Because biology and culture have always shaped human experience, it can be a challenge to separate the influences of each of these factors on human practices. For example, in the 1950s paleoanthropologists developed the theory that human childbirth is particularly difficult compared to birth in other mammals. This theory was based in part on the observation of a "tight fit" between the human mother's birth canal and the baby's head, though several other primates also possess similarly tight fits between the newborn's head or shoulders and the birth canal. Nevertheless, changes in the birth canal associated with bipedalism were held responsible for difficult birth in humans.

At the same historical moment, North American childbirth practices were changing. In one generation from the 1920s to the 1950s, birth shifted from the home to the hospital. In the process childbirth was transformed from something a woman normally accomplished at home, perhaps with the help of a midwife or relatives, into the high-tech delivery of a *neonate* (the medical term for a newborn) with the assistance of medically trained personnel. During the 1950s women were generally fully anesthetized during the birth process. Paleoanthropological theories mirrored the cultural norms, providing a scientific explanation for the change in North American childbirth practices.

As a scientific theory, the idea of especially difficult human birth stands on shaky ground. No fossil neonates have ever been recovered, and only a handful of complete pelves (the bones forming the birth canal) exist. Instead, scientists must examine the birth process in living humans and nonhuman primates to reconstruct the evolution of the human birth pattern. Cultural beliefs and practices, however, shape every aspect of birth. Cultural factors determine where a birth occurs, the actions of the individuals present, and beliefs about the nature of the experience.

When paleoanthropologists of the 1950s and 1960s asserted that human childbirth is more difficult than birth in other mammals, they may have been drawing upon their own North American cultural beliefs that childbirth is dangerous and belongs in a hospital. A quick look at global neonatal mortality statistics indicates that in countries such as the Netherlands and Sweden, healthy, well-nourished women give birth successfully outside of hospitals as they did throughout human evolutionary history. In other countries, deaths related to childbirth reflect malnutrition, infectious disease, and the low social status of women, rather than an inherently faulty biology. ■

Biocultural Question

Though well-nourished, healthy women successfully birth their babies outside the hospital setting, caesarean section (C-section) rates have been rising in industrial and postindustrial societies. In the United States, one in three births is by C-section. The C-section rates in many Latin American countries are greater than 50 percent of all births. What cultural factors have led to this practice? Would your personal approach to birth change with the knowledge that humans have successfully adapted to childbirth?

brain expansion—rely upon a feedback loop between brain size and behavior. The behaviors made possible by larger brains confer advantages to large-brained individuals, contributing to their increased reproductive success. Over time, gene frequencies shift such that individuals with larger brains become more common in successive generations, and the population gradually evolves to acquiring a larger-brained form.

Paleoanthropologists debate whether the evolution of the genus *Homo* from australopithecine ancestors was a gradual process or a sudden development, or some combination of the two. Recently, researchers at the University of Pennsylvania announced the discovery of a genetic mutation, shared by all humans but absent in apes, that acts to prevent growth of powerful jaw muscles. Applying the theory of punctuated equilibria or sudden evolutionary transformation (discussed in Chapter 2), they calculate that the mutation arose between 2.1 and 2.7 million years ago, the period when *H. habilis* first appeared. They argue that without heavy jaw muscles attached to the outside of the braincase, a significant constraint to brain growth was removed. In other words, humans may have developed large brains as an accidental byproduct of jaw-size reduction.[10]

Natural selection added to the effects of the sudden change of the jaw through the gradual brain expansion that continued in the genus *Homo* until some 200,000 years ago. By then, brain size had approximately tripled and reached the levels of today's humans. Tool making preserved in the archaeological record provides us with tangible data concerning our ancestors' cultural abilities

---

[10]Stedman, H. H., et al. (2004). Myosin gene mutation correlates with anatomical changes in the human lineage. *Nature 428,* 415–418.

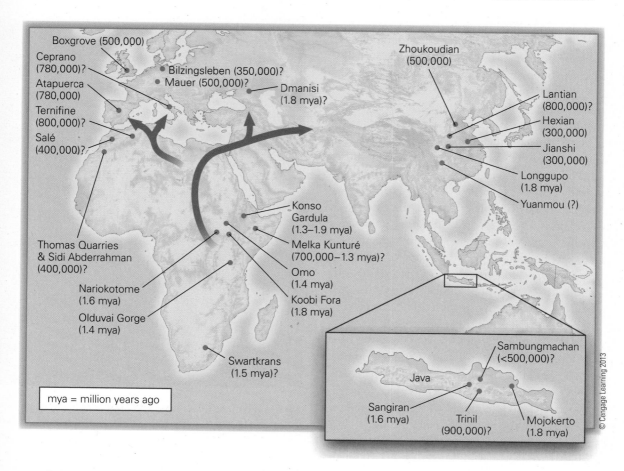

Figure 4.7 *Homo erectus* Sites *Homo erectus* sites are shown here with their dates. The arrows indicate the proposed routes by which *Homo* spread from Africa to Eurasia. The question marks indicate the uncertain dating for particular sites.

according with the simultaneous biological expansion of the brain. Beginning with *H. habilis* in Africa around 2.5 million years ago, human evolution followed a sure course of increasing brain size relative to body size and increasing cultural development, each acting upon and thereby promoting the other.

Homo erectus

Shortly after 2 million years ago, by which time *Homo habilis* and Oldowan tools had become widespread in Africa, a new species, ***Homo erectus*** ("upright human"), appeared on that continent. Unlike *H. habilis,* however, *H. erectus* did not remain confined to Africa. In fact, evidence of *H. erectus* fossils almost as old as those discovered in Africa have been found in the Caucasus Mountains of Georgia (between Turkey and Russia), in southern and central China, and on the island of Java, Indonesia. In other words, members of the genus *Homo* spread widely and relatively quickly throughout much of Asia and eventually Europe as well (▶ **Figure 4.7**).

The emergence of *H. erectus* as a new species in the long course of human evolution coincided with the

beginning of the Pleistocene epoch, which spanned from 12,000 to 1.8 million years ago. During this time of periodic global cooling, Arctic cold conditions and abundant snowfall in the earth's northern hemisphere created vast ice sheets that temporarily covered much of Eurasia and North America. These fluctuating major glacial periods often lasted tens of thousands of years, separated by intervening warm periods. During interglacial periods, the world warmed up to the point that the ice sheets melted and sea levels rose, but sea levels were generally much lower than today, exposing large surfaces of low-lying lands now under water.

The Pleistocene epoch, with its dramatic climatic shifts, is the time during which humans—from *H. erectus* to *H. sapiens*—evolved and spread all across the globe.

▲▲▲▲▲▲▲▲▲▲▲▲▲▲▲▲▲▲▲▲▲▲▲▲▲▲▲▲▲▲▲▲▲▲▲▲▲

Homo erectus "Upright human." A species within the genus *Homo* first appearing just after 2 million years ago in Africa and ultimately spreading throughout the Old World.

▼▼▼▼▼▼▼▼▼▼▼▼▼▼▼▼▼▼▼▼▼▼▼▼▼▼▼▼▼▼▼▼▼▼▼▼▼

Confronted by environmental changes due to climatic fluctuations or movements into different geographic areas, our early human ancestors were constantly challenged to make biological and, more especially, cultural adaptations in order to survive and successfully reproduce. In the course of this long evolutionary process, random mutations introduced new characteristics into evolving populations in different regions of the world. As we shall see below, great debate surrounds the question of whether one or all of these populations contributed to modern humanity.

According to the principle of natural selection, certain characteristics provided adaptive benefits within particular environmental conditions. At the same time, other characteristics that conferred no particular advantage or disadvantage also appeared by random mutation in geographically removed populations. The end result was a gradually growing physical variation in the genus *Homo*. In this context, it is not surprising that *H. erectus* fossils found in Africa, Asia, and Europe reveal levels of physical variation similar to those seen in modern human populations living across the globe today. Many paleoanthropologists believe that the physical variation in the genus *Homo* was too great to consider all these specimens a single species, and they advocate instead splitting *H. erectus* into a variety of distinct species.

Available fossil evidence indicates that *H. erectus* had body size and proportions similar to modern humans, though with heavier musculature. Differences in body size between the sexes diminished considerably compared to earlier bipeds, perhaps to facilitate successful childbirth.[11] Based on fossil skull evidence, *H. erectus* average brain size ranked within the higher range of *H. habilis* and within the lower range of modern human brains. The dentition was fully human, though relatively large by modern standards. As one might expect, given its larger brain, *H. erectus* outstripped its predecessors in cultural abilities.

In Africa and most of Eurasia, more sophisticated hand axes replaced Oldowan choppers, marking a tool industry known as the Acheulean. At first, hand axes—shaped by regular blows giving them a larger and finer cutting edge than chopper tools—probably served as all-purpose implements for food procurement and processing and for defense. But *H. erectus* also developed cleavers (like hand axes but without points) and various scrapers to process animal hides for bedding and clothing. In addition, these early humans relied on flake tools used "as is" to cut meat and process vegetables, or refined by "retouching" into points and borers for drilling or punching holes in materials. *Homo erectus'* use of raw materials also demonstrates improved technological efficiency.

Instead of making a few large tools out of big pieces of stone, *Homo erectus* placed a new emphasis on smaller

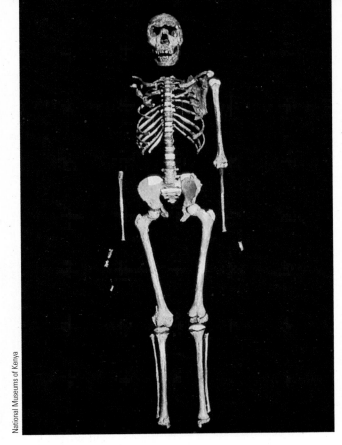

National Museums of Kenya

▲▲▲ One of the oldest and certainly one of the most complete *Homo erectus* fossils is the Nariokotome Boy from Lake Turkana, Kenya. How can scientists determine the age and sex of this specimen? Age comes from an examination of the degree to which bones have finished their growth and the emergence of the molar teeth; sex is determined from the shape of the pelvis, due to adaptations in the female pelvis that accommodate childbirth. Even though these remains come from a tall adolescent boy, this pelvis has been used to reconstruct theories about the evolution of human birth.

tools, thus economizing their raw materials. Some of these raw materials continue even today to have practical value, as the Anthropology Applied feature illustrates.

Remains found in southern Africa also suggest that *Homo erectus* may have learned to use fire by 1 million years ago. Fire gave our ancestors more control over their environment. It permitted them to continue activities after dark and provided a means to frighten away predators. It supplied them with the warmth and light needed for cave-dwelling, and it enabled them to cook their food. The ability to modify food culturally through cooking may have played a role in the reduction of the tooth size and jaws of later fossil groups since tough raw foods require more chewing. However, cooking has several other benefits: It detoxifies a number of otherwise poisonous plants; it allows for the absorption of important vitamins, minerals, and proteins that would otherwise pass unused through the

---

[11]Hager, L. (1989). *The evolution of sex differences in the hominid bony pelvis.* Ph.D. dissertation, University of California, Berkeley.

ANTHROPOLOGY APPLIED

Stone Tools for Modern Surgeons

When anthropologist Irven DeVore of Harvard University needed to have some minor melanomas removed from his face, he did not leave it up to the surgeon to supply his own scalpels. Instead, he had graduate student John Shea make a scalpel. Making a blade of obsidian (a naturally occurring volcanic glass) by the same techniques used by Upper Paleolithic peoples to make blades, he then hafted this in a wooden handle, using melted pine resin as glue and then lashing it with sinew. After the procedure, the surgeon reported that the obsidian scalpel was superior to metal ones.[a]

DeVore was not the first to undergo surgery performed with stone scalpels. In 1975, Don Crabtree, then at Idaho State University, prepared the scalpels that his surgeon would use in Crabtree's heart surgery. In 1980, Payson Sheets at the University of Colorado prepared obsidian

scalpels that were used successfully in eye surgery. And in 1986, David Pokotylo of the Museum of Anthropology at the University of British Columbia underwent reconstructive surgery on his hand with blades he himself had made (the hafting was done by his museum colleague, Len McFarlane).

Using scalpels modeled on ancient stone tools arose because anthropologists realized that obsidian is superior in almost every way to materials normally used to make scalpels: It is 210 to 1,050 times sharper than surgical steel, 100 to 500 times sharper than a razor blade, and 3 times sharper than a diamond blade (which not only costs much more, but cannot be made with more than 3 millimeters of cutting edge). It is easier to cut with obsidian blades, and these blades do less damage in the process (under a microscope, incisions made with the sharp-

est steel blades show torn, ragged edges and are littered with bits of displaced flesh).[b] A surgeon using an obsidian blade has better control, and the incision heals faster with less scarring and pain.

Because of the superiority of obsidian scalpels, Sheets went so far as to form a partnership with eye surgeon Dr. Firmon Hardenbergh of Boulder, Colorado. Together, they developed a means of producing cores of uniform size from molten glass, as well as a machine to detach blades from the cores. ■

[a]Shreeve, J. (1995). *The Neandertal enigma: Solving the mystery of modern human origins* (p. 134). New York: William Morrow.

[b]Sheets, P. D. (1987). Dawn of a New Stone Age in eye surgery. In R. J. Sharer & W. Ashmore (Eds.), *Archaeology: Discovering our past* (p. 231). Palo Alto, CA: Mayfield.

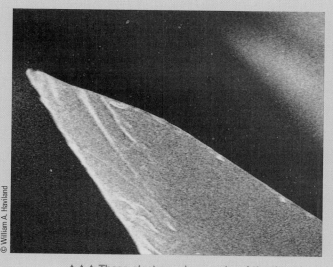 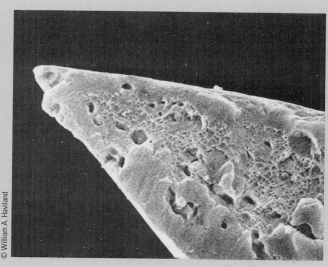

▲▲▲ These electron micrographs of the tips of an obsidian blade (*left*) and a modern steel scalpel (*right*) illustrate the superiority of the obsidian.

© William A. Haviland

body; it makes high-energy complex carbohydrates, such as starch, digestible.

In addition, without controlled use of fire, early humans could not have moved successfully into regions where winter temperatures regularly dropped below 50 degrees Fahrenheit (10 degrees Celsius)—as they must have in northern China or the mountain highlands of Central Asia, or most of Europe, where the genus *Homo* spread some 780,000 years ago. Although considerable variation exists, studies of modern humans indicate that most people can remain reasonably comfortable down to 50 degrees Fahrenheit with minimal clothing so long as they keep active. Below that temperature, hands and feet cool to the point of pain. In short, when our human ancestors learned to employ fire to warm and protect themselves and to cook their food, they dramatically increased their geographic range and nutritional options.

With *H. erectus* we also begin to have evidence of organized hunting as the means for procuring meat, animal hides, horn, bone, and sinew. Early evidence demonstrating the hunting technology of these ancestors includes 400,000-year-old wooden spears discovered in a peat bog (originally marsh or swamp land) in northern Germany, although evolving humans likely had begun to hunt before then. Prehistoric sites such as Ambrona in Spain preserve evidence of increased organizational ability: Fires were used to drive a variety of large animals (including elephants) into a swamp for killing,[12] although others have proposed natural grass fires as an alternative explanation.

With *H. erectus,* then, we find a clearer demonstration of the complex interplay of biological, cultural, and ecological factors. Changes in social organization and technology paralleled an increase in brain size and complexity and a reduction in tooth and jaw size. In turn, cultural adaptations such as controlled use of fire, cooking, and more complex toolkits may have facilitated language development. Analysis of the tools made by early *Homo* indicates that the toolmakers were overwhelmingly right-handed, handedness being a trait associated with language abilities. Moreover, the size of the opening for the nerve that controls tongue movement, so important for spoken language, equals that of modern humans.

Improvements in communication and social organization brought about by language undoubtedly contributed to better methods for food gathering and hunting, to a population increase, and to territorial expansion. Continuous biological and cultural changes through natural selection through the course of hundreds of thousands of years gradually transformed *H. erectus* into the next emerging species: *Homo sapiens.*

Lumpers or Splitters

Various sites in Africa, Asia, and Europe have yielded fossils dating to between roughly 200,000 and 400,000 years

ago. The best population sample, bones of about thirty individuals of both sexes and all ages (but none older than about 40), comes from Atapuerca, a 400,000-year-old site in Spain. Overall, these bones depict a mixture of characteristics of *Homo erectus* with those of early *Homo sapiens,* exactly what one would expect of fossil remains transitional between the two. For example, brain size overlaps the upper end of the *H. erectus* range and the lower end of the range for *H. sapiens.*

Whether one chooses to call these or any other contemporary fossils early *Homo sapiens,* late *Homo erectus,* or *Homo antecessor,* as did the Spanish anthropologists who discovered them, is more than a name game. Fossil names indicate researchers' perspectives about evolutionary relationships among groups. Giving specimens separate species names signifies that they form part of a reproductively isolated group. But were they isolated? Some argue that the evidence does not support such an assumption. There are two basic approaches to naming species in the fossil record: lumping and splitting.

This textbook takes the lumping approach because of its simplicity and emphasis on general trends appropriate for an introduction to the field. Paleoanthropologists who argue for the impossibility of demonstrating whether or not a collection of ancient bones and teeth represents a distinctive species tend to be "lumpers." They place similar-looking fossil specimens together in more inclusive groups. "Splitters," by contrast, focus on the variation in the fossil record, interpreting fine-grained differences in the shape of skeletons or skulls as evidence of distinctive biological species with corresponding cultural capacities. Referring to the variable shape of the bony ridge above ancient eyes, South African paleoanthropologist Philip Tobias has quipped, "Splitters will create a new species at the drop of a brow ridge." Splitting has the advantage of specificity, whereas lumping has the advantage of simplicity.

The Neandertals

Closer to the present, the fossil record provides us with many more ancestral humans compared to earlier periods. The record is particularly rich when it comes to **Neandertals,** perhaps the most controversial ancient members of the genus *Homo.* Typically, they are represented as the classic cavemen, stereotyped in Western popular media and even in museum displays as wild and hairy club-wielding brutes.

Extremely muscular members of the genus *Homo* living from about 30,000 to approximately 125,000 years

---

[12]Freeman, L. G. (1992). *Ambrona and Torralba: New evidence and interpretation.* Paper presented at the 91st annual meeting, American Anthropological Association.

▲▲▲ As seen in these skulls of various human ancestors, arranged from most ancient on the left to most recent on the right, brain size increased dramatically over the course of time. This increase began about 2.5 million years ago and coincides with the first appearance of stone tools in the archaeological record. From left to right, these specimens are: (1) a gracile australopithecine, (2) *Homo habilis*, (3) *Homo erectus*, (4) an archaic *Homo sapiens* from Africa (Kabwe), (5) a Neandertal, and (6) an anatomically modern *Homo sapiens*. The continuous feedback loop between culture and brain expansion up until 200,000 years ago complicates the discernment of species in the fossil record. Could changes such as the reduction in the brow ridges and skull shape be associated with distinct cultural abilities?

ago in Europe and parts of Asia, Neandertals appear more regularly in the fossil record because they buried their dead. Although they had modern-sized brains, Neandertal faces and skulls differ considerably from those of later fossilized remains known as anatomically modern humans. Large Neandertal noses and teeth protrude forward more than do the smaller noses and teeth of modern humans.

Neandertals generally had a sloping forehead and a prominent bony brow ridge over their eyes, a receding chin, and a bony mass on the back of the skull that allowed for attachment of powerful neck muscles. These features, while not exactly in line with modern ideals of European beauty, are also common in Norwegian and Danish skulls dating to about 1,000 years ago—the time of the Vikings[13]—and remain to a certain degree in some humans today. Nevertheless, these anatomical similarities do little to negate the popular image of Neandertals as cave-dwelling brutes. Their rude reputation may also derive from the time of their discovery, as the first widely publicized Neandertal skull was found in

1856, well before scientific theories to account for human origins had gained acceptance.

This odd-looking old skull, found in Germany's Neander Valley (*tal* in German), took scientists by surprise. Initially, they explained its extraordinary features as evidence of some disfiguring disease in an invading "barbarian" from the east who had crawled into a deep cave to die. Although we now know that many aspects of the Neandertals' unique skull shape and body form represent their biological adaptation to an extremely cold climate, and that their brain size and capacity for cultural adaptation were noticeably superior to those of earlier members of the genus *Homo*, controversy still surrounds the Neandertals.

A SEPARATE SPECIES?

Were Neandertals a separate species that became extinct about 30,000 years ago? Or were they a subspecies of

▲▲

Neandertals A distinct group within the genus *Homo* inhabiting Europe and Southwest Asia from approximately 30,000 to 125,000 years ago.

▼▼

[13]Ferrie, H. (1997) An interview with C. Loring Brace. *Current Anthropology 38*, 861.

Homo sapiens? And if they were not a dead end, not an unsuccessful side branch in human evolution, did they actually contribute to our modern human gene pool? In that case, so the argument goes, their direct descendants walk the earth today. Neandertals' place in human evolutionary history remains contentious.

With their large brain size, the Neandertal capacity for cultural adaptation was predictably superior to that of earlier species. For example, Neandertals survived the cold climate of Europe during the various glacial periods through an extensive use of fire. They lived in small bands or single-family units, both in the open and in caves, probably communicating through language. Deliberate burials of the dead reflect a measure of ritual behavior in their communities.

Moreover, the fossil remains of an amputee discovered in Iraq and an arthritic man excavated in France imply that Neandertals cared for the disabled, something not seen previously in the human fossil record. The toolmaking tradition of all but the latest Neandertals is called the **Mousterian tool tradition** after a site (Le Moustier) in the Dordogne region of southern France. *Mousterian* refers to a tradition of the Middle Paleolithic or Middle Stone Age tool industries of Europe and Southwest Asia and North Africa, generally dating from about 40,000 to 125,000 years ago.

Generally lighter and smaller than those of earlier traditions, Mousterian toolkits also contained a greater variety of tool types. While previous techniques obtained only two or three flakes from an entire stone core, Mousterian toolmakers created many smaller flakes, which they skillfully retouched and sharpened. Hand axes, flakes, scrapers, borers, notched flakes for shaving wood, and many types of points that could be attached to wooden shafts to make spears facilitated more effective use of food resources and enhanced the quality of clothing and shelter. Mousterian stone tools were used by *all* peoples, Neandertals and their contemporaries elsewhere, including Europe, western Asia, and North Africa, during this time period. By the time that classic Neandertals were disappearing between 30,000 and 40,000 years ago, their technology was comparable to the tool complexes used by anatomically modern *Homo sapiens* during that same period.[14]

THE GENUS *HOMO* ELSEWHERE

Meanwhile, archaic *H. sapiens* variants, without the midfacial projection and massive muscle attachments on the back of the skull common among Neandertals, inhabited other parts of the world during this time period. For example, human fossil skulls found near the Solo River in Java dating from the middle to late Pleistocene possess modern-sized brains. The fossils display certain features

of *H. erectus* combined with those of archaic as well as more modern *H. sapiens*.

Further, a controversial discovery on the Indonesian island of Flores illustrates that geographic isolation can account for an unusual amount of variation in morphology for members of the genus *Homo*. A small-bodied, small-brained adult specimen—dated to between 18,000 and 38,000 years ago, no more than 1 meter (3 feet) tall, with humanlike skull and teeth—was designated as the new species *Homo floresiensis* in 2004.[15]

The paleoanthropologists who discovered this specimen, along with various stone tools and the bones of other animal species dated back to 90,000 years ago, suggest that *Homo floresiensis* is "the end product of a long period of evolution on a comparatively small island where environmental conditions placed small body size at a selective advantage."[16] Some paleoanthropologists argue that the skeleton represents an individual with microcephaly, a disease that causes small headedness, and a variety of other medical conditions. However, recent studies indicate a ratio of brain size to body size in this specimen similar to australopithecines, with a brain shaped like a dwarf version of *Homo erectus*.[17] Additional discoveries in the region have supported this theory.

Fossils from various parts of Africa, including the famous Kabwe skull from Zambia (see photo on page 89, third from right) also show a combination of ancient and modern traits. Finally, similar remains have been found at several places in China. For these members of the genus *Homo*, improved cultural adaptive abilities relate to the fact that the brain had achieved modern size. Generally classified as archaic *Homo sapiens*, like Neandertals, these specimens possess large brains, but their skull shape differs from that of later specimens.

Large brains promote sophisticated technology as well as conceptual thought of considerable intellectual complexity. Decorative pendants and objects with carved

---

[14]Mellars, P. (1989). Major issues in the emergence of modern humans. *Current Anthropology 30*, 356–357.

[15]Brown, P., et al. (2004). A new small bodied hominin from the Late Pleistocene of Flores, Indonesia. *Nature 431*, 1055–1061.

[16]Brown, et al., p. 1060.

[17]Falk, D., et al. (2005). The brain of LB1, *Homo floresiensis. Science 308*, 242–245.

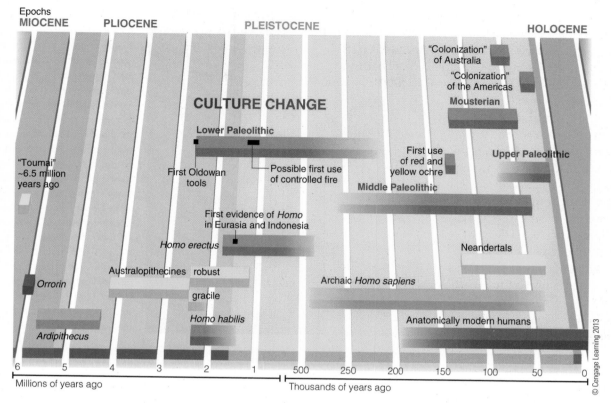

Figure 4.8 Timeline of Human Evolutionary History Paleoanthropologists debate the exact relationship among the bipedal species, along with the number of species that existed, over the past 5 to 8 million years. This timeline takes a "lumping" approach, limiting the number of fossil groups represented. The time spans for the Lower, Middle, and Upper Paleolithic vary tremendously by region. Note also that the time scale is expanded for the most recent 250,000 years.

and engraved markings also appear in the archaeological record from this period, often colored with pigments such as manganese dioxide and red or yellow ochre. The ceremonial burying of the dead and nonutilitarian decorative objects provide additional evidence of symbolic thinking and language use in these ancient populations.

Complications surround the establishment of a one-to-one relationship between anatomical change and culture change over the course of human evolutionary history (▶ **Figure 4.8**). Beginning around 200,000 years ago, individuals with a more anatomically modern human appearance began to appear in Africa and southwestern Asia. While the earliest of these fossils appear with the same Mousterian tool industries used by the Neandertals, over time new tool industries and other forms of cultural expression emerged. Whether these changes in skull shape account for a new species with superior cultural abilities lies at the heart of the modern human origins debate.

The Upper Paleolithic

A veritable explosion of tool types and other forms of cultural expression began about 40,000 years ago. Known as the *Upper Paleolithic transition*, the toolkits

of this period include increased prominence of "blade" tools: long, thin, precisely shaped pieces of stone demonstrating the considerable skill of their creators. The **Upper Paleolithic**, lasting until about 10,000 years ago, marks the beginning of behavioral modernity. Best known from archaeological evidence found in Europe where numerous distinctive tool complexes from successive time periods, the period is also known for its art. Cave wall paintings, engravings, and bas-relief sculptures, as well as many portable nonutilitarian artifacts, abound.

In Upper Paleolithic times, humans began to manufacture tools for more effective hunting, fishing, and gathering. Cultural adaptation also became

▲▲▲

Mousterian tool tradition The tool industry of the Neandertals and their contemporaries of Europe, Southwest Asia, and North Africa from 40,000 to 125,000 years ago.

Upper Paleolithic A period of time from about 40,000 until about 10,000 years ago that marks the beginning of behavioral modernity. The tool industries of this time are characterized by long, slim blades that produced an explosion of creative symbolic forms.

▼▼▼

AP Images/Jean Clottes

more highly specific and regional, thus enhancing human chances for survival under a wide variety of environmental conditions. Instead of manufacturing all-purpose tools, Upper Paleolithic populations inhabiting a wide range of environments—mountains, marshlands, tundra, forests, lake regions, river valleys, and seashores—all developed specialized devices suited to the resources of their particular habitat and to the different seasons. Our ancestors found ways and means to travel across icy Arctic regions and open waters to reach places never previously inhabited by humans. Humans reached Australia between 40,000 and 60,000 years ago and the Americas between about 15,000 and 30,000 years ago.

This degree of regional specialization required improved manufacturing techniques. The blade method of manufacture, invented by archaic *H. sapiens* and later used widely in Europe and western Asia, required fewer raw materials than before and resulted in smaller and lighter tools with a better ratio between weight of flint and length of cutting edge. The pressure-flaking technique—in which a bone, antler, or wooden tool is used to press off small flakes from a larger flake or blade—gave the Upper Paleolithic toolmaker greater control over the shape of the tool than was possible with percussion flaking (▶ **Figure 4.9**).

Invented by Mousterian toolmakers, the *burin* (a stone tool with chisel-like edges) came into common use in the Upper Paleolithic. The burin provided an excellent means of working bone and antler into tools such as fishhooks and harpoons. The spear-thrower or *atlatl* (a Nahuatl word used by Aztec Indians in Mexico, referring to a wooden device, 1 to 2 feet long, with a hook on the end for throwing a spear) also appeared at this time. By effectively elongating the arm, the atlatl gave hunters increased force behind the throw.

In addition to the creativity evident in their tools and weapons, Upper Paleolithic peoples produced representational artwork. In some regions, tools and weapons were engraved with beautiful animal figures; pendants were made of bone and ivory, as were female figurines; and small sculptures were modeled out of clay. Spectacular paintings and engravings depicting humans and animals of this period have been found on the walls of caves and rock shelters in southwestern Europe, Australia, and Africa.

The southern African rock art tradition spanned 27,000 years and lasted into historic times; from this continuity, we know that much of it depicts artists' visions when in altered states of consciousness related to spiritual practices. Along with the animals, the art also includes a variety of geometric motifs reminiscent of visual hallucinations spontaneously generated by the human nervous system when in a trancelike state.

Australian cave art, some of it older than European cave art and also associated with trancing, includes similar motifs. The occurrence of the same geometric designs in the cave art of Europe suggests that trancing was a part of these prehistoric foraging cultures as well. Some argue that geometric motifs in Paleolithic art were interpreted as stylized human figures and patterns of descent. Although this is speculative, the great importance of kinship in all historically known communities of hunters, fishers, and gatherers makes such a suggestion plausible.

Mousterian Tools

Upper Paleolithic Tools

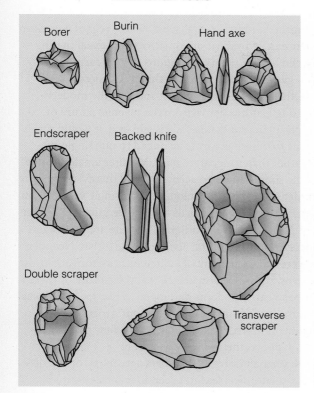

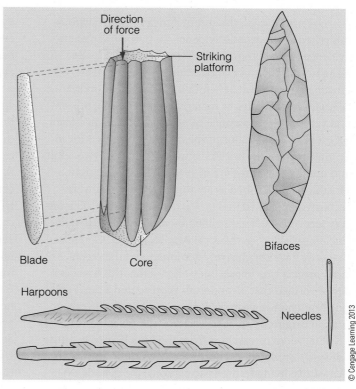

Figure 4.9 Mousterian Versus Upper Paleolithic Tool-Making Techniques and Tools Compared to Mousterian tools, Upper Paleolithic tools are more varied and use raw materials more efficiently. Upper Paleolithic techniques allowed for the production of blade tools. In particular, pressure-flaking techniques let toolmakers work with bone and antler, as well as stone, forming it into very fine shapes.

Paleoanthropologists debate whether this cultural explosion required a new kind of human, anatomically modern with correspondingly superior intellectual and creative abilities. After all, new kinds of humans were not associated with subsequent cultural explosions such as the Neolithic revolution (Chapter 5). The biological and cultural evidence preserved in fossil and archaeological records do not give a simple answer to this question.

The Modern Human Origins Debate

On a biological level, the modern human origins debate distills down to a question of whether one, some, or all populations of the archaic groups played a role in the evolution of modern *Homo sapiens*. Those supporting the multiregional hypothesis argue that the fossil evidence suggests a simultaneous local transition from *H. erectus* to modern *H. sapiens* throughout all the parts of the world inhabited by early members of the genus *Homo*. By contrast, those supporting the recent African origins hypothesis (also known as the *Eve hypothesis* or

the *out of Africa hypothesis*) argue that all anatomically modern humans living today descend directly from a more recent single population of archaic *H. sapiens* in Africa. This hypothesis asserts that improved cultural capabilities allowed members of this group to replace other archaic human forms as they began to spread out of Africa sometime after 100,000 years ago. So while both models place human origins firmly in Africa, the first argues that our human ancestors began moving into Asia and Europe as early as 1.8 million years ago, whereas the second maintains that anatomically modern *H. sapiens* evolved only in Africa, completely replacing

multiregional hypothesis The hypothesis that modern humans originated through a process of simultaneous local transition from *Homo erectus* to *Homo sapiens* throughout the inhabited world.

recent African origins hypothesis The hypothesis that modern humans are all derived from one single population of archaic *Homo sapiens* who migrated out of Africa after 100,000 years ago, replacing all other archaic forms due to their superior cultural capabilities; also known as the *Eve hypothesis* or the *out of Africa hypothesis*.

other members of the genus *Homo* as they spread throughout the world.

For many years, the recent African origins hypothesis relied upon genetic evidence. In particular, genetic evidence seemed to point to a single mother or "Eve" for all anatomically modern humans by tracing human origins through DNA that is found in the mitochondria—a cellular structure that is maternally inherited. Until several years ago, the absence of good fossil evidence from Africa has been a major problem for the recent African origins hypothesis. In 2003, however, skulls of two adults and one child (discovered in 1997 in the Afar region of Ethiopia) described as anatomically modern were reconstructed and dated to 160,000 years ago.[18] The discoverers of these fossils called them *Homo sapiens idaltu* (meaning "elder" in the local Afar language). Convinced that they have conclusively demonstrated the recent African origins hypothesis, they argued that this fossil evidence verified that Neandertals represented a dead-end side branch of human evolution. Until 2010, the recent African origins hypothesis was the mainstream position.

But when researchers from the Max Planck Institute released a study comparing the Neandertal genome to that of five living human populations, the genetic evidence shifted to supporting the multiregional hypothesis.[19] This new study documents a significant proportion of Neandertal genes persisting among contemporary non-African populations, indicating mating between the Neandertals and the anatomically modern humans who appeared in Africa some 200,000 years ago.

Proponents of multiregionalism had already critiqued the recent African origins model on several grounds. For example, the molecular evidence upon which it is based has been strongly criticized as other genetic studies had also indicated that Africa was not the sole source of DNA in modern humans.[20]

Recent African origins proponents argue that anatomically modern people coexisted for a time with archaic populations until the superior cultural capacities of the moderns resulted in extinction of the archaic peoples. This may help explain its popularity with some Western scholars, as it resonates with European experience of colonial expansion; the difference is that Africa, rather than Europe, is the origin of the supposedly superior people. It also harmonizes with the historical discomfort of considering Neandertals as fully human.

Some have argued that evidence from Europe, where Neandertals and "anatomically moderns" cohabited between 30,000 and 40,000 years ago, supports a model of coexistence and replacement. However, defining some fossils as either Neandertal or anatomically modern is difficult. The latest Neandertals show features (such as chins) more commonly seen in anatomically modern humans, while "early moderns" show features (such as brow ridges and bony masses at the back of the

skull) reminiscent of Neandertals. This mix of modern and Neandertal features in a child's skeleton found in Portugal prompted several specialists to regard it as clear evidence of hybridization, or successful sexual mating between both human populations.[21] The current Neandertal genome study supports this conclusion.

Other specialists argue that some of the modern-appearing features derive from the juvenile nature of this specimen. But if this child is a hybrid, it would mean that the two human forms belonged to one single species rather than to separate ones. Multiregionalists argue that the simplest way to account for all this evidence is to consider these fossils as belonging to a single varied population, with some individuals showing features more typical of Neandertals than others. They cite archaeological evidence that the cultural achievements of late Neandertals were not fundamentally different from those of early moderns,[22] as well as evidence that the culture of these European early moderns developed in Europe[23] and was not introduced from outside, as recent African origins proponents assert. They argue that the new genetic evidence supports their position precisely.

Nevertheless, by 30,000 years ago, many of the distinctive anatomical features seen in archaic groups like Neandertals seem to disappear from the fossil record in Europe. Instead, individuals with higher foreheads, smoother brow ridges, and more distinct chins seem to have had Europe to themselves. However, if one looks at the full range of contemporary human variation across the globe, one can find living peoples who do not meet the anatomical definition of modernity proposed in the recent African origins model.[24]

The modern human origins debate raises fundamental questions about the complex relationship between biological and cultural human variation. As we reviewed the human fossil record throughout this chapter, we

[18]White, T., et al. (2003). Pleistocene *Homo sapiens* from the Middle Awash, Ethiopia. *Nature 423*, 742–747.

[19]Green, R. E., et al. (2010, May 7). A draft sequence of the Neandertal genome. *Science 328*, 710–722.

[20]Templeton, A. R. (1995). The "Eve" hypothesis: A genetic critique and reanalysis. *American Anthropologist 95* (1), 51–72; Gibbons, A. (1997). Ideas on human origins evolve at anthropology gathering. *Science 276*, 535–536; Pennisi, E. (1999). Genetic study shakes up out of Africa theory. *Science 283*, 1828.

[21]Holden, C. (1999). Ancient child burial uncovered in Portugal. *Science 283*, 169.

[22]d'Errico, F., et al. (1998). Neandertal acculturation in western Europe? *Current Anthropology 39*, 521. See also Henry, D. O., et al. (2004). Human behavioral organization in the Middle Paleolithic: Were Neandertals different? *American Anthropologist 107* (1), 17–31.

[23]Clark, G. A. (2002). Neandertal archaeology: Implications for our origins. *American Anthropologist 104* (1), 50–67.

[24]Wolpoff, M., & Caspari, R. (1997). *Race and human evolution* (pp. 344–345, 393). New York: Simon & Schuster.

made inferences about the cultural capabilities of our ancestors partially based on biological features. For instance, the argument of a significantly increased brain size of *Homo habilis* 2.5 million years ago compared to earlier australopithecines was used to support the claim that these ancestors were capable of more complex cultural activities, including the manufacture of stone tools. Can we make the same kinds of assumptions about other more recent biological developments? Can we say that only anatomically modern humans with higher foreheads and reduced brow ridges were capable of making sophisticated tools and beautiful art due to fundamental biological differences?

Supporters of the multiregional hypothesis have long argued that we cannot. They propose instead that the human evolutionary history consists of a long period of a single evolving human species without geographically distinct biological types. Paleoanthropologists looking at the fossil evidence can recognize distinctive suites of features possessed by fossil groups, but whether these groups constitute distinct species or variation within a single species is far more difficult to determine.

Without isolation, gene flow tends to keep populations from differentiating into distinct species. As we shall see in the following chapters, since the end of the Ice Age into today's era of globalization, most populations did not live in extreme isolation. The integrating effects of gene flow have become so powerful that dramatic regional variations for suites of traits no longer exist. Whatever the path in the more recent years of our long evolutionary history, we have become an amazingly diverse and yet still unified single species inhabiting the entire earth. ❋

Chapter Checklist

What is the basic outline of mammalian primate evolution?

✔ The first mammals that appeared over 200 million years ago were small nocturnal creatures.

✔ The mass extinction of the dinosaurs about 65 million years ago allowed for an adaptive radiation of mammals that ultimately included the origins of the primates.

✔ The earliest primates were small arboreal nocturnal insect eaters.

✔ Old World and New World primate species separated by about 40 million years ago. Many of the Old World anthropoid species became ground-dwellers.

✔ About 23 million years ago, hominoids, the broad-shouldered tailless primates that include all living and extinct apes and humans, began to appear throughout Asia, Africa, and Europe.

✔ Genetic studies have confirmed that the African apes—chimpanzees, bonobos, and gorillas—are our closest living relatives.

What is the anatomy of bipedalism, and how do we recognize the human line in the fossil record?

✔ Bipedal locomotion and larger brains constitute the most striking differences between humans and our closest primate relatives.

✔ Bipedalism preceded brain expansion by several million years and played a pivotal role in setting us apart from the apes.

✔ The earliest members of the bipedal human line diverged from the African apes (chimpanzees, bonobos, and gorillas) sometime between 5 and 8 million years ago.

✔ Skeletal changes from the skull down to the toes accompany bipedalism.

How do we differentiate the earliest bipeds from one another?

✔ The forest-dwelling ardipithecines seem to be the earliest definite biped.

✔ Australopithecines, well equipped for generalized foraging in a relatively open savannah environment, came next and included two basic types: the robust vegetarian australopithecines, a line that went extinct, and the gracile australopithecines who ultimately evolved into the genus *Homo*.

✔ Although many theories propose that bipedalism reinforced brain expansion by freeing the hands for activities other than locomotion, the increase in brain size did not appear in human evolutionary history until much later with the appearance of the genus *Homo*.

What is the course of evolution in the genus *Homo*?

✔ With the first members of genus *Homo*—*Homo habilis*—about 2.5 million years ago, stone tools begin to appear in the archaeological record. Possible earlier tools made of perishable materials such as plant fibers are not preserved.

✔ Slightly larger brain size and the reduction of the face characterized early *Homo*.

✔ Throughout the course of the evolution of the genus *Homo*, the critical importance of culture as the human mechanism for adaptation imposed selective pressures favoring a larger brain, which in turn made possible improved cultural adaptation.

✔ *Homo erectus,* appearing about 2 million years ago, had a brain close in size to that of modern humans and sophisticated behaviors including controlled use of fire for warmth, cooking, and protection.

✔ *H. erectus* remains are found throughout Africa, Asia, and Europe, reaching the colder northern areas about 780,000 years ago.

✔ The technological efficiency of *H. erectus* is evidenced in improved tool making—first the hand axe and later specialized tools for hunting, butchering, food processing, hide scraping, and defense.

When did *Homo sapiens* appear and how do we define ourselves in the fossil record?

✔ Between 200,000 and 400,000 years ago, evolving humans achieved the brain capacity of contemporary *Homo sapiens.*

✔ Several local variations of the genus *Homo* existed around this time period all with comparable technological capabilities.

✔ The large-brained Neandertals fit into this group. They used fire extensively to adapt to their Arctic climate, lived in small bands, and communicated through language. Remains testify to ritual behavior and caretaking for the aged and infirm.

✔ Determining the place of Neandertals in the human evolutionary line is one of the major debates of paleoanthropology.

What is the Upper Paleolithic and how does this link to the modern human origins debate?

✔ The Upper Paleolithic was a creative explosion consisting of richly varied tool industries with fine-blade tools predominating, along with new tool-making techniques and materials and expressive art.

✔ The stone tool industries and artwork of Upper Paleolithic cultures surpassed any previously undertaken by humans. Cave paintings and rock art found in Spain, France, Australia, and Africa served a religious purpose and attest to a highly sophisticated aesthetic sensibility.

✔ Humans came to inhabit the entire globe during this period, developing watercraft and other technologies suitable for adaptation to a variety of environments.

✔ Paleoanthropologists link changes in cultural capacity to changes in brain size and skull shape over most of the course of human evolutionary history.

✔ As we get closer to the present, and fossil specimens possess brains the size of contemporary humans, paleoanthropologists debate whether a particular skull shape can be linked to cultural abilities and a behavioral repertoire.

✔ With the gene flow that has existed since at least the end of the Ice Age, it is not possible to divide humans into a series of distinct types.

What are the various theories to account for modern human origins?

✔ This debate distills to the question of whether one, some, or all populations of the archaic groups played a role in the evolution of modern *Homo sapiens.*

✔ The recent African origins hypothesis proposes that modern humans evolved in Africa about 200,000 years ago, replacing other populations as they spread throughout the globe because of their superior cultural capabilities.

✔ The multiregional hypothesis proposes that humans originated in Africa some 2 million years ago and that ancient populations throughout the globe are all ancestors of modern humans, unified as a single species maintained through gene flow.

Questions for Reflection

1. Over the course of the past 2.5 million years, the fossil evidence shows that changes in skull shape came with increasing brain size. These changes are associated with culture in the form of the earliest stone tools, coordinated hunting efforts, the controlled use of fire, language, and eventually an explosion of innovations and symbolic expression in the Upper Paleolithic. As our discussion gets closer to the present, how do the two major hypotheses for modern human origins relate skull size and shape to cultural differences? Can skull shape and size account for cultural differences among contemporary peoples?

2. Do you think evidence from a single bone is enough to determine whether an organism from the past was bipedal?

3. Paleoanthropologists can be characterized as either lumpers or splitters depending upon their approach to recognizing species in the fossil record. Which of these approaches do you prefer and why?

4. How do you feel about the possibility of having Neandertals as part of your ancestry? How might you relate the Neandertal debate to stereotyping or racism in contemporary society?

5. Do you think that gender has played a role in anthropological interpretations of the behavior of our ancestors and the way that paleoanthropologists and archaeologists conduct their research? Do you believe that feminism has a role to play in the interpretation of the past?

Key Terms

continental drift
bipedalism
Ardipithecus
Australopithecus
robust australopithecines
gracile australopithecines

Oldowan tool tradition
Lower Paleolithic
Homo habilis
Homo erectus
Neandertals
Mousterian tool tradition

Upper Paleolithic
multiregional hypothesis
recent African origins
   hypothesis

Online Study Resources

Login to **www.cengagebrain.com** to access the resources your instructor has assigned and to purchase materials. For this book, you can access:

CourseMate
Access chapter-specific learning tools including flashcards, glossaries, practice quizzes, videos, and more in your Anthropology CourseMate.

Lok Samiti (translation: People's Committee) of Mehdiganj, India. Photograph by Nandal Master.

पेप्सी कोला भारत छोड़ो
कोका कोला भारत
छोड़ो पी. एम.
एन. एच.

VISUAL ESSENCE

Over the course of human evolutionary history, both our cultural and biological capabilities have contributed to our adaptability as a species. But since the start of the Neolithic era some 10,000 years ago—when some humans shifted to farming and to the domestication of animals and to village life—cultural adaptations have presented serious biological consequences. Human diets limited by reliance on single crops sometimes led to malnutrition and even famine when these crops failed. Crowded living conditions and close contact with animals in Neolithic villages promoted the spread of infectious disease. Competition for critical resources began to intensify. Today the struggles set in motion at the start of the Neolithic take place on a global scale and place untenable pressures on the world's natural resources. Here, women in Mehdiganj, India, hold water urns called *gharas* with the words "Water Is Life" written on them to protest the nearby Coca-Cola bottling plant. As the plant uses up the local fresh water, nearby farmers lose their livelihood and way of life. In a competition for resources such as this, global corporations like Coca-Cola have advantages over local inhabitants. But ultimately, for all of us to win, strategies must be implemented to ensure a planet in balance.

5 The Neolithic Revolution

throughout the Paleolithic, people depended exclusively on wild sources of food for their survival. They hunted and trapped wild animals, fished and gathered shellfish, eggs, berries, nuts, roots, and other plant foods, relying on their wits and muscles to acquire what nature provided. Whenever favored sources of food became scarce, people adjusted by increasing the variety of foods they ate and incorporating less desirable foods into their diets.

Over time, the subsistence practices of some peoples began to change in ways that radically transformed their way of life as they became food producers rather than food foragers.[1] For some human groups, a more sedentary existence accompanied food production. This in turn permitted a reorganization of the workload in society: Some individuals could be freed from the food quest to devote their energies to other tasks. Over the course of thousands of years, these changes brought about an unforeseen way of life. With good reason, the **Neolithic** era (literally, the New Stone Age), when this change took place, has been called revolutionary in human history.

The Mesolithic Roots of Farming and Pastoralism

As seen in the previous chapter, by the end of the Paleolithic humans had spread throughout the globe. During this period glaciers covered much of the northern hemisphere. By 12,000 years ago, warmer climates prevailed, and these glaciers receded, causing changes in human habitats globally. As sea levels rose throughout the world, many areas flooded that had been dry land during periods of glaciation, such as the Bering Strait, parts of the North Sea, and an extensive land area that had joined the eastern islands of Indonesia to mainland Asia.

In this chapter you will learn to:

- Identify the Mesolithic roots of farming and pastoralism.

- Recognize the mechanisms of and evidence for plant and animal domestication.

- Define the Neolithic revolution and describe theories about the reasons for this shift in lifeways.

- Identify the various centers of domestication globally.

- Examine the effects of food production on population size.

- Recognize how the means of subsistence affect other aspects of social organization.

- Describe the health consequences of the Neolithic transition.

- Compare the cultural changes of the Neolithic to hunter-gatherer lifeways and to hierarchical notions of progress.

---

[1]Rindos, D. (1984). *The origins of agriculture: An evolutionary perspective* (p. 99). Orlando: Academic Press.

In some northern regions, warmer climates brought about particularly marked changes, allowing the replacement of barren tundra with forests. In the process, the herd animals—upon which northern Paleolithic hunting peoples had depended for much of their food, clothing, and shelter—disappeared from many areas. Some, like the caribou and musk ox, moved to colder climates; others, like the mammoths, died out completely. In the new forests, animals were often more solitary in their habits. As a result, large cooperative hunts were less productive than before. Diets shifted to abundant plant foods as well as fish and other foods in and around lakes, bays, and rivers. In Europe, Asia, and Africa, anthropologists call this transitional period between the Paleolithic and the Neolithic the **Mesolithic,** or Middle Stone Age. In the Americas, comparable cultures are referred to as **Archaic cultures**.

New technologies accompanied the changed postglacial environment. Toolmakers began to manufacture ground stone tools, shaped and sharpened by grinding the tool against sandstone, often using sand as an additional abrasive. Once shaped and sharpened, these stones were set into wooden or sometimes antler handles to make effective axes and adzes (cutting tools with a sharp blade set at right angles to a handle). Though such implements take longer to make, they rarely break even with heavy use, unlike tools made of chipped stone. Thus they were helpful in clearing forest areas and in the woodwork needed for the creation of dugout canoes and skin-covered boats. Evidence of seaworthy watercraft at Mesolithic sites indicates that human foraging for food took place on the open water—coastal areas, rivers, and lakes—as well as on the land.

The **microlith**—a small but hard, sharp blade—tradition flourished in the Mesolithic. Although microlithic ("small stone") tools existed in Central Africa by about 40,000 years ago,[2] they did not become common elsewhere until the Mesolithic. Microliths could be produced in mass quantities because they were small, easy to make, and could be fashioned from sections of blades. This tool could be attached to an arrow or another tool shaft by using melted resin (from pine trees) as a binder.

Microliths provided Mesolithic people with an important advantage over their Upper Paleolithic forebears: The small size of the microlith enabled them to devise a wider array of composite tools made out of stone and wood or bone. Thus they could make sickles, harpoons, arrows, knives, and daggers by fitting microliths into slots in wood, bone, or antler handles. Later experimentation with these forms led to more sophisticated tools and weapons, such as bows to propel sharp-pointed arrows.

Dwellings from the Mesolithic provide evidence of a somewhat more settled lifestyle during this period. People subsisting on a dietary mixture of wild game, seafood, and plants in the now milder forested environments of the north did not need to move regularly over large geographic areas in pursuit of migratory herds.

In the warmer parts of the world, wild plant foods were more readily available, and so collection already had complemented hunting in the Upper Paleolithic. Thus, in areas like Southwest Asia, the Mesolithic represents less of a changed way of life than was true in Europe. Here, the important **Natufian culture** flourished.

The Natufians lived between 10,200 and 12,500 years ago at the eastern end of the Mediterranean Sea in caves, rock shelters, and small villages with stone- and mud-walled houses. They are named after Wadi en-Natuf, a ravine near Jerusalem, Israel, where the remains of this culture were first found. Natufians buried their dead in communal cemeteries, usually in shallow pits without any other objects or decorations. One of their villages, a 10,500-year-old settlement at Jericho in the Jordan River Valley, contained a small shrine. Basin-shaped depressions in the rocks found outside homes and plastered storage pits beneath the floors of the houses indicate that the Natufians stored plant foods. Natufians also used sickles—small stone blades set in straight handles of wood or bone—to cut grain.

The new way of life and abundant food supplies of the various Mesolithic and Archaic cultures permitted peoples in some parts of the world to live in larger and more sedentary groups. Some of these settlements went on to expand into the first farming villages, towns, and ultimately cities.

The Neolithic Revolution

The Neolithic, or New Stone Age, named for the polished stone tools characteristic of this period, represents a major cultural change. The transition from a foraging economy based on hunting, gathering, and fishing to one based on food production outweighs the importance of the tool type for which this period gets its name. Food foragers and village-dwellers alike used these Neolithic tools.

The **Neolithic revolution** (also known as the *Neolithic transition*) was by no means smooth or instantaneous; in fact, the switch to food production spread over

---

[2]Bednarik, R. G. (1995). Concept-mediated marking in the Lower Paleolithic. *Current Anthropology 36*, 606.

many centuries—even millennia—and grew directly from the preceding Mesolithic. Where to draw the line between the two periods is not always clear. Food production in the early Neolithic included both **horticulture,** the cultivation of crops carried out with simple hand tools such as digging sticks and hoes, and **pastoralism,** breeding and managing migratory herds of domesticated grazing animals, such as goats, sheep, cattle, llamas, and camels.

The ultimate source of all cultural change is **innovation**: any new idea, method, or device that gains widespread acceptance in society. **Primary innovation** refers to the creation, invention, or discovery by chance of a completely new idea, method, or device. For example, consider the discovery that clay permanently hardens when exposed to high temperatures. Presumably, accidental firing of clay took place around numerous ancient campfires. This chance occurrence became a primary innovation when someone perceived its potential use. This perception allowed our ancestors to begin to make figurines of fired clay some 35,000 years ago.

A **secondary innovation** involves a deliberate application or modification of an existing idea, method, or device. For example, ancient peoples applied the knowledge about fired clay to make pottery containers and cooking vessels. Recent evidence from Yuchanyan Cave, located in the southwest of China's Hunan Province, indicates the presence of the earliest pottery vessels; these are radiocarbon dated to between about 15,000 and 18,000 years ago.

The shift to relatively complete reliance on domesticated plants and animals took several thousand years. While this transition has been particularly well studied in Southwest Asia, archaeological evidence for food production also exists from other parts of the world such as China and Central America and the Andes at similar or somewhat younger dates. Human groups throughout the globe independently, but more or less simultaneously, invented food production.

What Is Domestication?

Domestication takes place as humans modify, intentionally or unintentionally, the genetic makeup of a population of wild plants or animals, sometimes to the extent that members of the population are unable to survive and/or reproduce without human assistance. Domestication resembles the interdependence between different species frequently seen in the natural world, where one species depends on another (that feeds upon it) for its protection and reproductive success.

For example, certain ants native to the American tropics grow fungi in their nests, and these fungi provide the ants with most of their nutrition. Like human farmers, the ants add manure to stimulate fungal growth and eliminate competing weeds, both mechanically and through use of antibiotic herbicides. The fungi are protected and ensured reproductive success while providing the ants with a steady food supply.[3]

In plant–human interactions, domestication ensures the plants' reproductive success while providing humans

▲▲▲▲▲▲▲▲▲▲▲▲▲▲▲▲▲▲▲▲▲▲▲▲▲▲▲▲▲▲▲▲▲▲▲▲▲

Neolithic The New Stone Age; a prehistoric period beginning about 10,000 years ago in which peoples possessed stone-based technologies and depended on domesticated crops and/or animals for subsistence.

Mesolithic The Middle Stone Age of Europe, Asia, and Africa beginning about 12,000 years ago.

Archaic cultures The term used to refer to Mesolithic cultures in the Americas.

microlith A small blade of flint or similar stone, several of which were hafted together in wooden handles to make tools; widespread in the Mesolithic.

Natufian culture A Mesolithic culture from the lands that are now Israel, Lebanon, and western Syria, between about 10,200 and 12,500 years ago.

Neolithic revolution The domestication of plants and animals by peoples with stone-based technologies, beginning about 10,000 years ago and leading to radical transformations in cultural systems; sometimes referred to as the *Neolithic transition*.

horticulture The cultivation of crops carried out with simple hand tools such as digging sticks and hoes.

pastoralism The breeding and managing of migratory herds of domesticated grazing animals, such as goats, sheep, cattle, llamas, and camels.

innovation Any new idea, method, or device that gains widespread acceptance in society.

primary innovation The creation, invention, or discovery by chance of a completely new idea, method, or device.

secondary innovation The deliberate application or modification of an existing idea, method, or device.

domestication An evolutionary process whereby humans modify, intentionally or unintentionally, the genetic makeup of a population of wild plants or animals, sometimes to the extent that members of the population are unable to survive and/or reproduce without human assistance.

▼▼▼▼▼▼▼▼▼▼▼▼▼▼▼▼▼▼▼▼▼▼▼▼▼▼▼▼▼▼▼▼▼▼▼▼▼

[3]Diamond, J. (1998). Ants, crops, and history. *Science 281,* 1974–1975.

with food. Selective breeding eliminates thorns, toxins, and bad-tasting chemical compounds, which in the wild had served to ensure a plant species' survival, at the same time producing larger, tastier edible parts attractive to humans. U.S. environmentalist Michael Pollan suggests that domesticated plant species successfully exploit human desires so that they are able to out-compete other plant species; he has even proposed that agriculture is "something grasses did to people to conquer trees."[4]

Evidence of Early Plant Domestication

Domesticated plants generally differ from their wild ancestors in ways favored by humans. These features include increased size (at least of edible parts); reduction or loss of natural means of seed dispersal; reduction or loss of protective devices (such as husks or distasteful chemical compounds); loss of delayed seed germination (important to wild plants for survival in times of drought or other temporarily adverse conditions); and development of simultaneous ripening of the seed or fruit.

For example, wild cereals have a very fragile stem, whereas domesticated ones have a tough stem. Under natural conditions, plants with fragile stems scatter their seed for themselves, whereas those with tough stems do not. At harvest time, the grain stalks with soft stems would shatter at the touch of a sickle or flail, scattering the seeds to the wind. Inevitably, though unintentionally, most of the seeds that people were able to harvest would have come from the tough plants. Early domesticators probably also tended to select seed from plants having few husks or none at all—eventually breeding them out—because husking prior to pounding the grains into meal or flour required extra labor.

Many of the distinguishing characteristics of domesticated plants can be seen in remains from archaeological sites. Paleobotanists can often tell the fossil of a wild plant species from a domesticated one, for example, by studying the shape and size of various plant structures (▶ **Figure 5.1**).[5]

Evidence of Early Animal Domestication

Domestication also produced changes in the skeletal structure of some animals. For example, the horns of wild goats and sheep differ from those of their domesticated counterparts. Some types of domesticated sheep have no horns at all. Similarly, the size of an animal or its parts can vary with domestication as seen in the smaller size of certain teeth of domesticated pigs compared to those of wild ones.

The age and sex ratios of butchered animals at an archaeological site can indicate the presence of animal domestication. For example, archaeologists found that

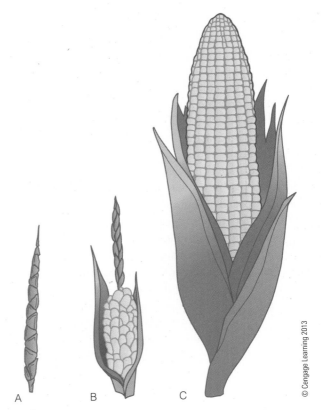

Figure 5.1 The Domestication of Maize Increased size of edible parts is a common feature of domestication. The large ear of corn or maize (C) that we know today is a far cry from the tiny ears (about an inch long) characteristic of 5,500-year-old maize (B). Maize may have arisen when a simple gene mutation transformed male tassel spikes of the wild grass called teosinte (A) into the small, earliest versions of the female maize ear. Teosinte, a wild grass from highland Mexico, is far less productive than maize and does not taste good. Like most plants that were domesticated, it was not a favored food for foraging people. Domestication transformed this plant into something highly desirable.

© Cengage Learning 2013

the age and/or sex ratios at the 10,000-year-old site in the Zagros Mountains of Iran differed from those of wild herds. A sharp rise in the number of young male goats killed indicates that people were slaughtering the young males for food and saving the females for breeding. Although such herd management does not prove that the goats were fully domesticated, it indicates a step in that direction.[6] Similarly, the archaeological sites in the Andean highlands of South America, dating to around 6,300 years ago, contain evidence that these animals were penned up, indicating the beginning of domestication.

[4]Pollan, M. (2001). *The botany of desire: A plant's-eye view of the world*. New York: Random House.

[5]Gould, S. J. (1991). *The flamingo's smile: Reflections in natural history* (p. 368). New York: Norton.

[6]Zeder, M. A., & Hesse, B. (2000). The initial domestication of goats (*Capra hircus*) in the Zagros Mountains 10,000 years ago. *Science 287*, 2254–2257.

Why Humans Became Food Producers

Although it might seem that a sudden flash of insight about the human ability to control plants and animals underlies the rise of domestication, the evidence points us in different directions. Contemporary foragers, for example, choose to forgo food production, even though they know full well the role of seeds in plant growth and that plants grow better under certain conditions than others. In fact, U.S. biologist Jared Diamond aptly describes contemporary food foragers as "walking encyclopedias of natural history with individual names for as many as a thousand or more plant and animal species, and with detailed knowledge of those species' biological characteristics, distribution, and potential uses."[7]

Lack of knowledge clearly is not the reason for avoiding food production, as foragers frequently apply their expertise to actively manage the resources on which they depend. For example, indigenous peoples living in northern Australia deliberately alter the runoff channels of creeks to flood extensive tracts of land, converting them into fields of wild grain. Indigenous Australians choose to continue to forage while also managing the land.

One reason that food foragers may avoid food production is that it does not free people from hard work. In fact, available ethnographic data indicate just the opposite—that farmers, by and large, work far longer hours compared to most food foragers.

Also, food production is not necessarily a more secure means of subsistence than food foraging. Low species diversity makes highly productive seed crops—of the sort originally domesticated in Southwest Asia, Central America, and the Andean highlands—unstable from an ecological perspective. Without constant human attention, their productivity suffers.

For these reasons, contemporary food foragers do not necessarily regard farming and animal husbandry as superior to hunting, gathering, or fishing. Farming ushers in whole new systems of relationships that disturb an age-old balance between humans and nature. As long as existing practices work well, food foragers have no need to abandon them, especially if they provide an eminently satisfactory way of life. Noting that food foragers have more time for play and relaxation than food producers, anthropologist Marshall Sahlins has labeled hunter-gatherers the "the original affluent society."[8] Nevertheless, as food-producing peoples (including postindustrial societies) have deprived them of more and more of the land base necessary for their way of life, foraging has become more difficult. The competition for resources ushered in during the Neolithic favors those cultures that develop concepts of land ownership.

Given the above, we may well ask why any human group abandoned food foraging in favor of food production. Several theories account for this change in human subsistence practices. The desiccation or oasis theory, first championed by Australian archaeologist V. Gordon Childe in the mid-20th century, suggests environmental determinism. Glacial cover over Europe and Asia caused a shift in rain patterns from Europe to North Africa and Southwest Asia so that when the glaciers retreated northward, so did the rain. As a result, North Africa and Southwest Asia became dryer, and people were forced to congregate at oases for water.

Relative food scarcity in such an environment drove people to collect the wild grasses and seeds growing around the oases, congregating in a part of Southwest Asia known as the Fertile Crescent (▶ Figure 5.2). Eventually they began to cultivate the grasses to provide enough food for the community. According to this theory, animal domestication began because the oases attracted hungry animals, such as wild goats, sheep, and cattle, which came to graze on the stubble of the grain fields and to drink. Finding that these animals were often too thin to eat, people began to fatten them up.

Although Childe's work can be critiqued on a number of grounds and many other theories have been proposed to account for the shift to domestication, the oasis theory remains historically significant as the first scientifically testable explanation for the origins of food production. Childe's theory set the stage for the development of archaeology as a science. Later theories developed by archaeologists built on Childe's ideas and took into account the role of chance environmental circumstances of the specific region along with other cultural factors that may be driving the change.

The Fertile Crescent

Present evidence indicates that the earliest plant domestication took place gradually in the Fertile Crescent, the long arc-shaped sweep of river valleys and coastal plains extending from the Upper Nile (Sudan) to the Lower Tigris (Iraq). Archaeological data suggest the domestication of rye as early as 13,000 years ago by people living at a site (Abu Hureyra) east of Aleppo, Syria, although wild plants and animals continued to be their major food sources. Over the next several millennia they became full-fledged farmers, cultivating rye and wheat.[9] By 10,300 years ago, others in the region were also growing crops.

[7]Diamond, J. (1997). *Guns, germs, and steel* (p. 143). New York: Norton.

[8]Sahlins, M. (1972). *Stone age economics*. Chicago: Aldine.

[9]Pringle, H. (1998). The slow birth of agriculture. *Science 282*, 1446–1449.

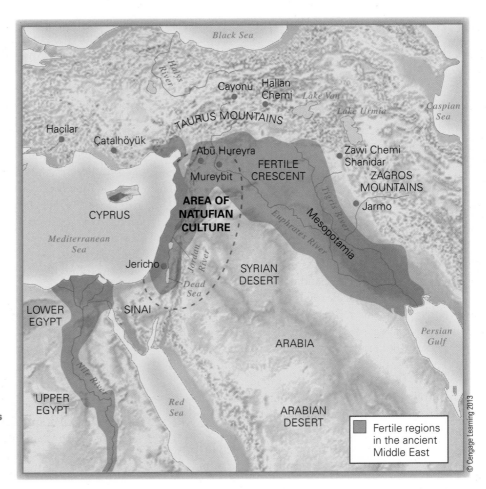

Figure 5.2 The Fertile Crescent This area of Southwest Asia and North Africa shows the Fertile Crescent, the site of the beginning of domestication.

The domestication process was a consequence of a chance convergence of independent natural events and other cultural developments.[10] The Natufians, whose culture we looked at earlier in this chapter, illustrate this process. These people lived at a time of dramatically changing climates in Southwest Asia. With the end of the last glaciation, temperatures not only became significantly warmer but markedly seasonal as well. Between 6,000 and 12,000 years ago, the region experienced the most extreme seasonality in its history, with dry summers significantly longer and hotter than today. As a consequence of increased evaporation, many shallow lakes dried up, leaving just three in the Jordan River Valley.

At the same time, the region's plant cover changed dramatically. Among plants, the annuals, including wild cereal grains and legumes (such as peas, lentils, and chickpeas), adapt well to environmental instability and seasonal dryness. Because they complete their life cycle in a single year, annuals can evolve very quickly under unstable conditions. Moreover, they store their reproductive abilities for the next wet season in abundant seeds, which can remain dormant for prolonged periods.

The Natufians, who lived where these conditions were especially severe, adapted by modifying their subsistence practices in two ways: First, they probably burned the landscape regularly to promote browsing by red deer and grazing by gazelles, the main focus of their hunting activities. Second, they placed greater emphasis on the collection and storage of wild seeds from the annual plants that they used for food through the dry season. The importance of stored foods, coupled with the scarcity of reliable water sources, promoted more sedentary living patterns, reflected in the substantial villages of late Natufian times. Because the Natufians already possessed sickles (originally used to cut reeds and sedges for baskets) for harvesting grain and grinding stones for processing a variety of wild foods, they had an easier shift to their reliance on seed.[11]

The Natufians' use of sickles to harvest grain turned out to have important if unexpected consequences. In the course of harvesting, the easily dispersed seeds fell at the harvest site, while those that clung to the stems came back to the settlement where people processed and stored them.[12] The periodic burning of vegetation

---

[10]McCorriston, J., & Hole, F. (1991). The ecology of seasonal stress and the origins of agriculture in the Near East. *American Anthropologist 93*, 46–69.

[11]Olszewski, D. I. (1991). Comment. *Current Anthropology 32*, 43.

[12]Blumer, M. A., & Byrne, R. (1991). The ecological genetics and domestication and the origins of agriculture. *Current Anthropology 32*, 30.

carried out to promote the deer and gazelle herds may have also affected the development of new genetic variation. Heat impacts mutation rates. Also, fire removes individuals from a population, which changes the genetic structure of a group drastically and quickly.

Inevitably some seeds from nondispersing variants were carried back to settlements, where they germinated and grew on dump heaps and other disturbed sites (latrines, areas cleared of trees, or burned-over terrain). Certain variants, known as *colonizers*, do particularly well in disturbed habitats, making them ideal candidates for domestication. Moreover, sedentism disturbs habitats as resources closer to settlements were depleted over time. Thus variants of plants particularly susceptible to human manipulation had more opportunities to flourish where people were living. Under such circumstances, people began to actively promote the growth of these plants, even by deliberately sowing them. Ultimately, humans realized that they could play a more active role in the process by deliberately trying to breed the strains they preferred. With this, domestication shifted from an unintentional to an intentional process.

The development of animal domestication in Southwest Asia seems to have proceeded along somewhat similar lines in the hilly country of southeastern Turkey, northern Iraq, and the Zagros Mountains of Iran. Large herds of wild sheep and goats, as well as rich environmental diversity, characterized these regions. From the flood plains of the valley of the Tigris and Euphrates rivers, for example, travel to the north or east takes one into high country through three other ecological zones: first steppe; then oak and pistachio woodlands; and finally high plateau country with grass, scrub, or desert vegetation. Valleys that run at right angles to the mountain ranges afford relatively easy access across these zones. Today, a number of peoples in the region still graze their herds of sheep and goats on the low steppe in the winter and move to high pastures on the plateaus in the summer.

Food foragers inhabited these regions prior to the domestication of plants and animals. Each ecological zone contained distinct plant species, and because of the variation in altitude, plant foods matured at different times in different zones. These ancient peoples hunted a variety of animal species for meat and hides. The bones of hoofed animals—deer, gazelles, wild goats, and wild sheep—dominate the human refuse piles from these periods. Most of these hoofed animals naturally move back and forth from low winter pastures to high summer pastures. People followed the animals in their seasonal migrations, making use of other wild foods as they passed through different zones: palm dates in the lowlands; acorns, almonds, and pistachios higher up; apples and pears higher still; wild grains maturing at different times in different areas; woodland animals in the forested region between summer and winter grazing lands. All in all, it was a rich, varied fare.

The archaeological record indicates that, at first, the people of the southwestern Asian highlands hunted animals of all ages and sexes. But, beginning about 11,000 years ago, the percentage of immature sheep consumed increased to about 50 percent of the total. At the same time, the percentage of females among animals eaten decreased. (Feasting on male lambs increases yields by sparing the females for breeding.) This marks the beginning of human management of sheep.

The human management of flocks shielded sheep from the effects of natural selection, affording the variants preferred by humans to have increased reproductive success. Variants attractive to humans did not arise out of need but at random, as mutations do. But then humans selectively bred the varieties they favored. In such a way, those features characteristic of domestic sheep—such as greater fat and meat production, excess wool, and so on—began to develop (▶ **Figure 5.3**). By 9,000 years ago, the shape and size of the bones of domestic sheep had become distinguishable from those of wild sheep. At about the same time and by similar means, ancient humans domesticated pigs in southeastern Turkey and the lower Jordan River Valley.[13]

Some researchers link animal domestication to the development of fixed territories and settlements. They suggest that resource ownership promotes postponing the short-term gain of killing prey for the long-term gain of continued access to animals in the future.[14] Eventually, ancient peoples introduced animal species domesticated in one area to regions outside their natural habitat.

To sum up, unaware of the long-term and revolutionary cultural consequences of their actions, the domesticators of plants and animals sought only to maximize their available food sources. But as the domestication process continued, the productivity of the domestic species increased relative to wild species. Thus these species became increasingly more important to subsistence, resulting in further domestication and further increases in productivity.

Other Centers of Domestication

In addition to Southwest Asia, the domestication of plants and, in some cases, animals took place independently in Southeast Asia, parts of the Americas (Central America, the Andean highlands, the tropical forests of South America, and eastern North America), northern

---

[13]Pringle, p. 1448.

[14]Alvard, M. S., & Kuznar, L. (2001). Deferred harvest: The transition from hunting to animal husbandry. *American Anthropologist* 103 (2), 295–311.

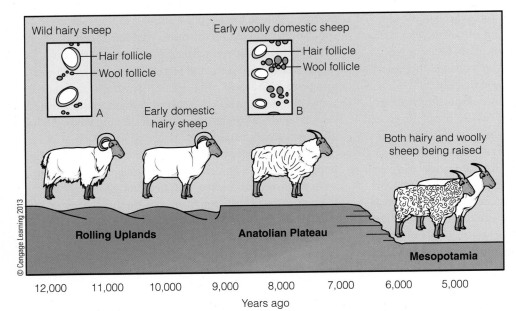

Figure 5.3 Domestication of Sheep Domestication of sheep resulted in evolutionary changes that created more wool. Inset A shows a section of the skin of wild sheep as seen through a microscope, with the arrangement of hair and wool follicles. Inset B shows how this arrangement changed with domestication so that the sheep produced more wool.

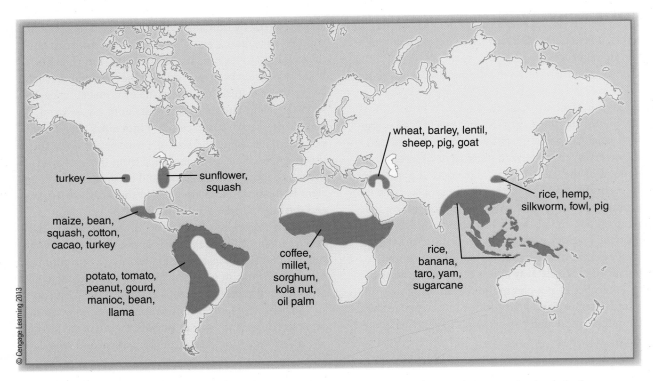

Figure 5.4 Early Plant and Animal Domestication Independent domestication of plants and animals took place in widely scattered areas more or less simultaneously (in a period spanning several thousand years). The figure indicates some of the domesticates typical to each area such as wheat and sheep in Southwest Asia; sorghum and millet in Central Africa, rice and pigs in China; taro and bananas in Southeast Asia; maize and cacao in Central America; potatoes and llamas in South America; and squash and sunflowers in North America. Although the domesticated plants and animals appeared independently in distinct regions, today humans use all of them throughout the globe.

China, and Africa (▶ **Figure 5.4**). In China, domestication of rice was underway along the middle Yangtze River by about 11,000 years ago.[15] It was not until 4,000 years later, however, that domestic rice dominated wild rice to become the dietary staple.

Similarly, decorations on pottery dated to between 5,000 and 8,800 years ago document rice as the earliest

domesticated species of Southeast Asia. Other domesticates, particularly root crops such as yams and taro, dominate this region. Root crop farming, or **vegeculture**, typically involves growing many different species together in a single field. Because this approximates the

---

[15]Pringle, p. 1449.

© maggiegowan.co.uk/Alamy

▲▲▲ The Dani people of Papua New Guinea, specialize in growing sweet potatoes through vegeculture, or root crop farming. While vegeculture typically involves many species of root crop planted together in one area, the Dani fill vast irrigated fields exclusively with more than seventy varieties of sweet potato. The Dani have incorporated this important food into many of their rituals. Here Dani women roast sweet potatoes on a fire as part of a ceremonial pig roast.

complexity of the natural vegetation, vegeculture tends to be more stable than seed crop cultivation. Propagation or breeding of new plants usually occurs through vegetative means—the planting of cuttings—rather than the planting of seeds.

In the Americas, the domestication of plants began about as early as it did in these other regions. Evidence for one species of domestic squash appears as early as 10,000 years ago in the coastal forests of Ecuador, the same time that another species independently appeared in an arid region of highland Mexico.[16] The ecological diversity of the highland valleys of Mexico, like the hill country of Southwest Asia, provided an excellent environment for domestication. Movement of people through a variety of ecological zones as they changed altitude brought plant and animal species into new habitats, providing opportunities for humans and colonizing species alike.

Domestication in the Andean highlands of Peru, another environmentally diverse region, emphasized root

crops, the best known being potatoes (of which about 3,000 varieties were grown, versus the mere 250 grown today in North America). South Americans also domesticated guinea pigs, llamas, alpacas, and ducks, whereas peoples in the Mexican highlands never did much with domestic livestock. They limited themselves to dogs, turkeys, and bees. American Indians living north of Mexico developed some of their own indigenous domesticates. These included local varieties of squash and sunflowers.

Ultimately, American Indians domesticated over 300 food crops, including two of the four most important ones in the world today: potatoes and maize (the other two are wheat and rice). In fact, America's indigenous peoples first cultivated 60 percent of the crops grown in the world today; they not only developed the world's largest array of nutritious foods but also contributed the most to the world's varied cuisines.[17] After all, where would Italian cuisine be without tomatoes? Thai

---

[16]Pringle, p. 1447.

[17]Weatherford, J. (1988). *Indian givers: How the Indians of the Americas transformed the world* (pp. 71, 115). New York: Fawcett Columbine.

▲▲▲

vegeculture The cultivation of domesticated root crops, such as yams and taro.

▼▼▼

cooking without peanuts? Russian cooking without potatoes? Small wonder American Indians have been called the world's greatest farmers.[18]

As plant species became domesticated, horticultural societies came into being. Small communities of gardeners worked together with simple hand tools and used neither irrigation nor the plow. Horticulturists typically cultivate a variety of crops in small gardens they have cleared by hand. Indians in the Amazon rainforest used sophisticated farming methods, as is evident in the research conducted by an international team of archaeologists and other scientists. These ancient methods, which left behind rich dark soils, may have important current applications as shown in this chapter's Original Study. Reviving these ancient soil-enrichment techniques could contribute to better global management of rainforests and climate today.

[18]Weatherford, p. 95.

ORIGINAL STUDY

The Real Dirt on Rainforest Fertility

By Charles C. Mann

IRANDUBA, AMAZÔNAS STATE, BRAZIL—Above a pit dug by a team of archaeologists here is a papaya orchard filled with unusually vigorous trees bearing great clusters of plump green fruit. Below the surface lies a different sort of bounty: hundreds, perhaps thousands, of burial urns and millions of pieces of broken ceramics, all from an almost unknown people who flourished here before the conquistadors. But surprisingly, what might be most important about this central Amazonian site is not the vibrant orchard or the extraordinary outpouring of ceramics but the dirt under the trees and around the ceramics. A rich, black soil known locally as *terra preta do Indio* (Indian dark earth), it sustained large settlements on these lands for 2 millennia, according to the Brazilian-American archaeological team working here.

Throughout Amazonia, farmers prize *terra preta* for its great productivity—some farmers have worked it for years with minimal fertilization. Such long-lasting fertility is an anomaly in the tropics. Despite the exuberant growth of rainforests, their red and yellow soils are notoriously poor: weathered, highly acidic, and low in organic matter and essential nutrients. In these oxisols, as they are known, most carbon and nutrients are stored not in the soil, as in temperate regions, but in the vegetation that covers it. When loggers, ranchers, or farmers clear the vegetation, the intense sun and rain quickly decompose the remaining organic matter in the soil, making the land almost incapable of sustaining life—one reason ecologists frequently refer to the tropical forest as a "wet desert."

Because *terra preta* is subject to the same punishing conditions as the surrounding oxisols, "its existence is very surprising," says Bruno Glaser, a chemist at the Institute of Soil Science and Soil Geography at the University of Bayreuth, Germany. "If you read the textbooks, it shouldn't be there." Yet according to William I. Woods, a geographer at Southern Illinois University, Edwardsville, *terra preta* might cover as much as 10 percent of Amazonia, an area the size of France. More remarkable still, *terra preta* appears to be the product of intensive habitation by precontact Amerindian populations. "They practiced agriculture here for centuries," Glaser says. "But instead of destroying the soil, they improved it—and that is something we don't know how to do today."

In the past few years, a small but growing group of researchers—geographers, archaeologists, soil scientists, ecologists, and anthropologists—has been investigating this "gift from the past," as *terra preta* was called by the late anthropologist James B. Petersen, a founding member of the Iranduba team. By understanding how indigenous groups created Amazonian dark earths, these researchers hope, today's scientists might be able to transform some of the region's oxisols into new *terra preta*. Indeed, experimental programs to produce "*terra preta* nova" have already begun. Population pressure and government policies are causing rapid deforestation in the tropics, and poor tropical soils make much of the clearing as economically nonviable in the long run as it is ecologically damaging.

The Good Earth

Terra preta is scattered throughout Amazonia, but it is most frequently found on low hills overlooking rivers—the kind of terrain on which indigenous groups preferred to live. According to Eduardo Neves, an archaeologist at the University of São Paulo who is part of the Iranduba team, the oldest deposits date back more than 2,000 years and occur in the lower and central Amazon; *terra preta* then appeared to spread to cultures upriver. By AD 500 to 1000, he says, "it appeared in almost every part of the Amazon Basin."

Typically, black-soil regions cover 1 to 5 hectares, but some encompass 300 hectares or more. The black soils are generally 40 to 60 centimeters deep but can reach more than 2 meters. Almost always they are full of broken ceramics. Although they were created centuries ago—probably for agriculture, researchers such as Woods believe—patches of *terra preta* are still among the most desirable land in the Amazon. Indeed, *terra preta* is valuable enough that locals sell it as potting soil. To the consternation of archaeologists, long planters full of *terra preta*, complete with pieces of pre-Columbian pottery, greet visitors to the airport in the lower Amazon town of Santarém.

As a rule, *terra preta* has more "plant-available" phosphorus, calcium, sulfur, and nitrogen than surrounding oxisols; it also has much more organic matter, retains moisture and nutrients better, and is not rapidly exhausted by agricultural use when managed well.

The key to *terra preta*'s long-term fertility, Glaser says, is charcoal: *Terra preta* contains up to 70 times as much as adjacent oxisols. "The charcoal prevents organic matter from being rapidly mineralized," Glaser says. "Over time, it partly oxidizes, which keeps providing sites for nutrients to bind to." But simply mixing charcoal into the ground is not enough

CONTINUED

ORIGINAL STUDY CONTINUED

to create *terra preta*. Because charcoal contains few nutrients, Glaser says, "high nutrient inputs via excrement and waste such as turtle, fish, and animal bones were necessary." Special soil microorganisms are also likely to play a role in its persistent fertility, in the view of Janice Thies, a soil ecologist who is part of a Cornell University team studying *terra preta*. "There are indications that microbial biomass is higher in *terra preta*," she says, which raises the possibility that scientists might be able to create a "package" of charcoal, nutrients, and microfauna that could be used to transform oxisols into *terra preta*.

Slash-and-Char

Surprisingly, *terra preta* seems not to have been created by the "slash-and-burn" agriculture famously practiced in the tropics. In slash-and-burn, farmers clear and then burn their fields, using the ash to flush enough nutrients into the soil to support crops for a few years; when productivity declines, they move on to the next patch of forest. Glaser, Woods, and other researchers believe that the long-ago Amazonians created *terra preta* by a process that Christoph Steiner, a University of Bayreuth soil scientist, has dubbed "slash-and-char."

Instead of completely burning organic matter to ash, in this view, ancient farmers burned it only incompletely, creating charcoal, then stirred the charcoal directly into the soil. Later they added nutrients and, in a process analogous to adding sourdough starter to bread, possibly soil previously enriched with microorganisms. In addition to its potential benefits to the soil, slash-and-char releases much less carbon into the air than slash-and-burn, which has potential implications for climate change. ■

Adapted from Mann, C. C. (2002, August). The real dirt on rainforest fertility. *Science, 297,* 920–923. Copyright © 2002 by the American Association for the Advancement of Science. Reprinted with permission from AAAS.

While plant domestication took place independently across the globe, at the same time people everywhere developed the same categories of foods—starchy grains (or root crops) accompanied by one or more legumes: for example, wheat and barley with peas, chickpeas, and lentils in Southwest Asia; maize with various kinds of beans in Mexico. Together the amino acids (building blocks of proteins) in these starch and legume combinations provide humans with sufficient protein.

The starchy grains eaten at every meal in the form of bread, some sort of food wrapper (like a tortilla), or a gruel or thickening agent in a stew along with one or more legumes, form the core of the diet. Each culture combines these rather bland sources of carbohydrates and proteins with flavor-giving substances that help the food go down.

In Mexico, for example, the chili pepper serves as the flavor enhancer par excellence; in other cuisines a bit

© Bettmann/Corbis

◀ Mexicans have used chili peppers for millennia. Chili peppers enhance the flavors of food and aid in digestion by helping with the breakdown of cellulose in diets heavy in plant foods. Chilies have other uses as well: This illustration from a 16th-century Aztec manuscript shows a mother threatening to punish her child with the smoke from chili peppers. Chili smoke was also used as a chemical weapon in warfare.

VISUAL COUNTERPOINT

▲▲▲ The higher fertility of the Amish, conservative Protestant farmers in North America, compared to that of the Ju/'hoansi foragers from the Kalahari Desert, was originally attributed to nutritional stress among the hunter-gatherers. We now know that childrearing beliefs and practices account for these differences. The Ju/'hoansi fertility pattern derives from beliefs that a crying baby should be breastfed, an action that biologically suppresses fertility. In farming communities, families view children as assets to help with the work, and infant feeding practices reinforce high fertility rates. Children are weaned at young ages and transitioned to soft foods, a practice that promotes the next pregnancy. All human activity includes a complex interplay between human biology and culture.

of meat or fat, a dairy product, or mushrooms adds the flavor. U.S. anthropologist Sidney Mintz refers to this as the *core-fringe-legume pattern* (CFLP), noting its stability until the recent worldwide spread of processed sugars and high-fat foods.[19]

Food Production and Population Size

Human population has been growing steadily since the Neolithic. The exact relationship between population growth and food production resembles the old chicken and egg question: Does population growth create the pressures that result in innovations, such as food production, or is population growth a consequence of food production? As already noted, domestication inevitably leads to higher yields, and higher yields make it possible to feed more people, albeit at the cost of more work.

Across human populations, increased dependence on farming and increased fertility seem to go hand in hand: Farming populations tend to have higher rates of fertility compared to food foragers.[20] Foraging mothers have their children about four to five years apart while some contemporary farming populations not

practicing any form of birth control have another baby every year and a half. A complex interplay between human biology and culture lies at the heart of this difference. Some researchers suggest that the availability of soft foods for infants brought about by farming promoted population growth. In humans, frequent breastfeeding has a dampening effect on mothers' ovulation, inhibiting pregnancy in nursing mothers who breastfeed exclusively. Because breastfeeding frequency declines when soft foods are introduced, fertility tends to increase.

However, the introduction of soft foods is an oversimplification of the explanation for changes in fertility. Many other pathways can also lead to fertility changes. For example, farming cultures tend to view numerous children as assets to help out with the many household chores. Further, higher fertility rates among farmers might derive from higher mortality rates due to infectious diseases brought about by the sedentary lifestyles and narrow diets characteristic of the Neolithic. High

[19]Mintz, S. (1996). A taste of history. In W. A. Haviland & R. J. Gordon (Eds.), *Talking about people* (2nd ed., pp. 81–82). Mountain View, CA: Mayfield.

[20]Sellen, D. W., & Mace, R. (1997). Fertility and mode of subsistence: A phylogenetic analysis. *Current Anthropology 38*, 886.

infant mortality, in turn, could raise the cultural value placed on fertility.

Another pitfall in the explanation of fertility differences among peoples is the culture of the anthropologist. Early anthropologists viewed the migratory foraging lifestyle as inferior and interpreted the differences in fertility to be consequences of nutritional stress among the foragers.

This theory was based in part on the observation that humans and many other mammals require a certain percentage of body fat in order to reproduce successfully. However, detailed studies among the !Kung or Ju/'hoansi (pronounced "zhutwasi") of the Kalahari Desert in southern Africa disproved this nutritional theory (another example of the self-correcting nature of science). Low fertility among the Ju/'hoansi ultimately derives from cultural beliefs about the right way to handle a baby: The Ju/'hoansi mother responds rapidly to her baby, breastfeeding whenever the infant shows any signs of fussing, day or night.[21] On a biological level, the Ju/'hoansi pattern of breastfeeding in short, very frequent bouts suppresses ovulation, or the release of a new egg into the womb for fertilization. Biology and culture interact in all aspects of the human experience.

The Spread of Food Production

Paradoxically, although domestication increases productivity, it also increases instability. As humans increasingly focus on varieties with the highest yields, other varieties become less valued and ultimately ignored. As a result, farmers depend on a rather narrow choice of resources, compared to the wide range utilized by food foragers. Today, modern agriculturists rely on a mere dozen species for about 80 percent of the world's annual tonnage of all crops.[22]

This dependence on fewer varieties means that when a crop fails, for whatever reason, farmers have

less to fall back on compared to food foragers. Furthermore, the common farming practice of planting crops together in one locality increases the likelihood of failure because proximity promotes the spread of disease among neighboring plants. Moreover, by relying on seeds from the most productive plants of a species to establish next year's crop, farmers favor genetic uniformity over diversity. In turn, some virus, bacterium, or fungus could wipe out vast fields of genetically identical organisms all at once. This is what happened in the terrible Irish potato famine of 1845–1850, which caused the deaths of about 1 million people due to hunger and disease and forced another 2 million to abandon their homes and emigrate. The population of Ireland dropped from 8 million to 5 million as a result of the famine.

The Irish potato famine illustrates how the combination of increased productivity and vulnerability may contribute to the geographic spread of farming. Time and again in the past, population growth followed by crop failure triggered movement of peoples from one place to another, where they have reestablished their familiar subsistence practices.

Once farming came into existence, its instability more or less guaranteed that it would spread to neighboring regions through such migrations. From Southwest Asia, for instance, farming spread north westward eventually to all of Europe, westward to North Africa, and eastward to India. Domesticated variants also spread from China and Southeast Asia westward. Those who brought crops to new locations brought other things as well, including languages, beliefs, and new alleles for human gene pools. The spread of certain ideas, customs, or practices from one culture to another is known as **diffusion**.

A similar diffusion occurred from West Africa to the southeast, creating the modern far-reaching distribution of speakers of Bantu languages. Crops including sorghum (so valuable today it is grown in hot, dry areas on all continents), pearl millet, watermelon, black-eyed peas, African yams, oil palms, and kola nuts (the source of modern cola drinks) were first domesticated in West Africa but began spreading eastward by 5,000 years ago. Between 2,000 and 3,000 years ago, Bantu speakers with their crops reached the continent's east coast and a few centuries later reached its southern tip.

---

[21]Konner, M., & Worthman, C. (1980). Nursing frequency, gonadal function, and birth spacing among !Kung hunter-gatherers. *Science 207*, 788–791; Shostak, M. (1983). *Nisa: The life and words of a !Kung woman.* New York: Random House.

[22]Diamond, *Guns, germs, and steel*, p. 132.

diffusion The spread of certain ideas, customs, or practices from one culture to another.

The Culture of Neolithic Settlements

Excavations of Neolithic settlements have revealed much about the daily activities of their former inhabitants. Archaeologists can reconstruct the pattern of their lives from structures, artifacts, and even the food debris found at these sites. Jericho, an early farming community located on the Jordan River's West Bank in the Palestinian territories, provides an excellent case in point.

Jericho: An Early Farming Community

Excavations at the Neolithic settlement that later grew to become the biblical city of Jericho have revealed the remains of a sizable farming community inhabited as early as about 10,300 years ago. Here, in the Jordan River Valley, crops could be grown almost continuously due to the presence of a bounteous spring and the rich soils of an Ice Age lake that had dried up some 3,000 years earlier. In addition, floodborne deposits originating in the Judean highlands to the west regularly renewed the fertility of the soil.

To protect their settlement against floods and associated mudflows, as well as invaders, the people of Jericho built massive stone walls around the settlement.[23] Within these walls (6½ feet wide and 12 feet high), as well as a large rock-cut ditch (27 feet wide and 9 feet deep), an estimated 400 to 900 people lived in houses of mud brick with plastered floors arranged around courtyards. Jericho's inhabitants also built a stone tower inside one corner of the wall, near the spring. It would have taken 100 people 104 days to build this tower. A staircase inside it probably led to a building on top. The village also included storage facilities as well as ceremonial structures, all made of mud brick. A village cemetery reflects the sedentary life of these early people. Nomadic groups, with few exceptions, rarely buried their dead in a single central location.

Common features in art, ritual, use of prestige goods, and burial practices indicate close contact between the farmers of Jericho and other nearby villages. Discovered inside the walls of Jericho, obsidian and turquoise from Sinai and marine shells from the coast document trade among neighboring villages.

Neolithic Material Culture

Life in Neolithic villages included various innovations in the realms of tool making, pottery, housing, and clothing. These aspects of material culture illustrate the dramatic social changes that took place during the Neolithic.

TOOL MAKING

Early harvesting tools consisted of razor-sharp flint blades inserted into handles of wood or bone. Later toolmakers added grinding and polishing the hardest stones to this tool-making technique. Scythes, forks, hoes, and simple plows replaced basic digging sticks. Later, when domesticated animals became available for use as draft animals, these early farmers redesigned their plows. Villagers used mortars and pestles to grind and crush grain. Along with the development of diverse technologies, individuals acquired specialized skills for creating a variety of craft specialties including leatherworks, weavings, and pottery.

POTTERY

Hard work on the part of those producing the food supported other members of the society who could then apply their skills and energy to various craft specialties such as pottery. In the Neolithic, different forms of pottery developed for transporting and storing food, water, and various material possessions. Impervious to damage by insects, rodents, and dampness, pottery vessels could be used for storing small grains, seeds, and other materials. Moreover, villagers could boil their food in pottery vessels over the fire instead of cooking by dropping fire-heated stones directly into food. Neolithic peoples used pottery for pipes, ladles, lamps, and other objects; some cultures even used large pottery vessels for disposal of the dead. Significantly, pottery containers remain important for much of humanity today.

Widespread use of pottery made of clay and fired in very hot ovens likely indicates a sedentary community. Archaeologists have found pottery in abundance in all but a few of the earliest Neolithic settlements. Its fragility and weight make it less practical for use by nomads and hunters, who more typically use woven bags, baskets, and containers made of animal hide. Nevertheless, some modern nomads make and use pottery, just as there are farmers today who do not. In fact, food foragers in East Asia were making pottery vessels by about 15,000 years ago, long before pottery appeared in Southwest Asia.

The manufacture of pottery requires artful skill and some technological sophistication. To make a useful vessel requires knowledge of clay: how to remove impurities, how to shape it into desired forms, and how to dry it so that it does not crack. Proper firing requires knowledge and care so that the clay heats enough to

---

[23]Bar-Yosef, O. (1986). The walls of Jericho: An alternative interpretation. *Current Anthropology 27*, 160.

▲▲▲ Ancient pottery provides evidence of animal domestication as well as the craft specializations that developed as a consequence of the Neolithic revolution. This howling canine came from Remojadas, a culture that flourished between 1,000 and 2,100 years ago along the Gulf Coast of present-day Mexico. Dogs, one of the few domesticated animal species found in Mesoamerica, were frequently incorporated into vessels or freestanding pieces such as this hollow ceramic figure.

harden and resists future disintegration from moisture yet does not crack or even explode as it heats and later cools down.

Neolithic peoples decorated their pottery in various ways. Some engraved designs on the vessel before firing while others shaped special rims, legs, bases, and other details separately and fastened them to the finished pot. Painting, the most common form of pottery decoration, accounts for literally thousands of unique designs found among the pottery remains of ancient cultures.

HOUSING

Food production and the new sedentary lifestyle brought about another technological development—house building. Because most food foragers move around frequently, they care little for permanent housing. Cave shelters, pits dug in the earth, and simple lean-tos made of hides and wooden poles serve the purpose of keeping the weather out. In the Neolithic, however, dwellings became more complex in design and more diverse in type. Some were constructed of wood, while others included more elaborate shelters made of stone, sun-dried brick, or branches plastered together with mud or clay.

Although permanent housing frequently goes along with food production, some cultures created substantial housing without shifting to food production. For example, on the northwestern coast of North America, people lived in sturdy houses made of heavy planks hewn from cedar logs, yet their food consisted entirely of wild plants and animals, especially salmon and sea mammals.

CLOTHING

The Neolithic also marked the widespread use of clothing made of woven textiles. The raw materials and technology necessary for the production of clothing came from several sources: flax and cotton from farming; wool from domesticated sheep, llamas, or goats; silk from silkworms. Human invention contributed the spindle for spinning and the loom for weaving.

Social Structure

The economic and technological developments listed thus far enabled archaeologists to draw certain inferences concerning the organization of Neolithic societies. Although there are indications of ceremonial and spiritual activity, village life seemed to lack central organization and hierarchy. Burials, for example, reveal a marked absence of social differentiation. Only rarely did early Neolithic peoples use stone slabs to construct or cover graves or include elaborate objects with the dead. Evidently, no person had attained the kind of exalted status that required an elaborate funeral. The smallness of most villages and the absence of elaborate buildings suggest that the inhabitants knew one another very well and were even related, so that most of their relationships were probably highly personal ones,

◀
◀
◀ Sometimes Neolithic peoples organized themselves to carry out large projects, such as constructing Stonehenge, the famous ceremonial and astronomical center built in England some 4,500 years ago. Used as a burial ground long before the massive stone circle was erected, Stonehenge reflects the builders' understanding of the forces of nature and their impact upon food production. For instance, the opening of the stone circles aligns precisely with the sunset of the summer solstice. This careful alignment indicates that Neolithic peoples were paying close attention to the movement of the sun and to the seasonal growing cycle.

© Johannes Kerhoven

with equal emotional significance. Still, Neolithic peoples sometimes organized themselves to carry out impressive communal works preserved in the archaeological record, such as the site of Stonehenge in England.

The general picture of early Neolithic social structure is one of a relatively egalitarian society with minimal division of labor but some development of new and more specialized social roles. Villages consisted of several households, each providing for most of its own needs. Kinship groups probably met the organizational needs of society beyond the household level.

Neolithic Cultures in the Americas

In the Americas the shape and timing of the Neolithic revolution differed compared to other parts of the world. For example, Neolithic farming villages were common in Southwest Asia between 8,000 and 9,000 years ago, but similar villages did not appear in the Americas until about 4,500 years ago, in **Mesoamerica** (the region from central Mexico to the northern regions of Central America) and the Andean highlands. Moreover, pottery, which developed in Southwest Asia shortly after plant and animal domestication, did not emerge in the Americas until about 4,500 years ago. Early Neolithic peoples in the Americas did not use the potter's wheel. Instead, they manufactured elaborate pottery by hand. Looms and the hand spindle appeared in the Americas about 3,000 years ago.

None of these absences indicate backwardness on the part of Native American peoples, many of whom,

as we have already seen, were highly sophisticated farmers and plant breeders. Instead, we can surmise that many Neolithic peoples in the Americas were satisfied with existing practices. When food production developed in Mesoamerica, the Andean highlands, and North America, it did so wholly independently of Europe and Asia, with different crops, animals, and technologies.

Outside Mesoamerica and the Andean highlands, hunting, fishing, and the gathering of wild plant foods remained important to the economy of Neolithic peoples in the Americas. Apparently, most American Indians continued to emphasize a food-foraging rather than a food-producing mode of life, even though maize and other domestic crops came to be cultivated just about everywhere that climate permitted. These groups, like hunter-gatherers in other parts of the world, opted not to take on the challenges of food production. These cultures remained stable until the arrival of European explorers, which instigated a pattern of disease and domination.[24]

The Neolithic and Human Biology

Although we tend to think of the invention of food production in terms of its cultural consequences, it obviously had a biological impact as well. Physical anthropologists studying human skeletons from Neolithic burial grounds

[24]Mann, C. C. (2005). *1491: New revelations of the Americas before Columbus*. New York: Knopf.

Paleolithic Prescriptions for the Neolithic and Beyond

U.S. anthropologists George Armelagos and Mark Nathan Cohen suggest that the downward trajectory for human health began with the earliest human village settlements some 10,000 years ago.[a] When humans began farming rather than gathering, they often switched to single-crop diets. In addition, settlement into villages led directly to the increase in infectious disease. The health consequences of the Neolithic range from increased mortality to dental decay to substance abuse. Though recent scientific discoveries have cured some of the problems brought about by the shift to food production, a series of health problems connect us to our Neolithic forebears.

Throughout most of our evolutionary history, humans led more physically active lives and ate a more varied low-fat diet than we do now. Our ancestors did not drink alcohol or smoke. They spent their days scavenging or hunting for animal protein while gathering vegetable foods, with some insects thrown in for good measure. They stayed fit through traveling great distances each day over the savannah and beyond.

Though we hail increased life expectancy as one of modern civilization's greatest accomplishments, this phenomenon, brought about in part by the discovery of antibiotics during the middle of the twentieth century, is quite recent. The chronic diseases that linger—such as diabetes, heart disease, substance abuse, and high blood pressure—have their roots in the Neolithic.

The prevalence of these diseases of civilization has increased rapidly over the past sixty-five years. Anthropologists Melvin Konner and Marjorie Shostak and physician Boyd Eaton have suggested that our Paleolithic ancestors left us with a prescription for a cure. They propose that as "stone-agers in a fast lane," people's health will improve by returning to the lifestyle to which their bodies are adapted.[b] Such Paleolithic prescriptions are an example of evolutionary medicine—a branch of medical anthropology that uses evolutionary principles to contribute to human health.

Evolutionary medicine bases its prescriptions on the idea that rates of cultural change exceed the rates of biological change. Our food-forager physiology was shaped over millions of years, while the cultural changes leading to contemporary lifestyles have occurred rapidly. For example, tobacco was domesticated in the Americas only a few thousand years ago and was widely used as both a narcotic and an insecticide. Alcoholic beverages, which depend on the domestication of a variety of plant species such as hops, barley, and corn, also could not have arisen without village life, as the fermentation process requires time and watertight containers. The high-starch diets and sedentary lifestyle of the Neolithic contribute to diabetes and heart disease.

Our evolutionary history offers clues about the diet and lifestyle to which our bodies evolved. By returning to our ancient lifeways, we can make the health consequences of the Neolithic transition a thing of the past. ∎

Biocultural Question

Can you imagine what sort of Paleolithic prescriptions our evolutionary history would contribute for modern behaviors, such as childrearing practices, sleeping, and work patterns? Are there any ways that your culture or personal lifestyle is well aligned with past lifeways?

[a]Cohen, M. N., & Armelagos, G. J. (Eds.). (1984). *Paleopathology at the origins of agriculture.* Orlando: Academic Press.

[b]Eaton, S. B., Konner, M., & Shostak, M. (1988). Stone-agers in the fast lane: Chronic degenerative diseases in evolutionary perspective. *American Journal of Medicine 84* (4), 739–749.

---

have found evidence for a somewhat lessened mechanical stress on peoples' bodies and teeth. Although exceptions exist, the teeth of Neolithic peoples generally show less wear, their bones are less robust, and compared to the skeletons of Paleolithic and Mesolithic peoples, they had less osteoarthritis (the result of stressed joint surfaces).

On the other hand, other skeletal features provide clear evidence for a marked deterioration in health and mortality. Skeletons from Neolithic villages show evidence of severe and chronic nutritional stress as well as pathologies related to infectious and deficiency diseases.

High-starch diets led to increased dental decay during the Neolithic as well. Scientists have recently documented dental drilling of teeth in a 9,000-year-old Neolithic site in Pakistan.[25] This resembles the high frequency of dental decay seen in contemporary populations when they switch from a varied hunter-gatherer diet to a high-starch diet. In fact, as this chapter's Biocultural Connection explores, the Neolithic revolution had devastating consequences for human health.

▲▲▲▲▲▲▲▲▲▲▲▲▲▲▲▲▲▲▲▲▲▲▲▲▲▲▲▲▲▲▲▲▲▲▲▲▲▲

Mesoamerica The region extending from central Mexico to northern Central America.

---

[25]Coppa, A., et al. (2006). Early Neolithic tradition of dentistry. *Nature 440*, 755–756.

▼▼▼▼▼▼▼▼▼▼▼▼▼▼▼▼▼▼▼▼▼▼▼▼▼▼▼▼▼▼▼▼▼▼▼▼▼▼

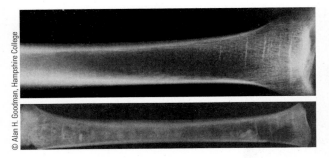

▲▲▲ The ends of these thighbones, found in a prehistoric farming community in Arizona, exhibit Harris lines, which indicate that the young individual recovered after a period of arrested growth caused by famine or disease. The bones document the health consequences attributed to the ecological instability of food production.

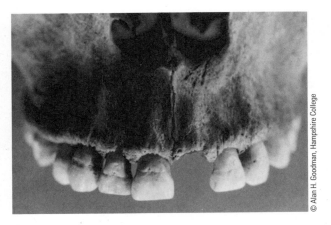

▲▲▲ Enamel hypoplasias (visible pitting), such as shown on these teeth, indicate arrested growth caused by famine or disease. These teeth are from an adult who lived in a prehistoric farming community in Arizona.

Domestication encourages a sedentary lifestyle with the great potential for overpopulation relative to the resource base. Under these conditions, even minor environmental fluctuations can lead to widespread hunger and malnutrition. Evidence of stress and disease increased proportionally with population density and the reliance on intensive agriculture.[26] Further, the crowded conditions in settlements led to competition for resources with other villages, increasing the mortality rate due to warfare.

For the most part, Neolithic peoples depended on crops selected for their higher productivity and storability rather than for nutritional balance. Moreover, as already noted, the crops' nutritional shortcomings would have been exacerbated by their susceptibility to periodic failure, particularly as populations grew in size. Thus it comes as no surprise that Neolithic peoples experienced worsened health and higher mortality compared to their Paleolithic forebears. Some have gone so far as to assert that the switch from food foraging to food production was the worst mistake that humans ever made!

Sedentary life in fixed villages likely increased the incidence of disease and mortality characteristic of the Neolithic. With sedentism comes a sanitation problem as garbage and human waste accumulate. Small groups of people, who move about from one campsite to another, leave their waste behind. Moreover, transmission of airborne diseases increases where people are gathered into villages. As we saw in Chapter 2, farming practices also created the ideal environment for the species of mosquito that spreads malaria.

The close association between humans and their domestic animals facilitated the transmission of some animal diseases to people. A host of life-threatening diseases—including smallpox, chicken pox, and in fact all of the infectious diseases of childhood overcome by medical science only in the latter half of the 20th century—came to humans through their close association with domestic

animals (▶ **Table 5.1**). Again we see that domestication and the changes of the Neolithic revolution had unforeseen biological consequences for the human population.

The Neolithic and the Idea of Progress

Although the overall health of Neolithic peoples suffered as a consequence of this cultural shift, many view the transition from food foraging to food production as a great step upward on a ladder of progress. In part this interpretation derives from one of the more widely held beliefs of Western culture—that humans and their lifeways have progressed steadily over time. To be sure, farming allowed people to increase the size of their populations, to live together in substantial sedentary communities, and to reorganize the workload in ways that permitted craft specialization. However, this is not progress in a universal sense but, rather, a set of cultural beliefs about the nature of progress. Each culture defines progress (if it does so at all) in its own terms.

Whatever the benefits of food production, Neolithic humans paid a substantial price for the development of **agriculture**—intensive crop cultivation, employing plows, fertilizers, and/or irrigation. As U.S. anthropologists Mark Cohen and George Armelagos put it, "Taken as a whole, indicators fairly clearly suggest an overall decline in the quality—and probably in the length—of human life associated with the adoption of agriculture."[27]

---

[26]Cohen, M. N., & Armelagos, G. J. (1984). *Paleopathology at the origins of agriculture*. Orlando: Academic Press; Goodman, A., & Armelagos, G. J. (1985). Death and disease at Dr. Dickson's mounds. *Natural History 94* (9), 12–18.

[27]Cohen, M. N., & Armelagos, G. J. (1984). Paleopathology at the origins of agriculture: Editors' summation. In *Paleopathology at the origins of agriculture* (p. 594). Orlando: Academic Press.

Table 5.1 Diseases Acquired from Domesticated Animals

Disease	Animal with Most Closely Related Pathogen	Deaths Globally According to WHO (Year)	Prevention Strategies
Measles	Cattle (rinderpest)	197,000 (2007)	Immunization
Tuberculosis	Cattle	1.6 million (2005)	Treatment of infected individuals to prevent spread
Smallpox	Cattle (cowpox) or other livestock with related pox viruses	Eradicated as of December 1979; between 1900 and eradication, smallpox killed 300–500 million people	Immunization
Influenza	Pigs, ducks	Several different types; all are seasonal and variable, with 250,000 to 500,000 deaths estimated annually	Immunization
Pertussis (whooping cough)	Pigs, dogs	297,000 (2000)	Immunization

Close contact with animals provides a situation in which variants of animal pathogens may establish themselves in humans. For example, humans have developed symptoms from infection with avian influenza (bird flu) following contact with domesticated birds.

© Cengage Learning 2013

Source: Diamond, J. (1997). Table 11.1 Deadly Gifts From Our Animal Friends. In *Guns, germs, and steel: The fates of human societies*. Copyright © 1997 by Jared Diamond. Used by permission of W.W. Norton & Company, Inc.

Rather than imposing ethnocentric notions of progress on the archaeological record, anthropologists view the advent of food production as part of the diversification of cultures, something that began in the Paleolithic. Although some societies continued to practice various forms of hunting, gathering, and fishing, others became horticultural. But the resource competition that began in the Neolithic has, over time, pushed hunter-gatherers into increasingly marginalized territories that possess fewer natural resources.

Some horticultural societies developed agriculture. Technologically more complex than horticultural societies, agriculturalists practice intensive crop cultivation, employing plows, fertilizers, and possibly irrigation. They may use a wooden or metal plow pulled by one or more harnessed draft animals, such as horses, oxen, or water buffaloes, to produce food on larger plots of land. The distinction between horticulturalist and intensive agriculturalist is not always easy to make. For example, the Hopi Indians of the North American Southwest traditionally employed irrigation in their farming while at the same time using basic hand tools.

Pastoralism arose in environments that were too dry, too grassy, too steep, too cold, or too hot for effective horticulture or intensive agriculture. Pastoralists breed and manage migratory herds of domesticated grazing animals, such as goats, sheep, cattle, llamas, or camels. For example, without plows early Neolithic peoples could not farm the heavy grass cover of the Russian steppe, but they could graze their animals there. Thus, a number of peoples living in the arid grasslands and deserts that stretch from northwestern Africa into Central Asia kept large herds of domestic animals, relying on their neighbors for plant foods. Finally, some societies went on to develop civilizations—the subject of the next chapter.

▲▲

agriculture Intensive crop cultivation, employing plows, fertilizers, and/or irrigation.

▼▼

Chapter Checklist

What is the Mesolithic?

✔ The period between the Paleolithic and Neolithic, this period of warming after the last glacial period included rising sea levels, changes in vegetation, and the disappearance of herd animals from many areas.

✔ The Mesolithic included a shift from hunting big game to hunting smaller game and gathering a broad spectrum of plants and aquatic resources.

✔ Increased reliance on seafood and plants allowed some people to become more sedentary.

✔ Ground-stone tools, including axes and adzes, met the needs for new technologies in the postglacial world. Many Mesolithic tools in the Old World were made with microliths—small, hard, sharp blades of flint or similar stone that could be produced in quantity and hafted with others to produce implements like sickles.

✔ In the Americas, the Archaic is comparable to the Old World Mesolithic.

What are the characteristics of the Neolithic?

✔ A shift to food production through the domestication of plants and animals constitutes most of the change of this period.

✔ Settlement in permanent villages accompanied food production in many cases, though some Neolithic peoples who depended on domesticated animals did not become sedentary. Still others maintained a hunter-gatherer lifestyle.

✔ During the Neolithic, stone that was too hard to be chipped was ground and polished for tools. People developed scythes, forks, hoes, and plows to replace simple digging sticks.

✔ Village life allowed for a reorganization of the workload, letting some individuals pursue specialized tasks.

When, how, and why did the shift to food production and village life take place?

✔ The change to food production took place independently and more or less simultaneously in various regions of the world including Southwest and Southeast Asia, highland Mexico and Peru, South America's Amazon forest, eastern North America, China, and Africa. In all cases, people developed food complexes based on starchy grains and/or roots that were consumed with protein-containing legumes plus flavor enhancers.

✔ Southwest Asia contains the earliest known Neolithic sites, consisting of small villages of mud huts with individual storage pits and clay ovens along with evidence of food production and trade. At ancient Jericho, remains of tools, houses, and clothing indicate that Neolithic peoples occupied the oasis as early as 10,300 years ago. At its height, Neolithic Jericho had a population of 400 to 900 people. Comparable villages developed independently in Mexico and Peru by about 4,500 years ago.

✔ The most probable theory to account for the Neolithic revolution is that domestication came about as a consequence of a chance convergence of separate natural events and cultural developments.

What is domestication and how can we recognize it?

✔ A domesticated plant or animal is one that has become genetically modified as an intended or unintended consequence of human manipulation.

✔ Analysis of plant and animal remains at a site usually indicates whether its occupants were food producers. Wild cereal grasses, for example, typically have fragile stems, whereas cultivated ones have tough stems. Domesticated plants can also be identified because their edible parts are generally larger than those of their wild counterparts.

✔ Domestication produces skeletal changes in some animals. The horns of wild goats and sheep, for example, differ from those of domesticated ones. Age and sex imbalances in herd animals may also indicate manipulation by human domesticators.

✔ Domesticated crops are more productive but also more vulnerable. Food production requires more labor compared to hunting and gathering.

How did the Neolithic revolution impact social structure?

✔ Human population sizes have increased steadily since the Neolithic. Some scholars argue that pressure from increasing population size led to innovations such as intensive agriculture. Others suggest that these innovations allowed population size to grow.

✔ Periodic crop failures forced Neolithic peoples to move into new regions, spreading farming from one region to another, such as into Europe from Southwest Asia. Sometimes, food foragers adopted the cultivation of crops from neighboring peoples in response to a shortage of wild foods.

✔ Trade specializations came about due to the increased yields of food production. This included the extensive manufacture and use of pottery, the building of permanent houses, and the weaving of textiles.

✔ Archaeological evidence indicates that social organization was probably relatively egalitarian, with minimal division of labor and little development of specialized social roles. No evidence has been found indicating that religion or government *was* yet a centrally organized institution.

What were the biological consequences of the Neolithic revolution?

✔ New diets, living arrangements, and farming practices led to increased incidence of disease and higher mortality rates. Increased fertility, however, more than offset mortality, and globally human population has grown since the Neolithic.

✔ Many of the health problems humans face today originated in the Neolithic.

✔ Increased competition for resources began in the Neolithic. Hunter-gatherers have become increasingly marginalized over time due to this competition.

Questions for Reflection

1. The changed lifeways of the Neo-lithic included the domestication of plants and animals as well as settlement into villages. What were the costs and benefits of this new way of life? Did the Neolithic set into motion problems that are still with us today?

2. Why do you think some people of the past chose not to make the change from food foraging to food producing? What problems existing in today's world

have their origins in the lifeways of the Neolithic?

3. Consider the reduction of diversity and the vulnerability to disease brought about by the domestication of wild spe-cies during the Neolithic. Are these same factors relevant to today's genetically modified foods? Who benefits most di-rectly from genetically modified foods?

4. Why are the changes of the Neo-lithic sometimes mistakenly associated

with progress? Why have the social forms that originated in the Neolithic come to dominate the earth?

5. Although the archaeological record indicates some differences in the timing of domestication of plants and animals in different parts of the world, why is it incorrect to say that one region was more advanced than another?

Key Terms

Neolithic
Mesolithic
Archaic cultures
microlith
Natufian culture
Neolithic revolution

horticulture
pastoralism
innovation
primary innovation
secondary innovation
domestication

vegeculture
diffusion
Mesoamerica
agriculture

Online Study Resources

Login to **www.cengagebrain.com** to access the resources your instructor has assigned and to purchase materials. For this book, you can access:

CourseMate
Access chapter-specific learning tools including flashcards, glossaries, practice quizzes, videos, and more in your Anthropology CourseMate.

VISUAL ESSENCE

With the emergence of cities and states, human societies began to develop organized central governments and concentrated power that made it possible to build monumental structures such as the magnificent 12th-century Angkor Wat temple complex in Cambodia. But cities and states also ushered in a series of problems, many of which we still face today such as large-scale warfare. Like monumental civic works, warfare requires elaborate organization under a centralized authority, both to mount attacks and for defense. Within decades of the dedication of this 500-acre temple to the Hindu god Vishnu, a neighboring group sacked it. The original Khmer rulers then took the temple back and restored it, ultimately dedicating the temple to Buddhism. In more recent times, this temple again was the site of violence when the army of Khmer Rouge, a murderous regime responsible for the deaths of at least 1.5 million Cambodians, retreated to the sacred ruins as they were ousted from power in 1979. Although the Khmer Rouge professed a doctrine of "complete eradication of the past" to justify their policy of genocide, in an ironic twist, international concern for preservation of these ancient remains protected the Khmer army from massive bombings by international forces. Today peace has returned to Cambodia, and collective global infrastructure protects the temple of Angkor Wat for all of us.

6 The Emergence of Cities and States

a walk down a busy street of a city such as Cairo or New York brings us in contact with numerous activities essential to life in contemporary urban society. People going to and from offices and stores fill crowded sidewalks. Heavy traffic of cars, taxis, and trucks periodically comes to a standstill. A brief two-block stretch may contain a grocery store; shops selling clothing, appliances, or books; a restaurant; a newsstand; a gasoline station; and a movie theater. Other features such as a museum, a police station, a school, a hospital, or a church distinguish some neighborhoods.

Each of these services or places of business depends on others from outside this two-block radius. A butcher shop, for instance, depends on slaughterhouses and beef ranches. A clothing store could not exist without designers, farmers who produce cotton and wool, and workers who manufacture synthetic fibers. Restaurants rely on refrigerated trucking and vegetable and dairy farmers. Hospitals need insurance companies, pharmaceutical companies, and medical equipment industries to function. All institutions, finally, depend on the public utilities—the telephone, gas, water, and electric companies. Although not perceptible at first glance, interdependence defines modern cities.

The interdependence of goods and services in a big city makes a variety of products readily available. But interdependence also creates vulnerability. If strikes, bad weather, or acts of violence cause one service to stop functioning, other services can deteriorate.

At the same time, cities respond to stresses with resilience. When one service breaks down, others take over its functions. A long newspaper strike in New York City in the 1960s, for example, opened opportunities for several new news magazines as well as expanded television coverage of news and events. This phenomenon also occurred with the explosion of reality television programs in the United States during the 2007–2008 Hollywood writers' strike.

In many parts of the world, wars have caused extensive damage to basic infrastructure, leading to the development of alternative systems to cope with everything from the most basic tasks such as procuring food to

In this chapter you will learn to:

- **Define civilization, cities, and states and identify their global origins.**

- **Identify the elements of archaeological exploration of ancient civilizations through a case study of the Maya city of Tikal.**

- **Examine the four major cultural changes that mark the transition from the Neolithic to life in urban centers.**

- **Compare theories for the development of states.**

- **Identify the problems that accompany the development of cities and states.**

▲▲▲ Since the U.S. invasion of Iraq in 2003, the infrastructure of the city of Baghdad has sustained serious damage from bombing and pillaging. When the city experiences heavy rains, the sewer system collapses, which floods the streets with contaminated water. The city's inhabitants cope by creating makeshift bridges and alternative travel routes to avoid the contaminated water.

communication within global political systems. People coping with the aftermath of a natural disaster such as Hurricane Katrina in 2005 or the massive earthquake and tsunami that hit Japan in 2011 must also find such alternatives.

With the interconnectedness of modern life due to the Internet and globalization, the interdependence of goods and services transcends far beyond city limits. New social media such as Facebook and Twitter allow for instantaneous communication about geopolitical events. Social media mobilized global support for the 2011 revolutions in Tunisia and Egypt, which contributed to relatively peaceful outcomes in these cases.

On the surface, city life seems so orderly that we take it for granted. A moment's reflection, however, reminds us that the intricate metropolitan fabric of life did not always exist, and the concentrated availability of diverse goods developed only very recently in human history.

Defining Civilization

The word *civilization* comes from the Latin *civis,* an inhabitant of a city, and *civitas,* the urban community in which one dwells. In everyday North American and European usage, the word *civilization* connotes refinement and progress and may imply ethnocentric judgments about cultures. In anthropology, by contrast, the term has a more precise meaning that avoids culture-bound notions. As used by anthropologists, **civilization** refers to societies in which large numbers of people live in cities, are socially stratified, and are governed by a ruling elite working through centrally organized political systems called states. We shall elaborate on all of these points in this chapter.

As Neolithic villages grew into towns, the world's first cities developed. This happened between 4,500 and 6,000 years ago, first in Mesopotamia (modern-day Iraq and Syria), then in Egypt's Nile Valley and the Indus Valley (today's India and Pakistan). In China, civilization was underway by 5,000 years ago. Independent of these developments in Eurasia and Africa, the first American Indian cities appeared in Peru around 4,000 years ago and in Mesoamerica about 2,000 years ago (▶ **Figure 6.1**).

What characterized these first cities? Why are they called the birthplaces of civilization? The most obvious feature of cities—and of civilization—is their large size and population. But cities are more than overgrown towns.

Consider the case of Çatalhöyük, a compact 9,500-year-old settlement in south-central Turkey.[1] The tightly packed residences for more than 5,000 inhabitants left no room for streets. People traversed the tops of neighboring houses and dropped through a hole in the roof to get to their own home. Although house walls were covered with paintings and bas-reliefs, the houses were structurally similar to one another. People grew

▲▲▲▲▲▲▲▲▲▲▲▲▲▲▲▲▲▲▲▲▲▲▲▲▲▲▲▲▲▲▲▲▲▲▲▲▲▲▲

civilization In anthropology, societies in which large numbers of people live in cities, are socially stratified, and are governed by a ruling elite working through centrally organized political systems called states.

▼▼▼▼▼▼▼▼▼▼▼▼▼▼▼▼▼▼▼▼▼▼▼▼▼▼▼▼▼▼▼▼▼▼

[1]Material on Çatalhöyük is drawn from Balter, M. (1998). Why settle down? The mystery of communities. *Science 282,* 1442–1444; Balter, M. (1999). A long season puts Çatalhöyük in context. *Science 286,* 890–891; Balter, M. (2001). Did plaster hold Neolithic society together? *Science 294,* 2278–2281; Kunzig, R. (1999). A tale of two obsessed archaeologists, one ancient city and nagging doubts about whether science can ever hope to reveal the past. *Discover 20* (5), 84–92.

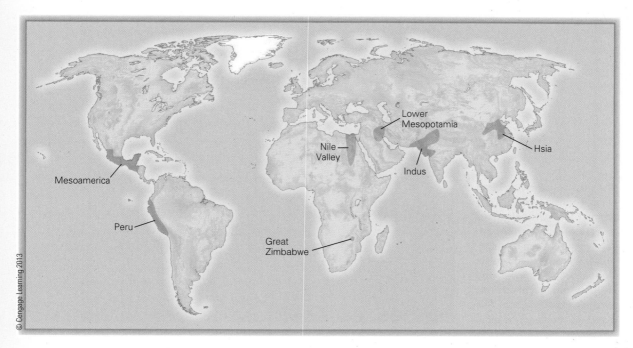

Figure 6.1 Map of Early Civilizations The major early civilizations sprang from Neolithic villages in various parts of the world. Those of the Americas developed wholly independently of those in Africa and Eurasia; Chinese civilization seems to have developed independently of Southwest Asia, including the Nile and Indus civilizations.

some crops and tended livestock but also collected significant amounts of food from wild plants and animals, never intensifying their agricultural practices. There is no evidence of public architecture and only minimal evidence of a division of labor or a centralized authority. It was as if several Neolithic villages were crammed together in one place at Çatalhöyük.

Archaeological evidence from early urban centers, by contrast, demonstrates organized planning by a central authority, technological intensification, and social stratification. For example, flood control and protection were vital components of the great ancient cities of the Indus River Valley, located in today's India and Pakistan. Mohenjo-Daro, an urban center at its peak some 4,500 years ago with a population of at least 20,000, was built on an artificial mound, safe from floodwaters. The city streets were laid out in a grid pattern with sophisticated drainage systems for individual homes, indicating further centralized planning.

Ancient peoples incorporated their spiritual beliefs and social order into the cities they built. For example, the layout of the great Mesoamerican city Teotihuacan, founded 2,200 years ago, translated the solar calendar into a unified spatial pattern. Ancient city planners oriented the Avenue of the Dead—a grand north-south axis running from the Pyramid of the Moon and bordered by the Pyramid of the Sun and the royal palace compound—to an astronomical marker, east of true north. They even channeled the San Juan River to conform to their pattern where it runs through the city. Thousands of apartment compounds surrounded this core, separated from one another by a grid of narrow streets, maintaining the east-of-north orientation throughout the city. Archaeologists estimate that over 100,000 people inhabited this great city until its sudden collapse possibly in the 7th century.

There is clear evidence of both social and economic diversity in Teotihuacan. Variation in size and quality of apartment rooms indicates some six levels of society. Those at the top of the social scale

The view looking south down Teotihuacan's principal avenue, the Avenue of the Dead, was unequaled in scale until the construction of such modern-day avenues as the Champs-Élysées in Paris. Archaeologists estimate that 100,000 people lived in this city in various neighborhoods according to their social position. This major boulevard was home to the elite.

© William A. Haviland

lived on or near the Avenue of the Dead. The Pyramid of the Sun, built along this street above a cave, was seen as a portal to the underworld and as the home of deities associated with death. Teotihuacan artisans worked on exotic goods and raw materials imported from afar, and at least two neighborhoods housed people with foreign affiliations—one for those from Oaxaca, the other (the "merchant's quarter") for those from the Gulf and Maya lowlands. Farmers, whose labor in fields (some of them irrigated) supplied the food to fellow city-dwellers, also resided in the city.[2]

Mohenjo-Daro and Teotihuacan, like other early cities throughout the globe, represent far more than expanded Neolithic villages. Some consider the array of changes accompanying the emergence of urban living as one of the great developments in human culture. The following case study provides a glimpse into another of the world's ancient cities and reveals how archaeologists went about studying this city—from the first exploratory surveys, to the excavations, to the theories proposed about its development.

Tikal: A Case Study

The ancient city of Tikal, one of the largest lowland Maya centers in existence, is situated in Central America about 300 kilometers north of Guatemala City. Here, on a broad limestone terrace in a rainforest, the Maya settled 3,000 years ago. Because archaeologists have correlated the Maya calendar precisely with our own, we know that their civilization flourished until 1,100 years ago.

At its height, Tikal covered about 120 square kilometers (km²). The Great Plaza, a large paved area surrounded by about 300 major structures and thousands of houses,

stood at Tikal's center or nucleus (▶ **Figure 6.2**). Starting from a small, dispersed population, Tikal swelled to at least 45,000 people. By 1,550 years ago, its population density had reached 600 to 700 persons per square kilometer, which was three times that of the surrounding region.

Archaeologists explored the greater Tikal region under the joint auspices of the University of Pennsylvania Museum and the Guatemalan government from 1956 through the 1960s. At the time, it was the most ambitious archaeological project undertaken in the western hemisphere.

In the first few years of the Tikal Project, archaeologists investigated only the major temple and palace structures found in the vicinity of the Great Plaza, at the site's epicenter. But in 1959, aiming to gain a balanced view of Tikal's development and composition, they turned

© Cengage Learning 2013

their attention to the hundreds of small mounds, thought to be the remains of dwellings, that surrounded larger buildings. This represented a shift in the practice of archaeology toward studying the complexities of everyday life. Imagine trying to get a realistic view of life in a major city such as Chicago or Beijing by looking only

---

[2]Cowgill, G. L. (1997). State and society at Teotihuacan, Mexico. *Annual Review of Anthropology 26*, 129–161.

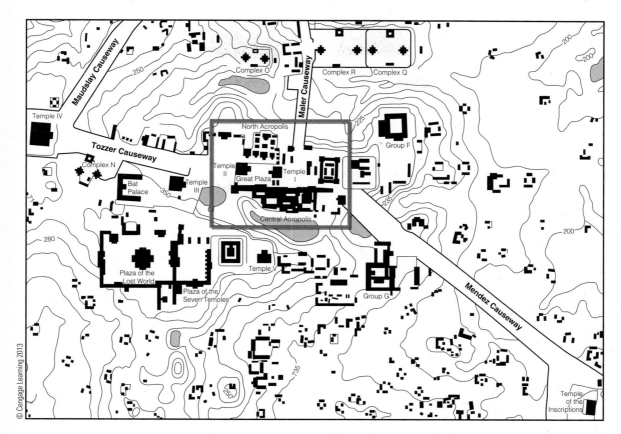

Figure 6.2 Detailed Map of Tikal Tikal spreads far beyond the Great Plaza and the monumental buildings that have been excavated and are mapped here. Archaeologists used surveying techniques, test pits, and other strategies to define the city's boundaries and to understand the full spectrum of lifeways that took place there. The red outline in the center of the map delineates the royal court, royal burial ground, and central marketplace. In addition to what is pictured here, Tikal extends several kilometers outward in every direction. Those familiar with the original *Star Wars* movie will be interested to know that the aerial views of the rebel camp were filmed at Tikal, where monumental structures depicted in this map rise high above the forest canopy.

at their monumental public buildings. Similarly, archaeologists realized that they needed to examine the full range of ruins at Tikal in order to accurately reconstruct past lifeways.

With data from the excavation of small structures, most of which were probably houses, archaeologists estimated Tikal's population size and density. In turn, this information allowed archaeologists to test the conventional assumption that the subsistence practices of the Maya inhabitants could not sustain large population concentrations.

Extensive excavation also provided a sound basis for a reconstruction of the everyday life and social organization of the Maya, a people who had been known almost entirely through the study of ceremonial remains. For example, differences in architecture, house construction, and associated artifacts and burials suggest differences in social class. Features of house distribution might reflect the existence of extended families or other types of kin groups. The excavation of both large and small structures revealed the social structure of the total population of Tikal.[3]

Surveying and Excavating the Site

Mapping crews extensively surveyed 6 square kilometers of forested land surrounding the Great Plaza, providing a preliminary map to guide the small-structure excavation process.[4] The dense, tall rainforest canopy prevented the use of aerial photography for this mapping. Trees obscured all but the tallest temples. Many of the small ruins remain practically invisible even to observers on the ground. Four years of mapping revealed that ancient Tikal extended far beyond the original 6 km² surveyed. More time and money allowed continued surveying of the area in order to fully define the city's boundaries and calculate its overall size.[5]

---

[3]Haviland, W. A. (2002). Settlement, society and demography at Tikal. In J. Sabloff (Ed.), *Tikal*. Santa Fe: School of American Research.

[4]Haviland, W. A., et al. (1985). *Excavations in small residential groups of Tikal: Groups 4F-1 and 4F-2*. Philadelphia: University Museum.

[5]Puleston, D. E. (1983). *The settlement survey of Tikal*. Philadelphia: University Museum.

The initial excavation of six structures, two plazas, and a platform revealed new structures not visible before excavation, the architectural complexity of the structures, and an enormous quantity of artifacts. Some structures were partially excavated, and some remained uninvestigated. Following this initial work, the archaeological team excavated over a hundred additional small structures in different parts of the site in order to ensure investigation of a representative sample. The team also sank numerous test pits in various other small-structure groups to supplement the information gained from more extensive excavations. They also washed and catalogued every artifact recovered.

Evidence from the Excavation

Excavation at Tikal produced considerable evidence about the social organization, technology, and diversity in this ancient city, as well as the relationship between people in Tikal and other regions. For example, the site provides evidence of trade in nonperishable items. Granite, quartzite, hematite, pyrite, jade, slate, and obsidian all were imported, either as raw materials or finished products. Marine materials came from Caribbean and Pacific coastal areas. In turn, Tikal residents exported chert (a flintlike stone used to manufacture tools) both in its raw form and as finished objects. Tikal's location between two river systems may have facilitated an overland trade route. Evidence of trade in perishable goods—such as textiles, feathers, salt, and cacao—indicated the presence of full-time traders among the Tikal Maya.

In the realm of technology, archaeologists found specialized woodworking, pottery, obsidian, and shell workshops. The skillful carving displayed on stone monuments suggests that occupational specialists did this work. Similarly, the fine artwork glazed into ceramic vessels demonstrates that ancient artists could envision the transformation of their pale, relatively colorless ceramics into their finished fired form.

To control the large population, some form of bureaucratic organization must have existed in Tikal. From Maya written records (glyphs), we know that the government was headed by a hereditary ruling dynasty with sufficient power to organize massive construction and maintenance. This included a system of defensive ditches and embankments on the northern and southern edges of the city. The longest of these ran for a distance of perhaps 19 to 28 kilometers. Although we do not have direct evidence, clues indicate the presence of textile workers, dental workers, makers of bark cloth "paper," scribes, masons, astronomers, and other occupational specialists.

Archaeologists suggest that the religion of the Tikal Maya developed initially as a means to cope with the uncertainties of agriculture. With thin soils and no streams, Tikal residents depended on rainwater collected in reservoirs. Rain in the region is abundant, but the onset of the season is unreliable. The ancient Maya may have perceived Tikal, with a high elevation relative to surrounding terrain, as a "power place," especially suited for making contact with supernatural forces and beings.

The Maya priests tried not only to win over and please the deities in times of drought but also to honor them in times of plenty. Priests—experts on the Maya calendar—determined the most favorable time to plant crops and were involved with other agricultural matters. This tended to keep people in or near the city so that they could receive guidance on their crops. The population in and around Tikal depended upon their priests to influence supernatural beings and forces on their behalf.

As the population increased, land for agriculture became scarce, forcing the Maya to find new methods of food production that could sustain Tikal's dense population. They added the planting and tending of fruit trees and other crops that could be grown around their houses in soils enriched by human waste. (Unlike houses at Teotihuacan, those at Tikal were not built close to one another.) Along with increased reliance on household gardening, the Maya constructed artificially raised fields in areas that flooded during the rainy season. Careful maintenance allowed for intensive cultivation of these

▲▲▲ Archaeologists have proposed that Tikal emerged as an important religious center due its relative altitude in the region. Altitude may have created a perception of power and access to supernatural forces. Today Tikal remains an important religious center for local Maya, who gather in front of the acropolis for a traditional ceremony.

raised fields, year after year. By converting low areas into reservoirs and constructing channels to carry runoff from plazas and other architecture into these reservoirs, the Maya at Tikal maximized the collection of water for the dry season.

As these agricultural changes took place, a class of artisans, craftspeople, and other occupational specialists emerged to serve the needs of an elite consisting of the priesthood and a ruling dynasty. The Maya built numerous temples, public buildings, and various kinds of houses appropriate to the distinct social classes of their society.

For several hundred years, Tikal sustained its ever-growing population. When the pressure for food and land reached a critical point, population growth stopped. At the same time, warfare with other cities had increasingly destructive effects on Tikal. Archaeologists are able to diagnose the damage to the city from warfare by looking at specific evidence from the excavations: abandoned houses situated on prime lands in rural areas, nutritional problems visible in skeletons recovered from burials, and construction of the previously mentioned defensive ditches and embankments. The archaeological record indicates a period of readjustment directed by an already strong central authority. Activities then continued as before, but without further population growth for another 250 years or so.

As this case study shows, excavations at Tikal demonstrate the splendor, the social organization, the belief systems, and the agricultural practices of the ancient Maya civilization.

Cities and Cultural Change

If a person who grew up in a rural North American village today moved to Philadelphia, Montreal, or Los Angeles, she or he would experience a very different way of life. The same would be true for a Neolithic village-dweller who moved into one of the world's first cities in Mesopotamia 5,500 years ago. As we will explore in depth in Chapter 8, every culture is a dynamic and integrated system of adaptation that responds to external and internal factors. As humans turned to food production and from there to living in urban centers, the social structure and ideology changed as well. Four basic changes mark the transition from Neolithic village life to life in the first urban centers: agricultural innovation, diversification of labor, central government, and social stratification.

Agricultural Innovation

Changes in farming methods distinguished early civilizations from Neolithic villages. The ancient Sumerians, for example, built an extensive system of dikes, canals,

and reservoirs to irrigate their farmlands. With such a system, they could control water resources at will; water could be held and then run off into the fields as necessary.

Irrigation was important for crop yield, because not having to depend upon the seasonal rain cycles allowed farmers to harvest more crops in one year. Increased crop yields, resulting from agricultural innovations, contributed to the high population densities of ancient civilizations.

Diversification of Labor

Diversified labor activity also characterized early civilizations. In a Neolithic village without irrigation or plow farming, every family member participated in the raising of crops. In contrast, the high crop yields made possible by new farming methods and the increased population of civilizations permitted a sizable number of people to pursue nonagricultural activities on a full-time basis.

Ancient public records document a variety of specialized workers. For example, an early Mesopotamian document from the old Babylonian city of Lagash (modern-day Tell al-Hiba, Iraq) lists the artisans, craftspeople, and others paid from crop surpluses stored in the temple granaries. These lists included coppersmiths, silversmiths, sculptors, merchants, potters, tanners, engravers, butchers, carpenters, spinners, barbers, cabinetmakers, bakers, clerks, and brewers.

With specialization came the expertise that led to the invention of new ways of making and doing things. In Eurasia and Africa, civilization ushered in the **Bronze Age**, a period marked by the production of tools and ornaments made of this metal alloy. Metals were in great demand for the manufacture of farmers' and artisans' tools, as well as for weapons. Copper and tin (the raw materials from which bronze is made) were smelted, or separated from their ores, then purified and cast to make plows, swords, axes, and shields. Later, with the invention of improved methods of heating metals, such tools were made from smelted iron. In wars, stone knives, spears, and slings could not stand up against metal spears, arrowheads, swords, helmets, or armor.

▲▲▲

Bronze Age In the Old World, the period marked by the production of tools and ornaments of bronze; began about 5,000 years ago in China and Southwest Asia and about 500 years earlier in Southeast Asia.

▼▼▼

The indigenous civilizations of the Americas also used metals. South American peoples used copper, silver, and gold for tools as well as for ceremonial and ornamental objects. The Aztecs and Maya used the same soft metals for ceremonial and ornamental objects while continuing to rely on stone for their everyday tools. To those who assume the inherent superiority of metal, this seems puzzling. However, the ready availability of obsidian (a glass formed by volcanic activity), its extreme sharpness (many times sharper than the finest steel), and the ease with which toolmakers can work it made it perfectly suited to their needs. Moreover, unlike bronze—and especially iron—copper, silver, and gold are soft metals and have limited practical use. Obsidian tools provide some of the sharpest cutting edges ever made (recall Chapter 4's Anthropology Applied, "Stone Tools for Modern Surgeons").

Early civilizations developed extensive trade systems to procure the raw materials needed for their technologies. In many parts of the world, boats provided greater access to trade centers, transporting large loads of imports and exports between cities at lower costs than if they had been carried overland. A one-way trip from the ancient Egyptian cities along the Nile River to the Mediterranean port city of Byblos in Phoenicia (not far from the present city of Beirut, Lebanon) took far less time by rowboat compared to the overland route. With a sailboat, it was even faster.

Egyptian kings, or pharaohs, sent expeditions in various directions for prized resources: south to Nubia (the Egypt-Sudan border area) for gold; east to the Sinai Peninsula for copper; to Arabia for spices and perfumes; to Asia for lapis lazuli (a blue semiprecious stone) and other jewels; north to Lebanon for cedar, wine, and funerary oils; and southwest to Central Africa for ivory, ebony, ostrich feathers, leopard skins, cattle, and the captives they enslaved. Evidence of trading from Great Zimbabwe in southern Africa indicates that by the 11th century these trading networks extended throughout the Old World. Increased contact with foreign peoples through trade brought new information to trading economies, furthering the spread of innovations and bodies of knowledge such as geometry and astronomy.

Central Government

A governing elite also emerged in early civilizations. The challenges new cities faced because of their size and complexity required a strong central authority. The governing elite saw to it that different interest groups, such as farmers or craft specialists, provided their respective services and did not infringe on one another.

Just as they do today, governments of the past ensured that cities were safe from their enemies by constructing fortifications and raising an army. They levied taxes and appointed tax collectors so that construction workers, the army, and other public expenses could be paid. They saw to it that merchants, carpenters, or farmers who made legal claims received justice according to their legal system's standards. They guaranteed safety for the lives and property of ordinary people and assured them that any harm done to one person by another

◀ The construction of elliptical granite walls held together without any mortar at Great Zimbabwe in southern Zimbabwe, Africa, attests to the skill of the people who built these structures. When European explorers, unwilling to accept the notion of civilization in sub-Saharan Africa, discovered these magnificent ruins, they wrongly attributed them to white non-Africans. This false notion persisted until archaeologists demonstrated that these structures were part of a city with 12,000 to 20,000 inhabitants that served as the center of a Bantu state.

© Robert Holmes/Corbis

would be justly handled. In addition, they arranged for storage of surplus food for times of scarcity and supervised public works such as extensive irrigation systems and fortifications.

EVIDENCE OF CENTRALIZED AUTHORITY

Evidence of centralized authority in ancient civilizations comes from such sources as law codes, temple records, and royal chronicles. Excavation of the city structures themselves provides additional evidence because these remains can show definitive signs of city planning. The precise astronomical layout of the Mesoamerican city Teotihuacan, described earlier, attests to strong, centralized control.

Monumental buildings and temples, palaces, and large sculptures are usually found in ancient civilizations. For example, the Great Pyramid for the tomb of Khufu, the Egyptian pharaoh, is 755 feet long (236 meters) and 481 feet high (147 meters); it contains about 2.3 million stone blocks, each with an average weight of 2.5 tons. The Greek historian Herodotus claimed that it took 100,000 men twenty years to build this tomb. Such gigantic structures could be built only because a powerful central authority was able to harness the considerable labor force, engineering skills, and raw materials necessary for their construction.

Writing or some form of recorded information provides another indicator of the existence of centralized authority. With writing, central authorities could disseminate information and store, systematize, and deploy memory for political, religious, and economic purposes.

Scholars attribute the initial motive for the development of writing in Mesopotamia to recordkeeping of state affairs. Writing allowed early governments to track accounts of their food surplus, tribute records, and other business receipts. Some of the earliest documents appear to be just such records—lists of vegetables and animals bought and sold, tax lists, and storehouse inventories.

Before 5,500 years ago, records consisted initially of "tokens," ceramic pieces with different shapes indicative of different commercial objects. Thus a cone shape could represent a measure of grain or a cylinder could be an animal. As the system became more sophisticated, tokens came to represent different animals, as well as processed foods (such as oil, trussed

ducks, or bread) and manufactured or imported goods (such as textiles and metal).[6] Ultimately, clay tablets with impressed marks representing objects replaced these tokens.

By 5,000 years ago, in the Mesopotamian city of Uruk in Iraq (which likely derives its modern country name from this ancient place), a new writing technique emerged. Writers would use a reed stylus to make wedge-shaped markings on a tablet of damp clay. Originally, each marking stood for a word. Because most words in this language were monosyllabic, over time the markings came to stand for syllables (▶ **Figure 6.3**).

Controversy surrounds the question of the earliest evidence of writing (▶ **Figure 6.4**). Traditionally, the earliest writing was linked to Mesopotamia. However, in 2003 archaeologists working in the Henan Province of central China discovered signs carved into 8,600-year-old tortoise shells; these markings resemble later-written characters and predate the Mesopotamian evidence by about 2,000 years.[7]

In the Americas, writing systems came into use among various Mesoamerican peoples, but the Maya system was particularly sophisticated. Like other aspects of that culture, the writing system appears to have roots in the earlier writing system of the Olmec civilization.[8] The Maya hieroglyphic system had less to do with keeping track of state properties than with extravagant celebrations of the accomplishments of their rulers. Maya lords glorified themselves by recording their dynastic genealogies, important conquests, and royal marriages; by using grandiose titles to refer to themselves; and by associating their actions with important astronomical events. Different though this may be from the recordkeeping of ancient Mesopotamia, all writing systems share a concern with political power and its maintenance.

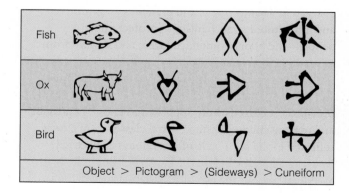

Figure 6.3 Cuneiform Writing Cuneiform writing developed from representational drawings of objects. Over time the drawings became simplified and more abstract, as well as being wedge-shaped so that they could be cut into a clay tablet with a stylus.

Source: Courtesy of the Penn Museum.

[6]Lawler, A. (2001). Writing gets a rewrite. *Science 292*, 2419.

[7]Li, X., et al. (2003). The earliest writing? Sign use in the seventh millennium BC at Jiahu, Henan Province, China. *Antiquity 77*, 31–44.

[8]Pohl, M. E. D., Pope, K. O., & von Nagy, C. (2002). Olmec origins of Mesoamerican writing. *Science 298*, 1984–1987.

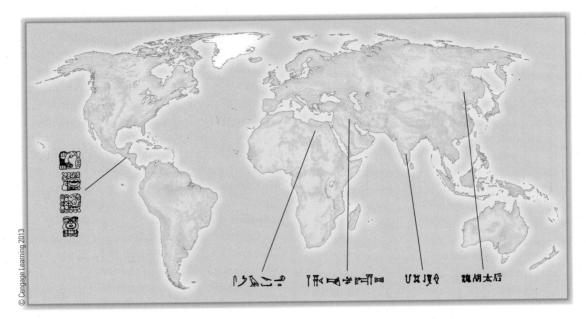

© Cengage Learning 2013

Figure 6.4 Origins of Written Language The transience of spoken words contrasts with the relative permanence of written records. In all of human history, writing has been independently invented at least five times.

THE EARLIEST GOVERNMENTS

A king and his advisors typically headed the earliest city governments although a few ancient queens also ruled. Of the many ancient kings known, one stands out as truly remarkable for the efficient government organization and highly developed a legal system characterizing his reign: Hammurabi, the Babylonian king who lived in Mesopotamia (modern Iraq) between 3,700 and 3,950 years ago. From Babylon, the capital of his empire, he issued a set of laws now known as the Code of Hammurabi, notable for its thorough detail and standardization. It prescribed the correct form for legal procedures and determined penalties for perjury and false accusation. It contained laws applying to property rights, loans and debts, family rights, and even damages paid for malpractice by a physician. It defined fixed rates to be charged in various trades and branches of commerce, and it instituted a mechanism to protect vulnerable people—the poor, women, children, and slaves—from injustice.

Officials had the code publicly displayed on huge stone slabs so that no one could plead ignorance. Even the neediest citizens were supposed to know their rights and responsibilities. Distinct social classes were clearly reflected in the law ("rule of law" does not necessarily mean "equality before the law"). For example, if an aristocrat put out the eye of a fellow aristocrat, the law required that his own eye be put out in turn; hence the saying "an eye for an eye." However, if the aristocrat put out the eye of a commoner, he simply owed this person a payment of silver.[9]

© Cengage Learning 2013

Although some civilizations flourished under a single ruler with extraordinary governing abilities, other civilizations prospered with a widespread governing bureaucracy that was very efficient at every level. The government of the Inca empire is one such example.

The Inca civilization of Peru and its surrounding territories reached its peak 500 years ago, just before the arrival of the Spanish invaders. By 1525, it stretched 4,000 kilometers (2,500 miles) from north to south and 800 kilometers (500 miles) from east to west, making it one of the largest empires of its time. Its population, which numbered in the millions, was composed of people of many different ethnic groups. In the achievements of its governmental and political system, Inca civilization surpassed every other civilization of the Americas and most of those of Africa and Eurasia. An emperor, regarded as the divine son of the Sun God, headed the government. Below him came the royal family, the aristocracy, imperial administrators, and lower nobility, and below them

[9]Moscati, S. (1962). *The face of the ancient orient* (p. 90). New York: Doubleday.

the masses of artisans, craftspeople, farmers, laborers, and servants.

The empire was divided into four administrative regions, further subdivided into provinces, and so on down to villages and families. Governmental agriculture and tax officials closely supervised farming activities such as planting, irrigation, and harvesting. Teams of professional relay runners could carry messages up to 400 kilometers (250 miles) in a single day over a network of roads and bridges that remains impressive even today.

Despite the complexity of the Inca civilization, they had no known form of conventional writing. Instead, public records and historical chronicles were kept in the form of an ingenious coding system of colored strings with knots known as *quipus* (the Quechua word for "knot").

© Cengage Learning 2013

Social Stratification

The rise of large, economically diversified populations presided over by centralized governing authorities brought with it the fourth cultural change characteristic of civilization: social stratification, or the emergence of social classes. For example, symbols of special status and privilege that ranked people according to the kind of work they did or the family into which they were born appeared in the ancient cities of Mesopotamia.

A social position at or near the head of government conferred high status. Although specialists—metalworkers, tanners, traders, or the like—generally outranked farmers, the people engaged in these kinds of economic activities were either members of the lower classes or outcasts.[10] Merchants of the past could sometimes buy their way into a higher class. With time, the possession of wealth and the influence it could buy became their own prerequisites for high status, as seen in some contemporary cultures.

How do archaeologists know that different social classes existed in ancient civilizations? As described earlier, laws and other written documents, as well as archaeological features including dwelling size and location, can reflect social stratification. Burial customs also provide evidence of social stratification. Graves excavated at early Neolithic sites consist mostly of simple pits dug in the

◄ The Inca civilization spanned a vast territory and was responsible for monumental structures such as Machu Picchu, located high in the Andes Mountains at an altitude of almost 2,500 meters (nearly 8,000 feet). Generally thought to have been built as the estate for the Inca ruler Pachacuti (1438–1472), the archaeological record indicates Machu Picchu may have been a sacred site as well. By the time of the Spanish conquistadores, the Inca people had abandoned the site, possibly because of a smallpox epidemic that had been brought to the Americas by Europeans.

Aram Bingham

[10]Sjoberg, G. (1960). *The preindustrial city* (p. 325). New York: Free Press.

▲▲▲ Grave goods frequently indicate the status of deceased individuals in stratified societies. For example, China's first emperor was buried with 7,000 life-size terra cotta figures of warriors.

ground. They contained few, if any, **grave goods**—utensils, figurines, and personal possessions, symbolically placed in the grave for the deceased person's use in the afterlife. The uniformity of early Neolithic gravesites indicates essentially classless societies. In contrast, graves excavated in civilizations vary widely in size, mode of burial, and the number and variety of grave goods. This reflects a stratified society, divided into social classes. The graves of important people contain not only various artifacts made from precious materials, but sometimes, as in some early Egyptian burials, the remains of servants evidently killed to serve their master in the afterlife.

Skeletons from the gravesites also provide evidence of stratification. Age at death, nutritional stress during childhood, as well as presence of certain diseases can be determined from skeletal remains. In stratified societies of the past, the dominant groups usually lived longer, ate better, and enjoyed an easier life than lower-ranking members of society, just as they do today.

grave goods Items such as utensils, figurines, and personal possessions, symbolically placed in the grave for the deceased person's use in the afterlife.

hydraulic theory The theory that explains civilization's emergence as the result of the construction of elaborate irrigation systems, the functioning of which required full-time managers whose control blossomed into the first governing body and elite social class; also known as *irrigation theory*.

The Making of States

From Africa to China to the South American Andes, ancient civilizations have created magnificent palaces built high above the ground, sculptures beautifully rendered using techniques that continue into the present, and vast, awe-inspiring engineering projects. These impressive accomplishments could indicate that civilization is better than other cultural forms, particularly when civilizations have come to dominate peoples with other social systems. But domination reflects aggression, size, and power—not cultural superiority. In other words, the emergence of centralized governments, characteristic of civilizations, has allowed some cultures to dominate others and for civilizations to flourish. Anthropologists have proposed several theories to account for the transition from small, egalitarian farming villages to large urban centers in which population density, social inequality, and diversity of labor required a centralized government.

Ecological Theories

Ecological approaches emphasize the role of the environment in the development of states. Among these, the **hydraulic theory**, or *irrigation theory*, holds that civilizations developed when Neolithic peoples realized that the best farming occurred in the fertile soils of river valleys, provided that they could control the periodic flooding.[11] The centralized effort to

[11]Wittfogel, K. A. (1957). *Oriental despotism, a comparative study of total power.* New Haven, CT: Yale University Press.

ANTHROPOLOGY APPLIED

Tell It to the Marines: Teaching Troops about Cultural Heritage

By Jane C. Waldbaum

The need to protect ancient sites, museums, and antiquities in war-torn Iraq and Afghanistan has led the Archaeological Institute of America (AIA) to begin an innovative program to help educate troops soon to be sent to those countries. Conceived by AIA vice president C. Brian Rose, the program sends experienced lecturers to military bases to teach the basics of Middle Eastern archaeology and the importance of protecting the evidence of past cultures. The class, taken by both officers and enlisted men and women, is mandatory.

The effort is a supplement to the AIA's longstanding, nationwide lecture program in which scholars in archaeology and related fields present the latest research and developments to more than 102 local societies in the United States and Canada. The lectures for the troops focus on the areas where military personnel will be deployed and on the specific sites, monuments, museums, and artifacts that they might be called upon to protect.

The current lectures, funded in part by the Packard Humanities Institute, emphasize Mesopotamia's role in the development of writing, schools, libraries, law codes, calendars, and astronomy, as well as connections with familiar biblical figures such as Abraham and Daniel and ancient sites such as Ur and Babylon. Afghanistan's position as a crossroads of ancient civilizations and the route of Alexander the Great through the region is discussed. Troops also learn about basic archaeological techniques, the importance of preserving context, the necessity of working with archaeologists and conservators, and the most effective ways to protect sites against looters.

The first series of lectures was given at the Marine Corps base at Camp Lejeune, North Carolina, and there are plans to expand the program to other bases and services in the near future. "Many of the officers have M.A. degrees; some are reservists and high-school history teachers," says Rose, who delivered the inaugural lectures last spring. "They care a great deal about the history of the areas in which they serve; some of them have actually lived in or near Babylon on earlier tours of duty. All of us have been struck by their thirst for knowledge during and after our lectures."

Many have helped get this program up and running, including U.S. Marine Colonel Matthew Bogdanos, who was instrumental in securing the return of many antiquities stolen from the Iraq Museum. "When it comes to clearing a building, neutralizing a land mine, or making a neighborhood safe for children, we know what to do," says Bogdanos. "When it comes to protecting a country's cultural heritage, we are just as eager to do the right thing—we just don't always know the best way to do it. This is where Brian Rose's groundbreaking program will pay dividends for generations." ∎

Source: Waldbaum, J. C. (2005, Nov/Dec). Tell it to the Marines, *Archaeology Magazine, 58*(6), Reprinted by permission of the publisher.

control the irrigation process blossomed into the first governing body, elite social class, and civilization.

Another theory suggests that in regions of ecological diversity, trade is necessary to procure scarce resources. In Mexico, for example, trade networks distributed chilies grown in the highlands, cotton and beans from intermediate elevations, and salt from the coasts to people throughout the region. Some form of centralized authority developed to organize the procurement and redistribution of these commodities.

A third theory developed by U.S. anthropologist Robert Carneiro suggests that states develop where populations are hemmed in by environmental barriers such as mountains, deserts, seas, or other human populations as an outcome of warfare and conflict in these circumscribed regions.[12] As these populations grow, they have no space in which to expand, and so they begin to compete for increasingly scarce resources. Internally, this may result in the development of social stratification, in which an elite controls important resources to which lower classes have limited access. Externally, this leads to warfare and even conquest, which, to be successful, require elaborate organization under a centralized authority. This chapter's Anthropology Applied feature examines another kind of relationship between archaeology and war as contemporary centralized authorities such as the U.S. military turn to archaeologists in order to protect cultural resources.

---

[12]Carneiro, R. L. (1970). A theory of the origin of the state. *Science* *169*, 733–738.

◀ Although the Ancient Pueblo cultures did not develop sprawling, crowded cities with vast monumental structures, their housing and farming methods both demonstrate remarkable sophistication. They built a series of linked enclaves, with about 100 inhabitants each, into the dramatic cliff faces and farmed the top of the mesa they inhabited by using reservoirs and irrigation channels. They also built shrines within their villages of the sort still used by their descendants in the U.S. Southwest today. Other native North Americans built large cities such as Cahokia, a city with an estimated population of about 30,000 people dating from 650 to 1400, located in southern Illinois. Until 1800, when Philadelphia surpassed it, Cahokia was the largest city in the land that is now the United States. The development of civilization does not make a people better—just better able to dominate.

Amory Ledyard

There are problems with each of these ecological theories. Across the globe and through time, anthropologists find cultures that do not fit these models. For example, some of the earliest large-scale irrigation systems developed in highland New Guinea, where strong centralized governments never emerged. North American Indians possessed trade networks that extended from Labrador in northeastern Canada to the Gulf of Mexico and the Yellowstone region of the Rocky Mountains and even to the Pacific—all without centralized control.[13] And in many of the cultures that do not fit the theories of ecological determinism, neighboring cultures learned to coexist rather than pursuing warfare to the point of complete conquest.

Although few anthropologists would deny the importance of the human–environment relationship, many are dissatisfied with approaches that do not take into account beliefs and values.[14] For example, as described in the case study of Tikal, even though Maya religion had some ties to natural cycles, the beliefs and power relations that developed within that culture were not environmentally determined. Human societies past and present bring their beliefs and values into their interactions with the environment.

Action Theory

Scholars have criticized the above theories because they fail to recognize the capacity of ambitious, charismatic leaders to shape the course of human history. Accordingly, U.S. anthropologists Joyce Marcus and Kent Flannery have developed what they call **action theory**.[15] This theory acknowledges the relationship of society to the environment in shaping social and cultural behavior, but it also recognizes that forceful leaders strive to advance their positions through self-serving actions. In so doing, they may create change.

In the case of Maya history, for example, local leaders, who once relied on personal charisma for the economic and political support needed to sustain them in their positions, may have seized upon religion to solidify their power. Through religion they developed an ideology that endowed them and their descendants with supernatural ancestry and gave them privileged access to the gods, on which their followers depended. In this case, certain individuals could monopolize power and emerge as divine kings, using their power to subjugate any rivals.

The above example demonstrates the importance of the context in which a forceful leader operates. In the case of the Maya, the combination of existing cultural and ecological factors opened the way to the emergence of political dynasties. Thus explanations

---

[13]Haviland, W. A., & Power, M. W. (1994). *The original Vermonters* (2nd ed., chs. 3 & 4). Hanover, NH: University Press of New England.

[14]Adams, R. M. (2001). Scale and complexity in archaic states. *Latin American Antiquity 11*, 188.

[15]Marcus, J., & Flannery, K. V. (1996). *Zapotec civilization: How urban society evolved in Mexico's Oaxaca Valley*. New York: Thames & Hudson.

of civilization's emergence tend to involve multiple causes, rather than just one. Furthermore, we may have the cultural equivalent of what biologists call *convergence*, where similar societies come about in different ways. Consequently, a theory that accounts for the rise of civilization in one place may not account for its rise in another.

Civilization and Its Discontents

Living in the context of civilization ourselves, we are inclined to view its development as a great step up on a so-called ladder of progress. Whatever benefits civilization has brought, these cultural changes have produced new problems. Among them is the challenge of waste disposal and its consequences. In fact, waste disposal probably began to be a difficulty in settled farming communities even before civilizations emerged. But as villages grew into towns and towns grew into cities, the situation became far more serious, as crowded conditions and the buildup of garbage and sewage created optimal environments for infectious diseases such as bubonic plague, typhoid, and cholera. As a result, early cities were disease-ridden places, with relatively high death rates.

Genetic adaptation to disease has influenced the course of history globally. In northern Europeans, for example, the mutation of a gene on chromosome 7 makes carriers resistant to cholera, typhoid, and other bacterial diarrheas.[16] Because of the mortality caused by these diseases, selection favored spread of this allele among northern Europeans. But, as with sickle-cell anemia, protection comes at a price: cystic fibrosis, a usually fatal disease present in people who are homozygous for the altered gene.

Other acute infectious diseases accompanied the rise of towns and cities. In a small population, diseases such as chicken pox, influenza, measles, mumps, pertussis, polio, rubella, and smallpox will kill or immunize so high a proportion of the population that the virus cannot continue to propagate. Measles, for example, tends to die out in any human population with fewer than half a million people.[17] The continued existence of such diseases depends upon the presence of a large population, as found in cities. Survivors possessed immunity to these deadly diseases.

Other conditions unique to cities also promote disease. For example, the bacteria that cause tuberculosis (TB) cannot survive in the presence of sunlight and fresh air. Before industrialization, when people began working and living in dark, crowded urban centers, if an infected individual coughed and released the TB bacteria into the air, sunlight would prevent the spread of infection. TB, like many other sicknesses, can be called a disease of civilization.

Social Stratification and Disease

Civilization affects disease in another powerful way. Social stratification impacts who gets sick as much as any bacterium, past or present. For example, Ashkenazi Jews of eastern Europe were forced into urban ghettos over several centuries, becoming especially vulnerable to the TB thriving in crowded, dark, confined neighborhoods. As with the genetic response to malaria (the sickle-cell allele) and bacterial diarrheas (the cystic fibrosis gene), TB triggered a genetic response in the form of the Tay-Sachs allele, which protects heterozygous individuals from TB.[18]

Unfortunately, homozygotes for the Tay-Sachs allele develop a lethal, degenerative condition that remains common in Ashkenazi Jews. Without the selective pressure of TB, the frequency of the Tay-Sachs allele would never have increased. Similarly, without the strict social rules confining poor Jews to the ghettos (compounded by social and religious rules about marriage), the frequency of the Tay-Sachs allele would never have increased.

Today, not only are poor individuals more likely to become infected with TB, they are also less likely to be able to afford the medicines to treat this disease. For people in poor countries and for disadvantaged people in wealthier countries, TB—like AIDS—can be an incurable, fatal, infectious disease. As a World Health Organization expert has said, "Both TB and HIV thrive on poverty."[19] The poor of the world have borne a higher disease burden since the development of stratified societies characteristic of cities and states.

Colonialism and Disease

Infectious disease played a major role in European colonization of the Americas. When Europeans with immunity to so-called Old World diseases came to the

[16] Ridley, M. (1999). *Genome: The autobiography of a species in 23 chapters* (p. 142). New York: HarperCollins.

[17] Diamond, J. (1997). *Guns, germs, and steel* (p. 203). New York: Norton.

[18] Ridley, p. 191.

[19] Sawert, H. (2002). *TB and poverty in the context of global TB control.* World Health Organization. Satellite Symposium on TB & Poverty, 11–12 October 2002.

▲▲▲

action theory The theory that self-serving action by forceful leaders plays a role in civilization's emergence.

▼▼▼

BIOCULTURAL CONNECTION

Perilous Pigs: The Introduction of Swine-Borne Disease to the Americas

By Charles C. Mann

On May 30, 1539, Hernando de Soto landed his private army near Tampa Bay, in Florida. . . . Half warrior, half venture capitalist, Soto had grown very rich very young by becoming a market leader in the nascent trade for Indian slaves. The profits had helped to fund Pizarro's seizure of the Incan empire, which had made Soto wealthier still. Looking quite literally for new worlds to conquer, he persuaded the Spanish Crown to let him loose in North America. . . . He came to Florida with 200 horses, 600 soldiers, and 300 pigs.

From today's perspective, it is difficult to imagine the ethical system that would justify Soto's actions. For four years his force, looking for gold, wandered through what is now Florida, Georgia, North and South Carolina, Tennessee, Alabama, Mississippi, Arkansas, and Texas, wrecking almost everything it touched. The inhabitants often fought back vigorously, but they had never before encountered an army with horses and guns. . . . Soto's men managed to rape, torture, enslave, and kill countless Indians. But the worst thing the Spaniards did, some researchers say, was entirely without malice—bring the pigs.

According to Charles Hudson, an anthropologist at the University of Georgia, . . . The Spaniards approached a cluster of small cities, each protected by earthen walls, sizeable moats, and deadeye archers. In his usual fashion, Soto brazenly marched in, stole food, and marched out.

After Soto left, no Europeans visited this part of the Mississippi Valley for more than a century. Early in 1682 whites appeared again, this time Frenchmen in canoes. . . . area[s] where Soto had found cities cheek by jowl . . . [were] deserted [without an] Indian village for 200 miles. About fifty settlements existed in this strip of the Mississippi when Soto showed up, according to Anne Ramenofsky, an anthropologist at the University of New Mexico. . . . Soto "had a privileged glimpse" of an Indian world, Hudson says. "The window opened and slammed shut. When the French came in and the record opened up again, it was a transformed reality. A civilization crumbled. The question is, how did this happen?"

The question is even more complex than it may seem. Disaster of this magnitude suggests epidemic disease. In the view of Ramenofsky and Patricia Galloway, an anthropologist at the University of Texas, the source of the contagion was very likely not Soto's army but its ambulatory meat locker: his 300 pigs. Soto's force itself was too small to be an effective biological weapon. Sicknesses like measles and smallpox would have burned through his 600 soldiers long before they reached the Mississippi. But the same would not have held true for the pigs, which multiplied rapidly and were able to transmit their diseases to wildlife in the surrounding forest. When human beings and domesticated animals live close together, they trade microbes with abandon. Over time mutation spawns new diseases: Avian influenza becomes human influenza, bovine rinderpest becomes measles. Unlike Europeans,

Americas for the first time, they brought these devastating diseases with them. Millions of Native Americans—who had never been exposed to influenza, smallpox, typhus, and measles—died as a result. The microbes causing these diseases and the human populations upon which they depend developed in tandem over thousands of years of urban life in Eurasia, and before that in village life with a variety of domesticated animal species. Thus, anyone who survived had acquired immunity in the process. See this chapter's Biocultural Connection for more on the death and disease Europeans brought with them when they colonized the Americas.

Very few diseases traveled back to Europe from the Americas. Instead, these colonizers brought back the riches that they had pillaged and papers that gave them ownership of the lands they had claimed.

Anthropology and Cities of the Future

Not until relatively recent times did public health measures reduce the risk of living in cities, and had it not been for a constant influx of rural peoples, areas of high population density might not have persisted. Europe's urban population, for example, did not become self-sustaining until early in the 20th century.[20]

What led humans to live in such unhealthy places? Most likely, the same things that lure people to cities today attracted our ancestors. Cities are vibrant, exciting

---

[20]Diamond, p. 203.

Indians did not live in close quarters with animals—they domesticated only the dog, the llama, the alpaca, the guinea pig, and, here and there, the turkey and the Muscovy duck. . . . [W]hat scientists call zoonotic disease was little known in the Americas. Swine alone can disseminate anthrax, brucellosis, leptospirosis, taeniasis, trichinosis, and tuberculosis. Pigs breed exuberantly and can transmit diseases to deer and turkeys. Only a few of Soto's pigs would have had to wander off to infect the forest.

Indeed, the calamity wrought by Soto apparently extended across the whole Southeast. The Coosa city-states, in western Georgia, and the Caddoan-speaking civilization, centered on the Texas-Arkansas border, disintegrated soon after Soto appeared. The Caddo had had a taste for monumental architecture: public plazas, ceremonial platforms, mausoleums. After Soto's army left, notes Timothy K. Perttula, an archaeological consultant in Austin, Texas, the Caddo stopped building community centers and began digging community cemeteries. . . . [After] Soto's . . . visit, Perttula believes, the Caddoan population fell from about 200,000 to about 8,500—a drop of nearly 96 percent. . . . "That's one reason whites think of Indians as nomadic hunters," says Russell Thornton, an anthropologist at the University of California at Los Angeles. "Everything else—all the heavily populated urbanized societies—was wiped out."

How could a few pigs truly wreak this much destruction? . . . One reason is that Indians were fresh territory for many plagues, not just one. Smallpox, typhoid, bubonic plague, influenza, mumps, measles, whooping cough—all rained down on the Americas in the century after Columbus. . . .

To Elizabeth Fenn, the smallpox historian, the squabble over numbers obscures a central fact. Whether one million or 10 million or 100 million died, . . . the pall of sorrow that engulfed the hemisphere was immeasurable. Languages, prayers, hopes, habits, and dreams—entire ways of life hissed away like steam. . . . In the long run, Fenn says, the consequential finding is not that many people died but that many people once lived. The Americas were filled with a stunningly diverse assortment of peoples who had knocked about the continents for millennia. "You have to wonder," Fenn says. "What were all those people *up* to in all that time?" ∎

Biocultural Question

Does the history of the decimation of American Indians through infectious disease have any parallels in the contemporary globalized world? Do infectious diseases impact all peoples equally?

Adapted from Mann, C. C. (2005). *1491: New revelations of the Americas before Columbus.* New York: Knopf.

places that provide new opportunities and protection in times of warfare. Of course, people's experience in the cities did not always live up to expectations, particularly for the poor.

In addition to health problems, many early cities faced social problems strikingly similar to those found in cities all over the world today. Dense population and the inequalities of class systems and oppressive centralized governments created internal stress. The poor saw that the wealthy had all the things that they themselves lacked. It was not just a question of luxury items; the poor did not have enough food or space in which to live with comfort, dignity, and health.

In addition to these challenges, abundant archaeological evidence also documents warfare in early civilizations. Cities were fortified. Ancient documents list battles, raids, and wars between groups. Cylinder seals, paintings, and sculptures depict battle scenes, victorious kings, and captured prisoners of war. Increasing population and the accompanying scarcity of fertile farming land often led to boundary disputes and quarrels between civilized states or between so-called tribal peoples and a state. When war broke out, people crowded into walled cities for protection and for access to irrigation systems.

It is discouraging to note that many of the problems associated with the first civilizations are still with us. Waste disposal, pollution-related health problems, crowding, social inequities, and warfare continue to challenge humanity. Through the study of past civilizations, and through comparison of contemporary societies, we now stand a chance of understanding these problems. Such understanding represents a central part of the anthropologist's mission and can contribute to the ability of our species to transcend human-made problems. ✳

Chapter Checklist

When did the first cities and states develop and what were they like?

✔ The world's first cities grew out of Neolithic villages between 4,500 and 6,000 years ago—first in Mesopotamia, then in Egypt and the Indus Valley. In China, the process was underway by 5,000 years ago. Somewhat later, and completely independently, similar changes took place in Mesoamerica and the central Andes.

✔ Four basic cultural changes mark the transition from Neolithic village life to life in civilized urban centers: agricultural innovation, diversification of labor, emergence of centralized government, and social stratification.

✔ Agricultural innovation involved the development of new farming methods, such as irrigation, that increased crop yields. Agricultural innovations brought about other changes such as increased population size.

✔ Diversification of labor occurred as a result of population growth in cities. Some people could provide sufficient food for everyone so that others could devote themselves to specialization as artisans and craftspeople. Specialization led to the development of new technologies and the beginnings of extensive trade systems.

✔ The emergence of a central government provided an authority to deal with the complex problems associated with cities. Monumental public structures and other signs of centralized planning provide evidence of centralized governments. With the invention of writing, governments could keep records of their transactions and/or boast of their own power and glory.

✔ With social stratification, or the emergence of social classes, symbols of status and privilege appeared. Individuals were ranked according to the work they did or the position of their families. Graves, burial customs, grave goods, skeletons, the size of dwellings, and preserved records in writing and in art provide evidence of social stratification.

Why did cities and states develop?

✔ Ecological theories emphasize the interrelation of the actions of ancient peoples with their environment. According to these theories, civilizations developed as centralized governments began to control irrigation systems, trade networks, and/or scarce resources.

Action theory proposes that the actions of forceful, dynamic leaders, promoting their own interests, may play a role in social change.

✔ These theories omit the importance of the beliefs and values of the cultures of the past. Several factors probably acted together to bring about the emergence of cities and states.

What problems beset early cities?

✔ Poor sanitation in early cities, coupled with large numbers of people living in close proximity, created environments in which infectious diseases were rampant.

✔ Early urban centers also faced social problems strikingly similar to those persisting in the world today. Dense population, class systems, and a strong centralized government created internal stress.

✔ Warfare was common; cities were fortified, and armies served to protect the state.

✔ European city-dwellers had already adapted to urban diseases that decimated both urban and rural Indian populations when the European colonial explorers arrived in the Americas.

Questions for Reflection

1. Since the origins of cities and states, humans have engaged in large-scale elaborate warfare. Is warfare an inevitable outcome to this form of social organization?

2. In large-scale societies of the past and present, elite classes have disproportionate access to and control of all resources. Is this social stratification an inevitable consequence of the emergence of cities and states? How can the study of social stratification in the past contribute to the resolution of contemporary issues of social justice?

3. What are some of the ways that differences in social stratification are expressed in your community? Does your community have any traditions surrounding death that serve to restate the social differentiation of individuals? Does your community have traditions that serve to redistribute the wealth so that it is shared more evenly?

4. With today's global communication and economic networks, will it be possible to shift away from social systems involving centralized governments, or is a global, centralized authority inevitable?

5. With many archaeological discoveries there is a value placed on "firsts," such as the earliest writing, the first city, or the earliest government. Given the history of the independent emergence of cities and states throughout the world, do you think that scientists should place more value on these events just because they are older?

Key Terms

civilization
Bronze Age

grave goods
hydraulic theory

action theory

Online Study Resources

Login to **www.cengagebrain.com** to access the resources your instructor has assigned and to purchase materials. For this book, you can access:

CourseMate
Access chapter-specific learning tools including flashcards, glossaries, practice quizzes, videos, and more in your Anthropology CourseMate.

VISUAL ESSENCE

Racism, a doctrine of superiority by which one group justifies the dehumanization of others based on their distinctive physical characteristics, is fueled by the false belief that so-called racial groups are natural and separate divisions within our species. Although visible physical differences reflect some aspects of human diversity, biological evidence demonstrates unequivocally that separate races do not exist. Broadly defined, geographic racial groupings differ from one another in only 7 percent of their genes. Here, Yao Ming, the world-famous basketball star from China, trains at a track in Beijing, along with other athletes. This image shows the variation in height within a single so-called racial category. In his role as a Special Olympics Global Ambassador, Ming devotes much of his time off the courts to inspiring and assisting young Chinese athletes with disabilities. Specific genetic sequences contribute to some of the Special Olympic athlete's disabilities just as they do to Yao Ming's height, or a person's skin tone, or any other physical characteristic, but for every individual, these components are a miniscule fraction of their genetic humanity. Although cultures past and present have created social and political barriers to separate us, gene flow throughout evolutionary history has maintained all of humankind as a single species. The best scientific evidence demonstrates our biological unity.

7 Modern Human Diversity—Race and Racism

from male to female, short to tall, light to dark, we can categorize biological variation in a number of ways, but in the end we are all members of the same species. Minute variations of our DNA give each of us a unique genetic fingerprint, yet this variation remains within the bounds of human genetics. Any visible differences among modern humans exist within the framework of biological features shared throughout the species, and as a species, humans vary. Although the terms *black, white,* and *race* are used in this chapter, they signify purely cultural concepts.

Human genetic variation generally is distributed across the globe in a continuous fashion. From a biological perspective, this variation sometimes follows a pattern imposed by interaction with the environment through the evolutionary process of natural selection. Random genetic drift accounts for the remainder. But the significance we give our biological variation is anything but random because cultures determine the way we perceive variation—in fact, whether we perceive it at all. For example, in many Polynesian cultures, where skin color bears no relationship to social status, people pay little attention to this physical characteristic. By contrast, in countries such as the United States, Brazil, and South Africa, people notice skin color immediately because the range from light to dark is historically associated with the ranking from high to low in the social, economic, and political order. Therefore, the study of biological diversity requires an awareness of the cultural dimensions that shape the questions asked about diversity as well as an understanding of how this knowledge has been used historically.

When European scholars first began their systematic study of human variation in the 18th and 19th centuries, they focused on documenting differences among human groups in order to divide them hierarchically into progressively "better" types of humans. Today, this hierarchical approach has been appropriately abandoned. Before exploring how we study contemporary biological variation today, let's examine the effects of social ideas about race and racial hierarchy on the interpretation of biological variation, past and present.

In this chapter you will learn to:

- **Describe the history of human classification.**

- **State how the biological concept of race cannot be applied to humans.**

- **Recognize the conflation of biological race into cultural race in theories that attempt to link race to behavior and intelligence.**

- **Discuss physical anthropological approaches to the study of human biological variation.**

- **Describe the role of adaptation in human variation in skin color.**

- **Examine the interaction between biological and cultural components of the human adaptive complex.**

The History of Human Classification

Early European scholars tried to systematically classify *Homo sapiens* into subspecies, or races, based on geographic location and phenotypic features such as skin color, body size, head shape, and hair texture. The 18th-century Swedish naturalist Carolus Linnaeus (recall him from Chapter 2) originally divided humans into subspecies based on geographic location and classified all Europeans as white, Africans as black, American Indians as red, and Asians as yellow.

The German physician Johann Blumenbach (1752–1840) introduced some significant and insidious changes to this four-race scheme in the 1795 edition of his book *On the Natural Variety of Mankind*. Most notably, this book formally introduced a hierarchy of human types. Blumenbach considered the skull of a woman from the Caucasus Mountain range (located between the Black and the Caspian seas of southeastern Europe and southwestern Asia) the most beautiful in his collection. More symmetrical than the others, he saw it as a reflection of nature's ideal form: the circle. Surely, Blumenbach reasoned, this "perfect" specimen resembled God's original creation. Moreover, he thought that the living inhabitants of the Caucasus region were the most beautiful in the world. Based on these criteria, he concluded that this high mountain range, that included lands mentioned in the Bible, was the place of human origins.

Blumenbach argued that all light-skinned peoples in Europe and adjacent parts of western Asia and northern Africa belonged to the same race. On this basis, he dropped the "European" race label and replaced it with "Caucasian." Although he continued to distinguish American Indians as a separate race, he regrouped dark-skinned Africans as Ethiopian and split those Asians not considered Caucasian into two separate races: Mongolian (referring to most inhabitants of Asia, including China and Japan) and Malay (indigenous Australians, Pacific Islanders, and others).

Convinced that Caucasians were closest to the original ideal humans supposedly created in God's image, Blumenbach ranked them as superior. The other races, he argued, were the result of "degeneration"; by moving away from their place of origin and adapting to different environments and climates, they had degenerated physically and morally into what many Europeans came to think of as inferior races.[1]

We now clearly recognize the factual errors and ethnocentric prejudices embedded in Blumenbach's work, as well as others, with respect to the concept of race. Political leaders have used this notion of superior and inferior races to justify brutalities ranging from repression to slavery to mass murder to genocide. The tragic story of Ota Benga, a Twa Pygmy man who in the early 1900s was caged in a New York zoo with an orangutan, painfully illustrates the disastrous impact of this dogma.

---

[1]Gould, S. J. (1994). The geometer of race. *Discover 15* (11), 65–69.

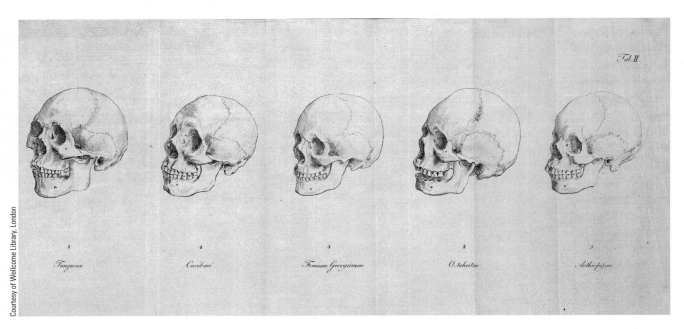

Courtesy of Wellcome Library, London

▲▲▲ Johann Blumenbach ordered humans into a hierarchical series with Caucasians (his own group) ranked the highest and created in God's image. He suggested that the variation seen in other races was a result of "degeneration" or movement away from this ideal type. The five types he identified from left to right are: Mongolian, American Indian, Caucasian, Malay, and Ethiopian. This view is both racist and an oversimplification of the expression of human variation in the skeleton. Although people from one part of the world might be more likely to possess a particular nuance of skull shape, every population exhibits significant variation. Humans do not exist as discrete types.

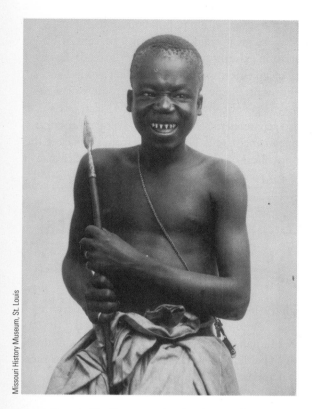

▲▲▲ Here is Ota Benga posing for the camera when he was part of the African exhibit at the St. Louis World's Fair in 1904. Several years later he was put on display at the Bronx Zoo in the monkey house.

Captured in a raid in Congo, Ota Benga came into the possession of a North American businessman Samuel Verner, who was looking for exotic "savages" for exhibition in the United States. In 1904, Ota and a group of fellow Twa were shipped across the Atlantic and exhibited at the World's Fair in St. Louis, Missouri. About 23 years old at the time, Ota was 4 feet 11 inches in height and weighed 103 pounds. Throngs of visitors came to see displays of dozens of indigenous peoples from around the globe, shown in their traditional dress and living in replica villages doing their customary activities. The fair was a success for the organizers, and all the Twa Pygmies survived to be shipped back to their homeland. Verner also returned to Congo and with Ota's help collected artifacts that he intended to sell to the American Museum of Natural History in New York City.

In the summer of 1906, Ota came back to the United States with Verner, who soon went bankrupt and lost his entire collection. Left stranded in the big city, Ota was placed in the care of the museum and then taken to the Bronx Zoo and exhibited in the monkey house, with an orangutan as company. Ota's sharpened teeth (a cultural practice among his own people) were seen as evidence of his supposedly cannibal nature. After intensive protest, zoo officials released Ota from his cage and let him roam free in the park during the day, where teasing visitors often harassed him. Ota (usually referred to as a "boy") was then turned over to an orphanage for African American children. In 1916, upon hearing that he would never

return to his homeland, he took a revolver and shot himself through the heart.[2]

The racist display at the Bronx Zoo a century ago was by no means unique. Ota's tragic life was the manifestation of a powerful ideology in which one small part of humanity sought to demonstrate and justify its claims of biological and cultural superiority. Indeed, such false notions have resulted in the oppression and genocide of millions of humans because of the color of their skin or the shape of their skull.

This ideology had particular resonance in North America, where people of European descent colonized lands originally inhabited by Native Americans and then went on to exploit African slaves and (later) Asians imported as a source of cheap labor. According to U.S. anthropologist Audrey Smedley, the earliest settlers who came over from England had already refined this dehumanizing ideology in their dealings with the Irish, whom they imported as slaves and indentured servants.[3] Indeed, in Bacon's Rebellion, an uprising in colonial Virginia in 1676, Irish and African slaves fought side by side (ironically, to drive out American Indians). Only later did North American slavery become the exclusive burden of Africans.

Although the Emancipation Proclamation officially ended slavery in 1863, dismantling its pseudo-scientific foundations took much longer, and some argue that these false notions continue today. In the early 20th century, scholars began to challenge the concept of racial hierarchies. Among the strongest critics was Franz Boas (1858–1942), a Jewish scientist who immigrated to the United States to avoid rising antisemitism in his German homeland and who became a founder of North America's four-field anthropology. As president of the American Association for the Advancement of Science, Boas criticized false claims of racial superiority in an important speech titled "Race Problems in America," published in the prestigious journal *Science* in 1909.[4] Boas's scholarship in both cultural and biological anthropology contributed to the depth of his critique.

Ashley Montagu (1905–1999), a student of Boas and one of the best-known anthropologists of his time, devoted much of his career to combating scientific racism. Born Israel Ehrenberg to a working-class Jewish family in England, he also felt the sting of antisemitism. After changing his name in the 1920s, he immigrated to the United States, where he went on to fight racism in his writing and in academic and public lectures. Of all his works, none is more important than his book *Man's Most Dangerous Myth: The Fallacy of Race*. Published in 1942, it took the lead in debunking the "social myth" of clearly

[2]Bradford, P. V., & Blume, H. (1992). *Ota Benga: The Pygmy in the zoo.* New York: St. Martin's Press.

[3]Smedley, A. (1998). *Race in North America: Origin and evolution of a worldview.* Boulder, CO: Westview Press.

[4]Boas, F. (1909, May 28). Race problems in America. *Science 29* (752), 839–849.

bounded races. The book is now in its sixth edition, published in 1998.[5] Montagu's once controversial ideas have now become mainstream, and his text remains one of the most comprehensive treatments of its subject.

Race as a Biological Concept

To understand why the racial approach to human variation has been so unproductive and even damaging, we must first understand the race concept in strictly biological terms. Biologists define **race** as a subspecies, or a population of a species differing geographically, morphologically, or genetically from other populations of the same species.

As simple and straightforward as such a definition may seem, there are three very important aspects to note about it. First, the definition is arbitrary; no scientific criteria exist on how many differences are required to constitute a race. For example, if one researcher emphasizes skin color while another emphasizes blood group differences, the researchers will not classify people in the same way.

Second, this biological definition of race does not mean that any one race has exclusive possession of any particular variant of a gene. In human terms, the frequency of a trait like the type O blood group, for example, may be high in one population and low in another, but it is present in both. In other words, populations are genetically *open*, meaning that genes flow between them. The only reproductive barriers that exist for humans are the cultural rules some societies impose regarding appropriate mates. As President Obama's family illustrates (Luo father from western Kenya and Anglo-American mother born in Kansas, who became an anthropologist as we see in Chapter 11's Anthropology Applied), these social barriers change as cultures change.

Third, the biological definition of race does not apply to humans because the differences among individuals *within* a so-called racial population are greater than the differences *among* separate populations. U.S. evolutionary biologist Richard Lewontin demonstrated this through genetic analyses in the 1970s. He compared the amount

of genetic variation within populations and among so-called racial groups, finding a mere 7 percent of human variation existing among groups.[6] Instead, the vast majority of genetic variation exists *within* groups. As the science writer James Shreeve puts it, "most of what separates me genetically from a typical African or Eskimo also separates me from another average American of European ancestry."[7] This follows from the fact of the genetic openness of races; no one race has an exclusive claim to any particular form of a gene or trait.

The Conflation of the Biological into the Cultural Category of Race

Although the biological race concept does not pertain to human variation, race is a significant cultural category. Human groups frequently insert a false notion of biological difference into the cultural category of race to make it appear more factual and objective. In various ways, cultures define religious, linguistic, and ethnic groups as races, thereby confusing linguistic and cultural traits with physical traits.

For example, people in many Latin American countries classify one another as Indian, Mestizo (mixed), or Ladino (of Spanish descent). But despite the biological connotations of these terms, random cultural criteria define these categories—such as whether individuals wear shoes, sandals, or go barefoot; whether they speak Spanish or an Indian language; and whether they live in a thatched hut or a European-style house. By speaking Spanish, wearing Western-style clothes, and living in a house in a non-Indian neighborhood, Indian people shed their indigenous identity and acquire a national identity as citizens of the country.

Similarly, the ever-changing racial categories used by the U.S. Census Bureau both reflect and reinforce the conflation of the biological with the cultural. The 2010 list includes large catchall political groupings such as white and black as well as specific tribal affiliations of American Indians or Alaskan Natives, a designation that comes much closer to a population in the biological sense. The Census Bureau asks people to identify Hispanic ethnicity, independent of the category of race, but considers Arabs and Christians of Middle Eastern ancestry as white (Caucasian) despite the political relevance of their ancestry. The observation that the purported race of an individual

▲▲▲ **Fingerprint patterns of loops, whorls, and arches are genetically determined. Grouping people on this basis would place most Europeans, sub-Saharan Africans, and East Asians together as "loops." Australian Aborigines and the people of Mongolia would be together as "whorls." The Bushmen of southern African would be grouped as "arches."**

[5]Montagu, A. (1998) *Man's most dangerous myth: The fallacy of race* (6th ed.). Lanham, MD: Rowman & Littlefield.

[6]Lewontin, R. C. (1972). The apportionment of human diversity. In T. Dobzhansky et al. (Eds.), *Evolutionary biology* (pp. 381–398). New York: Plenum Press.

[7]Shreeve, J. (1994). Terms of estrangement. *Discover 15* (11), 60.

can vary over the course of his or her lifetime speaks to the fact that cultural forces shape the designation of membership in a particular racial category.[8]

The Census Bureau gathers health statistics by so-called racial categories for the purposes of correcting health disparities among social groups. Unfortunately, the false biological concept of race gets inferred in these analyses. As a result, the increased risk of dying from a heart attack for African Americans compared to whites is falsely attributed to biological differences rather than to health-care disparities or other social factors.

Similarly, medical genetics research is regularly over-simplified to fit into the comparisons among the racial types defined in the 18th and 19th centuries. Whether this genetic research will avoid the trap of recreating false genetic types that do not reflect the true nature of human variation remains to be seen. The recent claims made for race-specific drugs and vaccines based on lim-ited scientific data indicate that the social category of race may again be interfering with our understanding of the true nature of human genetic diversity.

Against a backdrop of prejudice, the conflation of the social with the biological has historically provided "scientific" justification for excluding whole categories of people from certain roles or positions in society. For example, in colonial North America, a racial world-view assigned American Indians and Africans imported as slaves to perpetual low status. A supposed biological inferiority was used to justify this subordinate ranking, whereas access to privilege, power, and wealth was reserved for favored groups of European descent.[9] The more subtle forms of discrimination that exist today demand extreme vigilance when notions of biolog-ical difference enter into discussions of race and health.

Because of the colonial association of lighter skin with greater power and higher social status, people whose history includes domination by lighter-skinned Europeans have sometimes valued this phenotype. In Haiti, for example, the "color question" has been the dominant force in social and political life. Skin texture, facial features, hair color, and socioeconomic class collectively influence the ranking. According to Haitian anthropologist Michel-Rolph Trouillot, "a rich black becomes a mulatto, a poor mulatto becomes black."[10]

The Nazis in Germany elevated a racialized worldview to state policy with particularly evil consequences. The

[8]Hahn, R. A. (1992). The state of federal health statistics on racial and ethnic groups. *Journal of the American Medical Association 267* (2), 268–271.

[9]American Anthropological Association. (1998, May 17). State-ment on "race." http://www.aaanet.org/stmts/racepp.htm (retrieved August 29, 2011).

[10]Trouillot, M. R. (1996). Culture, color, and politics in Haiti. In S. Gregory & R. Sanjek (Eds.), *Race*. New Brunswick, NJ: Rutgers University Press.

▲▲▲ In colonial Mexico, sixteen different *castas* ("castes") were named, giving specific labels to individuals who were of various combinations of Spanish, Indian, and African ances-try. These paintings of *castas* are traditionally arranged from light to dark as a series and reflect an effort to impose hierar-chy despite the fluid social system in place. Especially in the southeastern United States the hierarchy was more rigid; the "one drop rule," also known as *hypodescent*, would ascribe the "lower" position to individuals if they had even one drop of blood from a "lower" grouping within the hierarchy.

Nuremberg race laws of 1935 codified prevailing beliefs: the superiority of the Aryan race and the inferiority of the Gypsy and Jewish races. The Nazi doctrine justified, on supposed biological grounds, their policy of extermination. In all, 11 million people (Jews, Gypsies, homosexuals, and other so-called inferior peoples, as well as political oppo-nents of the Nazi regime) were deliberately put to death.

Tragically, human history contains many atrocities on the scale of the Nazi Holocaust (from the Greek word for

▲▲▲▲▲▲▲▲▲▲▲▲▲▲▲▲▲▲▲▲▲▲▲▲▲▲▲▲▲▲▲▲▲▲▲▲▲

race In biology, the taxonomic category of subspecies that is not applicable to humans because the division of humans into discrete types does not represent the true nature of human biological vari-ation. In some societies, race is an important social category.

▼▼▼▼▼▼▼▼▼▼▼▼▼▼▼▼▼▼▼▼▼▼▼▼▼▼▼▼▼▼▼▼▼▼▼▼▼▼▼

"wholly burnt" or "sacrificed by fire"). Such *genocides*—programs of extermination of one group by another—have a long history predating World War II and continuing today. Recent and ongoing genocide in parts of South America, Africa, Europe, and Asia, like previous genocides, are accompanied by dehumanizing rhetoric that depicts those being exterminated as somehow less human.

The Social Significance of Race: Racism

Scientific facts, unfortunately, have been slow to change what people think about race. **Racism,** a doctrine of superiority by which one group justifies the dehumanization of others based on their distinctive physical characteristics, persists as a major political problem. Indeed, politicians have often exploited this concept as a means of mobilizing support, demonizing opponents, and eliminating rivals. Racial conflicts result from social stereotypes, not scientific facts.

Race and Behavior

The assumption that behavioral differences exist among human races remains an issue to which many people still cling tenaciously. Throughout history, certain characteristics have been attributed to groups of people under a variety of names—national character, spirit, temperament—all of them vague and representative of concepts unrelated to any biological phenomena. Common myths involve the coldness of Scandinavians or the rudeness of Americans or the fierceness of the Yanomami Indians. Such unjust characterizations rely upon a false notion of biological difference.

To date, no inborn behavioral characteristic can be attributed to any group of people (which the nonscientist might call a "race") that cannot be explained in terms of cultural practices. If the Chinese happen to exhibit exceptional visual-spatial skills, it is probably because the business of learning to read Chinese characters requires a kind of visual-spatial learning not required by mastery of Western alphabets.[11] Similarly, the almost complete absence of non-whites from honors and awards in the sport of golf (until Tiger Woods) had everything to do with the social rules of country clubs and the sport's expense.[12] All such differences or characteristics can be explained in terms of culture.

In the same vein, high crime rates, alcoholism, and drug use among certain groups can be understood with reference to culture rather than biology. Individuals alienated and demoralized by poverty, injustice, and unequal opportunity tend to abandon the traditional paths to success of the dominant culture because these paths are blocked. In a racialized society, poverty and all its ill consequences affect some groups of people much more severely than others. Slowly, some of this systemic racism, a form of *structural violence*—a concept discussed in detail in Chapter 16—is becoming rectified. For example, in 2010 the U.S. Congress passed the Fair Sentencing Act, legislation aimed at redressing many years of harsher penalties associated with crack cocaine use; crack is primarily associated with African Americans, as compared to the more expensive, equally potent powdered form of cocaine more often associated with white drug users. Before this legislation, the typical white user would have had to possess 100 times the amount of powdered cocaine to receive the same prison sentence as his or her African American crack-using counterpart.[13]

Race and Intelligence

Scholars and laypeople alike, unfamiliar with the fallacy of biological race in humans, have asked whether some races are inherently more intelligent than others. To address this issue we first must clarify the term *intelligence*. Unfortunately, deciding what abilities or talents actually make up what we call intelligence remains contentious. Some psychologists insist that it is a single quantifiable thing measured by IQ tests. Many more psychologists consider intelligence to be the product of the interaction of different sorts of cognitive abilities: verbal, mathematical-logical, spatial, linguistic, musical, bodily kinesthetic, social, and personal.[14] Each of these kinds of intelligence seems unrelated to the others in that individuals possess unique combinations of strengths in each of these areas. Just as humans independently inherit height, blood type, skin color, and so forth, it seems likely that to the degree that intelligence is heritable, each of these kinds of intelligence would be inherited independently.

Furthermore, scholars have shown the limits of IQ tests as a fully valid measure of inborn intelligence. An IQ test measures *performance* (something that one does) rather than *genetic disposition* (something that the

---

[11]Chan, J. W. C., & Vernon, P. E. (1988). Individual differences among the peoples of China. In J. W. Berry (Ed.), *Human abilities in cultural context* (pp. 340–357). Cambridge, UK: Cambridge University Press.

[12]Before Tiger Woods came Charles Sifford (b. 1922), the first African American to win honors in golf. Sifford did so at a time when desegregating the sport meant being subjected to threats and racial abuse. In 2004, the World Golf Hall of Fame inducted him as their first African American member.

[13]King, J. (n.d.). Reducing the crack and powder cocaine sentencing disparity should also reduce racial disparities in sentences and prisons. *NACDL news release.* http://www.nacdl.org/public.nsf/NewsReleases/2010mn23?OpenDocument (retrieved September 9, 2011).

[14]Jacoby, R., & Glauberman, N. (Eds.). (1995). *The Bell Curve debate* (pp. 7, 55–56, 59). New York: Random House.

individual was born with). Performance reflects past experiences and present motivational state, as well as innate ability.

Despite these limits, for at least a century some researchers have used IQ tests to try to prove the existence of significant differences in intelligence among human populations. In the United States systematic comparisons of intelligence between so-called whites and blacks began in the early 20th century and were frequently combined with data gathered by physical anthropologists about skull shape and size.

During World War I, for example, a series of IQ tests, known as Alpha and Beta, were regularly given to draftees. The results showed that, on average, Euramericans attained higher scores compared to African Americans. Even though African Americans from the urban northern states scored higher than Euramericans from the rural South, and some African Americans scored higher than most Euramericans, many people took this as proof of the intellectual superiority of white people. But all that the tests really showed was that, on average, whites outperformed blacks in the social situation of IQ testing. The tests did not measure intelligence per se, but the ability, conditioned by culture, of certain individuals to respond appropriately to certain questions conceived by Americans of European descent for comparable middle-class whites. These tests frequently require knowledge of white middle-class values and linguistic behavior.

For such reasons, intelligence tests continue to be the subject of controversy. Many psychologists as well as anthropologists have shown that the tests have only limited application in particular cultural circumstances.

---

[15]Sanday, P. R. (1975). On the causes of IQ differences between groups and implications for social policy. In M. F. A. Montagu (Ed.), *Race and IQ* (pp. 232–238). New York: Oxford University Press.

In turn, holding cultural and environmental factors constant results in African and European Americans scoring equally well.[15]

Nevertheless, some researchers still argue that there are significant differences in intelligence among human populations. Richard Herrnstein, a psychologist, and Charles Murray, a political scientist and longtime fellow of the American Enterprise Institute, a conservative think tank, are among these researchers. In a lengthy (and highly publicized) book entitled *The Bell Curve*, they argue for immutable genetic origins for the difference in IQ scores among Americans of African, Asian, and European descent.

Scholars have criticized Herrnstein and Murray's book on many grounds, including violation of basic rules of statistics and their practice of utilizing studies, no matter how flawed, that appear to support their thesis while ignoring or barely mentioning those that contradict it. In addition, the basic laws of heredity also discredit their argument. As Mendel discovered with his pea plants back in the late 19th century, genes are inherited independently of one another. Whatever the alleles that may be associated with intelligence, they bear no relationship to the ones for skin pigmentation or to any other aspect of human variation such as blood type.

Further, the expression of genes always occurs in an environment, and among humans, culture shapes all aspects of that environment. In the following Original Study, U.S. physical anthropologist Jonathan Marks extends the discussion of race and intelligence to stereotypes about athletic abilities of different so-called races.

▲▲

racism A doctrine of superiority by which one group justifies the dehumanization of others based on their distinctive physical characteristics.

▼▼

ORIGINAL STUDY

A Feckless Quest for the Basketball Gene

By Jonathan Marks

You know what they say about a little knowledge. Here's some: The greatest sprinters and basketball players are predominantly black. Here's some more: Nobel laureates in science are predominantly white.

What do we conclude? That blacks have natural running ability, and whites have natural science ability? Or perhaps

that blacks have natural running ability, but whites don't have natural science ability, because that would be politically incorrect?

Or perhaps that we can draw no valid conclusions about the racial distribution of abilities on the basis of data like these.

That is what modern anthropology would say.

But it's not what a new book, *Taboo: Why Black Athletes Dominate Sports and Why We're Afraid to Talk about It,* says. It says that blacks dominate sports because of their genes and that we're afraid to talk about it on account of a cabal of high-ranking politically correct postmodern

CONTINUED

professors—myself, I am flattered to observe, among them.

The book is a piece of good old-fashioned American anti-intellectualism (those dang perfessers!) that plays to vulgar beliefs about group differences of the sort we recall from *The Bell Curve* (1994). These are not, however, issues that anthropologists are "afraid to talk about"; we talk about them a lot. The author, journalist and former television producer Jon Entine, simply doesn't like what we're saying. But to approach the subject with any degree of rigor, as anthropologists have been trying to do for nearly a century, requires recognizing that it consists of several related questions.

First, how can we infer a genetic basis for differences among people? The answer: Collect genetic data. There's no substitute. We could document consistent differences in physical features, acts, and accomplishments until the Second Coming and be entirely wrong in thinking they're genetically based. A thousand Nigerian Ibos and a thousand Danes will consistently be found to differ in complexion, language, and head shape. The first is genetic, the second isn't, and the third we simply don't understand.

What's clear is that, developmentally, the body is sufficiently plastic that subtle differences in the conditions of growth and life can affect it profoundly. Simple observation of difference is thus not a genetic argument.

Which brings us to the second question: How can we accept a genetic basis for athletic ability and reject it for intelligence? The answer: We can't. Both conclusions are based on the same standard of evidence. If we accept that blacks are genetically endowed jumpers because "they" jump so well, we are obliged to accept that they are genetically unendowed at schoolwork because "they" do so poorly.

In either case, we are faced with the scientifically impossible task of drawing conclusions from a mass of poorly controlled data. Controls are crucial in science: If every black schoolboy in America knows he's supposed to be good at basketball and bad at algebra, and we have no way to measure schoolboys outside the boundaries of such an expectation, how can we gauge their "natural" endowments? Lots of things go into the observation of excellence or failure, only one of which is genetic endowment.

But obviously humans differ. Thus, the last question: What's the relationship between patterns of human genetic variation and groups of people? The answer: It's complex.

All populations are heterogeneous and are built in some sense in opposition to other groups. Jew or Muslim, Hutu or Tutsi, Serb or Bosnian, Irish or English, Harvard or Yale—one thing we're certain of is that the groups of most significance to us don't correspond to much in nature.

Consider, then, the category "black athlete"—and let's limit ourselves to men here. It's broad enough to encompass Arthur Ashe, Mike Tyson, and Kobe Bryant.

When you read about the body of the black male athlete, whose body do you imagine? Whatever physical gift these men share is not immediately apparent from looking at them.

Black men of highly diverse builds enter athletics and excel.

Far more don't excel. In other words, there is a lot more to being black and to being a prominent athlete than mere biology. If professional excellence or overrepresentation could be regarded as evidence for genetic superiority, there would be strong implications for Jewish comedy genes and Irish policeman genes.

Inferring a group's excellence from the achievements of some members hangs on a crucial asymmetry: To accomplish something means that you had the ability to do it, but the failure to do it doesn't mean you didn't have the ability. And the existing genetic data testify that known DNA variations do not respect the boundaries of human groups.

To be an elite athlete, or elite anybody, presumably does require some kind of genetic gift. But those gifts must be immensely diverse, distributed broadly across the people of the world—at least to judge from the way that the erosion of social barriers consistently permits talent to manifest itself in different groups of people.

In an interview with *The Philadelphia Daily News* in February, Mr. Entine observed that Jews are overrepresented among critics of the views he espouses. But is that a significantly Jewish thing? Or is it simply a consequence of the fact that among any group of American intellectuals you'll find Jews overrepresented because they are a well-educated minority? There's certainly no shortage of non-Jews who find the ideas in "Taboo" to be demagogic quackery.

Of course, Jewish academics may sometimes be speaking as academics, not as Jews. Likewise black athletes may perform as athletes, not just as embodied blackness.

How easy it is to subvert Michael Jordan, the exceptional and extraordinary man, into merely the representative of the black athlete.

The problem with talking about the innate superiority of the black athlete is that it is make-believe genetics applied to naïvely conceptualized groups of people. It places a spotlight on imaginary natural differences that properly belongs on real social differences.

More important, it undermines the achievements of individuals as individuals. Whatever gifts we each have are far more likely, from what we know of genetics, to be unique individual constellations of genes than to be expressions of group endowments. ■

From Marks, J. (2000, April 8). A feckless quest for the basketball gene. *New York Times.* Copyright © 2000 by the New York Times Co. Reprinted by permission.

Separating genetic components of intelligence (or any other continuous trait) from environmental contributors poses enormous problems.[16] Most studies of intelligence rely on comparisons between identical twins, genetically identical individuals raised in the same or different environments. A host of problems plague twin studies: inadequate sample sizes, biased subjective judgments, failure to make sure that "separated" twins really were raised separately, unrepresentative samples of adoptees to serve as controls, untested assumptions about similarity of environments. In fact, children reared by the same mother resemble her in IQ to the same

---

[16]Andrews, L. B., & Nelkin, D. (1996). The bell curve: A statement. *Science 271,* 13.

SOUTHERN WHITES ARE THE NEGROES' BEST FRIENDS BUT NO INTEGRATION

© Bettmann/Corbis

◄ Any discussion of race and behavior or intelligence in the United States must include the history of slavery and legal segregation in the South, as well as other forms of structural violence that favored the white race at the expense of minorities. These social, political, and historical facts influence race relations in the United States today far more than minute genetic differences.

degree, whether or not they share her genes.[17] Clearly, the degree to which intelligence is inherited through genes is far from understood.[18]

Undoubtedly, the social environment contributes substantially to intelligence. This should not surprise us, as environmental factors influence other genetically determined traits. Height in humans, for example, has a genetic basis, but it also depends upon both nutrition and health status (severe illness in childhood arrests growth, and renewed growth never makes up for this loss). Moreover, scientists have not yet teased apart the exact relative contributions of genetic and environmental factors on either the height or the intelligence of an individual.

Research on the importance of the environment in the expression of intelligence further exposes the problems with generalizations about IQ and race. For example, IQ scores of all groups in the United States, as in most industrial and postindustrial countries, have risen some 15 points since World War II. In addition, the gap between Americans of African and European descent has narrowed in recent decades. Other studies show impressive IQ scores for African American children from socially deprived and economically disadvantaged backgrounds who have been adopted into highly edu-

cated and prosperous families. Studies have shown that underprivileged children adopted into such privileged homes can boost their IQs by 20 points. Also, IQ scores rise in proportion to the test-takers' amount of schooling.

More such cases could be cited, but these suffice to make the point and lead to three conclusions. First, there is a bias in IQ testing based on social class. Second, the assertion that IQ is biologically fixed and immutable is clearly false. Third, ranking human beings with respect to their intelligence scores in terms of racial difference is doubly false.

Over the past 2.5 million years, all populations of the genus *Homo* have adapted primarily through culture—actively inventing solutions to the problems of existence rather than relying only on biological adaptation. Thus we would expect a comparable degree of intelligence in all present-day human populations. The only way to be sure that individual human beings develop their innate abilities and skills to the fullest is to ensure that they have access to the necessary resources and the opportunities to do so.

Studying Human Biological Diversity

Considering the problems, confusion, and horrendous consequences, anthropologists have abandoned the race concept as being of no utility in understanding human biological variation. Instead, they have found it more

[17]Lewontin, R. C., Rose, S., & Kamin, L. J. (1984). *Not in our genes* (pp. 100, 113, 116). New York: Pantheon.

[18]Lewontin, Rose, & Kamin, pp. 9, 121.

productive to study *clines* (see Chapter 2), the distribution and significance of single, specific, genetically based characteristics and continuous traits related to adaptation. In fact, skin color—the trait that has been used so often to separate people into groups—provides an excellent example of the role of natural selection in shaping human variation.

Skin Color: A Case Study in Adaptation

Several key factors impact variation in skin color: the transparency or thickness of the skin; a copper-colored pigment called carotene; reflected color from the blood vessels (responsible for the rosy color of lightly pigmented people); and, most significantly, the amount of melanin (from *melas*, a Greek word meaning "black")—a dark pigment in the skin's outer layer. People with dark skin have more melanin-producing cells than those with light skin, but everyone (except those with albinism) has a measure of melanin. Exposure to sunlight increases melanin production, causing skin color to deepen.

Melanin protects skin against damaging ultraviolet solar radiation, conferring less susceptibility to skin cancer and sunburn on darker-sakinned peoples compared to those with less melanin.[19] Dark skin also helps to protect certain vitamins that would be destroyed under intense exposure to sunlight. Because the highest concentrations of dark-skinned people tend to be found in the tropical regions of the world, it appears that natural selection has favored heavily pigmented skin as a protection against exposure where ultraviolet radiation is most constant.[20] High altitude also increases exposure to damaging ultraviolet radiation such that pigmented skin is also favored in this environment.

The inheritance of skin color involves several genes (rather than variants of a single gene), each with several alleles, thus creating a continuous range of expression for this trait. In addition, the geographic distribution of skin color tends to be continuous (▶ **Figure 7.1** and **Figure 7.2**). In northern latitudes, light skin has an adaptive advantage related to the skin's important biological function as the manufacturer of vitamin D through a chemical reaction dependent upon sunlight. Vitamin D maintains the balance of calcium in the body. In northern climates with little sunshine, light skin allows enough sunlight to penetrate the skin and stimulate the formation of vitamin D, essential for healthy bones and balance in the nervous system. Dark pigmentation interferes with this process in environments where sunlight is limited.

Cultural practices can help alleviate the severe consequences of vitamin D deficiency. Until fairly recently, parents in northern Europe and northern North America fed their children a spoonful of cod liver oil, rich in vitamin D, during the dark winter months. Today, pasteurized milk is often fortified with vitamin D.

Given what we know about the adaptive significance of human skin color and the fact that, until 800,000 years

ago, members of the genus *Homo* were exclusively creatures of the tropics, lightly pigmented skin is likely a recent development in human history. Conversely, and consistent with humanity's African origins, darkly pigmented skin is probably quite ancient. The enzyme tyrosinase, which converts the amino acid tyrosine into the compound that forms melanin, is present in lightly pigmented people in sufficient quantity to make them very "black." But this does not occur because lighter-skinned people also have genes that inactivate or inhibit the enzyme.[21]

Human skin, liberally endowed with sweat glands and lacking heavy body hair compared to other primates, effectively eliminates excess body heat in a hot climate. This would have been especially advantageous to our ancestors on the savannah, who could have avoided confrontations with large carnivorous animals by carrying out most of their activities in the heat of the day. For the most part, tropical predators rest during this period, hunting primarily from dusk until early morning. Without much hair to cover their bodies, selection would have favored dark skin in our human ancestors. In short, based on available scientific evidence, all humans appear to have a black ancestry, no matter how white some of them may appear to be today.

One should not conclude that, because it is newer, lightly pigmented skin is better or more highly evolved than heavily pigmented skin. Darker skin better suits the conditions of life in the tropics or at high altitudes, although with cultural adaptations like protective clothing, hats, and sunscreen lotions lightly pigmented people can survive in these climates. Conversely, the availability of supplementary sources of vitamin D allows more heavily pigmented people to do well far away from the tropics. In both cases, culture has rendered skin color differences largely irrelevant from a purely biological perspective. With time and effort, skin color may eventually lose its social significance as well.

Culture and Biological Diversity

Although cultural adaptation has reduced the importance of biological adaptation and physical variation, cultural forces do impose their own selective pressures. For example, take the reproductive fitness of individuals with diabetes—a disease with a known genetic predisposition. Ready medication in North America and Europe makes people with diabetes as biologically fit as anyone else. However, without access to the needed medication, a situation that is all too common globally, diabetes results in death. In fact, one's financial status affects one's access to medication, and so, however unintentional it may be, financial status determines biological fitness.

---

[19]Neer, R. M. (1975). The evolutionary significance of vitamin D, skin pigment, and ultraviolet light. *American Journal of Physical Anthropology 43*, 409–416.

[20]Branda, R. F., & Eatoil, J. W. (1978). Skin color and photolysis: An evolutionary hypothesis. *Science 201*, 625–626.

[21]Wills, C. (1994). The skin we're in. *Discover 15* (11), 79.

BIOCULTURAL CONNECTION

Beans, Enzymes, and Adaptation to Malaria

Some human adaptations to the deadly malarial parasite are biological while others are strictly tied to cultural practices such as local cuisine. The phenotype of the sickle-cell allele, for example, manifests specifically in red blood cells. Biological and dietary adaptations to malaria converge with the interaction between one form of the glucose-6-phosphate-dehydrogenase (G-6-PD) enzyme and fava bean consumption.

The fava bean is a broad flat bean (*Vivia faba*) that is a dietary staple in malaria-endemic areas along the Mediterranean coast. G-6-PD is an enzyme that serves to reduce one sugar, glucose-6-phosphate, to another sugar—in the process releasing an energy-rich molecule. The malaria parasite lives in red blood cells off of energy produced via G-6-PD. Individuals with a mutation in the G-6-PD gene, so-called G-6-PD deficiency, produce energy by an alternate pathway not involving this enzyme that the parasite cannot use. Furthermore, G-6-PD-deficient red blood cells seem to turn over more quickly, thus allowing less time for the parasite to grow and multiply. While a different form of G-6-PD deficiency is also found in some sub-Saharan African populations, the form found in Mediterranean populations is at odds with an adaptation embedded in the cuisine of the region.

Enzymes naturally occurring in fava beans also contain substances that interfere with the development of the malarial parasite. In cultures around the Mediterranean Sea, where malaria is common, fava beans are incorporated into the diet through foods eaten at the height of the malaria season. However, if an individual with G-6-PD deficiency eats fava beans, the result is that the substances toxic to the parasite become toxic to humans. With G-6-PD deficiency, fava bean consumption leads to *hemolytic crisis* (Latin for "breaking of red blood cells") and a series of chemical reactions that release free radicals and hydrogen peroxide into the bloodstream. This condition is known as *favism*.

The toxic effect of fava bean consumption in G-6-PD individuals has prompted a rich folklore around this simple food, including the ancient Greek belief that fava beans contain the souls of the dead. The link between favism and G-6-PD deficiency has led parents of children with this condition to limit consumption of this favorite dietary staple.

Unfortunately, apprehension about the fava bean has sometimes led to a generalized fear about many excellent sources of protein such as peanuts, lentils, chickpeas, soy beans, and nuts. Another biocultural connection is again at the root of this unnecessary deprivation. The Arabic name for fava beans is *foul* (pronounced "fool"), while the soy beans are called *foul-al-Soya,* and peanuts are *foul-al-Soudani*; in other words, the plants are linked linguistically even though they are unrelated biologically.[a]

An environmental stressor as potent as malaria has led to a number of human adaptations. In the case of fava beans and G-6-PD deficiency, these adaptations can work at cross-purposes. Cultural knowledge of the biochemistry of these interactions will allow humans to adapt, regardless of their genotype. ∎

Biocultural Question

How does what you have learned from this chapter about the falsehood of the biological category of race relate to the way the varied adaptations to malaria, described here, work against one another?

[a]Babiker, M. A., et al. (1996). Unnecessary deprivation of common food items in glucose-6-phosphate dehydrogenase deficiency. *Annals of Saudi Arabia 16* (4), 462–463.

© Charles O. Cecil/Alamy

▲▲▲ Fava beans, a dietary staple in the countries around the Mediterranean Sea, also provide some protection against malaria. However, in individuals with G-6-PD deficiency, the protective aspects of fava beans turn deadly. This dual role has led to a rich folklore surrounding fava beans.

In view of the consequences for human biology of such seemingly benign innovations as dairying or farming, we may wonder about many recent practices—for example, the effects of increased exposure to radiation from use of x-rays, nuclear accidents, production of radioactive wastes, ozone depletion (which increases human exposure to solar radiation), and the like. In addition to exposure to radiation, humans also face increased exposure to other known mutagenic agents, including a wide variety of chemicals.

Hormone-disrupting chemicals raise serious concerns because they interfere with the reproductive process. For example, in 1938 the synthetic estrogen DES (diethylstilbestrol) was developed and subsequently prescribed for a variety of ailments ranging from acne to prostate cancer. Moreover, DES was routinely added to animal feed. Then, in 1971 researchers realized that DES causes vaginal cancer in young women. Subsequent studies have also shown that DES causes problems with the male reproductive system and can produce deformities of the female reproductive tract of individuals exposed to DES in utero. DES mimics the natural hormone, binding with appropriate receptors in and on cells, and thereby turns on biological activity associated with the hormone.[25]

DES is not the only danger. Scientists have identified at least fifty-one chemicals—many of them in common use—that disrupt hormones, and even this could be the tip of the iceberg. Some of these chemicals mimic estrogens in the manner of DES, while others interfere with other parts of the endocrine system, such as thyroid and testosterone metabolism. The list includes such supposedly benign and inert substances as plastics widely used in laboratories and chemicals added to polystyrene and polyvinyl chloride (PVCs) to make them more stable and less breakable. These plastics are widely used in plumbing, food processing, and food packaging.

In addition, many detergents and personal care products, contraceptive creams, the giant jugs used to bottle drinking water, and plastic linings in cans contain hormone-disrupting chemicals. Plastics line about 85 percent of food cans in the United States. Similarly, after years of plastics use in microwave ovens, we now know the deleterious health consequences of the release of compounds from plastic wrap and plastic containers during microwaving. Most concerning is bisphenol A (BPA)—a chemical widely used in the manufacturing of water bottles and baby bottles (hard plastics). Researchers have documented an association between BPA and higher rates of chronic diseases such as heart disease and diabetes. It also disrupts a variety of other reproductive and metabolic processes. Infants and fetuses are at the greatest risk from exposure to BPA.[26]

Consensus in the scientific community has led governments to start taking action (the Canadian government declared BPA a toxic compound). However, removing the compound from the food industry may be easier that ridding the environment of the contaminant. For decades billions of pounds of BPA have been produced each year, and in turn it has been dumped into landfills and into bodies of water. As with the Neolithic revolution and the development of civilization, each invention creates new challenges for humans.

The implications of these developments are sobering. We know that pathologies result from extremely low levels of exposure to harmful chemicals. Besides those used domestically, the United States exports millions of pounds of these chemicals to the rest of the world.[27] Hormone disruptions may be at least partially responsible for certain trends that now concern scientists. These range from increasingly early onset of puberty in human females to dramatic declines in human sperm counts. With respect to the latter, some sixty-one separate studies confirm that sperm counts dropped almost 50 percent from 1938 to 1990. More recent studies confirm these results.[28] Most of these studies were carried out in the United States and Europe, but some from Africa, Asia, and South America show that it is a worldwide phenomenon. If the trend continues, it will have profound results.

One of the difficulties with predicting trends is that serious health consequences of new cultural practices are often not apparent until years or even decades later. By then, of course, these practices are fully embedded in the cultural system, and huge financial interests are at stake. Think, for example, of how the human dependence on fossil fuels has jeopardized the health of the world's oceans, as demonstrated by the 2010 British Petroleum disaster in the Gulf of Mexico.

More than ever in our history, today's cultural practices impact human gene pools. The long-term effects on the human species as a whole remain to be seen. Poor people and people of color disproportionately bear these burdens, demonstrating that racism and classism still exert their negative effects globally. ✳

[25]Colburn, T., Dumanoski, D., & Myers, J. P. (1996). Hormonal sabotage. *Natural History 3*, 45–46.

[26]Lang, I. A., et al. (2008). Association of urinary bisphenol A concentration with medical disorders and laboratory abnormalities in adults. *Journal of the American Medical Association 300* (11), 1303–1310; vom Saal, F. S., & Myers, J. P. (2008). Bisphenol A and risk of metabolic disorders. *Journal of the American Medical Association 300* (11), 1353–1355; Richter, C. A., et al. (2007). In vivo effects of bisphenol A in laboratory rodent studies. *Reproductive Toxicology 24* (2), 199–224.

[27]Colburn, Dumanoski, & Myers, p. 47.

[28]Merzenich, H., Zeeb, H., & Blettner, M. (2010). Decreasing sperm quality: A global problem? *BMC Public Health*. doi: 10.1186/1471-2458-10-24 (retrieved September 11, 2011).

Chapter Checklist

What is the history of human classification?

✔ Scientists of the past placed humans into discrete races and then ordered them hierarchically. This work was dismantled and discredited beginning in the early 20th century with the work of anthropologist Franz Boas and his student Ashley Montagu.

✔ Despite scientific evidence demonstrating no biological races, folk beliefs about different biological types of human beings persist.

Does the biological concept of race apply to human variation?

✔ Humans are a single, highly variable species inhabiting the entire globe. Though biological processes are responsible for human variation, the biological concept of race or subspecies cannot be applied to human diversity. No discrete racial types exist.

✔ Individual traits appear in continuous gradations (clines) from one population to another without sharp breaks. Traits are inherited independently, and populations are genetically open.

✔ The vast majority of human variation exists within populations rather than between populations.

How does the race concept function within cultures?

✔ In many countries such as the United States, Haiti, Brazil, and South Africa, the sociopolitical category of race contributes significantly to social identity and opportunity.

✔ Racial conflicts result from social stereotypes and not scientific facts.

✔ Racists of the past and present frequently invoke the notion of biological difference to support unjust social practices.

✔ Behavioral characteristics attributed to race can be explained in terms of experience as well as a hierarchical social order affecting the opportunities and challenges faced by different groups of people, rather than biology.

What are the flaws with studies that attempt to link race and intelligence?

✔ These studies imply a biological basis for variations and do not take into account that biological race does not exist.

✔ The inherited components of intelligence cannot be separated from those that are culturally acquired.

✔ There is still no consensus on what intelligence really is, but it is generally agreed that intelligence is made up of several different talents and abilities.

✔ The cultural and environmental specificity of IQ testing makes it invalid for broad comparisons.

Why does human skin color vary across the globe?

✔ Subject to tremendous variation, skin color is a function of several factors: transparency or thickness of the skin, distribution of blood vessels, and amount of carotene and melanin in the skin.

✔ Exposure to sunlight increases the amount of melanin, darkening the skin.

✔ Natural selection has favored heavily pigmented skin as protection against the strong solar radiation of equatorial latitudes.

✔ In northern latitudes, natural selection has favored relatively depigmented skin, which can utilize relatively weak solar radiation in the production of vitamin D.

✔ Cultural factors such as selective mating, as well as geographic location, play a part in skin color distribution globally.

How have human cultures shaped human biology?

✔ Cultural practices shape human environments, which in turn can act on gene pools.

✔ Peoples with a dairying tradition possess the ability to digest milk sugars (lactose) into adulthood.

✔ Foods and activity patterns are a complete adaptive package.

✔ In populations with dietary traditions of "slow release" foods and high activity, the incidence of obesity and diabetes skyrockets when these groups assume Western-style diets characterized by abundant foods that are high in sugar content.

✔ Hormone-disrupting chemicals used in plastics and other industries interfere with reproductive and metabolic processes and are associated with higher rates of chronic disease.

✔ The serious health consequences of new cultural practices are often not apparent until decades later. By then, these practices are fully embedded in the cultural system.

Questions for Reflection

1. As a species, humans are extremely diverse, and yet our biological diversity cannot be partitioned into discrete types, subspecies, or races. At the same time, race functions as a social and political category that imposes inequality in some societies. How have cultural beliefs about race affected the interpretation of biological diversity in the past? What are the cultural beliefs about biological diversity in your community today?

2. While we can see and scientifically explain population differences in skin color, why is it invalid to use the biological concept of subspecies or race when referring to humans? Can you imagine another species of animal, plant, or microorganism for which the subspecies concept makes sense?

3. Globally, health statistics are gathered by country. In addition, some countries such as the United States gather health statistics by race. How are these two endeavors different and similar? Should statisticians gather health statistics by grouping?

4. How do you define the concept of intelligence? Do you think scientists will ever be able to discover the genetic basis of intelligence?

5. Cultural practices affect microevolutionary changes in the human species and often have dramatic effects on human health. Do you see examples of structural violence in your community that make some individuals more vulnerable to disease than others? Do you see examples globally?

Key Terms

race
racism

thrifty genotype
lactose

lactase

Online Study Resources

Login to **www.cengagebrain.com** to access the resources your instructor has assigned and to purchase materials. For this book, you can access:

CourseMate
Access chapter-specific learning tools including flashcards, glossaries, practice quizzes, videos, and more in your Anthropology CourseMate.

VISUAL ESSENCE

Each culture is distinct, expressing its unique qualities in numerous ways—by the clothes we wear, the way we speak, what we eat, where we find our food, when we rest, and with whom we live. Although culture goes far beyond what meets the eye, it is inscribed everywhere we look. Here we see a Uyghur family eating together on carpets woven with traditional Uyghur designs. The Uyghur, a Turkic-speaking Muslim ethnic minority in China, live in the country's northwestern province of Xinjiang. Politically dominated by China's Han ethnic majority, who comprise 90 percent of the population, Uyghurs are proud of their cultural identity and hold onto their traditional heritage. In public spaces, most are easily recognized by their distinctive dress, even from a distance. The fabrics, forms, designs, and colors of their clothes, rugs, and other objects mark the social identity of the group. Such particular and shared presentation of the self as a member of a community is one of many features of culture.

8 The Characteristics of Culture

An introductory anthropology course presents what may seem like endless variety of human societies, each with its own distinctive way of life, manners, beliefs, arts, and so on. Yet for all this diversity, these societies have one thing in common: Each is a group of human beings cooperating to ensure their collective survival and well-being.

Group living and cooperation are impossible unless individuals know how others are likely to behave in any given situation. Thus some degree of predictable behavior is required of each person within the society. In humans, it is culture that sets the limits of behavior and guides it along predictable paths that are generally acceptable to those who fall within the culture. The culturally specified ways in which we learn to act so that we conform to the social expectations in our community did not develop randomly. Among the major forces guiding how each culture has developed in its own distinctive way is a process known as adaptation.

In this chapter you will learn to:

- **Explain culture as a dynamic form of adaptation.**

- **Distinguish between culture, society, and ethnicity.**

- **Identify basic characteristics common to all cultures.**

- **Describe the connections among culture, society, and the individual.**

- **Define and question ethnocentrism.**

Culture and Adaptation

From generation to generation, humans, like all animals, have continually faced the challenge of adapting to their environment, its conditions and its resources, as well as to changes over time. As discussed in Chapter 2, the term *adaptation* refers to a gradual process by which organisms adjust to the conditions of the locality in which they live. Organisms have generally adapted biologically as the frequency of advantageous anatomical and physiological features increases in a population through the process of natural selection. For example, body hair protects mammals from extremes of temperature, specialized teeth help them to procure the kinds of food they need, and so on. Short-term physiological responses to the environment—along with responses that become incorporated into an organism through interaction with the environment during growth and development—are other kinds of biological adaptations.

BIOCULTURAL CONNECTION

Pig Lovers and Pig Haters

By Marvin Harris

In the Old Testament of the Bible, the Israelite's God (Yahweh) denounced the pig as an unclean beast that pollutes if tasted or touched. Later, Allah conveyed the same basic message to his prophet Muhammad. Among millions of Jews and Muslims today, the pig remains an abomination, even though it can convert grains and tubers into high-grade fats and protein more efficiently than any other animal.

What prompted condemnation of an animal whose meat is relished by the greater part of humanity? For centuries, the most popular explanation was that the pig wallows in its own urine and eats excrement. But linking this to religious abhorrence leads to inconsistencies. Cows kept in a confined space also splash about in their own urine and feces.

These inconsistencies were recognized in the 12th century by Maimonides, a widely respected Jewish philosopher and physician in Egypt, who said God condemned swine as a public health measure because pork had "a bad and damaging effect upon the body." The mid-1800s discovery that eating undercooked pork caused trichinosis appeared to verify Maimonides's reasoning. Reform-minded Jews then renounced the taboo, convinced that if well-cooked pork did not endanger public health, eating it would not offend God. But others held to it.

Scholars have suggested this taboo stems from the idea that the animal was once considered divine—but this explanation falls short since sheep, goats, and cows were also once worshiped in the Middle East, and their meat is enjoyed by all religious groups in the region.

I think the real explanation lies in the fact that pig farming threatened the integrity of the basic cultural and natural ecosystems of the Middle East. Until their conquest of the Jordan Valley in Palestine over 3,000 years ago, the Israelites were nomadic herders, living almost entirely from sheep, goats, and cattle. Like all pastoralists, they maintained close relationships with sedentary farmers who held the oases and the great rivers. With this mixed farming and pastoral complex, the pork prohibition constituted a sound ecological strategy. The pastoralists could not raise pigs in their arid habitats, and among the semi-sedentary farming populations pigs were more of a threat than an asset.

Humans, however, have increasingly come to depend on cultural adaptation, a complex of ideas, technologies, and activities that enables them to survive and even thrive in their environment. Biology has not provided people with built-in fur coats to protect them in cold climates, but it has given us the ability to make our own coats, build fires, and construct shelters to shield ourselves against the cold. We may not be able to run as fast as a cheetah, but we are able to invent and build vehicles that can carry us faster and farther than any other creature. Through culture and its many constructions, the human species has secured not just its survival but its expansion as well—at great cost to other species and, increasingly, to the planet at large. And by manipulating environments through cultural means, people have been able to move into a vast range of environments, from the icy Arctic to the searing Sahara Desert.

This is not to say that everything human beings do is *because* it is adaptive to a particular environment. For one thing, people do not just react to an environment as given; rather, people react to it as they perceive it, and different groups of people may perceive the same environment in radically different ways. People also react to things other than the environment: their own biological natures, their beliefs and attitudes, and the short- and long-term consequences of their behavior for themselves and other people and life forms that share their habitats. (See the Biocultural Connection feature for a particular cultural adaptation.)

Although people maintain cultures to deal with problems, some cultural practices have proved to be maladaptive and have actually created new problems—such as toxic water and air caused by certain industrial practices or North America's obesity epidemic spurred on by the mass production of cars, fast food, television, and computers.

A further complication is the relativity of any particular adaptation: What is adaptive in one context may be seriously maladaptive in another. For example, the hygiene practices of food-foraging peoples—their toilet habits and methods of garbage disposal—are appropriate to contexts of low population densities and some degree of residential mobility. But, as discussed in Chapter 5, these same practices become serious health hazards in the context of large, fully sedentary populations.

Similarly, behavior that is adaptive in the short run may be maladaptive over a longer period of time. For

The basic reason for this is that the world zones of pastoral nomadism correspond to unforested plains and hills that are too arid for rainfall agriculture and that cannot easily be irrigated. The domestic animals best adapted to these zones are ruminants (including cattle, sheep, and goats), which can digest grass, leaves, and other cellulose foods more effectively than other mammals.

The pig, however, is primarily a creature of forests and shaded riverbanks. Although it is omnivorous, its best weight gain is from foods low in cellulose (nuts, fruits, tubers, and especially grains), making it a direct competitor of man. It cannot subsist on grass alone and is ill-adapted to the hot, dry climate of the grasslands, mountains, and deserts in the Middle East. . . .

Among the ancient mixed farming and pastoralist communities of the Middle East, domestic animals were valued primarily as sources of milk, cheese, hides, dung, fiber, and traction for plowing. Goats, sheep, and cattle provided all of this, plus an occasional supplement of lean meat. From the beginning, therefore, pork must have been a luxury food, esteemed for its succulent, tender, and fatty qualities.

Between 4,000 and 9,000 years ago, the human population in the Middle East increased sixty-fold. Extensive deforestation accompanied this rise, largely due to damage caused by sheep and goat herds. Shade and water, the natural conditions appropriate for raising pigs, became ever more scarce, and pork became even more of a tempting luxury. . . . People find it difficult to resist such temptations on their own. Hence Yahweh and Allah were heard to say that swine were unclean—unfit to eat or touch.

In short, in the Middle East it was ecologically maladaptive . . . to raise pigs in substantial numbers, and small-scale production would only increase the temptation. Better then, to prohibit the consumption of pork entirely. ■

Biocultural Question
Consider a taboo you follow and come up with an explanation for it other than the conventional one that most people accept.

Adapted from Harris, M. (1989). *Cows, pigs, wars, and witches: The riddles of culture* (pp. 35–60). New York: Vintage/Random House.

---

instance, the development of irrigation in ancient Mesopotamia (southern Iraq) made it possible for people to increase food production, but it also caused a gradual accumulation of salt in the soil, which contributed to the downfall of that civilization about 4,000 years ago.

Today, in many parts of the world, the development of prime farmland for purposes other than food production increases dependency on food raised in less than optimal environments. Marginal farmlands can produce high yield with costly technology. However, over time these yields will not be sustainable due to loss of topsoil, increasing salinity of soil, and silting of irrigation works, not to mention the high cost of fresh water and fossil fuel.

All told, for a culture to be successful, it must produce collective human behavior that is generally adaptive to the natural environment. Successful adaptation has been, and continues to be, a major challenge facing every society in its quest for survival, from generation to generation. In response to this challenge, our species has developed a great variety of cultures, each with its own unique features befitting the particular needs of societies located in different corners of the globe. So, what do we mean by culture?

The Concept of Culture

Anthropologists conceived the modern concept of culture toward the end of the 19th century. The first comprehensive definition came from the British anthropologist Sir Edward Tylor. Writing in 1871, he defined culture as "that complex whole which includes knowledge, belief, art, law, morals, custom, and any other capabilities and habits acquired by man as a member of society."[1]

▲▲

cultural adaptation A complex of ideas, activities, and technologies that enable people to survive and even thrive in their environment.

▼▼

[1]Tylor, E. B. (1871). *Primitive culture: Researches into the development of mythology, philosophy, religion, language, art and customs* (p. 1). London: Murray.

▲▲▲ What is adaptive at one time may not be at another. In the Central Plains of North America, irrigation systems and chemical fertilizers have resulted in large but unsustainable crop yields in a principal region of grain cultivation. Here we see crop fields in western Kansas that are watered by a center-pivot irrigation system fed by the Ogallala aquifer. The aquifer, which underlies eight states from southern South Dakota to northwestern Texas, provides about 30 percent of the nation's groundwater used for irrigation, plus drinking water to 82 percent of the people who live within the aquifer boundary. However, over the past five decades, the aquifer's water table has dropped dramatically, and some experts estimate it will dry up in as little as twenty-five years. Moreover, in semi-arid regions steady winds hasten evaporation of surface water. This leads to a buildup of salts in the soil, eventually resulting in toxic levels for plants. Chemical fertilizers also contribute to the pollution problem.

Recent definitions tend to distinguish more clearly between actual behavior and the abstract ideas, values, and perceptions of the world that inform that behavior. To put it another way, **culture** goes deeper than observable behavior; it is a society's shared and socially transmitted ideas, values, and perceptions that are used to make sense of experience and generate behavior and are reflected in that behavior.

Characteristics of Culture

Through the comparative study of many human cultures, past and present, anthropologists have gained an understanding of the basic characteristics evident in all

▲▲▲▲▲▲▲▲▲▲▲▲▲▲▲▲▲▲▲▲▲▲▲▲▲▲▲▲▲▲▲▲▲▲▲▲▲▲

culture A society's shared and socially transmitted ideas, values, and perceptions that are used to make sense of experience and generate behavior and are reflected in that behavior.

enculturation The process by which a society's culture is passed on from one generation to the next and individuals become members of their society.

▽▽▽▽▽▽▽▽▽▽▽▽▽▽▽▽▽▽▽▽▽▽▽▽▽▽▽▽▽▽▽▽▽▽▽▽▽▽

of them: Every culture is socially learned, shared, based on symbols, integrated, and dynamic. A careful study of these characteristics helps us to see the importance and the function of culture itself.

Culture Is Learned

All culture is socially learned rather than biologically inherited. One learns one's own culture by growing up with it, and the process by which culture is passed on from one generation to the next is called **enculturation**.

Most animals eat and drink whenever the urge arises. Humans, however, are enculturated to do most of their eating and drinking at certain culturally prescribed times and feel hungry as those times approach. These eating times vary from culture to culture, as does what is eaten, how it is prepared, how it is consumed, and where. To add complexity, food is used to do more than merely satisfy nutritional requirements. When used to celebrate rituals and religious activities, food "establishes relationships of give and take, of cooperation, of sharing, of an emotional bond that is universal."[2]

Through enculturation every person learns socially appropriate ways of satisfying the basic biologically determined needs of all humans: food, sleep, shelter, companionship, self-defense, and sexual gratification. It is important to distinguish between the needs themselves, which are not learned, and the learned ways in which they are satisfied—for each culture determines in its own way how these needs will be met. For instance, a French Canadian fisherman's ideas of a great dinner and a comfortable way to sleep may vary greatly from those of a nomadic cattle herder in East Africa.

Learned behavior is exhibited to some degree by most, if not all, mammals. Several species may even be said to have elementary culture, in that local populations share patterns of behavior that, as among humans, each generation learns from the one before and that differ from one population to another. For example, research shows a distinctive pattern of behavior among lions of southern Africa's Kalahari Desert—behavior that fostered nonaggressive interaction with the region's indigenous hunters and gatherers and that each generation of lions passed on to the next.[3] Moreover, Kalahari lion behavior changed over a thirty-year period in response to new circumstances. That said, it is important to note that

not all learned behavior is cultural. For instance, a pigeon may learn tricks, but this behavior is reflexive, the result of conditioning by repeated training, not the product of enculturation.

Beyond our species, examples of socially learned behavior are particularly evident among other primates. A chimpanzee, for example, will take a twig, strip it of all leaves, and smooth it down to fashion a tool for extracting termites from their nest. Such tool making, which juveniles learn from their elders, is unquestionably a rudimentary form of cultural behavior once thought to be exclusively human. In Japan, macaque monkeys have learned the advantages of washing sweet potatoes before eating them and teach the next generation the same practice.

Within any given primate species, one population's way of life often differs from that of others, just as it does among humans. We have discovered both in captivity and in free nature that primates in general and apes in particular "possess a near-human intelligence generally, including the use of sounds in representational ways, a rich awareness of the aims and objectives of others, the ability to engage in tactical deception, and the ability to use symbols in communication with humans and each other."[4]

Our increasing awareness of such traits in our primate relatives has spawned numerous movements to extend some fundamental human rights to apes—rights such as freedom from living in fear, respect for dignity, and not being subjected to incarceration (caging), exploitation (medical experimentation), or other mistreatment. The movement reached a milestone in 2008 when Spain's parliament approved a resolution committing the country to the "Declaration on Great Apes," applying some human rights to gorillas, chimpanzees, bonobos, and orangutans.[5]

---

[2]Caroulis, J. (1996). Food for thought. *Pennsylvania Gazette 95* (3), 16.

[3]Thomas, E. M. (1994). *The tribe of the tiger: Cats and their culture* (pp. 109–186). New York: Simon & Schuster.

[4]Reynolds, V. (1994). Primates in the field, primates in the lab. *Anthropology Today 10* (2), 4.

[5]O'Carroll, E. (2008, June 27). Spain to grant some human rights to apes. *Christian Science Monitor*.

◀
◀
◀ Culture is passed on from one generation to the next. Here we see Meregeta Zewde Tadesi teaching his son the art of writing a prayer book in their village on the outskirts of Lalibela, one of Ethiopia's holiest cities. The village and town are located in northern Ethiopia's Amhara region, which is populated mostly by Ethiopian Orthodox Christians. Lalibela's population of about 15,000 includes more than 1,000 priests, deacons, and monks. Tadesi trained as a scribe in the ancient city of Gondar, a center of religious learning about 200 kilometers (125 miles) from their home.

© Sean Sprague/The Image Works

Culture Is Shared

As a shared set of ideas, values, perceptions, and standards of behavior, culture is the common denominator that makes the actions of individuals intelligible to other members of their society. Culture enables members of a group to predict how other individuals are most likely to behave in a given circumstance, and it tells them how to react accordingly. **Society** may be defined as an organized group or groups of interdependent people who generally share a common territory, language, and culture and who act together for collective survival and well-being. The ways in which these people depend upon one another can be seen in features such as their economic, communication, and defense systems. They are also bound together by a general sense of common identity.

Because culture and society are such closely related concepts, anthropologists study both. Obviously, there can be no culture without a society. Conversely, there are no known human societies that do not exhibit culture. This cannot be said for all other animal species. Ants and bees, for example, instinctively cooperate in a manner that clearly indicates a remarkable degree of social organization, yet this instinctual behavior is not a culture.

Although members of a society share a culture, it is important to realize that all is not uniform. For one thing, no two people share the exact same version of their culture. And there are other variations. At the very least, there is some difference between the roles of men and women. This stems from the fact that women give birth and men do not and that there are obvious differences between male and female reproductive anatomy and physiology. Every society gives cultural meaning to biological sex differences by explaining them in a particular way and specifying what their significance is in terms of social roles and expected patterns of behavior.

Because each culture does this in its own way, there can be tremendous variation from one society to another. Anthropologists use the term **gender** to refer to the cultural elaborations and meanings assigned to the biological differentiation between the sexes. So, although one's *sex* is biologically determined, one's *gender* is socially constructed within the context of one's particular culture.

Apart from sexual differences directly related to reproduction, biological underpinnings for contrasting gender roles have largely disappeared in modern industrialized and postindustrial societies. For example, men and women are equally capable of accomplishing tasks requiring muscular strength, such as moving heavy automobile engines, because assembly lines use hydraulic lifts for the job. Nevertheless, all cultures exhibit at least some

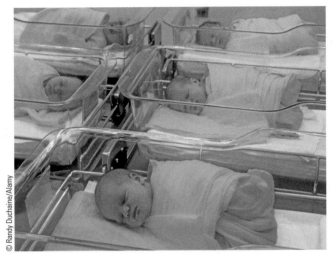

© Randy Duchaine/Alamy

▲▲▲ In U.S. hospital nurseries, newborn girls are wrapped in pink blankets and boys in blue blankets. This is in response to popular expectations in the United States and many other countries that newborn infants be assigned a gender identity of either male or female. Yet significant numbers of infants are born each year whose genitalia do not conform to cultural expectations. Because only two genders are recognized, the usual reaction is to make the young bodies conform to cultural requirements through gender assignment surgery that involves constructing male or female genitalia. This is in contrast to many Native American cultures (among others), which have traditionally recognized more than two genders.[6]

role differentiation related to biology—some far more so than others.

In addition to cultural variation associated with gender, there is also variation related to age. In any society, children are not expected to behave as adults, and the reverse is equally true. But then, who is a child and who is an adult? Again, although age differences are "natural," cultures give their own meaning and timetable to the human life cycle.

SUBCULTURES: GROUPS WITHIN A LARGER SOCIETY

Besides gender and age differentiation, there may be cultural variation between subgroups in societies that share an overarching culture. These may be occupational groups in societies where there is a complex division of labor, or social classes in a stratified society, or ethnic groups in other societies. When such groups exist within a society—each functioning by its own distinctive set of ideas, values, and behavior patterns while still sharing some common standards—we call them **subcultures**.

---

[6]For statistics on this, see Blackless, M., et al. (2000). How sexually dimorphic are we? Review and synthesis. *American Journal of Human Biology 12*, 151–166.

◀◀
◀ The Amish people have held onto their traditional agrarian way of life in the midst of industrialized North American society. Their strong community spirit—reinforced by close social ties between family and neighbors, common language, traditional customs, and shared religious beliefs that set them apart from non-Amish people—is also expressed in a traditional barn raising, a large collective construction project.

Amish communities are an example of a subculture in North America. Specifically, the Amish are an **ethnic group**—people who collectively and publicly identify themselves as a distinct group based on cultural features such as shared ancestry and common origin, language, customs, and traditional beliefs. The Amish originated in western Europe during the Protestant revolutions of the 16th century. Today, members of this group number about 100,000 and live mainly in the United States—in Pennsylvania, Ohio, Illinois, and Indiana—as well as in Ontario, Canada.

These rural pacifists base their lives on their traditional Anabaptist beliefs, which hold that only adult baptism is valid and that "true Christians" (as they define them) should not hold government office, bear arms, or use force. They prohibit marriage outside their faith, which calls for obedience to radical Christian teachings, including social separation from what they see as the wider "evil world" and rejection of material wealth as "vainglorious."

Among themselves they usually speak a German dialect known as Pennsylvania Dutch (from *Deutsch,* meaning "German"). They use formal German for religious purposes, although children learn English in school. Valuing simplicity, hard work, and a high degree of neighborly cooperation, the Amish dress in a distinctive plain garb and even today rely on the horse for transportation as well as agricultural work.[7] In sum, the Amish share the same **ethnicity**. This term, rooted in the Greek word *ethnikos*

("nation") and related to *ethnos* ("custom"), is the expression of the set of cultural ideas held by an ethnic group.

The goal of Amish education is to teach youngsters reading, writing, and arithmetic, as well as Amish values. Adults in the community reject what they regard as "worldly" knowledge and the idea of schools producing good citizens for the state. Resisting all attempts to force their children to attend regular public schools, they insist that education take place near home and that teachers be committed to Amish ideals.

Amish nonconformity to mainstream culture has frequently resulted in conflict with state authorities, as well as legal and personal harassment from people outside their communities. Pressed to compromise, they have introduced "vocational training" beyond the middle school

▲▲▲

society An organized group or groups of interdependent people who generally share a common territory, language, and culture and who act together for collective survival and well-being.

gender The cultural elaborations and meanings assigned to the biological differentiation between the sexes.

subculture A distinctive set of ideas, values, and behavior patterns by which a group within a larger society operates, while still sharing common standards with that larger society.

ethnic group People who collectively and publicly identify themselves as a distinct group based on cultural features such as common origin, language, customs, and traditional beliefs.

ethnicity A term rooted in the Greek word *ethnikos* ("nation") and related to *ethnos* ("custom") that is the expression of the set of cultural ideas held by an ethnic group.

[7]Hostetler, J., & Huntington, G. (1971). *Children in Amish society.* New York: Holt, Rinehart & Winston.

▼▼▼

or junior high school level to fulfill state requirements, but they have managed to retain control of their schools and to maintain their way of life.

Confronted with economic challenges that make it impossible for most to subsist solely on farming, some Amish work outside their communities. Many more have established cottage industries and actively market home-made goods to tourists and other outsiders. Yet, while their economic separation from mainstream society has declined somewhat, their cultural separation has not.[8] They remain a reclusive community, more distrustful than ever of the dominant North American culture surrounding them and mingling as little as possible with non-Amish people.

The Amish are but one example of the way a sub-culture may develop and be dealt with by the larger society within which it functions. Different as they are, the Amish actually put into practice many values that other North Americans respect in the abstract: thrift, hard work, independence, a close family life. The degree of tolerance accorded to them, in contrast to some other ethnic groups, is also due to the fact that the Amish are white Europeans; they are viewed as being of the same race as those who historically comprise dominant mainstream society. As we discussed in Chapter 7, the concept of race has no scientific biological validity when applied to humans, yet it persists as a powerful social classification. This can be seen in the spatial organization of many U.S. cities in which certain neighborhoods are predominantly Asian, black, white, or Hispanic. This organizational pattern conforms to the racial categories long imposed by U.S. government bureaucracies, which officially reinforce and culturally reproduce a historical race-based ideology in U.S. society.

Implicit in our discussion thus far is that subcultures may develop in different ways. On the one hand, Amish subculture in the United States developed gradually in response to how these members of a strict evangelical Protestant sect have adapted to survive within the wider North American society, while holding tightly to the traditional way of life of their European ancestors. In contrast, North American Indian subcultures are distinctive ways of life rooted in traditions of formerly independent societies. The Native Americans endured invasion of their own territories and colonization by European settlers and were brought under the control of federal governments in the United States, Canada, and Mexico.

Although all American Indian groups have experienced enormous changes due to colonization, many have retained traditions significantly different from those of the dominant Euramerican culture surrounding them. This makes it difficult to determine whether they persevere as distinct cultures as opposed to subcultures. In this sense, *culture* and *subculture* represent opposite ends of a continuum, with no clear dividing line between them. This chapter's Anthropology Applied feature examines the intersection of culture and subculture with an example concerning Apache Indian housing.

PLURALISM

Our discussion raises the issue of the multi-ethnic or **pluralistic society** in which two or more ethnic groups or nationalities are politically organized into one territorial state but maintain their cultural differences. Pluralistic societies emerged after the first politically centralized states arose a mere 5,000 years ago. With the rise of the state, it became possible to bring about the political unification of two or more formerly independent societies, each with its own culture, thereby creating a more complex order that transcends the theoretical one culture–one society linkage.

Pluralistic societies, which are common in the world today (▶ **Figure 8.1**), all face the same challenge: They are comprised of groups that, by virtue of their high degree of cultural variation, are all essentially operating by different sets of rules. Since social living requires predictable behavior, it may be difficult for the members of any one subgroup to accurately interpret and follow the different standards by which the others operate.

Unfortunately, the lack of understanding among different subgroups within a pluralistic society can intensify to the point of anger and violence. There are many examples of troubled pluralistic societies in the world today, including Bolivia, India, and Kenya, where central governments face major challenges in maintaining peace and lawful order.

Culture Is Based on Symbols

Much of human behavior involves **symbols**—sounds, gestures, marks, or other signs that are arbitrarily linked to something else and which they represent in a meaningful way. Because often there is no inherent or necessary relationship between a thing and its representation, symbols are arbitrary, acquiring specific meanings when people agree on usage in their communications.

In fact, symbols—ranging from national flags to wedding rings to money—enter into every aspect of culture, from social life and religion to politics and economics. We are all familiar with the fervor and devotion that a religious symbol can elicit from a believer. An Islamic crescent, Christian cross, or a Jewish Star of David—as well as the sun among the Inca, a cow among the Hindu,

---

[8]Kraybill, D. B. (2001). *The riddle of Amish culture* (pp. 1–6, 244, 268–269). Baltimore: Johns Hopkins University Press.

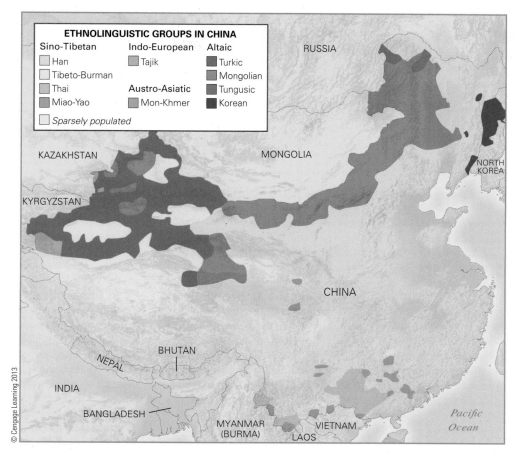

Figure 8.1 Ethnolinguistic Groups in China China is the largest country in the world, with a population of 1.3 billion people. A pluralistic society, it has fifty-five officially recognized nationalities. By far the largest ethnic group is the Han, comprising about 90 percent of the population. However, there are many ethnic minorities speaking radically different languages and having different cultural traditions. For example, the Uyghur (shown in this chapter's opening photo), numbering over 8 million, are a Turkic-speaking people in Xinjiang Province in northwestern China. Unlike most Han, who are Buddhists, most Uyghur are Sunni Muslims. Historically dominating the Chinese state, the Han typically see themselves as the "real" Chinese and ignore the ethnic minorities or view them with contempt. This ethnocentrism is also reflected in names historically used for these groups.

a white buffalo calf among Plains Indians, or any other object of worship—may bring to mind years of struggle and persecution or may stand for a whole philosophy or religion.

The most important symbolic aspect of culture is language—using words or signs to represent objects and ideas. Through language humans are able to transmit culture from one generation to another. In particular, language makes it possible to learn from cumulative, shared experience. Without it, one could not inform others about events, emotions, and experiences. Language is so important that one of the four main subfields of anthropology is dedicated to its study.

Culture Is Integrated

The breadth and depth of every culture is remarkable. It includes what people do for a living, the tools they use, the ways they work together, how they transform their environments and construct their dwellings, what they eat and drink, how they worship, what they believe is right or wrong, what gifts they exchange and when they exchange them, who they marry, how they raise their children, and how they deal with misfortune, sickness, death, and so on. Moreover, culture provides ways to pass on knowledge and enculturate new members so they can contribute to their community as well-functioning adults. And it facilitates social interaction and offers ways for

▲▲▲▲▲▲▲▲▲▲▲▲▲▲▲▲▲▲▲▲▲▲▲▲▲▲▲▲▲▲▲▲▲▲▲▲▲

pluralistic society A society in which two or more ethnic groups or nationalities are politically organized into one territorial state but maintain their cultural differences.

symbol A sound, gesture, mark, or other sign that is arbitrarily linked to something else and represents it in a meaningful way.

▼▼▼▼▼▼▼▼▼▼▼▼▼▼▼▼▼▼▼▼▼▼▼▼▼▼▼▼▼▼▼▼▼▼▼▼▼

© Cengage Learning 2013

ANTHROPOLOGY APPLIED

New Houses for Apache Indians

By George S. Esber

The United States, in common with other industrialized countries of the world, contains a number of more or less separate subcultures. Those who live by the standards of one particular subculture have their closest relationships with one another, receiving constant reassurance that their perceptions of the world are the only correct ones and coming to take it for granted that the whole culture is as they see it. As a consequence, members of one subculture frequently have trouble understanding the needs and aspirations of other such groups. For this reason anthropologists, with their special understanding of cultural differences, are frequently employed as go-betweens in situations requiring interaction between peoples of differing cultural traditions.

As an example, while I was still a graduate student in anthropology, one of my professors asked me to work with architects and a community of Tonto Apache Indians to research housing needs for a new Apache community. Although the architects knew about cross-cultural differences in the use of space, they had no idea how to get relevant information from the Indian people. For their part,

the Apaches had no explicit awareness of their needs, for these were based on unconscious patterns of behavior. For that matter, few people are consciously aware of the space needs for their own social patterns of behavior.

My task was to persuade the architects to hold back on their planning long enough for me to gather, through participant observation and a review of written records, the data from which Apache housing needs could be abstracted. At the same time, I had to overcome Apache anxieties over an outsider coming into their midst to learn about matters as personal as their daily lives as they are acted out, in and around their homes. With these hurdles overcome, I was able to identify and successfully communicate to the architects those features of Apache life having importance for home and community design. At the same time, discussions of my findings with the Apaches enhanced their own awareness of their unique needs.

As a result of my work, the Apaches moved into houses that had been designed with *their* participation, for *their* specific needs. Among my findings was

the realization that the Apaches preferred to ease into social interactions rather than to shake hands and begin interacting immediately, as is more typical of the Anglo pattern. Apache etiquette requires that people be in full view of one another so each can assess the behavior of others from a distance prior to engaging in social interaction with them. This requires a large, open living space. At the same time, hosts feel compelled to offer food to guests as a prelude to further social interaction. Thus, cooking and dining areas cannot be separated from living space. Nor is standard middle-class Anglo kitchen equipment suitable, since the need for handling large quantities among extended families requires large pots and pans, which in turn calls for extra-large sinks and cupboards. Built with such ideas in mind, the new houses accommodated long-standing native traditions. ∎

Adapted from Esber, G. S. (1987). Designing Apache houses with Apaches. In R. M. Wulff & S. J. Fiske (Eds.), *Anthropological praxis: Translating knowledge into action.* Boulder, CO: Westview. 2007 update by Esber. Reprinted by permission of the author.

people to avoid or resolve conflicts within their group as well as with outsiders.

Because these and all other aspects of a culture must be reasonably well integrated for the culture to function properly, anthropologists seldom focus on a distinctive cultural element or feature in isolation. Instead, they view each in terms of its larger context and carefully examine its connections to related features.

For purposes of comparison and analysis, anthropologists customarily imagine a culture as a well-structured

system made up of particular parts that function together as an organized whole. While they may sharply distinguish each part as a clearly defined unit with its own characteristics and special place within the larger system, anthropologists recognize that reality is complex and that divisions among cultural features are often not clear-cut.

Broadly speaking, a society's cultural features fall within three categories: social structure, infrastructure, and superstructure, as depicted in our "barrel model" (▶ **Figure 8.2**).

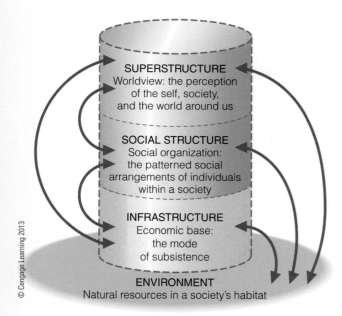

Figure 8.2 The Barrel Model of Culture Every culture is an integrated and dynamic system of adaptation that responds to a combination of internal factors (economic, social, ideological) and external factors (environmental, climatic). Within a cultural system, there are functional relationships among the economic base (infrastructure), the social organization (social structure) and the ideology (superstructure). A change in one often leads to a change in the others.

To ensure a community's biological continuity, a culture must provide a social structure for reproduction and mutual support. **Social structure** concerns rule-governed relationships—with all their rights and obligations—that hold members of a society together. Households, families, associations, and power relations, including politics, are all part of social structure. It establishes group cohesion and enables people to consistently satisfy their basic needs, including food and shelter for themselves and their dependents, by means of work.

There is a direct relationship between a group's social structure and its economic foundation, which includes subsistence practices and the tools and other material equipment used to make a living. Because subsistence practices involve tapping into available resources to satisfy a society's basic needs, this aspect of culture is known as **infrastructure.** It includes strategies for the production and distribution of goods and services considered necessary for life.

Supported by this economic foundation, society is held together by a collective body of ideas, beliefs, and values by which a group of people makes sense of the world—its shape, challenges, and opportunities. This

shared worldview is known as **superstructure.** Including religion and political ideology, superstructure comprises a people's overarching ideas about themselves and the world around them—and it gives meaning and direction to their lives.

Features in a culture's superstructure, or worldview, provide its members with certain customary ideas and rituals that enable them to think creatively about the meaning of life and death. For example, many cultures even make it possible for people to imagine an afterlife. Invited to suspend disbelief and engage in such imaginings, people find the means to deal with the grief of losing a loved one.

Influencing and reinforcing one another—and continually adapting to changing environmental, demographic, technological, political-economic, and ideological factors—the interconnected features in these three interdependent structures together form part of a cultural system. Each cultural system not only offers a shared design for thought and action, but brings some predictability to collective life, thereby helping to ensure the group's physical, psychological, and emotional well-being.

KAPAUKU CULTURE AS AN INTEGRATED SYSTEM

The integration of economic, social, and ideological aspects of a culture can be illustrated by the Kapauku

Papua, a mountain people of Western New Guinea, studied in 1955 by U.S. anthropologist Leopold Pospisil.[9] The Kapauku economy traditionally relies on plant cultivation, along with pig breeding, hunting, and fishing. Although plant cultivation provides

▲▲

social structure The rule-governed relationships—with all their rights and obligations—that hold members of a society together. This includes households, families, associations, and power relations, including politics.

infrastructure The economic foundation of a society, including its subsistence practices and the tools and other material equipment used to make a living.

superstructure A society's shared sense of identity and worldview. The collective body of ideas, beliefs, and values by which a group of people makes sense of the world—its shape, challenges, and opportunities—and their place in it. This includes religion and national ideology.

▼▼

[9]Pospisil, L. (1963). *The Kapauku Papuans of West New Guinea.* New York: Holt, Rinehart & Winston.

most of the people's food, it is through pig breeding that men achieve political power and positions of legal authority.

Among the Kapauku, living in an area now claimed by Indonesia, pig breeding is a complex business. Raising a lot of pigs requires a lot of food to feed them. The primary fodder is sweet potatoes, grown in garden plots. According to Kapauku culture, certain garden activities and the caring of pigs are tasks that fall exclusively in the domain of women's work. Thus to raise many pigs, a man needs numerous women in the household. As a result, in Kapauku society multiple wives are not only permitted, they are highly desired. For each wife, however, a man must pay a bride-price, and this can be expensive. Furthermore, wives have to be compensated for their care of the pigs. Put simply, it takes pigs, by which wealth is measured, to get wives, without whom pigs cannot be raised in the first place. Needless to say, this requires considerable entrepreneurship. It is this ability that produces leaders in Kapauku society.

The interrelatedness of these elements with various other features of Kapauku culture is even more complicated. For example, one condition that encourages men to marry several women is a surplus of adult females, sometimes caused by loss of males through warfare. Among the Kapauku, recurring warfare has long been viewed as a necessary evil. By the rules of Kapauku warfare, men may be killed but women may not. This system works to promote the imbalanced sex ratio that fosters the practice of having more than one wife. Having multiple wives tends to work best if all of them come to live in their husband's village, and so it is among the Kapauku. With this arrangement, the men of a village are typically blood relatives of one another, which enhances their ability to cooperate in warfare.

Considering all of this, it makes sense that the Kapauku typically trace descent (ancestry) through the men, which, coupled with near-constant warfare, tends to promote male dominance. So it is not surprising to find that only men hold the positions of leadership in Kapauku society, as they appropriate the products of women's labor in order to play their political games. Such male dominance is by no means characteristic of all human societies. Rather, as in the Kapauku case, it arises only under particular sets of circumstances that, if changed, will alter the way in which men and women relate to each other.

Culture Is Dynamic

Cultures are dynamic systems that respond to motions and actions within and around them. When one element or feature within the system shifts or changes, the entire system strives to adjust, just as it does when an outside force applies pressure. To function adequately, a culture must be flexible enough to allow such adjustments in the face of unstable or changing circumstances.

All cultures are, of necessity, dynamic, but some are far less so than others. When a culture is too rigid or static and fails to provide its members with the means required for long-term survival under changing conditions, it is not likely to endure. On the other hand, some cultures are so fluid and open to change that they may lose their distinctive character. The Amish, mentioned earlier in this chapter, typically resist change as much as possible but are constantly making balanced decisions to adjust when absolutely necessary. North Americans in general, however, have created a culture in which change has become a positive ideal, reflecting the ongoing technological, demographic, and social transformations in their society.

Every culture is dynamically designed, not unlike a thermostat regulating room temperature, enabling it to cope with recurrent strains and tensions, even dangerous disruptions and deadly conflicts. Sharing a culture, members of a society are capable of dealing with crises, solving their conflicts, and restoring order. Sometimes, however, the pressures are so great that the cultural features in the system are no longer adequate or acceptable, and the established order is changed.

Culture and Change

Cultures have always changed over time, although rarely as rapidly or as massively as many are doing today. Change takes place in response to events such as population growth, technological innovation, environmental crisis, the intrusion of outsiders, or modification of behavior and values within the culture. In our current age of globalization, we are witnessing a much accelerated pace of widespread and radical change, discussed in detail in the last chapter of this book.

While cultures must have some flexibility to remain adaptive, change can also bring unexpected and often disastrous results. For example, consider the relationship between culture and the droughts that periodically afflict so many people living in African countries just south of the Sahara Desert. The lives of some 14 million nomadic herders native to this region are centered on cattle and other grazing animals, migrating from place to place as needed to provide them with pasture and water.

For thousands of years these migratory herders have efficiently utilized vast areas of arid lands in ways that allowed them to survive many severe droughts. Unfortunately, the non-settled way of life is frowned upon by

▲▲▲ Climate and politics have conspired to create serious cultural change among migratory herders. Moving across vast territories to provide pasture and water for their livestock, these nomadic peoples have long depended upon seasonal mobility for survival. Difficult to control by central governments trying to impose taxes on them, they now face major obstacles in pursuing their ancestral way of life. Such herders are increasingly restricted from moving across their traditional grazing territories and are hit all the harder when droughts occur. So it is in the arid African grassland regions of Kenya pictured here, where the limited grazing lands and severe drought have resulted in the death of many animals and turned others into "bones on hoofs." Such catastrophes have forced many herders in Kenya and elsewhere to give up their old lifeways entirely.

the central governments of modern states in the region. These governments dislike nomadism for several reasons. For instance, it often involves people moving back and forth across remote international boundaries that are impossible to guard, and it makes people difficult to track for purposes of taxation and other governmental controls.

Viewing the nomads as evading their authority, many governments have established policies to keep migratory herders from ranging through their traditional grazing territories and to convert them into sedentary villagers. Simultaneously, governments have aimed to press them into a market economy by giving them incentives to raise many more animals than required for their own needs so that the surplus could be sold to increase the tax base. Combined, these policies have led to overgrazing, erosion, and a lack of reserve pasture during recurring droughts. Thus droughts are even more disastrous than in the past because when they occur, they jeopardize the nomads' very existence.

Culture, Society, and the Individual

Ultimately, a society is no more than a union of individuals, all of whom have their own special needs and interests. To survive, it must succeed in balancing the immediate self-interest of its individual members against the needs and demands of the collective well-being of society as a whole. To accomplish this, a society offers rewards for adherence to its culturally prescribed standards. In most cases, these rewards assume the form of social approval. For example, in contemporary North American society a person who holds a good job, takes care of family, pays taxes, and does volunteer work in the neighborhood may be spoken of as a "model citizen" in the community. To ensure the survival of the group, each person must learn to postpone certain immediate personal satisfactions. Yet the needs of the individual cannot be overlooked entirely or emotional stress and growing resentment may erupt in the form of protest, disruption, and even violence.

Consider, for example, the matter of sexual expression, which, like anything that people do, is shaped by culture. Sexuality is important in every society, for it helps to strengthen cooperative bonds among members, ensuring the perpetuation of the social group itself. Yet sex can be disruptive to social living. Without clear rules of who has sexual access to whom, competition for sexual privileges can destroy the cooperative bonds on which human survival depends. In addition, uncontrolled sexual activity can result in reproductive rates that cause a society's population to outstrip its resources. Hence, as it shapes sexual behavior, every culture must balance the needs of society against the individual's sexual needs and desires so that frustration does not build up to the point of being disruptive in itself.

© AP Images/Sergey Ponomarev

◀ Many people in the world consider their own nation superior to others, framing their nationalist pride by proclaiming to be a "master race," "divine nation," or "chosen people" and viewing their homeland as sacred. Such nationalist ideology is associated with militant ethnocentrism and dislike, fear, or even hatred of foreigners, immigrants, and ethnic minorities. For instance, most Russians now agree with the nationalist slogan "Russia for the Russians," and almost half believe their nation has a natural right to dominate as an empire. The photo shows Russian Nationalists, right-wing extremists, 10,000 of whom recently marched to St. Petersburg to protest the immigration of Azeri Tajiks, Turks, and other foreigners into Russia.

Cultures vary widely in the way they go about this. On one end of the spectrum, societies such as the Amish in North America or the Muslim Brotherhood in Egypt have taken an extremely restrictive approach, specifying no sex outside of marriage. On the other end are societies such as the Norwegians in northern Europe who generally accept premarital sex and often choose to have children outside marriage, or even more extreme, the Canela Indians in Brazil's Amazon region, whose social codes guarantee that, sooner or later, everyone in a given village has had sex with just about everyone of the opposite sex. Yet, even as permissive as the latter situation may sound, the system nonetheless has strict operational rules.[10] In all life issues, not just sexual matters, cultures must strike a balance between the needs and desires of individuals and those of society as a whole.

Ethnocentrism and the Evaluation of Culture

There are numerous highly diverse cultural solutions to the challenges of human existence. Anthropologists have been intrigued to find that people in most cultures tend to see their own way of life as the best of all possible worlds. This is reflected in the way individual societies refer to themselves: Typically, a society's traditional name for itself translates roughly into "true human beings." In contrast, their names for outsiders commonly trans-

late into various versions of "subhumans," including "monkeys," "dogs," "weird-looking people," "funny talkers," and so forth. As we touched on in Chapter 1, any adequately functioning culture regards its own ways in positive terms, and often as the only proper ones, a view known as *ethnocentrism.*

Anthropologists have been actively engaged in the fight against ethnocentrism ever since they started to study and actually live among traditional peoples with radically different cultures—thus learning by personal experience that these "others" were no less human than anyone else. Resisting the common urge to rank cultures, anthropologists have instead aimed to understand individual cultures and the general concept of culture. To do so, they have examined each culture on its own terms, discerning whether or not the culture satisfies the needs and expectations of the people themselves. If a people practiced human sacrifice or capital punishment, for example, anthropologists asked about the circumstances that made the taking of human life acceptable according to that particular group's values.

This brings us to **cultural relativism**—the idea that one must suspend judgment of other peoples' practices in order to understand those practices in their own cultural terms. Only through such an approach can one gain a meaningful view of the values and beliefs that underlie the behaviors and institutions of other peoples and societies as well as clearer insights into the underlying beliefs and practices of one's own society.

Cultural relativism is essential as a research tool. However, employing it for research does not mean

cultural relativism The idea that one must suspend judgment of other people's practices in order to understand them in their own cultural terms.

---

[10]Crocker, W. A., & Crocker, J. (1994). *The Canela: Bonding through kinship, ritual, and sex* (pp. 143–171). Fort Worth: Harcourt Brace.

suspending judgment forever, nor does it require that anthropologists defend a people's right to engage in any cultural practice, no matter how destructive. All that is necessary is that we avoid *premature* judgments until we have a full understanding of the culture in which we are interested. Then and only then may anthropologists adopt a critical stance and an informed way to consider the advantages and disadvantages of particular beliefs and behaviors for a society and its members.

A valid question to ask is this: How well does a given culture satisfy the biological, social, and psychologi-

cal needs of those whose behavior it guides?[11] Specific indicators to determine this are to be found in the nutritional status and general physical and mental health of its population; the incidence of violence, crime, and delinquency; the demographic structure, stability, and tranquility of domestic life; and the group's relationship to its resource base.

The culture of a people who experience high rates of malnutrition (including obesity), violence, crime, delinquency, suicide, emotional disorders and despair, and environmental degradation may be said to be operating less well than that of another people who exhibit few such problems. In a well-working culture, people "can be proud, jealous, and pugnacious, and live a very

---

[11]Bodley, J. H. (1990). *Victims of progress* (3rd ed., p. 138). Mountain View, CA: Mayfield.

◀ High rates of crime and delinquency are signs that a culture is not adequately satisfying a people's needs and expectations. This San Quentin Prison cellblock in California can be seen as such evidence. It is sobering to note that 25 percent of all imprisoned people in the world are incarcerated in the United States. In the past ten years the country's jail and prison population jumped by more than 700,000—from 1.6 to 2.3 million. Ironically, people in the United States think of their country as "the land of the free," yet it has the highest incarceration rate in the world (751 per 100,000 inhabitants). The median among all nations is about 125, roughly a sixth of the U.S. rate.

satisfactory life without feeling anxiety, 'alienation,' 'anomie,' 'depression,' or any of the other pervasive ills of our own inhuman and civilized way of living."[12] When traditional ways of coping no longer seem to work and people feel helpless to shape their own lives in their own societies, symptoms of cultural breakdown become prominent.

In short, a culture is essentially a maintenance system to ensure the continued well-being of a group of people. It may be deemed successful as long as it secures the survival of a society in a way that its members find to be reasonably fulfilling. What complicates matters is that any society is made up of groups with different interests, raising the possibility that some people's interests may be served better than those of others. Therefore, a culture that is quite fulfilling for one group within a society may be less so for another. For this reason, anthropologists must always ask *whose* needs and *whose* survival are best served by the culture in question. Only by looking at the overall situation can a reasonably objective judgment be made as to how well a culture is working.

Anthropologists today recognize that few peoples still exist in total or near-total isolation; globalization affects the dynamics of culture in almost every corner of our global village. Accordingly, as will be detailed in many of the following chapters, we must widen our scope and develop a truly worldwide perspective that enables us to appreciate cultures as increasingly open and interactive systems.

[12] Fox, R. (1968). *Encounter with anthropology* (p. 290). New York: Dell.

Chapter Checklist

What is culture, and what characteristics are common to all cultures?

✔ Culture is a society's shared and socially transmitted ideas, values, and perceptions that are used to make sense of experience and generate behavior and are reflected in that behavior.

✔ While every culture involves a group's shared values, ideas, and behavior, this does not mean that everything within a culture is uniform. For instance, in all cultures people's roles vary according to age and gender. (Anthropologists use the term *gender* to refer to the cultural elaborations and meanings assigned to the biological differences between sexes.) And in some cultures there are other subcultural variations. A subculture (for example, the Amish) shares certain overarching assumptions of the larger culture, while observing its own set of distinct rules. Pluralistic societies are those in which two or more ethnic groups or nationalities are politically organized into one territorial state but maintain their cultural differences.

✔ In addition to being shared, all cultures are learned, with individual members learning the accepted norms of social behavior through the process of enculturation. Also, every culture is based on symbols—transmitted through the communication of ideas, emotions, and desires—especially language. And culture is integrated, so that all aspects function as an integrated whole (albeit not without tension, friction, and even conflict). Finally, all cultures are dynamically designed to adjust to recurrent strains and tensions.

✔ As illustrated in the barrel model, all aspects of a culture fall into one of three broad, interrelated categories: infrastructure (the subsistence practices or economic system), social structure (the rule-governed relationships), and superstructure (the ideology or worldview).

✔ Cultural change takes place in response to such events as population growth, technological innovation, environmental crisis, intrusion of outsiders, or modification of values and behavior within the culture. Although cultures must change to adapt to new circumstances, sometimes the unforeseen consequences of change are disastrous for a society.

What is cultural adaptation?

✔ Cultural adaptation—a complex of ideas, activities, and technologies that enables people to survive and even thrive in their environment—has enabled humans to survive and expand into a wide variety of environments.

✔ Cultures have always changed over time, although rarely as rapidly or massively as many are doing today. Sometimes what is adaptive in one set of circumstances or over the short run is maladaptive over time.

What are the connections between culture, society, and the individual?

✔ As a union of individuals, a society must strike a balance between the self-interest of individuals with the needs and demands of the collective well-being of the group. To accomplish this, a society rewards adherence to its culturally prescribed standards in the form of social approval.

✔ When individual needs and desires are eclipsed by those of society, the result may be stress and mental illness expressed in "antisocial" behavior such as alienation, substance abuse, or violence.

What is ethnocentrism, and what is the measure of a society's success?

✔ Ethnocentrism is the belief that one's own culture is superior to all others. To avoid making ethnocentric judgments, anthropologists adopt the approach of cultural relativism, which requires suspending judgment in order to understand each culture in its own terms.

✔ The least biased measure of a culture's success may be based on answering this question: How well does a particular culture satisfy the physical and psychological needs of those whose behavior it guides? The following indicators provide answers: the nutritional status and general physical and mental health of the population, the incidence of violence, the stability of domestic life, and the group's relationship to its resource base.

Questions for Reflection

1. An often overlooked first step for developing an understanding of another culture is having knowledge and respect for one's own cultural traditions. Do you know the origins of the worldview commonly held by most people in your community? How do you think it developed over time and what makes it so accepted or popular in your group today?

2. Although all cultures across the world display some degree of ethnocentrism, some are more ethnocentric than others. In what ways is your own society ethnocentric? Considering today's globalization (as described in Chapter 1), do you think ethnocentrism poses more of a problem than in the past?

3. Like everyone else in the world, you are meeting daily challenges of survival through your culture. And since you are made "fully human" by your own culture, how do you express your individual identity in your community? What do your hairstyle, clothes, shoes, jewelry, and so on communicate about who you are?

4. Many large modern societies are pluralistic. Are you familiar with any subcultures in your own society? Could you make friends with or even marry someone from another subculture? What kind of problems would you be likely to encounter?

5. The barrel model offers you a simple framework to imagine what a culture looks like from an analytical point of view. How would you apply that model to your own community?

Key Terms

cultural adaptation
culture
enculturation
society
gender

subculture
ethnic group
ethnicity
pluralistic society
symbol

social structure
infrastructure
superstructure
cultural relativism

Online Study Resources

Login to **www.cengagebrain.com** to access the resources your instructor has assigned and to purchase materials. For this book, you can access:

CourseMate
Access chapter-specific learning tools including flashcards, glossaries, practice quizzes, videos, and more in your Anthropology CourseMate.

© James Michael Dorsey

VISUAL ESSENCE

As social creatures depending upon one another for survival, humans can communicate clearly in a multiplicity of situations about countless things connected to our well-being. We do this with a variety of distinctive gestures, sounds, touches, and body postures. Our most sophisticated means of sharing large amounts of complex information is language—a foundation stone of every human culture. As shown in this photo of a Tuareg nomad talking on his satellite phone while astride a camel in the Sahara Desert, modern technology enables people to communicate instantly from even the most remote corners of the earth. But no matter how sophisticated our electronic gadgets, we must share a language to make sense of messages. What we cannot see is what language he is speaking. It may be his native tongue Tamasheq, a Berber language common in northwestern Africa. However, living in a former French colony, he could be speaking French. Or perhaps he is a tour guide using the language that appears on the label of his plastic water jug—a recycled "Camel Super Diesel Oil" container produced in the United Arab Emirates where the official language is Arabic but English is common.

9 Language and Communication

the human ability to communicate through language rests squarely on our biological makeup. We are "programmed" for language, be it through sounds or gestures. (Sign languages, such as American Sign Language or ASL, used by many who are mute or hearing impaired, are fully developed languages in their own right.) Beyond the cries of babies, which are not learned but do communicate, humans must learn their language. So it is that a normal child from anywhere in the world readily learns the language of his or her culture.

Language is a system of communication using symbolic sounds, gestures, or marks that are put together according to certain rules, resulting in meanings that are intelligible to all who share that language. As we discussed in the previous chapter, these sounds, gestures, and marks are *symbols*—signs that are arbitrarily linked to something else and represent it in a meaningful way. For example, the word *crying* is a symbol, a combination of sounds to which we assign the meaning of a particular action and which we can use to communicate that meaning, whether or not anyone around us is actually crying.

Signals, unlike culturally learned symbols or meaningful signs, are instinctive sounds and gestures that have a natural or self-evident meaning. Screams, sighs, and coughs, for example, are signals that convey some kind of emotional or physical state. Throughout the animal kingdom, species communicate essential information by means of signals.

Today's language experts differ on how much credit to give to animals, such as dolphins or chimpanzees, for the ability to use symbols as well as signals. Over the past few decades, researchers aiming to understand the biological basis, social use, and evolutionary development of language have investigated a fascinating array of animal communication systems, including dolphin whistles, whale songs, elephant rumbles, bee dances, and chimpanzee gestures. Some have investigated language acquisition aptitude among apes by teaching them to communicate using ASL or "lexigrams" (symbols) on keyboard devices. Public interest in such research has turned some of these apes into media stars—most notably, Koko the gorilla who is credited

In this chapter you will learn to:

- **Define language and the three branches of language study within anthropology.**

- **Describe the various aspects of body language and paralanguage.**

- **Recount the origins of language, speech, and writing.**

- **Analyze the impact of culture on language and of language on culture.**

- **Discuss the roles of literacy and telecommunication in today's world.**

◄ Koko making the sign for "fake." For nearly four decades this lowland gorilla has been a key figure at the Gorilla Foundation headquarters in Woodside, California, an institute dedicated to protecting and preserving gorillas through interspecies communication research and education. Taught American Sign Language by U.S. developmental psychologist Penny Patterson, Koko combines her working vocabulary of over 1,000 signs into statements averaging three to six signs in length. She initiates the majority of her conversations with humans and often signs to herself. For 24 years Koko had the company of a younger gorilla named Michael, also trained to sign. They signed to each other, using human language to supplement their own natural communicative gestures and vocalizations. When Michael died in 2000, Koko expressed grief by signing "sorry" and "cry." She often went to his room and smelled his blankets. Today she has a new male companion named Ndume.

© The Gorilla Foundation

with having a working vocabulary of 1,000 signs and the ability to use that vocabulary in complex statements and questions.[1]

More knowledge about the various systems of animal communication must be gained before it becomes clear what the implications of those systems are for our understanding of the nature and evolution of language. Meanwhile, even as debate continues over how human and animal communication relate to each other, we cannot dismiss communication among nonhuman species as a set of simple instinctive reflexes or fixed action patterns.[2]

While language studies such as the one involving Koko are fascinating and reveal much about primate cognition, the fact remains that human culture depends on an elaborate system of communication far more complex than that of any other species—including our fellow primates. The reason for this is the sheer amount of knowledge that must be learned by each person from other individuals in order to fully participate in society. Of course, a significant amount of learning can and does take place in the absence of language by way of observation and imitation, guided by a limited number of meaningful signs or symbols. However, all known human cultures are so rich in content that they require communication systems that not only can give precise labels to various classes of phenomena but also permit people to think and talk about their own and others' experiences and expectations—past, present, and future.

The central and most highly developed human system of communication is language. Knowledge of the workings of language, then, is essential to a full understanding of what culture is about and how it operates.

Linguistic Research and the Nature of Language

Any human language—Chinese, English, Swahili, or whatever—is a means of transmitting information and sharing with others both collective and individual experiences. It is a system that enables us to translate our concerns, beliefs, and perceptions into symbols that can be understood and interpreted by others.

In spoken language, this is done by taking sounds—no language uses more than about fifty—and developing rules for putting them together in meaningful ways. Sign languages, such as American Sign Language, do the same—not with sound, but with shaping and moving the hands and other parts of the body and with facial expressions, including mouthing. The vast array of languages in the world—some 6,000 or so different ones—may well astound and mystify us by their great variety and complexity, yet language experts have found that all languages, as far back as we can trace them, are organized in the same basic way.

The roots of **linguistics**—the systematic study of all aspects of language—go back a long way, to the works of an-

[1]Among many references on this, see Bekoff, M., et al. (Eds.). (2002). *The cognitive animal: Empirical and theoretical perspectives on animal cognition*. Cambridge, MA: MIT Press; Hobaiter, C., & Byrne, R. W. (2011, July). The gestural repertoire of the wild chimpanzee. *Animal Cognition 14* (4); Patterson, F. G. P., & Gordon, W. (2002). Twenty-seven years of Project Koko and Michael. In B. Galdikas et al. (Eds.), *All apes great and small* (vol. 1): *Chimpanzees, bonobos, and gorillas* (pp. 165–176). New York: Kluwer Academic.

[2]Armstrong, D. F., Stokoe, W. C., & Wilcox, S. E. (1993). Signs of the origin of syntax. *Current Anthropology 34*, 349–368; Burling, R. (1993). Primate calls, human language, and nonverbal communication. *Current Anthropology 34*, 25–53.

cient language specialists in India more than 2,000 years ago. The European age of exploration, from the 16th through the 18th centuries, set the stage for a great leap forward in the scientific study of language. Explorers, invaders, and missionaries accumulated information about a huge diversity of languages from all around the world. An estimated 12,000 languages still existed when they began their inquiries.

Linguists in the 19th century, including anthropologists, made a significant contribution in comparative research—discovering patterns, relationships, and systems in the sounds and structures of different languages and tentatively formulating laws and regular principles concerning language. In the 20th century, while still collecting data, these researchers made considerable progress in unraveling the reasoning process behind language construction, testing and working from new and improved theories.

Insofar as theories and facts of language are verifiable by independent researchers looking at the same materials, it can now be said that we have a science of linguistics. This science has three main branches: descriptive linguistics, historical linguistics, and a third branch that focuses on language in relation to social and cultural settings.

Descriptive Linguistics

How can an anthropologist, a trader, a missionary, a diplomat, or any other outsider research a foreign language that has not yet been described and analyzed, or for which there are no readily available written materials? There are hundreds of such undocumented languages in the world. Fortunately, effective methods have been developed to help with the task. Descriptive linguistics involves unraveling a language by recording, describing, and analyzing all of its features. It is a painstaking process, but it is ultimately rewarding in that it provides deeper understanding of a language—its structure, its unique linguistic repertoire (figures of speech, word plays, and so on), and its relationship to other languages.

The process of unlocking the underlying rules of a spoken language requires a trained ear and a thorough understanding of the way multiple different speech sounds are produced. Without such know-how, it is extremely difficult to write out or make intelligent use of any data concerning a particular language. To satisfy this preliminary requirement, most people need special training in phonetics, discussed below.

Phonology

Rooted in the Greek word *phone* (meaning "sound"), **phonetics** is defined as the systematic identification and description of the distinctive sounds of a language. Phonetics is basic to **phonology**, the study of language sounds. In order to analyze and describe any language, one first needs an inventory of all its distinctive sounds.

While some of the sounds used in other languages may seem very much like those of the researcher's own speech pattern, others may be unfamiliar. For example, the *th* sound common in English does not exist in the Dutch language and is difficult for most Dutch speakers to pronounce, just as the *r* sound used in numerous languages is tough for Japanese speakers. And the unique "click" sounds used in Bushmen languages in southern Africa are difficult for speakers of just about every other language.

While collecting speech sounds or utterances, the linguist works to isolate the **phonemes**—the smallest units of sound that make a difference in meaning. The linguist performs this isolation and analysis through a process called the *minimal-pair test*. The researcher tries to find two short words that appear to be exactly alike except for one sound, such as *bit* and *pit* in English. If the substitution of *b* for *p* in this minimal pair makes a difference in meaning, as it does in English, then those two sounds have been identified as distinct phonemes of the language and will require two different symbols to record. If, however, the linguist finds two different pronunciations (as when "butter" is pronounced "budder") and then finds that there is no difference in their meaning for a native speaker, the sounds represented will be considered variants of the same phoneme. In such cases, for economy of representation only one of the two symbols will be used to record that sound wherever it is found.

Morphology, Syntax, and Grammar

While making and studying an inventory of distinctive sounds, linguists also look into **morphology**, the study of the patterns or rules of word formation in a language, including the guidelines for verb tense, pluralization, and compound words. They do this by marking out specific sounds and sound combinations that

▲▲

language A system of communication using symbolic sounds, gestures, or marks that are put together according to certain rules, resulting in meanings that are intelligible to all who share that language.

signals Instinctive sounds or gestures that have a natural or self-evident meaning.

linguistics The modern scientific study of all aspects of language.

phonetics The systematic identification and description of distinctive speech sounds in a language.

phonology The study of language sounds.

phonemes The smallest units of sound that make a difference in meaning in a language.

morphology The study of the patterns or rules of word formation in a language, including the guidelines for verb tense, pluralization, and compound words.

▽▽

seem to have meaning. These are called **morphemes**—the smallest units of sound that carry a meaning in a language. Morphemes are distinct from phonemes, which can alter meaning but have no meaning by themselves. For example, a linguist studying English in a North American farming community would soon learn that *cow* is a morpheme—a meaningful combination of the phonemes *c, o,* and *w.* Pointing to two of these animals, the linguist would elicit the word *cows* from local speakers. This would reveal yet another morpheme—the *s*—which can be added to the original morpheme to indicate plural.

The next step in unraveling a language is to identify its **syntax**—the patterns or rules by which morphemes, or words, are arranged into phrases and sentences. The **grammar** of the language will ultimately consist of all observations about its morphemes and syntax.

One of the strengths of modern descriptive linguistics is the objectivity of its methods. For example, English-speaking linguistic anthropologists do not approach a language with the idea that it must have nouns, verbs, prepositions, or any other of the form classes identifiable in English. Instead they see what turns up in the language and attempt to describe it in terms of its own inner workings. This allows for unanticipated discoveries. For instance, unlike many other languages, English does not distinguish between feminine and masculine nouns. So it is that English speakers use the definite article *the* in front of any noun, while French requires two types of such definite articles: *la* for feminine nouns and *le* for masculine—as in *la lune* (the moon) and *le soleil* (the sun).

German speakers go one step farther, utilizing three types of articles: *der* in front of masculine nouns, *die* for feminine, and *das* for neutral. It is also interesting to note that in contrast to their French neighbors, Germans consider the moon to be masculine, so they say *der Mon,* and the sun to be feminine, which makes it *die Sonne.* In another part of the world, the highlands of Peru and Bolivia in South America, indigenous peoples who speak Quechua are not concerned about whether nouns are gendered or neutral, for their language has no definite articles.

Historical Linguistics

While descriptive linguistics focuses on all features of a particular language as it exists at any one moment in time, historical linguistics deals with the fact that languages change. In addition to deciphering "dead" languages that are no longer spoken, specialists in this field investigate relationships between earlier and later forms of the same language, study older languages to track processes of change into modern ones, and examine interrelationships among older languages. For example, they attempt to sort out the development of Latin (as spoken almost 1,500 years ago in southern Europe) into Italian, Spanish, Portuguese, French, and Romanian by identifying natural shifts in the original language, as well as modifications brought on by direct

contact during the next few centuries with Germanic-speaking invaders from northern Europe.

When focusing on long-term processes of change, historical linguists depend on written records of languages. They have achieved considerable success in working out the relationships among different languages, and these are reflected in classification schemes. For example, English is one of approximately 140 languages classified in the larger Indo-European language family (▶ **Figure 9.1**). A **language family** is a group of languages descended from a single ancestral language. This family is subdivided into eleven subgroups, which reflects the fact that there has been a long period (6,000 years or so) of **linguistic divergence** from an ancient unified language (reconstructed as Proto-Indo-European) into separate "daughter" languages. English is one of several languages in the Germanic subgroup (▶ **Figure 9.2**), all of which are more closely related to one another than they are to the languages of any other subgroup of the Indo-European family.

So, despite differences, the languages of one subgroup share certain features when compared to those of another. As an illustration, the word for "father" in the Germanic languages always starts with an *f* or closely related *v* sound (Dutch *vader,* German *Vater,* Gothic *Fadar*). Among the Romance languages, by contrast, the comparable word always starts with a *p:* French *père,* Spanish and Italian *padre*—all derived from the Latin *pater.* The original Indo-European word for "father" was *p'te¯r,* so in this case, the Romance languages have retained the earlier pronunciation, whereas the Germanic languages have diverged.

Historical linguists are not limited to the faraway past, for even modern languages are constantly transforming—adding new words, dropping others, or changing meaning. Studying them in their specific cultural context can help us understand the processes of change that may have led to linguistic divergence in the past.

Processes of Linguistic Divergence

Clearly, one force for change is selective borrowing between languages. This is evident in the many French words present in the English language—and in the growing number of English words cropping up in languages all around the world due to globalization. Technological breakthroughs resulting in new equipment and products also prompt linguistic shifts. For instance, the electronic revolution that brought us radio, television, computers, and mobile phones has created entirely new vocabularies.

Increasing professional specialization is another driving force. We see one of many examples in the field of biomedicine where today's students must learn the specialized vocabulary and idioms of the profession—over 6,000 new words in the first year of medical school.

There is also a tendency for any group within a larger society to create its own unique vocabulary,

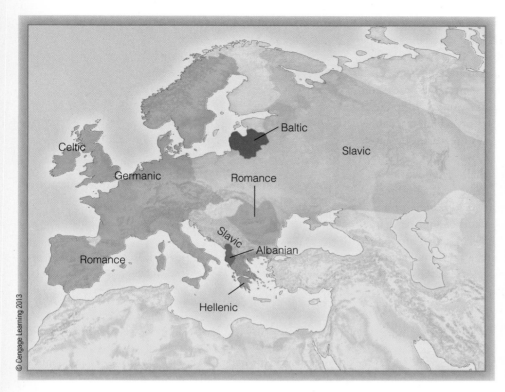

Figure 9.1 Indo-European Language Subgroups in Europe Not all languages spoken in Europe are part of the Indo-European family. For example, Basque—an isolated language also known as Euskara—is still spoken in the French-Spanish borderland. Moreover, languages spoken by Hungarians, Estonians, Finns, Komi (in northeast Russia), and Saami (in northern Scandinavia) belong to the Uralic language family.

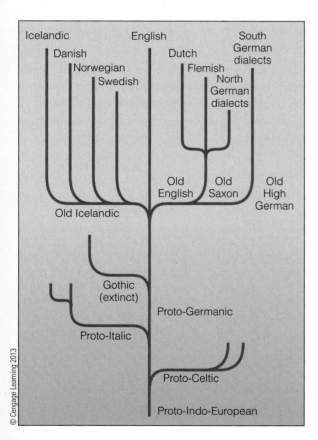

Figure 9.2 The English Language Family Tree English is one of a group of languages in the Germanic subgroup of the Indo-European family. This diagram shows its relationship to other languages in the same subgroup. The root is Proto-Indo-European, an ancestral language originally spoken by early farmers and herders who spread north and west over Europe, bringing with them both their customs and their language.

whether it is a street gang, sorority, religious group, a platoon of soldiers, or prison inmates. By changing the meaning of existing words or inventing new ones, members of the in-group can communicate with fellow members while effectively excluding outsiders who may be within hearing range. Finally, there seems to be a human tendency to admire and copy the person who comes up with a new and clever idiom, a useful word, or a particularly stylish pronunciation. All of this means that no language stands still.

Language Loss and Revival

Perhaps the most powerful force for linguistic change is the domination of one society over another, as demonstrated during 500 years of European colonialism.

▲▲

morphemes The smallest units of sound that carry a meaning in language. They are distinct from phonemes, which can alter meaning but have no meaning by themselves.

syntax The patterns or rules by which words are arranged into phrases and sentences.

grammar The entire formal structure of a language, including morphology and syntax.

language family A group of languages descended from a single ancestral language.

linguistic divergence The development of different languages from a single ancestral language.

▼▼

Imposed external rule persists today in many parts of the world, such as Taiwan's indigenous peoples being governed by Mandarin-speaking Chinese, Tarascan Indians by Spanish-speaking Mexicans, or Bushmen by English-speaking Namibians. In many cases, foreign political control has resulted in linguistic erosion or even complete disappearance, sometimes leaving only a faint trace in old, indigenous names for geographic features such as hills and rivers.

Over the last 500 years about half of the world's 12,000 or so languages have become extinct as a direct result of warfare, epidemics, and forced assimilation brought on by colonial powers and other aggressive outsiders. Most of the remaining 6,000 languages are spoken by very few people, and many of the surviving languages are losing speakers rapidly due to globalization. In fact, half have fewer than 10,000 speakers each, and fewer than 1,000 speak the rest. Put another way, half of the world's languages are spoken by just 2 percent of the world's population.[3]

In North America, only 150 of the original 300 indigenous languages still exist, and many of these are moving toward extinction at an alarming rate. Thousands of indigenous languages elsewhere in the world are also threatened. For example, fewer than ten people still speak N|uu, a "click" language traditionally spoken in South Africa's Kalahari Desert. N|uu is the only surviving member of the !Ui branch of the Tuu language family (previously called Southern Khoisan).

Anthropologists predict that the number of languages still spoken in the world today will be cut in half by the year 2100, in large part because children born in ethnic minority groups no longer use the ancestral language when they go to school, migrate to cities, join the larger workforce, and are exposed to printed and electronic media. The printing press, radio, satellite television, Internet, and text messaging on mobile phones are driving the need for a shared language that many understand, and increasingly that is English. In the past 500 years, this language—originally spoken by about 2.5 million people living only in part of the British Isles in northwestern Europe—has spread around the world. Today some 375 million people (5.4 percent of the global population) claim English as their native tongue. About a billion others (nearly 15 percent of humanity) speak it as a second or foreign language.

While a common language allows people from different ethnic backgrounds to communicate, there is the risk that a global spread of one language may contribute to the disappearance of others. And with the extinction of each language, we lose "hundreds of generations of traditional knowledge encoded in these ancestral tongues"[4]—a vast repository of knowledge about the natural world, plants, animals, ecosystems, and cultural traditions.

© Bonny Sands

▲▲▲ Several linguistic anthropologists are collaborating on field research with speakers of endangered Khoisan "click" languages such as N|uu in southern Africa. Using a portable ultrasound-imaging machine, they can capture the tongue movements of the click consonants. Here, U.S. linguist Johanna Brugman holds an ultrasound probe under the chin of one of the ten remaining N|uu speakers, Ouma Katrina Esau, who is helping to document how click sounds are made. Clicks are produced by creating suction within a cavity formed between the front and back parts of the tongue—except in the case of bilabial clicks in which the cavity is made between the lips and the back of the tongue. N|uu is one of only three languages remaining in the world that use bilabial clicks as consonants. The vertical bar in the word *N|uu* indicates a click sound.

A key issue in language preservation efforts today is the impact of electronic media, such as the Internet, where content still exists in relatively few languages, and more than 80 percent of Internet users are native speakers of just ten of the world's 6,000 languages. In 2001, the United Nations Educational, Scientific, and Cultural Organization (UNESCO) established Initiative B@bel, which uses information and communication technologies to support linguistic and cultural diversity. Promoting multilingualism on the Internet, this initiative aims to bridge the digital divide—to make access to Internet content and services more equitable for users worldwide (▶ **Figure 9.3**).

Sometimes, in reaction to a real or perceived threat of cultural dominance by powerful foreign societies, ethnic groups and even entire countries may seek to maintain or reclaim their unique identity by purging their vocabularies of "foreign" terms. Emerging as a significant force for linguistic change, such **linguistic nationalism** is particularly characteristic of the former colonial countries of Africa and Asia today. It is not limited to those countries, however, as one can see by periodic French attempts to purge their language of such

---

[3]Crystal, D. (2002). *Language death* (pp. 2–6, 69). Cambridge, UK: Cambridge University Press; see also Knight, C., et al. (Eds.). (2000). *The evolutionary emergence of language: Social function and the origins of linguistic form* (p. 393). Cambridge, UK: Cambridge University Press.

[4]Living Tongues. http://www.livingtongues.org/ (retrieved August 31, 2011).

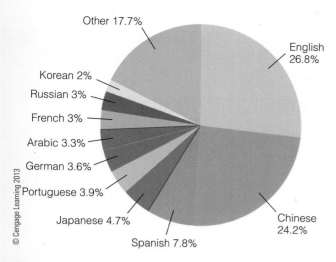

© Cengage Learning 2013

Other 17.7%

English 26.8%

Korean 2%

Russian 3%

French 3%

Arabic 3.3%

German 3.6%

Portuguese 3.9%

Chinese 24.2%

Japanese 4.7%

Spanish 7.8%

Figure 9.3 Language Use on the Internet Although the world's digital divide is diminishing, it is still dramatic. As illustrated here, over 80 percent of today's 2 billion Internet users are native speakers of just ten of the world's 6,000 languages. Among the fastest-growing Internet language groups today are Arabic, Chinese, and Russian. (Figures shown in pie chart are rounded.)

Source: www.internetworldstats.com (retrieved September 12, 2011).

Americanisms as *le hamburger.* Another example of this is France's decision to substitute the word *e-mail* with the government-approved term *couriel.*

For many ethnic minorities, efforts to counter the threat of linguistic extinction or to resurrect already extinct languages form part of their struggle to maintain a sense of cultural identity and dignity. A prime means by which powerful groups try to assert their dominance over minorities living within their borders is to actively suppress their languages. Examples of this include 20th-century government-sanctioned efforts to repress Native American cultures in Canada and the United States and to fully absorb them into mainstream society. Government policies included taking Indian children away from their parents and putting them in boarding schools where only English was allowed, and students were often punished for speaking their traditional languages. Upon returning to their homes, many could no longer communicate with their own close relatives and neighbors.

While now abolished, these institutions and the historical policies that shaped them did lasting damage to American Indian groups striving to maintain their cultural heritage. Especially over the past three decades, many of these besieged indigenous communities have been actively involved in language revitalization efforts. Among numerous examples of this is the work of S. Neyooxet Greymorning, a Southern Arapaho, who has devoted three decades to developing and implementing ways to revive indigenous languages, including his own. Greymorning, a professor of anthropology and Native American studies at the University of Montana, tells his story in the Anthropology Applied feature on the next page.

Language in Its Social and Cultural Settings

As discussed in the section on descriptive linguistics, language is not simply a matter of combining sounds according to certain rules to come up with meaningful utterances. It is important to remember that languages are spoken by people who are members of distinct societies. In addition to the fact that most societies have their own unique cultures, individuals within each society tend to vary in the ways they use language based on social factors such as gender, age, class, and ethnicity.

We choose words and sentences to communicate meaning, and what is meaningful in one community or culture may not be in another. Our use of language reflects, and is reflected by, the rest of our culture. For that reason, linguistic anthropologists also research language in relation to its various distinctive social and cultural contexts. This third branch of linguistic study falls into two categories: sociolinguistics and ethnolinguistics.

Sociolinguistics

Sociolinguistics, the study of the relationship between language and society, examines how social categories—such as age, gender, ethnicity, religion, occupation, and class—influence the use and significance of distinctive styles of speech.

LANGUAGE AND GENDER

As a major factor in personal and social identity, gender is often reflected in language use, so it is not surprising that numerous thought-provoking sociolinguistic topics fall under the category of language and gender. These include research on **gendered speech**—distinct male and female speech patterns that vary across social and cultural settings.

One of the first in-depth studies in this vein, done in the early 1970s, asserted that neither language nor gender could be studied independently of the socially constructed communities in which we live. Exploring the relationship of gender and power, this study examined the social factors said to contribute to North American women exhibiting less decisive speech styles than men. This study

▲▲

linguistic nationalism The attempt by ethnic minorities and even countries to proclaim independence by purging their language of foreign terms.

sociolinguistics The study of the relationship between language and society through examining how social categories—such as age, gender, ethnicity, religion, occupation, and class—influence the use and significance of distinctive styles of speech.

gendered speech Distinct male and female speech patterns that vary across social and cultural settings.

▼▼

ANTHROPOLOGY APPLIED

When Bambi Spoke Arapaho: Preserving Indigenous Languages

By S. Neyooxet Greymorning

In life, there are experiences later recognized as defining moments. For me, a moment like that happened in my second year of college when some mysterious individual stood over me and asked, "What are you doing to help your people?" I remember getting up, going to the library, and walking along the stacks. Trailing my fingers over books, I randomly stopped and pulled one out. It was about the overall status of American Indian languages in the United States. Curious, I opened it, looked up Arapaho, and read that it was among the healthiest Native languages. Comforted by this, it didn't occur to me that a rapidly dwindling number of young Arapaho speakers was signaling the demise of my ancestral tongue. Years later when I told tribal Elder Francis Brown about this, he said, "The Elders called your name."

Perhaps they continued to call. When I went on to graduate school and studied anthropology, I felt driven to take almost every linguistic class available. By 1981, I understood that to lose a language is to lose aspects of how a people make sense of themselves and the world they live in, and the values that culturally and psychologically bind a people together shaping their identity. Feeling the need to do something, I decided to spend the summer on the Wind River Reservation in central Wyoming putting together an Arapaho dictionary. Then I learned that University of Massachusetts professor Dr. Zdeněk Salzmann, a Czech anthropologist who did linguistic work with the Arapaho, had the same idea. I called him, and he suggested we work together.

As a graduate student I dedicated myself to gaining the knowledge, skills, and experience that could contribute to revitalizing languages. Upon completing my doctorate, in 1992, I was invited to direct

Dr. S. Neyooxet Greymorning, University of Montana

and a subsequent wave of related scholarly works have produced new insights about language as a social speech "performance" in both private and public settings.[5]

Gendered speech research also includes the study of distinct male and female syntax exhibited in various languages around the world, such as the Lakota language, still spoken at the Pine Ridge and Rosebud Indian reservations in South Dakota. When a Lakota woman asks someone, "How are you?" she says, "Tonikt*hkahe*?" But when her brother poses the same question, he says, "Tonikt*ukahwo*?" As explained by Michael Two Horses, "Our language is gender-specific in the area of commands, queries, and a couple of other things."[6]

SOCIAL DIALECTS

Sociolinguists are also interested in **dialects**—varying forms of a language that reflect particular regions, occupations, or social classes and that are similar enough to be mutually intelligible.

Distinguishing dialects from languages and revealing the relationship between power and language, the noted U.S. linguist Noam Chomsky often quoted the saying that a dialect is a language without an army.[7] Technically, all dialects are languages—there is nothing partial or sublinguistic about them—and the point at which two dialects become distinctly different languages is roughly the point at which speakers of one are unable to communicate with speakers of the other.

Dialect boundaries may be geographical, ethnic, or social-economic and they are not always very sharp. In the

---

[5]See Lakoff, R. T. (2004). *Language and woman's place.* M. Bucholtz (Ed.). New York: Oxford University Press.

[6]Personal communication, April 2003.

[7]See biographical entry for Chomsky in Shook, J. R., et al. (Eds.). (2004). *Dictionary of modern American philosophers, 1860–1960.* Bristol, UK: Thoemmes Press. The saying is attributed to Yiddish linguist Max Weinreich.

a language and culture program on the Wind River Reservation where Arapaho language instruction had been introduced within the public school system in the late 1970s. By 1993, although Arapaho was taught from kindergarten to high school, my assessment revealed students were only able to say a few basic phrases and vocabulary words having to do with food, animals, colors, and numbers—nothing near fluency and the goal of keeping Arapaho alive.

Recognizing the need for a different approach, I began laying the groundwork to establish one of the first full-day language immersion preschools on a reservation: Hinono'eitiino'oowu'—the Arapaho Language Lodge. The aim was for language "providers" to only speak Arapaho and use a multifaceted approach that included not only word and phrase acquisition, but also response exercises, visual association, and interaction with videos and audio cassettes of songs.

Around this time I contacted Disney Studios and convinced them to allow us to translate *Bambi* into Arapaho as a learning aid.[a] *Bambi* seemed like a good choice because it echoed traditional stories in which animals speak, it was a story that most children on the reservation knew,

and as the story unfolds Bambi uses simple childlike language as he learns to talk.

However, even a multifaceted approach that included Bambi speaking Arapaho was not turning the tide of language demise, so I began to think through the challenges with increased focus. From 1996 to 2002 I gradually developed a new approach, Accelerated Second Language Acquisition (ASLA©™). During 2003, using my children as language learners, I tested and honed ASLA into a workable methodology that helps re-tune the brain so people learn to visualize the language rather than continually translate back and forth in their minds between the language they know and the one they're learning.

In an effort to encourage language teachers on the reservation to adopt this approach, I have modeled teaching Arapaho through ASLA at the University of Montana with remarkable results. Beyond efforts to help preserve Arapaho, I'm regularly asked to give ASLA workshops for others who are committed to Indigenous language revitalization. To date, I have had contact with over 1,200 individual language instructors from more than 60 different communities in the US,

Canada, and Australia, representing over 40 different languages.[b]

The challenge of preserving languages (and the countless keys to life that each one holds) is daunting in our age of globalization. But something my uncle told me during a boyhood visit with him encourages me to be counted among those who keep trying. He woke me at dawn and took me to a pond. There was no wind, and the water was like glass. After instructing me to pick up a small stone, he said, "Now drop it in the pond and tell me what you see." Releasing the stone, I watched it make ever-widening circles on the water. "I want you to always remember," said my uncle, "that nothing is so small that it can't put something larger than itself into motion." ■

[a]See Greymorning, S. N. (2001). Reflections on the Arapaho Language Project or, when Bambi spoke Arapaho and other tales of Arapaho language revitalization efforts. In K. Hale & L. Hinton, *The green book of language revitalization in practice* (pp. 287–297). New York: Academic Press.
[b]For video examples of students of ASLA speaking Arapaho, plus written comments from language instructors and students about ASLA, go to www.nsilc.org.

case of regional dialects, there is frequently a transitional territory, or perhaps a buffer zone, where features of both are found and understood, as between central and southern China. However, if you learn the Chinese of Beijing, you will find that a Chinese person from Guangzhou (Canton) or Hong Kong will understand almost nothing of what you say, although both languages—or dialects—are usually lumped together as Chinese by outsiders.

A classic example of the kind of dialect that may set one group apart from others within a single society is one spoken by many inner-city African Americans. Technically known as African American Vernacular English (AAVE), it has often been referred to as *black English* and *Ebonics*. Unfortunately, there is a widespread misperception among non-AAVE speakers that this dialect is somehow

substandard or defective. A basic principle of linguistics is that the selection of a so-called prestige dialect—in this case, what we may call Standard English as opposed to AAVE—is determined by social and historical forces such as wealth and power and is not dependent on virtues or shortcomings of the dialects themselves. In fact, AAVE is a highly structured mode of speech with patterned rules of sounds and sequences like any other language or dialect. Many of its distinctive features stem from the retention of sound patterns, grammatical rules concerning verbs, and even words of the West African languages spoken by the ancestors of present-day African Americans.[8]

dialects The varying forms of a language that reflect particular regions, occupations, or social classes and that are similar enough to be mutually intelligible.

[8]Monaghan, L., Hinton, L., & Kephart, R. (1997). Can't teach a dog to be a cat? The dialogue on ebonics. *Anthropology Newsletter 38* (3), 1, 8, 9.

In many societies where different dialects or languages are spoken, individuals often know more than one and become skilled at switching back and forth, depending on the situation in which they are speaking. Without being conscious of it, we all do the same sort of thing when we switch from formality to informality in our speech, depending on where we are and to whom we are talking. The process of changing from one mode of speech to another as the situation demands, whether from one language to another or from one dialect of a language to another, is known as **code switching**, and it has been the subject of a number of sociolinguistic studies.

Ethnolinguistics

The study of the dynamic relationship between language and culture, and how they mutually influence and inform each other, is the domain of **ethnolinguistics**. In this type of research, anthropologists may investigate how a language reflects the culturally significant aspects of a people's environment. For example, Aymara Indians living in the Bolivian highlands depend on the potato (or *luki*) as their major source of food, and their language has over 200 words for this vegetable, reflecting the many varieties they traditionally grow and the many different ways that they preserve and prepare it. Similarly,

Americans in a car-manufacturing city like Detroit most likely possess a rich vocabulary allowing them to precisely distinguish between many different types of cars, categorized by model, year, and manufacturer.

Another example concerns cultural categories of color. Languages have different ways of dividing and naming elements of the color spectrum, which is actually a continuum of multiple hues with no clear-cut boundaries between them. In English we speak of red, orange, yellow, green, blue, indigo, and violet, but other languages mark out different groupings. For instance, Indians in Mexico's northwestern mountains speaking Tarahumara have just one word for both green and blue—*siyoname.*

The idea that the concepts (words such as names and verbs) and grammar (such as sentence structure) of a language affect how people perceive and think about the world is known as the theory of **linguistic relativity**. This theory is associated with the pioneering ethnolinguistic research carried out by anthropologist Edward Sapir and his student Benjamin Lee Whorf during the 1930s. Their work resulted in what is now known as the *Sapir-Whorf hypothesis*—the idea that each language provides particular grooves of linguistic expression that predispose speakers of that language to perceive the world in a certain way.

Whorf gained many of these insights while translating English into Hopi, a North American Indian language

© Kazuyoshi Namachi/Corbis

▲▲▲ Aymara Indians living in the highlands of Bolivia and Peru in South America depend on the potato as their major source of food. Their language has over 200 words for this vegetable, reflecting the many varieties they traditionally grow and the many different ways they preserve and prepare it. This is an example of linguistic relativity.

still spoken in Arizona. Doing this work, he discovered that Hopi differs from English not only in vocabulary but also in terms of its grammatical categories such as nouns and verbs. For instance, Hopi use numbers for counting and measuring things that have physical existence, but they do not apply numbers in the same way to abstractions like time. They would have no problem translating an English sentence such as, "I see fifteen sheep grazing on three acres of grassland," but an equally simple sentence such as, "Three weeks ago, I enjoyed my fifteen minutes of fame" would require a much more complex translation into Hopi.

It is also of note that Hopi verbs express tenses differently than English verbs. Rather than marking past, present, and future, with *-ed, -ing,* or *will,* Hopi requires additional words to indicate if an event is completed, is still ongoing, or is expected to take place. So instead of saying, "Three strangers stayed for fifteen days in our village," a Hopi would say something like, "We remember three strangers stay in our village until the sixteenth day." In addition, Hopi verbs do not express tense by their forms. Unlike English verbs that change form to indicate past, present, and future, Hopi verbs distinguish among a statement of fact (if the speaker actually witnesses a certain event), a statement of expectation, and a statement that expresses regularity. For instance, when you ask an English-speaking athlete "Do you run?" he may answer "Yes," when in fact he may at that moment be sitting in an armchair watching TV. A Hopi athlete asked the same question in his own language might respond "No," because in Hopi the statement of fact "he runs" translates as *wari* ("running occurs"), whereas the statement that expresses regularity "he runs" (such as, on the track team) translates as *warikngwe* ("running occurs characteristically").

This shows that the Hopi language structures thinking and behavior with a focus on the present—on getting ready and carrying out what needs to be done right now. Whorf summed it up like this: "A characteristic of Hopi behavior is the emphasis on preparation. This includes announcing and getting ready for events well beforehand, elaborate precautions to insure persistence of desired conditions, and stress on good will as the preparer of good results."[9] Based on his research on the Hopi language and culture, Whorf developed his important theoretical insight "that the structure of the language one habitually uses influences the manner in which one understands his environment. The picture of the universe shifts from tongue to tongue."[10]

In the 1990s linguistic anthropologists devised new research strategies to actually test Sapir and Whorf's original

hypothesis.[11] One study found that speakers of Swedish and Finnish (neighboring peoples who speak radically different languages), working at similar jobs in similar regions under similar laws and regulations, show significantly different rates of on-the-job accidents. The rates are substantially lower among the Swedish speakers. What emerges from comparison of the two languages is that Swedish (one of the Indo-European languages) emphasizes information about movement in three-dimensional space. Finnish (a Ural-Altaic language unrelated to Indo-European languages) emphasizes more static relations among coherent temporal entities. As a consequence, it seems that Finns organize the workplace in a way that favors the individual person over the temporal organization in the overall production process. This in turn leads to frequent production disruptions, haste, and (ultimately) accidents.

If language does mirror cultural reality, it would follow that changes in a culture will sooner or later be reflected in changes in the language. We see this happening all around the world today, including in the English language.

Language Versatility

In many societies throughout the world, it is not unusual for individuals to be fluent in two, three, or more different languages. They succeed in this in large part because they experience training in multiple languages as children—not as high school or college students, which is the educational norm in the United States.

In some regions where groups speaking different languages coexist and interact, people often understand one another but may choose not to speak the other's language. Such is the case in the borderlands of northern Bolivia and southern Peru where Quechua-speaking and Aymara-speaking Indians are neighbors. When an Aymara farmer speaks to a Quechua herder in Aymara, the Quechua will reply in Quechua, and vice versa, each knowing that the other understands both languages even if speaking just one. The ability to comprehend two languages but express oneself in only one is known as *receptive* or *passive bilingualism.*

In the United States, perhaps reflecting the country's enormous size and power, many citizens are not inter-

▲▲▲▲▲▲▲▲▲▲▲▲▲▲▲▲▲▲▲▲▲▲▲▲▲▲▲▲▲▲▲▲▲▲▲▲▲▲▲

code switching The practice of changing from one mode of speech to another as the situation demands, whether from one language to another or from one dialect of a language to another.

ethnolinguistics A branch of linguistics that studies the relationships between language and culture and how they mutually influence and inform each other.

linguistic relativity The idea that language to some extent shapes the way in which people perceive and think about the world.

▼▼

[9] Carroll, J. B. (Ed.). (1956). *Language, thought and reality: Selected writings of Benjamin Lee Whorf* (p. 148). Cambridge, MA: MIT Press.

[10] Ibid., p. vi in foreword by Stuart Chase.

[11] Lucy, J. A. (1997). Linguistic relativity. *Annual Review of Anthropology 26,* 291–312.

ested in learning a second or foreign language. This is especially significant—and troubling—since the United States is not only one of the world's most ethnically diverse countries, but it is also the world's largest economy and heavily dependent on international trade relations. In our globalized world, being bilingual or multilingual may open doors of communication not only for trade but for work, diplomacy, art, and friendship. Ironically, reluctance to learn another language prevails in the United States despite the fact that the majority language in the Americas is not English but Spanish; Spanish is not only the majority language of the hemisphere, but the fastest-growing language in the United States.

Beyond Words: The Gesture-Call System

As efficient as they are at naming and talking about ideas, actions, and things, all languages are to some degree inadequate at communicating certain kinds of information that people need to know in order to fully understand what is being said. For this reason, human speech is always embedded within a gesture-call system of a type that we share with nonhuman primates.

The various sounds and gestures of this system serve to "key" speech, providing listeners with the appropriate frame for interpreting what a speaker is saying. Messages about human emotions and intentions are effectively communicated by this gesture-call system: Is the speaker happy, sad, mad, enthusiastic, tired, or in some other emotional state? Is he or she requesting information, denying something, reporting factually, or lying? Very little of this information is conveyed by spoken language alone. In English, for example, at least 90 percent of emotional information is transmitted not by the words spoken but by body language and tone of voice.

Nonverbal Communication

The **gesture** component of the gesture-call system consists of facial expressions and bodily postures and motions that convey intended as well as subconscious messages. The study of such nonverbal signals in *body language* is known as **kinesics**.

Humanity's repertoire of body language is enormous. This is evident if you consider just one aspect of it: the fact that a human being has about fifty facial muscles and is thereby capable of making more than 7,000 facial expressions! Thus, it should not be surprising to hear that at least 60 percent of our total communication takes place nonverbally. Often, gestural messages complement spoken messages—for instance, nodding the head while affirming something verbally, raising eyebrows when asking a question, or using hands to illustrate or emphasize what is being talked about. However, nonverbal signals

are sometimes at odds with verbal ones, and they have the power to override or undercut them. For example, a person may say the words "I love you" a thousand times to another, but if it is not true, the nonverbal signals will likely communicate that falseness.

Anthropologists paid little attention to the analysis of nonverbal communication prior to the 1950s, but since then a great deal of research has been devoted to this intriguing subject. Cross-cultural studies in kinesics have shown that there are many similarities around the world in such basic facial expressions as smiling, laughing, crying, and displaying shock or anger. The smirks, frowns, and gasps that we have inherited from our primate ancestry require little learning and are harder to fake than customary or socially obtained gestures that are shared by members of a group, albeit not always consciously so.

Routine greetings are also similar around the world. Europeans, Balinese, Papuans, Samoans, Bushmen, and at least some South American Indians all smile and nod, and if the individuals are especially friendly, they will raise their eyebrows with a rapid movement, keeping them raised for a fraction of a second. By doing so, they signal a readiness for contact. The Japanese, however, suppress the eyebrow flash, regarding it as indecent, showing that there are important cross-cultural differences as well as similarities.

Another example can be found in gestural expressions for yes and no. In North America, one nods the head down then up for yes or shakes it left and right for no. The people of Sri Lanka also nod to answer yes to a factual question, but if asked to do something, a slow sideways movement of the head means yes. In Greece, the nodded head means yes, but no is indicated by jerking the head back so as to lift the face, usually with the eyes closed and the eyebrows raised.

Another aspect of nonverbal communication has to do with social space: how people position themselves physically in relation to others. **Proxemics**, the cross-cultural study of people's perception and use of space, came to the fore through the work of U.S. anthropologist Edward Hall (1914–2009), who coined the term.[12]

As a young man in the 1930s, Hall worked on construction crews with Hopi and Navajo Indians, building roads and dams. After earning his doctorate, he worked with the U.S. State Department to develop the new field of intercultural communication at the Foreign Service Institute. While training some 2,000 Foreign Service workers, his ideas about nonverbal communication began to crystallize.

Hall's research showed that people from different cultures have different frameworks for defining and organizing space—the personal space they establish around their bodies, as well as the macrolevel sensibilities that shape cultural expectations about how streets, neighborhoods, and cities should be arranged. Among other things, his investigation

---

[12]Hall, E. T. (1963). A system for the notation of proxemic behavior. *American Anthropologist* 65, 1003–1026.

VISUAL COUNTERPOINT

▲▲▲ Cultures around the world have noticeably different attitudes concerning proxemics or personal space—how far apart people should be positioned in nonintimate social encounters. How does the gap between the U.S. businessmen pictured here compare with that of the robed men of Saudi Arabia?

of personal space revealed that every culture has distinctive norms for closeness. You can see this for yourself if you are watching a foreign film, visiting a foreign country, or find yourself in a multicultural group. How close do people stand to one another when talking in the street or riding in a subway or elevator? Does the pattern match the one you are accustomed to in your own cultural corner?

Hall identified four categories of proxemically relevant spaces or body distances: intimate (0–18 inches), personal-casual (1½– 4 feet), social-consultive (4–12 feet), and public distance (12 feet and beyond). He warned that different cultural definitions of socially accepted use of space within these categories can lead to serious miscommunication and misunderstanding in cross-cultural settings.[13] His research has been a foundation stone for the present-day training of international businesspeople, diplomats, and others involved in intercultural work.

Paralanguage

The second component of the gesture-call system is **paralanguage**—specific voice effects that accompany speech and contribute to communication. These include vocalizations such as giggling, groaning, or sighing, as well as voice qualities such as volume, intensity, pitch and tempo.

The importance of paralanguage is suggested by the comment, "It's not so much *what* was said as *how* it

was said." Obviously, whispering or shouting can make a big difference in meaning, even though the uttered words would be the same when written down. Minor differences in pitch, tempo, and phrasing may seem less obvious, but they still impact how words are perceived. Studies show, for example, that subliminal messages communicated below the threshold of conscious perception by seemingly minor differences in phrasing, tempo, length of answers, and the like are far more important in courtroom proceedings than even the most perceptive trial lawyer may have realized. Among other things, *how* a witness gives testimony alters the reception it gets from jurors and influences the witness's credibility.[14]

Communication has changed radically over the past two decades with the rise of e-mail, text messaging, and Twitter. These technologies resemble the spontaneity and speed of face-to-face communication but lack the body signals and voice qualifiers that nuance what is being said (and hint at how it is being received). Studies show that the intended tone of e-mail messages is perceived

▲▲

gestures Facial expressions and bodily postures and motions that convey intended as well as subconscious messages.

kinesics The study of nonverbal signals in body language including facial expressions and bodily postures and motions.

proxemics The cross-cultural study of people's perception and use of space.

paralanguage Voice effects that accompany language and convey meaning. These include vocalizations such as giggling, groaning, or sighing, as well as voice qualities such as pitch and tempo.

▼▼

[13]Hall, E. T. (1990). *The hidden dimension* (pp.114–130). New York: Anchor Books.

[14]O'Barr, W. M., & Conley, J. M. (1993). When a juror watches a lawyer. In W. A. Haviland & R. J. Gordon (Eds.), *Talking about people* (2nd. ed., pp. 42–45). Mountain View, CA: Mayfield.

correctly only 56 percent of the time. Misunderstood messages can quickly create problems and even hostility. Since the risk of miscommunication with these technologies abounds, despite interpretation signals such as LOL (laugh out loud) or the smiley face ☺, certain sensitive exchanges are better made in person.[15]

Tonal Languages

There is an enormous diversity in the ways languages are spoken. In addition to hundreds of vowels and consonants, sounds can be divided into tones—rises and falls in pitch that play a key role in distinguishing one word from another. About 70 percent of the world's languages are **tonal languages** in which the various distinctive sound pitches of spoken words are not only an essential part of their pronunciation but are also key to their meaning.

Worldwide, at least one-third of the population speaks a tonal language, including many in Africa, Central America, and East Asia. For example, Mandarin Chinese, the most common language in China, has four contrasting tones: flat, rising, falling, and falling then rising. These tones are used to distinguish among normally stressed syllables that are otherwise identical. Thus, depending on intonation, *ba* can mean "to uproot," "to hold," "eight," or "a harrow" (farm tool).[16] Cantonese, the primary language in Guagdong and surroundings in southern China, uses six contrasting tones, and some Chinese dialects have as many as nine.

In nontonal languages, such as English, tone can still be used to convey an attitude or to change a statement into a question. But tone alone does not change the meaning of individual words as it does in Mandarin, where careless use of tones with the syllable *ma* could cause one to call someone's mother a horse!

Telecommunication: Talking Drums and Whistled Speech

Even a very loud human voice has its natural limits beyond which our ears cannot pick up the sound. Of course, sounds carry farther in some environments than in others. For example, shouts across a lake or canyon are more easily heard than those passing through a thick forest.

Until the telecommunication inventions of the 19th century, acoustic space was limited by natural factors. Yet long ago people found ways to expand their acoustic range, sounding information far beyond their loudest vocal reach. One example is the *talking drum*. Widespread among tonal-speaking peoples in West Africa, these large drums can transmit coded information that can be heard from as far away as 12 kilometers (7½ miles).

Another traditional telecommunication system used to expand acoustic space is **whistled speech,** an exchange of whistled words using a phonetic emulation of the sounds produced in spoken voice.[17] Whistling sounds are generated by blowing, producing air vibrations at the mouth's aperture; the faster the air stream, the higher the noise. Whistled speech can be more effective across great distances than shouted talk because it occurs at a higher pitch or frequency range.

Whistling techniques vary. Some involve both lips, others use lips and teeth or a retroflexed tongue with various finger combinations. Two-finger whistling can produce very loud sounds and in a ravine can be picked up by the human ear from as far away as 8 kilometers (5 miles).

Although whistled speech tends to be an abridged form of everyday spoken language, its vocabulary can be considerable. In Silbo, for instance, traditionally used by Spanish-speaking inhabitants of La Gomera off the northwest African coast, islanders can whistle some 2,000 words.

While its precise origins are not known, whistled speech still occurs in more than thirty languages around the world. Like the talking drum, it is an endangered tradition—disappearing in part because the communities where the practice once thrived are no longer isolated or because the ancestral lifeways are vanishing or already gone. Moreover, the ever-expanding reach of mobile phones and other electronic telecommunication technologies have contributed to the demise of whistled language.[18]

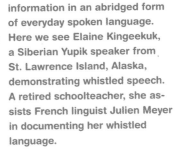

▲▲▲ Whistled speech, occurring in about thirty languages around the world, allows community members to exchange essential information in an abridged form of everyday spoken language. Here we see Elaine Kingeekuk, a Siberian Yupik speaker from St. Lawrence Island, Alaska, demonstrating whistled speech. A retired schoolteacher, she assists French linguist Julien Meyer in documenting her whistled language.

© Rolex/Jacques Belat

[15]Kruger, J., et al. (2005, December). Egocentrism over e-mail: Can people communicate as well as they think? *Journal of Personality and Social Psychology* 89 (6), 925–936.

[16]Catford, J. C. (1988). *A practical introduction to phonetics* (p. 183). Oxford: Clarendon Press.

[17]Meyer, J., Meunier, F., & Dentel, L. (2007). Identification of natural whistled vowels by non-whistlers. *Proceedings of Interspeech 2007* (pp. 1593–1596). Antwerpen, Belgium.

[18]Meyer J., & Gautheron, B. (2006). Whistled speech and whistled languages. In K. Brown (Ed.), *Encyclopedia of language & linguistics* (2nd ed., vol. 13, pp. 573–576). Oxford, UK: Elsevier; Meyer, J. (2008). Typology and acoustic strategies of whistled languages: Phonetic comparison and perceptual cues of whistled vowels. *Journal of the International Phonetic Association* 38, 69–94.

The Origins of Language

Cultures all around the world have sacred stories or myths addressing the age-old question of the origin of human languages. Anthropologists collecting these stories have often found that cultural groups tend to locate the place of origin in their own ancestral homelands and believe that the first humans also spoke their language.

For example, the Incas of Peru tell the story of Pacha Camac ("Earth Maker"), the divine creator, who came to the valley of Tiwanaku in the Andean highlands in ancient times. As the myth goes, Pacha Camac drew people up from the earth, making out of clay a person of each nation, painting each with particular clothing, and giving each a language to speak and songs to sing.

On the other side of the globe, ancient Israelites believed that it was Yahweh, the divine creator, who had given them Hebrew, the original tongue spoken in paradise. Later, when humans began building the high Tower of Babel to signify their own power and to link earth and heaven, Yahweh intervened. He created a confusion of tongues so that people could no longer understand one another, and he scattered them all across the face of the earth, leaving the massive tower unfinished.

Early scientific efforts to explain the origin of language suffered from a lack of solid data. Today there is more scientific evidence, including genetic information, to work with—better knowledge of primate brains, new studies of primate communication, more information on the development of linguistic competence in children, more human fossils that can be used to tentatively reconstruct what ancient brains and vocal tracts were like, and a better understanding of the lifeways of early human ancestors. We still cannot conclusively prove how, when, and where human language first developed, but we can now theorize reasonably on the basis of more and better information.

The fossil record shows that the archaic humans known as Neandertals (living from 28,000 to 125,000 years ago in Europe and southwestern Asia) had the neurological and anatomical features necessary for speech. Fossilized brain casts from earlier members of the genus *Homo* provide evidence of specializations in the left hemisphere of the brain associated with the development of language. The observation that the earliest stone tools were made predominantly by right-handed individuals also supports the idea that lateral specialization had occurred by this time.

Because human language is embedded within a gesture-call system of a type that we share with nonhuman primates (especially great apes), anthropologists have gained considerable insight on human language by observing the communication systems of fellow primates. Like humans, apes are capable of referring to events removed in time and space, a phenomenon known as **displacement** and one of the distinctive features of human language.[19]

Since there is continuity between gestural and spoken language, the latter could have emerged from the former through increasing emphasis on finely controlled movements of the mouth and throat. This scenario is consistent with the appearance of neurological structures underlying language in the earliest representatives of the genus *Homo* and steady enlargement of the human brain 200,000 to 2.5 million years ago. The soft tissues of the vocal tract related to speech are not preserved in the fossil record. But as outlined in the Biocultural Connection on the next page, a comparison of the vocal anatomy of chimps and humans allows paleoanthropologists to identify the anatomical differences responsible for human speech that appeared over the course of human evolution.[20]

There are obvious advantages to spoken over gestural language for a species increasingly dependent on tool use for survival. To talk with your hands, you must stop whatever else you are doing with them; speech does not interfere with that. Other benefits include being able to talk in the dark, past opaque objects, or among speakers whose attention is diverted. Although we do not know precisely when the changeover to spoken language took place, all would agree that spoken languages are at least as old as the species *Homo sapiens*.

From Speech to Writing

When anthropology developed as an academic discipline over a century ago, it concentrated its attention on small traditional communities that relied primarily on personal interaction and oral communication for survival. Cultures that depend on talking and listening often have rich traditions of storytelling and speechmaking, which play a central role in education, conflict resolution, political decision making, spiritual or supernatural practices, and many other aspects of life.

---

[19]For a discussion covering thirty years of chimpanzee sign language studies and some neurological and behavior data accounting for the similarity between human and nonhuman communication systems, see Fouts, R. S., & Waters, G. (2001). Chimpanzee sign language and Darwinian continuity: Evidence for a neurology continuity of language. *Neurological Research 23*, 787–794.

[20]Evolutionary theorist Philip Lieberman argues that the human language ability is the confluence of a succession of separate evolutionary developments rigged together by natural selection for an evolutionarily unique ability. See Lieberman, P. (2006). *Toward an evolutionary biology of language*. Cambridge, MA: Belknap Press.

▲▲▲

tonal language A language in which the sound pitch of a spoken word is an essential part of its pronunciation and meaning.

whistled speech An exchange of whistled words using a phonetic emulation of the sounds produced in spoken voice.

displacement A term referring to things and events removed in time and space.

▼▼▼

BIOCULTURAL CONNECTION

The Biology of Human Speech

While other primates have shown some capacity for language (a socially agreed-on code of communication), actual speech is unique to humans; this ability is linked to humans' distinct anatomical development of the vocal organs.

Of particular importance are the positions of the human larynx (voice box) and the epiglottis. The larynx—situated in the respiratory tract between the pharynx (throat) and trachea (windpipe)—contains the vocal chords. The epiglottis is the structure that separates the esophagus or food pipe from the windpipe as food passes from the mouth to the stomach. (See the figure for comparative diagrams of the anatomy of this region in chimps and humans.)

As humans mature and develop the neurological and muscular coordination for speech, the larynx and epiglottis shift to a downward position. The human tongue bends at the back of the throat and is attached to the pharynx, the region of the throat where the food and airways share a common path. Sound occurs as air exhaled from the lungs passes over the vocal cords and causes them to vibrate.

Through continuous interactive movements of the tongue, pharynx, lips, and teeth, as well as nasal passages, the sounds are alternately modified to produce speech—the uniquely patterned sounds of a particular language. Based on longstanding socially learned patterns of speech, different languages stress certain distinctive types of sounds as significant and ignore others. For instance, languages belonging to the Iroquoian family, such as Mohawk, Seneca, and Cherokee, are among the few in the world that have no bilabial stops (*b* and *p* sounds). They also lack the labiodental spirants (*f* and *v* sounds), leaving the bilabial nasal *m* sound as the only consonant requiring lip articulation.

It takes many years of practice for people to master the muscular movements needed to produce the precise sounds of any particular language. But no human could produce the finely controlled speech sounds without a lowered position of the larynx and epiglottis. ▪

Biocultural Question

Sharing a capacity for speech, humans say and understand many thousands of words. Since macaws and other parrots also learn many words, do they have speech? And if so, do they actually think? Do they have language?

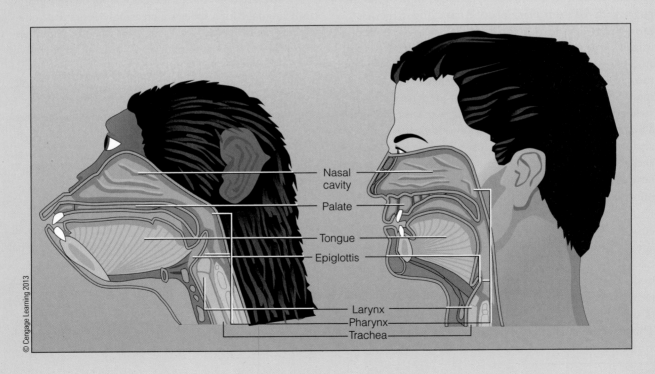

Nasal cavity
Palate
Tongue
Epiglottis
Larynx
Pharynx
Trachea

© Cengage Learning 2013

Traditional orators (from the Latin *orare* "to speak") are usually trained from the time they are very young. They often enhance their extraordinary memorization skills through rhyme, rhythm, and melody. Orators may also employ special objects to help them remember—notched sticks, knotted strings, bands embroidered with shells, and so forth. Traditional Iroquois Indian orators often performed their formal speeches with wampum belts made of hemp string with white and bluish-purple shell beads woven into distinctive patterns that symbolize a variety of important messages or agreements, including treaties with other nations.

Thousands of languages, past and present, have existed only in spoken form, but many others have been documented in graphic symbols of some sort. Over time, simplified pictures of things (pictographs) evolved into more stylized symbolic forms.

Although different peoples invented a variety of graphic styles, anthropologists distinguish an actual **writing system** as a set of visible or tactile signs used to represent units of language in a systematic way. Symbols carved into 8,600-year-old tortoise shells recently discovered in western China may represent the world's earliest evidence of elementary writing.[21]

A fully developed early writing system is Egyptian hieroglyphics, developed some 5,000 years ago and in use for about 3,500 years. Another very old system is *cuneiform*, an arrangement of wedge-shaped imprints developed primarily in Mesopotamia (southern Iraq), which lasted nearly as long. Cuneiform writing stands out among other early forms in that it led to the first phonetic writing system (that is, an **alphabet** or series of symbols representing the sounds of a language), ultimately spawning a wide array of alphabetic writing systems. About two millennia after these systems were established, others began to appear, developing independently in distant locations around the world.[22] The word *alphabet* comes from the first two letters in the Greek writing system, *alpha* and *beta*.

Literacy and Modern Telecommunication in Our Globalizing World

Thousands of years have passed since literacy first emerged, yet today nearly 800 million adults worldwide cannot read or write. Two-thirds of them are women, with

▲▲▲ The telecommunication revolution is reaching even the most remote places on earth thanks to satellite phones and cell phone towers powered by fossil fuel, the sun, or the wind. Those without phones of their own can often find mobile phone stands such as this one in Kampala, Uganda, in East Africa.

© Charles Sturge/Alamy

rural women topping the list. For example, fewer than half of the rural women in India can read and write, and in some of the country's northeastern districts only one in five is literate. Looking at the next generation, 75 million children around the world are not enrolled in school.[23]

Illiteracy condemns already disadvantaged people to ongoing poverty—migrant rural workers, refugees, ethnic minorities, and those living in rural backlands and urban slums. Declaring literacy a human right, the United Nations established September 8 as International Literacy Day and proclaimed the period 2003 to 2012 as the Literacy Decade with the objective of extending literacy to all humanity.[24]

While many people in the world still rely on others to write and read for them, the global telecommunication revolution has reached the most remote villages on earth. The demand for cell phones is high, even among the poor in rural backlands and urban slums—and they

▲▲▲

writing system A set of visible or tactile signs used to represent units of language in a systematic way.

alphabet A series of symbols representing the sounds of a language arranged in a traditional order.

▼▼▼

[21]Li, X., et al. (2003). The earliest writing? Sign use in the seventh millennium BC at Jiahu, Henan Province, China. *Antiquity 77*, 31–44.

[22]del Carmen Rodríguez Martínez, M., et al. (2006). Oldest writing in the New World. *Science 313* (5793), 1610–1614.

[23]UNESCO Institute for Statistics. http://www.uis.unesco.org/Literacy/Pages/default.aspx (retrieved September 1, 2011).

[24]UNESCO Literacy Decade. http://www.unesco.org/new/en/education/themes/education-building-blocks/literacy/un-literacy-decade/ (retrieved September 1, 2011).

make long-distance communication possible without literacy. Many use these phones only for voice calls. But others also use them to download e-mails, exchange text messages, and explore the Internet.

Beyond maintaining social networks, mobile phones are increasingly used in everyday subsistence strategies. For example, they enable tens of millions of poor rural-dwellers in developing countries to locate the best prices for their produce—making it possible for growers to deal directly with district markets rather than going through intermediaries.[25]

In today's fast-changing globalizing world, the mobile phone is more than a means of communication. It has become a survival tool—perhaps nowhere more so than in Japan, which now ranks as the world's top cellular nation. On the move and surrounded by strangers, people use their mobiles to get and give information, to express their individuality, and to stay in touch—Twittering instead of whistling to avoid feeling lost in the global jungle. ✳

---

[25] See Horst, H., & Miller, D. (2006). *The cell phone: An anthropology of communication*. New York: Berg.

Chapter Checklist

What is language, and does the term apply only to humans?

✓ Language is a system of communication using symbolic sounds, gestures, or marks that are put together according to a set of rules. It is through language that people in every society are able to share their experiences, concerns, and beliefs, over the past and in the present, and to communicate these to the next generation. Language makes communication of infinite meanings possible to fellow speakers.

✓ Today's language experts differ on how much credit to give to animals, such as various dolphin and ape species, for the ability to use symbols as well as signals, even though these animals and many others have been found to communicate in remarkable ways. Several chimpanzees, gorillas, and orangutans have been taught American Sign Language.

What areas of language study or linguistics do anthropologists pursue?

✓ The three branches of language study in anthropology are descriptive linguistics, historical linguistics, and a third branch that focuses on language in relation to social and cultural settings.

✓ Descriptive linguists mark out and explain the features of a language at a particular time in its history. Their work includes phonology (the study of language sound patterns) and the investigation of grammar—all rules concerning

morphemes (the smallest units of meaningful combinations of sounds) and syntax (the principles according to which phrases and sentences are built).

✓ Historical linguists investigate relationships between earlier and later forms of the same language—including identifying the forces behind the changes that have taken place in languages in the course of linguistic divergence. Their work provides a means of roughly dating certain migrations, invasions, and people's intercultural interactions.

✓ The third area of linguistic anthropology is the study of language as it relates to society and culture—research areas known as sociolinguistics and ethnolinguistics. Sociolinguists study the relationship between language and society, examining how social categories (such as age, gender, ethnicity, religion, occupation, and class) influence the use and significance of distinctive styles of speech. Ethnolinguists study the dynamic relationship between language and culture and how they mutually influence and inform each other.

How have languages evolved through time, and why have so many disappeared?

✓ All languages change—borrowing terms from other languages or inventing new words for new technologies or social realities. A major cause of language change is the domination of one society over another, which over the last 500 years led to the disappearance of about

half of the world's 12,000 languages. A reaction to this loss and to the current far-reaching spread and domination of the English language is linguistic nationalism— purging foreign terms from a language's vocabulary and pressing for the revitalization of lost or threatened languages.

✓ Many of the world's languages have become extinct as a direct result of warfare, epidemics, and forced assimilation brought on by colonial powers and other aggressive outsiders. Most people in the world today speak one of the dominant languages; very few people speak each of the remaining languages, and many of them are losing speakers rapidly due to globalization.

✓ A social dialect is the language of a group of people within a larger one, all of whom may speak more or less the same language.

Is language more than words?

✓ Human language is embedded in a gesture-call system inherited from our primate ancestors that serves to "key" speech, providing the appropriate frame for interpreting linguistic form.

✓ The gesture component consists of facial expressions and bodily postures and motions that convey intended as well as subconscious messages. The study of such nonverbal signals in body language is known as kinesics. Proxemics is the study of how people perceive and use space.

✔ The call component of the gesture-call system is represented by paralanguage, consisting of various voice qualities such as pitch and tempo and vocalizations such as giggling or sighing.

✔ About 70 percent of the world's languages are tonal, in which the musical pitch of a spoken word is an essential part of its pronunciation and meaning.

What are the origins of spoken and written language, and how do modern telecommunication systems impact literacy around the world?

✔ Cultures around the world have sacred stories or myths about the origin of human languages. All agree that spoken languages are at least as old as the species *Homo sapiens*.

✔ The first writing systems—Egyptian hieroglyphics and cuneiform—developed about 5,000 years ago. Recently discovered symbols carved into 8,600-year-old tortoise shells found in western China may represent the world's earliest evidence of elementary writing.

✔ The global telecom industry reaches into the most remote corners of the world, not only transforming how people communicate, but with whom and about what.

Questions for Reflection

1. In what ways do you feel prepared or unprepared to meet the challenge of communicating effectively in our increasingly globalized world?

2. Over the last 500 years, half of the world's 12,000 languages vanished. It is now estimated that about 30 languages per year will become extinct during the current century. Do you see this demise as positive or negative?

3. Applying the principle of linguistic relativity to your own language, consider how your perceptions of objective reality might have been shaped by your language. How might your sense of time be different if you grew up speaking Hopi?

4. What distinguishes us from apes like Koko the gorilla? What words might Koko choose to tell us about her confined existence as a subject of scientific research?

5. Since much of our communication is nonverbal, how effective do you think text message codes like OJ (only joking), XD (excited), VSF (very sad face), or G (grin) are in digital communication when e-mailing or texting? Have your digital messages ever been misunderstood? If so, what do you think was at the root of the miscommunication, and how was it resolved?

Key Terms

language
signals
linguistics
phonetics
phonology
phonemes
morphology
morphemes
syntax
grammar

language family
linguistic divergence
linguistic nationalism
sociolinguistics
gendered speech
dialects
code switching
ethnolinguistics
linguistic relativity
gestures

kinesics
proxemics
paralanguage
tonal language
whistled speech
displacement
writing system
alphabet

Online Study Resources

Login to **www.cengagebrain.com** to access the resources your instructor has assigned and to purchase materials. For this book, you can access:

CourseMate
Access chapter-specific learning tools including flashcards, glossaries, practice quizzes, videos, and more in your Anthropology CourseMate.

VISUAL ESSENCE

Every society reproduces itself biologically as well as culturally. From generation to generation, children learn the values, social codes, and skills that condition them for their future social status as adult men and women. Most traditional communities raise their children in ways that ensure they have the appropriate appearance, clothing, attitude, and other culturally significant features that indicate gender differences. Here we see a Kazakh father and son setting out on a hunting expedition with a golden eagle in the Altai Mountains of western Mongolia. Kazakhs are seminomadic herders living in northern regions of Central Asia. For centuries, they have trained these fast birds of prey, equipped with extremely powerful talons and a wingspan of well over 2 meters (more than 7 feet), to partner them in hunting rabbit, fox, goat, and even wolf—primarily for meat and hides. Eagle hunting is a male tradition. Boys learn from their fathers and uncles how to capture, raise, train, and confidently handle an eagle from fledgling to maturity—how to ride high and proud on their horse stirrups with this huge raptor on their arm; when and how to release the bird to pursue the prey; and how to gallop across the steppe as fast as the wind to claim it.

10 Social Identity, Personality, and Gender

in 1690 English philosopher John Locke presented the *tabula rasa* theory in *An Essay Concerning Human Understanding*. This notion holds that a newborn human is like a blank slate, and what the individual becomes in life is written on the slate by his or her life experiences. The implication is that at birth all individuals are basically the same in their potential for character development and that their adult personalities are exclusively the products of their postnatal experiences, which differ from culture to culture.

Locke's idea offered high hopes for the all-embracing impact of intellectual and moral instruction on a child's character formation, but it missed the mark, as we now know, for it did not take into consideration genetic contributions to human behavior. Based on recent breakthroughs in human genetic research, anthropologists have come to recognize that an identifiable portion of our behavior is genetically influenced.[1] This means each person is born with a particular set of inherited tendencies that help mark out his or her adult personality. While this genetic inheritance sets certain broad potentials and limitations, an individual's cultural environment, gender, social status, and unique life experiences, particularly in the early childhood years, also play a significant role in personality formation.

Since different cultures handle the raising and education of children in different ways, these practices and their effects on adult personalities are important subjects of anthropological inquiry. Such cross-cultural studies gave rise to the specialization of psychological anthropology and are the subjects of this chapter.

In this chapter you will learn to:

- **Discuss the distinctive cultural forces that shape personality and social identity.**

- **Explain how cultures are learned and passed to new generations.**

- **Distinguish between sex and gender from a cross-cultural perspective.**

- **Give examples that illustrate the cultural relativity of normality and abnormality.**

- **Describe culturally specific mental disorders.**

Enculturation: The Self and Social Identity

From the moment of birth, a person faces multiple survival challenges. Obviously, newborns cannot take care of their own biological needs. Only in myths and romantic fantasies do we encounter stories about children successfully coming of age alone in the wilderness or accomplishing this feat having been raised by animals in the wild. Millions of children around the world have been

◀ ◀ ◀ Recognizing herself in the mirror, this young girl has developed the self-awareness necessary to understand that she is a distinct individual. In modern industrial and postindustrial societies, self-awareness is typically established by about age 2.

© Laura Dwight/Corbis

fascinated by stories about Tarzan and the apes or the jungle boy Mowgli and the wolves. Moreover, young and old alike have been captivated by newspaper hoaxes about "wild" children, such as a 10-year-old boy reported found running among gazelles in the Syrian Desert in 1946.

Fanciful ideas aside, human children are biologically ill equipped to survive without culture. This point has been driven home by several documented cases of feral children (*feral* comes from *fera*, which is Latin for "wild animal") who grew up deprived of human contact. None of them had a happy ending. For instance, there was nothing romantic about the girl Kamala, supposedly rescued from a wolf den in India in 1920: She moved about on all fours and could not feed herself. And Parisians considered the naked "wild boy" captured in the woods outside Aveyron village in 1800 an incurable idiot.

Worse still is the true story of Genie, the "wild child" of Los Angeles, who spent her entire childhood in near total isolation. Imprisoned alone by her deranged father in a room with covered windows, she was infantile and emaciated when her nearly blind mother dragged the 13-year-old girl into a welfare office in 1970. Bounced back and forth between her mother, foster parents, and institutions, Genie never mastered the rudiments of language and now lives in a home for retarded adults.[2] Clearly, the biological capacity for what we think of as human, which entails culture, must be nurtured to be realized.

Because culture is socially constructed and learned rather than biologically inherited, all societies must somehow ensure that culture is adequately transmitted from one generation to the next—a process we have already defined as *enculturation*. Since each group lives by a particular set of cultural rules, a child will have to learn the rules of his or her society in order to survive. Most of that learning takes place in the first few years when a child learns how to feel, think, speak, and ultimately act like an adult who embodies being Japanese, Kikuyu, Lakota, Norwegian, or whatever ethnic or national group into which it is born.

The first agents of enculturation in all societies are the members of the infant's household, especially the child's mother. (In fact, cultural factors are at work even before birth through what a pregnant mother eats, drinks, and inhales, as well as the sounds, rhythms, and activity patterns of her daily life.) Who the other members are depends on how households are structured in each particular society.

As the young person matures, people outside the household are brought into the enculturation process. These usually include other relatives and certainly the individual's peers. In some societies, professionals are brought into the process to provide formal instruction. In others, children are allowed to learn through observation and participation, at their own speed.

Self-Awareness

Enculturation begins with the development of **self-awareness**—the ability to identify oneself as an individual creature, to reflect on oneself, and to evaluate oneself. Humans do not have this ability at birth, even though it is essential for their successful social func-

─────────────

[1]Harpending, H., & Cochran, G. (2002). In our genes. *Proceedings of the National Academy of Sciences USA 99* (1), 10–12.

[2]Rymer, R. (1994). *Genie: A scientific tragedy*. New York: HarperCollins.

tioning. It is self-awareness that permits one to assume responsibility for one's conduct, to learn how to react to others, and to assume a variety of roles in society. An important aspect of self-awareness is the attachment of positive value to one's self. Without this, individuals cannot be motivated to act to their advantage.

Self-awareness does not come all at once. In modern industrial and postindustrial societies, for example, self and non-self are not clearly distinguished until a child is about 2 years of age, lagging somewhat behind other cultures.[3] Self-awareness develops in concert with neuromotor development, which is known to proceed at a slower rate in infants from industrial societies than in infants in many, perhaps even most, small-scale farming or foraging communities. The reasons for this slower rate are not yet clear, although the amount of human contact and stimulation that infants receive seems to play an important role.

As noted earlier in this text, infants in the United States, for example, generally do not sleep with their parents, most often being put in rooms of their own. This is seen as an important step in making them into individuals, "owners" of themselves and their capacities. As a consequence, they do not experience the steady stream of personal stimuli, including smell, movement, and warmth, that they would if co-sleeping. Private sleeping also takes away the opportunity for frequent nursing through the night.

In the majority of the world's human societies, infants routinely sleep with their parents, or at least their mothers. Also, they are carried or held most other times, usually in an upright position, often in the company of other people and amid various activities. The mother typically responds to a cry or "fuss" within seconds, usually offering the infant her breast.

This steady stream of contact and varied stimuli is significant, for studies show that stimulation plays a key role in the hardwiring of the brain; it is necessary for development of the neural circuitry. Looking at breast-feeding in particular, the longer a child is breastfed, the better his or her overall health, the higher he or she will score on cognitive tests, and the lower the risk of obesity, allergies, and attention deficit hyperactivity disorder.[4] Because our biological heritage as primates has programmed us to develop in response to social stimuli, it is not surprising that self-awareness and a variety of other beneficial qualities develop more rapidly in response to close contact with other humans.

Social Identity Through Personal Naming

Personal names are important devices for self-definition in all cultures. It is through naming that a social group acknowledges a child's birthright and establishes its social identity. Among the many cultural rules that exist in each society, those having to do with naming are unique because they individualize a person and at the same time identify one as a group member. In fact, names often express and represent multiple aspects of one's group identity—ethnic, gender, religious, political, or even rank, class, or caste. Without a name, an individual has no identity, no self. For this reason, many cultures consider name selection to be an important issue and mark the naming of a child with a special event or ritual known as a **naming ceremony**.

NAMING PRACTICES ACROSS CULTURES

Worldwide, there are countless contrasting approaches to naming. For example, Aymara Indians in the Bolivian highland community of Laymi do not consider an infant truly human until they have given it a name. Naming does not happen until the child begins to speak the Aymara language, typically around the age of 2. Once the child shows the ability to speak like a human, he or she is considered fit to be recognized as such with a proper name. A naming ceremony marks the child's social transition from a state of nature to culture and consequently to full acceptance into the Laymi community.

Unlike the Aymara, Icelanders name their babies at birth. Following ancient custom Icelandic infants receive the father's personal given name as their last name. The suffix *sen* is added to a boy's name and *dottir* to a girl's name. Thus, a brother and sister whose father is named Sven Olafsen would have the last names Svensen and Svendottir. Although such *patronyms* are common in Iceland, sometimes the mother's first name is chosen for her child's surname. Such *matronyms* (surnames based on mother's names) may be preferred for a boy or girl whose mother remains unmarried, is divorced, or simply prefers her own name identifying family status. Such is the case with an Icelandic woman named Eva, with a daughter named Gudrun Evasdottir and son Gunnar Evason. Matronymic traditions occur in several other parts of the world, including the Indonesian island of

▲▲

self-awareness The ability to identify oneself as an individual, to reflect on oneself, and to evaluate oneself.

naming ceremony A special event or ritual to mark the naming of a child.

▼▼

[3]Rochat, P. (2001). Origins of self-concept. In G. Bremner & A. Fogel (Eds.), *Blackwell handbook of infant development* (pp. 191–212). Malden, MA: Blackwell.

[4]Dettwyler, K. A. (1997, October). When to wean. *Natural History,* 49; World Health Organization. (2003). *Global strategy on infant and young child feeding.* Geneva: WHO.

◀ Navajo babies begin to learn the importance of community at a special First Laugh Ceremony (*Chi Dlo Dil*). At this event, the person who prompted an infant's first laugh teaches the child (and reminds the community) about the joy of generosity by helping the baby to give symbolic gifts of sweets and rock salt to each guest. Pictured here is the baby daughter of a pediatrician working at a remote clinic on the reservation. She celebrates her first laugh wearing a Navajo dress and jewelry given to her by her mother's Navajo patients.

Sumatra, homeland of the Minangkabau. In this ethic group of several million people, children are members of their mother's clan, inheriting her family name.

Among the Netsilik Inuit in Arctic Canada, a mother experiencing a difficult delivery would call out the names of deceased people of admirable character. The name being called at the moment of birth was thought to enter the infant's body and help the delivery, and the child would bear that name thereafter. Inuit parents may also name their children for deceased relatives in the belief that the spiritual identification will help shape their character.[5]

In many cultures, a person receives a name soon after birth but may acquire new names during subsequent life phases. Navajo Indians from the southwestern United States name a child at birth, but traditionalists often give the baby an additional ancestral clan name after the child laughs for the first time. Among the Navajo, laughter is seen as the earliest expression of human language, a signal that life as a social being has started. Thus it is an occasion for celebration. The person who prompted that very first laugh invites family and close friends to a First Laugh Ceremony. At the gathering, the party sponsor places rock salt in the baby's hand and helps slide the salt all over the little one's body. Representing tears—of both laughter and sadness—the salt is said to provide strength and protection, leading to a long, happy life. Then the ancestral name is given.[6]

NAMING AND IDENTITY POLITICS

Because names symbolically express and represent an individual's cultural self, they may gain particular significance in personal and collective identity politics. For instance, when an ethnic group or nation falls under the control of a more powerful and expanding neighboring group, its members may be forced to assimilate and give up their cultural identity. Name-change stories are also common among immigrants hoping to avoid racial discrimination or ethnic stigmatization. For instance, it was not uncommon for Jewish immigrants and their U.S.-born children to Americanize their names: Comedian Joan Molinsky became Joan Rivers and fashion designer Ralph Lifshitz became Ralph Lauren.

In identity politics, naming can also be a resistance strategy by a minority group asserting its cultural pride or even rights of self-determination against a dominant society. In the United States, for instance, African Americans with inherited Christian names that were imposed upon their enslaved ancestors have, in growing numbers, rejected those names. Many have also abandoned the faith tradition represented by those names to become members of the Nation of Islam (Black Muslims). An enduringly famous example of this is champion boxer Cassius Clay, who converted to Islam in the mid-1960s. Like others, he rejected his "slave name" and adopted the name Muhammad Ali.

Self and the Behavioral Environment

The development of self-awareness requires basic orientations that structure the psychological field in which the self acts. These include object orientation, spatial orientation, temporal orientation, and normative orientation.

[5] Balikci, A. (1970). *The Netsilik Eskimo.* Garden City, NY: Natural History.

[6] Authors' participant observation at traditional Navajo First Laugh ceremony of Wesley Bitsie-Baldwin; personal communication, LaVerne Bitsie-Baldwin and Anjanette Bitsie.

Every individual must learn about a world of objects other than the self. Through this *object orientation,* each culture singles out for attention certain environmental features, while ignoring others or lumping them together into broad categories. A culture also explains the perceived environment. This is important, for a cultural explanation of one's surroundings imposes a measure of order and provides the individual with a sense of direction needed to act meaningfully and effectively.

Behind this lies a powerful psychological drive to reduce uncertainty—part of the common human need for a balanced and integrated perspective on the relevant universe. When confronted with ambiguity and uncertainty, people invariably strive to clarify and give structure to the situation; they do this in ways that their particular culture deems appropriate. Thus our observations and explanations of the universe are largely culturally constructed and mediated symbolically through language. Everything in the physical environment varies in the way it is perceived and experienced by humans. In short, we perceive the world around us through a cultural lens.

The behavioral environment in which the self acts also involves *spatial orientation,* or the ability to get from one object or place to another. In all societies, the names and significant features of places are important references for spatial orientation. Finding your way to class, remembering where you left your car keys, directing someone to the nearest bus stop, or traveling through deep underground networks in subway tunnels are examples of highly complex cognitive tasks based on spatial orientation and memory. So is a desert nomad's ability to travel long distances from one remote oasis to another—determining the route by means of a mental map of the vast open landscape and gauging location by the position of the sun in daytime, the stars at night, and even by the winds and smell of the air.

Technological revolutions in the past few decades have led to the invention of a newly created media environment, where we learn to orient ourselves in cyberspace. Without our spatial orientations, whether in physical or virtual reality, navigating through daily life would be impossible.

Temporal orientation, which gives people a sense of their place in time, is also part of the behavioral environment. Connecting past actions with those of the present and future provides a sense of self-continuity. This is the function of a calendar. Derived from the Latin word *kalendae,* which originally referred to a public announcement at the first day of a new month or moon, such a chart gives people a framework for organizing their days, weeks, months, and even years. Just as the perceived environment of objects is organized in cultural terms, so too are time and space.

A final aspect of the behavioral environment is the *normative orientation.* Moral values, ideals, and principles, which are purely cultural in origin, are as much a part of the individual's behavioral environment as are trees, rivers, and mountains. Without them people would have nothing by which to gauge their own actions or those of others. Normative orientation includes standards that indicate what ranges of behavior are acceptable for males, females, and whichever additional gender roles exist in a particular society.

Culture and Personality

In the process of enculturation, each individual is introduced to a society's natural and human-made environment along with a collective body of ideas about the self and others. The result is the creation of a kind of internalized cultural map of the world in which the individual will feel, think, and act as a social being. It is each person's particular guide of how to run the maze of life. When we speak of someone's personality, we are generalizing about that individual's internalized map over time. Thus personalities are products of enculturation, as experienced by individuals, each with his or her distinctive genetic makeup.

Personality does not lend itself to a formal definition, but for our purposes we may take it as the distinctive way a person thinks, feels, and behaves. Derived from the Latin word *persona,* meaning "mask," the term relates to the idea of learning to play one's role on the stage of daily life. Gradually, the mask, as it is placed on a child, begins to shape that person until there is little sense of the mask as a superimposed alien force. Instead it feels natural, as if one were born with it. The individual has successfully internalized the culture.

Personality Development: A Cross-Cultural Perspective on Gender

Although *what* one learns is important to personality development, most anthropologists assume that *how* one learns is no less important. Along with psychological theorists, anthropologists view childhood experiences as strongly influencing adult personality, and they are most interested in analyses that seek to prove, modify, or at least shed light on the cultural differences in shaping personality.

For example, the traditional ideal in Western societies has been for men to be tough, aggressive, assertive, dominant, and self-reliant, whereas women have been expected to be gentle, passive, obedient, and caring. To

personality The distinctive way a person thinks, feels, and behaves.

many, these personality contrasts between the sexes seem so natural that they are thought to be biologically grounded and therefore fundamental, unchangeable, and universal. But are they? Have anthropologists identified any psychological or personality characteristics that universally differentiate men and women?

U.S. anthropologist Margaret Mead is well known as a pioneer in the cross-cultural study of both personality and gender. In the early 1930s she studied three ethnic groups in Papua New Guinea—the Arapesh, the Mundugamor, and the Tchambuli. This comparative research suggested that whatever biological differences exist between men and women, they are extremely malleable. In short, she concluded, biology is not destiny. Mead found that among the Arapesh, relations between men and women were expected to be equal, with both genders exhibiting what most North Americans traditionally consider feminine traits (cooperative, nurturing, and gentle). She also discovered gender equality among the Mundugamor (now generally called Biwat); however, in that community both genders displayed supposedly masculine traits (individualistic, assertive, volatile, aggressive). Among the Tchambuli (now called Chambri), however, Mead found that women dominated men.[7]

More recent anthropological research suggests that some of Mead's interpretations of gender roles were incorrect—for instance, Chambri women neither dominate Chambri men nor vice versa. Yet, overall her research generated new insights into the human condition, showing that male dominance is not genetically fixed in our human nature. Instead, it is socially constructed in the context of particular cultural adaptations, and, consequently, alternative gender arrangements can be created. Although biological influence in male–female behavior cannot be ruled out, it has nonetheless become clear that each culture provides different opportunities and has different expectations for ideal or acceptable behavior.[8]

CHILDREARING AND GENDER AMONG THE JU/'HOANSI

To understand the importance of childrearing practices for the development of gender-related personality characteristics, consider the Ju/'hoansi Bushmen, native to the Kalahari Desert in the borderlands of Namibia and Botswana in southern Africa. Traditionally subsisting as nomadic hunter-gatherers (foragers), in the past three decades many Ju/'hoansi have been forced to settle down—tending small herds of goats, planting gardens for their livelihood, and engaging in occasional wage labor on white-owned farms.[9]

Among those Ju/'hoansi who traditionally forage for a living, equality is stressed, and dominance and aggressiveness are not tolerated in either gender. Males are as mild-mannered as females, and females are as energetic and self-reliant as males. By contrast, among the

Ju/'hoansi who have recently settled in permanent villages, males and females exhibit personality characteristics resembling those traditionally thought of as typically masculine and feminine in North America and other industrial societies.

Among the food foragers, each newborn child receives extensive personal care from its mother during the first few years of life, for the space between births is typically four to five years. This is not to say that mothers are constantly with their children. For instance, when women go to collect wild plant foods in the bush, they do not always take their offspring along. At such times, children are supervised by their fathers or other community adults, one-third to one-half of whom are always found in camp on any given day. Because these include men as well as women, children are as much habituated to the male as to the female presence.

Traditional Ju/'hoansi fathers spend much time with their offspring, interacting with them in nonauthoritarian ways. Although they may correct their children's behavior, so may women who neither defer to male authority nor use the threat of paternal punishment. Among these foragers, no one grows up to respect or fear male authority any more than female authority. In fact, instead of being punished, a child who misbehaves will simply be carried away and introduced to some other more agreeable activity.

Children of both sexes do equally little work. Instead, they spend much of their time in playgroups that include boys and girls of widely different ages. And when it comes to older children keeping an eye out for the younger ones, this is done spontaneously rather than as an assigned task, and the burden does not fall more heavily on girls than boys. In short, Ju/'hoansi children in traditional foraging groups have few experiences that set one gender apart from the other.

---

[7]Mead, M. (1950). *Sex and temperament in three primitive societies.* New York: New American Library. (orig. 1935)

[8]Errington, F. K., & Gewertz, D. B. (2001). *Cultural alternatives and a feminist anthropology: An analysis of culturally constructed gender interests in Papua New Guinea.* Cambridge, UK, and New York: Cambridge University Press.

[9]Draper, P. (1975). !Kung women: Contrasts in sexual egalitarianism in foraging and sedentary contexts. In R. Reiter (Ed.), *Toward an anthropology of women* (pp. 77–109). New York: Monthly Review.

▲▲▲ In traditional Ju/'hoansi society, fathers as well as mothers show great indulgence to children, who do not fear or respect men more than they do women.

But for those Ju/'hoansi who have been forced to abandon their traditional foraging life and who now reside in permanent settlements, the situation is very different. Women spend much of their time at home preparing food, doing other domestic chores, and tending the children. Men, meanwhile, spend many hours outside the household growing crops, raising animals, or doing wage labor. As a result, children are less habituated to their presence. This remoteness of the men, coupled with their more extensive knowledge of the outside world and their access to money, tends to strengthen male influence in the household.

Within these village households, gender typecasting begins early. As soon as girls are old enough, they are expected to attend to many of the needs of their younger siblings, thereby allowing their mothers more time to deal with other domestic tasks. This shapes and limits the behavior of girls, who cannot range as widely or explore as freely as they could without little brothers and sisters in tow. Boys, by contrast, have little to do with babies and toddlers, and when they are assigned work, it generally takes them away from the household. Thus the space that village girls occupy becomes restricted, and they are trained in behaviors that promote passivity and nurturance, whereas village boys begin to learn the distant, controlling roles they will later play as adult men.

When comparing childrearing traditions in different cultures, we find that a group's economic organization and the social relations in its subsistence practices impact the way a child is brought up, and this, in turn, affects the adult personality. Cross-cultural comparisons also show that there are alternative practices for raising children, which means that changing the societal conditions in which one's children grow up can alter significantly the way men and women act and interact.

With this in mind, we turn to a brief discussion of different childrearing practices, contrasting dependence and independence training. There are cultural variations within each of these types, and many societies exhibit a mixture of both styles.

DEPENDENCE TRAINING

Some years after Margaret Mead's pioneering comparative research on gender, psychological anthropologists carried out a significant and wide-ranging series of cross-cultural studies on the relationship between childrearing and personality. Among other things, their work distinguished two general patterns of childrearing. These patterns stem from a number of practices that, regardless of the reason for their existence, have the effect of emphasizing dependence on the one hand and independence on the other. For convenience, we describe these as *dependence training* and *independence training*.[10]

Dependence training socializes people to think of themselves in terms of the larger whole. Its effect is to create community members whose idea of selfhood transcends individualism, promoting compliance in the performance of assigned tasks and keeping individuals within the group. This pattern is typically associated with extended families, which consist of several husband-wife-children units within the same household. It is most likely to be found in societies with an economy based on subsistence farming but also in foraging groups where several family groups may live together for at least part of the year.

Big extended families are important, for they provide the labor force necessary to till the soil, tend whatever flocks are kept, and carry out other part-time economic pursuits considered necessary for existence. But built into these large families are potentially disruptive tensions. For example, important family decisions must be collectively accepted and followed. In addition, the in-marrying spouses—husbands and/or wives who come from other groups—must conform themselves to the group's will, something that may not be easy for them.

▲▲▲

dependence training Childrearing practices that foster compliance in the performance of assigned tasks and dependence on the domestic group, rather than reliance on oneself.

▼▼▼

[10]Whiting, J. W. M., & Child, I. L. (1953). *Child training and personality: A cross-cultural study.* New Haven, CT: Yale University Press.

Dependence training helps to keep these potential problems under control and involves both supportive and corrective aspects. On the supportive side, permissiveness is shown to babies and toddlers, particularly in the form of breastfeeding, which is provided on demand and continues for several years. They may interpret this as a reward, one that reinforces that the family is the main agent in providing for one's needs. Also on the supportive side, at a relatively young age children begin participating in a number of child-care and domestic tasks, all of which make significant and obvious contributions to the family's welfare. Thus, children learn early on that it is normal for family members to share and actively help one another.

On the corrective side, adults actively discourage selfish or aggressive behavior. Moreover, they tend to be insistent on overall obedience, which commonly inclines the individual toward being subordinate to the group. This combination of encouragement and discouragement in the socialization process teaches individuals to put the group's needs above their own—to be compliant, supportive, noncompetitive, and generally responsible, to stay within the fold and not do anything potentially disruptive. Indeed, a person's very definition of self comes from the individual being a part of a larger social whole rather than from his or her mere individual existence.

INTERDEPENDENCE AMONG THE BENG OF WEST AFRICA

Recognizing that dependence training comes in many unique cultural variations, we now briefly turn to the Beng, a group of about 20,000 Mande-speaking farmers living in twenty-two villages in the tropical woodlands of Côte d'Ivoire, West Africa. Each family forms a large household, which includes the spirits of deceased ancestors. These spirits, known as *wru*, spend nights with their living relatives but depart at dawn for their invisible spirit village called *wrugbe*.

Believing in reincarnation, the Beng look upon infants not as new creatures but as reincarnated spirit ancestors gradually emerging from *wrugbe* back into everyday life. For this reason, Beng babies are embraced as profoundly spiritual beings who at first are only tentatively attached to life on earth. Their cries are interpreted as a longing for something from *wrugbe*, and good parents do everything within their power to make earthly life so comfortable and appealing that the child will not be tempted to return there. This includes extensive grooming of the little one to help attract additional care and love from relatives and neighbors. Held much of the

© Cengage Learning 2013

day by an array of caretakers, Beng babies develop a broad variety of social ties and emotional attachments and appear generally free of stranger anxiety. Also, since they are thought to be living partly in the spirit world, these tiny "old souls" are allowed to determine their own sleeping and nursing schedules, and, notably, the biological mother is just one of many potential breastfeeders.

Having studied childrearing practices among these West African farmers, U.S. anthropologist Alma Gottlieb concludes that in Beng communities, the social goal is to promote interdependence rather than independence, in contrast to what is the normal practice in most North American families today. In short, Beng babies are made to feel "constantly cherished by as many people as possible," learning early on that individual security comes through the intertwining of lives, collectively sharing joys and burdens.[11]

INDEPENDENCE TRAINING

Independence training fosters individual self-reliance and personal achievement. It is typically associated with societies in which a basic social unit consisting of parent(s) and offspring fends for itself. Independence training is particularly characteristic of mercantile (trading), industrial, and postindustrial societies where self-sufficiency and personal achievement are important traits for success, if not survival—especially for men, and increasingly for women.

This pattern also involves both encouragement and discouragement. On the negative side, the schedule dictates infant feeding more than does demand. In North America, as already noted, babies are rarely nursed for more than a year, if that. Many parents resort to an artificial nipple (pacifier) to satisfy the baby's sucking instincts—typically doing so to calm the child rather than out of an awareness that infants need sucking to strengthen and train coordination in the muscles used for feeding and speech.

---

[11]Gottlieb, A. (2005). Non-Western approaches to spiritual development among infants and young children: A case study from West Africa. In P. L. Benson et al. (Eds.), *The handbook of spiritual development in childhood and adolescence* (pp. 150–162). Thousand Oaks, CA: Sage; Gottlieb, A. (2004). Babies as ancestors, babies as spirits: The culture of infancy in West Africa. *Expedition 46* (3), 13–21; see also Gottlieb's 2003 book, *The afterlife is where we come from: The culture of infancy in West Africa*. Chicago: University of Chicago Press.

independence training Childrearing practices that foster independence, self-reliance, and personal achievement.

North American parents are comparatively quick to start feeding infants baby food and even try to get them to feed themselves. Many are delighted if they can prop their infants up in the crib or playpen so that they can hold their own bottles. Moreover, as soon after birth as possible, children are commonly given their own private space, away from their parents. Collective responsibility is not pushed upon children; they are not usually given significant domestic tasks until later in childhood; and these are often carried out for personal benefit (such as to earn an allowance to spend as they wish) rather than as contributions to the family's welfare.

Displays of individual will, assertiveness, and even aggression are encouraged or at least tolerated to a greater degree than in those cultures where dependence training is the rule. In schools, and even in the family, competition and winning are emphasized. Schools in the United States, for example, devote considerable resources to competitive sports. Competition is fostered within the classroom as well—overtly through practices such as spelling bees and awards and covertly through customs such as grading on a curve. In addition, there are various popularity contests, such as crowning a prom queen and king or holding an election to choose the classmate who is "best looking" or "most likely to succeed." By the time individuals have grown up in U.S. society, they have received a clear message: Life is about winning or losing, and losing is equal to failure.[12]

In sum, independence training generally encourages individuals to exert dominance and to seek help and attention rather than to give it. Such qualities are useful in societies with hierarchical social structures that emphasize personal achievement and where individuals are expected to look out for their own interests. Its socialization patterns match cultural values and expectations increasingly common in the spread of global capitalism.

One kind of training—independence, dependence, or a combination of both—is not inherently better or worse than any other. Compliant adults who are accepting of authority serve very well in a society that values cooperation and service toward the needs of the group. On the other hand, self-reliant, independent adults who are eager to explore new ways of doing things fit other societies that put a premium on individualism. Building on this basic cross-cultural dichotomy in childrearing practices, comparative research by psychological anthropologists has greatly added to our increasingly sophisticated understanding of the complex relationship between culture and personality.

Group Personality

From the holistic perspective that anthropologists bring to the comparative study of childrearing, it is clear that customary practices, personality formation, and other aspects of culture are systemically interrelated. This insight has prompted research to explore whether whole societies might be analyzed in terms of particular personality types. Certainly, common sense suggests that personalities fitting for one culture may be less suitable for others. For example, an egocentric, aggressive personality would be out of place where self-effacement, cooperation, and sharing are the keys to success.

---

[12]Turnbull, C. M. (1983). *The human cycle* (p. 74). New York: Simon & Schuster.

© N. Chagnon/Anthro-Photo

◄
◄
◄ Yanomami Indians living in the Amazon rainforest of Venezuela show off as *waiteri* in a public performance of a cultural ideal: being courageous, ferocious, humorous, and generous all wrapped in one heroic male personhood.

Unfortunately, common sense, like conventional wisdom in general, can be wrong. Anthropologists asked themselves whether it would be possible to describe a group personality without falling into the trap of stereotyping. The answer is a qualified yes, especially with respect to traditional communities. The larger and more complex a society becomes, the greater its variegation in personalities. In an abstract way, we may speak of a generalized *cultural personality* for a society, as long as we do not expect to find a uniformity of personalities within that society.

Consider for example the Yanomami Indians, (pictured on the previous page) who subsist on foraging and food gardens in the tropical forests of northern Brazil and southern Venezuela. Commonly, Yanomami men strive to achieve a reputation for fierce courage as *waiteri*, and they defend that heroic reputation at the risk of serious personal injury and death.[13] Yet among the Yanomami there are men who have quiet and less combative personalities. It is all too easy for an outsider to overlook these individuals when other, more "typical" Yanomami are in the front row, pushing and demanding attention.

Modal Personality

Obviously, any productive approach to the problem of group personality must recognize that each individual is unique to a degree in both genetic inheritance and life experiences, and it must leave room for a range of different personality types in any society. In addition, personality traits that may be regarded as appropriate in men may not be so regarded in women, and vice versa. Given all this, we may focus our attention on the **modal personality** of a group, defined as those character traits that occur with the highest frequency in a social group and are therefore the most representative of its culture.

Modal personality is a statistical concept rather than the personality of an average person in a particular society. As such, it raises other questions for investigation: How do more complex societies organize diversity? How does diversity relate to cultural change? Such questions are easily missed if one associates a certain type of personality with one particular culture, as did some earlier anthropologists. At the same time, modal personalities of different groups still can be compared.

National Character

Several years ago, Italy's tourism minister publicly commented on "typical characteristics" of Germans, referring to them as "hyper-nationalistic blondes" and "beer-drinking slobs" holding "noisy burping contests" on his country's beaches.[14] Outraged (and proud of his country's excellent beer), Germany's chancellor canceled his planned vacation to Italy and demanded an official apology. Of course, many Germans think of Italians as

© Simon Kwong/Corbis

▲▲▲ The collectively shared core values of Chinese culture promote the integration of the individual into a larger group, as we see in this large gathering of Hong Kong residents practicing tai chi.

dark-eyed, hot-blooded spaghetti eaters. To say so in public, however, would cause uproar.

Unflattering stereotypes about foreigners are deeply rooted in cultural traditions everywhere. Many Japanese believe Koreans are stingy, crude, and aggressive, while many Koreans see the Japanese as cold and arrogant. Similarly, we all have in mind some image, perhaps not well defined, of the typical citizen of Russia or Mexico or England. And when people from the United States travel abroad, they may be hurt or insulted that some Europeans hold the negative image of loud, brash, and arrogant Yankees. Although these are simply stereotypes, we might ask if they have any basis in fact. In reality, does such a thing as *national character* exist?

Some anthropologists once thought that the answer might be yes. They embarked upon national character studies in the 1930s and 1940s, aiming to discover basic personality traits shared by the majority of the people of modern state societies. In what came to be known as the *culture and personality* movement, their research

---

[13]See Chagnon, N. (1990). On Yanomamo violence: Reply to Albert. *Current Anthropology 31* (2), 49–53; Ramos, A. R. (1987). Reflecting on the Yanomami: Ethnographic images and the pursuit of the exotic. *Current Anthropology 2* (3), 284–304.

[14]Italy-Germany verbal war hots up. (2003, July 9). *Deccan Herald* (Bangalore, India).

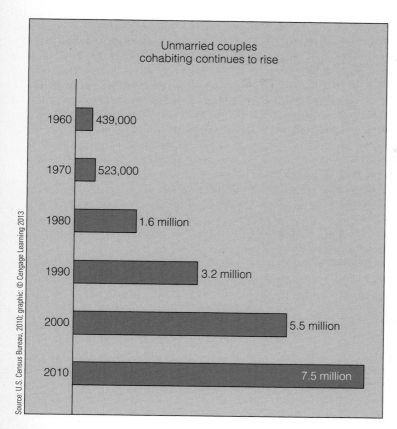

Figure 10.1 **Cohabitation Rate in the United States** The number of unmarried opposite-sex couples cohabiting in the United States continues to rise. These couples now make up 12 percent of all opposite-sex U.S. couples, married and unmarried.

emphasized childrearing practices and education as the factors theoretically responsible for such characteristics.

Early on it was recognized that the national character studies were flawed, mainly because they made overgeneralized conclusions based on limited data, relatively small samples of informants, and questionable assumptions about developmental psychology. These flaws notwithstanding, national character studies were important in that they helped change the anthropological focus from traditional small-scale communities of foragers, herders, and farmers in exotic places to large-scale contemporary state societies. Moreover, they prompted new theoretical and methodological approaches to serious interdisciplinary group research.[15]

[15]See Beeman, W. O. (2000). Introduction: Margaret Mead, cultural studies, and international understanding. In M. Mead & R. Métraux (Eds.), *The study of culture at a distance* (pp. xiv–xxxi). New York and Oxford, UK: Berghahn.

[16]Observations on North American culture in this section are drawn primarily from Natadecha-Sponsal, P. (1993). The young, the rich and the famous: Individualism as an American cultural value. In P. R. DeVita & J. D. Armstrong (Eds.), *Distant mirrors: America as a foreign culture* (pp. 46–53). Belmont, CA: Wadsworth. See also Morello, C. (2011, May 18). Number of long-lasting marriages in U.S. has risen, Census Bureau reports. *Washington Post*; Noack, T. (2001). Cohabitation in Norway: An accepted and gradually more regulated way of living. *International Journal of Law, Policy, and the Family 15* (1), 102–117.

Core Values

An alternative approach to national character—one that allows for the fact that not all personalities will conform to cultural ideals—is that of Chinese American anthropologist Francis Hsu. His approach studies **core values** (values especially promoted by a particular culture) and related personality traits. The Chinese, Hsu suggests, value kin ties and cooperation above all else. To them, mutual dependence is the very essence of personal relationships and has been for thousands of years. Compliance and subordination of one's will to that of family and kin transcend all else, while self-reliance is neither promoted nor a source of pride.

Perhaps the core value held in highest esteem by North Americans of European descent is rugged individualism—traditionally for men but in recent decades for women as well. Each person is supposed to be able to achieve anything he or she likes, given a willingness to work hard enough. From their earliest years, individuals are subjected to relentless pressures to excel, and as we have already noted, competition and winning are seen as crucial to this. Undoubtedly, this contributes to the restlessness and drive seen as characteristic for much of North American society today—and increasingly common wherever people compete for survival, wealth, and power in the global market.

Also, to the degree that it motivates individuals to work hard and to go where the jobs are, it fits well with the demands of a modern economy. Whereas individuals in Chinese traditional society are firmly bound into a larger group to which they have lifelong obligations, most urban North Americans and western Europeans live isolated from relatives other than their young children and spouse—and even the commitment to marriage has lessened. Many people in western Europe, North America, and other industrial or postindustrial societies choose singlehood or cohabitation over marriage (▶ **Figure 10.1**). Among those who do wed, many do so later in life, often prompted by the birth of a child. This growing individualism is also indicated by high divorce rates. In the United States those rates have leveled off since peaking in the 1980s, but more than 40 percent of U.S. marriages still fail.[16]

modal personality Those character traits that occur with the highest frequency in a social group and are therefore the most representative of its culture.

core values Those values especially promoted by a particular culture.

Alternative Gender Models

As touched on earlier, the gender roles assigned to each sex vary from culture to culture and have an impact on personality formation. But what if the sex of an individual is not self-evident? As revealed in this chapter's Original Study, written when its author was an undergraduate student, this narrative offers a compelling personal account of the emotional difficulties associated with intersexuality and gender ambiguity.[17]

---

[17]For scholarly accounts of the issues presented here, readers may turn to several excellent books, including the one mentioned in the Original Study: Roscoe, W. (1991). *The Zuni man-woman.* Albuquerque: University of New Mexico Press.

ORIGINAL STUDY

The Blessed Curse

By R. K. Williamson

One morning not so long ago, a child was born. This birth, however, was no occasion for the customary celebration. Something was wrong: something very grave, very serious, very sinister. This child was born between sexes, an "intersexed" child. From the day of its birth, this child would be caught in a series of struggles involving virtually every aspect of its life. Things that required little thought under "ordinary" circumstances were, in this instance, extraordinarily difficult. Simple questions now had an air of complexity: "What is it, a girl or a boy?" "What do we name it?" "How shall we raise it?" "Who (or what) is to blame for this?"

A Foot in Both Worlds

The child referred to in the introductory paragraph is myself. As the great-granddaughter of a Cherokee woman, I was exposed to the Native American view of people who were born intersexed, and those who exhibited transgendered characteristics. This view sees such individuals in a very positive and affirming light. Yet my immediate family (mother, father, and brothers) were firmly fixed in a negative Christian Euramerican point of view. As a result, I was presented with two different and conflicting views of myself. This resulted in a lot of confusion within me about what I was, how I came to be born the way I was, and what my intersexuality meant in terms of my spirituality as well as my place in society.

I remember, even as a small child, getting mixed messages about my worth as a human being. My grandmother, in keeping with Native American ways, would tell me stories about my birth. She would tell me how she knew when I was born that I had a special place in life,

given to me by God, the Great Spirit, and that I had been given "a great strength that girls never have, yet a gentle tenderness that boys never know" and that I was "too pretty and beautiful to be a boy only and too strong to be a girl only." She rejoiced at this "special gift" and taught me that it meant that the Great Spirit had "something important for me to do in this life." I remember how good I felt inside when she told me these things and how I soberly contemplated, even at the young age of 5, that I must be diligent and try to learn and carry out the purpose designed just for me by the Great Spirit.

My parents, however, were so repulsed by my intersexuality that they would never speak of it directly. They would just refer to it as "the work of Satan." To them, I was not at all blessed with a "special gift" from some "Great Spirit," but was "cursed and given over to the Devil" by God. My father treated me with contempt, and my mother wavered between contempt and distant indifference. I was taken from one charismatic church to another in order to have the "demon of mixed sex" cast out of me. At some of these "deliverance" services I was even given a napkin to cough out the demon into!

In the end, no demon ever popped out of me. Still I grew up believing that there was something inherent within me that caused God to hate me, that my intersexuality was a punishment for this something, a mark of condemnation.

Whenever I stayed at my grandmother's house, my fears would be allayed, for she would once again remind me that I was fortunate to have been given this special gift. She was distraught that my parents were treating me cruelly and

pleaded with them to let me live with her, but they would not let me stay at her home permanently. Nevertheless, they did let me spend a significant portion of my childhood with her. Had it not been for that, I might not have been able to survive the tremendous trials that awaited me in my walk through life.

A Personal Resolution

For me, the resolution to the dual message I was receiving was slow in coming, largely due to the fear and self-hatred instilled in me by Christianity. Eventually, though, the spirit wins out. I came to adopt my grandmother's teaching about my intersexuality. Through therapy, and a new, loving home environment, I was able to shed the constant fear of eternal punishment I felt for something I had no control over. After all, I did not create myself.

Because of my own experience, and drawing on the teaching of my grandmother, I am now able to see myself as a wondrous creation of the Great Spirit—but not only me. All creation is wondrous. There is a purpose for everyone in the gender spectrum. Each person's spirit is unique in her or his or her-his own way. It is only by living true to the nature that was bestowed upon us by the Great Spirit, in my view, that we are able to be at peace with ourselves and be in harmony with our neighbor. This, to me, is the Great Meaning and the Great Purpose. . . . ■

Adapted from Williamson, R. K. (1995). The blessed curse: Spirituality and sexual difference as viewed by Euramerican and Native American cultures. *The College News* 18 (4). Reprinted with permission of the author.

The biological facts of human nature are not always as clear-cut as most people assume. As described in Chapter 2, at the level of chromosomes, biological sex is determined according to whether a person's 23rd chromosomal set is XX (female) or XY (male). Some of the genes on these chromosomes control sexual development. This standard biological package does not apply to all humans, for a considerable number are **intersexuals**—people who are born with reproductive organs, genitalia, and/or sex chromosomes that are not exclusively male or female. These individuals do not fit neatly into a binary gender standard.[18]

For example, some people are born with a genetic disorder that results in them having only one X chromosome instead of the usual two. A person with this chromosomal complex, known as Turner syndrome, develops female external genitalia but has nonfunctional ovaries and is therefore infertile. Other individuals are born with the XY sex chromosomes of a male but have an abnormality on the X chromosome that affects the body's sensitivity to androgens (male hormones). This is known as androgen insensitivity syndrome (AIS). An adult XY person with complete AIS appears fully female with a normal clitoris, labia, and breasts. Internally, these individuals possess testes (up in the abdomen, rather than in their usual descended position in the scrotal sac), but they are otherwise born without a complete set of either male or female internal genital organs. They generally possess a short, blind-ended vagina.

"Hermaphrodites" comprise a distinct category of intersexuality—although the terms *male pseudohermaphrodite* and *female pseudohermaphrodite* are often used to refer to a range of intersex conditions.[19] More obviously intersexed individuals ("true hermaphrodites") have both testicular and ovarian tissue. They may have a separate ovary and testis, but more commonly they have an ovotestis—a gonad containing both sorts of tissue. About 60 percent of these individuals possess XX (female) sex chromosomes, and the remainder may have XY or a mosaic (a mixture). Their external genitalia may be ambiguous or female, and they may have a uterus or (more commonly) a hemi-uterus (half uterus).[20]

U.S. biologist Anne Fausto-Sterling, a specialist in this area, notes that the concept of intersexuality is rooted in "an idealized biological world in which our species is perfectly divided into two kinds:

> That idealized story papers over [that] some women have facial hair, some men have none; some women speak with deep voices, some men veritably squeak. Less well known is the fact that on close inspection, absolute dimorphism disintegrates even at the level of basic biology. Chromosomes, hormones, the internal sex structures, the gonads and external genitalia all vary more than most people realize. Those born outside of the . . . dimorphic mold are called intersexuals.[21]

Intersexuality may be unusual, but it is not uncommon. In fact, about 1 percent of all humans are intersexed in some not necessarily visible way—in other words, nearly 70 million people worldwide.[22] Until recently, it was rarely discussed publicly in many societies. Since the mid-20th century, individuals with financial means in technologically advanced parts of the world have had the option of reconstructive surgery and hormonal treatments to alter such conditions, and many parents faced with raising a visibly intersexed child in a culture intolerant of such minorities have chosen this option. However, there is a growing movement to put off such irreversible procedures indefinitely or at least until the child becomes old enough to make the choice. Obviously, a society's attitude toward these individuals can impact their personality, their fundamental sense of self and how they express it.

In addition to people who are biologically intersexed, throughout history some individuals have been subjected to a surgical removal of some of their sexual organs. In many cultures, male prisoners or war captives have undergone forced castration, crushing or cutting the testicles. Castration may limit the sex drive, but it does not eliminate it or the possibility of having an erection.

---

[18]This section is based on several sources: Chase, C. (1998). Hermaphrodites with attitude. *Gay and Lesbian Quarterly 4* (2), 189–211; Dumurat-Dreger, A. (1998, May/June). "Ambiguous sex" or ambivalent medicine? *The Hastings Center Report 28* (3), 2435 (posted on the Intersex Society of North America website: www.isna.org); Fausto-Sterling, A. (1993). The five sexes: Why male and female are not enough. *The Sciences 33* (2), 20–24; the Mayo Clinic website: http://www.mayoclinic.com/.

[19]The term *hermaphrodite*, objected to by many, comes from a figure in Greek mythology: Hermaphroditus (son of Hermes, messenger of the gods, and Aphrodite, goddess of beauty and love) became half male and half female when he fell in love with a nymph, and his body fused with hers. The Intersex Society of North America suggests using DSD (disorders of sexual development) rather than hermaphrodites, urging clinicians to shift from focusing on gender and genitals to the exclusion of the real medical problems people with DSD face.

[20]Fausto-Sterling, A. (2000, July). The five sexes revisited. *The Sciences*, 20–24.

[21]Ibid.

[22]Fausto-Sterling, A. (2003, August 2). Personal e-mail communication from this recognized expert on the subject. For published statistics, see her article co-authored with Blackless, M., et al. (2000). How sexually dimorphic are we? Review and synthesis. *American Journal of Human Biology 12*, 151–166.

▲▲▲▲▲▲▲▲▲▲▲▲▲▲▲▲▲▲▲▲▲▲▲▲▲▲▲▲▲▲▲▲▲▲▲▲▲▲

intersexuals People born with reproductive organs, genitalia, and/or sex chromosomes that are not exclusively male or female.

▼▼▼▼▼▼▼▼▼▼▼▼▼▼▼▼▼▼▼▼▼▼▼▼▼▼▼▼▼▼▼▼▼▼▼▼▼▼

© AP Images/Anja Niedringhaus

◄
◄ Caster Semenya is a South African middle-distance runner. At age 18, after winning the women's 800-meter race at the 2009 World Championships in Berlin, Semenya faced a barrage of media reports with headlines such as "Gold Awarded amid Dispute over Runner's Sex." The International Association of Athletics Federations (IAAF) subsequently ordered gender testing that revealed that the runner has internal male sexual organs. After being withdrawn from international competitions, she was officially cleared by the IAAF in July 2010 and resumed her athletic career.

It does, however, put an end to the production of sperm necessary for reproduction.

Archaeological evidence from ancient Egypt, Iraq, Iran, and China suggests that the cultural practice of castrating war captives began several thousand years ago. Young boys captured during war or slave-raiding expeditions were often castrated before being sold and shipped off to serve in foreign households, including royal courts. In the Ottoman empire of the Turks, where they could occupy a variety of important functions in the sultan's household from the mid-15th century onward, they became known as *eunuchs*. As suggested by the original meaning of the word, which is Greek for "guardian of the bed," castrated men were often put in charge of a ruler's harem, the women's quarters in a household. Eunuchs could also rise to high status as priests and administrators and were even appointed to serve as army commanders. Some powerful lords, kings, and emperors kept hundreds of eunuchs in their castles and palaces.[23]

Other than forced castration, there were also men who engaged in self-castration or underwent voluntary castration. For example, early Christian monks in Egypt and neighboring regions voluntarily abstained from sexual relationships and sometimes castrated themselves for the sake of the kingdom of heaven. Such genital mutilation was also practiced among Coptic monks in Egypt and Ethiopia, until the early 20th century.[24]

In the late 15th century, Europe saw the emergence of a category of musical eunuchs known as *castrati*. These eunuchs sang female parts in church choirs after Roman Catholic authorities banned women singers on the basis of Saint Paul's instruction, "Let your women keep silence in the churches." Without functioning testes to produce male sex hormones, physical development

into manhood is aborted, so deeper voices—as well as body hair, semen production, and other usual male attributes—were not part of a castrati's biology.[25]

Mapping the sexual landscape, anthropologists have come to realize that gender bending exists in many cultures all around the world, playing a significant role in shaping behaviors and personalities. For example, indigenous communities in the Great Plains and the southwestern United States created social space for **transgenders**—people who cross over or occupy an alternative position in the binary male–female gender construction. The Lakota of the northern Plains had a third gender category of culturally accepted transgendered males who dressed as women and were thought to possess both male and female spirits. They called (and still call) these third-gender individuals *winkte*, applying the term to a male "who wants to be a woman." Thought to have special curing powers, *winktes* traditionally enjoyed considerable prestige in their communities. Among the neighboring Cheyenne, such a person was called *hemanah*, literally meaning "half-man, half-woman."[26] The preferred term among most North American Indians today is "two-spirits."[27]

[23]Herdt, G. (Ed.). (1996). *Third sex, third gender: Beyond sexual dimorphism in culture and history.* New York: Zone.

[24]Abbot, E. (2001). *A history of celibacy.* Cambridge, MA: Da Capo Press.

[25]Taylor, G. (2000). *Castration: Abbreviated history of western manhood* (pp. 38–44, 252–259). New York: Routledge.

[26]Medicine, B. (1994). Gender. In M. B. Davis (Ed.), *Native America in the twentieth century.* New York: Garland.

[27]Jacobs, S. E. (1994). Native American two-spirits. *Anthropology Newsletter 35* (8), 7.

Such third-gender individuals are well known in Samoa, where males who take on the identity of females are referred to as *fa'afafines* ("the female way"). Becoming a *fa'afine* is an accepted option for boys who prefer to dance, cook, clean house, and care for children and the elderly. In large families, it is not unusual to find two or three boys being raised as girls to take on domestic roles in their households. As U.S. anthropologist Lowell Holmes reports,

> In fact, they tend to be highly valued because they can do the heavy kinds of labor that most women find difficult. A Samoan nun once told me how fortunate it is to have a *fa'afine* in the family to help with the household chores. [There] is also the claim made that *fa'afines* never have sexual relations with each other but, rather, consider themselves to be "sisters." [They] are religious and go to church regularly dressed as women and . . . some are even Sunday school teachers. *Fa'afines* often belong to women's athletic teams, and some even serve as coaches.[28]

Transgenders cannot simply be lumped together as homosexuals. For example, the Tagalog-speaking people in the Philippines use the word *bakla* to refer to a man who views himself "as a male with a female heart." These individuals cross-dress on a daily basis, often becoming more female than females in their use of heavy makeup, in the clothing they wear, and in the way they walk. Like the Samoan *fa'afafines*, they are generally not sexually attracted to other *bakla* but are drawn to heterosexual men instead. And the Bugis of Sulawesi Island in Indonesia acknowledge five genders: *oroané* (male-men), *makunrai* (female-women), *calalai* (transgendering females), *calabai* (transgendering males), and *bissu* (androgynous shamans imagined to embody female and male elements).[29]

Clearly, the cross-cultural sex and gender scheme is complex. In the course of thousands of years, human cultures have creatively dealt with a wide range of inherited and artificially imposed sexual features. Studying multifaceted categories involving intersexuality and transgendering enables us to recognize the existing range of gender alternatives and to debunk false stereotypes. It is one more piece of the human puzzle—an important one that prods us to rethink social codes and the range of forces that shape personality as well as each society's definition of normal.

▲▲▲ Transgendering occurs in many cultures, but it is not always publicly tolerated. Among Polynesians inhabiting Pacific Ocean islands such as Tonga and Samoa, however, such male transvestites are culturally accepted. Samoans refer to these third-gender individuals as *fa'afafines* ("the female way").

Normal and Abnormal Personality in Social Context

The cultural standards that define normal behavior for any society are determined by that society itself. Although the societies just noted have accepted transgender behaviors, many other societies regard them as culturally abnormal and do not tolerate those who deviate from commonly accepted social standards of sexual behavior. For instance, according to a recent global report, state-sponsored homophobia, the irrational fear of humans with same-sex preferences, thrives in many countries, with its resulting aggressive intolerance:

> With Panama decriminalising homosexuality in 2008 and Burundi for the first time in its history criminal-

▲▲▲

transgenders People who cross over or occupy a culturally accepted intermediate position in the binary male–female gender construction; also identified as third gender people or by various culturally specific names such as "two spirits," used in many Native American groups.

▼▼▼▼▼▼▼▼▼▼▼▼▼▼▼▼▼▼▼▼▼▼▼▼▼▼▼▼▼▼▼▼▼▼▼

[28]Holmes, L. D. (2000). *Paradise bent* (film review). *American Anthropologist 102* (3), 604–605.

[29]Davies, S. G. (2007). *Challenging gender norms: Five genders among the Bugis in Indonesia.* Belmont, CA: Thomson Wadsworth.

© Photography Hugh Hartshorne/ReAngle Pictures

izing homosexuality in 2009, the world now counts 80 countries with State-sponsored homophobic laws: 72 countries and 3 entities (Turkish Cyprus, Gaza and Cook Islands) punish consenting adults with imprisonment, while 5 countries (Iran, Mauritania, Saudi Arabia, Sudan, Yemen and parts of Nigeria and Somalia) punish them with the death penalty.[30]

If a male in one of these sexually restrictive societies dresses as a woman, he is widely viewed as emotionally troubled or even mentally ill, and his abnormal behavior may lead to punitive measures or psychiatric intervention.

What seems normal and acceptable (if not always popular) in one society is often considered abnormal and unacceptable—ridiculous, shameful, and sometimes even criminal—in another. As well, the standards that define normal behavior may shift over time. In England, for instance, homosexuality was decriminalized in 1967. And six years later, the American Psychiatric Association finally removed same-sex orientation from its authoritative list of clinical mental disorders.[31]

In short, the boundaries that distinguish the normal from the abnormal vary across cultures and time, as do the standards of what is socially acceptable. In many cultures, individuals may stand out as "different" without being considered "abnormal" in the strictest sense of the word—and without suffering social rejection, ridicule, censure, condemnation, imprisonment, or some other penalty. Moreover, there are cultures that not only tolerate or accept a much wider range of diversity than others, but may actually accord special status to the deviant or eccentric as unique, extraordinary, or even sacred, as illustrated by the following example.

Sadhus: Holy Men in Hindu Cultures

A fascinating ethnographic example of a culture in which abnormal individuals are socially accepted and even

honored is provided by religious mystics in India and Nepal. Surrendering all social, material, and even sexual attachments to normal human pleasures and delights, these ascetic monks, or *sadhus,* dedicate themselves to achieving spiritual union with the divine or universal Soul. This is done through intense meditation (chanting sacred hymns or mystical prayer texts—mantras) and yoga (an ascetic and mystic discipline involving prescribed postures and controlled breathing). The goal is to become a fully enlightened soul, liberated from the physical limits of the individual mortal self, including the cycle of life and death.

The life of the *sadhu* demands extraordinary concentration and near superhuman effort, as can be seen in the most extreme yoga postures. This chosen life of suffering may even include self-torture as a form of extreme penance. For instance, some *sadhus* pierce their tongue or cheeks with a long iron rod, stab a knife through their arm or leg, or stick their head into a small hole in the ground for hours on end.

Most Hindus revere and sometimes even fear *sadhus.* When they encounter one—by a temple or cemetery, or perhaps near a forest, riverbank, or mountain cave—they typically offer him food or other alms. Sightings are not uncommon since an estimated 5 million *sadhus* live in India and Nepal.[32] Of course, if one of these bearded, longhaired Hindu monks decided to practice his extreme yoga exercises and other sacred devotions in western Europe or North America, observers would consider such a holy man to be severely mentally disturbed.

Mental Disorders Across Time and Cultures

No matter how eccentric or even bizarre certain behaviors might seem in a particular place and time, it is possible for the abnormal to become socially accepted in cultures that are changing. Such is the case with manic depression (now more properly called *bipolar disorder*) and attention deficit hyperactivity disorder (ADHD), both previously regarded as dreaded problems.

In western Europe and North America, the manic and hyperactivity aspects of these conditions are gradually becoming viewed as assets in the quest for success. More and more, they are interpreted as indicative of "finely wired, exquisitely alert nervous systems" that make one highly sensitive to signs of change, able to fly from one thing to another while pushing the limits of everything, and doing it all with an intense level of energy focused totally in the future. These are extolled as high virtues in the corporate world, where being

[30]International Lesbian, Gay, Bisexual, Trans, and Intersex Association (ILGA). (2009). *The 2009 report on state-sponsored homophobia.* See also the Pew Research Center. (2007). *Global attitudes survey.*

[31]Bayer, R. (1987). *Homosexuality and American psychiatry: The politics of diagnosis.* Princeton, NJ: Princeton University Press.

[32]See Kelly, T. L. (2006). *Sadhus, the great renouncers.* Photography exhibit, Indigo Gallery, Naxal, Kathmandu, Nepal. http://www.asianart.com/exhibitions/sadhus/index.html (retrieved September 2, 2011); see also Heitzman, J., & Wordem, R. L. (Eds.). (2006). *India: A country study* (sect. 2, 5th ed.). Washington, DC: Federal Research Division, Library of Congress.

◀
◀
◀ **This Shaivite *sadhu* of the Aghori sub-sect drinks from a human skull bowl (symbolizing human mortality). He is a strict follower of the Hindu god Shiva, whose image can be seen behind him.**

considered "hyper" or "manic" is increasingly an expression of approval.[33]

Just as social attitudes concerning a wide range of both psychological and physical differences change over time within a society, they also vary across cultures (see Biocultural Connection on the following page).

CULTURAL RELATIVITY AND ABNORMALITY

Does this suggest that normalcy is a meaningless concept when applied to personality? Within the context of a particular culture, the concept of normal personality is quite significant. Irving Hallowell, a major figure in the development of psychological anthropology, ironically observed that it is normal to share the delusions traditionally accepted by one's society. Abnormality involves the development of a delusional system of which the culture does not approve. The individual who is disturbed because he or she cannot adequately measure up to the norms of society and be happy may be termed "neurotic." When a person's delusional system is so different that it in no way reflects his or her society's norms, the individual may be termed "psychotic."

If severe enough, culturally induced conflicts can produce psychosis and also determine its particular form. In a culture that encourages aggressiveness and suspicion, the insane person may be the one who is passive and trusting. In a culture that encourages passivity and trust, the insane person may be the one who is aggressive and suspicious. Just as each society establishes its own norms, each individual is unique in his or her perceptions.

Although it is true that each particular culture defines what is and is not normal behavior, the situation is complicated by findings suggesting that major categories of mental disorders may be universal types of human affliction. Take, for example, schizophrenia—probably the most common of all psychoses and one that may be found in any culture, no matter how it is manifested. Individuals afflicted by schizophrenia experience distortions of reality that impair their ability to function adequately, so they often withdraw from the social world into their own psychological shell.

While environmental factors play a role, evidence suggests that schizophrenia is caused by a biochemical disorder for which there is an inheritable tendency. One of its more severe forms is paranoid schizophrenia. Those suffering from it fear and mistrust nearly everyone. They hear voices that whisper dreadful things to them, and they are convinced that someone is "out to get them." Acting on this conviction, they engage in bizarre sorts of behaviors, which lead to their removal from society.

CULTURE-BOUND SYNDROME

A **culture-bound syndrome**, or ethnic psychosis, is a mental disorder specific to a particular cultural group.[34] A historical example is Windigo psychosis, limited to northern Algonquian groups such as the Cree and

[33]Martin, E. (1999). Flexible survivors. *Anthropology News 40* (6), 5–7. See also Martin, E. (2009). *Bipolar expeditions:* Mania and depression in American culture. Princeton, NJ: Princeton University Press.

[34]Simons, R. C., & Hughes, C. C. (Eds.). (1985). *The culture-bound syndromes: Folk illnesses of psychiatric and anthropological interest.* Dordrecht, Netherlands: Reidel.

▲▲▲

culture-bound syndrome A mental disorder specific to a particular ethnic group; also known as *ethnic psychosis.*

▼▼▼

BIOCULTURAL CONNECTION

Down Syndrome Across Cultures

By Katherine A. Dettwyler

U.S. biological anthropologist
Katherine Dettwyler compares the cultural experience of Down syndrome, the biological state of having an extra 21st chromosome, in Peter, her son, and in Abi, a child she meets while doing fieldwork in Mali, West Africa.

Down syndrome children are often (though not always!) sweet, happy, and affectionate kids. Many families of children with Down syndrome consider them to be special gifts from God and refer to them as angels. . . .

A little girl had just entered the hut, part of a large family with many children. She had a small round head, and all the facial characteristics of a child with Down syndrome—Oriental-shaped eyes with epicanthic folds, a small flat nose, and small ears. There was no mistaking the diagnosis. Her name was Abi, and she was about 4 years old, the same age as Peter.

I knelt in front of the little girl. "Hi there, sweetie," I said in English. "Can I have a hug?" I held out my arms, and she willingly stepped forward and gave me a big hug.

I looked up at her mother. "Do you know that there's something 'different' about this child?" I asked, choosing my words carefully.

"Well, she doesn't talk," said her mother, hesitantly, looking at her husband for confirmation.

"That's right," he said. "She's never said a word."

"But she's been healthy?" I asked.

"Yes," the father replied. "She's like the other kids, except she doesn't talk. She's always happy. She never cries. We know she can hear, because she does what we tell her to. Why are you so interested in her?"

"Because I know what's the matter with her. I have a son like this." Excitedly, I pulled a picture of Peter out of my bag and showed it to them. They couldn't see any resemblance, though. The difference in skin color swamped the similarities in facial features. But then, Malians think all white people look alike. And it's not true that all kids with Down syndrome look the same. They're "different in the same way," but they look most like their parents and siblings.

"Have you ever met any other children like this?" I inquired, bursting with curiosity about how rural Malian culture dealt with a condition as infrequent as Down syndrome. Children with Down syndrome are rare to begin with, occurring about once in every 700 births. In a community where thirty or forty children are born each year at the most, a child with Down syndrome might be born only once in twenty years. And many of them would not survive long enough for anyone to be able to tell that they were different. Physical defects along the midline of the body (heart, trachea, intestines) are common among kids with Down syndrome; without immediate surgery and neonatal intensive care, many

© Cengage Learning 2013

Ojibwa. In their traditional belief systems, these Indians recognized the existence of cannibalistic monsters called Windigos. Individuals afflicted by the psychosis developed the delusion that, falling under the control of these monsters, they were themselves transformed into Windigos, with a craving for human flesh. As this happened, the psychotic individuals perceived people around them turning into edible animals—fat beavers, for instance. Although there are no known instances where sufferers of Windigo psychosis actually devoured humans, they were acutely afraid of doing so, and people around them feared that they might.

Windigo psychosis may seem different from clinical cases of paranoid schizophrenia found in Euramerican cultures, but a closer look suggests otherwise. The disorder was merely being expressed in ways compatible with traditional northern Algonquian cultures. Ideas of persecution, instead of being directed toward other humans, were directed toward supernatural beings (the Windigo monsters); cannibalistic panic replaced panic expressed in other forms.

Windigo behavior has seemed exotic and dramatic to Euramericans, but psychotic individuals draw upon whatever imagery and symbolism their culture has to offer. For instance, the delusions of Irish schizophrenics draw upon would not survive. Such surgery is routine in American children's hospitals but nonexistent in rural Mali. For the child without any major physical defects, there are still the perils of rural Malian life to survive: malaria, measles, diarrhea, diphtheria, and polio. Some, like Peter, have poor immune systems, making them even more susceptible to childhood diseases. The odds against finding a child with Down syndrome, surviving and healthy in a rural Malian village, are overwhelming.

Not surprisingly, the parents knew of no other children like Abi. They asked if I knew of any medicine that could cure her. "No," I explained, "this condition can't be cured. But she will learn to talk, just give her time. Talk to her a lot. Try to get her to repeat things you say. And give her lots of love and attention. It may take her longer to learn some things, but keep trying. In my country, some people say these children are special gifts from God." There was no way I could explain cells and chromosomes and nondisjunction to them, even with a translator's help. And how, I thought to myself, would that have helped them anyway? They just accepted her as she was.

We chatted for a few more minutes, and I measured the whole family, including Abi, who was, of course, short for her age. I gave her one last hug and a balloon and sent her out the door after her siblings. . . .

I walked out of the hut, . . . trying to get my emotions under control. Finally I gave in, hugged my knees close to my chest, and sobbed. I cried for Abi—what a courageous heart she must have; just think what she might have achieved given all the modern infant stimulation programs available in the West. I cried for Peter—another courageous heart; just think of what he might achieve given the chance to live in a culture that simply accepted him, rather than stereotyping and pigeonholing him, constraining him because people didn't think he was capable of more. I cried for myself—not very courageous at all; my heart felt as though it would burst with longing for Peter, my own sweet angel.

There was clearly some truth to the old adage that ignorance is bliss. Maybe pregnant women in Mali had to worry about evil spirits lurking in the latrine at night, but they didn't spend their pregnancies worrying about chromosomal abnormalities, the

moral implications of amniocentesis, or the heart-wrenching exercise of trying to evaluate handicaps, deciding which ones made life not worth living. Women in the United States might have the freedom to choose not to give birth to children with handicaps, but women in Mali had freedom from worrying about it. Children in the United States had the freedom to attend special programs to help them overcome their handicaps, but children in Mali had freedom from the biggest handicap of all—other people's prejudice.

I had cried myself dry. I splashed my face with cool water from the bucket inside the kitchen and returned to the task at hand. ∎

Biocultural Question

Given cross-cultural differences in childrearing, do children with certain genetic handicaps have a better chance of growing up with a normal personality in some societies than in others?

Adapted from Dettwyler, K. A. (1994) *Dancing skeletons: Life and death in West Africa* (pp. 97–99). Long Grove, IL: Waveland Press. Reprinted with permission of Waveland Press. All rights reserved.

---

the images and symbols of Irish Catholicism and feature Virgin and Savior motifs. In short, the underlying biological structure of the mental disorder may be the same in all cases, but its expression is culturally specific.

In more recent decades, Western society and several other parts of the world have seen the rise of two related culture-bound syndromes associated with consumer capitalism: *bulimia nervosa* and *anorexia nervosa*. Bulimia

is characterized by frequent binge eating followed by vomiting or other frantic efforts to avoid gaining weight. Anorexia is an obsession to remain thin, evidenced in self-starvation that may result in death. This neurotic "fear of fatness" manifests itself in Western consumer societies where a growing percentage of the population is overweight or obese. Bulimia and anorexia are primarily diagnosed in female adolescents who reside in a culture that exalts thinness, even as fast food and leisure snacking are ever more prevalent. With the globalization of consumer society's fat–thin contradiction, its associated psychological eating disorders are also crossing borders.[35]

[35]Littlewood, R. (2004). Commentary: Globalization, culture, body image, and eating disorders. *Culture, Medicine, and Psychiatry* 28 (4), 597–602.

Today, Japan is just behind the United States in deaths related to psychological eating disorders.[36]

Personal Identity and Mental Health in Globalizing Society

Anthropologists view childrearing, gender issues, social identity, and emotional and mental health issues in their cultural context; this perspective recognizes that each individual's unique personality, feelings of happiness, and overall sense of health are shaped or influenced by the particular culture within which the person is born and raised to function as a valued member of the community. These communities, however, are seldom stable.

As illustrated by the spread of consumer culture and its associated psychological disorders, people all across the world face sometimes bewildering challenges hurled at them by globalization. These forces impact how people raise their children, how their personalities are influenced, and how they maintain their individual and collective social, psychological, and mental health.

In the past few decades, medical and psychological anthropologists have made valuable contributions to improving health care, not only in so-called developing countries far away but also in their own societies. However, mental health practices prevailing in Europe and North America remain ethnocentric when theorizing and treating psychological disorders—a problem reinforced by a reductionist biomedical mindset that largely ignores the role of cultural factors in the etiology, expression, course, and outcome of mental disorders. Furthermore, commercial pressures on the health-care establishment favor bioscience and pharmacotherapy, with drug companies providing a quick and cheap fix for the problem.[37]

Informed by cultural relativist views on normality and deviance, anthropological perspectives on identity, mental health, and psychiatric disorders are especially useful in pluralistic societies where people from different ethnic groups, each with a distinctive culture, coexist and interact. Intensified by globalization, this multi-ethnic convergence drives home the need for a medical pluralism providing multiple healing modalities suited for the cultural dynamics of the 21st century. ✤

---

[36]World Health Organization. (2004). Statistical information system. http://www.who.int/whosis/en/ (retrieved September 2, 2011); see also Eating disorders (most recent) by country. Nationmaster.com. http://www.nationmaster.com/graph/mor_eat_dis-mortality-eating-disorders (retrieved September 19, 2011).

[37]Luhrmann, T. M. (2001). *Of two minds: An anthropologist looks at American psychiatry.* New York: Vintage; Marsella, A. J., & White, G. (1982). *Cultural conceptions of mental health and therapy.* New York: Springer.

Chapter Checklist

What is enculturation, and how does it shape a person's personality and identity?

✔ Enculturation, the process by which individuals become members of their society, begins soon after birth. Its first agents are the members of an individual's household, and then it involves other members of society. For enculturation to proceed, a person must possess self-awareness, the ability to identify oneself as an individual, to reflect on oneself, and to evaluate oneself.

✔ A child's birthright and social identity are established through personal naming, a universal practice with numerous cross-cultural variations. A name is an important device for self-definition—without one, an individual has no identity, no self. Many cultures mark the naming of a child with a special ceremony.

✔ For self-awareness to emerge and function, four basic orientations are necessary to structure the behavioral environment in which the self acts: object orientation (learning about a world of objects other than the self), spatial orientation, temporal orientation, and normative orientation (an understanding of the values, ideals, and standards that constitute the behavioral environment).

How do a society's childrearing practices and concepts of sex and gender influence a person's behavior, personality, and identity?

✔ Gender behaviors and relations are malleable and vary cross-culturally. Each culture presents different opportunities and expectations concerning ideal or acceptable male–female behavior. In some cultures, male–female relations are based on equal status, with both genders expected to behave similarly. In others, however, male–female relations are based on inequality and are marked by different standards of expected behavior. Anthropological research demonstrates that gender dominance is a cultural construct and, consequently, that alternative male–female social arrangements can be created if so desired.

✔ Through cross-cultural studies psychological anthropologists have established the interrelation of personality, childrearing practices, and other aspects of culture. For example, dependence training, usually associated with traditional farming societies, stresses compliance in the performance of assigned tasks and dependence on the domestic group, rather than reliance on oneself. At the opposite extreme, independence training, typical of societies characterized by small, independent families, puts a premium on self-reliance, independent behavior, and personal achievement. Although a society may emphasize one sort of behavior over the other, it may not emphasize it to the same degree in both sexes.

✔ Some psychological anthropologists contend that childrearing practices have their roots in a society's customs for meeting the basic physical needs of its members and that these practices produce particular kinds of adult personalities.

✔ Intersexuals—individuals born with reproductive organs, genitalia, and/or sex chromosomes that are not exclusively male or female—do not fit neatly into either a male or female biological standard or into a binary gender standard. Numerous cultures in the course of history have created social space for intersexuals, as well as transgenders—physically male or female persons who cross over or occupy an alternative social position in the binary male–female gender construction.

What determines cultural norms, and is there such a thing as group personality or national character?

✔ Early on, anthropologists worked on the problem of whether it is possible to delineate a group personality without falling into stereotyping. Each culture chooses, from the vast array of possibilities, those traits that it sees as normative or ideal. Individuals who conform to these traits are rewarded; the rest are not. The modal personality of a group is the body of character traits that occur with the highest frequency in a culturally bounded population. As a statistical concept, it opens up for investigation how societies organize the diverse personalities of their members, some of which conform more than others to the modal type.

✔ National character studies have focused on the modal characteristics of modern countries. Researchers have attempted to determine the childrearing practices and education that shape such a group personality. Many anthropologists believe national character theories are based on unscientific and overly generalized data; others focus on the core values promoted in particular societies while recognizing that success in instilling these values in individuals may vary considerably.

✔ What defines normal behavior in any culture is determined by the culture itself, and what may be acceptable or even admirable in one may not be regarded in the same way in another. Abnormality involves developing personality traits not accepted by a culture.

Does culture play a role in a person's mental health?

✔ Culturally induced conflicts not only can produce psychological disturbance but can also determine the form of the disturbance. Similarly, mental disorders that have a biological cause, like schizophrenia, will be expressed by symptoms specific to the culture of the afflicted individual.

✔ Culture-bound syndromes, or ethnic psychoses, are mental disorders specific to a particular ethnic group.

✔ Multi-ethnic convergence, intensified by globalization, drives home the need for a medical pluralism providing multiple healing modalities suited for the cultural dynamics of the 21st century.

Questions for Reflection

1. Every society faces the challenge of humanizing its children, teaching them the values and social codes that will enable them to be functioning and contributing members in the community. What childrearing practices did you experience that embody the values and social codes of your society?

2. Do you fit within the acceptable range of your society's modal personality? How so?

3. Given that nearly 70 million people in today's world are intersexed, and in light of the fact that a very small fraction of these people have access to reconstructive sexual surgery, what do you think of societies that have created cultural space for alternative gender options beyond the strictly male or female categories?

4. Margaret Mead's cross-cultural research on gender relations suggests that male dominance is a cultural construct and, consequently, that alternative gender arrangements can be created. Looking at your grandparents, parents, and siblings, do you see any changes in your own family? What about your own community? Do you think such changes are positive?

5. Do you know someone in your family, neighborhood, or school who is "abnormal"? What is the basis for that judgment, and do you think everyone shares that opinion? Can you imagine that personal habits you consider normal would be viewed as deviant in the past or in another country?

Key Terms

self-awareness
naming ceremony
personality
dependence training

independence training
modal personality
core values
intersexuals

transgenders
culture-bound syndrome

Online Study Resources

Login to **www.cengagebrain.com** to access the resources your instructor has assigned and to purchase materials. For this book, you can access:

CourseMate
Access chapter-specific learning tools including flashcards, glossaries, practice quizzes, videos, and more in your Anthropology CourseMate.

VISUAL ESSENCE

In making a living, humans must gather, produce, exchange, buy, or otherwise obtain essential resources—food, water, shelter, and fuel. Almost everywhere on earth throughout time, our species has managed this in a wide range of highly contrasting natural environments. We have done so by means of various biological and cultural adaptations. Inventing or borrowing various technologies, humans have developed distinctive subsistence arrangements to harness energy and process resources. Thus we may find hunter-gatherers in Namibia's desert, fishers in Norway, manioc planters in Colombia's rainforest, goat herders in Iran's mountains, steel-mill laborers in South Korea, and computer techs in India. All human activities impact their environments, some radically transforming the landscape. Here we see peasant farmers practicing wet-rice cultivation on the steep slopes of southern China's Guangxi Province. They have carved out terraces to capture rainwater, prevent soil erosion, and increase food production. This is only part of the story. How will the crop be harvested in this challenging terrain? Who will process and package it? Where will it be shipped and how? What will determine its price?

11 Subsistence and Exchange

all living beings must satisfy certain basic needs to stay alive—including food, water, and shelter. Moreover, because these needs must be met on a regular basis, no creature could long survive if its relations with the environment were random and chaotic. People have a huge advantage over other animals in this regard. We have culture. With the passing of time, culture has become our primary means of adapting to the limitations and possibilities within any given environment.

Adaptation

In previous chapters, we noted that *adaptation* is the process organisms undergo to achieve a beneficial adjustment to a particular environment. What makes human adaptation unique among all other species is our capacity to produce and reproduce culture, enabling us to creatively adapt to an extraordinary range of radically different environments. The biological underpinnings of this capacity include large brains and a long period of growth and development.

How humans adjust to the burdens and opportunities presented in daily life is the basic concern of all cultures. As defined in Chapter 8, a people's *cultural adaptation* consists of a complex of ideas, activities, and technologies that enable them to survive and even thrive; in turn, that adaptation impacts their natural environment.

Through their distinctive cultures, different human groups have managed to adapt to a very diverse range of natural environments—from Arctic snowfields to Polynesian coral islands, from the Sahara Desert to the Amazon rainforest. Adaptation occurs not only when humans make all kinds of changes in their natural environment, but also when their natural environment biologically changes them, as illustrated in the following Biocultural Connection.

In this chapter you will learn to:

- Recognize the relationship between cultural adaptation and long-term cultural change.

- Identify the three major types of subsistence strategies.

- Distinguish various economic arrangements for producing, distributing, and consuming goods.

- Compare forms of gift exchange, redistribution, and trade.

- Summarize the impact of global markets on local communities.

BIOCULTURAL CONNECTION

Surviving in the Andes: Aymara Adaptation to High Altitude

However adaptable we are as a species through our diverse cultures, some natural environments pose such extreme climatic challenges that the human body must make physical adaptations to survive successfully. The central Andean highlands of Bolivia offer an interesting example of complex biocultural interaction, where a biologically adapted human body type has emerged due to natural selection.

Known as the *altiplano*, this high plateau has an average elevation of 4,000 meters (13,000 feet). Many thousands of years ago, small groups of human foragers in the warm lowlands climbed up the mountain slopes in search of game and other food. The higher they moved, the harder it became to breathe due to decreasing molecular concentration, or partial pressure, of oxygen in the inspired air. However, upon reaching the cold and treeless highlands, they found herds of llamas and hardy food plants, including potatoes—reasons to stay. Eventually (about 4,000 years ago) their descendants, known as the Aymara, domesticated both the llamas and the potatoes and developed a new way of life as high-altitude agropastoralists.

The llamas provided meat and hides, as well as milk and wool. And the potatoes, a rich source of carbohydrates, became their staple food. In the course of many centuries, the Aymara selectively cultivated more than 200 varieties of these tubers on small family-owned tracts of land. They boiled them fresh for immediate consumption and also freeze-dried and preserved them as *chuño*, which is the Aymara's major source of nutrition to this day.

Still surviving as highland subsistence farmers and herders, these Aymara Indians have adapted culturally and biologically to the cold and harsh conditions of Bolivia's altiplano. They live and go about their work at extremely high altitudes (up to 4,800 meters/15,600 feet), where the partial pressure of oxygen in the air is far lower than that to which most humans are biologically accustomed.

Experiencing a marked hypoxemia (insufficient oxygenation of the blood), a person's normal physiological response to being active at such heights is quick and heavy breathing. Most outsiders visiting the altiplano typically need several days to acclimatize to these conditions. Going too high too quickly can cause *soroche* (mountain sickness), with physiological problems such as pulmonary hypertension, increased heart rates, shortness of breath, headaches, fever, lethargy, and nausea. These symptoms usually disappear when one becomes fully acclimated, but most people will still be quickly exhausted by otherwise normal physical exercise.

For the Aymara Indians whose ancestors have inhabited the altiplano for many thousands of years, the situation is different. Through generations of natural selection, their bodies have become biologically adapted to the low oxygen levels. Short-legged and barrel-chested, their small bodies have an unusually large thoracic volume compared to their tropical lowland neighbors and most other humans. Remarkably, their expanded heart and lungs possess about 30 percent greater pulmonary diffusing capacity to oxygenate blood. In short, the distinctly broad chests of the Aymara Indians are biological evidence of their adaptation to the low-oxygen atmosphere of a natural habitat in which they survive as high-altitude agropastoralists. ∎

Biocultural Question

If a group of Aymara Indians abandons their high-altitude homeland in the Bolivian altiplano and settles for a new life in the coastal lowlands, will their descendants still living in this low-altitude environment a dozen generations later have smaller chests?

For more information see Baker, P. (Ed.). (1978). *The biology of high altitude peoples*. London: Cambridge University Press; Rupert, J. L., & Hochachka, P. W. (2001). The evidence for hereditary factors contributing to high altitude adaptation in Andean natives: A review. *High Altitude Medicine & Biology 2* (2), 235–256.

© Victor Englebert

The Unit of Adaptation

The unit of adaptation includes both organisms and their environment. Organisms, including human beings, exist as members of a population; populations, in turn, must have the flexibility to cope with variability and to change within the natural environment that sustains them. In biological terms, this flexibility means that different organisms within the population have somewhat different genetic endowments. In cultural terms, it means that variation occurs among individual skills, knowledge, and personalities. Indeed, organisms and environments form dynamic interacting systems. And although environments do not determine culture, they do present certain possibilities and limitations: People might just as easily farm as fish, but we do not expect to find farmers in Siberia's frozen tundra or fishermen in the middle of North Africa's Sahara Desert.

Some anthropologists have adopted the ecologists' concept of **ecosystem,** defined as a system, or functioning whole, composed of both the natural environment and all the organisms living within it. The system is bound by the activities of the organisms, as well as by such physical processes as erosion and evaporation.

Adaptation in Cultural Evolution

Human groups adapt to their environments by means of their cultures. However, cultures may change over the course of time; they evolve. This is called **cultural evolution.** The process is sometimes confused with the idea of **progress**—the notion that humans are moving forward to a better, more advanced stage in their development toward perfection. Yet not all changes turn out to be positive in the long run, nor do they improve conditions for every member of a society even in the short run. Notably, complex urban societies are not more highly evolved than those of food foragers. Rather, both are highly evolved, but in quite different ways.

Cultural adaptation must also be understood from a long-term historical point of view. To fit into an ecosystem, humans (like all organisms) must have the potential to adjust to or become a part of it. A good example of this is the Comanche, whose history begins in the highlands of southern Idaho.[1] Living in that harsh, arid region, these North American Indians traditionally subsisted on wild plants, small animals, and occasionally larger game. Their material equipment was simple and limited to what they (and their dogs) could carry or pull. The size of their groups was restricted, and what little social power could develop was in the hands of the shaman, who was a combination of healer and spiritual guide.

At some point in their nomadic history, the Comanche moved east onto the Great Plains, attracted by enormous bison herds. As much larger groups could be supported by the new and plentiful food supply, the Comanche needed a more complex political organization. Eventually they acquired horses and guns from European and neighboring Indian traders. This enhanced their hunting capabilities significantly and led to the emergence of powerful hunting chiefs.

The Comanche became raiders in order to get more horses (which they did not breed for themselves), and their hunting chiefs evolved into war chiefs. The once materially poor and peaceful hunter-gatherers of the dry highlands became wealthy, and raiding became a way of life. In the late 18th and early 19th centuries, they dominated the southern plains (now primarily Texas and Oklahoma). In moving from one regional environment to another and in adopting a new technology, the Comanche were able to take advantage of existing cultural capabilities to thrive in their new situation.

Sometimes societies that developed independently of one another find similar solutions to similar problems. For example, the Cheyenne Indians moved from the woodlands of the Great Lakes region to the Great Plains and took up a form of Plains Indian culture resembling that of the Comanche, even though the cultural historical backgrounds of the two groups differed significantly. Before they transformed into horse-riding bison hunters, the Cheyenne had cultivated crops and gathered wild rice, which fostered a distinct set of social, political, and religious practices. This is an example of **convergent evolution**—the development of similar cultural adaptations to similar environmental conditions by different peoples with different ancestral cultures.

Especially interesting is that the Cheyenne gave up crop cultivation completely and focused exclusively on hunting and gathering after their move into the vast grasslands of the northern High Plains. Contrary to the popular notion of evolution as a progressive movement toward increased manipulation of the environment, this ethnographic example shows that cultural historical

▲▲

ecosystem A system, or a functioning whole, composed of both the natural environment and all the organisms living within it.

cultural evolution Cultural change over time—not to be confused with progress.

progress The ethnocentric notion that humans are moving forward to a higher, more advanced stage in their development toward perfection.

convergent evolution In cultural evolution, the development of similar cultural adaptations to similar environmental conditions by different peoples with different ancestral cultures.

▼▼

[1]Wallace, E., & Hoebel, E. A. (1952). *The Comanches.* Norman: University of Oklahoma Press.

changes in subsistence practices do not always go from dependence on wild food to farming; they may go the other way as well.

Related to the phenomenon of convergent evolution is **parallel evolution,** in which similar cultural adaptations to similar environmental conditions are achieved by peoples whose ancestral cultures were already somewhat alike. For example, the development of farming in Southwest Asia and Mesoamerica (discussed in Chapter 5) took place independently, as people in both regions, whose lifeways were already comparable, became dependent on a narrow range of plant foods that required human intervention for their protection and reproductive success. Both developed intensive forms of agriculture, built large cities, and created complex social and political organizations.

It is important to recognize that stability as well as change is involved in cultural adaptation and evolution; episodes of major adaptive change may be followed by long periods of relative stability in a cultural system.

Moreover, not everybody benefits from changes, especially if change is forced upon them. As history painfully demonstrates, all too often humans have made changes that have had disastrous results, leading to the deaths of thousands, even millions, of people—not to mention other creatures—and to the destruction of the natural environment. In short, we must avoid falling into the ethnocentric trap of equating change with progress or seeing everything as adaptive.

Modes of Subsistence

Human societies all across the world have developed a cultural infrastructure compatible with the natural resources they have available to them and within the limitations of their various habitats. Each mode of subsistence involves not only resources but also the technology required to effectively capture and utilize them, as well as the kinds of work arrangements that are developed to best suit a society's needs. In the next few pages, we will discuss the major types of cultural infrastructure, beginning with the oldest and most universal mode of subsistence: food foraging.

Food-Foraging Societies

Before the domestication of food plants and animals, all people supported themselves through **food foraging,** a mode of subsistence involving some combination of hunting, fishing, and gathering wild plant foods. When food foragers had the earth to themselves, they had their pick of the best environments. But gradually areas with rich soils and ample supplies of water were appropriated by farming societies and more recently by industrial

societies, in which human labor, hand tools, and animal power were largely replaced by machines. As a result, small foraging communities were edged out of their traditional habitats by these expanding groups.

Today at most a quarter of a million people—less than 0.005 percent of the world population of close to 7 billion—still subsist mainly as foragers. They are found only in the world's most marginal areas (frozen Arctic tundra, deserts, and inaccessible forests) and typically lead a migratory existence that makes it impractical to accumulate many material possessions. Because foraging cultures have nearly disappeared in areas having a natural abundance of food and fuel resources, anthropologists are necessarily cautious when it comes to making generalizations about the ancient human past based on in-depth studies of still-existing foraging groups that have adapted to more marginal habitats.

Characteristics of Food-Foraging Societies

Typically, foragers have ample and balanced diets and are less likely to experience severe famine than farmers. Their material possessions are limited, but so is their desire to amass things. Notably, they have plenty of leisure time for concentrating on family ties, social life, and spiritual development—apparently far more than people living in farming and industrial societies. Such findings clearly challenge the once widely held view that food foragers live a miserable existence.

Present-day peoples who subsist by hunting, fishing, and wild plant collection are not following an ancient way of life because they do not know any better. Rather, they have been forced by circumstances into situations where foraging is the best means of survival or they simply prefer to live this way. In fact, foraging constitutes a rational response to particular ecological, economic, and sociopolitical realities. Moreover, for at least 2,000 years, hunters, fishers, and gatherers have met the demands for commodities such as furs, hides, feathers, ivory, pearls, fish, nuts, and honey within larger trading networks. Like everyone else, most food foragers are now part of a larger system with social, economic, and political relations extending far beyond regional, national, or even continental boundaries.

Among the hallmarks of food-foraging societies (particularly those few that still survive in marginal areas that are not naturally rich in food and fuel) is mobility. Foragers move as needed within a circumscribed region that is their home range to tap into naturally available food sources. A crucial factor in this mobility is availability of water. The distance between the food supply and water must not be so great that more energy is required to fetch water than can be obtained from the food.

Another characteristic of the food-foraging adaptation is the small size of local groups, typically fewer than a hundred people. No completely satisfactory explanation for this has been offered, but both ecological and social factors are involved. Among the ecological factors is the number of people that the available resources can support at a given level of food-getting techniques. This requires adjusting to seasonal and long-term changes in resource availability. The population density of foraging groups surviving in marginal environments today rarely exceeds one person per square mile—a very low density.

Other key features are egalitarianism, food sharing, communal property, flexible division of labor by gender, and rarity of warfare.

Food-Producing Societies

As described in Chapter 5, the domestication of plants and animals began about 10,000 years ago with the *Neolithic revolution*. This led to radical transformations in cultural systems, with foragers developing new social and economic patterns based either on plant cultivation or pastoralism. Although food production gave people alternative sources for nutrition and some control over vital resources, the new ways of life were not always more reliable than foraging.

Producing Food in Gardens: Horticulture

With the advent of plant domestication, some societies took up **horticulture** (from the Latin *hortus*, meaning "garden"), in which small communities of gardeners cultivate crops with simple hand tools, using neither irrigation nor the plow. Typically, horticulturists cultivate several varieties of food plants in small, hand-cleared gardens. Because they do not usually fertilize the soil, they use a given garden plot for only a few years before abandoning it in favor of a new one. Often horticulturists can grow enough food for their subsistence, and occasionally they produce a modest surplus that can be used for purposes such as intervillage feasts and exchange. Although their major food supplies may come from their gardens, many horticulturalists will also fish, hunt game, and collect wild plants foods when need and opportunity arise.

One of the most widespread forms of horticulture, especially in the tropics, is **slash-and-burn cultivation,** or *swidden farming*, in which the natural vegetation is cut, the slash is subsequently burned, and crops are then planted among the ashes. This is an ecologically sophisticated and sustainable way of raising food, especially in the tropics, when carried out under the right conditions: low population densities and adequate amounts of land. It mimics the diversity of the natural ecosystem, growing

▲▲▲ Although food foragers such as the Ju/'hoansi Bushmen in southern Africa have a flexible division of labor, men usually do the hunting and women much of the gathering. Here Ju/'hoansi women prepare a three-pound ostrich egg omelet (equivalent to about two dozen chicken eggs). Traditionally, the bird's large, hard shell serves as a very useful water container. If it is broken, the shell's pieces are fashioned into jewelry.

several different crops in the same field. Mixed together, the crops are less vulnerable to pests and plant diseases than a single crop.

Not only is the system ecologically sound, but it is far more energy efficient than modern farming methods used in developed countries such as the United States, where natural resources such as land and fuel are still

▲▲

parallel evolution In cultural evolution, the development of similar cultural adaptations to similar environmental conditions by peoples whose ancestral cultures are already somewhat alike.

food foraging A mode of subsistence involving some combination of hunting, fishing, and gathering of wild plant foods.

horticulture The cultivation of crops in food gardens, carried out with simple hand tools such as digging sticks and hoes.

slash-and-burn cultivation An extensive form of horticulture in which the natural vegetation is cut, the slash is subsequently burned, and crops are then planted among the ashes; also known as *swidden farming*.

▼▼

relatively cheap and abundant, and many farms operate with financial support in the form of government subsidies or tax breaks. While high-tech farming requires more energy input than it yields, slash-and-burn farming produces between 10 and 20 units of energy for every unit expended.

Producing Food on Farms: Agriculture

In contrast to horticulture, **agriculture** (from the Latin *agri*, meaning "field") is growing food plants like grains, tubers, fruits, and vegetables in soil prepared and maintained for crop production. This form of more intensive food production involves using technologies other than hand tools, such as irrigation, fertilizers, and plows pulled by harnessed draft animals. In the developed countries of the world, agriculture relies on fuel-powered tractors to produce food on larger plots of land.

Among agriculturists, surplus crop cultivation is generally substantial—providing food not only for their own needs but also for those of various full-time specialists and nonproducing consumers. This surplus may be traded or sold for cash, or it may be coerced out of the farmers through taxes, rent, or tribute (forced gifts acknowledging submission or protection) paid to landowners or other dominant groups. These landowners and specialists—such as traders, carpenters, blacksmiths, sculptors, basket makers, and stonecutters—typically reside in substantial towns or cities, where political power is centralized in the hands of a socially elite class. Dominated by more powerful groups and markets, much of what the farmers do is governed by political and economic forces over which they have little control.

CHARACTERISTICS OF CROP-PRODUCING SOCIETIES

One of the most significant correlates of crop cultivation was the development of fixed settlements, in which farming families reside together near their cultivated fields. The task of food production lent itself to a different kind of social organization. Because the hard work of some members of the group could provide food for all, others became free to devote their time to inventing and manufacturing the equipment needed for a new sedentary way of life. Tools for digging and harvesting, pottery for storage and cooking, clothing made of woven textiles, and housing made of stone, wood, or sun-dried bricks all grew out of the new sedentary living conditions and the altered division of labor.

The Neolithic revolution also brought important changes in social structure. At first, social relations were egalitarian and hardly different from those that prevailed among food foragers. As settlements grew, however, and large numbers of people had to share important resources such as land and water, society became more elaborately organized.

Mixed Farming: Crop Growing and Animal Breeding

Indigenous food-producing cultures in the western hemisphere depended primarily on growing domesticated indigenous crops such as manioc, corn, and beans. With some exceptions, including the Aymara and Quechua, who traditionally also keep llamas and alpacas in their high-altitude homeland in the Andes Mountains of South America (as described in the Biocultural Connection on page 222), American Indians obtained sufficient meat, fat, leather, and wool from wild game.

In contrast, Eurasian and African food-producing peoples often do not have an opportunity to obtain enough vitally important animal proteins from wild game, fish, or fowl. Many have developed a subsistence strategy that combines crop cultivation with raising animals for food, labor, or trade. Depending on cultural traditions, ecological circumstances, and animal habits, some species are kept in barns or fenced-off fields, while others range freely in and around the settlement or designated pastures, albeit under supervision, branded or otherwise marked by their owners as private property.

Likewise, many ancient agricultural communities adapted to mountainous environments from the Alps to the Himalayas have traditionally herded livestock (cows, sheep, horses, and so on) in high summer pastures, leaving their narrow lowland valleys for alternative use—farming grains, keeping orchards, and growing vegetables and hay to feed animals in the winter. After the crop harvest, before the weather turns cold and snow covers the higher pastures, those who left the village to tend the herds bring the animals back to the valley and settle in for the winter season. This "vertical" seasonal movement of herders and their livestock between high-altitude summer pastures and lowland valleys is an example of *transhumance* (*trans* means "across"; *humus* means "earth").

In contrast to transhumance, in which a number of men from the village annually move with their herds to seasonal pastures while other community members remain home in the settlement, there are also cultures in which the entire community migrates with the herds to their alternate grazing grounds—as described in the next section.[2]

---

[2]Cole, J. W., & Wolf, E. R. (1999). *The hidden frontier: Ecology and ethnicity in an alpine valley* (with a new introduction). Berkeley: University of California Press; see also Jones, S. (2005). Transhumance re-examined. *Journal of the Royal Anthropological Institute 11* (4), 841–842.

▲▲▲ In the Zagros Mountains region of Iran, pastoral nomads follow seasonal pastures, migrating vast distances with their huge herds of goats and sheep over rugged terrain that includes perilously steep snowy passes and fast ice-cold rivers.

Herding Grazing Animals: Pastoralism

One of the more striking examples of human adaptation to the environment is **pastoralism**—breeding and managing large herds of domesticated herbivores (grazing and browsing animals), such as goats, sheep, cattle, horses, llamas, and camels. Unlike the forms of animal husbandry just discussed, pastoralism is a specialized way of life centered on breeding and herding animals.

Dependent on livestock for survival, families in pastoral cultures own herds of grazing animals whose needs for food and drink determine their everyday routines. When a dozen or more herding families join together, their collective herds may number in the thousands and sometimes even a few hundred thousand. Unlike crop cultivators who need to remain close to their fields, pastoral peoples do not usually establish permanent settlements since they must follow or lead their large herds to new pastures on a regular basis. Like their animals, most pastoralists must be mobile and have adjusted their way of life accordingly.

Nomadic pastoralism is an effective way of living—far more so than sheep or cattle ranching—in environments that are too dry, cold, steep, or rocky for farming, such as the vast, arid grasslands that stretch eastward from northern Africa through the Arabian Desert, across the plateau of Iran and into Turkistan and Mongolia. Today, in Africa and Asia alone, more than 21 million people are pastoralists, still migrating with their herds. These nomadic groups regard movement as a natural part of life.

Although pastoral nomads depend greatly on animals to meet their daily needs, they also trade surplus animals, leather, wool (and various crafts such as woven rugs) with farmers or merchants. In exchange they receive crops and valued commodities such as flour, dried fruit, spices, tea, metal knives, pots and kettles, cotton or linen textiles, guns, and (more recently) lightweight plastic containers, sheets, and so on. In other words, there are many ties that connect them to surrounding agricultural and industrial societies.

Labor division among pastoral nomads is mainly according to age and gender. Typically, the chief task of the adult men and older boys is tending the herds. Although women and older girls in many pastoral societies are involved in herding as well, they primarily cook, sew, weave, care for the children, and carry fuel and water.

Intensive Agriculture: Urbanization and Peasantry

As discussed in Chapter 6, with the intensification of agriculture, some farming settlements grew into towns and even cities. With urbanization came greater complexity—labor specialization, the formation of elite groups, public management, taxation, and policing. For food and fuel, urbanized populations depended on what was

▲▲▲

agriculture Intensive crop cultivation, employing plows, fertilizers, and/or irrigation.

pastoralism The breeding and managing of migratory herds of domesticated grazing animals, such as goats, sheep, cattle, llamas, and camels.

▼▼▼

produced or foraged in surrounding areas. Thus the urban ruling class sought to widen its territorial power and political control over rural populations.

Once a powerful group managed to dominate a community of farmers, it also imposed its rules on them, forcing them to work harder and obliging them to make payments in farm produce or labor services as fees for land use and protection and/or as acknowledgment of submission. Burdened by taxes to feed those repressing them, these farmers were left with little for their own families and lost their independence. Subjected to an ever-more dominant group, they became **peasants.** These small-scale producers of crops or livestock live on land self-owned or rented in exchange for labor, crops, or money and are usually exploited by more powerful groups in a complex society.[3]

And so it continues in many parts of the world today. No matter how hard they work, peasants typically possess too little land of their own to go beyond meeting the most basic needs of their families. Unable to produce enough of a surplus to sell for cash, they rarely have capital to buy the laborsaving equipment that could increase their production. So, most peasants remain stuck in poverty, struggling to make ends meet. Meanwhile big landowners and wealthy merchants have the means to expand their holdings and invest in new machinery that leads to increased productivity and profitability.

Industrial Food Production

Until about 200 years ago, human societies all across the world had developed cultural infrastructures based on foraging, horticulture, agriculture, or pastoralism. This changed with the invention of the steam engine in England, which brought about an industrial revolution that quickly spread to other parts of the globe. Replacing animal and human labor, as well as hand tools, new machines were invented, first powered by steam, then by biofuels (coal, gas, oil), sharply increasing factory production and boosting mass transportation. Throughout the 1800s and 1900s, this resulted in large-scale **industrial societies.** Technological inventions utilizing electricity and, since the 1940s, nuclear energy brought about more dramatic changes in social and economic organization on a worldwide scale.

Modern industrial technologies have transformed food production. In contrast to traditional farms and plantations, which historically rely on human labor (often forced) and on animal power in many places, modern agriculture depends on newly invented labor-saving devices such as tractors, combine harvesters, milk machines, and so on. With large machines plowing, seeding, weeding, mowing, and harvesting crops, the need for farmhands and other rural workers is sharply diminished. This has

also happened with livestock production—in particular, hogs, cattle, and poultry.

Industrial food production may be defined as large-scale businesses involved in mass food production, processing, and marketing, which primarily rely on laborsaving machines. It has had far-reaching economic, social, and political consequences, not all of which are readily recognized as related and intertwined. Today, large food-producing corporations own enormous tracts of land on which they mass-produce tons of mechanically harvested crops and/or raise huge quantities of meat animals. Crops and animals alike are harvested, processed, packed, and shipped with ever-greater efficiency to supermarkets to feed largely urban masses. Profits are often considerable, especially for corporate owners and shareholders.

Although meat, poultry, and other agricultural products are relatively cheap and thus affordable, industrial food production by agribusiness has often been a disaster for millions of peasants and small farmers. Even medium-sized farms growing corn, wheat, or potatoes or raising cows, hogs, and chickens can rarely compete without government subsidies. For that reason, the number of family-owned farms in western Europe, North America, and other parts of the world has dramatically declined in the past few decades. This process has led to huge drops in many rural populations, decimating many farming communities.

For the family farms that have managed to survive, there is seldom enough income to cover the costs of a large household, including education, health care, farm and household insurance, and taxes. This situation forces individuals to seek money-earning opportunities elsewhere, often far away. Ironically, some hire on as cheap wage laborers in poultry- or meat-packing plants where working conditions are distasteful and often dangerous.

Maximizing profits, industrial food production systems streamline operations, increase output, and reduce costs, including human labor (by trimming the number of workers, minimizing benefits, and driving down wages). Pushing for market expansion, the largest have gone global. The United States is the world's largest producer of chicken meat—some 36 billion pounds per year. On average, each American consumes 85 pounds of chicken a year, but much of the country's production is exported. Over 900,000 tons go to Russia (mostly legs—more than a billion of them), and another 400,000 to China (primarily chicken feet—about 1.2 billion). The country's largest processing plant, located in Mississippi, slaughters about 2.5 million chickens per week. Today's

---

[3]Wolf, E. R. (1966). *Peasants* (pp. 4–5). Englewood Cliffs, NJ: Prentice-Hall.

Chickens ready for butchering are usually grabbed by their feet, stuffed in crates, and trucked off to the slaughterhouse. But some farmers use mechanical harvesters. Moving through a chicken barn, a harvester can pick up about 200 birds in 30 seconds. Once full, it places the birds in holding containers. From there, the chickens are mechanically transferred to a "packing unit," which automatically counts them and places them into drawers that are stacked, loaded onto a truck, and transported to a processing plant. There the chickens are mass-killed, cut up, and packaged.

industrial food production and global marketing complex, involving a network of interlinked distribution centers, is made possible by an electronic-digital revolution that began in the late 20th century.[4]

Subsistence and Economics

An **economic system** is an organized arrangement for producing, distributing, and consuming goods. In pursuing a particular means of subsistence, people necessarily produce, distribute, and consume things, so it is obvious that our discussion of subsistence patterns involves economic matters. Yet economic systems encompass much more than we have covered so far.

Although anthropologists have adopted theories and concepts from economists, most recognize that theoretical principles derived from the study of capitalist market economies have limited applicability to economic systems in societies that are not industrialized and where people do not produce and exchange goods for private profit. This is because, in these non-state societies, the economic sphere of behavior is not separate from the social, religious, and political spheres.

In every society, particular customs and rules govern the kinds of work done, who does the work, attitudes toward the work, how it is accomplished, and who controls the resources necessary to produce desired goods, knowledge, and services. The primary resources in any culture are raw materials, technology, and labor. The rules directing the use of these are embedded in a people's culture and determine the way the economy operates within any given natural environment.

[4]Ritzer, G. (2007). *The coming of post-industrial society* (2nd ed.). New York: McGraw-Hill.

Land and Water Resources

All societies regulate allocation of valuable natural resources—especially land and water. Food foragers must determine who will hunt game and gather plants in their home range and where these activities take place. Groups that rely on fishing or growing crops need to make similar decisions concerning who carries out which task on which stretch of water or land. Farmers must have some means of determining title to land and access to water supplies for irrigation. Pastoralists require a system that determines rights to watering places and grazing land, as well as the rights to land where they move their herds.

In Western capitalist societies, a system of private ownership of land and rights to natural resources generally prevails. Although elaborate laws have been enacted to regulate the buying, owning, and selling of land and water resources, if individuals wish to reallocate valuable farmland to some other purpose, they generally can.

▲▲▲

peasant A small-scale producer of crops or livestock living on land self-owned or rented in exchange for labor, crops, or money and exploited by more powerful groups in a complex society.

industrial society A society in which human labor, hand tools, and animal power are largely replaced by machines, with an economy primarily based on big factories.

industrial food production Large-scale businesses involved in mass food production, processing, and marketing, which primarily rely on labor-saving machines.

economic system An organized arrangement for producing, distributing, and consuming goods.

▼▼▼

In traditional nonindustrial societies, land is often controlled by kinship groups such as the family or band rather than by individuals. For example, among the Ju/'hoansi Bushmen of the Kalahari Desert, each band of ten to thirty people lives on roughly 250 square miles of land, which they consider to be their territory—their own country. These territories are not defined by boundaries but in terms of waterholes that are located within them. The land is said to be owned by those who have lived the longest in the band, usually a group of brothers and sisters or cousins. Their concept of landholding, however, is not something easily translated in modern Western terms of private ownership. Within their traditional worldview, no part of their homeland can be sold for money or traded away for goods. Outsiders must ask permission to enter the territory, but denying the request would be unthinkable.

The practice of defining territories on the basis of *core features*—waterholes (as among the Ju/'hoansi), watercourses or waterways (as among Indians of the northeastern United States), unique sites in the landscape where ancestral spirits are thought to dwell (as among the Aborigines in Australia), or something else—is typical of food foragers. Territorial boundaries tend to be vaguely defined, and to avoid friction foragers may designate part of their territory as a buffer zone between them and their neighbors. The adaptive value of this is obvious: The size of band territories, as well as the size of the band, can adjust to keep in balance with availability of resources in any given place. Such adjustment would be more difficult under a system of individual ownership of clearly bounded land.

Technology Resources

All societies have some means of creating and allocating tools that are used to produce goods, as well as traditions concerning passing them on to succeeding generations.

A society's **technology**—the number and types of tools employed, combined with knowledge about how to make and use them—is directly related to the lifestyles of its members. Food foragers and pastoral nomads who are frequently on the move are apt to have fewer and more portable tools than more settled peoples such as sedentary farmers. A great number of heavier tools would hinder mobility. Thus the average weight of an individual's personal belongings among the Ju/'hoansi foragers is just under 25 pounds, limited to the barest essentials such as implements for hunting, gathering, fishing, building, and cooking. Pastoral nomads, aided by pack animals, typically have more material possessions than foragers, but still less than people who live in permanent settlements.

Food foragers make and use a variety of tools, many of which are ingenious in their effectiveness. Some of these they make for their individual use, but codes of generosity are such that a person may not refuse to give or loan what is requested. Tools may be given or loaned to others in exchange for the products resulting from their use. For example, a Ju/'hoansi who gives his arrow to another hunter has a right to a share of any animals the hunter kills. Game is considered to belong to the man whose arrow killed it, even when he is not present on the hunt. In this context, it makes little sense for them to accumulate luxuries or surplus goods, and the fact that no one owns significantly more than another helps to limit status differences.

Among horticulturists, the axe, digging stick, and hoe are the primary tools. Since these are relatively easy to produce, almost everyone can make them. Whoever makes a tool has first rights to it, but when he or she is not using it, any family member may ask to use it, and the request is rarely denied. Refusal would cause people to treat the tool owner with scorn for this singular lack of concern for others. If a relative helps raise the crop traded for a particular tool, that relative becomes part owner of the implement, and it may not be traded or given away without his or her permission.

In permanently settled agricultural communities, tools and other productive goods are more complex, heavier, and costlier to make. In such settings, individual ownership tends to be more absolute, as are the conditions under which people may borrow and use such equipment. It is easy to replace a knife lost by a relative during palm cultivation but much more difficult to replace an iron plow or a diesel-fueled harvesting machine. Rights to the ownership of complex tools are more rigidly applied; generally the person who has funded the purchase of a complex piece of machinery is considered the sole owner and may decide how and by whom it will be used.

Labor Resources and Patterns

In addition to raw materials and technology, labor is a key resource in any economic system. A look around the world reveals many different labor patterns, but two features are almost always present in human cultures: a basic division of labor by gender and by age.

DIVISION OF LABOR BY GENDER

Anthropologists have studied extensively the social division of labor by gender in cultures of all sorts. Whether men or women do a particular job varies from group to group, but typically work is divided into the tasks of either one or the other. For example, the practices most commonly regarded as "women's work" tend to be those that can be carried out near home and that are easily resumed after interruption. The tasks historically often regarded as "men's work" tend to be those requiring physical strength, rapid mobilization of high bursts of energy, frequent travel at some distance from home, and assumption of high levels of risk and danger.

Many exceptions occur, however, as in those societies where women regularly carry burdensome loads or put in long hours of hard work cultivating crops in the fields. In some societies, women perform almost three-quarters of all work, and in several societies they have served as warriors. For example, in the 19th-century West African kingdom of Dahomey (in what is now called Benin), thousands of women served in the armed forces of the Dahomean king. Also, there are references to female warriors in ancient Ireland, and archaeological evidence indicates their presence among the Vikings.

During World War II in the early 1940s, some 58,000 Soviet Russian women engaged in frontline combat defending their homeland against German invaders, and during the Vietnam War in the 1960s and early 1970s, North Vietnamese women fought in mixed-gender communist army units. Today, women serve in the military of most countries, but only Canada, Denmark, France, Germany, and a few others permit them to join combat units.

Instead of looking for key biological factors to explain the social division of labor, a more useful strategy is to examine the kinds of work that men and women do in the context of specific societies to see how they relate to other cultural and historical factors. Researchers find a continuum of patterns, ranging from flexible integration of men and women to rigid segregation by gender.[5]

The *flexible/integrated pattern* is exemplified by the Ju/'hoansi discussed above and is seen most often among food foragers (as well as communities where crops are traditionally cultivated primarily for family consumption). In such societies, men and women perform up to 35 percent of activities with approximately equal participation, and tasks deemed especially appropriate for one gender may be performed by the other without loss of face, as the situation warrants. Where these practices prevail, boys and girls grow up in much the same way, learn to value cooperation over competition, and become equally habituated to adult men and women, who interact with one another on a relatively equal basis.

Societies following a *segregated pattern* define almost all work as either masculine or feminine, so men and women rarely engage in joint efforts of any kind. In such societies, it is inconceivable that someone would even think of doing something considered the work of the opposite sex. This pattern is frequently seen in pastoral nomadic, intensive agricultural, and industrial societies, where men's work keeps them outside the home for much of the time. Typically, men in such societies are expected to be tough, aggressive, and competitive—and this often involves assertions of male superiority, and hence authority, over women. Historically, societies segregated by gender often have imposed their control on societies featuring integration, upsetting the egalitarian nature of the latter.

In the third pattern of labor division by gender, men and women carry out their work separately, as in societies segregated by gender, but the relationship between them is one of balanced complementarity rather than inequality. Although each gender manages its own affairs, the interests of both men and women are represented at all levels. Thus, as in integrated societies, neither gender exerts dominance over the other. This pattern may be seen among certain American Indian peoples with economies based on subsistence farming, as well as among several West African kingdoms, including that of the aforementioned Dahomeans.

In postindustrial societies, the division of labor by gender becomes blurred and even irrelevant, resembling the flexible/integrated pattern of traditional foragers briefly discussed above. Although gender preferences and discrimination in the workplace exist in societies making the economic transition, cultural ideas more fitting to agricultural or industrial societies predictably change in due time, adjusting to postindustrial challenges and opportunities.

▲▲▲▲▲▲▲▲▲▲▲▲▲▲▲▲▲▲▲▲▲▲▲▲▲▲▲▲▲▲▲▲▲▲▲▲

[5]Sanday, P. R. (1981). *Female power and male dominance: On the origins of sexual inequality* (pp. 79–80). Cambridge, UK: Cambridge University Press.

technology Tools and other material equipment, together with the knowledge of how to make and use them.

▼▼▼▼▼▼▼▼▼▼▼▼▼▼▼▼▼▼▼▼▼▼▼▼▼▼▼▼▼▼▼▼▼▼▼▼

DIVISION OF LABOR BY AGE

Division of labor according to age is also typical of human societies. Among the Ju/'hoansi, for example, children are not expected to contribute significantly to subsistence until they reach their late teens. Indeed, until they possess adult levels of strength and endurance, many "bush" foods are difficult for them to gather.

The Ju/'hoansi equivalent of retirement comes somewhere around the age of 60. Elderly people, while they will usually do some foraging for themselves, are not expected to contribute much food. However, older men and women alike play an essential role in spiritual matters. Freed from food taboos and other restrictions that apply to younger adults, they may handle ritual substances considered dangerous to those still involved with hunting or having children. By virtue of their old age, they have memories of customary practices and events that happened far in the past. Thus they are repositories of accumulated wisdom—the libraries of a nonliterate people—and are able to suggest solutions for problems younger adults have never before had to face. Considered useful for their knowledge, they are far from being unproductive members of society.

In many traditional farming societies, children as well as older people may make a greater contribution to the economy in terms of work and responsibility than is common in industrial or postindustrial societies. For instance, in Maya peasant communities in southern Mexico and Guatemala, children not only look after their younger brothers and sisters but also help with housework. Girls begin to make a substantial contribution to the work of the household by age 7 or 8. By age 11 they are constantly busy with an array of chores—grinding corn, making tortillas, fetching wood and water, sweep-

ing, and so forth. Young boys have less to do but are given small tasks, such as bringing in the chickens or playing with a baby. However, by age 12 they are carrying toasted tortillas to the men out working in the fields and returning with loads of corn.[6]

Children also work in industrial societies, where poor families depend on every possible contribution to the household. There, however, economic desperation may easily lead to the cold exploitation of children in factory settings. The use of child labor has become a matter of increasing concern as large capitalist corporations rely more and more on the low-cost manufacture of goods in the world's poorer countries.

UNICEF estimates that nearly 160 million children ages 5 to 14 are engaged in child labor—1 in 6 children in the world. Almost all live in Third World countries where their families depend on the extra income they bring home. Millions are working in hazardous conditions, such as in mines or with chemicals and pesticides in agriculture. Others toil away in workshops or as domestic servants. Often working full-time from dawn to dusk for extremely low wages, they have no opportunity for education.[7] Although the United States long ago passed laws prohibiting institutionalized child labor, the country imports at least $100 million worth of products manufactured by poorly paid children, ranging from rugs and carpets to clothing and soccer balls.[8]

COOPERATIVE LABOR

Cooperative work groups can be found everywhere—from foraging societies to food-producing ones, and from nonindustrial societies to industrial ones. Often, if the effort involves the whole community, a festive spirit permeates the work. For example, in some parts of East Africa, work parties begin with the display of a pot of beer to be consumed after the tasks have been finished. Home-brewed from millet, their major cereal crop, the beer is not really payment for the work; indeed, the labor involved is worth far more than the beer consumed. Rather, drinking the low-alcohol but highly nutritious beverage together is more of a symbolic activity to celebrate the spirit of friendship and mutual support. Recompense comes as individuals sooner or later participate in work parties for others. In rural areas all around the world, farmers commonly help one another during harvest and haying seasons, often sharing major pieces of equipment.

Feng Li/Getty Images

▲▲▲ Many of the soccer balls that children play with in the United States and Europe are handstitched by children in India who work under brutal conditions for pennies a day. After past scandals about soccer ball factories using child labor, many companies started adding labels stating that the balls were not made with child labor—but those labels are often sewn on the balls by children as young as 6 years old.

[6]Vogt, E. Z. (1990). *The Zinacantecos of Mexico: A modern Maya way of life* (2nd ed., pp. 83–87). Fort Worth: Holt, Rinehart & Winston.

[7]UNICEF. (2011, February 23). Child protection from violence, exploitation, and abuse. www.unicef.org/protection/index_child-labour.html (retrieved September 15, 2011).

[8]It's the law: Child labor protection. (1997, November/December). *Peace and Justice News*, 11; Smith, M. D. (2008, September 16). Indian child labor exploited in production of soccer balls. *Huffington Post.*

In most human societies, the basic unit within which cooperation takes place is the household. Traditionally—and still in many parts of the world—it is a unit of both economic production (working together in support of a livelihood) and consumption (sharing meals, domestic comfort, and so on). In industrial and postindustrial societies, these two activities are now usually separated.

TASK SPECIALIZATION

In contemporary industrial and postindustrial societies, there is a great diversity of specialized tasks to be performed, and no individual can even begin to know all of those customarily seen as fitting for his or her age and gender. However, although specialization continues to increase, modern technologies are making labor divisions based on gender less relevant. By contrast, in small-scale foraging and traditional crop-cultivating societies, where division of labor typically occurs along lines of age and gender, each person has knowledge and competence in all aspects of work appropriate to his or her age and gender. Yet, even in these nonindustrial societies there is a measure of task specialization.

An example of task specialization can be found among the Afar people of the Danakil Depression in the borderlands of Eritrea and Ethiopia, one of the lowest and hottest places on earth.[9] The desolate landscape features sulphur fields, smoking fissures, volcanic tremors, and vast salt plains. Since ancient times, groups of Afar men periodically mine the salt, hacking blocks from the

© Cengage Learning 2013

plain's crust. The work is backbreaking, all the more so with temperatures soaring to 140 degrees Fahrenheit.

Along with the physical strength required for such work under the most trying conditions, successful mining demands specialized planning and organization skills for getting to and from the worksite.[10] Pack camels have to be fed in advance, since importing sufficient fodder for them interferes with their ability to carry out salt. Food and water, packed by Afar women at the desert's edge, must be carried in for the thirty or forty miners that typically work together. Travel is arranged for nighttime to avoid the scorching sun.

Distribution and Exchange

In societies without a money economy, the rewards for labor are usually direct. The workers in a family group consume what they harvest, eat what the hunter or gatherer brings home, and use the tools they themselves make. But even where no formal medium of exchange such as money exists, some distribution of goods takes place. Anthropologists often classify the cultural systems of distributing material goods into three modes: reciprocity, redistribution, and market exchange.[11]

Reciprocity

Reciprocity refers to the exchange of goods and services, of roughly equal value, between two parties. This may involve gift giving. Notably, individuals or groups in most cultures like to think that the main point of the transaction is the gift itself, yet what actually matters are the social ties that are created or reinforced between givers and receivers. Because reciprocity is about a relationship between the self and others, gift giving is seldom really selfless. The overriding, if unconscious, motive is to fulfill social obligations, reinforce relationships, and perhaps to gain a bit of prestige in the process.

Cultural traditions dictate the occasion, location, and manner of exchange. For example, when indigenous hunters in Australia kill an animal, the meat is divided among the hunters' families and other relatives. Each person in the camp gets a share, the size depending on the nature of the person's kinship tie to the hunters. The giving and receiving is obligatory, as is the particularity of the distribution. Such sharing of food reinforces community bonds and ensures that everyone eats.

[9] Nesbitt, L. M. (1935). *Hell-hole of creation.* New York: Knopf.

[10] Mesghinua, H. M. (1966). Salt mining in Enderta. *Journal of Ethiopian Studies 4* (2); O'Mahoney, K. (1970). The salt trade. *Journal of Ethiopian Studies 8* (2).

[11] Polanyi, K. (1968). The economy as instituted process. In E. E. LeClair Jr. & H. K. Schneider (Eds.), *Economic anthropology: Readings in theory and analysis* (pp. 127–138). New York: Holt, Rinehart & Winston.

▲▲▲▲▲▲▲▲▲▲▲▲▲▲▲▲▲▲▲▲▲▲▲▲▲▲▲▲▲▲▲▲▲▲▲▲

reciprocity The exchange of goods and services, of approximately equal value, between two parties.

▼▼▼▼▼▼▼▼▼▼▼▼▼▼▼▼▼▼▼▼▼▼▼▼▼▼▼▼▼▼▼▼▼▼▼▼

▲▲▲ Once covered by the Red Sea, the Danakil Desert in northeastern Africa is now a deep, dry depression with enormous salt flats. Afar nomads come here periodically to quarry this rock salt. With camels, they haul the heavy slabs to the interior highlands for trade. Traveling at night, they avoid the scorching sun.

Reciprocity falls into several categories. The Australian food distribution example just noted constitutes an example of **generalized reciprocity**—exchange in which the value of what is given is not calculated, nor is the time of repayment specified. Gift giving, in the unselfish sense, also falls in this category. So, too, does the act of a kindhearted soul who stops to help a stranded motorist or someone else in distress and refuses payment with the admonition: "Pass it on to the next person in need."

Most generalized reciprocity, however, occurs among close kin or people who otherwise have intimate ties with one another. Within such circles, people give to others when they have the means and can count on receiving from others in time of need. Typically, participants will not consider such exchanges in economic terms but will couch them explicitly in terms of family and friendship social relations.

Balanced reciprocity differs in that it is not part of a long-term process. The giving and receiving, as well as the time involved, are more specific. One has a direct obligation to reciprocate promptly in equal value in order for the social relationship to continue. Examples of balanced reciprocity in contemporary North American society include customary practices such as hosting a baby shower for young friends expecting their first baby, giving presents at birthdays and various other culturally prescribed special occasions, or buying drinks when one's turn comes at a gathering of friends or associates.

Giving, receiving, and sharing as so far described constitute a form of social security or insurance. A family contributes to others when they have the means and can count on receiving from others in time of need—promoting an egalitarian distribution of wealth over the long run. Exchanges that occur within a group of relatives or between friends generally take the form of generalized or balanced reciprocity.

Negative reciprocity is a third form of exchange in which the aim is to get something for as little as possible. The parties involved have opposing interests and are not usually closely related; they may be strangers or even enemies. They are people with whom exchanges are often neither fair nor balanced and are usually not expected to be such. The exchange may involve hard bargaining, manipulation, or outright cheating. An extreme form of negative reciprocity is to take something by force, while realizing that one's victim may seek compensation or retribution for losses.

TRADE AND BARTER

Trade refers to a transaction in which two or more people are involved in an exchange of something—a quantity of food, fuel, clothing, jewelry, animals, or money, for example—for something else of equal value. In such a transaction, the value of the trade goods can be fixed by previous agreements or negotiated on the spot by the trading partners.

When there is no money involved in the transaction and the parties negotiate a direct exchange of one trade good for another, we use the term *barter*. In barter, arguing about the price and conditions of the deal may well be in the form of negative reciprocity, with each party aiming to get the better end of the transaction. Relative value is calculated, and despite an outward show of indifference, sharp trading is generally the rule, when compared to the more balanced nature of exchanges within a group.

© Terry O'Sullivan

KULA RING: GIFT GIVING AND TRADING IN THE SOUTH PACIFIC

Balanced reciprocity can take more complicated forms, whereby mutual gift giving serves to facilitate social interaction, smoothing social relations between traders wanting to do business. One classic ethnographic example of balanced reciprocity between trading partners seeking to be friends and do business at the same time is the **Kula ring** in the southwestern Pacific Ocean. Involving thousands of seafarers going to great lengths to establish and maintain good trade relations, this centuries-old ceremonial exchange system continues to this day.[12]

Kula participants are men of influence who travel to islands within the Trobriand ring to exchange prestige items—red shell necklaces (*soulava*), which are circulated around the ring of islands in a clockwise direction, and white shell armbands (*mwali*), which are carried in the opposite direction (▶ **Figure 11.1**). Each man in the Kula is linked to partners on the islands that neighbor his own. To a partner residing on an island in the clockwise direction, he offers a *soulava* and receives in return a *mwali*. He makes the reverse exchange of a *mwali* for a *soulava* to a partner living in the counterclockwise direction. Each of these trade partners eventually passes the object on to a Kula partner further along the chain of islands. *Soulava* and *mwali* are ranked according to their size, their color, how finely they are polished, and their particular histories. Some *soulava* and *mwali* are so famous that they create a sensation when they appear in a village.

Traditionally, men make their Kula journeys in elaborately carved dugout canoes, sailing and paddling these boats, which are 6 to 7.5 meters (20 to 25 feet) long, across open waters to shores some 100 kilometers (about 60 miles) or more away. The adventure is often dangerous and may take men away from their homes for several weeks, sometimes even months. Although men on Kula voyages may use the opportunity to trade for practical goods, acquiring such goods is not always the reason for these voyages—nor is Kula exchange a necessary part of regular trade expeditions.

Perhaps the best way to view the Kula is as an indigenous insurance policy in an economic order fraught with danger and uncertainty. It establishes and reinforces social partnerships between traders doing business on distant shores, ensuring a welcome reception from people who have similar vested interests. This ceremonial exchange network does more than simply smooth the trade of foods and other goods essential for survival. Melanesians participating in the Kula ring know that

their social position depends upon the company they keep and the circles in which they move. They derive their social prestige from the reputations of their partners and the valuables that they circulate. By giving and receiving armbands and necklaces that accumulate the histories of their travels and the names of those who have possessed them, men proclaim their individual fame and talent, gaining considerable influence for themselves in the process.

Like other forms of currency, *soulava* and *mwali* must flow from hand to hand; once they stop flowing, they lose their value. A man who takes these valuables out of their interisland circuit invites criticism. He loses not only prestige or social capital as a man of influence, but may become a target of sorcery for unraveling the cultural fabric that holds the islands together as a functioning social and economic order.

▲▲▲

generalized reciprocity A mode of exchange in which the value of the gift is not calculated, nor is the time of repayment specified.

balanced reciprocity A mode of exchange in which the giving and the receiving are specific as to the value of the goods and the time of their delivery.

negative reciprocity A mode of exchange in which the aim is to get something for as little as possible. Neither fair nor balanced, it may involve hard bargaining, manipulation, outright cheating, or theft.

Kula ring A form of balanced reciprocity that reinforces trade and social relations among the seafaring Melanesians who inhabit a large ring of islands in the southwestern Pacific Ocean.

▼▼▼

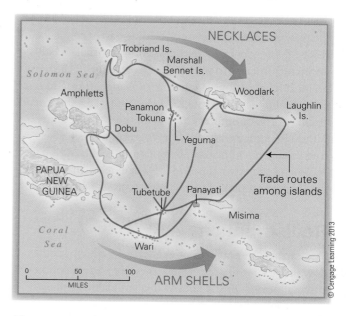

Figure 11.1 Kula Ring The ceremonial gift exchanges of shell necklaces and armbands in the Kula ring encourage trade and barter throughout the Melanesian islands.

[12]Malinowski, B. (1922). *Argonauts of the western Pacific* (p. 94). London: Routledge & Kegan Paul; and see Weiner, A. B. (1988). *The Trobrianders of Papua New Guinea* (p. 156). New York: Holt, Rinehart & Winston; Mason, J. A. (1957). *The ancient civilizations of Peru*. Baltimore: Penguin.

As this example from the South Pacific illustrates, the potential tension between trading partners may be resolved or lessened by participation in a ritual of balanced reciprocity. As an elaborate complex of ceremony, political relationships, economic exchange, travel, magic, and social integration, the Kula ring illustrates the inseparability of economic matters from the rest of culture. Although perhaps difficult to recognize, this is just as true in modern industrial societies as it is in traditional Trobriand society—as is evident when heads of state engage in ceremonial gift exchanges at official visits.

Redistribution

Redistribution is a form of exchange in which goods flow into a central place where they are sorted, counted, and reallocated. In societies with a sufficient surplus to support some sort of government, goods in the form of gifts, tribute, taxes, and the spoils of war are gathered into storehouses controlled by a chief or some other leader. From there they are handed out again. The leadership has three motives in redistributing this income: The first is to gain or maintain a position of power through a display of wealth and generosity; the second is to assure those who support the leadership an adequate standard of living by providing them with desired goods; and the third is to establish alliances with leaders of other groups by hosting them at lavish parties and giving them valuable goods.

Taxes imposed by central governments of countries all around the world today are one form of redistribution—required payments typically based on a percentage of one's income and property value. Typically, a portion of the taxes goes toward supporting the government itself while the rest is redistributed either in cash (such as welfare payments and government loans or subsidies to businesses) or in services (such as military defense, law enforcement, food and drug inspection, schools, highway construction, and the like). Tax codes vary greatly among countries. In many European countries, wealthy citizens are taxed at a considerably higher percentage of their income than are U.S. citizens. While tax fluctuations, exemptions, and evasions make it impossible to be precise, the highest rates applied to the taxable income of individuals are 15 to 20 percentage points greater than in the United States in countries such as Denmark, Sweden, and the Netherlands. On the other hand, there are many countries in the world where the highest tax rates are much lower, such as Bulgaria, Kazakhstan and Paraguay.[13]

SPENDING WEALTH TO GAIN PRESTIGE

In societies where people devote most of their time to subsistence activities, gradations of wealth are small, kept that way through various cultural mechanisms and systems of reciprocity that spread quite fairly what little wealth exists. It is a different situation in ranked societies where substantial surpluses are produced, and the gap between the have-nots and the have-lots can be considerable. In these societies, the social prestige that comes from showy displays—known as **conspicuous consumption**—is a strong motivator for the distribution of wealth.

Excessive efforts to impress others with one's wealth or status also play a prominent role in industrial and postindustrial societies. The display of symbolic prestige items particular to these societies—designer clothes, expensive jewelry, mansions, luxury cars, private planes—fits neatly into an economy based on consumer wants.

A form of conspicuous consumption also occurs in some crop-cultivating and foraging societies. Various American Indian groups living along the Pacific Northwest coast—including the Tlingit, Haida, and Kwakwaka'wakw (Kwakiutl)—illustrate this through potlatches hosted by their chiefs. A **potlatch** is a ceremonial event in which a village chief publicly gives away stockpiled food and other goods that signify wealth. (The term comes from the Chinook Indian word *patshatl,* which means "gift.")

Traditionally, a chief whose village had built up enough surplus to host such a feast for other villages in the region would give away large piles of sea otter furs, dried salmon, blankets, and other valuables while making boastful speeches about his generosity, greatness, and glorious ancestors. While other chiefs became indebted to him, he reaped the glory of successful and generous leadership and saw his prestige rise. In the future, his own village might face shortages, and he would find himself on the receiving end of a potlatch. Should that happen, he would have to listen to the self-serving and pompous speeches of rival chiefs. Obliged to receive, he would temporarily lose prestige and status.

In extreme displays of wealth, chiefs even destroyed some of their precious possessions. This occurred with some frequency in the second half of the 19th century, after European contact triggered a process of cultural change that included new trade wealth. Outsiders might view such grandiose displays as wasteful in the extreme. However, these extravagant giveaway ceremonies have played an ecologically adaptive role in a coastal region where villages alternately faced periods of scarcity and abundance and relied upon alliances and trade relations with one another for long-term survival. The potlatch provided a ceremonial opportunity to strategically redistribute surplus food and goods among allied villages in

---

[13]Taxation statistics. (2011). *NationMaster.com.* http://www.nationmaster.com/graph/tax_hig_mar_tax_rat_ind_rat-highest-marginal-tax-rate-individual (retrieved September 20, 2011); Tax rates around the world. (2011). *Wikipedia.* http://en.wikipedia.org/wiki/Tax_rates_around_the_world (retrieved September 20, 2011).

▲▲▲ Among Native Americans living along the Pacific Northwest coast of North America, one gains prestige by giving away valuables at the potlatch feast. Here we see Tlingit clan members dressed in traditional Chilkat and Raven's Tail robes during a recent potlatch in Sitka, Alaska.

response to periodic fluctuations in fortune. A strategy that features this sort of accumulation of surplus goods for the express purpose of displaying wealth and giving it away to raise one's status is known as a **prestige economy**.

LEVELING MECHANISMS

The potlatch is an example of a **leveling mechanism**—a cultural obligation compelling prosperous members of a community to give away goods, host public feasts, provide free service, or otherwise demonstrate generosity so that no one permanently accumulates significantly more wealth than anyone else. With leveling mechanisms at work, greater wealth brings greater social pressure to spend and give generously. In exchange for such demonstrated altruism, a person not only increases his or her social standing in the community, but may also keep disruptive envy at bay.

Underscoring the value of collective well-being over individual self-interest, leveling mechanisms are important in the long-term survival of traditional communities. The potlatch is just one of many cultural varieties of leveling mechanisms.

By pressuring members into sharing their wealth in their own community rather than hoarding it or privately investing it elsewhere, leveling mechanisms keep resources in circulation. They also reduce social tensions among relatives and fellow villagers, promoting a collective sense of togetherness. An added practical benefit is that they ensure that necessary services within the community are performed.

Market Exchange and the Marketplace

Typically, until well into the 20th century, **market exchange**—the buying and selling of goods and services, with prices set by rules of supply and demand—was carried out in specific localities or *marketplaces*. This is still the case in much of the nonindustrial world and even in numerous centuries-old European and Asian towns and cities. In food-producing societies, marketplaces overseen

▲▲

redistribution A mode of exchange in which goods flow into a central place, where they are sorted, counted, and reallocated.

conspicuous consumption A showy display of wealth for social prestige.

potlatch On the northwestern coast of North America, a ceremonial event in which a village chief publicly gives away stockpiled food and other goods that signify wealth.

prestige economy The creation of a surplus for the express purpose of displaying wealth and giving it away to raise one's status.

leveling mechanism A cultural obligation compelling prosperous members of a community to give away goods, host public feasts, provide free service, or otherwise demonstrate generosity so that no one permanently accumulates significantly more wealth than anyone else.

market exchange The buying and selling of goods and services, with prices set by rules of supply and demand.

▼▼

by a centralized political authority provide the opportunity for farmers or peasants in the surrounding rural territories to exchange some of their livestock and produce for needed items manufactured in factories or in the workshops of craft specialists, who usually live in towns and cities. Thus markets require some sort of complex division of labor as well as centralized political organization.

The traditional market is local, specific, and contained. Prices are typically set on the basis of face-to-face bargaining rather than by unseen forces wholly removed from the transaction itself. Notably, sales do not necessarily involve money; instead, goods may be directly exchanged through some form of barter among the specific individuals involved.

In industrializing and industrial societies, many market transactions still take place in a specific identifiable location—including international trade fairs such as the semi-annual Canton Trade Fair in Guangzhou, China. In the spring of 2011, 24,000 enterprises participated in the event, offering some 150,000 products and generating nearly $40 billion in sales; more than 200,000 buyers from over 50 countries attended the fair.[14]

It is increasingly common for people living in technologically wired parts of the world to buy and sell everything from cattle to cars without ever being in the same city, let alone the same space. For example, think of Internet companies such as eBay and craigslist where all buying and selling occur electronically and irrespective of geographic distance. When people talk about a market in today's industrial or postindustrial world, the particular geographic location where something is bought or sold is often not at all important.

The faceless market exchanges that take place in industrial and postindustrial societies stand in stark contrast to experiences in the marketplaces of nonindustrial societies, which have much of the excitement of a fair. Traditional exchange centers are colorful places where sights, sounds, and smells awaken the senses. Typically, vendors and/or their family members produced the goods they are selling, thereby personalizing the transactions. Dancers and musicians may perform, and feasting and fighting may mark the end of the day. In these markets social relationships and personal interactions are key elements, and noneconomic activities may overshadow economic ones. In short, such markets are gathering places where people renew friendships, see relatives, gossip, and keep up with the world, while procuring needed goods they cannot produce for themselves.[15]

MONEY AS MEANS OF EXCHANGE

Although there are marketplaces without money of any sort, money does facilitate trade. **Money** may be defined as a means of exchange used to make payments for other goods and services as well as to measure their value. Its critical attributes are durability, transportability, divisibility, recognizability, and interchangeability. Items that have

been used as money in various societies include salt, shells, precious stones, cacao beans, special beads, livestock, and valuable metals such as iron, copper, silver, and gold.

About 5,000 years ago, merchants and others in Mesopotamia (a vast area between the rivers Tigris and Euphrates, encompassing much of present-day Iraq and neighboring border areas) began using precious metal such as silver in transactions. Once they agreed on the value of these pieces as a means of exchange (money), more complex commercial developments followed. As the means of exchange were standardized in terms of value, it became easier to accumulate, lend, or borrow money for specified amounts and periods against payment of interest. In due time, some began to deal in money itself and became bankers.

As the use of money became widespread, the metal units were adapted to long-term use, easy storage, and long-distance transportation. In some cultures, such pieces of iron, copper, or silver were cast as miniature models of valuable implements like sword blades, axes, or spades. But some 2,600 years ago in the ancient kingdom of Lydia (southwestern Turkey), they were molded into small flat discs conforming to different sizes and weights.[16] Over the next few centuries, metal coins were also standardized in terms of the metal's purity and value, such as 100 units of copper equals 10 units of silver or 1 of gold.

By about 2,000 years ago, commercial use of such coins had spread throughout much of Europe and become common in parts of Asia and Africa, especially along trade routes and in urban centers. Thus money set into motion radical economic changes in many traditional societies and introduced what has been called *merchant capitalism* in many parts of the world.[17]

Local Economies and Global Capitalism

Imposing market production schemes on other societies and ignoring cultural differences can have unintended negative economic consequences, especially in this era of

---

[14]Canton Fair ends with trade volume growth. (2011, May 6). *Xinhua News Agency.* http://english.peopledaily.com.cn/90001/90778/90861/7371496.html (retrieved September 4, 2011); see also The 109th Canton Fair —New services and products lead to increased trade. (2011, May 5). *PR Newswire.* http://www.prnewswire.com/news-releases/the-109th-canton-fair-new-services-and-products-lead-to-increased-trade-122821239.html (retrieved September 4, 2011).

[15]Plattner, S. (1989). Markets and marketplaces. In S. Plattner (Ed.), *Economic anthropology* (p. 171). Stanford, CA: Stanford University Press.

[16]Davies, G. (2005). *A history of money from the earliest times to present day* (3rd ed.). Cardiff: University of Wales Press.

[17]See also Wolf, E. R. (1982). *Europe and the people without history* (pp. 135–141). Berkeley: University of California Press.

globalization. For example, it has led prosperous countries to impose inappropriate development programs in parts of the world that they regard as economically underdeveloped. Typically, these schemes focus on increasing the target country's gross national product through large-scale production that all too often boosts the well-being of a few but results in poverty, poor health, discontent, and a host of other ills for many.

Among many examples of this situation is the global production of soy, which has increased greatly in many parts of the world. Of particular note is Paraguay, where big landowners, in cooperation with large agribusinesses (most of which are owned by neighboring Brazilians) now produce soy from genetically modified seeds, developed and marketed by foreign companies, especially the U.S.-based multinational corporation Monsanto. Although these large landowners and agribusinesses possess just 1 percent of the total number of farms in Paraguay, they now own almost 80 percent of the country's agricultural land. Exporting the soy, they make hefty profits because production costs are low and international demand is high for cattle feed and biofuel. But the victims of progress are the rural poor—hundreds of thousands of small farmers, landless peasants, rural laborers, and their families. Traditionally growing much of their own food (plus a bit extra for the local market) on small plots, many of them have been edged out and forced to work for hunger wages or to migrate to the city, or even abroad. Those who stay face malnutrition and other hardships, for they lack enough fertile land to feed their families and do not earn enough to buy basic foodstuffs.[18]

Because every culture is an integrated system (as illustrated by the barrel model in Chapter 8), a shift in the infrastructure, or economic base, impacts interlinked elements of the society's social structure and superstructure. As the ethnographic examples of the potlatch and the Kula ring show, economic activities in traditional cultures are intricately intertwined with social and political relations and may also involve spiritual elements. Agribusinesses and other large-scale economic operations or development schemes that do not take such structural complexities into consideration may have unintended negative consequences on a society.

Fortunately, there is now a growing awareness on the part of economic development officials that future projects are unlikely to achieve sustainable success without the appropriate experts to guide them. Anthropologists have this expertise, as they have conducted research among people impacted by such projects. For example, criticized of insensitivity to powerless communities, many of which are ethnic minorities, large banks investing in rural development projects in Africa, Asia, or Latin America now consult with or employ experts academically trained in cultural anthropology as chronicled in this chapter's Anthropology Applied on the next page.

Informal Economy and the Escape from State Bureaucracy

Powerful business corporations promote their profit-making agendas through slogans such as "free trade," "free markets," and "free enterprise." But the commercial success of such enterprises, foreign or domestic, does not come without a price, and all too often that price is paid by still surviving indigenous foragers, small farmers, herders, fishermen, local artisans such as weavers and carpenters, and so on. From their viewpoint, such slogans of freedom have the ring of "savage capitalism," a term now commonly used in Latin America to describe a world order in which the powerless are often condemned to poverty and misery.

Many of these powerful corporations are successful, at least in part, because they manage to avoid the taxes imposed on smaller businesses. The same is often true for the wealthy, who have special access to loopholes and other opportunities to reduce or eliminate taxes that others are obliged to pay. Some of those less privileged, though, have found creative ways to avoid paying taxes and to "beat the system." The system, in this case, refers to the managing bureaucracy in a state-organized society politically controlled by an elected or appointed governing elite.

State bureaucracies seek to manage and control economic activities for regulation and taxation purposes. However, they do not always succeed in these efforts for a variety of reasons, including insufficient government resources; underpaid, unskilled, or unmotivated inspectors and administrators; and a culture of corruption. In state-organized societies where large numbers of people habitually avoid bureaucratic regulators seeking to monitor and tax their activities, there is a separate, undocumented economic system known as the **informal economy**—a network of producing and circulating marketable commodities, labor, and services that for various reasons escape government control (enumeration, regulation, or other types of public monitoring or auditing).

This informal sector may encompass a range of activities: house cleaning, child care, gardening, repair or construction work, making and selling alcoholic beverages, street peddling, money lending, begging, prostitution,

▲▲

money A means of exchange used to make payments for other goods and services as well as to measure their value.

informal economy A network of people producing and circulating marketable commodities, labor, and services that for various reasons escape government control.

▼▼

[18]Fogel, R., & Riquelme, M. A. (2005). *Enclave sorjero. Merma de soberania y pobreza*. Ascuncion: Centro de Estudios Rurales Interdisciplinarias; Bodley, J. H. (1990). *Victims of progress* (3rd ed., p. 141). Mountain View, CA: Mayfield.

ANTHROPOLOGY APPLIED

Anthropologist S. Ann Dunham, Mother to a U.S. President

By Nancy I. Cooper

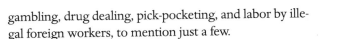

As our plane descended over the island of Java, the most spectacular sight of my life came into view: a full-blown eruption of Merapi volcano billowing clouds of ash straight up into the sky. On the lower slopes of this exploding "mountain of fire" (*gunung api*) hundreds of thousands of people would have to flee their homes and farms. My thoughts were with them—and with my friend Ann Dunham. She had researched and worked with rural people in this region as an applied anthropologist before her untimely death at age 52 in 1995. I had known her while doing my own research here on Indonesia's most populated island. I was returning to meet some of the people she had known.

Stanley Ann Dunham's life started out ordinary enough in an American working-class family from Kansas. They lived in several states before settling in the ethnically diverse state of Hawai'i. As a teen Ann thrived there, embracing the common humanity in cultural differences. At the University of Hawai'i in Honolulu, she

met and married an economics student from Kenya, East Africa. In 1961, she gave birth to his namesake, Barack Obama Jr., who would grow up to be the 44th president of the United States. The marriage was short-lived, and Ann became a single parent.

While studying anthropology, Ann met and married Lolo Soetoro, a geography student from Java. In 1967 she and her young son joined him in Jakarta, Indonesia's capital city. Befriending local boys, "Barry" happily roamed nearby fields among goats and water buffalo. Ann gave birth to daughter Maya and became interested in handmade crafts like basketry, ceramics, and leatherwork, trying her own hand at weaving and batik. This interest grew into concern about the welfare of small enterprises embedded within larger, more powerful economic systems.

Soon, Ann began working as a consultant, hired by what became a long list of mostly foreign aid and economic development organizations. At the Ford Foundation's Southeast Asia regional of-

fice in Jakarta, for example, she oversaw grants in the Women and Employment branch and collaborated on a study of rural women in the outlying islands of Indonesia. In the 1980s, as a cottage industries development consultant with the Agricultural Development Bank of Pakistan, she arranged credit for low-income handicraft castes in the Punjab, including blacksmiths.

Next, Ann became a research coordinator (funded by USAID and the World Bank) at Bank Rakyat Indonesia, helping implement a microcredit project for owners of small rural businesses. Today this bank has one of the largest microfinance programs in the world, and microcredit is widely recognized as a significant means of lessening poverty. In between appointments, Ann returned to Hawai'i to settle her children in school and continue her own studies. She also did a brief stint with Women's World Banking based in New York City.

The data Ann and her research teams collected during these years, combined

gambling, drug dealing, pick-pocketing, and labor by illegal foreign workers, to mention just a few.

These off-the-books activities, including fraud and trade in stolen or smuggled goods on the black market, have been known for a long time but generally have been dismissed by economists as of marginal importance. Yet in many countries of the world the informal economy is, in fact, more important than the formal economy, and may involve more than half the labor force and up to 40 percent of a country's gross national product (GNP). In many places, large numbers of under- and unemployed people who have only limited access to the formal economic sector in effect improvise, "getting by" on scant resources. Meanwhile, more affluent members of society

may dodge various regulations in order to maximize returns and/or vent their frustrations at their perceived loss of self-determination in the face of increasing government regulation.

And now that globalization is connecting national, regional, and local markets in which natural resources, commodities, and human labor are bought and sold, people everywhere in the world face new economic opportunities and confront new challenges. Not only are natural environments more quickly and radically transformed by new powerful technologies, but long-established subsistence practices, economic arrangements, social organizations, and associated ideas, beliefs, and values are also under increasing pressure. ✳

Provided by Nancy Cooper, Anthropology Dept., University of Hawaii

▲▲▲ Ann Dunham turns the wheel of an agricultural machine in Pakistan in 1987.

with her anthropological fieldwork, culminated in her 1992 doctoral dissertation on peasant blacksmithing, published by Duke University Press in 2009.[a]

In both words and action, Ann argued against Western modernization theories that insisted that all developing economies must go through the same stages Western capitalist economies experienced in order to succeed in the global market environment. Recognizing the disturbing effects that rapid modernization often has on indigenous populations with colonial histories, she refuted such damaging notions and sought ways to solve the real challenges of emerging economies with sensitivity and analytical prowess.

Ann Dunham's contributions were formally recognized 15 years after her death when she was awarded Indonesia's highest civilian honor. Accepting the prize on behalf of his mother from President Susilo Bambang Yudhoyono, President Obama said, "In honoring her, you honor the spirit that led her to travel into villages throughout the country."

I felt that spirit as I traveled through Java's limestone hills where we had worked years earlier. Word spread quickly through the village of Kajar that Ann's friend was visiting, and I was greeted warmly. I sat with the family of the late owner of the blacksmithing cooperative featured in Ann's book, swapping stories about her and looking at photos she had taken of them and fellow villagers. And I spent long hours visiting with blacksmiths as they hammered hot scrap metal into useful tools.

All too soon, it was time to leave. Volcanic ash had shut down the airport where I had landed, so I left the region by rail. As the train pulled away from the station, images of blacksmithing and new friends danced in my head, along with renewed memories of an engaged anthropologist whose work changed people's lives for the better. ■

[a]Ann died before having an opportunity to revise her dissertation for publication, as she had planned; her adviser Alice G. Dewey and I, her fellow graduate student, carried it to completion at the request of Ann's daughter Maya.

Chapter Checklist

What are cultural adaptation and cultural evolution?

✔ Cultural adaptation is the complex of ideas, activities, and technologies that enables people to survive in a certain environment and in turn to impact the environment.

✔ The unit of adaptation includes both organisms and their environment; an ecosystem is a functioning whole composed of the natural environment and all the organisms living in it.

✔ Cultural evolution (the changing of cultures over time) should not be confused with the idea of progress (the notion that humans are moving forward to a better, more advanced stage in their development toward perfection).

✔ Convergent evolution is the development of similar cultural adaptations to similar environmental conditions by different peoples with different ancestral cultures. Parallel evolution is the same phenomenon, but it emerges with peoples whose ancestral cultures were already similar.

What are the major subsistence strategies and the characteristics of the societies that practice them?

✓ The oldest and most universal mode of subsistence or adaptation among humans is food foraging. It requires people to move their residence according to changing food sources. Local group size is kept small, possibly because small numbers fit the land's capacity to sustain the group. A habitat rich in natural resources can sustain more people than marginal lands that are home to the world's few surviving foragers. Another characteristic of food-foraging societies is egalitarianism.

✓ The shift from food foraging to food production began about 10,000 years ago. Known as the Neolithic revolution, it involved the domestication of plants and animals.

✓ Horticulture is the cultivation of crops in gardens using simple hand tools. It includes slash-and-burn cultivation—cutting and burning the natural vegetation and planting crops among the ashes. Agriculture involves growing crops on farms with irrigation, fertilizers, and/or animal-powered plows. Crop-producing societies led to fixed settlements, new technologies, and altered division of labor.

✓ Mixed farming involves a combination of crop growing and animal breeding; it may occur in mountainous environments where farmers practice transhumance, moving their livestock between high-altitude summer pastures and winter pastures in lowland valleys.

✓ Pastoralism is a subsistence mode that relies on breeding and managing large herds of domesticated herbivores, such as cattle, sheep, and goats. Pastoralists are usually nomadic, moving as needed to provide animals with pasture and water.

✓ Intensive agriculture led to urbanization and peasantry. Farm settlements grew into towns and cities, and social complexity grew to include labor spe-

cialization, elite classes, public management, taxation, and policing.

✓ Industrial food production features large-scale businesses involved in mass food production, processing, and marketing, and relying on laborsaving machines. It is rooted in the industrial revolution, which began 200 years ago with the invention of the steam engine. Human labor, animal power, and hand tools replaced machines and resulted in massive cultural change in many societies.

✓ Today's industrial food production and global marketing complex, involving a network of interlinked distribution centers, are made possible by an electronic-digital revolution that began in the late 20th century.

What is an economic system, relative to subsistence?

✓ An economic system is an organized arrangement for producing, distributing, and consuming goods. Each society allocates natural resources (especially land, water, and fuel), technology, and labor according to its own priorities.

✓ In nonindustrial societies, kinship groups, such as the band, generally control natural resources. This provides flexibility since the size of a band and its territories can be adjusted according to the availability of resources in any particular place. The technology of a people (the tools they use and the knowledge about them) is related to their mode of subsistence. All societies have some means of creating and allocating the tools used to produce goods.

✓ Labor is a major productive resource, and the allotment of work is commonly governed by rules according to gender and age. Cross-culturally, only a few broad generalizations can be made covering the kinds of work performed by men and women. A more productive strategy is to examine the kinds of work that men and women do in the context of specific societies to see how it relates to other cultural and historical factors. The cooperation of many people working together is a typical feature of both nonindustrial and industrial societies. Task specialization is important even in societies with very simple technologies.

How are goods distributed?

✓ The processes of distribution may be distinguished as reciprocity, redistribution, and market exchange. Reciprocity, the exchange of goods and services of roughly equal value, comes in three forms: generalized (in which the value is not calculated, nor the time of repayment specified); balanced (in which one has an obligation to reciprocate promptly); and negative (in which the aim is to get something for as little as possible). A classic ethnographic example of balanced reciprocity between trading partners seeking to maintain social ties while also doing business is the Kula ring among islanders of the southwestern Pacific Ocean.

✓ Trade refers to a transaction in which two or more people are involved in an exchange of something for something else of equal value. Such exchanges have elements of reciprocity but involve a greater calculation of the relative value of goods exchanged. Barter is a form of trade in which no money is involved, and the parties negotiate a direct exchange of one trade good for another. It may well be in the form of negative reciprocity, as each party aims to get the better end of the deal. The Kula ring example involves both balanced reciprocity and sharp trading.

✓ Redistribution requires a strong, centralized political organization. A government assesses a tax or tribute on each citizen to support its activities, leaders, and religious elite and then redistributes the rest, usually in the form of public services. The system of tax collection and delivery of government services and subsidies in the United States is a form of redistribution.

✓ Conspicuous consumption, or display for social prestige, is a motivating force in societies that produce a surplus of goods. The prestige comes from publicly giving away one's valuables, as in the potlatch ceremony, which is also an example of a leveling mechanism.

What is market exchange, and where is the marketplace?

✓ In nonindustrial societies, the marketplace is usually a specific site where people exchange produce, livestock, and material items they have made. It also functions as a social gathering place and a news medium.

✔ Although market exchanges may take place through bartering and other forms of reciprocity, money (something used to make payments for goods and services as well as to measure their value) makes market exchange more efficient.

How does global capitalism impact local economies?

✔ When powerful countries impose market production schemes on other societies, the impact can be negative—as in the global production of soy in Paraguay where big landowners in cooperation with large agribusinesses have edged out small farmers and landless peasants.

✔ In state-organized societies with market economies, the informal economy—comprised of economic activities set up to avoid official scrutiny and regulation—may be more important than the formal sector.

Questions for Reflection

1. In capturing essential natural resources, humans often modify their environments. Have you seen any examples of landscapes radically transformed for economic reasons? Who do you think benefits or loses most?

2. What were the radical changes during the Neolithic period, prompting some to refer to it as a revolution? Can you think of any equally radical changes in subsistence practices going on in the world today?

3. As the potlatch ceremony shows, prestige may be gained by giving away wealth. Does such a prestige-building mechanism exist in your own society? If so, how does it work?

4. What do you think is the future for the world's hundreds of millions of independent herders, farmers, and peasants trying to make a living off the land as their ancestors did?

5. Technological development in industrial societies often results in highly productive machines effectively replacing animal and human workers. Can you think of a useful mechanical device and describe its benefits and costs, to you as well as to others?

Key Terms

ecosystem	peasant	redistribution
cultural evolution	industrial society	conspicuous consumption
progress	industrial food production	potlatch
convergent evolution	economic system	prestige economy
parallel evolution	technology	leveling mechanism
food foraging	reciprocity	market exchange
horticulture	generalized reciprocity	money
slash-and-burn cultivation	balanced reciprocity	informal economy
agriculture	negative reciprocity	
pastoralism	Kula ring	

Online Study Resources

Login to **www.cengagebrain.com** to access the resources your instructor has assigned and to purchase materials. For this book, you can access:

CourseMate
Access chapter-specific learning tools including flashcards, glossaries, practice quizzes, videos, and more in your Anthropology CourseMate.

VISUAL ESSENCE

Every society has rules and customs concerning sexual relations, marriage, household and family structures, and child-rearing practices. Most people think of these social regulations as simply the natural way of doing things. But in fact they are cultural constructs and play vital roles in establishing and maintaining social alliances, allocating resources, and assigning social obligations. Because marriage and family, in various forms, play a fundamental role in any society, wedding rituals are especially significant social events. Whether private or public, sacred or secular, weddings reveal, confirm, and underscore important ideas and values of culture. Symbolically rich, they usually feature particular speech rituals, along with prescribed apparel, postures and gestures, food and drink, songs and dances passed down through many generations. Here we see a traditional Japanese wedding at Tokyo's sacred Meiji shrine, dedicated to the deified spirits of the ancestral emperor and his wife. Conforming to the ancient tradition of Shinto ("the way of the spirits"), the bride wears a white silk kimono as a profession of purity. Her hood symbolically hides "horns of jealousy" from her new mother-in-law, who will have authority over her in the household she is joining. The red umbrella represents protection from evil spirits.

12 Sex, Marriage, and Family

Unlike individuals raised in traditional Shinto Japanese families, such as those featured in this chapter's opening photo, young people in the Trobriand Islands of the South Pacific are traditionally unconstrained in premarital sexual explorations. By age 7 or 8, they begin playing erotic games and imitating adult seductive attitudes. Within another four or five years they start pursuing sexual partners in earnest—experimenting erotically with a variety of individuals.

Since attracting sexual partners is an important matter among young Trobrianders, they spend considerable time making themselves look appealing and seductive. Their daily conversations are loaded with sexual hints, and magical spells as well as small gifts are used to entice a prospective sex partner to the beach at night or to the house in which boys sleep apart from their parents. Because girls, too, sleep apart from their parents, adolescents have considerable freedom in arranging their erotic escapades. Boys and girls play this game as equals, with neither having an advantage over the other.[1]

In this chapter you will learn to:

- **Discuss how different cultures permit or restrict sexual relations.**

- **Distinguish several marriage forms and understand their determinants and functions.**

- **Contrast family and household forms across cultures.**

- **Explain a range of marital residence patterns.**

- **Weigh the impact of globalization and reproductive technology on marriage and family.**

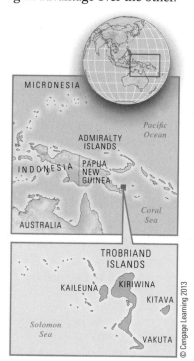

---

[1]Weiner, A. B. (1988). *The Trobrianders of Papua New Guinea* (p. 17). New York: Holt, Rinehart & Winston.

▲▲▲ To attract lovers, young Trobriand women and men must look as attractive and seductive as possible. This young woman's beauty has been enhanced by face painting and adornments given to her by her father.

By the time Trobrianders are in their mid-teens, meetings between lovers may take up most of the night, and affairs are apt to last for several months. Ultimately, a young islander begins to meet the same partner again and again, rejecting the advances of others. When the couple is ready, they appear together one morning outside the young man's house as a way of announcing their intention to be married.

Until the latter part of the 20th century, the Trobriand attitude toward adolescent sexuality was in marked contrast to that of most Western cultures in Europe and North America where individuals were not supposed to have sexual relations before or outside of marriage. Since then, practices in much of Europe and North America have converged toward those of the Trobrianders, even though the traditional ideal of premarital abstinence has not been abandoned entirely.

Control of Sexual Relations

In the absence of effective birth control, the usual outcome of sexual activity between fertile individuals of the opposite sex is that, sooner or later, the woman becomes pregnant. Given the intricate array of social responsibilities involved in rearing the children that are born of sexual relations—and the potential for violent conflict resulting from unregulated sexual competition—it is not surprising that all societies have cultural rules intended to regulate those relations, although those rules vary considerably across cultures.

For instance, in some societies sexual intercourse during pregnancy is taboo, while in others it is looked upon positively as something that promotes the growth of the fetus. And while some cultures sharply condemn same-sex acts or relations, many others are indifferent and do not even have a special term to distinguish homosexuality as significant in its own right. In several cultures same-sex acts are not only accepted but even prescribed.

Such is the case in some Papua societies in New Guinea, for example, where certain prescribed male-to-male sexual acts are part of initiation rituals required of all boys to become respected adult men.[2] In those cultures, people traditionally see the transmission of semen from older to younger boys, through oral sex, as vital for building up the strength needed to protect against the supposedly debilitating effects of adult heterosexual intercourse.[3]

Despite longstanding culture-based opposition to homosexuality in many areas of the world, this sexual orientation exists within the wide range of human sexual relations, emotional attractions, and social identities, and it is far from uncommon. Homosexuality is found in diverse contexts—from lifelong loving relationships to casual sexual encounters and from being fully open to being utterly private and secretive. During the past few decades, public denigration and condemnation of homosexuality have diminished in numerous countries, and same-sex relationships have become a publicly accepted part of the cosmopolitan lifestyle in metropolitan centers such as Amsterdam, Paris, Rio de Janeiro, and San Francisco. As recently as 2009, India decriminalized homosexuality.[4] Clearly, the social rules and cultural meanings of all sexual behavior are subject to great variability—not only across cultures but also across time.

Marriage and the Regulation of Sexual Relations

In much of America, Asia, Europe, and northern Africa, the traditional ideal was (and in many communities still is) that all sexual activities outside of marriage were disapproved or even forbidden. Individuals were expected to

---

[2]Kirkpatrick, R. C. (2000). The evolution of human homosexual behavior. *Current Anthropology 41,* 385.

[3]Herdt, G. H. (1993). Semen transactions in Sambia culture. In D. N. Suggs & A. W. Mirade (Eds.), *Culture and human sexuality* (pp. 298–327). Pacific Grove, CA: Brooks/Cole.

[4]Timmons, H., & Kumar, H. (2009, July 3). Indian court overturns gay sex ban. *New York Times.*

establish a family through marriage, by which one gains an exclusive right of sexual access to another person. The main purpose of sexual intercourse was not erotic pleasure but reproduction.

Recognizing the potential risks of unregulated sexual relations, including unplanned pregnancies by a man other than the lawful husband, these societies often criminalized *extramarital* affairs as adultery. According to strict Judeo-Christian law as prescribed in the Book of Leviticus (20:10), adultery was punishable by death: "And the man that committeth adultery with another man's wife . . . the adulterer and the adulteress shall surely be put to death." Deuteronomy (22:24) adds: "Then ye shall bring them both out unto the gate of that city, and ye shall stone them with stones that they die."

Many centuries later, among Christian colonists in 17th- and 18th-century New England, a woman's participation in adultery remained a serious crime. While it did not lead to stoning, women so accused were shunned by the community and could even be imprisoned. As recounted in *The Scarlet Letter* by Nathaniel Hawthorne, the adulteress was forced to have the letter "A" stitched on her dress, publicly signifying her transgression.

Such restrictions exist today in many traditional Muslim societies in northern Africa and western Asia, where age-old Shariah law continues or has been reinstated to regulate social behavior in strict accordance with religious standards of morality. Under this law, women found guilty of having sexual relations outside marriage can be sentenced to death by stoning. In northern Nigeria, for example, a Muslim woman who committed adultery and had a child outside marriage was sentenced to death in 2002. An Islamic appeals court ultimately overturned her sentence, but the case nonetheless drove home the rule of Shariah law. More recent incidents include that of Sakineh Mohammadi Ashtiani, an Iranian woman sentenced to death by stoning on adultery charges in 2006. The sentence was dropped in 2010 after her case drew international protests.[5] Turning legal transgressions into a public spectacle, authorities reinforce public awareness of the rules of social conduct, even if a sentence is dropped or changed.

A positive side effect of such restrictive rules is that they may contribute to limiting the spread of sexually transmitted diseases. For instance, the global epidemic of HIV/AIDS has had dramatically less impact in northern Africa's Muslim countries than in the non-Muslim states of sub-Saharan Africa, where the average infection rate among adults is almost 17 times higher. Statistics vividly illustrate the impact of religious and cultural prohibitions (although other factors may also be involved): The reported percentage of adults infected by the HIV/AIDS virus is about 0.1 percent in Algeria, Morocco, and Tunisia, in contrast to some 17 percent in South Africa, 25 percent in Botswana, and 26 percent in Swaziland.[6] Communities devastated by this sexually transmitted disease not only confront a serious public health problem but also face a cultural challenge in that they must create a new public awareness and adjust attitudes about sexual pleasure so that they do not endanger their collective well-being.

Yet, most cultures in the world do not sharply regulate an individual's sexual practices. Indeed, a majority of cultures are considered sexually permissive or semipermissive (the former having few or no restrictions on sexual experimentation before marriage, the latter allowing some experimentation but less openly). A minority of known societies—about 15 percent—have rules requiring that sexual involvement take place only within marriage.

This brings us to an anthropological definition of **marriage**—a culturally sanctioned union between two or more people that establishes certain rights and obligations between the people, between them and their children, and between them and their in-laws. Such marriage rights and obligations most often include, but are not limited to, sex, labor, property, childrearing, exchange, and status. Thus defined, marriage is universal. Notably, our definition of marriage refers to "people" rather than to "a man and a woman" because in some countries same-sex marriages are considered socially acceptable and allowed by law, even though opposite-sex marriages are far more common. We will return to this point later in the chapter.

Incest Taboo

Just as marriage in its various forms is found in all cultures, so is the **incest taboo**—the prohibition of sexual contact between certain close relatives. But what is defined as "close" is not the same in all cultures. Moreover,

[5]Sakineh Mohammadi Ashtiani. (2011, January 18). *New York Times*. http://topics.nytimes.com/top/reference/timestopics/people/a/sakineh_mohammadi_ashtiani/index.html (retrieved September 5, 2011).

[6]UNAIDS. (2009). 2009 AIDS epidemic update, p. 7. http://www.unaids.org/en/dataanalysis/epidemiology/2009aidsepidemicupdate/ (retrieved September 5, 2011); see also Gray, P. B. (2004, May). HIV and Islam: Is HIV prevalence lower among Muslims? *Social Science & Medicine 58* (9), 1751–1756. Note: Because sexuality is a taboo discussion topic in Muslim societies, many may not seek appropriate counseling, testing, and treatment for HIV/AIDS. For this reason, the actual infection rate may be somewhat higher than reported. See Hasnain, M. (2005, October 27). Cultural approach to HIV/AIDS harm reduction in Muslim countries. *Harm Reduction Journal 2*, 23.

marriage A culturally sanctioned union between two or more people that establishes certain rights and obligations between the people, between them and their children, and between them and their in-laws. Such marriage rights and obligations most often include, but are not limited to, sex, labor, property, childrearing, exchange, and status.

© Marie Labbancz

▲▲▲ Tory receives a celebratory kiss from her father alongside her new spouse Monica at their wedding in Connecticut, where same-sex marriage became legal in 2008.

such definitions may be subject to change over time. While the scope and details of the taboo vary across cultures and time, almost all societies past and present strongly forbid sexual relations at least between parents and children and nearly always between siblings. In some societies the taboo extends to other close relatives, such as cousins, and even some relatives linked through marriage.

Anthropologists have long been fascinated by the incest taboo and have proposed many explanations for its cross-cultural existence and variation. The simplest explanation is that our species has an "instinctive" repulsion for incest. It has been documented that human beings raised together have less sexual attraction for one another. However, by itself this "familiarity breeds contempt" argument may substitute the result for the cause. The incest taboo ensures that children and their parents, who are constantly in close contact, avoid regarding one another as sexual objects. Besides this, if an instinctive horror of incest exists, how do we account for the far from rare violations of the taboo? In the United States, for instance, an estimated 10 to 14 percent of children under 18 years of age have been involved in incestuous relations.[7]

Moreover, so-called instinctive repulsion does not explain institutionalized incest, such as marriage customs for divine rulers of the Inca empire in ancient Peru, who were required to marry their own (half) sister. Sharing the same father, both siblings belonged to the political dynasty that derived its sacred right to rule the empire from Inti, its ancestral Sun God. And by virtue of this royal lineage's godly origin, their children could claim the same sacred political status as their human god-father and god-mother. Ancient emperors in Egypt also practiced such religiously prescribed incest based on a similar claim to godly status.

Early students of genetics argued that the incest taboo prevents the harmful effects of inbreeding. While this is so, it is also true that, as with domestic animals, inbreeding can increase desired characteristics as well as detrimental ones. Furthermore, undesirable effects will show up sooner than without inbreeding, so whatever genes are responsible for them are quickly eliminated from the population. That said, a preference for a genetically different mate does tend to maintain a higher level of genetic diversity within a population, and in evolution this variation works to a species' advantage. Without genetic diversity a species cannot adapt biologically to environmental change.

The inbreeding or biological avoidance theory can be challenged on several fronts. Detailed census records made in Roman Egypt about 2,000 years ago show that brother–sister marriages were not uncommon among ordinary members of the farming class, and we have no evidence for linking this cultural practice to any biological imperatives.[8] To the contrary, some anthropologists have argued that the incest taboo exists as a cultural means to preserve the stability and integrity of the family, which is essential to maintaining social order. Sexual relations between members other than the husband and wife would introduce competition, destroying the harmony of a social unit fundamental to societal order.

[7]Whelehan, P. (1985). Review of incest, a biosocial view. *American Anthropologist 87*, 678; see also U.S. Department of Health and Human Services, Administration on Children, Youth, and Families. (2005). *Child maltreatment 2003*. Washington, DC: U.S. Government Printing Office.

[8]Leavitt, G. C. (1990). Sociobiological explanations of incest avoidance: A critical review of evidential claims. *American Anthropologist 92*, 982.

A truly convincing explanation of the incest taboo has yet to be advanced.[9]

Endogamy and Exogamy

Whatever its cause, the utility of the incest taboo can be seen by examining its effects on social structure. Closely related to prohibitions against incest are cultural rules against **endogamy** (from Greek *endon*, "within," and *gamos*, "marriage"), or marriage within a particular group of individuals (cousins and in-laws, for example). If the group is defined as one's immediate family alone, then societies generally prohibit or at least discourage endogamy, thereby promoting **exogamy** (from Greek *exo*, "outside," and *gamos*, "marriage"), or marriage outside the group. Yet, a society that practices exogamy at one level may practice endogamy at another. Among the Trobriand Islanders, for example, each individual has to marry outside of his or her own clan and lineage (exogamy). However, since eligible sex partners are to be found within one's own community, village endogamy is commonly practiced.

Interestingly, societies vary widely concerning which relatives are or are not covered by rules of exogamy. For example, first cousins are prohibited from marrying each other in many countries where the Roman Catholic Church has long been a dominant institution. Such marriages are also illegal in thirty-one of the United States. Yet, in numerous other societies, first cousins are preferred spouses,[10] and the *Journal of Genetic Counseling* concludes: "Cousins can have children together without running much greater risk than a 'normal' couple of their children having genetic abnormalities."[11] (See a discussion of U.S. marriage prohibitions in the Biocultural Connection on the page 250.)

Early anthropologists suggested that our ancestors discovered the advantage of intermarriage as a means of creating bonds of friendship or alliances between distinct communities. By widening the human network, a larger number of people could pool natural resources and cultural information, including technology and other useful knowledge.

Exogamy may also help build and maintain political alliances and promote trade between groups, thereby ensuring mutual protection and access to needed goods and resources not otherwise available. Forging wider kinship networks, exogamy also functions to integrate distinctive groups and thus potentially reduces violent conflict.

Distinction Between Marriage and Mating

Having defined marriage partly in terms of sexual access, we must make clear the distinction between marriage and mating. All mammals, including humans, form breeding pairs—some mate for life and some do not, some with a single individual and some with several or many. Among humans, mates are secured and held solely through individual effort and mutual consent.

In contrast to mating, which occurs when individuals join for purposes of sexual relations, marriage is a socially binding and culturally recognized relationship. Only marriage is backed by social, political, and ideological factors that regulate sexual relations as well as reproductive rights and obligations. Thus, while mating is biological, marriage is cultural. This is evident when we consider the various forms of marriage around the world.

Forms of Marriage

Within societies, and all the more so across cultures, we see contrasts in the constructs and contracts of marriage. Indeed, as evident in the definition of marriage given above, this institution comes in various forms—and these forms are distinct in terms of the number and gender of spouses involved.

Monogamy

Monogamy—marriage in which both partners have just one spouse—is the most common form of marriage worldwide. In North America and most of Europe, it is the only legally recognized form of marriage. In these places, not only are other forms of marriage prohibited, but systems of inheritance, whereby property and

---

[9]In a sample of 129 societies, anthropologist Nancy Thornhill (1993) found that only fifty-seven had specific rules against parent–child or sibling incest. Twice that number (114) had explicit rules to control activity with cousins, in-laws, or both (quoted in Haviland, W. A., & Gordon, R. J. (Eds.), *Talking about people* (p. 127). Mountain View, CA: Mayfield). Absence of specific incest rules, however, does not mean sexual relations with close relatives were either common or condoned.

[10]Ottenheimer, M. (1996). *Forbidden relatives: The American myth of cousin marriage* (pp. 116–133). Champaign: University of Illinois Press.

[11]Grossman, J. (2002, April 8). Should the law be kinder to kissin' cousins? A genetic report should cause a rethinking of incest laws. *Find Law.* http://writ.news.findlaw.com/grossman/20020408.html (retrieved September 5, 2011).

▲▲▲

incest taboo The prohibition of sexual relations between specified individuals, usually parent and child and sibling relations at a minimum.

endogamy Marriage within a particular group or category of individuals.

exogamy Marriage outside the group.

monogamy A marriage form in which both partners have just one spouse.

▼▼▼

BIOCULTURAL CONNECTION

Marriage Prohibitions in the United States

By Martin Ottenheimer

In the United States, every state has laws prohibiting the marriage of some relatives. All states forbid parent–child and sibling marriages, but there is considerable variation in prohibitions concerning more distant relatives. For example, although the majority of states ban marriage between first cousins, nineteen states allow it, and others permit it under certain conditions. Notably, the United States is the only country in the Western world that has prohibitions against first-cousin marriage.

Many people in the United States believe that laws forbidding marriage between family members exist because parents who are too close biologically run the risk of producing children with mental and physical defects. Convinced that first cousins fall within this "too close" category, they believe laws against first-cousin marriage were established to protect families from the effects of harmful genes.

There are two major problems with this belief: First, cousin prohibitions were enacted in the United States long before the discovery of the genetic mechanisms of disease. Second, genetic research has shown that offspring of first-cousin couples do not have any significantly greater risk of negative results than offspring of very distantly related parents.

Why, then, do some North Americans maintain this belief? To answer this question, it helps to know that laws against first-cousin marriage first appeared in the United States right after the mid-1800s when evolutionary models of human behavior became fashionable. In particular, a pre-Darwinian model that explained social evolution as dependent upon biological factors gained popularity. It supposed that "progress from savagery to civilization" was possible when humans ceased inbreeding. Cousin marriage was thought to be characteristic of savagery, the lowest form of human social life, and it was believed to inhibit the intellectual and social development of humans. It became associated with "primitive" behavior and dreaded as a threat to a civilized America.

Thus, a powerful myth emerged in American popular culture, which has since become embedded in law. That myth is held and defended to this day, sometimes with great emotion despite being based on a discredited social evolutionary theory and contradicted by the results of modern genetic research.

Recently, a group of geneticists published the result of a study of consanguineous ("shared blood") unions, estimating that there is "about a 1.7–2.8% increased risk for congenital defects above the population background risk."[a] Not only is this a high estimate, it is also well within the bounds of the margin of statistical error. But even so, it is a lower risk than that associated with offspring from women over the age of 40—who are not forbidden by the government to marry or bear children. ■

Biocultural Question

What do you think is the underlying cultural logic that makes some societies traditionally forbid first cousins from marrying each other, whereas others, equally familiar with genetics, accept or even prefer such marriages?

[a]Bennett, R. L., et al. (2002, April). Genetic counseling and screening of consanguineous couples and their offspring: Recommendations of the National Society of Genetic Counselors. *Journal of Genetic Counseling 11* (2), 97–119.

wealth are transferred from one generation to the next, are based on the institution of monogamous marriage. In some parts of the world, such as North America and Europe where divorce and remarriage rates are high, an increasingly common form of marriage is **serial monogamy**, whereby an individual marries a series of partners in succession.

Polygamy

While monogamy is the most common marriage form worldwide, it is not the most culturally preferred. That distinction goes to **polygamy** (one individual having multiple spouses)—specifically to **polygyny**, in which a man is married to more than one woman (*gyne* is Greek for "woman" and "wife"). Favored in about 80 to 85 percent of the world's cultures, polygyny is commonly practiced in parts of Asia and much of sub-Saharan Africa.[12]

Although polygyny is the favored marriage form in these places, monogamy exceeds it, but for economic rather than moral or legal reasons. In many polygynous societies, where a groom is usually expected to compensate a bride's family in cash or kind, a man must be fairly wealthy to be able to afford more than one wife. Recent multiple surveys of twenty-five sub-Saharan African countries where polygyny is common show that it declined by about 50 percent between the 1970s and 2001.

---

[12]Lloyd, C. B. (Ed.). (2005). *Growing up global: The changing transitions to adulthood in developing countries* (pp. 450–453). Washington, DC: National Academies Press, Committee on Population, National Research Council, and Institute of Medicine of the National Academies.

VISUAL COUNTERPOINT

▲▲▲ An American Christian polygamist with his three wives and children stand in front of their dormitory-style home in Utah (*left*), and a Baranarana man of Upper Guinea, Africa, poses with his two wives and children (*right*). Although this marriage form is legally prohibited in the United States, perhaps as many as 50,000 Americans live in polygamous households today.

This dramatic decline has many reasons, one of which is related to families making an economic transition from traditional farming and herding to wage labor in cities. Nonetheless, polygyny remains highly significant with an overall average of 25 percent of married women in such unions.[13]

Polygyny is particularly common in traditional food-producing societies that support themselves by herding grazing animals or growing crops and where women do the bulk of cultivation. Under these conditions, women are valued both as workers and as child bearers. Because the labor of wives in polygynous households generates wealth and little support is required from husbands, the wives have a strong bargaining position within the household. Often, they have considerable freedom of movement and some economic independence through the sale of crafts or crops. Wealth-generating polygyny is found in its fullest elaboration in parts of sub-Saharan Africa and southwestern Asia, though it is known elsewhere as well.[14]

In societies practicing wealth-generating polygyny, most men and women do enter into polygynous marriages, although some are able to do so earlier in life than others. This is made possible by a female-biased sex ratio and/or a mean age at marriage for females that is significantly below that for males. In fact, this marriage pattern is frequently found in societies where violence, including war, is common, resulting in many lives lost among young males. Their high combat mortality results in a population where women outnumber men.

By contrast, in societies where men are more heavily involved in productive work, generally only a small minority of marriages are polygynous. Under these circumstances, women are more dependent on men for support, so they are valued as child bearers more than for the work they do. This is commonly the case in pastoral nomadic societies where men are the primary owners and tenders of livestock. This makes women especially vulnerable if they prove incapable

▲▲▲▲▲▲▲▲▲▲▲▲▲▲▲▲▲▲▲▲▲▲▲▲▲▲▲▲▲▲▲▲▲▲▲▲▲▲

serial monogamy A marriage form in which a man or a woman marries or lives with a series of partners in succession.

polygamy A marriage form in which one individual has multiple spouses at the same time; from the Greek words *poly* ("many") and *gamos* ("marriage").

polygyny A marriage form in which a man is married to two or more women at the same time; a form of polygamy.

▼▼▼

---

[13]Ibid.

[14]White, D. R. (1988). Rethinking polygyny: Co-wives, codes, and cultural systems. *Current Anthropology 29*, 529–572.

of bearing children, which is one reason a man may seek another wife.

Another reason for a man to take on secondary wives is to demonstrate his high position in society. But where men do most of the productive work, they must work extremely hard to support more than one wife, and few actually do so. Usually, it is the exceptional hunter or male shaman ("medicine man") in a food-foraging society or a particularly wealthy man in a horticultural, agricultural, or pastoral society who is most apt to practice polygyny. When he does, it is usually of the *sororal* type, with the co-wives being sisters. Having lived their lives together before marriage, the sisters continue to do so with their husband, instead of occupying separate dwellings of their own.

Polygyny also occurs in a few places in Europe. In 1972, for example, English laws concerning marriage changed to accommodate immigrants who traditionally practiced polygyny. Since that time polygynous marriages have been legal in England for some specific religious minorities, including Muslims and Sephardic Jews. According to one family law specialist, the real impetus behind this law change was a growing concern that "destitute immigrant wives, abandoned by their husbands, [were] overburdening the welfare state."[15]

Even in the United States, where it is illegal, between 30,000 and 50,000 people in the Rocky Mountain states live in households made up of a man with two or more wives.[16] Most consider themselves Mormons, even though the official Mormon Church does not approve of the practice. A growing minority, however, call themselves "Christian polygamists," citing the Old Testament in the Bible as justification.[17] The Fundamentalist Church of Jesus Christ of the Latter-Day Saints (FLDS), the sect that split from the Mormon Church after it banned plural marriage, allows only adult males deemed godly by the church leader to enter into plural marriage. "Those later judged unworthy can have their wives and children reassigned to other men."[18]

Despite its illegality, regional law enforcement officials have generally adopted a "live and let live" attitude toward religious-based polygyny in their region. One woman—a lawyer and one of nine co-wives—expresses her attitude toward polygyny as follows:

> I see it as the ideal way for a woman to have a career and children. In our family, the women can help each other care for the children. Women in monogamous relationships don't have that luxury. As I see it, if this lifestyle didn't already exist, it would have to be invented to accommodate career women.[19]

Although monogamy and polygyny are the most common forms of marriage in the world today, other

▲▲▲ Polyandry—marriage between one woman and two or more men—occurs in fewer than a dozen societies, including among the Nyimba people living in northwest Nepal's Nyimba Valley in the Humla district near Tibet. From right: the older husband Chhonchanab with first daughter Dralma, the wife Shilangma, the younger husband KaliBahadur and second daughter Tsering.

forms do occur. **Polyandry** (*andros* in Greek means "man" or "husband"), the marriage of one woman to two or more men simultaneously, is known in only a few societies, perhaps in part because a woman's life expectancy is usually longer than a man's, and female infant mortality is somewhat lower, so a surplus of women in a society is likely.

Fewer than a dozen societies are known to have favored this form of marriage, but they involve people as widely separated from one another as the Marquesan Islanders of the Pacific and Tibetans in Central Asia. In

---

[15]Cretney, S. (2003). *Family law in the twentieth century: A history* (pp. 72–73). New York: Oxford University Press.

[16]Egan, T. (1999, February 28). The persistence of polygamy. *New York Times Magazine,* 52.

[17]Wolfson, H. (2000, January 22). Polygamists make the Christian connection. *Burlington Free Press,* 2c.

[18]Anderson, S. (2010, February). The polygamists. *National Geographic,* 36, 39. http://ngm.nationalgeographic.com/2010/02/polygamists/anderson-text (retrieved September 6, 2011).

[19]Johnson, D. (1996). Polygamists emerge from secrecy, seeking not just peace but respect. In W. A. Haviland & R. J. Gordon (Eds.), *Talking about people* (2nd ed., pp. 129–131). Mountain View, CA: Mayfield.

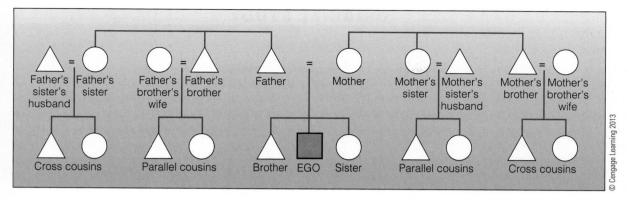

Figure 12.1 Kinship Relationships Anthropologists use diagrams of this sort to illustrate kinship relationships. This one shows the distinction between cross cousins and parallel cousins. In such diagrams, males are always shown with triangles, females with circles, marital ties with an equal sign (=), sibling relationships with a horizontal line, and parent–child relationships with a vertical line. Terms are given from the perspective of the individual labeled EGO, who can be male or female.

Tibet, where inheritance is through the male line and arable land is limited, the marriage of brothers to a single woman (*fraternal polyandry*) keeps the land together by preventing it from being repeatedly subdivided among sons from one generation to the next. Unlike monogamy, it also holds down population growth, thereby avoiding increased pressures on resources. Finally, among Tibetans who practice a mixed economy of farming, herding, and trading in the Trans Himalayas, fraternal polyandry provides the household with an adequate pool of male labor for all three subsistence activities.[20]

Group Marriage

Notable among several other marriage forms is **group marriage.** Also known as *co-marriage,* this is a rare arrangement in which several men and women have sexual access to one another. Until a few decades ago, Iñupiat Eskimos in northern Alaska, for instance, engaged in "spouse exchange" (*nuliaqatigiit*) between non-kin, with two conjugal husband–wife couples being united by shared sexual access. Highly institutionalized arrangements, these intimate relationships implied ties of mutual aid and support across territorial boundaries and were expected to last throughout the lifetime of the participants.[21] The ties between the couples were so strong that their children retained a recognized relationship to one another.[22]

Choice of Spouse

The Western egalitarian ideal that an individual should be free to marry whomever he or she chooses is a distinct arrangement, certainly not universally embraced. In many societies, marriage and the establishment of a family are considered far too important to be left to the whims of young people. The individual relationship of two people who are expected to spend their lives together and raise their children together is viewed as incidental to the more serious matter of allying two families through the marriage bond. Marriage involves a transfer of rights between families, including rights to property and rights over children, as well as sexual rights. Thus marriages tend to be arranged for the economic and political advantage of the family unit.

Although arranged marriages are rare in North American society, they do occur. Among ethnic minorities, they may serve to preserve traditional values that people fear might otherwise be lost. Among families of wealth and power, marriages may be arranged by segregating their children in private schools and carefully steering them toward appropriate spouses. The Original Study on pages 254–255 illustrates how marriages may be arranged in societies where such practices are commonplace.

---

[20]Levine, N. E., & Silk, J. B. (1997). Why polyandry fails. *Current Anthropology 38*, 375–398.

[21]Chance, N. A. (1990). *The Iñupiat and Arctic Alaska: An ethnography of development* (pp. 110–111). New York: Harcourt.

[22]Spencer, R. F. (1984). North Alaska Coast Eskimo. In D. Damas (Ed.), *Arctic: Handbook of North American Indians* (vol. 5, pp. 320–337). Washington, DC: Smithsonian Institution.

polyandry A marriage form in which a woman is married to two or more men at one time; a form of polygamy.

group marriage A marriage form in which several men and women have sexual access to one another; also called *co-marriage.*

parallel cousin The child of a father's brother or a mother's sister.

ORIGINAL STUDY

Arranging Marriage in India

By Serena Nanda

Six years [after my first field trip to India] I returned to do fieldwork among the middle class in Bombay, a modern, sophisticated city. From the experience of my earlier visit, I decided to include a study of arranged marriages in my project. By this time I had met many Indian couples whose marriages had been arranged and who seemed very happy. Particularly in contrast to the fate of many of my married friends in the United States who were already in the process of divorce, the positive aspects of arranged marriages appeared to me to outweigh the negatives. In fact, I thought I might even participate in arranging a marriage myself. I had been fairly successful in the United States in "fixing up" many of my friends, and I was confident that my matchmaking skills could be easily applied to this new situation, once I learned the basic rules. "After all," I thought, "how complicated can it be?"

An opportunity presented itself almost immediately. A friend from my previous Indian trip was in the process of arranging for the marriage of her eldest son. Since my friend's family was eminently respectable and the boy himself personable, well educated, and nice looking, I was sure that by the end of my year's fieldwork, we would have found a match.

The basic rule seems to be that a family's reputation is most important. It is understood that matches would be arranged only within the same caste and general social class, although some crossing of subcastes is permissible if the class positions of the bride's and groom's families are similar. Although dowry is now prohibited by law in India, extensive gift exchanges took place with every marriage. Even when the boy's family does not "make demands," every girl's family nevertheless feels the obligation to give the traditional gifts—to the girl, to the boy, and to the boy's family.

Particularly when the couple would be living in the joint family—that is, with the boy's parents and his married brothers and their families, as well as with unmarried siblings, which is still very common even among the urban, upper-middle class in India—the girl's parents are anxious to establish smooth relations between their family and that of the boy. Offering the proper gifts, even when not called "dowry," is often an important factor in influencing the relationship between the bride's and groom's families and perhaps, also, the treatment of the bride in her new home.

In a society where divorce is still a scandal and where, in fact, the divorce rate is exceedingly low, an arranged marriage is the beginning of a lifetime relationship not just between the bride and groom but between their families as well. Thus, while a girl's looks are important, her character is even more so, for she is being judged as a prospective daughter-in-law as much as a prospective bride....

My friend is a highly esteemed wife, mother, and daughter-in-law. She is religious, soft-spoken, modest, and deferential. She rarely gossips and never quarrels, two qualities highly desirable in a woman. A family that has the reputation for gossip and conflict among its womenfolk will not find it easy to get good wives for their sons....

Originally from North India, my friend's family had lived for forty years in Bombay, where her husband owned a business. The family had delayed in seeking a match for their eldest son because he had been an air force pilot for several years, stationed in such remote places that it had seemed fruitless to try to find a girl who would be willing to accompany him. In their social class, a military career, despite its economic security, has little prestige and is considered a drawback in finding a suitable bride....

The son had recently left the military and joined his father's business. Since he was a college graduate, modern, and well traveled, from such a good family, and, I thought, quite handsome, it seemed to me that he, or rather his family, was in a position to pick and choose. I said as much to my friend. While she agreed that there were many advantages on their side, she also said, "We must keep in mind that my son is both short and dark; these are drawbacks in finding the right match."...

An important source of contacts in trying to arrange her son's marriage was my friend's social club in Bombay. Many of the women had daughters of the right age, and some had already expressed an interest in my friend's son. I was most enthusiastic about the possibilities of one particular family who had five daughters, all of whom were pretty, demure, and well educated. Their mother had told my friend, "You can have your pick for your son, whichever one of my daughters appeals to you most." I saw a match in sight. "Surely," I said to my friend, "we will find one there. Let's go visit and make our choice." But my friend held back; she did not seem to share my enthusiasm, for reasons I could not then fathom.

When I kept pressing for an explanation of her reluctance, she admitted, "See, Serena, here is the problem. The family has so many daughters, how will they be able to provide nicely for any of them? ... Since this is our eldest son, it's best if we marry him to a girl who is the only daughter, then the wedding will truly be a gala affair." I argued that surely the quality of the girls themselves made up for any deficiency in the elaborateness of the wedding. My friend admitted this point but still seemed reluctant to proceed.

"Is there something else," I asked her, "some factor I have missed?" "Well," she finally said, "there is one other thing. They have one daughter already married and living in Bombay. The mother is always complaining to me that the girl's in-laws don't let her visit her own family often enough. So it makes me wonder, will she be that kind of mother who always wants her daughter at her own home? This will prevent the girl from adjusting to our house. It is not a good thing." And so, this family of five daughters was dropped as a possibility.

Somewhat disappointed, I neverthe-less respected my friend's reasoning and geared up for the next prospect. This was also the daughter of a woman in my friend's social club. There was clear interest in this family and I could see why. The family's reputation was excellent; in fact, they came from a subcaste slightly higher than my friend's own. The girl, who was an only daughter, was pretty and well educated and had a brother studying in the United States. Yet, after expressing an interest to me in this family, all talk of them suddenly died down and the search began elsewhere.

"What happened to that girl as a pros-pect?" I asked one day. "You never men-tion her anymore. She is so pretty and so educated, what did you find wrong?"

"She is too educated. We've decided against it. My husband's father saw the girl on the bus the other day and thought her forward. A girl who 'roams about' the city by herself is not the girl for our fam-ily." My disappointment this time was even greater, as I thought the son would have liked the girl very much. . . . I learned that if the family of the girl has even a slightly higher social status than the family of the boy, the bride may think herself too good for them, and this too will cause prob-lems. . . .

After one more candidate, who my friend decided was not attractive enough for her son, almost six months had passed and I had become anxious. My friend laughed at my impatience: "Don't be so much in a hurry," she said. "You Americans want everything done so quickly. You get married quickly and then just as quickly get divorced. Here we take marriage more seriously. We must take all the factors into account. It is not enough for us to learn by our mistakes. This is too serious a busi-ness. If a mistake is made we have not only ruined the life of our son or daughter, but we have spoiled the reputation of our family as well. And that will make it much harder for their brothers and sisters to get married. So we must be very careful."

What she said was true and I prom-ised myself to be more patient. I had re-ally hoped and expected that the match would be made before my year in India was up. But it was not to be. When I left India my friend seemed no further along in finding a suitable match for her son than when I had arrived.

Two years later, I returned to India and still my friend had not found a girl for her son. By this time, he was close to 30, and I think she was a little worried. Since she knew I had friends all over India, and I was going to be there for a year, she asked me to "help her in this work" and keep an eye out for someone suitable. . . .

It was almost at the end of my year's stay in India that I met a family with a mar-riageable daughter whom I felt might be a good possibility for my friend's son. . . . This new family had a successful business in a medium-sized city in central India and were from the same subcaste as my friend. The daughter was pretty and chic; in fact, she had studied fashion design in college. Her parents would not allow her to go off by herself to any of the major cities in India where she could make a career, but they had compromised with her wish to work by allowing her to run a small dress-making boutique from their home. In spite of her desire to have a ca-reer, the daughter was both modest and home-loving and had had a traditional, sheltered upbringing.

I mentioned the possibility of a match with my friend's son. The girl's parents were most interested. Although their daughter was not eager to marry just yet, the idea of living in Bombay—a sophisti-cated, extremely fashion-conscious city where she could continue her education in clothing design—was a great induce-ment. I gave the girl's father my friend's address and suggested that when they went to Bombay on some business or whatever, they look up the boy's family.

Returning to Bombay on my way to New York, I told my friend of this newly discovered possibility. She seemed to feel there was potential but, in spite of my urg-ing, would not make any moves herself. She rather preferred to wait for the girl's family to call upon them.

A year later I received a letter from my friend. The family had indeed come to visit Bombay, and their daughter and my friend's daughter, who were near in age, had be-come very good friends. During that year, the two girls had frequently visited each other. I thought things looked promising.

Last week I received an invitation to a wedding: My friend's son and the girl were getting married. Since I had found the match, my presence was particularly requested at the wedding. I was thrilled. Success at last! As I prepared to leave for India, I began thinking, "Now, my friend's younger son, who do I know who has a nice girl for him . . . ?" ■

Nanda, S. (2000). Arranging a marriage in India. From *Stumbling toward truth: anthropologists at work* (pp. 196–204). Long Grove, IL: Waveland Press. Reprinted by permission of the author.

Cousin Marriage

While cousin marriage is prohibited in some societies, certain cousins are the preferred marriage partners in oth-ers. A **parallel cousin** is the child of a father's brother or a mother's sister (▶ **Figure 12.1**). In some societies, the pre-ferred spouse for a man is his father's brother's daughter (or, from the woman's point of view, her father's brother's son). This is known as *patrilateral parallel-cousin marriage*.

Although not obligatory, such marriages have been favored historically among Arabs, the ancient Israelites, and the ancient Greeks. All of these societies are (or were) hier-archical in nature—that is, some people are ranked higher than others because they have more power and property—and although male dominance and descent are empha-sized, daughters as well as sons inherit property of value. Thus, when a man marries his father's brother's daughter (or a woman marries her father's brother's son), property is retained within the single male line of descent. In these societies, generally speaking, the greater the property, the more this form of parallel-cousin marriage is apt to occur.

A **cross cousin** is the child of a mother's brother or a father's sister (see Figure 12.1). Some societies favor *matrilateral cross-cousin marriage*—marriage of a man to his mother's brother's daughter, or a woman to her father's sister's son. This preference exists among food foragers (such as the Aborigines of Australia) and some farming cultures (including various peoples of South India). Among food foragers, who inherit relatively little in the way of property, such marriages help establish and maintain ties of solidarity between social groups. In agricultural societies, however, the transmission of property is an important determinant. In societies that trace descent exclusively in the female line, for instance, property and other important rights usually pass from a man to his sister's son; under cross-cousin marriage, the sister's son is also the man's daughter's husband.

Same-Sex Marriage

As noted earlier in this chapter, our definition of marriage refers to a union between "people" rather than between "a man and a woman" because in some societies same-sex marriages are socially acceptable and officially allowed by law. Marriages between individuals of the same sex may provide a way of dealing with problems for which opposite-sex marriage offers no satisfactory solution. This is the case with woman–woman marriage, a practice permitted in many societies of sub-Saharan Africa, although in none does it involve more than a small minority of all women.

Details differ from one society to another, but woman–woman marriages among the Nandi of western Kenya may be taken as representative of such practices in Africa.[23] The Nandi are a pastoral people who also do considerable farming. Control of most significant property and the primary means of production—livestock and land—is exclusively in the hands of men and may only be transmitted to their male heirs, usually their sons. Because polygyny is the preferred form of marriage, a man's property is normally divided equally among his wives for their sons to inherit. Within the household, each wife has her own home in which she lives with her children, but all are under the authority of the husband, who is a remote and aloof figure within the family. In such situations, the position of a woman who bears no sons is difficult; not only does she not help perpetuate her husband's male line—a major concern among the Nandi—but she has no one to inherit the proper share of her husband's property.

To get around these problems, a woman of advanced age who bore no sons may become a female husband by marrying a young woman. The purpose of this arrangement is for the young wife to provide the male heirs that her female husband could not. To accomplish this, the woman's wife enters into a sexual relationship with a man other than her female husband's male husband; usually it is one of his male relatives. No other obligations exist between this woman and her male sex partner, and her female husband is recognized as the social and legal father of any children born under these conditions.

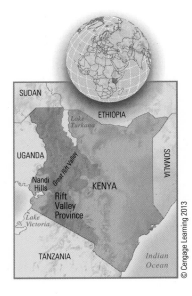

In keeping with her role as female husband, this woman is expected to abandon her female gender identity and, ideally, dress and behave as a man. In practice, the ideal is not completely achieved, for the habits of a lifetime are difficult to reverse. Generally, it is in the context of domestic activities, which are most highly symbolic of female identity, that female husbands most completely assume a male identity.

The individuals who are parties to woman–woman marriages enjoy several advantages. By assuming male identity, a barren or sonless woman raises her status considerably and even achieves near equality with men, who otherwise occupy a far more favored position in Nandi society than women. A woman who marries a female husband is usually one who is unable to make a good marriage, often because she (the female husband's wife) has lost face as a consequence of premarital pregnancy. By marrying a female husband, she too raises her status and also secures legitimacy for her children. Moreover, a female husband is usually less harsh and demanding, spends more time with her, and allows her a greater say in decision making than a male husband does. The one thing she may not do is engage in sexual activity with her marriage partner. In fact, female husbands are expected to abandon sexual activity altogether, including with their male husbands to whom they remain married even though the women now have their own wives.

In contrast to woman–woman marriages among the Nandi are same-sex marriages that include sexual activity between partners. Over the past decade, the legal recognition of such unions has become a matter of vigorous debate in some parts of the world. Several countries—including Argentina, Belgium, Canada, Iceland,

---

[23]The following is based on Obler, R. S. (1982). Is the female husband a man? Woman/woman marriage among the Nandi of Kenya. *Ethnology 19*, 69–88.

▲▲▲ In some societies, when a woman marries she receives her share of the family inheritance (her dowry), which she brings to her new family (unlike bride-price, which passes from the groom's family to the bride's family). Shown here are Slovakian women in a traditional farming village each carrying a trousseau (*výbava nevesty*)—consisting of the bride's clothes, linen, bedding, and other objects of her dowry—in a festive procession to her new home. Traditionally, the bride keeps her finer linen in a beautifully carved or painted dowry chest. In addition, her birth family contributes some livestock, land, or other form of wealth, which Slovaks call *veno,* to the new household. Held in her name, this property provides the woman with a measure of independence from her husband.

Netherlands, Norway, Portugal, South Africa, Spain, and Sweden—have passed laws legalizing gay marriages. Meanwhile numerous U.S. states have adopted constitutional amendments barring same-sex marriage, while others—including Connecticut, Iowa, Massachusetts, New Hampshire, New York, and Vermont—now legally recognize these unions. Additional states recognize same-sex marriage but do not allow official gay wedding ceremonies to take place within their boundaries.

The issue of same-sex marriage remains unsettled in many parts of the world, with official policies sometimes swinging back and forth—evidence of the fact that cultures are dynamic and capable of change. In addition, close to a dozen U.S. states and about two dozen countries around the world recognize civil unions (also known as *civil* or *domestic partnerships*), which offer a varying range of marriage benefits.

Among the arguments most commonly marshaled by opponents of same-sex unions is the claim that marriage has always been between males and females—but

as we have just seen, this is not true. Same-sex unions, from informal relationships to marriages, have been documented not only for a number of societies in Africa but in other parts of the world as well.[24] As among the Nandi, these unions provide acceptable positions in society for individuals who might otherwise be marginalized.

Marriage and Economic Exchange

Marriages in many human societies are formalized by some sort of economic exchange. This may take the form of a gift exchange known as **bridewealth** (sometimes called *bride-price*), which involves payments of money or valuable goods to a bride's parents or other close kin. This

▲▲▲▲▲▲▲▲▲▲▲▲▲▲▲▲▲▲▲▲▲▲▲▲▲▲▲▲▲▲▲▲▲▲▲▲▲

cross cousin The child of a mother's brother or a father's sister.

bridewealth The money or valuable goods paid by the groom or his family to the bride's family upon marriage; also called *bride-price*.

---

[24]Kuefler, M. (2007). The marriage revolution in late antiquity: The Theodosian Code and later Roman marriage law. *Journal of Family History 32* (4), 343–370.

▼▼▼▼▼▼▼▼▼▼▼▼▼▼▼▼▼▼▼▼▼▼▼▼▼▼▼▼▼▼▼▼▼▼▼▼▼▼

usually happens in patrilineal societies where the bride will become a member of the household in which her husband grew up; this household will benefit from her labor as well as from the offspring she produces. Thus her family must be compensated for their loss.

Bride-price is not a simple buying and selling of women; rather, it can contribute to the bride's household (through purchases of jewelry or furnishings) or can help finance an elaborate and costly wedding celebration. It also enhances the stability of the marriage, because it usually must be refunded if the couple separates. Other forms of compensation are an exchange of women between families—"My son will marry your daughter if your son will marry my daughter." Yet another exchange is **bride service**, a period of time during which the groom works for the bride's family.

In a number of societies, especially those where the economy is based on agriculture, women often bring a dowry with them at marriage. A **dowry** is a woman's share of parental property that, instead of passing to her upon her parents' death, is given to her at the time of her marriage. This does not mean that she retains control of this property after marriage. In some European and Asian countries, for example, a woman's property traditionally falls exclusively under her husband's control. Having benefited by what she has brought to the marriage, however, he is obligated to look out for her future well-being, including her security after his death. In the United States today, a form of dowry persists with the custom of the bride's family paying the wedding expenses.

One of the functions of dowry is to ensure a woman's support in widowhood (or after divorce), an important consideration in a society where men carry out the bulk of productive work, and women are valued for their reproductive potential rather than for the work they do. In such societies, women incapable of bearing children are especially vulnerable, but the dowry they bring with them at marriage helps protect them against desertion. Another function of dowry is to reflect the economic status of the woman in societies where differences in wealth are important. It also permits women, with the aid of their parents and kin, to compete through dowry for desirable (that is, wealthy) husbands.

Divorce

Like marriage, divorce in most societies is a matter of great concern to the couple's families as it impacts not only the individuals dissolving their marital relationship but also offspring, in-laws, other relatives, and sometimes entire communities. Indeed, divorce may have social, political, and economic consequences far beyond the breakup of a couple and their household.

Across cultures, divorce arrangements can be made for a variety of reasons and with varying degrees of difficulty. Among the Gusii farmers of western Kenya, for instance, sterility and impotence are grounds for a divorce. Among certain aboriginal peoples in northern Canada and Chenchu foragers in central India, divorce is traditionally discouraged after children are born; couples usually are urged by their families to adjust their differences. By contrast, in the southwestern United States, a traditional Hopi Indian woman in Arizona could divorce her husband at any time merely by placing his belongings outside the door to indicate he was no longer welcome. Among the most common reasons for divorce across cultures are infidelity, sterility, cruelty, and desertion.[25]

An adult unmarried woman is very rare in most non-Western societies where a divorced woman usually soon remarries. In many societies, economic considerations are often the strongest motivation to wed. On the island of New Guinea, a man does not marry because of sexual needs, which he can readily satisfy out of wedlock, but because there it is important to have a female partner to carry out tasks that traditionally fall to women—making pots and cooking his meals, fabricating nets, and weeding his plantings. Likewise, women in communities that depend on males for their fighting abilities need husbands who are able warriors as well as good hunters.

Although divorce has become common in various parts of the world, divorce rates have become so high in Western industrial and postindustrial societies that many worry about the future of traditional and familiar forms of marriage and family. It is interesting to note that although divorce was next to impossible in Western societies between 1000 and 1800, few marriages lasted more than about ten or twenty years, due to high mortality rates caused in part by inadequate health care and poor medical expertise.[26] For instance, women dying in childbirth ended many marriages. With increased longevity, separation by death has diminished, and separation by legal action has grown. In the United States divorce rates have leveled off since peaking in the 1980s, but over 40 percent of marriages still do not survive.[27]

[25]Goodwin, R. (1999). *Personal relationships across cultures* (pp. 86–89). New York: Routledge; see also Betzig, L. (1989). Causes of conjugal dissolution: A cross-cultural study. *Current Anthropology 30*, 654–676.

[26]Stone, L. (1998). *Kinship and gender: An introduction* (p. 235). Boulder, CO: Westview Press.

[27]Morella, C. (2011, May 18). Number of long-lasting marriages in U.S. has risen, Census Bureau reports. *Washington Post*.

Family and Household

Dependence on group living for survival is a basic human characteristic. We have inherited this from primate ancestors, although we have developed it in our own distinctly human way—through culture. However each culture may define what constitutes a family, this social unit forms the basic cooperative structure that ensures an individual's primary needs and provides the necessary care for children to develop as healthy and productive members of the group and thereby ensure its future.

Comparative historical and cross-cultural studies reveal a wide variety of family patterns, and these patterns may change over time. As a result, the definition of **family** is necessarily broad: two or more people related by blood, marriage, or adoption. The family may take many forms, ranging from a single parent with one or more children, to a married couple or polygamous spouses with or without offspring, to several generations of parents and their children.

For purposes of cross-cultural comparison, anthropologists define the **household** as the domestic unit of one or more persons living in the same residence. Other than family members, a household may include nonrelatives such as servants. Traditionally—and still in many parts of the world—this is the basic residential unit where economic production, consumption, inheritance, childrearing, and shelter are organized and carried out.

In the vast majority of human societies, most households are made up of families, but there are many other arrangements. For instance, among the Mundurucu Indians, a horticultural people living in the center of Brazil's Amazon rainforest, married men and women are members of separate households, meeting periodically for sexual activity. At age 13 boys join their fathers in the men's house. Meanwhile, their sisters continue to live with their mothers and the younger boys in two or three houses grouped around the men's house. Thus, the men's house constitutes one household inhabited by adult males and their sexually mature sons, and the women's houses, inhabited by adult women and prepubescent boys and girls, constitute others.

© Aldona Sablais/Photo Researchers, Inc.

▲▲▲ This is a celebration at the palace in the city of Yoruba in Oyo, Nigeria. As is usual in societies with nobility, the Yoruba royal household includes many individuals not related to the ruler, as well as the royal family.

An array of other domestic arrangements can be found in other parts of the world, including situations in which co-residents of a household are not related biologically or by marriage—such as the service personnel in an elaborate royal household, apprentices in the household of craft specialists, low-status clients in the household of rich and powerful patrons, or groups of children being raised by paired teams of adult male and female community members in an Israeli kibbutz (a collectively owned and operated agricultural settlement). So it is that *family* and *household* are not always synonymous.

▲▲▲

bride service A designated period of time when the groom works for the bride's family.

dowry A payment at the time of a woman's marriage that comes from her inheritance, made to either her or her husband.

family Two or more people related by blood, marriage, or adoption. The family may take many forms, ranging from a single parent with one or more children, to a married couple or polygamous spouses with or without offspring, to several generations of parents and their children.

household A domestic unit of one or more persons living in the same residence. Other than family members, a household may include nonrelatives, such as servants.

▼▼▼

Forms of the Family

To discuss the various forms families take in response to particular social, historical, and ecological circumstances, we must, at the outset, make a distinction between a **conjugal family** (in Latin *conjugere* means "to join together"), which is formed on the basis of marital ties, and a **consanguineal family** (based on the Latin word *consanguineus*, literally meaning "of the same blood"), which consists of related women, their brothers, and the women's offspring.

Consanguineal families are not common; examples of this form include the Musuo of southwestern China and the Tory Islanders—a Roman Catholic and Gaelic-speaking fishing people living off the coast of Ireland. Typically, Tory Islanders do not marry until they are in their late 20s or early 30s. By then, commented one local woman,

> It's too late to break up arrangements that you have already known for a long time. . . . You know, I have my sisters and brothers to look after, why should I leave home to go live with a husband? After all, he's got his sisters and his brothers looking after him.[28]

Notably, since the community numbers but a few hundred people, husbands and wives are within easy commuting distance of each other.

According to a cross-cultural survey of family types in 192 cultures around the world, the extended family is the most common, present in nearly half of those cultures, compared to the nuclear family at 25 percent, and the polygamous family at 22 percent.[29] Each of these is discussed below.

THE NUCLEAR FAMILY

The most basic family unit is the **nuclear family**, comprised of one or two parents and dependent offspring, which may include a stepparent, stepsiblings, and adopted children (▶ **Figure 12.2**). Until recently, the term *nuclear family* referred only to the mother, father, and child(ren) unit—the family form that most North Americans, Europeans, and many others regard as the normal or natural nucleus of larger family units. In the United States, traditional mother, father, child(ren) nuclear family households reached their highest frequency around 1950, when 60 percent of all households conformed to this model.[30] Today such families make up about 20 percent of U.S. households,[31] and the term *nuclear family* is used to cover the social reality of several types of small parent–child units, including single parents with children and same-sex couples with children.

Industrialization and market capitalism have played a historical role in shaping the nuclear family with which most of us are familiar today. One reason for this is that factories, mining and transportation companies, warehouses, shops, and other businesses generally only pay individual wage earners for the jobs they are hired to do. Whether these workers are single, married, divorced, have siblings, or have dependent children is really not a concern to the profit-seeking companies. Because jobs may come and go, individual wage earners must remain mobile to adapt to the labor markets. And since few wage earners have the financial resources to support large numbers of relatives without incomes of their own, industrial or postindustrial societies do not favor the continuance of larger extended families (discussed below), which are standard in most societies traditionally dependent on pastoral nomadism, agriculture, or horticulture.

Interestingly, the nuclear family is also likely to be prominent in traditional foraging societies such as that of the Inuit (formerly known as Eskimo) who live in the barren Arctic environments of eastern Siberia, Alaska, Greenland, and Canada. In the winter the traditional Inuit husband and

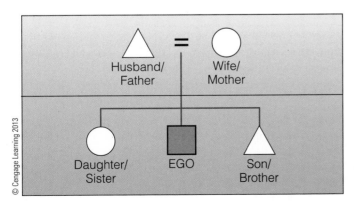

Figure 12.2 The Nuclear Family This diagram shows the relationships in a traditional nuclear family, a form that is common but declining in North America and much of Europe.

[28]Fox, R. (1981, December 3). [Interview]. Coast Telecourses, Inc., Los Angeles.

[29]Winick, C. (Ed.). (1970). *Dictionary of anthropology* (p. 202). Totowa, NJ: Littlefield, Adams.

[30]Stacey, J. (1990). *Brave new families* (pp. 5, 10). New York: Basic Books.

[31]Irvine, M. (1999, November 24). Mom-and-pop houses grow rare. *Burlington Free Press*; see also U.S. Census Bureau. (2008). *American Community Survey, 2006–2008*.

◄
◄
◄ **Extended family households exist in many parts of the world, including among the Maya of Central America and Mexico.**[32] In many of their communities, sons bring their wives to live in houses built on the edges of a small open plaza, on one edge of which their father's house already stands. Numerous household activities are carried out on this plaza—children play while adults do some productive work or socialize with guests. The head of the family is the sons' father, who makes most of the important decisions. All members of the family work together for the common good and deal with outsiders as a single unit.

wife, with their children, roam the vast Arctic Canadian snowscape in their quest for food. The husband hunts and makes shelters. The wife cooks, is responsible for the children, and makes the clothing and keeps it in good repair. Traditional chores include chewing her husband's boots to soften the leather for the next day so that he can resume his quest for game. The wife and her children could not survive without the husband, and life for a man is unimaginable without a wife.

Similar to nuclear families in industrial societies, those living under especially harsh environmental conditions must be prepared to fend for themselves. Such isolation comes with its own set of challenges, including the difficulties of rearing children without multigenerational support, and a lack of familial care for the elderly. Nonetheless, this form of family is well adapted to a mode of subsistence that requires a high degree of geographic mobility. For the Inuit in Canada, this mobility permits the hunt for food; for other North Americans, the hunt for jobs and improved social status require a mobile form of family unit.

THE EXTENDED FAMILY

When two or more closely related nuclear families cluster together into a large domestic group, they form a unit known as the **extended family**. This larger family unit—common in traditional horticultural, agricultural, and pastoral societies around the world—typically consists of siblings with their spouses and offspring, and often their parents. All of these kin, some related by blood and some by marriage, live and work together for the common good and deal with outsiders as a single unit.

Because members of the younger generation bring their husbands or wives to live in the family, extended families have continuity through time. As older members die off, new members are born into the family. By their nature, extended families have particular challenges. Among these are difficulties that the person marrying into the family is likely to experience in adjusting to his or her spouse's family.

Nontraditional Families and Nonfamily Households

In North America and parts of Europe, increasing numbers of people live in nonfamily households, either alone or with nonrelatives. In fact, about one-third of households in the United States fall into this category (▶ **Figure 12.3** on the next page). Many others live as members of what are often called *nontraditional families*.

Increasingly common are *cohabitation* households, comprised of unmarried couples. Since 1960, such households have dramatically increased in number, especially among young couples in their 20s and early 30s in North America and parts of Europe. In Norway, for example,

▲▲

conjugal family A family established through marriage.

consanguineal family A family of blood relatives, consisting of related women, their brothers, and the women's offspring.

nuclear family A group consisting of one or two parents and dependent offspring, which may include a stepparent, stepsiblings, and adopted children. Until recently this term referred only to the father, mother, and child(ren) unit.

extended family Two or more closely related nuclear families clustered together in a large domestic group.

▼▼

[32]Vogt, E. Z. (1990). *The Zinacantecos of Mexico, A modern Maya way of life* (2nd ed., pp. 30–34). Fort Worth: Holt, Rinehart & Winston.

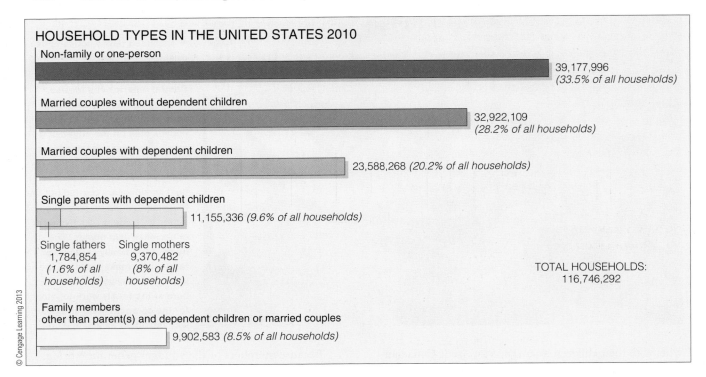

Figure 12.3 Household Types in the United States 2010 What has been traditionally considered the most prevalent household type, married couples with dependent children, is now only about 20 percent of the total number of households.

Source: U.S. Census Bureau, 2010.

over half of all live births now occur outside marriage. One reason is that Norwegian couples who have lived together for at least two years and who have children have many of the same rights and obligation as their married counterparts.[33] For many, however, cohabitation represents a relatively short-lived domestic arrangement, since most cohabiting couples either marry or separate within two years.[34]

Cohabitation breakup has contributed to the growing number of *single-parent* households—as have increases in divorce, sexual activity outside marriage, declining marriage rates among women of childbearing age, and the number of women preferring single motherhood. In the United States, more than a third of all births occur outside of marriage.[35] The proportion of U.S. single-parent households has grown to nearly 10 percent, while the number comprised of married couples with children has dropped to 20 percent. Although single-parent households account for about 10 percent of all U.S. households, they are home to 30 percent of all children (under 18 years of age) in the country.[36]

In the vast majority of cases, a child in a single-parent household lives with the mother. Single-parent households headed by women are neither new nor restricted to industrial or postindustrial societies. They have been studied for a long time in Caribbean countries, where men historically have been exploited as a cheap source of labor for sugar, coffee, or banana plantations. In more recent decades, many of these men are now also working as temporary migrant laborers in foreign countries, primarily in the United States—often living in temporary households comprised of fellow laborers.

Also significant today are the high numbers of *blended families,* comprised of a married couple together raising children from previous unions.

Residence Patterns

Where some form of conjugal or extended family is the norm, family exogamy requires that either the husband or the wife, if not both, must move to a new household

[33]Noack, T. (2001). Cohabitation in Norway: An accepted and gradually more regulated way of living. *International Journal of Law, Policy, and the Family 15* (1), 102–117.

[34]Forste, R. (2008). *Prelude to marriage, or alternative to marriage? A social demographic look at cohabitation in the U.S.* Working paper. Social Science Electronic Publishing, Inc. http://papers.ssrn.com/sol3/papers.cfm?abstract_id=269172 (retrieved September 7, 2011).

[35]Stein, R., & St. George, D. (2009, May 13). Babies increasingly born to unwed mothers. *Washington Post.*

[36]U.S. Census Bureau. (2010).

upon marriage. There are several common patterns of residence that a newly married couple may adopt—the prime determinant being ecological circumstances, although other factors enter in as well. Thus postmarital residence arrangements, far from being arbitrary, are adaptive in character.

Patrilocal residence is a pattern in which a married couple lives in the husband's father's place of residence. This residential arrangement is most often found in particular cultural situations, such as those where men play a predominant role in subsistence, and particularly if they own property that can be accumulated; where polygyny is customary; where warfare is prominent enough to make cooperation among men especially important; and where an elaborate political organization exists in which men wield authority. These conditions are most often found together in societies that rely on animal husbandry and/or intensive agriculture for their subsistence. Where patrilocal residence is customary, the bride often must move to a different band or community. In such cases, her parents' family is not only losing the services of a useful family member, but they are losing her potential offspring as well. Hence, some kind of compensation to her family, most commonly bride-price, is usual.

Matrilocal residence, in which a married couple lives in the wife's mother's place of residence, is a likely result if cultural ecological circumstances make the role of the woman predominate for subsistence. It is found most often in horticultural societies where political organization is relatively uncentralized and where cooperation among women is important. The Hopi Indians provide one example. Although it is the Hopi men who do the farming, the women control access to land and "own" the harvest. Indeed, men are not even allowed in the granaries. Under matrilocal residence, men usually do not move very far from the family in which they were raised, so they are available to help out there from time to time. Therefore, marriage usually does not involve compensation to the groom's family. Less common, but also found in matrilineal societies, is *avunculocal residence*, where the couple lives with the husband's mother's brother.

In **neolocal residence**, a married couple forms a household in a separate location. This occurs where the independence of the nuclear family is emphasized. In industrial societies such as the United States, where most economic activity occurs outside rather than inside the family and where it is important for individuals to be able to move where jobs can be found, neolocal residence is better suited than any of the other patterns.

Also noteworthy is ambilocal residence (*ambi* in Latin means "both"). In such an arrangement, the couple can join either the groom's or the bride's family, living wherever the resources look best or their presence is most needed or appreciated. Such a flexible pattern is particularly common among food-foraging peoples—if resources are scarce in the territorial range of the husband's family group, the couple may join the wife's relatives for more readily available food supplies in that domain.

Marriage, Family, and Household in Our Globalized and Technologized World

Large-scale emigration, modern technology, and multiple other factors in the emerging political economy of global capitalism also impact the cross-cultural mosaic of marriage, family, and household. For instance, electronic and digital communication by way of fiber optic cables and satellites has transformed how individuals express sexual attraction and engage in romantic courtship. Today, cross-cultural and transnational love relations bloom via the Internet. New technologies also permit the pursuit of traditionally prohibited relationships through clandestine text messaging of forbidden desires and tabooed intimacies—for example, across castes in India and between young unmarried men and women in traditional Muslim communities. Beyond sex and romance, many married couples and family members living far apart depend on satellite communications technology to stay in touch.

Adoption and New Reproductive Technologies

Although it has not been uncommon for childless couples in many cultures throughout human history to adopt children, including orphans and even captives, today it is a transnational practice for adults from industrial and postindustrial countries to travel across the world in search of infants to adopt, regardless of their ethnic heritage. Also increasingly common is open adoption, which makes it possible for a child to have a relationship with both the biological and the adoptive parents.

▲▲

patrilocal residence A residence pattern in which a married couple lives in the husband's father's place of residence.

matrilocal residence A residence pattern in which a married couple lives in the wife's mother's place of residence.

neolocal residence A residence pattern in which a married couple establishes its household in a location apart from either the husband's or the wife's relatives.

▼▼

© Edward Burtynsky

▲▲▲ Many of China's 114 million migrant laborers work in factories and live in factory dormitories such as this.

Among other contributing factors to the diversity of families and households are *new reproductive technologies* (NRTs), including various forms of *in vitro fertilization* (IVF) in which an egg is fertilized in a laboratory. The embryo is then transferred into the uterus to begin a pregnancy or is frozen for future use. In cases of IVF with a surrogate mother using donor egg and sperm, a newborn essentially has five parents: the birth parents who provided the egg and sperm, the surrogate mother who carried the baby, and the parents who will raise the baby.

Migrant Workforces

Another modern phenomenon changing the makeup of households and families worldwide is the ever-growing population of temporary and migrant workers. Today, China alone has 114 million of them, mostly young people who have quit the peasant villages of their childhood and traveled to fast-growing cities to work in factories, shops, restaurants, and businesses. Some pile into apartments with friends or co-workers, others live in factory dormitories—new, single-generation households that stand in stark contrast to the multigenerational extended family households in which they were raised.

Similar scenes are repeated all around the world as individuals in this transient workforce set up house together far away from home in order to make a living. Although many countries have passed legislation intended to provide migrants with protections concerning housing, as well as work conditions and pay (such as the 1983 Migrant and Seasonal Agricultural Worker Protection Act in the United States), living conditions for these workers are often miserable.[37]

As the various ethnographic examples in this chapter illustrate, our species has invented a wide variety of marriage, family, and household forms, each in correspondence with related features in the social structure and conforming to the larger cultural system. In the face of new challenges, we explore and tinker in search of solutions, sometimes resulting in finding completely new forms and other times returning to time-tested formulas of more traditional varieties.

---

[37]Chang, L. (2005, June 9). A migrant worker sees rural home in new light. *Wall Street Journal.*

Chapter Checklist

How do different cultures permit or restrict sexual relations?

✔ Every society has rules and customs concerning sexual relations, marriage, household and family structures, and childrearing practices, all of which play important roles in establishing and maintaining the social alliances and continuity that help ensure a society's overall well-being.

✔ A majority of cultures are sexually permissive and do not sharply regulate personal sexual practices. Others are restrictive and explicitly prohibit all sexual activity outside of marriage. Of these, a few punish adultery by imprisonment, social exclusion, or even death, as traditionally prescribed by some religious laws.

✔ Incest taboos forbid marriage and sexual relations between certain close relatives—usually between parent–child and between siblings at a minimum. A truly convincing explanation of the incest taboo has yet to be advanced, but it is related to the practices of endogamy (marrying within a group of individuals) and exogamy (marrying outside a group).

What is marriage?

✔ Marriage is a culturally sanctioned union between two or more people that establishes certain rights and obligations between them, them and their children, and them and their in-laws.

✔ Marriage falls into several broad categories. Monogamy, having one spouse, is the most common form of marriage. Serial monogamy, in which a man or woman marries a series of partners, has become common among Europeans and North Americans.

✔ Polygamy, in which one individual has multiple spouses, comes in two forms: polygyny and polyandry. A man must have a certain amount of wealth to be able to afford polygyny (marriage to more than one wife at the same time). Yet in societies where women do most of the productive work, polygyny may serve as a means of generating wealth for a household. Although few marriages in a given society may be polygynous, it is regarded as an appropriate, and even preferred, form of marriage in the majority of the world's societies.

✔ Since few communities have a surplus of men, polyandry (the custom of a woman having several husbands) is uncommon. Also rare is group marriage, in which several men and several women have sexual access to one another.

What determines who marries whom?

✔ In Western industrial and postindustrial countries, marriages are generally based on ideals of romantic love. In non-Western societies, economic considerations are of major concern in arranging marriages, and marriage serves to bind two families as allies.

✔ Preferred marriage partners in many societies are particular cross cousins (mother's brother's daughter if a man; father's sister's son if a woman) or, less commonly, parallel cousins on the paternal side (father's brother's son or daughter). Cross-cousin marriage is a means of establishing and maintaining solidarity between groups.

✔ Same-sex marriages exist in some societies. For example, woman–woman marriages as practiced in some African cultures provide a socially approved way to deal with problems for which heterosexual marriages offer no satisfactory solution. In recent years, several countries and some U.S. states have legalized same-sex marriage.

How does economics factor into marriage?

✔ In many human societies, marriages are formalized by economic exchange—such as a reciprocal gift exchange between the bride's and groom's relatives. More common is bridewealth, the payment of money or other valuables from the groom's to the bride's kin. Bride service occurs when the groom is expected to work for a period of time for the bride's family. A dowry is the payment of a woman's inheritance at the time of marriage to her or to her husband. Its purpose is to ensure support for women in societies where men do most of the productive work, and women are valued primarily for their reproductive potential.

What about divorce?

✔ Divorce is possible in all societies. Although reasons and frequency vary, the most common reasons for divorce across cultures are infidelity, sterility, cruelty, and desertion.

How do family and household differ, and what is the relationship between them?

✔ The family may take many forms, ranging from a single parent with one or more children, to a married couple or polygamous spouses with or without offspring, to several generations of parents and their children.

✔ A family is distinct from a household, which is the basic residential unit where economic production, consumption, inheritance, childrearing, and shelter are organized and carried out. In the vast majority of human societies, most households are made up of families or parts of families, but there are many other household arrangements.

✔ The most basic domestic unit is the nuclear family—a group consisting of one or two parents and dependent offspring, which may include a stepparent, stepsiblings, and adopted children. Until recently, the term referred solely to the mother, father, and child(ren) unit. This family form is common in the industrial and postindustrial countries of North America and Europe and also in societies, such as the Inuit, that live in harsh environments. It is well suited to the mobility required both in food-foraging groups and in industrial societies where job changes are frequent.

The extended family consists of several closely related nuclear families living and often working together in a single household.

What kinds of marital residence patterns exist across cultures?

Three common residence patterns are patrilocal (in which a married couple lives in the locality of the husband's father's place of residence), matrilocal (living in the locality of the wife's mother's place of residence), and neolocal (living in a locality apart from the husband's or wife's parents).

In North America and parts of Europe, increasing numbers of people live in nonfamily households, either alone or with nonrelatives. This includes the fast-growing category of unmarried couples who cohabitate. Many others live as members of what are often called nontraditional families, including single-parent households and blended families.

How do globalization and technology impact marriage and family?

New reproductive technologies, surrogacy, and international adoptions are adding new dimensions to familial relationships.

Another phenomenon changing the makeup of households and families worldwide is the ever-growing population of temporary and migrant workers.

Questions for Reflection

1. According to Shinto tradition in traditional Japanese society, the bridal dress is white as a symbolic expression of her purity. Many women living in less sexually restrictive societies also choose white for their wedding dress. Why do you think that is, and how is it in your own family and community? Also, why do you think the prescribed dress color for Japanese grooms is black and gray? Is that also true for your own culture?

2. Members of traditional communities in countries where the state is either weak or absent depend on relatives to help meet the basic challenges of survival. In such traditional societies, why would it be risky to choose marriage partners exclusively on the basis of romantic love? Can you imagine other factors that would play a role if your community's long-term survival were at stake?

3. Although most women in Europe and North America probably view polygyny as a marriage practice exclusively benefiting men, women in cultures where such marriages are traditional may stress more positive sides of sharing a husband with several co-wives. Under which conditions do you think polygyny could be considered as relatively beneficial for women?

4. Why do you think your own culture has historically prescribed restrictive rules about sexual relations, not only with respect to heterosexual contact outside marriage but also condemning same-sex relations? Do you expect economic and social changes in a society will further change ideas and attitudes toward sex and marriage? And if so, will they become more or less restrictive?

5. Many children in Europe and North America are raised in single-parent households. In contrast to the United States, where most children living with their unmarried mothers grow up in economically disadvantaged households, relatively few children raised by unmarried mothers in Norway face poverty. Why do you think that is?

Key Terms

marriage
incest taboo
endogamy
exogamy
monogamy
serial monogamy
polygamy
polygyny

polyandry
group marriage
parallel cousin
cross cousin
bridewealth
bride service
dowry
family

household
conjugal family
consanguineal family
nuclear family
extended family
patrilocal residence
matrilocal residence
neolocal residence

Online Study Resources

Login to **www.cengagebrain.com** to access the resources your instructor has assigned and to purchase materials. For this book, you can access:

CourseMate

Access chapter-specific learning tools including flashcards, glossaries, practice quizzes, videos, and more in your Anthropology CourseMate.

VISUAL ESSENCE

As social creatures, humans create and maintain networks that reach beyond immediate family or household to provide security and support. On a basic level these associations are arranged by kinship. For Scottish highlanders—and many traditional peoples around the world—large kin-groups called clans have been important units of social organization. Pictured here is the opening parade of the Clan Grant highland games in Spey Valley, Scotland. Clan members from around the world gather here to affirm their common identity based on kinship and regional origins. They express their membership by wearing kilts and shawls with a distinct tartan (plaid) pattern that identifies their particular clan. Historically, there were several dozen Scottish clans, with names often including the prefix "Mac" or "Mc" (from a Gaelic word meaning "son of"). For centuries, many Scots emigrated from their homelands in search of economic opportunity. Today their descendants are dispersed across the globe, especially in Australia, Canada, and the United States. Often sharing the same surname and aided by the Internet, widely scattered Scots seek to reestablish social ties of shared descent, traveling long distances to clan gatherings to celebrate their cultural heritage with traditional dancing, piping, games, and food.

13 Kinship and Other Forms of Grouping

all societies rely on some form of family or household organization to meet basic human needs: securing food, shelter, and protection against danger; coordinating work; regulating sexual activities; and organizing childrearing. As efficient and flexible as these socioeconomic units may be for meeting these challenges, many societies confront problems that are beyond the coping ability of family and household organization. For example, members of one independent local group often need some means of interacting with people outside their immediate circle for defense against natural disasters or outside aggressors and for securing vitally important resources for food, fuel, and shelter. A wider circle may also be necessary in forming a cooperative workforce for tasks that require more participants than households alone can provide.

Humans have come up with many ways to widen their circles of support to meet such challenges. One is through a formal political system, with personnel to make and enforce laws, keep the peace, allocate resources, and perform other regulatory and societal functions. But the predominant way to build this support in societies that are not organized as political states—especially foraging, crop-cultivating, and pastoral societies—is by means of **kinship**, a network of relatives within which individuals possess certain mutual rights and obligations.

Descent Groups

A common way of organizing a society along kinship lines is by creating what anthropologists call descent groups. Found in many societies, a **descent group** is any kin-group whose members share a direct line of descent from a real (historical) or fictional common ancestor. The addition of a few culturally meaningful obligations and taboos acts as a kind of glue to help hold the structured social group together.

Although many important functions of the descent group are taken over by other institutions when a society becomes politically organized as a state, elements of such kin-ordered groups may continue. We see this with

In this chapter you will learn to:

- **Discuss how kinship is the basis of social organization in every culture.**

- **Interpret kinship terminology as a cross-cultural key unlocking rules of human relations.**

- **Contrast cultures in which ancestry is traced through foremothers, forefathers, or both.**

- **Distinguish between different types of descent groups in kin-ordered societies.**

- **Explain how groups are formed beyond kinship, based on gender, common interest, and prestige.**

- **Describe the possibilities and limitations of upward and downward social mobility.**

BIOCULTURAL CONNECTION

Maori Origins: Ancestral Genes and Mythical Canoes

Anthropologists studying Maori people in New Zealand have been fascinated to find that the Maori oral traditions parallel and support modern scientific research on their genetic history. New Zealand, an island country with dramatic geography that served as the setting for the *Lord of the Rings* film trilogy, lies in a remote corner of the Pacific Ocean about 1,900 kilometers (1,200 miles) southeast of Australia. Named by Dutch seafarers who landed on its shores in 1642, it was claimed by the British as a colony about 150 years later. Maori, the country's indigenous people, fought back but were outgunned, outnumbered, and forced to lay down their arms in the early 1870s. Today, nearly 600,000 of New Zealand's 4.1 million citizens claim some Maori ancestry.

Maori have an age-old legend about how they came to Aotearoa ("Land of

▲▲▲ Traditional Maori *waka* (ocean-going canoe).

traditional indigenous societies that have become part of larger state societies yet endure as distinctive kin-ordered communities. So it is with the Maori of New Zealand, featured in this chapter's Biocultural Connection. Retaining key elements of their traditional social structure, they are still organized in about thirty large descent groups known as *iwi* ("tribes"), which form part of larger social and territorial units known as *waka* ("canoes").

Descent group membership must be sharply defined in order to operate effectively in a kin-ordered society. If membership is allowed to overlap, it is unclear where someone's primary loyalty belongs, especially when different descent groups have conflicting interests. Membership can be determined in a number of ways. The most common way is what anthropologists refer to as *unilineal descent*.

the Long White Cloud"), their name for New Zealand: More than twenty-five generations ago, their Polynesian ancestors arrived in a great fleet of sailing canoes from Hawaiki, their mythical homeland sometimes identified with Tahiti where the native language closely resembles their own. According to chants and genealogies passed down through the ages, this fleet consisted of at least seven (perhaps up to thirteen) seafaring canoes. Estimated to weigh about 5 tons each, these large dugouts had a single claw-shaped sail and may have carried 50 to 120 people, plus food supplies, plants, and animals.

As described by Maori anthropologist Te Rangi Hiroa (Peter Buck), the seafaring skills of these voyagers enabled them to navigate by currents, winds, and stars across vast ocean expanses.[a] Perhaps escaping warfare and tribute payments in Hawaiki, they probably made the 5-week-long voyage around 1350 CE, although there were earlier and later canoes as well.

Traditional Maori society is organized into about thirty different *iwis* ("tribes"), grouped into thirteen *wakas* ("canoes"), each with its own traditional territory. Today, prior to giving a formal talk, Maori still introduce themselves by identifying their *iwi*, their *waka*, and the major sacred places of their ancestral territory. Their genealogy connects them to their tribe's founding ancestor who was a crewmember or perhaps even a chief in one of the giant canoes mentioned in the legend of the Great Fleet.[b]

Maori oral traditions about their origins fit quite well with scientific data based on anthropological and more recent genetic research. Study by outsiders can be controversial because Maori equate an individual's genes to his or her genealogy, which belongs to one's *iwi* or ancestral community. Considered sacred and entrusted to the tribal elders, genealogy is traditionally surrounded by *tapu* ("sacred prohibitions").[c] The Maori term for genealogy is *whakapapa* ("to set layer upon layer"), which is also a word for gene. This Maori term captures something of the original *genous,* the Greek word for "begetting offspring." Another Maori word for gene is *ira tangata* ("life spirit of mortals"), and for them, a gene has *mauri* (a "life force"). Given these spiritual associations, genetic investigations of Maori human DNA could not proceed until the Maori themselves became actively involved in the research.

Together with other researchers, Maori geneticist Adele Whyte has examined sex-linked genetic markers, namely mitochondrial DNA in women and Y chromosomes in men.[d] She recently calculated that the number of Polynesian females required to found New Zealand's Maori population probably ranged between 170 and 230 women. If the original fleet sailing to Aotearoa consisted of seven large canoes, it may have carried a total of about 600 people (men, women, and children).

A comparison of the DNA of Maori with that of Polynesians across the Pacific Ocean and peoples from Southeast Asia reveals a genetic map of very ancient Maori migration routes. Mitochondrial DNA, which is passed along virtually unchanged from mothers to their children, provides a genetic clock linking today's Polynesians to southern Taiwan's indigenous coastal peoples, showing that female ancestors originally set out from that island off the southeast coast of China about 6,000 years ago.[e] In the next few thousand years, they migrated by way of the Philippines and then hopped south and east from island to island. Adding to their gene pool in the course of later generations, Melanesian males from New Guinea and elsewhere joined the migrating bands before arriving in Aotearoa. In short, Maori cultural traditions in New Zealand are generally substantiated by data from molecular biology as well as anthropology. ■

Biocultural Question

Why do you think the Maori view genealogy as sacred and attach certain prohibitions to it?

[a]Buck, P. H. (1938). *Vikings of the Pacific.* Chicago: University Press of Chicago.
[b]Hanson, A. (1989). The making of the Maori: Culture invention and its logic. *American Anthropologist 91* (4), 890–902.
[c]Mead, A. T. P. (1996). Genealogy, sacredness, and the commodities market. *Cultural Survival Quarterly 20* (2).
[d]Whyte, A. L. H. (2005). Human evolution in Polynesia. *Human Biology 77* (2), 157–177.
[e]Gene study suggests Polynesians came from Taiwan. (2005, July 4). Reuters.

Unilineal Descent

Unilineal descent (sometimes called *unilateral descent*) establishes descent group membership by a direct line from a common ancestor exclusively through one's male or female line. In this way, each individual is automatically assigned from the moment of birth to his or her mother's or father's group and to that group only.

kinship A network of relatives within which individuals possess certain mutual rights and obligations.

descent group Any kin-group whose members share a direct line of descent from a real (historical) or fictional common ancestor.

unilineal descent Descent traced exclusively through either the male or the female line of ancestry to establish group membership.

In non-Western societies, unilineal descent groups are quite common. Each newborn becomes part of a specific descent group traced by **matrilineal descent** through the female line or by **patrilineal descent** through the male line. In matrilineal societies females are culturally recognized as socially significant, for they are considered responsible for the group's continued existence. In patrilineal societies, this responsibility falls on the male members of the group, thereby enhancing their social importance.

The two major forms of a unilineal descent group (patrilineal or matrilineal) are the lineage and the clan. A **lineage** is a unilineal kin-group descended from a common ancestor or founder who lived four to six generations ago and in which relationships among members can be exactly stated in genealogical terms. A **clan** is an extended unilineal kin-group, often consisting of several lineages, whose members claim common descent from a remote ancestor, usually legendary or mythological.[1]

PATRILINEAL DESCENT AND ORGANIZATION

Patrilineal descent (sometimes called *agnatic* or *male descent*) is the more widespread of the two unilineal descent systems. Through forefathers, the male members of a

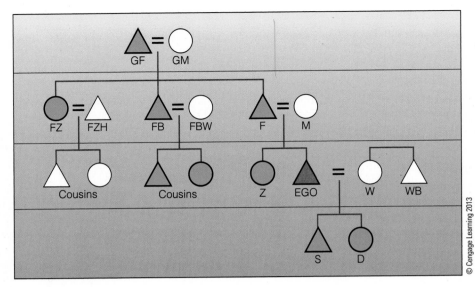

Figure 13.1 Tracing Patrilineal Descent Only the individuals symbolized by a filled-in circle or triangle are in the same descent group as EGO (the central person from whom the degree of each kinship relationship is traced). The abbreviation F stands for father, B for brother, H for husband, S for son, M for mother, Z for sister, W for wife, D for daughter, and G for grand.

© Cengage Learning 2013

patrilineal descent group trace their descent from a common ancestor (▶ **Figure 13.1**). Brothers and sisters belong to the descent group of their father's father, their father, their father's siblings, and their father's brother's children. A man's son and daughter also trace their descent back through the male line to their common ancestor. In the typical patrilineal group, authority over the children rests with the father or his elder brother. A woman belongs to the same descent group as her father and his brothers, but her children cannot trace their descent through them.

MATRILINEAL DESCENT AND ORGANIZATION

Matrilineal descent is traced exclusively through the female line (▶ **Figure 13.2**), just as patrilineal descent is through the male line. However, the matrilineal pattern differs from the patrilineal in that it does not automatically confer gender authority.

Although descent passes through the female line and women may have considerable power, they do not hold exclusive authority in the descent group. They share it with men. Usually, these are the brothers, rather

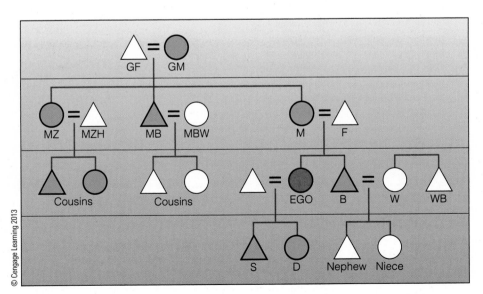

© Cengage Learning 2013

Figure 13.2 Tracing Matrilineal Descent This diagram can be compared with patrilineal descent in Figure 13.1. The two patterns are virtually mirror images. Note that a man cannot transmit descent to his own children.

[1]See Hoebel, E. A. (1949). *Man in the primitive world: An introduction to anthropology* (pp. 646, 652). New York: McGraw-Hill.

than the husbands, of the women through whom descent is traced. Apparently, the adaptive purpose of matrilineal systems is to provide continuous female solidarity within the female work group. Matrilineal systems are usually found in horticultural societies in which women perform much of the work in the house and nearby gardens. Matrilineal descent prevails partly because women's labor as crop cultivators is regarded as vital to the society.

In a matrilineal system, brothers and sisters belong to the descent group of the mother, the mother's mother, the mother's siblings, and the mother's sisters' children. Thus every male belongs to the same descent group as his mother, and his children belong to his wife's descent group, not his.

Although not true of all matrilineal systems, a common feature is the relative weakness of the social tie between wife and husband. A woman's husband lacks authority in the household they share. Her brother, and not the husband-father, distributes goods, organizes work, settles disputes, supervises rituals, and administers inheritance and succession rules. Meanwhile her husband fulfills the same role in his own sister's household. Furthermore, his sister's son rather than his own son inherits his property and status. Thus brothers and sisters maintain lifelong ties with one another, whereas marital ties are easily severed. In matrilineal societies, unsatisfactory marriages are more easily ended than in patrilineal societies.

Other Forms of Descent

Among Samoan Islanders (and many other cultures in the Pacific as well as in Southeast Asia), a person has the option of affiliating with either the mother's or the father's descent group. Known as *ambilineal descent*, such a kin-ordered system provides a measure of flexibility. However, this flexibility also introduces the possibility of dispute and conflict as unilineal groups compete for members. This problem does not arise under *double descent,* or double unilineal descent, a very rare system in which descent is matrilineal for some purposes and patrilineal for others.

Generally, where double descent is traced, the matrilineal and patrilineal groups take action in different spheres of society. For example, among the Yakö of eastern Nigeria, property is divided into both patrilineal possessions and matrilineal possessions.[2] The patrilineage owns perpetually productive resources, such as

▲▲▲ Unlike the Han, the dominant ethnic majority in China who are patrilineal, several ethnic minorities in southwestern China are matrilineal, including the Mosuo. The women in the Mosuo family shown here are blood relatives of one another, and the men are their brothers. Mosuo husbands live apart from their wives, in the households of their sisters.

land, whereas the matrilineage owns consumable property, such as livestock. The legally weaker matriline is somewhat more important in religious matters than the patriline. Through double descent, a Yakö might inherit grazing lands from the father's patrilineal group and certain ritual privileges from the mother's matrilineal group.

Finally, when descent derives from *both* the mother's and father's families equally, anthropologists use the term *bilateral descent*. In such a system people trace their descent from all ancestors, regardless of their gender or side of the family. We may recognize bilateral descent when individuals apply the same genealogical terms to identify similarly related individuals on both sides of the family. For instance, when they speak of a "grandmother" or "grandfather," no indication is given whether these relatives are on the paternal or maternal side of the family.

Bilateral descent exists in various foraging cultures and is also common in many contemporary state societies with agricultural, industrial, or postindustrial economies. For example, although most people in Europe, Australia, and

▲▲

matrilineal descent Descent traced exclusively through the female line of ancestry to establish group membership.

patrilineal descent Descent traced exclusively through the male line of ancestry to establish group membership.

lineage A unilineal kin-group descended from a common ancestor or founder who lived four to six generations ago and in which relationships among members can be exactly stated in genealogical terms.

clan An extended unilineal kin-group, often consisting of several lineages, whose members claim common descent from a remote ancestor, usually legendary or mythological.

▼▼

[2]Forde, C. D. (1968). Double descent among the Yakö. In P. Bohannan & J. Middleton (Eds.), *Kinship and social organization* (pp. 179–191). Garden City, NY: Natural History.

North America typically inherit their father's family name (indicative of a culture's history in which patrilineal descent is the norm), they usually consider themselves as much a member of their mother's family as of their father's.

Descent Within the Larger Cultural System

There is a close relationship between the descent system and a cultural system's infrastructure. Generally, patrilineal descent predominates where male labor is considered of prime importance, as among pastoralists and agriculturalists. Matrilineal descent predominates mainly among horticulturalists in societies where female work in subsistence is especially important. Numerous matrilineal societies are found in southern Asia, one of the earliest cradles of food production in the world. They are also prominent in areas of indigenous North America, South America's tropical lowlands, and parts of Africa.

In many societies an individual has no legal or political status except as a lineage member. Because citizenship is derived from lineage membership and legal status depends on it, political powers are derived from it as well. Lineage endures after the deaths of members with new members continually born into it, and so it has a continuing existence that enables it to act like a corporation, as in owning property, organizing productive activities, distributing goods and labor power, assigning status, and regulating relations with other groups. The descent group also may act as a repository of religious traditions. Ancestor worship, for example, is often a powerful force acting to enhance group solidarity. Thus it is a strong, effective base of social organization.

Whatever form of descent predominates, the kin of both mother and father are important components of the social structure in all societies. Just because descent may be traced patrilineally this does not mean that matrilineal relatives are necessarily unimportant. It simply means that, for purposes of group membership, the mother's relatives are excluded. Similarly, under matrilineal descent, the father's relatives are excluded for purposes of group membership.

By way of example, among the matrilineal Trobriand Islanders in the South Pacific (discussed in Chapter 12), children belong to their mother's descent groups, yet fathers play an important role in their upbringing. Upon marriage, the bride and groom's paternal relatives contribute to the exchange of gifts, and throughout life a man may expect his paternal kin to help him improve his economic and political position in society. Eventually, sons may expect to inherit personal property from their fathers.

As a traditional institution in a kin-ordered society, the descent group often endures in state-organized societies where political institutions are ineffective or weakly developed. Such is the case in many countries of the world today, especially in remote villages difficult to reach by state authorities. Also, because the cultural ideas, values, and practices associated with traditional descent groups may be deeply embedded, such patterns of culture often endure in *diasporic communities* among immigrants who have relocated from their ancestral homelands and retain their distinct cultural identities as ethnic minority groups in their new host countries.

Lineage Exogamy

A common characteristic of lineages is *exogamy*. As defined in the previous chapter, this means that lineage members must find their marriage partners in other lineages. One advantage of exogamy is that competition for desirable spouses within the group is curbed, promoting the group's internal cohesiveness. Lineage exogamy also means that each marriage is more than a union between two individuals; it is also a union that forges or reaffirms an alliance between lineages. This helps to maintain them as components of larger social systems. Finally, lineage exogamy promotes open communication within a society, facilitating the diffusion of knowledge from one lineage to another.

From Lineage to Clan

In the course of time, as generation succeeds generation and new members are born into the lineage, the kin-group's membership may become too large to manage or may outgrow the lineage's resources. When this happens **fission** occurs; that is, the original lineage splits into new, smaller lineages. Usually the members of the new lineages continue to recognize their original relationship to one another. The result of this process is the appearance of a larger kind of descent group: the clan (originally a *Gaelic word simply meaning "offspring"*).

As noted earlier, a clan—typically consisting of several lineages—is an extended unilineal descent group whose members claim common descent from a distant ancestor who may be legendary or mythological; as such, the members cannot trace the precise genealogical links back to that ancestor. This stems from the great genealogical depth of the clan, whose founding ancestor lived so far in the past that the links must be assumed rather than known in detail. A clan differs from a lineage in another respect: It lacks the residential unity that is generally (although not always) characteristic of a lineage's core members. As with the lineage, descent may be patrilineal, matrilineal, or ambilineal. Highland Scots, such as those pictured in this chapter's opening, provide an example of patrilineal clans (or patriclans), which typically trace descent through fathers from a distant founding male ancestor.

Because clan membership is dispersed rather than localized, it usually does not involve a shared holding of tangible property. Instead, it involves collective participation in ceremonial and political matters. Only on special occasions will the membership gather together for specific purposes.

Clans, however, may handle important integrative functions. Like lineages, they may regulate marriage through exogamy. Because of their dispersed membership, they give individuals the right of entry into associated local groups no matter where they are. Members usually are expected to give protection and hospitality to others in the clan.

Lacking the residential unity of lineages, clans frequently depend on symbols—of animals, plants, natural forces, colors, and special objects—to provide members with solidarity and a ready means of identification. These symbols, called *totems,* often are associated with the clan's mythical origin and reinforce for clan members an awareness of their common descent.

▲▲▲ Tsimishian people of Metlakatla, Alaska, raise a memorial totem pole gifted to the community by noted carver David Boxley, a member of the Eagle clan. The tradition of erecting totem poles to commemorate special events endures in several Native American communities in the Pacific Northwest. Carved from tall cedar trees, these spectacular monuments display a clan or lineage's ceremonial property and are prominently positioned as frontal house posts, as markers at gravesites, or at some other place of significance. Often depicting legendary ancestors and mythological animals, the painted carvings symbolically represent a descent group's cultural status and associated privileges in the community.

The word *totem* comes from the Ojibwa American Indian word *ototeman,* meaning "he is a relative of mine." **Totemism** was defined by the British anthropologist A. R. Radcliffe-Brown as a set of customary beliefs and practices "by which there is set up a special system of relations between the society and the plants, animals, and other natural objects that are important in the social life."[3] For example, Hopi Indian matrilineal clans in Arizona carry totemic names such as Bear, Bluebird, Butterfly, Lizard, Spider, and Snake.

Phratries and Moieties

Larger kinds of descent groups are phratries and moieties (▶ **Figure 13.3**). A *phratry* (after the Greek word for "brotherhood") is a unilineal descent group composed of at least two clans that supposedly share a common ancestry, whether or not they really do. Like individuals in the clan, phratry members cannot trace precisely their descent links to a common ancestor, although they firmly believe such an ancestor existed.

If the entire society is divided into only two major descent groups, whether they are equivalent to clans or phratries, each group is called a *moiety* (after the French word *moitié,* for "half"). Members of the moiety believe that they share a common ancestor but cannot prove it through definitive genealogical links. As a rule, the feelings of kinship among members of lineages and clans are stronger than those of members of phratries and moieties. This is primarily due to the much larger size and more diffuse nature of the latter groups.

Since feelings of kinship are often weaker between people from different clans, the moiety system is a cultural invention that keeps clan-based communities together by binding the clans into a social network of obligatory giving and receiving. By institutionalizing reciprocity between groups of clans, the moiety system binds together families who otherwise would not be sufficiently invested in maintaining the commonwealth.

Like lineages and clans, phratries and moieties are often exogamous and so are bound together by marriages between their members. And like clans, they

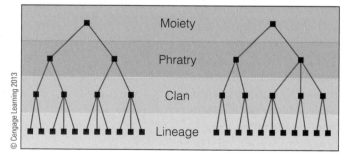

Figure 13.3 Descent Groups This diagram shows the organizational hierarchy of moieties, phratries, clans, and lineages. Each moiety is subdivided into phratries, each phratry is subdivided into clans, and each clan is subdivided into lineages.

▲▲▲▲▲▲▲▲▲▲▲▲▲▲▲▲▲▲▲▲▲▲▲▲▲▲▲▲▲▲▲▲▲▲▲▲▲▲▲

fission The splitting of a descent group into two or more new descent groups.

totemism The belief that people are related to particular animals, plants, or natural objects by virtue of descent from common ancestral spirits.

---

[3]Radcliffe-Brown, A. R. (1931). Social organization of Australian tribes. *Oceana Monographs 1,* 29.

▼▼▼▼▼▼▼▼▼▼▼▼▼▼▼▼▼▼▼▼▼▼▼▼▼▼▼▼▼▼▼▼▼▼▼▼▼▼▼

provide members rights of access to other communities. In a community that does not include one's clan members, one's phratry members are still there to turn to for hospitality. Finally, moieties may perform reciprocal services for one another. Among them, individuals depend on members of the opposite "half" in their community for the necessary mourning rituals when a member of their own moiety dies. Such interdependence between moieties serves to maintain the cohesion of the entire society.

Bilateral Kinship and the Kindred

Important as descent groups are, they are not found in all societies, nor are they the only kinds of extended kingroups to be found. *Bilateral kinship,* a characteristic of most contemporary European and American societies as well as a number of food-foraging cultures, affiliates a person with genetically close relatives (but not in-laws) through both sexes. In other words, the individual traces descent through both parents, all four grandparents, and so forth, recognizing multiple ancestors. Theoretically, one is associated equally with all blood relatives on both the mother's and father's sides of the family. This principle relates an individual lineally to all eight great-grandparents and laterally to all third and fourth cousins.

Since such a huge group is too big to be socially practical, it is usually reduced to a smaller circle of paternal and maternal relatives, called the kindred. The **kindred** is a group that includes an individual's close blood relatives on the maternal and paternal sides of his or her family. It is laterally rather than lineally organized—that is, **EGO,** or the central person from whom the degree of each relationship is traced, is the center of the group (▶ **Figure 13.4**). Thus, unlike a true descent group where the members trace descent from a common ancestor, the kindred is composed of people with a common living relative.

Most North Americans are familiar with the kindred;

those who belong are simply referred to as relatives. It includes those blood relatives on both sides of the family who are seen on important occasions, such as family weddings, reunions, and funerals. In the United States, for example, nearly everyone can identify the members of their kindred up to grandparents and first, if not always second, cousins.

Because of its bilateral structure, a kindred is never the same for any two people except siblings (brothers and sisters). And it is not self-perpetuating—it ceases with EGO's death. Unlike a descent group, it has no constant leader, nor can it easily hold, administer, or pass on property. Because of its vagueness, temporary nature, and changing affiliation, the kindred cannot function as a group except in relation to EGO. In most cases, it cannot organize work, nor can it easily administer justice or assign status.

It can, however, be turned to for aid. In non-Western societies, for example, raiding or trading parties may be composed of kindreds. The group comes together to perform some particular function, shares the results, and then disbands. It also can act as a ceremonial group for rites of passage, such as initiation ceremonies. Traditionally, the kindred is also of importance in many European cultures,

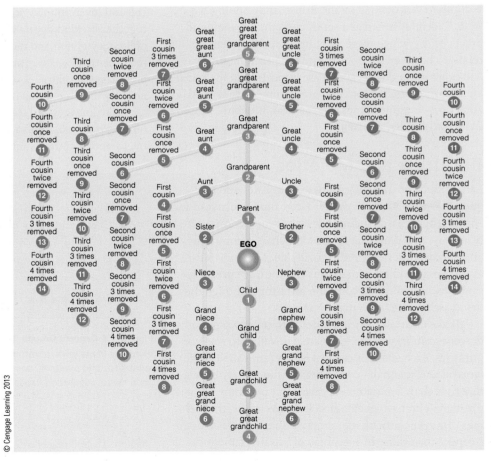

© Cengage Learning 2013

Figure 13.4 EGO and His or Her Kindred The kindred designates a person's exact degree of blood relatedness to other members of the family. This degree of blood relatedness determines not only one's social obligations toward relatives, but also one's rights. For instance, when EGO's wealthy, widowed, and childless great-aunt dies without a will, specific surviving members of her kindred will be legally entitled to inherit from her.

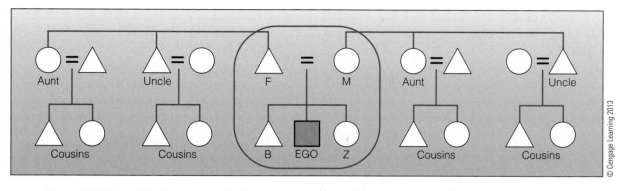

Figure 13.5 Eskimo Kinship System Kinship terminology in the Eskimo system emphasizes the nuclear family (circled). EGO's father and mother are distinguished from EGO's aunts and uncles, and siblings are distinguished from cousins.

where it may serve to help raise bail, compensate a victim's family, or carry out revenge for the murder or injury of a person in one's own kindred. Finally, kindreds also can regulate marriage through exogamy.

Kindreds are frequently found in industrial and postindustrial state societies. The capitalist wage labor conditions of these societies encourage mobility and promote individualism, thereby weakening the importance of a strong kinship organization.

Kinship Terminology and Kinship Groups

A system of organizing people who are relatives into different kinds of groups—whether kindreds, lineages, or clans—influences how relatives are labeled in any given society. Kinship terminology systems vary considerably across cultures, reflecting the positions individuals occupy within their respective societies and helping to differentiate one relative from another. Distinguishing factors include gender, generational differences, or genealogical differences. In the various systems of kinship terminology, any one of these factors may be emphasized at the expense of others.

By looking at the terms people in a particular society use for their relatives, an anthropologist can determine the structure of kin-groups, discern the most important relationships, and sometimes interpret the prevailing attitudes concerning various relationships. For instance, a number of languages use the same term to identify a brother and a cousin, and others have a single word for cousin, niece, and nephew. Some cultures find it useful to distinguish the oldest brother from his younger brothers and have different words for them. And unlike English, many languages discriminate between an aunt who is a mother's sister and one who is a father's sister.

Regardless of the factors emphasized, all kinship terminologies accomplish two important tasks. First, they classify similar kinds of individuals into single specific categories; second, they separate different kinds of individuals into distinct categories. Generally, two or more

kin are merged under the same term when the individuals have more or less the same rights and obligations with respect to the person referring to them as such. This is the case among most English-speaking North Americans, for instance, when someone refers to a mother's sister and a father's sister both as an "aunt." As far as the speaker is concerned, both relatives possess a similar status.

Several different systems of kinship terminology result from the application of the above principles, including the Eskimo, Hawaiian, Iroquois, Crow, Omaha, Sudanese, Kariera, and Aranda systems, each named after the ethnographic example first or best described by anthropologists. The last five of these systems are fascinating in their complexity and are found among only a few of the world's societies. However, to illustrate some of the basic principles involved, we will focus our attention on the first three systems.

The Eskimo System

The Eskimo system, comparatively rare among all the world's systems, is the one used by Euramericans, as well as by a number of food-foraging peoples (including the Inuit and other Eskimos; hence the name). Sometimes referred to as the *lineal system*, the **Eskimo system** emphasizes the nuclear family by specifically identifying mother, father, brother, and sister while lumping together all other relatives into a few large categories (▶ **Figure 13.5**). For example, the father is distinguished

▲▲▲

kindred An individual's close blood relatives on the maternal and paternal sides of his or her family.

EGO The central person from whom the degree of each relationship is traced.

Eskimo system Kinship reckoning in which the nuclear family is emphasized by specifically identifying the mother, father, brother, and sister, while lumping together all other relatives into broad categories such as uncle, aunt, and cousin; also known as the *lineal system*.

▼▼▼

from the father's brother (uncle); but the father's brother is not distinguished from the mother's brother (both are called "uncle"). The mother's sister and father's sister are treated similarly, both called "aunt." In addition, all the sons and daughters of aunts and uncles are called "cousin," thereby making a generational distinction but without indicating the side of the family to which they belong or even their gender.

Unlike other terminologies, the Eskimo system provides separate and distinct terms for the nuclear family members. This is probably because the Eskimo system is generally found in bilateral societies where the dominant kin-group is the kindred, in which only immediate family members are important in day-to-day affairs. This is especially true of modern European and North American societies, where many families are independent—living apart from, and not directly involved with, other relatives except on special occasions. Thus most North Americans (and others) generally distinguish between their closest kin (parents and siblings) but lump together (as aunts, uncles, cousins) other kin on both sides of the family.

The Hawaiian System

The **Hawaiian system** of kinship, common (as its name implies) in Hawaii and other islands in the central Pacific Ocean but found elsewhere as well, is the least complex system in that it uses the fewest terms. The Hawaiian system is also called the *generational system,* because all relatives of the same generation and sex are referred to by the same term (▶ **Figure 13.6**). For example, in one's parents' generation, the term used to refer to one's father is used as well for the father's brother and mother's brother. Similarly, one's mother, mother's sister, and father's sister are all lumped together under a single term. In EGO's generation, male and female cousins are distinguished by gender and are equated with brothers and sisters.

The Hawaiian system reflects the absence of strong unilineal descent, and members on both the father's and the mother's sides are viewed as more or less equal. The siblings of EGO's father and mother are all recognized as being similar relations and are merged under a single term appropriate for their gender. In like manner, the children belonging to the siblings of EGO's parents are related to EGO in the same way as a brother and a sister. Falling under the incest taboo, they are ruled out as potential marriage partners.

The Iroquois System

In the **Iroquois system** of kinship terminology, the father and father's brother are referred to by a single term, as are the mother and mother's sister; however, the father's sister and mother's brother are given separate terms (▶ **Figure 13.7**). In one's own generation, brothers, sisters, and parallel cousins (offspring of parental siblings of the same sex, that is, the children of the mother's sister or the father's brother) of the same sex are referred to by the same terms, which is logical enough considering that they are the offspring of people who are classified in the same category as EGO's actual mother and father. Cross cousins (offspring of parental siblings of opposite sex—that is, the children of the mother's brother or the father's sister) are distinguished by terms that set them apart from all other kin. In fact, cross cousins are often preferred as spouses, for marriage to them reaffirms alliances between related lineages or clans.

Iroquois terminology, named for the Iroquoian Indians of northeastern North America's woodlands, is in fact very widespread and is usually found with unilineal descent groups. It was, for example, the terminology in use until recently in rural Chinese society.

Kinship Terms and New Reproductive Technologies

If systems of kinship reckoning other than one's own seem strange and complex, consider the implications of an event that took place in 1978: the production of the world's first test tube baby, outside the womb, without sexual intercourse. Since then, several million babies have been created in this way, and all sorts of new technolo-

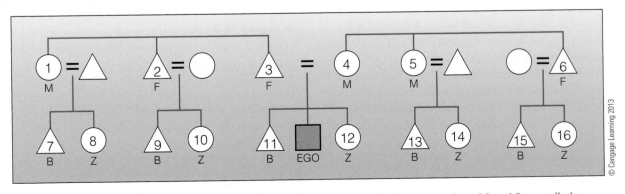

Figure 13.6 Hawaiian Kinship System In the Hawaiian kinship system the men numbered 2 and 6 are called by the same term as father (3); the women numbered 1 and 5 are called by the same term as mother (4). All cousins of EGO's own generation (7–16) are considered brothers (B) and sisters (Z).

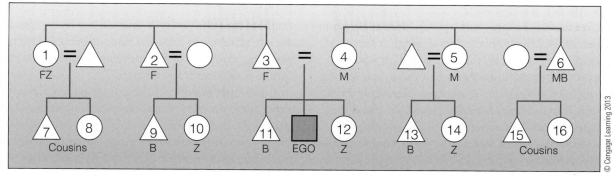

Figure 13.7 Iroquois Kinship System According to the Iroquois system of kinship terminology, EGO's father's brother (2) is called by the same term as the father (3); the mother's sister (5) is called by the same term as the mother (4); but the people numbered 1 and 6 are each referred to by a distinct term. Those people numbered 9–14 are all considered siblings, but 7, 8, 15, and 16 are considered cousins.

gies have become part of the reproductive repertoire. **New reproductive technologies (NRTs)** are alternative means of reproduction such as surrogate motherhood and *in vitro* (Latin for "in glass") fertilization.

These technologies have opened up a mind-boggling array of reproductive possibilities and social relations. For example, if a child is conceived from a donor egg, implanted in another woman's womb to be raised by yet another woman, who is its mother? To complicate matters further, the egg may have been fertilized by sperm from a donor not married to, or in a sexual relationship with, any of these women. Indeed, it has been suggested that we need nearly a dozen different kinship terms to cover the concepts of mother and father in today's changing societies.[4]

Clearly, NRTs challenge previously held notions of parenthood and of kinship. They force us to rethink what being biologically related to others really means. Moreover, they drive home the point that the human capacity for securing relatives is not only impressive and ingenious but also fascinating.

Grouping Beyond Kinship

Because ties of kinship and household are not always sufficient to handle all the challenges of human survival, people also form groups based on gender, age, common interest, and social status.

Grouping by Gender

As shown in preceding chapters, division of labor along gender lines occurs in all human societies. In some cultures, many tasks that men and women undertake may be shared or people may perform work normally assigned to the opposite sex without loss of face. In others, however, men and women are rigidly segregated in what they do. Such is the case in many maritime cultures, where seafarers aboard fishing, whaling, and trading ships are usually men. For instance, we find temporary all-male communities aboard ships of coastal Basque fishermen in northwest Spain, Yupik Eskimo whalers in Alaska, and Swahili merchants sailing along the East African coast. These seafarers commonly leave their wives, mothers, and daughters and young sons behind, sometimes for months at a time.

Clearly demarcated grouping by gender also occurs in many traditional horticultural societies. For instance, among the Mundurucu Indians of Brazil's Amazon rainforest, men and women work, eat, and sleep separately. From age 13 onward males live together in one large house, while women, girls, and preteen boys occupy two or three houses grouped around the men's house. For all intents and purposes, men associate with men, and women with women.

Grouping by Age

Age grouping is so familiar and so important that it and gender have been called the only universal factors that determine a person's positions in society. In North America today, for instance, a child's first friends are usually children of his or her own age. Starting preschool

▲▲▲

Hawaiian system Kinship reckoning in which all relatives of the same sex and generation are referred to by the same term; also known as the *generational system.*

Iroquois system Kinship reckoning in which a father and a father's brother are referred to by a single term, as are a mother and a mother's sister, but a father's sister and a mother's brother are given separate terms. Parallel cousins are classified with brothers and sisters, while cross cousins are classified separately but not equated with relatives of some other generation.

new reproductive technologies (NRTs) Alternative means of reproduction such as surrogate motherhood and in vitro fertilization.

[4]Stone, L. (1998). *Kinship and gender* (p. 272). Boulder, CO: Westview Press.

▼▼▼

or kindergarten with age mates, children typically move through a dozen or more years in the educational system together. At specified ages they are allowed to see certain movies, drive a car, and do things reserved for adults, such as voting, drinking alcoholic beverages, and serving in the military. Ultimately, North Americans retire from their jobs at a specified age and, increasingly, spend the final years of their lives in retirement communities, segregated from the rest of society. As North Americans age, they are labeled "teenagers," "middle-aged," and "senior citizens," whether they like it or not and for no other reason than the number of years they have lived.

Age classification also plays a significant role in non-Western societies that, at a minimum, make distinctions among immature, mature, and older people whose physical powers are waning. In these societies old age often has profound significance, bringing with it the period of greatest respect (for women, it may mean the first social equality with men). Rarely are the elderly shunted aside or abandoned. Even the Inuit of the Canadian Arctic, who are often cited as a people who literally abandon their aged relatives, do so only in truly desperate circumstances, when the group's physical survival is at stake. In all oral tradition societies, elders are the repositories of accumulated wisdom for their people. Recognized as such and no longer expected to carry out many subsistence activities, they play a major role in passing on cultural knowledge to their grandchildren.

All human societies recognize a number of life stages. The demarcation and duration of these stages vary across cultures. Each successive life stage provides distinctive social roles and comes with certain cultural features such as specific patterns of activity, attitudes, obligations, and prohibitions.

In many cultures, the social position of an individual in a specific life stage is also marked by outward appearance in terms of dress, hairstyle, body paint, tattoos, insignia, or some other symbolic distinction. Typically, these stages are designed to help the transition from one age to another, to teach needed skills, or to lend economic assistance. Often they are taken as the basis for the formation of organized groups.

AGE GRADE

An organized category of people with membership on the basis of age is known as an **age grade**. Entry into and transfer out of age grades may be accomplished individually, either by a biological distinction, such as puberty, or by a socially recognized status, such as marriage or childbirth.

Members of an age grade may have much in common—engaging in similar activities, cooperating with one another, and sharing the same orientation and aspirations. A specific time is often ritually established for moving from a younger to an older grade. An example of this is the traditional Jewish ceremony of the *bar mitzvah*

(a Hebrew term meaning "son of the commandment"), marking the time that a 13-year-old boy has reached the age of religious duty and responsibility. *Bat mitzvah,* meaning "daughter of the commandment," is the term for the equivalent ritual for a girl.

Although members of senior groups commonly expect deference from and acknowledge certain responsibilities to their juniors, this does not necessarily mean that one grade is seen as better, or worse, or even more important than another. There can be standardized competition (opposition) between age grades, such as that traditionally between first-year students and sophomores on U.S. college campuses.

AGE SET

In addition to age grades, some societies feature age sets (sometimes referred to as *age classes*). An **age set** is a formally established group of people born during a certain time span who move through the series of age-grade categories together. Members of an age set usually remain closely associated throughout their lives. This is akin to but distinct from the broad and informal North American practice of identifying generation clusters comprised of all individuals born within a particular time frame—such as baby boomers (1946–1960), gen-Xers (1961–1980), and the millennial or Internet generation (1981–2000) (year spans approximate).

The notion of an age set implies strong feelings of loyalty and mutual support. Because such groups may possess property, songs, shield designs, and rituals and are internally organized for collective decision making and leadership, age sets are distinct from simple age grades. Although age is a criterion for group membership in many parts of the world, its most varied and elaborate use is found in several pastoral nomadic groups in East Africa.[5]

Grouping by Common Interest

The rise of urban, industrialized societies in which individuals are often separated from their kin has led to a proliferation of **common-interest associations**—associations that result from the act of joining and are based on sharing particular activities, objectives, values, or beliefs, sometimes rooted in common ethnic, religious, or regional background. Moreover, common-interest associations help people meet a range of needs from companionship to safe work conditions to learning a new language and customs when moving to another country.

Common-interest associations are not, however, restricted to modernizing societies alone. They also are

---

[5]Among numerous references on this, see Sangree, W. H. (1965). The Bantu Tiriki of western Kenya. In J. L. Gibbs Jr. (Ed.), *Peoples of Africa* (pp. 69–72). New York: Holt, Rinehart & Winston.

▲▲▲ The opening parade, shown here, of the elaborate *eunoto* ceremony begins the coming of age of *morans* (warriors) for Maasai subclans of western Kenya. At the end of the ceremony, these men will be in the next age grade—junior adults—ready to marry and start families. Members of the same age set, they were initiated together into the warrior age grade as teenagers. They spent their warrior years raiding cattle (an old tradition that is now illegal but nonetheless still practiced) and protecting their community homes and animal enclosures (from wild animals and other cattle raiders). The *eunoto* ceremony includes a ritual in which mothers shave the warrior's heads, marking the end of many freedoms and the passage to manhood.

found in many traditional societies, and there is some evidence that they arose with the emergence of the first horticultural villages. Furthermore, associations in traditional societies may be just as complex and highly organized as those of countries such as the United States and Canada.

The variety of these associations is astonishing. In the United States, they include sport, hobby, and civic service clubs; religious and spiritual organizations; political parties; labor unions; environmental organizations; urban gangs; private militias; women's and men's clubs of all sorts—the list could go on and on. Their goals may include the pursuit of friendship, recreation, and the promotion of certain values, as well as governing, seeking peace on a local or global scale, and the pursuit or defense of economic interests.

A striking example of a common-interest association that focuses on economic well-being is India's Self-Employed Women's Association (SEWA), headquartered in the northwestern city of Ahmedabad. With more than half a million members, it is the single largest union of informal sector workers in the country. Working with 200 cooperatives and thousands of individual artisans, it has helped to establish support services vital to helping women achieve the goals of full employment and self-reliance, such as savings and credit, health care, child care, insurance, legal aid, capacity building, and communication services. SEWA's Trade Facilitation Centre is currently being expanded into a global network aimed at making women's voices and contributions significant factors in world trade decisions.

Associations also have served to preserve traditional songs, history, language, moral beliefs, and other customs among members of various ethnic minorities. So it is among North American Indians. Since the late 1960s, American Indians have been experiencing a resurgence of ethnic pride after generations of forced assimilation and schooling designed to stamp out their cultural identity. One satisfying way of publicly expressing pride in their ethnic identity and cultural heritage is by way of ceremonial gatherings known as *powwows*, which take place not only on reservations but also in cities where most American Indians now live.[6]

▲▲

age grade An organized category of people based on age; every individual passes through a series of such categories over his or her lifetime.

age set A formally established group of people born during a certain time span who move together through the series of age-grade categories.

common-interest association An association that results from the act of joining, based on sharing particular activities, objectives, values, or beliefs.

▼▼

[6]Ellis, C. (2006). *A dancing people: Powwow culture on the southern plains*. Lawrence: University Press of Kansas.

ASSOCIATIONS IN THE INTERNET AGE

Especially since the early 21st century, people are spending less time socializing face-to-face with others. Instead, millions spend their time with an ever-growing array of electronic and/or digital devices, communicating with others via the Internet and entertaining themselves.

Whether accessed by computer or mobile phone, social networking platforms—such as Facebook with nearly 700 million subscribers worldwide in 2011[7]—enable individuals to text message and exchange images with "friends," continually update their personal or other information, and engage in microblogging. In the United States, teenagers text message on average more than 100 times a day—a figure probably not much different from that of their age mates in Japan, Australia, and many other technologically advanced societies.

People in societies all across the globe now have direct access to an ever-expanding range of relatively cheap digital communication tools—especially mobile phones. Today there are over 4 billion mobile phone subscriptions worldwide, and 80 percent of the world's population is within mobile coverage.[8]

Excluding time spent texting or talking on phones, U.S. children ages 8 to 18 now spend more than 7½ hours a day using entertainment media. About 2 hours of this daily media consumption occurs on mobile devices—cell phones, iPods, or handheld video game players. Another hour consists of "old" content—TV or music—delivered through new pathways on a computer.[9]

These technologies are now also used by office managers, city mayors, law enforcers, and school principals for purposes of quick communication and have become instrumental in the functioning of many social groups. Importantly, in highly mobile societies and globally interconnected cultures, these new social media make it possible to build and expand social networks regardless of geographic distance and across international boundaries.

Grouping by Social Status in Stratified Societies

Social stratification is a common and powerful structuring force in many of the world's societies. Basically,

© David Sacks/Getty Images

▲▲▲ High-speed wireless networks in affluent Japan, as in many other parts of the world, make it possible for people to continually tap into information and exchange messages and images by means of portable computers or, increasingly, web-enabled mobile telephones. For Japanese commuters, who spend hours staring at tiny screens on their mobiles while riding the world's most extensive network of subways and commuter trains, blogging is especially popular.

stratified societies are those in which people are hierarchically divided and ranked into social strata, or layers, and do not share equally in basic resources that support income, status, and power. Members of the bottom layers (or strata) typically have fewer resources, lower prestige, and less power than those in top-ranked layers. In addition, they usually face greater or more oppressive restrictions and obligations and must work harder for far less material reward and social recognition.

In short, social stratification amounts to culturally institutionalized inequality. Stratified societies stand in sharp contrast to **egalitarian societies**, in which everyone has about the same rank and power and about the same access to basic resources. In these societies, social values of communal sharing are culturally emphasized and approved; wealth hoarding and elitist pretensions are despised, belittled, or ridiculed. As we saw in earlier chapters, foraging societies are characteristically egalitarian, although there are some exceptions.

---

stratified societies Societies in which people are hierarchically divided and ranked into social strata, or layers, and do not share equally in basic resources that support income, status, and power.

egalitarian societies Societies in which everyone has about the same rank and power and about the same access to basic resources.

[7]Lee, A. (2011, June 13). Facebook users DROP in U.S.: Millions left the social network in May 2011. *Huffington Post.* http://www.huffingtonpost.com/2011/06/13/facebook-users-members-us-growth-drops-may-2011_n_875810.html (retrieved September 14, 2011).

[8]Must, B., & Ludewig, K. (2010). Mobile money: Cell phone banking in developing countries. *Policy Matters Journal 7* (2), 26–33.

[9]Rideout, V. J., Foehr, U. G., & Roberts, D. F. (2010, January). Generation M²: Media in the lives of 8- to18-year-olds (p. 2). A Kaiser Family Foundation Study. Menlo Park, CA: Henry J. Kaiser Family Foundation. http://www.kff.org/entmedia/upload/8010.pdf (retrieved September 15, 2011).

SOCIAL CLASS AND CASTE

A **social class** may be defined as a category of individuals in a stratified society who have equal or nearly equal prestige according to the system of evaluation. The qualification "nearly equal" is important, for a certain amount of inequality may occur even within a given class. Class distinctions are not always clear-cut and obvious in societies that have a wide and continuous range of differential privileges.

A **caste** is a closed social class in a stratified society in which membership is determined by birth and fixed for life. The opposite of the principle that all humans are born equal, the caste system is based on the belief that humans are born and remain unequal until death. Castes are strongly endogamous, and offspring are automatically members of their parents' caste.

The classic ethnographic example of a caste system is the traditional Hindu caste system of India (also found in some other parts of Asia), which encompasses a complex ranking of social groups on the basis of "ritual purity." Each of some 2,000 different castes considers itself as a distinct community higher or lower than other castes, although their particular ranking varies among geographic regions and over time.

The different castes are associated with specific occupations and customs, such as food habits and styles of dress, along with rituals involving notions of purity and pollution. Ritual pollution is the result of contact such as touching, accepting food from, or having sex with a member of a lower caste. To remain pure, traditional Hindus are taught to avoid everyone and everything considered taboo to their caste. For this reason, castes are always endogamous. Differences in caste rankings are traditionally justified by the religious doctrine of *karma*, a belief that one's status in this life is determined by one's deeds in previous lifetimes.

All of these castes, or *jatis*, are organized into four basic orders or *varnas* (literally meaning "colors"), distinguished partly by occupation and ranked in order of descending religious status of purity (▶ **Figure 13.8**). The religious foundation for this social hierarchy comes from a 2,000-year-old sacred text, the Laws of Manu, which traditional Hindus consider to be the highest authority on their cultural institutions. It defines the Brahmans as the purest and therefore highest *varna*.

As priests and lawgivers, Brahmans represent the world of religion and learning. Next comes the order of

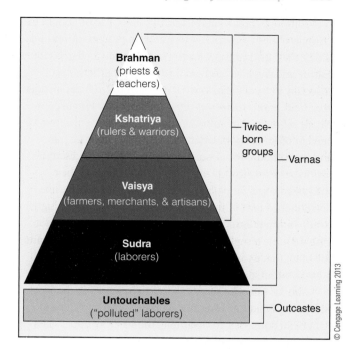

Figure 13.8 The Hindu Caste System Hindu castes are organized into four "grades of being" called *varnas* ("colors") that determine what members are permitted to do, touch, or eat; where they live; how they dress; and who they can marry. The highest-ranking order Brahman is associated with the color white, below which are the Kshatriya (red) and Vaisya (brown). Members born into these *varnas* are believed to have been reincarnated from a morally correct earlier life in a lower-ranked order. Below these three are the Sudra (black), who make a living as laborers. Lower still are the "polluted" laborers, the Untouchables, who are charged with cleaning the streets and with the collection and disposal of garbage, animal carcasses, and sewage. Brahmans and members of other *varnas* avoid direct contact with Untouchables, believing that touching or accepting food from them would result in ritual pollution.

fighters and rulers, known as the Kshatriyas. Below them are the Vaisyas (merchants and traders), who are engaged in commercial, agricultural, and pastoral pursuits. At the bottom are the Sudras (artisans and laborers), an order required to serve the other three *varnas* and who also make a living by handicrafts.

Falling outside the *varna* system is a fifth category of degraded individuals known as Untouchables. They do the dirty work in society—collecting garbage, removing animal carcasses, cleaning streets, and disposing of dung, sewage, and other refuse. Commonly associated with filth and regarded as impure by fellow Hindus, these "outcastes" can own neither land nor the tools of their trade. They constitute a large pool of cheap labor at the beck and call of those controlling economic and political affairs.

▲▲

social class A category of individuals in a stratified society who have equal or nearly equal prestige according to the system of evaluation.

caste A closed social class in a stratified society in which membership is determined by birth and fixed for life.

▼▼

Although India's national constitution of 1950 sought to officially abolish the caste system and the practice of untouchability, the caste system remains deeply entrenched in Hindu culture and is still widespread throughout southern Asia, especially in rural India. In what has been called India's hidden apartheid, entire villages in many Indian states remain completely segregated by caste. Untouchables represent about 15 percent of India's population—nearly 170 million people—and must endure social isolation, humiliation, and discrimination based exclusively on their birth status. Even their shadows are seen as polluting. They may not cross the line dividing their part of the village from that occupied by higher castes, may not drink water from public wells, and may not visit the same temples as the higher castes. Their children are still often made to sit at the back of classrooms, and in rural areas some are denied access to education altogether.[10]

Similar castelike situations exist elsewhere in the world. In Bolivia, Ecuador, and several other South and Central American countries, for example, the wealthy upper class is almost exclusively of European descent and rarely intermarries with people of American Indian or African descent. In contrast, the lower class of working poor in those countries is primarily made up of darker-skinned laborers and peasants. Likewise, most European stratified societies were historically organized in closed social classes known as *estates*—ranked as clergy, nobility, and citizens—each with distinctive political rights (privileges). Titles and forms of address hierarchically identified these estates, and they were publicly distinguished by dress and codes of behavior.

---

[10]Office of the United Nations Higher Commissioner for Human Rights, Committee on the Elimination of Racial Discrimination, India. (2007, March). Consideration of state reports (p. 3). www2. ohchr.org/english/bodies/cerd/cerds70.htm (retrieved September 15, 2011); see also Human Rights Watch and the Center for Human Rights and Global Justice. (2007). Hidden apartheid: Caste discrimination against India's "Untouchables." http://www.chrgj.org/docs/IndiaCERDShadowReport.pdf (retrieved September 15, 2011).

[11]Boshara, R. (2003, January/February). Wealth inequality: The $6,000 solution. *Atlantic Monthly.* See also Kennickell, A. B. (2003, November). *A rolling tide: Changes in the distribution of wealth in the U.S. 1989–2001.* Levy Economics Institute.

HISTORICAL RACIAL SEGREGATION IN SOUTH AFRICA AND THE UNITED STATES

Other than social class, caste, and estate, the hierarchy in a stratified society may be based on ethnic origin or skin color. For instance, dark-skinned individuals culturally classified as colored or black may encounter social rules excluding them from certain jobs or neighborhoods and making it difficult if not impossible to befriend or marry someone with a lighter skin color. (As we discussed in Chapter 7, the terms *race, black,* and *white* are purely social constructions, with no basis in biology. For simplicity, we use them here without quotation marks.)

One of the best-known historical examples of a pluralistic country with social stratification based on the notion of race is South Africa. From 1948 to 1992, a minority of 4.5 million people of European descent sought to protect its power and "racial purity" by means of a repressive regime of racial segregation and discrimination against 25 million indigenous black Africans. Known as *apartheid* (an Afrikaans-Dutch term meaning "segregation" or "separation"), this white superiority ideology officially relegated dark-skinned Africans to a low-ranking stratum.

Until the mid-20th century, institutionalized racial segregation also prevailed in the United States, where the country's ruling upper class was historically comprised exclusively of individuals of European (Caucasian or white) descent. For generations, it was against the law for whites to marry blacks or American Indians. Even after black slavery was abolished in 1863, such racial mixing prohibitions remained in force in many states from Maine to Florida. Today, despite significant steps toward equality since enactment of civil rights laws in the 1960s that officially prohibited race-based discrimination, American blacks as a racial minority (with notable individual exceptions) still rank lower in terms of wealth and health.[11] The following Original Study painfully illustrates the effects of this institutionalized racism—while also showing the role public education can play in challenging stereotypes and inequities.

ORIGINAL STUDY

African Burial Ground Project

By Michael Blakey

In 1991, construction workers in lower Manhattan unearthed what turned out to be part of a six-acre African burial ground containing remains of an estimated 10,000 enslaved African captives brought to New York in the 17th and 18th centuries to build the city and provide the labor for its thriving economy. The discovery sparked controversy as the African American public held protests and prayer vigils to stop the part of a federal building project that nearly destroyed the site. In 1993, the site was designated a National Historic Landmark, which opened the door to researching and protecting the site.

As a biological anthropologist and African American, I had a unique opportunity to work together with the descendant African American community to develop a plan that included both extensive biocultural research and the humane retention of the sacred nature of the site, ultimately through reburial and the creation of a fitting memorial. The research also involved archaeological and historical studies that used a broad African diasporic context for understanding the lifetime experiences of these people who were enslaved and buried in New York.

Studying a sample population of 419 individuals from the burial ground, our team used an exhaustive range of skeletal biological methods, producing a database containing more than 200,000 observations of genetics, morphology, age, sex, growth and development, muscle development, trauma, nutrition, and disease. The bones revealed an unmistakable link between biology and culture: physical wear and tear of an entire community brought on by the social institution of slavery.

We now know, based on this study, that life for Africans in colonial New York was characterized by poor nutrition, grueling physical labor that enlarged and often tore muscles, and death rates that were unusually high for 15- to 25-year-olds. Many of these young adults died soon after arriving on slaving ships. Few Africans lived past 40 years of age, and less than 2 percent lived beyond 55. Church records show strikingly different mortality trends for the Europeans of New York: About eight times as many English as Africans lived past 55 years of age.

Forty-percent of the remains unearthed were those of children under the age of 12. Skeletal research also showed that those Africans who died as children and were most likely to have been born in New York exhibited stunted and disrupted growth and exposure to high levels of lead pollution—unlike those who had been born in Africa (and were distinguishable because they had filed teeth). Fertility was very low among enslaved women in New York, and infant mortality was high. In these respects, this northern colonial city was very similar to South Carolina and the Caribbean to which its economy was tied—regions where conditions for African captives were among the harshest.

Individuals in this deeply troubling burial ground came from warring African states including Calibar, Asante, Benin, Dahomey, Congo, Madagascar, and many others—states that wrestled with the European demand for human slaves. They resisted their enslavement through rebellion, and they resisted their dehumanization by carefully burying their dead and preserving what they could of their cultures.

There is something about human remains that is so compelling. While many people find them disturbing, in the proper context science can give the public a chance to get close to these people, to imagine their lives, their era, their challenges—and what these have to tell us about our own lives and times.

The remains of certain individuals stood out to me and stirred my imagination. Among them is a man between 26 and 35 years old, who we labeled "101." His skull shape appears to be West African, and one of the chemicals we analyzed, strontium, points towards him having been born in Africa. And another chemical, lead, is somewhere intermediate between New York and West Africa. Given this and evidence of treponemal, a tropical disease, he may have been raised in the Caribbean. Also of note, he has elegant filed teeth, plus bone evidence of hard work and some healed fractures in his spine. But perhaps the most important thing about this particular individual is the heart-shaped symbol discovered on his coffin lid. That symbol nagged me for a while. I was sure that I had seen it somewhere before, but it was vague to me.

One day, early on in the project, I attended an African American cultural event at Howard University in Washington, DC. An image on the program cover grabbed my attention. It looked like the same symbol I had seen on 101's coffin. I asked a colleague at the New York burial ground lab to send me a drawing of the symbol found on the coffin. Then I took it to an art historian at Howard who specializes in this area—and tried my best not to appear excited. He too recognized it as a version of a symbol called the *sankofa*.

The meaning of this historic symbol is entirely fitting for an African burial site. It stands for the spiritual connection between the past and the present—the idea that we need to go back and search the past so that it can be a guide in the present. The *sankofa* symbolizes reverence for the ancestors and respect for elders. Disseminating knowledge of this symbol and its message, the African Burial Ground helps reverse the sort of historical amnesia that allows the repetition of social injustices.

As the largest bioarchaeological site of its kind, this African Burial Ground has provided significant opportunities to raise public awareness of colonial African heritage, especially in northern states. Of particular note is the 2003 Rites of Ancestral Return—a ceremony in which the remains of the 419 individuals excavated from the site were re-interred. The ceremony began with a procession of about 2,500 people walking in silence to the burial ground. I joined the researchers behind several hundred children, mostly of primary school age. These youngsters, dressed in little dark red uniforms and walking with a kind of reverent orderliness, really touched me. "They're the future," I thought to myself. One day they'll tell their children and grandchildren about the African Burial Ground. They are part of another step toward a more complete understanding of African American history—a more complete understanding of themselves and a more complete identity. ■

Adapted from Blakey, M. L. (2003). African Burial Ground Project, Department of Anthropology, College of William & Mary. Reprinted by permission of the author.

© A. J. Giordano/Corbis SABA

▲▲▲ Excavation in lower Manhattan revealed a burial ground with the remains of some 10,000 enslaved Africans brought to New York in the 17th and 18th centuries. The site is now a national monument featuring a distinctive memorial that commemorates and communicates the story of this all-important historical archaeological project. The memorial is operated by the U.S. National Park Service.

INDICATORS OF SOCIAL STATUS

Social classes are manifested in various ways, including *symbolic indicators*. For example, in the United States certain activities and possessions are indicative of class: occupation (a garbage collector has different class status than a medical specialist); wealth (rich people are generally in a higher social class than poor people); dress ("white collar" versus "blue collar"); form of recreation (upper-class people are expected to play golf rather than shoot pool down at the pool hall—but they can shoot pool at home or in a club); residential location (upper-class people do not ordinarily live in slums); kind of car; and so on. All sorts of status symbols are indicative of class position, including measures such as the number of bathrooms in a person's house. That said, class rankings do not fully correlate with economic status or pay scales. The earnings of a unionized car-factory laborer are historically above those of the average college humanities professor who has a doctorate.

MAINTAINING STRATIFICATION

In any system of stratification, those who dominate proclaim their supposedly superior status by means of a powerful ideology, commonly asserting it through intimidation or propaganda (in the form of gossip, media, religious doctrine, and so forth) that presents their position as normal, natural, hereditary, divinely guided, or at least well deserved. As U.S. anthropologist Laura Nader points out, "Systems of thought develop over time and reflect the interests of certain classes or groups in the society who manage to universalize their beliefs and values."[12]

So it is with certain religious ideologies that effectively assert that the social order is divinely fixed and therefore not to be questioned. In India, for example, Hindu belief in reincarnation and an incorruptible supernatural power that assigns people to a particular caste position, as a reward or punishment for the deeds and misdeeds of past lives, justifies one's position in this life. If, however, individuals faithfully perform the duties appropriate to their caste in this lifetime, then they can expect to be reborn into a higher caste in a future existence. Thus, in the minds of orthodox Hindus, one's caste position is something earned rather than the accident of birth that it appears to be to outside observers.

SOCIAL MOBILITY

Most stratified societies offer at least some **social mobility**—upward or downward change in one's social class position. The prospects of improving status and wealth help to ease the strains inherent in any system of inequality.

Social mobility is most common in societies made up of independent nuclear families where the individual is closely tied to fewer people—especially when neolocal residence is the norm, and it is assumed that individuals will leave their family of birth when they become adults. In such social settings—through hard work, occupational success, opportune marriage, and disassociation from the lower-class family in which they grew up—individuals can more easily move up in status and rank.

Societies that permit a great deal of upward and downward mobility are referred to as *open-class societies*—although the openness is apt to be less in practice than members hope or believe. In the United States, despite its rags-to-riches ideology, most mobility involves a move up or down only a notch; however, if this continues in a family over several generations, it may add up to a major change. Nonetheless, U.S. society makes much of relatively rare examples of great upward mobility consistent with its cultural values and does its best to overlook the numerous cases of little or no upward (not to mention downward) mobility.

Caste societies exemplify *closed-class societies* because of their severe institutionalized limits on social mobility. Yet even the Hindu caste system, with its guiding ideology that all social hierarchies within it are eternally fixed, has a degree of flexibility and mobility. Although individuals cannot move up or down the caste hierarchy, whole groups can do so depending on claims they assert for higher ranking and on how well they can convince or manipulate others into acknowledging their claims.

During the past half century, political activism has stirred among members of India's vast underclass of Untouchables and lowest Sudra castes—who refer to themselves collectively as *Dalits*, a Sanskrit name meaning "crushed" or "suppressed." Historically discriminated against and economically exploited, they now number about 200 million scattered all across this massive South Asian country of 1.15 billion people. A growing political force, Dalits are now organizing themselves on local, regional, and even national levels. Their movement for civil rights is facilitated by increased access to digital communication technology.

Within the vast underclass of Dalits, women and children are especially vulnerable, barely surviving at the very bottom of Indian society. In recent years, however, Dalit women in many parts of India have joined hands with the intention of claiming social justice. Perhaps best known among them is a group in India's northern province of Uttar Pradesh who vigorously protest government discrimination and official corruption and strive to create opportunities for women. Dressed in

---

[12]Nader, L. (1997). Controlling processes: Tracing the dynamic components of power. *Current Anthropology 38*, 271.

vibrant pink saris and wielding *lathi*, traditional Indian fighting sticks, they are known as the Gulabi ("Pink") Gang. They demand justice—shaming and intimidating abusive men and corrupt officials who deny them equal access to water, farming supplies, and other resources. As one of these "pink vigilantes" puts it, "On my own I have no rights, but together, as the Gulabi Gang, we have power."[13]

The Dalit women's movement in India illustrates that even long-established and culturally entrenched hierarchical orders are not immune to challenge, reform, or revolution. Great disparities in wealth, power, and privilege may persist and even grow in many parts of the world, but there are notable social changes in the opposite direction. In the course of the 19th century, slavery was abolished and declared illegal nearly everywhere in the world. And in the last century, civil rights, women's rights, and other human rights movements resulted in social and legal reforms, as well as changes in ideas and values regarding hierarchical social orders in many countries.

▲▲▲ India's Gulabi Gang, sometimes referred to as "pink vigilantes," challenge their country's repressive status quo. Most of them are Dalits (Untouchables and members of the lowest castes). Dressed in pink saris (*gulabi* means "pink" in Hindi), these poor rural women demand justice by shaming and intimidating abusive men as well as corrupt officials who deny them equal access to water, farming supplies, and other resources.

---

[13]Dunbar, P. (2008, January 19). The pink vigilantes: The Indian women fighting for women's rights. *Mail Online*. http://www.dailymail.co.uk/news/article-509318/The-pink-vigilantes-The-Indian-women-fighting-womens-rights.html (retrieved September 15, 2011).

social mobility An upward or downward change in one's social class position in a stratified society.

Chapter Checklist

What is kinship, and what role does it play in social organization?

✔ Kinship is a social network of relatives within which individuals possess certain mutual rights and obligations.

✔ In nonindustrial societies, kin-groups commonly deal with challenges that families and households cannot handle alone—challenges involving defense, resource allocation, and the need for cooperative labor. As societies become larger and more complex, formal political systems take over many of these matters.

What are the different types of descent groups in kin-ordered societies?

✔ A descent group is any kin-group whose members share a direct line of descent from a real (historical) or fictional common ancestor.

✔ Unilineal descent establishes kin-group membership exclusively through the male or female line. Patrilineal decent (agnatic or male descent) is traced through the male line and matrilineal through the female line. In all societies the kin of both mother and father are important elements in the social structure, regardless of how descent group membership is defined. However, unlike the patrilineal pattern, matrilineal descent does not automatically confer gender authority.

✔ There is a close relationship between the descent system and a cultural system's infrastructure. Generally, patrilineal descent predominates where male labor is considered of prime importance, as among pastoralists and agriculturalists. Matrilineal descent predominates mainly among horticulturalists where female work in subsistence is especially important.

✔ The two major forms of a unilineal descent group (patrilineal or matrilineal) are the lineage and the clan. A lineage is a unilineal kin-group descended from a common ancestor or founder who lived four to six generations ago and in which relationships among members can be exactly stated in genealogical terms. A clan is an extended unilineal kin-group, often consisting of several lineages, whose members claim common descent from a remote ancestor, usually legendary or mythological.

✔ Double descent is a very rare system in which descent is matrilineal for some purposes and patrilineal for others. Ambilineal descent provides a measure of flexibility in that an individual has the option of affiliating with either the mother's or father's descent group. When descent derives from both the mother's and father's families equally, anthropologists use the term *bilateral descent*.

✔ Since lineages are commonly exogamous (meaning that members must marry outside the lineage), sexual competition within the group is largely avoided. In addition, marriage of a group member represents an alliance of two lineages. Lineage exogamy also serves to maintain open communication within a society and fosters the exchange of information among lineages.

✔ Unlike lineages, clan residence is usually dispersed rather than localized. In the absence of residential unity, clan identification is often reinforced by totems: symbols from nature that remind members of their common ancestry. A phratry is a unilineal descent group of two or more clans that supposedly share a common ancestry. When a society is divided into two halves, each half consisting of one or more clans, these two major descent groups are called moieties.

✔ In a bilateral descent system, individuals are affiliated equally with the mother's and father's families. Such a large group is socially impractical and is usually reduced to a small circle of paternal and maternal relatives called the kindred. A kindred is never the same for any two people except siblings. Bilateral kinship and kindred organization are likely to prevail in societies where the nuclear family predominates.

What does kinship terminology reveal about human relations?

✔ Kinship terminology varies across cultures. The terms people use for their relatives can reveal the structure of kinship groups, the importance of certain relationships, and prevailing attitudes about specific kin. Some languages use the same term to identify a brother and a cousin, suggesting that these kin are of equal importance to an individual. Kin merged under the same term have the same basic rights and obligations with respect to the person referring to them as such.

✔ The Hawaiian system is the simplest system of kinship terminology, with all relatives of the same generation and gender referred to by the same term.

✔ The Eskimo system, also used by English-speaking North Americans and many others, emphasizes the nuclear family and merges all other relatives in a given generation into a few large, generally undifferentiated categories.

✔ In the Iroquois system, a single term is used for a father and his brother and another for a mother and her sister. Parallel cousins are equated with brothers and sisters but distinguished from cross cousins.

✔ New reproductive technologies separating conception from sexual intercourse and eggs from wombs challenge traditional notions of kinship and gender, resulting in new social categories.

Beyond kinship, what kinds of groups do humans form and why?

✔ Since ties of kinship and household are not always sufficient to handle all the challenges of human survival, people also form groups based on gender, age, common interest, and social status.

✔ Grouping by gender separates men and women to varying degrees in different societies; in some they may be together much of the time, while in others they may spend much of their time apart, even to the extreme of eating and sleeping separately.

✔ Age grouping is another form of association that may augment or replace kinship grouping. An age grade is a category of people organized by age. Some societies have age sets also, which are comprised of individuals who are initiated into an age grade at the same time and move together through a series of life stages. The most varied use of age grouping is found in African societies south of the Sahara. Among the Maasai of East Africa, for example, age sets pass through four successive age grades.

✔ Common-interest associations are linked with rapid social change and urbanization. They have increasingly assumed the roles formerly played by kinship or age groups. In urban areas they help new arrivals cope with the changes demanded by the move. Common-interest associations also are seen in traditional societies, and their roots may be found in the first horticultural villages.

✔ The Internet has lessened face-to-face interaction while opening up new forms of virtual communication through social media.

What is a stratified society, and what are the possibilities and limitations of upward and downward social mobility?

✔ A stratified society is divided into two or more categories of people who do not share equally in basic resources that support income, status, and power. Societies may be stratified by gender, age, social class, or caste.

✔ A social class is comprised of individuals who enjoy equal or nearly equal prestige according to a society's system of evaluation. Class distinctions are not always clear-cut and obvious in societies that have a wide and continuous range of differential privileges. Social classes can be expressed through symbolic indicators like activities and possessions that mark class position.

✔ A caste is a closed social class in which membership is determined by birth and fixed for life. The traditional Hindu caste system of India (also found in some other parts of Asia) is the classic ethnographic example of this system, which encompasses a complex ranking of some 2,000 castes associated with specific occupations and customs, including food habits and styles of dress and rituals involving notions of purity and pollution. These castes are organized into four basic orders or *varnas*.

✔ The hierarchy in a stratified society may also be based on ethnic origin or skin color. One example of stratification based on the notion of race is South Africa where people of European descent maintained power through apartheid—a repressive regime of racial segregation and discrimination against indigenous black Africans from 1948 to 1992.

✔ Caste societies exemplify closed-class societies because of their severe institutionalized limits on social mobility, yet even in these systems there is some flexibility through group action, as seen in the Dalit movement in India.

✔ Open-class societies are those with the easiest mobility, although the move is usually limited to one rung up or down the social ladder. The degree of mobility is related to social factors such as access to higher education or the prevailing type of family organization. Where the extended family is the norm, mobility tends to be severely limited. The independent nuclear family makes mobility easier.

Questions for Reflection

1. In some North American Indian languages, the English word for loneliness is translated as "I have no relatives." What does that tell you about the importance of kinship in these Native cultures?

2. Why do you think that one of the simplest kinship terminology systems, the Eskimo system, is functionally adequate for most Europeans, North Americans, and others living in complex modern societies?

3. One major reason anthropologists are so interested in understanding a culture's kinship terminology system is that it offers a quick but crucially important insight into a group's social structure. Why do you think this is especially true for traditional communities of foragers, herders, and farmers but is less so for urban neighborhoods in industrial and postindustrial societies?

4. Do you use a networking platform such as Facebook or Twitter to stay in touch with relatives, friends, schoolmates, or colleagues? Where are these individuals in your digital social network geographically located? How often do you see them in real space, and is your interaction with them different in person than online?

5. Slavery in the United States was officially abolished in 1863, caste-based discrimination of Untouchables was constitutionally outlawed in India in 1950, and race-based segregation in South Africa officially ended with the abolition of apartheid in 1992. Considering these important political changes, do you think that social repression against these groups has now ended for good?

Key Terms

kinship
descent group
unilineal descent
matrilineal descent
patrilineal descent
lineage
clan
fission

totemism
kindred
EGO
Eskimo system
Hawaiian system
Iroquois system
new reproductive technologies
(NRTs)

age grade
age set
common-interest association
stratified societies
egalitarian societies
social class
caste
social mobility

Online Study Resources

Login to **www.cengagebrain.com** to access the resources your instructor has assigned and to purchase materials. For this book, you can access:

CourseMate
Access chapter-specific learning tools including flashcards, glossaries, practice quizzes, videos, and more in your Anthropology CourseMate.

VISUAL ESSENCE

In all societies, from the largest to the smallest, people must figure out who gets what, when, where, and how. In the process, they try to mobilize, contest, and control power, and some are better at it than others. Fundamentally, this is what politics is about. Individuals, kin-groups, or larger coalitions defend or dispute an established social and economic order as they fight or negotiate with rival factions and foreign neighbors. Political organization takes many forms, of which the state is just one. In traditional kin-ordered societies, political power is neither centralized nor monopolized, but is shared by social networks of extended families, lineages, clans, or tribes. Representing their communities, leaders gather periodically to discuss and resolve collective problems and challenges. Among the Pashtun of Afghanistan and Pakistan, such a political assembly is called a *jirga*—as shown in this photo of tribal elders attending a Loya Jirga (Grand Assembly) in Afghanistan's capital city of Kabul. Like members of the U.S. Congress, French Parliament, or Japan Diet (legislature), these Pashtun delegates try to settle disputes, decide on treaties, discuss trade issues, and deal with other important political matters such as law and order in their war-torn homelands.

14 Politics, Power, and Violence

ironically, the groups formed to facilitate much-needed human cooperation also create dynamics that may lead to conflict within and between groups. We see this in a wide range of situations, from riots among fans rooting for different soccer teams to bloody conflicts between neighboring religious or ethnic groups. Therefore, every society must have ways and means for resolving internal conflicts and preventing the breakdown of its social order. Moreover, each society must possess the capacity to deal with neighboring societies in peaceful or troubled times.

Today, throughout the world, state governments play a central role in maintaining social order. Despite the predominance of state societies, there are still groups where political organization consists of flexible and informal kinship systems whose leaders lack real **power**—the ability of individuals or groups to impose their will upon others and make them do things even against their own wants or wishes. Between these two polarities of kin-ordered and state-organized political systems lies a world of variety.

Systems of Political Organization

The term **political organization** refers to the way power, as the capacity to do something, is accumulated, arranged, executed, and structurally embedded in society, whether in organizing a whale hunt, managing irrigated farmlands, or raising an army. In short, it is the means through which a society creates and maintains social order. It assumes a variety of forms among the peoples of the world, but anthropologists have simplified this complex subject by identifying four basic kinds of political systems: bands, tribes, chiefdoms, and states (▶**Figure 14.1**). The first two are uncentralized systems; the latter two are centralized.

Uncentralized Political Systems

Until recently, many non-Western peoples have had neither chiefs with established rights and duties nor any fixed form of government, as those who live in modern states understand the term. Instead, marriage and

In this chapter you will learn to:

- **Discuss how the issue of power is crucially important in every society.**

- **Distinguish between different types of political leadership and government.**

- **Analyze how politics, economics, and maintenance of (in)equality are linked.**

- **Contrast systems of justice and conflict resolution across cultures.**

- **Talk about war and peace with historical and cross-cultural insight.**

TYPES OF POLITICAL ORGANIZATION

The symbol → indicates that the attribute varies between less and more complex societies of that type.

	BAND	TRIBE	CHIEFDOM	STATE
MEMBERSHIP				
Number of people	Dozens and up	Hundreds and up	Thousands and up	Tens of thousands and up
Settlement pattern	Mobile	Mobile or fixed: 1 or more villages	Fixed: 2 or more villages	Fixed: Many villages and cities
Basis of relationships	Kin	Kin, descent groups	Kin, rank, and residence	Class and residence
Ethnicities and languages	1	1	1	1 or more
GOVERNMENT				
Decision making, leadership	Egalitarian	Egalitarian or Big Man	Centralized, hereditary	Centralized
Bureaucracy	None	None	None, or 1 or 2 levels	Many levels
Monopoly of force and information	No	No	No → Yes	Yes
Conflict resolution	Informal	Informal	Centralized	Laws, judges
Hierarchy of settlement	No	No	No → Paramount village or head town	Capital
ECONOMY				
Food production	No	No → Yes	Yes → Intensive	Intensive
Labor specialization	No	No	No → Yes	Yes
Exchanges	Reciprocal	Reciprocal	Redistributive (tribute)	Redistributive (taxes)
Control of land	Band	Descent group	Chief	Various
SOCIETY				
Stratified	No	No	Yes, ranked by kin	Yes, by class or caste
Slavery	No	No	Some, small-scale	Some, large-scale
Luxury goods for elite	No	No	Yes	Yes
Public architecture	No	No	No → Yes	Yes
Indigenous literacy	No	No	No → Some	Often

© Cengage Learning 2013

Figure 14.1 Four Types of Political Systems This figure outlines the four basic types of political systems: bands, tribes, chiefdoms, and states. Bands and tribes are uncentralized political organizations; chiefdoms and states are centralized.

kinship have formed their principal means of social organization. The economies of these societies are primarily of a subsistence type, and populations are typically small.

Leaders do not have real power to force compliance with the society's customs or rules, but if individuals do not conform, they may become targets of scorn and gossip or even be banished. Important decisions are usually made in a collective manner by agreement among adults. Dissenting members may decide to act with the majority, or they may choose to adopt some other course of action, including leaving the group.

This egalitarian form of political organization provides great flexibility, which in many situations offers an adaptive advantage. Because power in these kin-ordered communities is shared, with nobody exercising exclusive control over collective resources or public affairs, individuals typically enjoy much more freedom than those who are part of larger and more complex political systems.

BANDS

The **band** is a relatively small and loosely organized kin-ordered group that inhabits a specific territory and that may split periodically into smaller extended family groups that are politically and economically independent. Typically, bands are found among food foragers and other nomadic societies where people organize into politically autonomous family groups that usually camp together as long as environmental and subsistence circumstances are favorable. Bands periodically break up into smaller groups to forage for food or visit other relatives. The band is probably the oldest form of political organization, as all humans were once food foragers and remained so until the development of farming and pastoralism over the past 10,000 years.

Because bands are egalitarian and small, numbering at most a few hundred people, no real need exists for formal, centralized political systems. Everyone is related to—and knows on a personal basis—everyone else with whom dealings are required, so there is high value placed on getting along. Conflicts that do arise are usually settled informally through gossip, ridicule, direct negotiation, or mediation. When negotiation or mediation are used, the focus is on reaching a solution considered fair by all concerned parties, rather than on conforming to some abstract law or rule.

Decisions affecting a band are made with the participation of all its adult members, with an emphasis on achieving consensus—a collective agreement—rather than a simple majority. Individuals become leaders by virtue of their abilities and serve in that capacity only as long as they retain the confidence of the community. They have no real power to force people to abide by their decisions. A leader who exceeds what people are willing to accept quickly loses followers.

An example of the informal nature of band leadership is found among the Ju/'hoansi of the Kalahari Desert, mentioned in earlier chapters. Each Ju/'hoansi band is composed of a group of families that live together, linked through kinship to one another and to the headman (or, less often, headwoman).

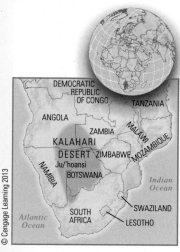

© Cengage Learning 2013

Although each band has rights to the territory it occupies and the resources within it, two or more bands may range over the same land. The headman, called the *kxau,* or "owner," is the focal point for the band's claims on the territory. He or she does not personally own the land or resources but symbolically represents the rights of band members to them. If the headman leaves the area to live elsewhere, people turn to someone else to lead them.

The headman coordinates band migration when resources are no longer adequate for subsistence in a particular habitat. This leader's major duty is to plan when and where the group will move, and when the move begins his or her position is at the beginning of the line. The leader selects the site for the new settlement and has the first choice of a spot for his or her own fire.

There are few other material rewards or duties. For example, a Ju/'hoansi headman is not a judge and does not punish other band members. Wrongdoers are judged and held accountable by public opinion, usually expressed by gossip, which can play an important role in curbing socially unacceptable behavior.

Another prime technique in small-scale societies for resolving disputes, or even avoiding them in the first place, is mobility. Those unable to get along with others of their group may choose or feel pressured to move to another group where existing kinship ties give them rights of entry.

TRIBES

The second type of uncentralized authority system is the tribe. In anthropology, the term **tribe** refers to a wide range of kin-ordered groups that are politically integrated by some unifying factor and whose members share a common ancestry, identity, culture, language, and territory. Tribes may develop when a number of bands group together, resolving conflicts with one another, for purposes of economic exchange and/or collective self-defense against common enemies.

Typically, though not invariably, a tribe has an economy based on some form of crop cultivation or herding. Because these subsistence methods usually yield more food than those of the food-foraging band, tribal membership is often larger than band membership. Although band population densities are usually less than one person per square mile, tribal population densities generally exceed that and may be as high as 250 per square mile. Greater population density introduces a new set of problems, as opportunities for bickering, begging, adultery, and theft increase markedly, especially among people living in permanent villages.

Each tribe consists of one or more self-supporting and self-governing local community (including smaller kin-groups discussed above as bands) that may then form alliances with others for various purposes. As in the band, political organization in the tribe is informal and temporary. Whenever a situation arises requiring political integration of all or several groups within the tribe—perhaps for defense, to carry out a raid, to pool resources in times of scarcity, or to capitalize on a windfall that must be distributed quickly lest it spoil—groups join to deal with the situation in a cooperative manner. When the

▲▲

power The ability of individuals or groups to impose their will upon others and make them do things even against their own wants or wishes.

political organization The way power, as the capacity to do something, is accumulated, arranged, executed, and structurally embedded in society; the means through which a society creates and maintains social order and reduces social disorder.

band A relatively small and loosely organized kin-ordered group that inhabits a specific territory and that may split periodically into smaller extended family groups that are politically independent.

tribe In anthropology, the term for a range of kin-ordered groups that are politically integrated by some unifying factor and whose members share a common ancestry, identity, culture, language, and territory.

▼▼

problem is satisfactorily solved, each group then resumes autonomy.

In many tribal societies the organizing unit and seat of political authority is the clan, comprised of people who consider themselves descended from a common ancestor. Within the clan, elders or headmen and/or headwomen regulate members' affairs and represent their clan in interactions with other clans. As a group, the elders of all the clans may form a council that acts within the community or for the community in dealings with outsiders. Because clan members usually do not all live together in a single community, clan organization facilitates joint action with members of related communities when necessary.

Leadership in tribal societies is also relatively informal, as evident in a wide array of past and present examples. The Navajo Indians in the southwestern United States, for example, traditionally did not think of government as something fixed and all-powerful, and leadership was not vested in a central authority. A local leader was a man respected for his age, integrity, and wisdom. Therefore, people sought his advice frequently, but he had no formal means of control and could not force any decision on those who asked for his help. Group decisions were made by public consensus, although the most influential man usually played a key role in reaching a decision. Social mechanisms that induced members to abide by group decisions included gossip, criticism, withdrawal of cooperation, and the belief that antisocial actions caused sickness and other misfortune.

Another example of tribal leadership is the Big Man. Common in the South Pacific, such men are leaders of localized descent groups or of a territorial group. The Big Man combines a small amount of interest in his tribe's welfare with a great deal of cunning and calculation for his own personal gain. His power is personal, for he holds no political office in any formal sense, nor is he elected. His prestige as a political leader is the result of strategic acts that raise him above most other tribe members and attract loyal followers who benefit from or depend on his success.

The Kapauku of Western New Guinea typify this form of political organization. Among them, the Big Man is called the *tonowi* ("rich one"). To achieve such a position of local leadership, one must be male, wealthy, generous, and eloquent. Physical bravery and an ability to deal with

▲▲▲ **This Big Man from New Guinea is wearing his official regalia.**

the supernatural are also common *tonowi* characteristics, but they are not essential.

The *tonowi* functions as the headman of the village unit in a wide variety of situations within and beyond the community. He represents his local group in dealing with outsiders and other villages and acts as negotiator and/or judge when disputes break out among his followers.

Notably, a *tonowi* who refuses to lend money to other villagers may be ostracized, ridiculed, and, in extreme cases, actually executed by a group of warriors. Such responses to tightfistedness ensure that economic wealth is distributed throughout the group. Also, because a *tonowi's* wealth comes from his success at breeding pigs (the focus of the entire Kapauku economy; see Chapter 8), it is not uncommon for a *tonowi* to lose his fortune rapidly due to poor management or bad luck with his pigs. Thus the Kapauku political structure shifts frequently; as one man loses wealth and consequently power, another gains it and becomes a *tonowi*. These changes prevent any one *tonowi* from holding political power for too long.

POLITICAL INTEGRATION BEYOND THE KIN-GROUP

Age sets, age grades, and common-interest groups discussed in the previous chapter are among the political integration mechanisms used by tribal societies. Cutting across territorial and kin groupings, these organizations link members from different lineages and clans. For example, among many Indian nations inhabiting North America's Great Plains in the 19th century, the band comprised the basic territorial and political unit. In addition, however, there were a number of military societies or warrior clubs.

Among the Cheyenne, for instance, there were seven military societies. A boy might be invited to join one of them when he achieved warrior status, whereupon he became familiar with the society's particular insignia, songs, and rituals. In addition to military functions, the warrior groups had ceremonial and social functions. The Cheyenne warriors' daily tasks consisted of overseeing activities in the village, protecting families as they moved to the next camping site, and enforcing buffalo hunting rules. Each warrior club had its own repertoire of dances, performed on special ceremonial occasions. Because each Cheyenne band had identical military societies bearing identical names, the societies served to integrate the entire tribe for military and political purposes.[1]

Centralized Political Systems

Political authority is not centralized in bands and tribes, but systems change when a society's social life becomes more complex. As populations grow, as technology becomes more intricate, and as specializations of labor and trade networks produce surplus goods, opportunities increase for some individuals or groups to exercise control at the expense of others. In such societies, political authority and power are concentrated in a single individual (the chief) or in a body of individuals (the state).

CHIEFDOMS

A **chiefdom** is a politically organized society in which several neighboring communities inhabiting a territory are united under a single ruling individual—the chief—who is at the head of a ranked hierarchy of people. Individuals' status in a chiefdom is determined by the closeness of their relationship to the chief. Those closest are officially superior and receive deferential treatment from those in lower ranks. The office of the chief is usually for life and often hereditary. Typically, it passes from a man to his son or his sister's son, depending on whether descent is traced patrilineally or matrilineally.

Unlike the headman or headwoman in bands and tribes, the leader of a chiefdom is generally a true authority figure, whose right to make final decisions, give commands, and enforce obedience serves to unite members in all affairs and at all times. For example, a chief can distribute land among community members and recruit people into military service.

Chiefdoms have a recognized hierarchy consisting of major and minor authorities who control major and minor subdivisions. Such an arrangement is, in effect, a chain of command, linking leaders at every level. It serves to bind groups in the heartland to the chief's headquarters, whether it is a hut made of mud and dung or a palace of marble. Although leaders of chiefdoms are almost always male, in some cultures a politically astute wife, sister, or single daughter of a deceased chief could also inherit such a powerful position.

Chiefs usually control the economic activities of those who fall under their political rule. Typically, chiefdoms involve redistributive systems, and the chief has control over surplus goods and perhaps even over the community's labor force. He (and sometimes she) may demand a quota of rice from farmers, which will then be redistributed to the entire community. Similarly, laborers may be recruited to build irrigation works, a palace, or a temple.

The chief may also amass a great amount of personal wealth and pass it on to offspring. Land, cattle, and luxury goods produced by specialists can be collected by the chief and become part of the power base. Moreover, high-ranking families of the chiefdom may engage in the same practice and use their possessions as evidence of noble status.

An example of this form of political organization may be seen among the Kpelle of Liberia, an ethnic group of Mande-speaking tropical farmers in West Africa.[2]

© Cengage Learning 2013

---

[1]Hoebel, E. A. (1960). *The Cheyennes: Indians of the Great Plains.* New York: Holt, Rinehart & Winston.

[2]Gibbs, J. L., Jr. (1965). The Kpelle of Liberia. In J. L. Gibbs Jr. (Ed.), *Peoples of Africa* (pp. 216–218). New York: Holt, Rinehart & Winston.

▲▲

chiefdom A politically organized society in which several neighboring communities inhabiting a territory are united under a single ruler, who is at the head of a ranked hierarchy of people.

▼▼

A Kpelle chief in Liberia, West Africa, listens to a dispute in his district. Settling disputes is one of several ongoing traditional tasks that fall to paramount chiefs among Kpelle people.

© Jacques Jangoux/Peter Arnold, Inc.

Among them is a class of *paramount chiefs*, each heading one of the Kpelle chiefdoms (which are now districts of the Liberian state). Presiding over lower-ranking chiefs, the paramount chiefs' traditional tasks are preserving order, hearing disputes, and performing various other supervisory functions.

In a ranked hierarchy beneath each Kpelle paramount chief are several lesser chiefs: one for each district within the chiefdom, one for each town within a district, and one for each quarter of all but the smallest towns. Each acts as a kind of lieutenant for his chief of the next higher rank and also serves as a liaison between him and those of lower rank.

Today, a paramount chief among the Kpelle is a salaried official of the Liberian government, mediating between it and the people in his district. He receives government commissions on taxes and court fees collected within his chiefdom, plus a commission for providing tappers and other laborers for the rubber plantations, the largest of which is owned by the Firestone Tire and Rubber Company, a U.S. corporation now a subsidiary of a Japanese-owned global rubber conglomerate. Moreover, he gets a stipulated amount of rice from each household and gifts from people who come to request favors and intercessions. In keeping with his high social status, a paramount chief has at his disposal uniformed messengers, a literate clerk, and the symbols of wealth: many wives, embroidered gowns, and freedom from manual labor.

Traditionally, chiefdoms in all parts of the world have been highly unstable, with lesser chiefs trying to take power from higher-ranking chiefs or paramount chiefs vying with one another for supreme power. In precolonial Hawaii, for example, war was the way to gain territory and maintain power; great chiefs set out to conquer one another in an effort to become paramount chief of all the islands. When one chief conquered another, the loser and his nobles were dispossessed of all property and were lucky if they escaped alive. The new chief then appointed his own supporters to positions of political power. As a consequence, there was very little continuity of governmental or religious administration.

STATES

The **state** is a political institution established to manage and defend a complex, socially stratified society occupying a defined territory. The most formal of political systems, it is organized and directed by a government that has the capacity and authority to manage and tax its subjects, make laws and maintain order, and use military force to defend or expand its territories. Some of the smallest states today measure less than 2.59 square kilometers (1 square mile), while the largest cover over 15.5 million square kilometers (6 million square miles).

Often states are ruled by coalitions of wealthy and well-connected individuals or groups that have accumulated and fought over power. Possessing the resources (including money, weapons, and manpower), these ruling elites exercise power by institutional means, such as a government and bureaucracy, which allow them to arrange and rearrange a society's social and economical order.

A large population in a state-organized society requires increased food production and wider distribution networks. Together, these lead to a transformation of the landscape by way of irrigation and terracing, carefully managed crop rotation cycles, intensive competition for clearly demarcated lands, roads, and enough farmers and other rural workers to support market systems and a specialized urban sector.

Under such conditions, corporate groups that stress exclusive membership proliferate, ethnic differentiation and ethnocentrism become more pronounced, and the potential for social conflict increases dramatically. Given these circumstances, state institutions—which minimally involve a bureaucracy, a military, and (often) an official religion—provide the means for numerous and diverse groups to function together as an integrated whole.

Since their first appearance some 5,000 years ago, political states have been anything but permanent. They are often unstable, and many have disappeared in the course of time, some temporarily and others forever. Some were annexed by other states, and others collapsed or fragmented into smaller political units. Although some present-day states are very old—such as Japan, which has endured as a state for almost 1,500 years—few are older than the United States. Nowhere have states even begun to exhibit the staying power of less centralized political systems.[3]

An important distinction to make at this point is between nation and state. As noted in Chapter 1, a **nation** is a people who share a collective identity based on a common culture, language, territorial base, and history.[4] Today, there are about 5,000 nations (including tribes) throughout the world, many of which have existed since before recorded history. By contrast, there are less than 200 internationally recognized states in the world today, most of which did not exist before the end of World War II (1945). Rarely do state and nation coincide, as they do, for example, in Iceland, Japan, and Swaziland.

About 75 percent of the world's states are *pluralistic societies,* defined in Chapter 8 as societies in which two or more ethnic groups or nationalities are politically organized into one territorial state but maintain their cultural differences.[5] Often, smaller nations (including tribes) and other groups find themselves at the mercy of one or more dominant nation or ethnic group controlling the state. Frequently facing discrimination or repression, some minority nations seek to improve their political position by founding an independent state. In the process, they usually encounter stiff opposition, which often leads to violent confrontations.

So it is with the Kurds, an Iranian-speaking Sunni Muslim nation whose homeland is subdivided among the modern states of Turkey, Iraq, and Iran. As members of a cross-border nation, many Kurds are willing to fight for political autonomy or even national independence, but they are forced to accept their minority status in these three neighboring states (▶**Figure 14.2**)

An important aspect of the state is its delegation of authority to maintain order within and outside its borders. Police, foreign ministries, war ministries, and other bureaucracies function to control and punish disruptive acts of crime, dissension, and rebellion. By such agencies

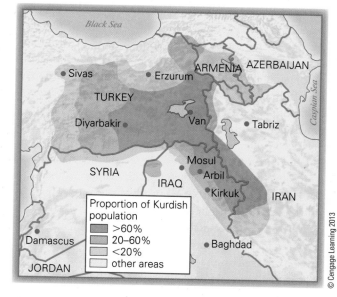

Figure 14.2 Kurdistan The Kurds—most of whom live in Turkey, Iran, and Iraq—are an example of a nation without a state. With a population of about 27 million, they are much more numerous than Australians, for example. In fact, the total population of the four Scandinavian countries—Denmark, Finland, Norway, and Sweden—is less than that of the Kurds, who have no independent country of their own, even though the region where they live is known as Kurdistan ("Land of the Kurds").

the state asserts authority impersonally and in a consistent, predictable manner. Western forms of government, like that of the United States, of course, are state governments, and their organization and workings are undoubtedly familiar to most everyone.

Political Systems and the Question of Legitimacy

Whatever a society's political system, it must find some way to obtain and retain the people's allegiance. In uncentralized systems, where every adult participates in all decision making, loyalty and cooperation are freely given, because each person is considered a part of the political system. As the group grows larger, however, and the organization becomes more formal, the problem of obtaining and keeping public support becomes greater.

---

[3]Diamond, J. (2005). *Collapse: How societies choose to fail or succeed.* New York: Viking Penguin.

[4]Clay, J. W. (1996). What's a nation? In W. A. Haviland & R. J. Gordon (Eds.), *Talking about people* (2nd ed., p. 188). Mountain View, CA: Mayfield.

[5]Van den Berghe, P. L. (1992). The modern state: Nation builder or nation killer? *International Journal of Group Tensions 22* (3), 193.

state A political institution established to manage and defend a complex, socially stratified society occupying a defined territory. It is organized and directed by a government that has the capacity make rules, impose order, tax its subjects, and use military force to defend or expand its territories.

nation A people who share a collective identity based on a common culture, language, territorial base, and history.

Centralized political systems may rely on coercion as a means of social control. This, however, can be risky because the personnel needed to apply force may be numerous and grow to be a political power. Also, the emphasis on force may create resentment and lessen cooperation. Thus police states are generally short-lived; most societies choose less extreme forms of social coercion. In the United States, this is reflected in the increasing emphasis placed on *cultural* control, as opposed to *social* control, which will be discussed in the sections on internalized and externalized controls a bit later in this chapter.

Also basic to the political process is the concept of legitimacy, or the right of political leaders to govern—to lawfully hold, use, and allocate power. Like force, legitimacy is a form of support for a political system; unlike force, it is based on the socially accepted customs, rules, or laws that bind and hold a people together as a collective whole. For example, among the Kapauku of Western New Guinea, discussed above, the legitimacy of the *tonowi*'s power comes from his wealth; the head of the traditional Dahomey state in what is now Benin, West Africa, acquired legitimacy through his age, as he was always the oldest living male; and the emperor of Japan (before being defeated by the Allies in 1945) was thought to have a divine right to rule.

Power based on legitimacy results in *authority*. It is distinct from power based solely on force: Obedience to authority follows from the belief that obedience is "right"; compliance to power based on force ensues from the fear of being deprived of liberty, physical well-being, life, or material property. Thus power based on legitimacy is symbolic and depends on the positive expectations of those who recognize and accept it. If the expectations are not met regularly (if the head of state fails to deliver economic prosperity or the leader is repeatedly unsuccessful in preventing or dealing with calamities), the legitimacy of the recognized power figure erodes or may collapse altogether.

Politics and Religion

Religion is often intricately connected to politics. Frequently it is religion that legitimizes the political order and the leadership. Religious beliefs may influence or provide authoritative approval to customary rules and laws. For example, acts that people believe to be sinful are often illegal as well.

In both industrial and nonindustrial societies, belief in the supernatural is important and is reflected in people's political institutions. Medieval Christian Europe well exemplifies the effect of religion on politics: Holy wars were fought over the smallest matter; labor was mobilized to build immense cathedrals in honor of the Virgin Mary and other saints; kings and queens ruled by "divine right," and they asked for the blessing of the pope (who claimed spiritual authority and political supremacy as head of the Roman Catholic Church) in important ventures, marital or martial.

In Peru, the divine ruler of the Inca empire proclaimed absolute authority based on the proposition that he was descended from the Sun God. Mexico's ancient Aztec political state was similarly based on religion, having a divine ruler and engaging in nearly constant warfare to procure captives for human sacrifices thought necessary to assuage or please the gods. Modern Iran was proclaimed an "Islamic republic," and its first head of state was the most holy of all Shiite Muslim holy men.

The fact that the president of the United States takes the oath of office by swearing on a Bible is another instance of the use of religion to legitimize political power, as is the phrase "one nation, under God" in the Pledge of Allegiance. U.S. coins are etched with the phrase "In God We Trust," many governmental meetings begin with a prayer or invocation, and the phrase "so help me God" is routinely used in legal proceedings. Despite the official separation of church and state, religious legitimization of government lingers.

Political Leadership and Gender

Irrespective of cultural configuration or type of political organization, women hold important positions of political leadership far less often than men. Furthermore, when they do occupy publicly recognized offices, their power and authority rarely exceed those of men. But significant exceptions occur. Historically, one might cite the female chiefs, or *sachems*, of Algonquian Indian communities in southern New England, as well as powerful queens in several Asian, African, and European monarchies.

Perhaps most notable is Queen Victoria, the long-reigning queen of England, Scotland, Wales, and Ireland. Also recognized as monarch in a host of colonies all over the world, Victoria even acquired the title "Empress of India." Ruling the British empire from 1837 until 1901, she was perhaps the world's wealthiest and most powerful leader.

In addition to inheriting high positions of political leadership, a growing number of women have been elected as presidents, chancellors, or prime ministers. Countries with elected female heads of state now or in recent years include, among others, Argentina, Brazil, Chile, Germany, India, Indonesia, Ireland, Liberia, Norway, the Philippines, and Sri Lanka. While such high-profile female leadership is still relatively rare, women regularly enjoy as much political power as men in a number of societies. In band societies, for example, it is common for females to have as much of a say in public affairs as males, even though more often than not men are the nominal leaders of their groups.

This was evident among the Iroquois nations of New York State, despite the fact that all leadership positions above the household and clan level were, without exception, filled by men. While holding all positions on the village and tribal councils, as well as on the great council of the Iroquois Confederacy, men were completely beholden to women, for only women could nominate them to high office. Moreover, women actively lobbied the men on the councils and could have someone removed from office whenever it suited them.

Lower visibility in politics does not necessarily indicate that women lack power in political affairs. And just as there are various ways in which women play a role behind the scenes, so it is when they have more visible roles, as in the dual-sex system of the Igbo in Nigeria, West Africa.

▲▲▲ Liberian President Ellen Johnson Sirleaf inspects members of the Liberian police after taking the presidential oath in January 2006. The first female president on the African continent, Sirleaf is a Harvard-educated economist who took the world by surprise when she won the elected head office in her war-torn and poverty-stricken country. Her leadership—recognized with a Nobel Peace Prize in 2011—has helped revitalize Liberia's economy, strengthen its rule of law, and provide basic services, including health, education, and infrastructure.

Among the Igbo, each political unit had separate political institutions for men and women, so that both had an autonomous sphere of authority, as well as an area of shared responsibility.[6] At the head of each political unit was a male *obi*, considered the head of government although in fact he presided over the male community, and a female *omu*, the acknowledged mother of the whole community but in practice concerned with the female section of the community. Unlike a queen (though both she and the *obi* were crowned), the *omu* was neither the wife of the *obi* nor the daughter of the previous *obi*.

Just as the *obi* had a council of dignitaries to advise him and to act as a check against any arbitrary exercise of power,

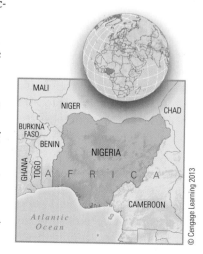

the *omu* was served by a similar council of women. The duties of the *omu* and her councilors involved such tasks as establishing rules and regulations for the community market (marketing was a woman's activity) and hearing cases involving women brought to her from throughout the town or village. If such cases also involved men, then she and her council would cooperate with the *obi* and his council.

In the Igbo system, then, women managed their own affairs, and their interests were represented at all levels of government. Moreover, they had the right to enforce their decisions and rules with sanctions similar to those employed by men, including strikes, boycotts, and "sitting on" someone, including a man:

> To "sit on" or "make war on" a man involved gathering at his compound, sometimes late at night, dancing, singing scurrilous songs which detailed the women's grievances against him and often called his manhood into question, banging on his hut with the pestles women used for pounding yams, and perhaps demol-

---

[6]Okonjo, K. (1976). The dual-sex political system in operation: Igbo women and community politics in midwestern Nigeria. In N. Hafkin & E. Bay (Eds.), *Women in Africa.* Stanford, CA: Stanford University Press.

legitimacy The right of political leaders to govern—to hold, use, and allocate power—based on the values a particular society embraces.

ishing his hut or plastering it with mud and roughing him up a bit. A man might be sanctioned in this way for mistreating his wife, for violating the women's market rules, or for letting his cows eat the women's crops. The women would stay at his hut throughout the day, and late into the night if necessary, until he repented and promised to mend his ways.[7]

When the British imposed colonial rule on the Igbo in the late 1800s, they failed to acknowledge the autonomy and power of the women. This is ironic because, as noted earlier, the long-reigning and powerful head of the British empire at the time was Queen Victoria. Nevertheless, British colonial administrators introduced "reforms" that destroyed traditional arrangements of female autonomy and power without providing alternative methods in exchange. As a result, Igbo women lost much of their traditional equality and became politically subordinate to men.

Political Organization and the Maintenance of Order

Political organization always includes means of maintaining order that ensure people behave in acceptable ways and define what action will be taken when they do not. In chiefdoms and states, some sort of authority has the power to regulate social affairs. In bands and tribes, however, people behave generally as they are expected to, without the direct intervention of any centralized political authority. To a large degree, gossip, criticism, fear of supernatural forces, and the like serve as effective deterrents to antisocial behavior.

Internalized Controls

Individuals who are well-socialized and enculturated members of their own society typically acquire an internalized set of shared beliefs and values about what is proper and what is not. These values are so deeply ingrained that each person becomes personally responsible for his or her own conduct. Cultural control may be thought of as an internalized form of self-control, as opposed to social control, which involves external enforcement through open coercion.

Cultural controls are embedded in our consciousness and may rely on deterrents such as fear of supernatural punishment—ancestral spirits sabotaging a hunt, for example—and magical retaliation. Like the devout Christian who avoids sinning for fear of hell, the individual expects some sort of punishment, even though no one in the community may be aware of the wrongdoing.

Cultural controls can also be framed in positive terms, with customary ways and means that encourage individual sacrifice for the common good. For example, many cultures honor traditions of giving to, or volunteering for, charitable or humanitarian institutions. Performed out of a desire to help those in need, such personal sacrifices may be motivated by a spiritual or religious worldview. Often deeply rooted in basic ideas of a wider community and reciprocity, they are also cultural controls against self-seeking, self-serving, greedy opportunism that threaten the well-being of a larger community.

Externalized Controls

Because internalized controls are not wholly sufficient even in bands and tribes, every society develops externalized social controls known as sanctions designed to encourage conformity to social norms. Operating within social groups of all sizes and involving a mix of cultural and social controls, sanctions may vary significantly within a given society, but they fall into one of two categories: positive or negative. Positive sanctions consist of incentives to conformity such as awards, titles, and recognition by one's neighbors. Negative sanctions consist of threats such as imprisonment, fines, corporal punishment, or ostracism from the community for violation of social norms.

For sanctions to be effective, they must be applied consistently, and they must be generally known among members of the society. Even if some individuals are not convinced of the advantages of social conformity, they are still more likely to obey society's rules than to accept the consequences of not doing so.

Sanctions may also be either formal or informal, depending on whether or not a legal statute is involved. In the United States, the man who goes shirtless in shorts to a church service may be subject to a variety of informal sanctions, ranging from disapproving glances from the clergy to the chuckling of other parishioners. If, however, he were to show up without any clothing at all, he would be subject to the formal negative sanction of arrest for indecent exposure. Only in the second instance would he have been guilty of breaking the law.

Formal sanctions, such as laws, are always organized, because they attempt to precisely and explicitly regulate people's behavior, whether they are peacefully trading with others or confronting them on a battlefield. Other examples of organized sanctions include, on the positive side, military decorations and monetary rewards. On the negative side are loss of face, exclusion from social life and its privileges, seizure of property, imprisonment, and even bodily mutilation or death.

---

[7]Van Allen, J. (1997). Sitting on a man: Colonialism and the lost political institutions of Igbo women. In R. Grinker & C. Steiner (Eds.), *Perspectives on Africa* (p. 450). Boston: Blackwell Press.

Informal sanctions emphasize cultural control and are diffuse in nature, involving spontaneous expressions of approval or disapproval by members of the group or community. They are, nonetheless, very effective in enforcing a large number of seemingly unimportant customs. Because most people want to be accepted, they are willing to acquiesce to the rules that govern dress, eating, and conversation, even in the absence of actual laws.

© Bryan & Cherry Alexander/ArcticPhoto

▲▲▲ Having a song duel is the traditional approach to dispute resolution among the Inuit of northern Canada.

Social Control Through Law

Among the Inuit of northern Canada, all offenses are considered to involve disputes between individuals; thus they must be settled between the disputants themselves. A traditional way of doing this is through a *song duel*, in which the individuals involved heap insults upon one another in songs specially composed for the occasion. Although society does not intervene, its interests are represented by spectators, whose applause determines the outcome. If, however, social harmony cannot be restored—and that is the goal, rather than assigning and punishing guilt—one or the other disputant may move to another band. Ultimately, there is no binding legal authority.

In Western society, by contrast, someone who commits an offense against another may become subject to a series of complex legal proceedings. In criminal cases the primary concern is to assign and punish guilt rather than to help the victim. The offender will be arrested by the police; tried before a judge and perhaps a jury; and, depending on the severity of the crime, may be fined, imprisoned, or even executed. Rarely does the victim receive restitution or compensation. Throughout this chain of events, the accused party is dealt with by police, judges, jurors, and jailers, who may have no personal acquaintance whatsoever with the plaintiff or the defendant.

Although rules enacted by an authorized legislative body and enforced by the judicial mechanisms of the state are fundamental features of Western jurisprudence, they are not the universal backbone of human law. Can any concept of law be applied to societies for whom the notion of a centralized judiciary is virtually meaningless? How shall we categorize Inuit song duels and other socially condoned forms of self-help that seem to meet some but not all of the criteria of law?

Ultimately, it is always of greatest value to consider each case within its cultural context. After all, law reflects a society's basic ideas about right and wrong, order and disorder, so to understand any society's laws, one must understand those underlying values and assumptions. Nonetheless, a working definition of law is useful for purposes of discussion and cross-cultural comparison, and for this **law** is adequately characterized as formal rules of conduct that, when violated, lead to corrective action in the form of *negative sanctions* (disapproval or punishment).

Functions of Law

Anthropologists recognize several basic functions of law, especially the following three: First, it defines relationships among society's members and marks out proper behavior under specified circumstances. Knowledge of the law permits each person to know his or her rights and duties with respect to every other member of society.

Second, law allocates the authority to employ coercion in the enforcement of sanctions. In societies with centralized political systems, such authority is generally vested in the government and its judiciary system. In societies that lack centralized political control, the authority to employ force may be allocated directly to the injured party.

Third, law functions to redefine social relations and to ensure social flexibility. As new situations arise, law must determine whether old rules and assumptions retain their validity and to what extent they must be altered. Law, if it is to operate efficiently, must allow room for change.

▲▲

cultural control Control through beliefs and values deeply internalized in the minds of individuals.

social control External enforcement through open coercion.

sanction An externalized social control designed to encourage conformity to social norms.

law Formal rules of conduct that, when violated, lead to negative sanctions.

▼▼

In practice, law is never as neat as this brief description suggests. This is because of the complexity of legal jurisdiction within each individual society.

Punishing Crimes and Settling Disputes

As we have observed, an important function of negative sanctions, legal or otherwise, is to discourage the breach of social norms. A person contemplating theft is aware of the possibility of being caught and punished. Yet, even in the face of severe sanctions, individuals in every society sometimes violate the norms and subject themselves to the consequences of their behavior.

In Western societies a clear distinction is made between offenses against the state and offenses against an individual. However, in non-state societies such as bands and tribes, all offenses are viewed as transgressions against individuals or kin-groups (families, lineages, clans, and so on).

Disputes between individuals or kin-groups may seriously disrupt the social order, especially in small groups where the number of disputants, though small in absolute numbers, may be a large percentage of the total population. For example, although the Inuit traditionally have no effective domestic or economic unit beyond the family, a dispute between two people will interfere with the ability of members of separate families to come to one another's aid when necessary and is consequently a matter of wider social concern. The goal of judicial proceedings in such instances is restoring social harmony rather than punishing an offender. When distinguishing between offenses of concern to the community as a whole and those of concern only to a few individuals, we may refer to them as *collective* or *personal*.

Disputes are generally settled in one of two ways. First, disputing parties may, through argument and compromise, voluntarily arrive at a mutually satisfactory agreement. This form of settlement is referred to as **negotiation** or, if it involves the assistance of an unbiased third party, **mediation**. In bands and tribes a third-party mediator has no coercive power and thus cannot force disputants to abide by such a decision, but as a person who commands great personal respect, the mediator frequently may help bring about a settlement.

Second, in chiefdoms and states, an authorized third party may issue a binding decision that the disputing parties will be compelled to respect. This process is referred to as **adjudication**. The difference between mediation and adjudication is a difference in authorization. In a dispute settled by adjudication, the disputing parties present their positions as compellingly as they can, but they do not participate in the ultimate decision making. Although the adjudication process is not universally characteristic,

every society employs some form of negotiation to settle disputes.

Often negotiation acts as a prerequisite or an alternative to adjudication. For example, in the resolution of U.S. labor disputes, striking workers may first negotiate with management, often with the mediation of a third party. If the state decides the strike constitutes a threat to the public welfare, the disputing parties may be forced to submit to adjudication. In this case, the responsibility for resolving the dispute is transferred to a presumably impartial judge. The judge's work is difficult and complex. In addition to sifting through the evidence presented, the judge must consider a wide range of norms, values, and earlier rulings to arrive at a decision that is considered just, not only by the disputing parties but by the public and other judges as well.

Restorative Justice and Conflict Resolution

Punitive justice, such as imprisonment, may be the most common approach to justice in North America, but it has not proven to be an effective way of changing criminal behavior. There are cultural alternatives.

In Canada, indigenous communities have successfully urged the federal government to reform justice services to make them more consistent with their values and traditions.[8] In particular, they have pressed for restorative justice techniques such as the Talking Circle, which is traditionally used in various forms by several Native American groups. For this, parties involved in a conflict come together in a circle with equal opportunity to express their views—one at a time, free of interruption. Usually, a "talking stick" (or an eagle feather or some other symbolic object) is held by whoever is speaking to signal that she or he has the right to talk at that moment and others have the responsibility to listen. The offender and victim(s) play active roles in the process, and rather than punishment, the aim is to repair the harm done through dialogue that evokes mutual empathy and prods accountability on the part of the offender.

In North America over the past three decades there has been significant movement away from the courts in favor of outside negotiation and mediation to resolve a wide variety of disputes. Many jurists see this as a means to clear overloaded court dockets so as to concentrate on more important cases. Today, leaders in the field of dispute resolution are finding effective ways to bring about balanced resolutions to conflict. An example of this appears in the Anthropology Applied feature.

---

[8]Criminal Code of Canada, §718.2(e).

ANTHROPOLOGY APPLIED

William Ury: Dispute Resolution and the Anthropologist

In an era when disputes quickly escalate into violence, conflict management is of growing importance. A world leader in this profession is anthropologist William L. Ury, an independent negotiations specialist.

In his first year at graduate school, Ury began looking for ways to apply anthropology to practical problems, including conflicts of all dimensions. He wrote a paper about the role of anthropology in peacemaking and on a whim sent it to Roger Fisher, a law professor noted for his work in negotiation and world affairs. Fisher, in turn, invited the young graduate student to co-author a kind of how-to book for international mediators. The book they researched and wrote together turned out to have a far wider audience, for it presented basic principles of negotiation that could be applied to household spats, manager–employee conflicts, or international crises. Titled *Getting to Yes: Negotiating Agreement Without Giving In* (1981), it sold millions of copies, was translated into twenty-one languages, and earned the nickname "the negotiator's bible."

While working on *Getting to Yes,* Ury and Fisher co-founded the Program on Negotiation (PON) at Harvard Law School, pulling together an interdisciplinary group of academics interested in new approaches to and applications of the negotiation process. Today this ap-

plied research center is a multi-university consortium that trains mediators, businesspeople, and government officials in negotiation skills. It has four key goals: (1) design, implement, and evaluate better dispute resolution practices; (2) promote collaboration among practitioners and scholars; (3) develop education programs and materials for instruction in negotiation and dispute resolution; (4) increase public awareness and understanding of successful conflict resolution efforts.

In 1982, Ury earned his doctorate in anthropology from Harvard with a dissertation titled "Talk Out or Walk Out: The Role and Control of Conflict in a Kentucky Coal Mine." Afterward, he taught for several years while maintaining a leadership role at PON. In particular, he devoted himself to PON's Global Negotiation Project (initially known as the Project on Avoiding War). Today, having left his teaching post at Harvard, Ury continues to serve as director of the Global Negotiation Project, writing, consulting, and running regular workshops on dealing with difficult people and situations.

Utilizing a cross-cultural perspective sharpened through years of anthropological research, he specializes in ethnic and secessionist disputes, including those between white and black South Africans, Serbs and Croats, Turks and Kurds, Catholics and Prot-

estants in Northern Ireland, and Russians and Chechens in the former Soviet Union.

Among the most effective tools in Ury's applied anthropology work are the books he continues to write on dispute resolution—from his 1993 *Getting Past No* to his 2007 title, *The Power of a Positive No.* His 1999 book, *Getting to Peace: Transforming Conflict at Home, at Work, and in the World,* examines what he calls the "third side," which is the role that the surrounding community can play in preventing, resolving, and containing destructive conflict between two parties.[a]

Like others in this field, Ury aims to create a culture of negotiation in a world where adversarial, win–lose attitudes are out of step with the increasingly interdependent relations among people. In writing and action, he challenges entrenched ideas that violence and war are inevitable, offering convincing evidence that human beings have as much inherent potential for cooperation and coexistence as they do for violent conflict. Certain that violence is a choice, Ury says, "Conflict is not going to end, but violence can."[b]

[a]Pease, T. (2000, Spring). Taking the third side. *Andover Bulletin.*
[b]Ury, W. (2002, Winter). A global immune system. *Andover Bulletin;* see also www.pon.harvard.edu/

Violent Conflict and Warfare

Although the regulation of a society's internal affairs is an important function of any political system, it is by no means the sole function. Another is the management of its external affairs—relations not just among different states but among different bands, lineages, clans, or whatever the largest autonomous political unit may be. And just as force, threatened or actual, may be

negotiation The use of direct argument and compromise by the parties to a dispute to arrive voluntarily at a mutually satisfactory agreement.

mediation The settlement of a dispute through negotiation assisted by an unbiased third party.

adjudication A mediation with an unbiased third party making the ultimate decision.

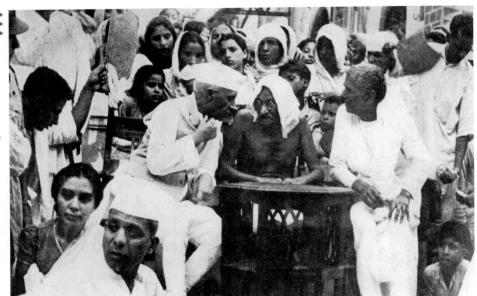

In contrast to cultures promoting militarism through marching songs, war games, and violent movies as public entertainment, there are cultures that value peace and tolerance. One of the world's most famous leaders preaching nonviolence in the political struggle was the Indian lawyer turned independence leader Mahatma Gandhi. (1869–1948). In this photo we see Gandhi (*center*) talking with Jawaharlal Nehru (in white cap), at a refugee camp in Uttar Pradesh, on June 1, 1947, a few months before India ceased to be a British colony and became an independent country.

used to maintain or restore order within a society, such powerful pressures are also used in the conduct of external affairs.

Humans have a horrific track record when it comes to violence. Far more lethal than spontaneous and individual outbursts of aggression, organized violence in the form of war is responsible for enormous suffering and deliberate destruction of life and property. In the past 5,000 years or so, some 14,000 wars have been fought, resulting in hundreds of millions of casualties. In the 20th century alone, an estimated 150 million people lost their lives due to human violence.

The scope of violent conflict is wide, ranging from individual fights, local feuds, raids, and piracy to formally declared international wars fought by professional armed forces. In addition, we may distinguish among various civil wars (in which armies from different geographic areas, ethnic or religious groups, or political parties within the same state are pitted against each other), rebellions, and guerrilla warfare involving small-scale hit-and-run tactical operations instead of pitched battles.

Why War?

In addition to the varying scales and methods of warfare, there are different motives, strategic objectives, and political or moral justifications for it. Some societies engage in defensive wars only and avoid armed confrontations with others unless seriously threatened or actually attacked. Others initiate aggressive wars to pursue particular strategic goals, including material benefits in the form of precious resources such as slaves, gold, or oil, as well as territorial expansion or control

over trade routes. In some cultures, aggressive wars are waged for ideological reasons, such as spreading one's own worldview or religion and defeating "evil" ideas or heresies elsewhere.

Beyond such explanations for warfare, is there something in our genetic makeup that makes it inevitable? Some argue that males of the human species are naturally aggressive. As evidence they point to aggressive group behavior exhibited by chimpanzees in Tanzania where researchers observed one group systematically destroy another and take over their territory.

Also, there is ample evidence that armed conflicts in the form of deadly feuds and raids have long existed in stateless societies such as foraging bands, horticultural villagers, or nomadic herders. However, warfare among humans is likely to be situation specific rather than an unavoidable expression of genetic predisposition for violent behavior (see this chapter's Biocultural Connection).

Moreover, war is not a universal phenomenon. In various parts of the world there are societies that do not practice warfare as we know it. Examples include people as diverse as the Ju/'hoansi Bushmen and Pygmy peoples of southern Africa, the Arapesh of New Guinea, the Jain of India, as well as the Amish of North America. Among societies that do practice warfare, levels of violence may differ dramatically.

We have ample reason to suppose that wars—not to be confused with more limited forms of deadly violence such as raids—have become a problem only in the last 10,000 years, since the invention of food-production techniques and especially since the formation of centralized states 5,000 years ago. Warfare has reached crisis propor-

BIOCULTURAL CONNECTION

Gender, Sex, and Human Violence

At the start of the 21st century, war and violence are no longer the strictly male domains that they were in many societies in the past. War has become embedded in the lives of noncombatants in many parts of the world and impacts the daily routines of elderly people, women, and children. Moreover, women now serve in the military forces of numerous states, although their participation in actual battlefield operations remains limited. Some female soldiers in the United States argue that gender should not limit their participation in combat, as they consider themselves as strong, capable, and well trained as their male counterparts. Others believe that biologically based sex differences make war a particularly male domain.

Scientists have long argued that males are biologically better suited to combat because natural selection has made them on average larger and more muscular than females. Charles Darwin first promoted this idea, known as *sexual selection*, in the 19th century. The British naturalist proposed that the physical specializations of males in animal species—such as horns, vibrant plumage, and, in the case of humans, intelligence and tool use—demonstrate selection acting upon males to aid in the competition for mates. In these scenarios, male reproductive success is thought to be optimized through a strategy of "spreading seed"—in other words, by being sexually active with as many females as possible.

Females, on the other hand, are considered "gatekeepers," who optimize their reproductive success through caring for individual offspring. According to Darwin's theory of sexual selection, in species where male–male competition is high, males will be considerably larger than females, and aggression will serve males well. In monogamous species, males and females will be of similar sizes.

British primatologist Richard Wrangham, a biological anthropologist at Harvard University, has taken the idea of sexual selection even farther. In his book *Demonic Males,* he explores the idea that both male aggression and patriarchy have an evolutionary basis. He states that humans, like our close cousins the chimpanzees, are "party gang" species characterized by strong bonds among groups of males who have dominion over an expandable territory. These features "suffice to account for natural selection's ugly legacy, the tendency to look for killing opportunities when hostile neighbors meet."[a] Violence in turn generates a male-dominated social order: "Patriarchy comes from biology in the sense that it emerges from men's temperaments out of their evolutionarily derived efforts to control women and at the same time have solidarity with fellow males in competition against outsiders."[b]

Some feminist scholars have pointed out that such scientific models are *gendered* in that they incorporate the norms derived from the scientists' culture. Darwin's original model of sexual selection incorporated the Victorian gender norms of the passive female and active male. Wrangham's more recent *Demonic Males* theory appears to be similarly shaped by the author's culture. It incorporates the dominant world order (military states) and the gender norms (aggressive males) it values. In both cases, scientific theory has provided a nature-based argument for a series of culture-based social customs.

This does not mean that biological differences between the sexes cannot be studied in the natural world. Instead, scientists studying sex differences must be especially aware of how they may project cultural beliefs onto nature. Meanwhile, the attitudes of female soldiers continue to challenge generalizations regarding military specialization by gender. ∎

Biocultural Question

Relate this essay to the Anthropology Applied feature about William Ury's conflict resolution work and his assertion that violence is a choice because human beings have as much inherent potential for cooperation and coexistence as they do for violent conflict.

[a] Wrangham, R., & Peterson, D. (1996). *Demonic males* (p. 168). Boston: Houghton Mifflin.

[b] Ibid., p. 125.

---

tions in the past 200 years, with the invention of modern weaponry and increased direction of violence against civilian populations.

Beginning in 1917 with military use of mustard gas—a chemical poison that causes blindness, large blisters on exposed skin, and (if inhaled) bleeding and blistering in mouth, throat, and lungs—the development of weapons of mass destruction has been lethally effective. Today, the chemical, biological, and atomic weapons arsenals stockpiled by many states are probably sufficient to wipe out all life on the planet, several times over.

Not surprisingly, given this development in the technology of death, casualties not just of civilians but also of *children* far outnumber those of soldiers. Indeed, because dangerous poisons, such as the anthrax bacterium or the nerve gas Sarin, are easy to produce and cheap, non-state groups (including terrorists) also seek to acquire them, if only to threaten to use them against more powerful opponents.

War is not so much an age-old problem as it is a relatively recent one. Among food foragers with their uncentralized political systems, violence may erupt sporadically, but warfare was all but unknown until recent times. Because territorial boundaries and membership among food-foraging bands are usually fluid and loosely defined, a man who hunts with one band today may hunt with a neighboring band next month. This renders warfare impractical.

So, too, does the systematic exchange of marriage partners among food-foraging groups, which makes it likely that someone in each band will have a sibling, parent, or cousin in a neighboring band. Moreover, the absence of a food surplus among foragers makes prolonged combat difficult. In sum, where populations are small, food surpluses are absent, property ownership is minimal, and state organization does not exist, the likelihood of organized violence by one group against another is small.[9]

Despite the traditional view of the gardener or farmer as a peaceful tiller of the soil, it is among such people, along with pastoralists, that warfare becomes prominent. One reason for this result is that food-producing peoples have a far greater tendency to grow in population; in contrast, populations of food foragers are generally maintained well below **carrying capacity**— the number of people that the available resources can support at a given level of food-getting techniques. This population growth, if unchecked, can lead to resource depletion—a problem commonly solved by seizing the resources of others.

In addition, the commitment to a fixed piece of land inherent in farming makes such societies somewhat less fluid in their membership than those of food foragers. Instead of marrying distantly, farmers marry locally, depriving them of long-distance kin networks. In rigidly matrilocal or patrilocal societies, each new generation is bound to the same territory, no matter how small it may be or how large the group trying to live within it.

The availability of unoccupied lands may not serve as a sufficient detriment to the outbreak of war. Among slash-and-burn farmers, for example, competition for land cleared of old growth forest frequently leads to hostility and armed conflict. The centralization of political control and the possession of valuable property among farming people provide many more stimuli for warfare.

It is among such peoples, especially those organized into states, where the violence of warfare is most apt to result in indiscriminate mass killing. This development has reached its peak in modern states. Indeed, much (but not all) of the warfare that has been observed in recent stateless societies (so-called tribal warfare) has been induced by states as a reaction to colonial expansion.[10]

Although competition for scarce resources may turn violent and lead to war, the motivations and justifications for war are often embedded in a society's worldview— the collective body of ideas that members of a culture generally share concerning the ultimate shape and substance of their reality. There are many examples of this, ranging from the Christian Crusades 700–900 years ago to Aztec Indian warfare some 500 years ago. More recently, the *jihad* (an Arabic word meaning "struggle" or "holy war") by Taliban Muslim fundamentalists in Afghanistan and Pakistan seeks to expel infidels (nonbelievers) from ancestral soil.

Wars Today

Currently, there are several dozen wars going on in the world. They occur not only *between* but also *within* states where the political leadership and government bureaucracy are corrupt, ineffective, or without popular support. Notably, many armies around the world recruit not only men, but also women and children. Today, more than 250,000 child soldiers, many as young as 12 years old, are participating in armed conflicts around the globe.[11]

The following examples offer some specific data on wars from the last decade of the 20th century to today. In the past two decades, about 2.5 million died and many millions more became refugees due to fighting in South Sudan, leading to that region's secession and political independence as a new state in 2011. And since warfare erupted in eastern Congo in 1998, almost 6 million people have died and millions more have been forced to flee their home villages. Involving eight African states and about twenty-five armed forces, this gruesome war with mass murder and rape is also known as Africa's World War.

Foreign military intervention is also a hallmark of long-lasting wars in regions that are strategically important or that are rich in natural resources, including Afghanistan and Iraq. In these countries, many hundreds of thousands of people, the vast majority of whom are noncombatants—children, women, and elders—have become casualties of war, and there has been massive destruction of roads, bridges, buildings, and livelihoods. When foreign armies leave, such battle-torn countries often remain mired in violent political turmoil between armed religious factions or rival ethnic groups and risk becoming dictatorships or failed states.

Beyond these wars there are numerous so-called low-intensity wars involving guerrilla organizations,

[9]Knauft, B. M. (1991). Violence and sociality in human evolution. *Current Anthropology 32*, 391–409.

[10]Whitehead, N. L., & Ferguson, R. B. (1993, November). Deceptive stereotypes about tribal warfare. *Chronicle of Higher Education*, A48.

[11]Study estimates 250,000 active child soldiers. (2006, July 26). Associated Press.

 Democratic Republic of Congo (formerly Zaire) is one of Africa's failed states, the consequence of a century of ruthless colonial exploitation, many decades of government mismanagement, and an ill-equipped bureaucracy. With a wealth of precious natural resources—including gold, diamonds, and uranium, especially in the eastern frontier provinces far from the capital—the country risks splintering. Since 1998, a gruesome war has devastated the peoples living in eastern Congo. In addition to the deaths of almost 6 million people, millions more are homeless. Here we see a small part of the 200,000 refugees fleeing from the horrors of mass murder, pillage, famine, and rape.

AP Images/Karel Prinsloo

rebel armies, resistance movements, terrorist cells, and a host of other armed groups engaged in violent conflict with official state-controlled armed forces. Every year, confrontations result in hundreds of hot spots and violent flashpoints, most of which are never reported in Western news media.[12]

As the above examples show, the causes of warfare are complex, involving economic, political, and ideological factors. The challenge of eliminating human warfare has never been greater—nor has the cost of *not* finding a way to do so. In the age of globalization, most countries now acknowledge a new category of violence—crimes against humanity—in order to punish those responsible for mass murder; these crimes may be prosecuted in an international court of justice.

Domination and Repression

In this chapter we have discussed how societies have grown in size, from bands to states, and how political power has grown from noncoercive leadership in small kin-groups to dictatorial regimes governing millions of subjects with little or no rights of self-determination. Today, only a quarter of all internationally recognized countries are inhabited by just one ethnic group or nationality. All others are occupied by more than one ethnic group, some even by multiple formerly independent nations whose territories have been joined, either by peaceful political means or as a result of military conquest and annexation.

As noted earlier, smaller or less powerful nations, as well as ethnic minorities, are often dominated by those who control the state and its armed forces. In such unequal power-sharing arrangements, ethnic or national minorities are often subjected to governmental rules and practices that the minorities find discriminatory or even repressive. And although the heyday of colonialism is now behind us, powerful groups still

expand and strengthen their control over societies and their territories far and near, primarily for coercive and exploitative purposes.

Acculturation

Acculturation is the massive cultural change that occurs in a society when it experiences intensive firsthand contact with a more powerful society. It always involves an element of force—either directly, as in conquests, or indirectly, as in the implicit or explicit threat that force will be used if people refuse to make the demanded changes. Other variables include degree of cultural difference; circumstances, intensity, frequency, and hostility of contact; relative social status of the agents of contact; and whether the nature of the flow is reciprocal or nonreciprocal.

In the course of cultural contact, any number of things may happen. Merger or fusion occurs when two cultures lose their separate identities and form a single culture, as historically expressed by the "melting pot" ideology in the United States. Sometimes, though, one of the cultures loses its autonomy but retains its identity as a subculture in the form of a caste, class, or ethnic group. This is typical of conquest or slavery situations, and the United States has examples of this despite its melting pot ideology of English-speaking, Protestant Euramerican culture—we need look no further than the nearest American Indian reservation.

The most extreme cases of forced cultural change, or acculturation, occur as a result of military conquest or massive invasion and breaking up of traditional political

▲▲▲

carrying capacity The number of people that the available resources can support at a given level of food-getting techniques.

acculturation The massive cultural change that occurs in a society when it experiences intensive firsthand contact with a more powerful society.

▼▼▼

[12]icasualties.org.

structures by dominant newcomers who know or care nothing about the culture they control. The indigenous people—unable to effectively resist imposed changes and hindered from carrying out many of their own social, religious, and economic activities—may be forced into new practices that tend to isolate individuals and destroy the integrity of their societies.

Ethnocide

A more vicious and radical form of acculturation is **ethnocide**—the violent eradication of an ethnic group's collective cultural identity as a distinctive people. This occurs when a state or more dominant nation deliberately sets out to destroy another society's cultural heritage in order to erase its collective identity as a distinct people. Ethnocide may take place when a powerful nation aggressively expands its territorial control by annexing neighboring peoples and their territories, incorporating the conquered groups as subjects.

A policy of ethnocide typically includes forbidding a subjugated nation's ancestral language, criminalizing their traditional customs, destroying their religion and demolishing sacred places and practices, breaking up their social organizations, and dispossessing or removing the survivors from their homelands. In essence, ethnocide includes everything short of physical extermination to remove all traces of a unique culture.

Among the many tragic examples of ethnocide is the experience of the Tibetan people in the Himalayan Mountains of Central Asia who could not defend themselves against an invasion by the Chinese communist army in 1950. The Chinese government then initiated ethnocidal policies by means of systematic attacks against traditional Tibetan culture. Seeking to stamp out deeply rooted religious beliefs and practices, it ordered the demolition of most Buddhist temples and monasteries. Following a mass uprising, hundreds of thousands of Tibetans were killed or forced into exile abroad.

Seeking to annihilate Tibetan identity, China tried to turn the surviving Tibetans into political subjects who would culturally identify themselves as Chinese nationals. Today more than 130,000 Tibetans live in exile, primarily in India and Nepal. The flow of Tibetans escaping Chinese oppression continues, with around 3,000 people fleeing their homes each year. They take great risks to do so—most crossing by foot over the dangerous Himalayas.[13]

Genocide

Prior to European invasions of the Amazon rainforest, more than 700 distinct ethnic groups inhabited this vast tropical region in South America. Their combined total population may have been as high as 5 million. However, after more than four centuries of colonial and capitalist pressures, the number of indigenous groups has dropped to about 270, and their collective total population has dwindled to some 200,000 people.[14] This dramatic decline did not happen by itself, and it raises the troubling issue of **genocide**—the physical extermination of one people by another, either as a deliberate act or as the accidental outcome of activities carried out by one people with little regard for their impact on others.

Genocide, like ethnocide, is not new in the world. In North America in 1637, for example, a deliberate attempt was made to destroy the Pequot Indians by setting fire to their village at Mystic, Connecticut, and then shooting all those—primarily unarmed elderly people, women, and children—who sought to escape the fire. To ensure that even their very memory would be stamped out, colonial authorities forbade the mention of the Pequot name. Numerous other massacres of Indian peoples occurred thereafter, up until the last one at Wounded Knee, South Dakota, in 1890. Of course, such acts were by no means restricted to the Americas. Among many now almost forgotten 19th-century acts of genocide is the extermination of the indigenous inhabitants of Tasmania, the large island just south of Australia.

The most widely known act of genocide in recent history was the attempt of the German Nazis during World War II to wipe out European Jews and Gypsies (especially Roma and Sinti). Together with almost 5 million other individuals whom the Nazis deemed abnormal and subhuman (homosexuals, those with physical or mental disabilities, and political and religious dissidents), these ethnic groups were targeted for extermination. About 500,000 Gypsies and 6 million Jews were all murdered in the name of improving the human species.

[13] Sachs, E., Rosenfeld, B., Lhewa, D., Rasmussen, A., & Keller, A. (2008). Entering exile: Trauma, mental health, and coping among Tibetan refugees arriving in Dharamsala, India. *Journal of Traumatic Stress 21* (2), 199–208. See also Avedon, J. F. (1997). *In exile from the land of snows: The definitive account of the Dalai Lama and Tibet since the Chinese conquest.* New York: Harper; and Wong, E. (2011, January 17). Tibetan who set himself afire dies. *New York Times.*

[14] Turner, T. (1991). Major shift in Brazilian Yanomami policy. *Anthropology Newsletter 32* (5), 1, 46.

On New Year's Day 1994, when the North American Free Trade Agreement (NAFTA) went into effect, 3,000 armed peasants belonging to the Zapatista revolutionary movement invaded towns in southern Mexico. Mostly Maya Indians, they declared war on the Mexican government, claiming that globalization was destroying their rural communities. Strong Internet presence helped them build an international network of political support. Now committed to nonviolent resistance to Mexican state control, Zapatistas have created 32 self-governing municipalities and established their own local health, justice, and education services.

© Matias Recart/AFP/Getty Images

In addition to this much-documented genocide, there are many other recent mass murders. For example, in 1994 more than half a million Tutsi people were slaughtered by their Hutu neighbors in the African country of Rwanda,[15] and more recently a genocidal campaign was waged against the non-Arab black peoples in the Darfur desert region of western Sudan. Estimates vary, but during the 20th century as many as 83 million people died of genocide and tyranny.[16]

Resistance to Domination and Repression

Indigenous peoples have varied considerably in their reactions to the radical upheavals brought about by foreign aggressors invading their ancestral homelands. Some have responded by moving to the nearest available forest, desert, or other remote site in hopes of being left alone. In Brazil, a number of communities once located near the coast took this option a few hundred years ago and were successful until the great push to invade, exploit, and destroy the Amazon tropical wilderness began in the 1960s. Others, like many Indians of North America, took up arms to fight back but were ultimately forced to sign treaties and surrender much of their territory, after which they were reduced to an impoverished underclass in their own land. Today, they continue to fight through nonviolent means to retain their identities as distinct peoples and to regain control over natural resources on their lands.

In addition, ethnic groups may try to retain their distinctive identities by maintaining cultural boundaries such as holding onto traditional language, festive ceremonies, customary dress, ritual songs and dances, unique food, and so on. Indeed, in opposing modernization, people often seek cultural protection and emotional comfort from **tradition**—customary ideas and practices passed on from generation to generation, which in a modernizing society may form an obstacle to new ways of doing things. When people are able to maintain some of their traditions in the face of powerful outside domination, the result may be **syncretism**—the creative blending of indigenous and foreign beliefs and practices into new cultural forms.

Violent Resistance: Rebellion and Revolution

When the scale of collective discontent and frustrated anger within a society reaches a critical level, the possibilities are high for **rebellion**—organized armed resistance to an established government or regime in power. There have been many peasant rebellions around the world in the course of history. Often such rebellions are triggered by repressive regimes imposing new taxes on the already

▲▲▲

ethnocide The violent eradication of an ethnic group's collective cultural identity as a distinctive people; occurs when a dominant society deliberately sets out to destroy another society's cultural heritage.

genocide The physical extermination of one people by another, either as a deliberate act or as the accidental outcome of activities carried out by one people with little regard for their impact on others.

tradition Customary ideas and practices passed on from generation to generation, which in a modernizing society may form an obstacle to new ways of doing things.

syncretism The creative blending of indigenous and foreign beliefs and practices into new cultural forms.

rebellion Organized armed resistance to an established government or authority in power.

[15]Human Rights Watch Report. (1999, March). Genocide in Rwanda: Leave none to tell the story. http://www.hrw.org/legacy/reports/1999/rwanda/ (retrieved September 16, 2011).

[16]White, M. (2001). *Historical atlas of the twentieth century.* http://users.erols.com/mwhite28/20centry.htm (retrieved September 16, 2011).

▼▼▼

struggling small farmers unable to feed their families under such unacceptable levels of exploitation.

In contrast to rebellions, which have relatively limited objectives, a **revolution**—a radical change in a society or culture—involves a more extreme transformation. Revolutions occur when the level of discontent in a society is very high. In the political arena, revolution involves the forced overthrow of an old government and the establishment of a completely new one.

The question of why revolutions erupt, as well as why they frequently fail to live up to the expectations of the people initiating them, is unsolved. It is clear, however, that the colonial policies of countries such as Britain, France, Spain, Portugal, and the United States during the 19th and early 20th centuries have created a world-wide situation in which revolution is nearly inevitable.

Despite the political independence most colonies have gained since World War II, powerful countries continue to exploit many of these "underdeveloped" countries for their natural resources and cheap labor, causing a deep resentment of rulers beholden to foreign powers. Further discontent has been caused as governing elites in newly independent states try to assert their control over peoples living within their boundaries. By virtue of a common ancestry, possession of distinct cultures, persistent occupation of their own territories, and traditions of self-determination, the peoples they aim to control identify themselves as distinct nations and refuse to recognize the legitimacy of what they regard as a foreign government.

Thus, in many former colonies, large numbers of people have taken up arms to resist annexation and absorption by imposed state governments run by people of other nationalities. As they attempt to make their multi-ethnic states into unified countries, ruling elites of one nationality set about stripping the peoples of other nations within their states of their lands, resources, and particular cultural identities.

One of the most important facts of our time is that the vast majority of the distinct peoples of the world have never consented to rule by the governments of states within which they find themselves living.[17] In many newly emerging countries, such peoples feel they have no other option than to take up weapons in armed protest.

Of the hundreds of armed conflicts in the world today, almost all are in the economically poor countries of Africa, Asia, and Central and South America, many of which were at one time under European colonial domination (▶**Figure 14.3**). Of these wars, the majority

---

[17]Nietschmann, B. (1987). The third world war. *Cultural Survival Quarterly 11* (3), 3.

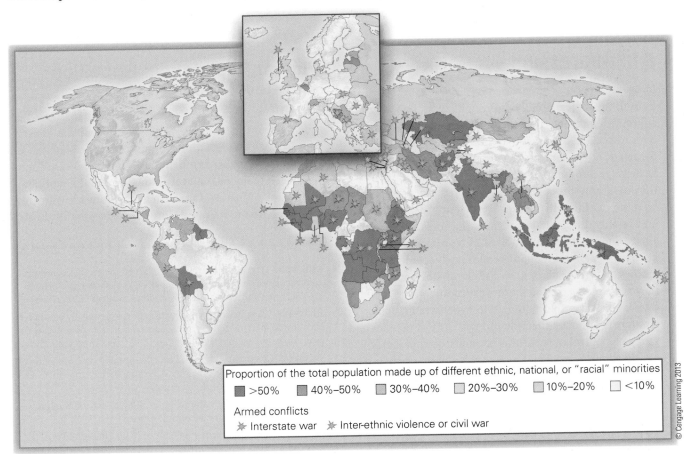

Proportion of the total population made up of different ethnic, national, or "racial" minorities

■ >50%   ■ 40%–50%   ■ 30%–40%   ■ 20%–30%   ■ 10%–20%   □ <10%

Armed conflicts
✳ Interstate war   ✳ Inter-ethnic violence or civil war

© Cengage Learning 2013

Figure 14.3 Political States of the World with Violent Conflicts In pluralistic societies in which two or more ethnic groups or nationalities form part of the same political state, violent conflict between neighboring groups is not uncommon.

are between the state and one or more nations or ethnic groups within the state's borders who are seeking to maintain or regain control of their personal lives, communities, lands, and resources in the face of what they regard as repression or subjugation by a foreign power.[18]

Nonviolent Resistance: Revitalization Movements

Not all suppressed, conquered, or colonized people eventually rise up against established authority, although why they do not is debatable. When they do, however, their political resistance may be nonviolent, such as, for instance, **civil disobedience**—refusal to obey civil laws in an effort to induce change in governmental policy or legislation, characterized by the use of passive resistance or other nonviolent means. Other nonviolent forms of resistance go far beyond politics.

Such is the case with **revitalization movements**, which are efforts for radical cultural reform in response to widespread social disruption and collective feelings of repression, anxiety, and despair. When primary ties of culture, social relationships, and activities are broken and meaningless activity is imposed by outside forces, individuals and groups characteristically react by rejecting newly introduced cultural elements, reclaiming historical roots and traditional identity, and sometimes by mustering spiritual imagination.

In the United States, revitalization movements have occurred often—whenever significant segments of the

population have found their life conditions to be at odds with the values of the American Dream. For example, the 1960s saw the emergence of revitalization movements among young people of middle-class and even upper-class families. In their case, the professed cultural values of peace, equality, and individual freedom were seen to be at odds with the realities of persistent war, poverty, and constraints on individual action imposed by a variety of impersonal institutions. Youths countered these realities by advocating free love, joining hippie communes, celebrating new forms of rock and folk music, using mind-altering drugs, challenging authority, growing their hair long, and wearing unconventional clothes.

Today there are revitalization movements in many parts of the world. These often arise where powerful forces of globalization have destabilized and culturally disrupted traditional societies without providing achievable alternatives for improving living standards for the majority of the populations so affected. ✳

▲▲

revolution Radical change in a society or culture. In the political arena, it involves the forced overthrow of an old government and establishment of a completely new one.

civil disobedience Refusal to obey civil laws in an effort to induce change in governmental policy or legislation, characterized by the use of passive resistance or other nonviolent means.

revitalization movement Efforts for radical cultural reform in response to widespread social disruption and collective feelings of great stress and despair.

▼▼

_____

[18]Ibid., p. 7.

Chapter Checklist

What is power, and why is it a crucially important issue in every society?

✔ Power is the ability of individuals or groups to impose their will upon others and make them do things even against their own wants and wishes. No group can function without persuading or coercing its members to conform to agreed-upon rules of conduct.

✔ A society's political organization establishes how power is accumulated, arranged, executed, and structurally embedded in that society. Power is fundamental in political organization,

because it is the means through which a society creates and maintains social order.

What are the different types of political organization?

✔ Four basic types of political systems are bands, tribes, chiefdoms, and states.

✔ The band is a relatively small (a few hundred people at most) and loosely organized kin-ordered group that inhabits a specific territory and that may split into smaller extended family groups that are politically and economically independent.

✔ Typically, bands are found among food foragers and other nomadic societies where people organize into politically autonomous family groups that usually camp together as long as environmental and subsistence circumstances are favorable. Political organization in bands is democratic, and informal control is exerted by public opinion in the form of gossip and ridicule. Leaders of bands are usually older men whose personal authority lasts only as long as members approve of their leadership.

✔ In anthropology, a tribe is a kin-ordered group politically integrated by a unifying factor and whose members share a common ancestry, identity, culture, language, and territory. With an economy usually based on crop cultivation or herding, the tribe's population is larger than that of the band, although family units within the tribe are still relatively autonomous and egalitarian. Political organization is transitory, and leaders have no coercive means of maintaining authority.

✔ In many tribal societies the organizing political unit is the clan, comprised of people who consider themselves descended from a common ancestor. Clan elders may regulate affairs and represent their group in relations with other clans. Another type of tribal leadership is the Big Man, who builds up his wealth and political power until he must be reckoned with as a leader.

✔ As societies grow and become more complex socially, politically, and economically, leadership becomes more centralized.

✔ A chiefdom is a politically organized society in which several neighboring communities inhabiting a territory are united under a chief who heads a ranked hierarchy of people. An individual's status is determined by his or her position in a descent group and distance of relationship to the chief, whose role is to unite his community in all matters. The chief may accumulate great personal wealth, which enhances his power base and which he may pass on to his heirs.

✔ The most centralized political organization is the state—an institution established to manage and defend a complex, socially stratified society occupying a defined territory. Its members are organized and directed by a formal government that has the capacity and authority to make laws and to use force to maintain the social order. The state is found in diverse, stratified societies, with unequal distribution of wealth and power.

✔ States are inherently unstable and transitory and differ from nations, which are communities of people who share a collective identity based on a common culture, language, territorial base, and history.

How do political organizations establish authority?

✔ Legitimacy—the right of political leaders to hold, use, and allocate power— is required to govern with authority. Legitimate government may be distinguished from rule based on intimidation or force. Most governments use some measure of ideology, including religion, to legitimize political power. Because religion is often intricately connected to politics, it may legitimize the political order and leadership.

✔ Historically, far fewer women than men have held important positions of political leadership. Nonetheless, women have at times enjoyed political equality with men in some societies, as among the Iroquoian peoples in northeastern North America. Lower visibility in politics does not necessarily indicate that women lack political power. Today, a growing number of women have been elected as president, chancellor, or prime minister.

How do political systems maintain social order and handle misconduct, crime, and conflict within the society?

✔ There are two kinds of social control. Internalized controls are cultural in nature, self-imposed by enculturated individuals who share beliefs and values about what is proper and what is not.

✔ Externalized controls (sanctions) mix cultural and social control. Positive sanctions are rewards or recognition by others, whereas negative sanctions include threat of imprisonment, fines, corporal punishment, or loss of face. Sanctions are either formal, including actual laws, or informal, involving norms.

✔ Law has formal rules of conduct that, when violated, lead to negative sanctions. In centralized political systems, this authority rests with the government and court system, whereas uncentralized societies give this authority directly to the injured party.

✔ In contrast to bands, tribes, and chiefdoms, state societies distinguish between offenses against the state (crimes) and offenses against an individual. A dispute may be settled in two ways: negotiation or adjudication.

✔ All societies use negotiation to settle individual disputes. In negotiation the parties to the dispute reach an agreement themselves, with or without the help of a third party. In adjudication, an authorized third party issues a binding decision. Punitive justice (such as imprisonment) stands in contrast to restorative justice.

What role do violence and warfare play in societies' efforts to regulate external affairs and conflicts?

✔ To regulate external affairs or relations between politically autonomous units, societies may resort to the threat or use of force. The wide scope of violent conflict includes individual fights, local feuds, and raids as well as formally declared international wars fought by professional armed forces.

✔ Some societies engage in defensive wars only and avoid armed confrontations with others unless seriously threatened or attacked. Others initiate aggressive wars to pursue material or ideological objectives. In the past 5,000 years, humans have fought some 14,000 wars resulting in many hundreds of millions of casualties, yet war is not a universal phenomenon.

✔ Acculturation, the massive cultural change that occurs in a society when it experiences intensive firsthand contact with a more powerful society, always involves an element of force.

✔ Ethnocide, the violent eradication of an ethnic group's collective identity as a distinctive people, occurs when a dominant society sets out to destroy another society's cultural heritage.

✔ Genocide is the physical extermination of one people by another, either as a deliberate act or as the accidental outcome of activities carried out by one people with little regard for the impact on others.

How do people resist domination and repression?

✔ Reactions of indigenous peoples to imposed changes vary considerably. Some have retreated to remote regions in hopes of being left alone, while others have lapsed into apathy. Some have reasserted their traditional culture's values by modifying foreign practices to conform to indigenous values, a phenomenon known as syncretism.

✔ Frustration and anger born of suppression and oppression may lead to rebellion—organized armed resistance to an established government or authority in power. And extreme dissatisfaction may lead to revolution—a radical change in a society or culture. In the political arena, revolution refers to the forced overthrow of an old government and the establishment of a new one.

✔ Suppression and oppression may spawn nonviolent civil disobedience and revitalization movements—collective efforts for radical cultural reform. Some revitalization movements try to speed up the acculturation process to get more of the benefits expected from the dominant culture. Others try to reconstitute a bygone but still remembered way of life. In other cases, a repressed group may try to introduce a new social order based on its ideology.

Questions for Reflection

1. In Afghanistan, a pluralistic society with many ethnic groups and tribes, political ties among communities are periodically reinforced by an ancient institution called the Loya Jirga, (Grand Assembly). These political leaders are all older men. Why do you think that is? Are women elected to important government positions in your society? If so, since when? Does gender in politics matter?

2. If political organization functions to impose or maintain order and to resolve conflicts, why do you think that a government in a country such as yours is so interested in legitimizing its power?

What happens when a government loses such legitimacy?

3. Which nationalities or ethnic groups do you know that are dominant, and which can you identify that are in a minority position or are repressed? What is the basis for this inequality?

4. In many states, political power is concentrated in the hands of a wealthy elite. Imagine you belong to a group that is losing its traditional freedom or quality of life due to government policies but feel that your political representatives are unwilling or unable to defend your interests. How would you challenge the state authorities?

5. In many Muslim countries, orthodox religious groups oppose modern developments that they associate with moral corruption and seek to maintain or return to a way of life more strictly based on Islamic traditions. Do you know Christian or Jewish fundamentalist groups with similar conservative values and ideas? What would be the future of your own family or community if a religious fundamentalist group became large enough to gain political power and rule the country?

Key Terms

power
political organization
band
tribe
chiefdom
state
nation
legitimacy
cultural control

social control
sanction
law
negotiation
mediation
adjudication
carrying capacity
acculturation
ethnocide

genocide
tradition
syncretism
rebellion
revolution
civil disobedience
revitalization movement

Online Study Resource

Login to **www.cengagebrain.com** to access the resources your instructor has assigned and to purchase materials. For this book, you can access:

CourseMate
Access chapter-specific learning tools including flashcards, glossaries, practice quizzes, videos, and more in your Anthropology CourseMate.

VISUAL ESSENCE

Wrestling with basic questions about life and death, people everywhere have an emotional and intellectual need to make sense of our place in the world. More broadly, we puzzle over human origin and destiny and truly big questions about time and space, the earth, and the universe. Throughout time and across the globe, people have creatively addressed these ponderings and worked out answers articulated in sacred narratives and rituals. Here we see Bugis from the island of Sulawesi, praying in front of their sailing ships anchored in the harbor of Jakarta, Indonesia. Famous for their colorful oceangoing schooners, these Muslim sailors have plied the seas between Malaysia and Australia and beyond for generations, transporting spices and other freight. This prayerful gathering took place on a holiday marking the end of Ramadan, the Islamic month of fasting, when Muslims refrain from eating, drinking water or any other liquids, smoking, and sexual activities, from sunrise to sunset. This taboo serves to purify thought and build restraint for the sake of Allah. Life on the open sea brings many risks—sudden storms, piracy, and other mishaps that may cause anxiety. Turning to their religion together, these sailors find a measure of psychological security.

15 Spirituality and Religion

from an anthropological point of view, spirituality and religion are part of a cultural system's *superstructure*, earlier defined as the collective body of ideas, beliefs, and values by which people make sense of the world and their place in it. In contrast to other disciplines—such as theology, for example, which may focus on questions concerning the nature of God, gods, or goddesses, and the interpretation of ancient sacred chants or texts—anthropology examines spirituality and religion in terms of a society's **worldview**—the collective body of ideas that members of a culture generally share concerning the ultimate shape and substance of their reality. In their cross-cultural studies of different religious and spiritual beliefs and practices, anthropologists seek to remain unbiased regarding the value of any particular historical tradition, belief, or ritual considered sacred by the people they study.

The Role of Spirituality and Religion

Among people in all cultures, particular spiritual or religious beliefs and practices fulfill numerous social and psychological needs, such as reducing anxiety by presenting an orderly view of the universe and answers to existential questions, including those concerning suffering and death. These beliefs and practices can provide the path by which people transcend their burdensome and mortal existence and attain, if only momentarily, spiritual hope and relief.

In addition, a traditional religion reinforces group norms, provides moral sanctions for individual conduct, and furnishes the ideology of common purpose and values that support social solidarity and the well-being of the community. Also of note, people often turn to religion or spirituality in the hope of reaching a specific goal, such as the healing of physical, emotional, or social ills.

The fact that belief in the supernatural fulfills so many social and psychological needs shared by humans across cultures offers an explanation for why it is universal. While recognizing that not all *individuals* believe in a

In this chapter you will learn to:

- **Define spirituality and religion and discuss their role in a cultural system.**

- **Provide a cross-cultural description of the range of supernatural beings and forces in which people believe.**

- **Identify religious specialists and analyze some of the rituals they oversee.**

- **Explain magic and witchcraft and their function in society, providing examples.**

- **Analyze the connection between social upheaval and new religious movements.**

◀◀
◀◀
◀ Members of the Church of Zion, an indigenous Christian church with a primarily Zulu congregation, perform a baptism in the Indian Ocean near Durban, South Africa. Over half of all Christian church members in South Africa belong to indigenous churches that combine some elements of their traditional African beliefs and rituals with those of Christianity.

supernatural force or entity, anthropologists know of no group of people anywhere on the face of the earth who, at any time over the past 100,000 years, has been without some manifestation of spirituality or religion.

In the 19th century the European intellectual tradition gave rise to the idea that scientific discoveries of proven facts and theoretical explanations would ultimately replace religion by demonstrating that myths and magic rituals were based on ignorance and fear. The expectation was that as science progressed religious mysteries would be solved, and people would abandon superstitions and even religion altogether. But to date, and despite tremendous scientific achievements, that has not occurred. In fact, in many places, the opposite trend seems to prevail, in particular where radical social and economic transformations destabilize the cultural order, challenge deeply embedded worldviews, and leave people feeling insecure and threatened by changes over which they have little or no control.

Although traditional, mainline Christian religions have shown some decline, nondenominational spirituality is on the rise. Also growing are fundamentalist religions, which often take a strong antiscience position. Examples include Islamic fundamentalism in countries such as Afghanistan, Algeria, and Iran; Jewish fundamentalism in Israel and the United States; and Hindu fundamentalism in India. Christian fundamentalism is represented in the surge of evangelical denominations in the United States, Central America, and sub-Saharan Africa.

Among the fastest-growing religious communities in the world are the indigenous churches of Africa. Over the last half century, the number of registered indigenous denominations in southern Africa alone has doubled from about 5,000 to about 10,000. There, it is estimated that more than half of Christian church members belong to indigenous churches, like the Amanazaretha church

founded by a Zulu prophet and popular among fellow Zulus in Natal.[1]

Within the United States, non-Christian religions are also growing. A recent study showed that among 225 million adults, 1.4 million were followers of Islam (up from 527,000 in 1990), 1.6 million of Buddhism (up from 401,000 in 1990), and nearly 1 million of Hinduism (up from 227,000 in 1990), not to mention various new age options such as Wicca (a modern, nature-oriented religion that draws upon ancient western European and pre-Christian beliefs and now counts as many as 675,000 adherents).[2]

Notably, just 16 percent of the adult population throughout the world claims to be nonreligious (▶ **Figure 15.1**). This is not to say that those calling themselves nonreligious are all atheists, because this miscellaneous category actually includes many millions who reject or do not fit under the label of any organized religion but who are metaphysically involved in creative arrangements of spiritual beliefs and practices of their own choosing.

An inventory of technological applications of modern science reveals the range of new anxieties now experienced by our species. These include fears of nuclear catastrophe, chemical or biological terrorism, and health hazards from pollution. People are also uneasy about personal data profiling, surveillance by bureaucracies and corporations, and the consequences of biotechnological developments including genetic engineering. Moreover, many people are dealing with emotional turmoil and psychological upheaval brought on by the destabilization or breakup of traditional communities due to globalization, plus invasions of foreign ideas and values through

---

[1]Gonzalez, J. (2002, January 11). Tracking Africa's fast-growing indigenous churches on DVD. *UA News.* http://uanews.org/node/5799 (retrieved September 16, 2011).

[2]Pew Forum on Religion and Public Life. (2008). *U.S. religious landscape survey.* Washington, DC: Pew Research Center.

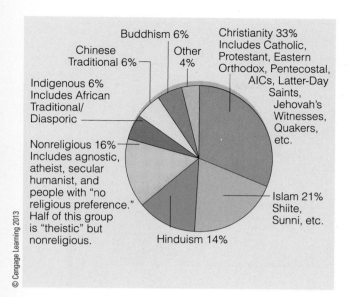

Figure 15.1 Major Religions of the World This chart shows the major religions of the world with their percentages of believers. Note that the total adds up to more than 100 percent due to rounding and due to the upper-bound estimates used for each group. As we go to press, more recent comparative figures for all these groups are not available. However, a 2009 study by the Pew Research Center reports that the number of Muslims has grown to 1.57 billion, representing about 23 percent of the total global population.

Source: Adherents.com. (2005). (retrieved September 29, 2011).

mass media controlled by unfamiliar powers. In the face of these and other modern worries, religion offers social and psychological support.

The Anthropological Approach to Religion

The continuing strength of religion in the face of scientific rationalism shows that faith remains a dominant and dynamic force in most contemporary societies. It is not the responsibility of anthropologists to pass judgment on the metaphysical truth of any particular faith system, but it is their task to show how each embodies a number of revealing facts about humanity and the particular cultural superstructure within which these religious or spiritual beliefs are ideologically embedded.

Although people in different cultures—each with their own beliefs about the ultimate shape and substance of the supernatural—have particular ideas about religion and spirituality, we offer a basic definition of both: **Religion** is an organized system of ideas about the spiritual sphere or the supernatural, along with associated ceremonial practices by which people try to interpret and/or influence aspects of the universe otherwise

beyond their control. Similar to religion, **spirituality** is also concerned with the sacred, as distinguished from material matters, but it is often individual rather than collective and does not require a distinctive format or traditional organization. Both indicate that many aspects of the human experience are thought to be beyond scientific explanation.

Since no known culture, including those of modern industrial societies, has achieved complete certainty in controlling existing or future conditions and circumstances, spirituality and/or religion play a role in all cultures. However, considerable variability exists globally (▶ **Figure 15.2**).

At one end of the spectrum are food-foraging peoples, whose technological ability to manipulate their environment is limited and who tend to see themselves as part of, rather than masters of, nature. This may be referred to as a *naturalistic worldview*. Among food foragers religion is likely to be inseparable from the rest of daily life. It also mirrors and confirms the egalitarian nature of social relations in their societies, in that individuals do not plead with high-ranking deities for aid the way members of stratified societies do.

At the other end of the spectrum is Western civilization, with its ideological commitment to overcoming problems through increasingly sophisticated technology and complex organizational skills. Here religion is usually less a part of daily activities and restricted to more specific occasions. Moreover, with its hierarchy of supernatural beings—for instance, God and (in some religions) the angels, saints, or holy figures—it reflects and confirms the stratified nature of the society in which it is embedded.

Religious activity may be less prominent in the lives of social elites, who may see themselves as more in control of their own destinies, than it is in the lives of peasants or members of lower classes. Among the latter, religion may afford some compensation for a dependent position in society. Yet religion is still important to elite members of society, in that it rationalizes the system in

▲▲▲

worldview The collective body of ideas that members of a culture generally share concerning the ultimate shape and substance of their reality.

religion An organized system of ideas about the spiritual sphere or the supernatural, along with associated ceremonial practices by which people try to interpret and/or influence aspects of the universe otherwise beyond their control.

spirituality Concern with the sacred, as distinguished from material matters. In contrast to religion, spirituality is often individual rather than collective and does not require a distinctive format or traditional organization.

▼▼▼

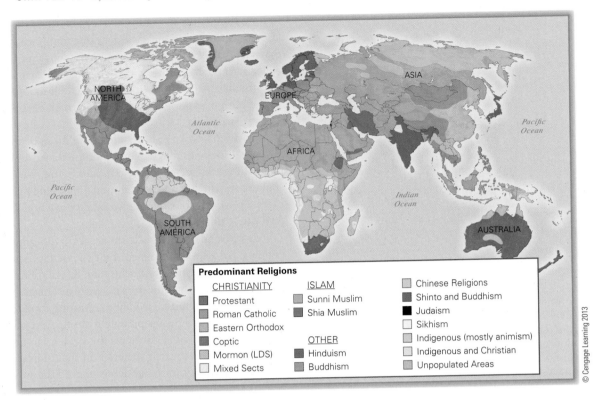

ASIA

EUROPE

NORTH
AMERICA

*Atlantic
Ocean*

AFRICA

*Pacific
Ocean*

*Pacific
Ocean*

*Indian
Ocean*

SOUTH
AMERICA

AUSTRALIA

Predominant Religions

CHRISTIANITY
- Protestant
- Roman Catholic
- Eastern Orthodox
- Coptic
- Mormon (LDS)
- Mixed Sects

ISLAM
- Sunni Muslim
- Shia Muslim

OTHER
- Hinduism
- Buddhism

- Chinese Religions
- Shinto and Buddhism
- Judaism
- Sikhism
- Indigenous (mostly animism)
- Indigenous and Christian
- Unpopulated Areas

© Cengage Learning 2013

Figure 15.2 The Global Distribution of Predominant Religions A half-page map cannot begin to convey the thousands of different religions and belief systems in the world or the complex dynamics of sectarian splinter groups. This one offers only a broad-stroke look at the global distribution of major religions, indicating where they predominate. In some areas, the mixture of different religions is such that no single faith is shared by most of that region's inhabitants. Notably, this map is not detailed enough to depict geographic pockets with significant numbers of a particular faith. For instance, even though New York City is the second-largest Jewish population center in the world and its 1.75 million Jewish adherents count for close to 10 percent of the population of the total metropolitan area, the city, like the state of New York, comprises mainly Roman Catholics (38 percent) and members of various Christian Protestant religions (30 percent). And many other significant religious groups are not individually represented here, such as Jehovah's Witnesses (a Christian sect with 7 million adherents), Cao Dai in Vietnam (5 million), which holds that all religions have the same divine origin, and Aladura in Nigeria (1 million), emphasizing faith healing and the power of prayer.

such a way that less advantaged people are not as likely to question the existing social order as they might otherwise be. With hope for a better existence after death, one may be more willing to put up with a disadvantaged position in life. Thus religious beliefs serve to influence and perpetuate certain ideas about the relationships, if not the actual relations, between different classes of people.

Myth

Members of a religion typically engage in the same ritual practices (such as pilgrimages or daily prayers), informed by shared beliefs that are encoded in special stories, or narratives, passed on from generation to generation. Known as **myths** (derived from the Greek word *mythos* meaning "speech" or "story"), these sacred narratives explain the fundamentals of human existence—where we and everything in our world came from, why we are here, and where we are going.

In cultures with a tradition of writing, such stories are often recorded in script. Among the oldest examples are the sacred texts of Hinduism known as Vedas, recorded in ancient Sanskrit some 3,500 years ago. Another is the Torah, sacred texts of Judaism recorded in ancient Hebrew script. Known as the Five Books of Moses, or Pentateuch, these texts are also foundational to Christianity (where they are referred to as the Old Testament) and to Islam.

Beyond their explanatory function, myths provide rationales for religious beliefs and practices and set cultural standards for "right" behavior. The following is a typical creation or origin myth, which has been orally passed on for generations by Abenaki Indians still residing in the U.S.–Canadian borderlands of Quebec and Vermont:

In the beginning, *Tabaldak*, "The Owner," created all living things but one—the spirit being who was to accomplish the final transformation of the earth.

Tabaldak made man and woman out of a piece of stone, but didn't like the result because their hearts were cold and hard. So he broke them up, and their remains today can be seen in the many stones that litter the landscape of the Abenaki homeland. Then *Tabaldak* tried again, this time using living wood, and from this came all later Abenakis. Like the trees from which they came, these people were rooted in the earth and could dance as gracefully as trees swaying in the wind.

The one living thing not created by *Tabaldak* was *Odzihózo*, "He Makes Himself from Something." This being seems to have created himself out of dust, but since he was a transformer, rather than creator, he wasn't able to accomplish it all at once. At first, he managed only his head, body, and arms; the legs came later, growing slowly as legs do on a tadpole. Not waiting until his legs were grown, he set out to transform the shape of the earth. He dragged his body about with his hands, gouging channels that became the rivers. To make the mountains, he piled dirt up with his hands. Once his legs grew, *Odzihózo's* task was made easier; by merely extending his legs, he made the tributaries of the main streams. . . .

Once he was finished, *Odzihózo* surveyed his handiwork and found it was good. The last work he made was Lake Champlain. . . . He liked it so well that he climbed onto a rock in Burlington Bay and changed himself into stone so that he could sit there and enjoy his masterpiece. . . . The Abenaki call the rock *Odzihózo*, since it is the Transformer himself.[3]

Such a myth, insofar as it is believed, accepted, and perpetuated in a culture, may be said to express part of a people's traditional worldview (as defined at the beginning of this chapter). Given the details of this particular Abenaki myth, we may conclude that these people recognize a kinship among all living things; after all, they were all part of the same creation, and human beings were even made from living wood. Moreover, an attempt to make them of nonliving stone was not satisfactory.

This idea of closeness among all living things led the Abenaki to show special respect to the animals they hunted in order to sustain their own lives. For example, after killing a beaver, muskrat, or waterfowl, one could not unceremoniously toss its bones into the nearest garbage pit. Proper respect required that the bones be returned to the water, with a request to continue its kind. Similarly, before eating meat, the Abenaki placed an offering of grease on the fire to thank Tabaldak. More generally, waste was to be avoided so as not to offend the animals. Failure to respect the rights of animals would result in them being unwilling to sacrifice their lives to help humans survive.

[3]Haviland, W. A., & Power, M. W. (1994). *The original Vermonters: Native inhabitants, past and present* (2nd ed., p. 193). Hanover, NH: University Press of New England.

Sacred stories about supernatural events or spiritual beings are told by cultures around the world. Myths like the creation myth of the Abenaki can be found in many variations across cultures.

Supernatural Beings and Spiritual Forces

A hallmark of religion is belief in supernatural beings and spiritual forces. In attempting to control by religious means what cannot be controlled in other ways, humans turn to prayer, sacrifice, and other religious or spiritual rituals. These presuppose the existence of spiritual forces that can be tapped into, or supernatural beings interested in human affairs and available for aid. In many cultures, these supernatural beings or spiritual forces are associated with unique places such as extraordinary rocks, lakes, wells, waterfalls, or other special geographic locations valued as sacred sites.

Beginning with supernatural beings, we may divide them into three categories: major deities (gods and goddesses), ancestral spirits, and other sorts of spirit beings. Although the variety of deities and spirits recognized by the world's cultures is tremendous, it is possible to make certain generalizations about them.

Gods and Goddesses

Gods and goddesses are the great and more remote beings. They are usually seen as controlling the universe. If more than one is recognized (known as **polytheism**), each has charge of a particular part of the universe. Such was the case with the gods and goddesses of ancient Greece: Zeus was lord of the sky, Poseidon was ruler of the sea, and Hades was lord of the underworld and ruler of the dead.

In addition to these three brothers, Greek mythology features a host of other deities, female as well as male, each similarly concerned with specific aspects of life and the universe. A **pantheon**, or collection of gods and goddesses such as those of the Greeks, is common in non-Western states as well. Because states typically have grown through conquest, often their pantheons have

▲▲▲

myth A sacred narrative that explains the fundamentals of human existence—where we and everything in our world came from, why we are here, and where we are going.

polytheism The belief in several gods and/or goddesses, as contrasted with monotheism—the belief in one god or goddess.

pantheon All the gods and goddesses of a people.

▼▼▼

◄ The patriarchal nature of traditional Euramerican society is culturally articulated and ideologically justified by its Judeo-Christian theology, in which a supreme male deity gives life to the first man, named Adam ("human being"), as depicted here on the ceiling of the Sistine Chapel in Rome. The first woman, named Eve, is created from her husband Adam's rib.

expanded as local deities of conquered peoples were incorporated into the official state pantheon.

Another frequent though not invariable feature of pantheons is the presence of a supreme deity, who may be all but totally ignored by humans. The Aztecs of the Mexican highlands, for instance, recognized a supreme pair to whom they paid little attention. After all, being so remote, this divine duo was unlikely to be interested in human affairs. The sensible practice, then, was to focus attention on less remote deities who were more directly concerned with human activities.

Whether or not a people recognize gods, goddesses, or both has to do with how men and women relate to each other in everyday life. Generally speaking, societies that subordinate women to men define the supreme deity in masculine terms. For instance, in traditional Christian religions believers speak of God as a father who had a divine son but do not entertain thoughts of God as a mother nor of a divine daughter. Such male-privileging religions developed in traditional societies with economies based upon the herding of animals or intensive agriculture primarily carried out or controlled by men.

Goddesses, by contrast, are likely to be most prominent in societies where women play a significant role in the economy, where women enjoy relative equality with men, and where men exercise limited authority over them and their children. Such societies are most often those that depend upon crop cultivation controlled and carried out solely or mostly by women.

Ancestral Spirits

A belief in ancestral spirits is consistent with the widespread notion that human beings are made up of two closely intertwined parts: a physical body and some mental component or spiritual self. For example, a traditional belief of the Penobscot Indians in Maine holds that each person has a vital spirit capable of traveling apart from the body. Given such a concept, the idea of the spirit being freed from the body in trance and dreams or by death, and having an existence thereafter, seems quite reasonable. Frequently, where a belief in ancestral spirits exists, these beings are seen as retaining an active interest and even membership in society.

Belief in ancestral spirits of one sort or another is found in many parts of the world, especially among people having unilineal descent systems with their associated ancestor orientation. In several such African societies, the concept is highly elaborate. Here one frequently finds ancestral spirits behaving just like humans. They are able to feel hot, cold, and pain, and they may be capable of dying a second death by drowning or burning. They even may participate in family and lineage affairs, and seats will be provided for them, even though the spirits are invisible. If they are annoyed, they may send sickness or death. Eventually, they are reborn as new members of their lineage, and, in societies that hold such beliefs, adults need to observe infants closely to determine just who has been reborn. Such beliefs provide a strong sense of continuity that links the past, present, and future.

Ancestor spirits played an important role in the patrilineal society of traditional China. For the gift of life, a boy was forever indebted to his parents, owing them obedience, deference, and a comfortable old age. Even after their death, he had to provide for them in the spirit world, offering them food, money, and incense on the anniversaries of their births and deaths. In addition, people collectively worshiped all lineage ancestors periodically throughout the year. Giving birth to sons was regarded as an obligation to the ancestors, because boys inherited their father's ancestral duties.

To fulfill his ancestors' needs for descendants (and his own need to be respectable in a culture that demanded satisfying the needs of one's ancestors), a man would go so far as to marry a girl who had been adopted into his family as an infant so she could be raised as a dutiful wife for him. Furthermore, a father readily would force his daughter to marry a man against her will. In fact, a female child raised to be cast out by her birth family might not find acceptance in her husband's family for years. Not until after death, when her vital spirit was carried in a tablet and placed in the shrine of her husband's family, was she an official member of it. As a consequence, once a son was born to her, a woman worked long and hard to establish the strongest possible tie between herself and her son to ensure she would be looked after in life.

Strong beliefs in ancestral spirits are particularly appropriate in a society of descent-based groups with their associated ancestor orientation. Moreover, as noted above, these beliefs provide a strong sense of continuity that links the past, present, and future.

Other Types of Supernatural Beings and Spiritual Forces

One of the most widespread concepts concerning supernatural beings is **animism**, a belief that nature is animated (enlivened or energized) by distinct personalized spirit beings separable from bodies. Spirits such as souls and ghosts are thought to dwell in humans, animals, and plants, as well as human-made artifacts and natural features such as stones, mountains, and wells; for animists, the world is filled with particular spirits.

The various spirits involved are a highly diverse lot. Generally speaking, though, they are less remote than gods and goddesses and are more involved in people's daily affairs. They may be benevolent, malevolent, or just plain neutral. They also may be awesome, terrifying, lovable, or mischievous. Because they may be pleased or irritated by human actions, people are obliged to be concerned about them.

Animism, a concept theoretically developed by the pioneering British anthropologist Sir Edward B. Tylor (1832–1917), is typical of those who see themselves as being a part of nature rather than superior to it. This includes most food foragers, as well as those food-producing peoples who acknowledge little qualitative difference between a human life and any living entity from turtles to trees, or even rivers and mountains. In such societies, gods and goddesses are relatively unimportant, but the woods are full of spirits. Gods and goddesses, if they exist at all, may be seen as having created the world and perhaps as making it fit to live in; but in animism, spirits are the ones to beseech when ill, the ones to help or hinder the shaman, and the ones whom the ordinary hunter may meet when off in the woods.

Although supernatural power is often thought of as being vested in supernatural beings, it does not have to be. Such is the case with **animatism**—the belief that nature is enlivened or energized by an impersonal spiritual force or supernatural energy, which may make itself manifest in any special place, thing, or living creature. This concept may not be universal, but it is found in cultures on every continent.

The Melanesians, for example, think of *mana* as a force inherent in all objects—not unlike the idea of a cosmic energy passing into and through everything, affecting living and nonliving matter alike (similar to "the force" in the *Star Wars* films). It is not in itself physical, but it can reveal itself physically. A warrior's success in fighting is not attributed to his own strength but to the *mana* contained in an amulet that hangs around his neck. Similarly, a farmer may know a great deal about horticulture, soil conditioning, and the correct time for sowing and harvesting but nevertheless depend upon *mana* for a successful crop, often building a simple altar to this power at one end of the field. If the crop is good, it is a sign that the farmer has in some way appropriated the necessary *mana*. Far from being a personalized spirit power, *mana* is abstract in the extreme; this force or energy always lies just beyond reach of the senses.

The concept of impersonal spirit force or energy was widespread among North American Indians. The Algonquins called it *manitou*; to the Iroquoians it was *orenda*; to the Lakota, *wakonda*.

In some cultures this impersonal spirit power or metaphysical energy is turned to for healing purposes. Notably, *animism* (as a belief in distinct spirit beings) and *animatism* (which lacks particular substance or individual form) are not mutually exclusive. They are often found in the same culture, as in Melanesian societies and also in the North American Indian societies just mentioned.

People trying to comprehend beliefs in the supernatural beings and powers that others recognize frequently ask how such beliefs are maintained. In part, the answer is through manifestations of power. Given a belief in animatism and/or the powers of supernatural beings, one is predisposed to see what appear to be results of the application of such powers. For example, if a Melanesian warrior is convinced of his power because he possesses the necessary *mana* and he is successful, he is likely to interpret this success as proof of the efficacy of *mana*: "After all, I would have lost had I not possessed it, wouldn't I?" Beyond this, because of his confidence in his *mana*, he may be willing to take more chances in his fighting, and this indeed could mean the difference between success or failure.

▲▲▲▲▲▲▲▲▲▲▲▲▲▲▲▲▲▲▲▲▲▲▲▲▲▲▲▲▲▲▲▲▲▲▲▲▲▲▲

animism The belief that nature is enlivened or energized by distinct personalized spirit beings separable from bodies.

animatism The belief that nature is enlivened or energized by an impersonal spiritual force or supernatural energy, which may make itself manifest in any special place, thing, or living creature.

▼▼▼▼▼▼▼▼▼▼▼▼▼▼▼▼▼▼▼▼▼▼▼▼▼▼▼▼▼▼▼▼▼▼▼▼▼▼▼

Mount Kailash in Tibet is the destination of many pilgrims every year. Rising 6,700 meters (about 22,000 feet), this mountain has been sacred for thousands of years to Hindus, Buddhists, Jains, and followers of Bön (Tibet's indigenous religion). They do not deify this peak, but they believe it to be the sacred abode of Lord Shiva, a member of the supreme divine trinity—so sacred that they would not even consider climbing it. Pilgrims follow the ancient tradition of circling the mountain on foot. The rugged, 52 kilometer (32 mile) trek, known as *parikarma*, is seen as a holy ritual that removes sins and brings good fortune. The most devout pilgrims make the journey lying down: Prostrating their bodies full-length, they extend their hands forward and make a mark on the ground with their fingers; then they rise, pray, crawl ahead on hands and knees to the mark, repeating the process again and again.

Failures, of course, do occur, but they can be explained. Perhaps one's prayer was not answered because a deity or spirit was still angry about some past insult. Or perhaps the Melanesian warrior lost his battle because he was not as successful in bringing *mana* to bear or his opponent had more of it. In any case, people generally emphasize successes over failures, and long after many of the latter have been forgotten, tales will still be told of striking cases of the workings of supernatural powers.

Sacred Places

In addition to revering supernatural figures such as deities, ancestral spirits, and other special beings, some religious traditions consider certain geographic places to be spiritually significant or even sacred. Typically, such sites are rivers, lakes, waterfalls, islands, forests, caves, and especially mountains. Their status is usually due to some unique shape or outstanding feature, such as a conical volcano capped with snow. Numerous mountains around the world fall into this category. Often they are associated with origin myths as splendid abodes of the gods. Or they are revered as dwelling places for the spirits of the dead, heights where

prophets received their divine directions, or retreats for prayer, meditation, and vision quests.

Three sacred mountains are shared by the Jewish, Christian, and Muslim traditions: Mount Ararat on the border between Armenia and Turkey in the Caucasus Mountains where the ark of the ancient patriarch Noah is said to have landed after the Great Flood; Mount Horeb, the "mountain of God" in the Sinai Desert, where the prophet Moses received the stone tablets with the ten sacred commandments from his god; and Mount Zion at the old city of Jerusalem where Solomon, the Israelite king, is believed to have been divinely ordered to build the Great Temple and where the Muslim sacred site Dome of the Rock (where the prophet Muhammad, accompanied by the angel Gabriel, ascended to heaven) is also located.

Symbolic of a supreme being, or associated with various important deities or ancestral spirits, sacred mountains may feature in religious ceremonies or spiritual rituals. In some religious traditions, these towering geographic features are places of worship, like shrines, or are sacred destinations for spiritual journeys or pilgrimages. For example, every year thousands of Buddhist and Hindu worshipers make a long pilgrimage to the foot of Mount Kailash in Tibet. They believe it to be the sacred abode of Lord Shiva, a member of the supreme divine trinity—so sacred that they would not even dream of trying to climb it.

Religious Specialists

Much of religion's value comes from the activities called for by its prescriptions and rules. Participation in religious ceremonies may bring a sense of personal lift—a wave of reassurance, a feeling of overwhelming joy, and even a sense of moving into a trancelike state—or a feeling of closeness to fellow participants. The beliefs and ceremonial practices of religions vary considerably, as do the individuals who guide others in these religious practices.

All human societies include individuals who guide and supplement the religious practices of others. Such individuals are seen to be highly skilled at contacting and influencing supernatural beings and manipulating supernatural forces. Often their qualification for this is that they have undergone special training. In addition, they may display certain distinctive personality traits that make them particularly well suited to perform these tasks.

Priests and Priestesses

In societies with the resources to support a full-time occupational specialist, a **priest** or **priestess** will have the role of guiding religious practices and influencing the supernatural. He or she is the socially initiated, ceremonially inducted member of a recognized religious organization, with a rank and function that belong to him or her as the holder of a position others have held before. The sources of power are the society and the institution within which the priest or priestess function.

The priest, if not the priestess, is a familiar figure in Western societies; he is the priest, minister, imam, lama, rabbi, or whatever the official title may be in an organized religion. Since Judaic, Christian, and Islamic religions all historically defined God in masculine, authoritarian terms, it is not surprising that the most important positions in these religions have been filled by men. Female religious specialists are likely to be found only in societies where women are acknowledged to contribute in a major way to the economy and where gods and goddesses are both recognized. In western Europe and North America, for instance, where women have become wage earners in almost every profession and occupy leadership positions in the workforce, they now have an increasing presence in the leadership of many Judeo-Christian religious groups.[4]

Although women still do not occupy the highest-ranking religious leadership positions in the Roman Catholic Church (headed by a male pope and his all-male council, the College of Cardinals), this Christian religion does recognize important female saints. Most significant among these is the Virgin Mary, held to be the human mother of God's son. In many places where Roman Catholicism has spread, worshipers have created cults around this female saint. Moreover, all around the world women devoted to a religious life have formed their own places for religious exclusion as nuns jointly belonging to a cloister or convent, headed by an abbess.

Such all-female religious institutions are not unique to Roman Catholicism. Convents of nuns are also part of Buddhist religious traditions. They can be found in several places around the world—in particular, Asian countries, including Thailand, as described by anthropologist Hillary Crane in this chapter's Biocultural Connection on the following page.

Shamans

Societies that lack full-time occupational specialization have existed far longer than those with such specialization, and they have always included individuals with special powers and skills that enable them to connect with and manipulate supernatural beings and forces. These powers have come to them through some personal experience, usually in solitude. In an altered state of consciousness, they receive a vision that empowers them to heal the sick, change the weather, control the movements of animals, and foretell the future. As they perfect these and related skills, they assume the role of shaman.

The word *shaman* originally referred to medical-religious specialists, or spiritual guides, among the Tungus and other Siberian pastoral nomads with animist beliefs. By means of various techniques such as fasting, drumming, chanting, or dancing, as well as hallucinogenic mushrooms, these Siberian shamans enter into a trance or altered state of consciousness. While in this waking dream state, they experience visions of an alternate reality inhabited by spirit beings such as guardian animal spirits who may assist in the healing.

Cross-cultural research of shamanism shows that similar medical-religious healing practices also exist in traditional cultures outside Siberia. For that reason, the

▲▲

priest or **priestess** A full-time religious specialist formally recognized for his or her role in guiding the religious practices of others and for contacting and influencing supernatural powers.

▼▼

---

[4]Lehman, E. C., Jr. (2002, Fall). Women's path into the ministry. *Pulpit & Pew Research Reports 1*, 4.

BIOCULTURAL CONNECTION

Change Your Karma and Change Your Sex?

By Hillary Crane

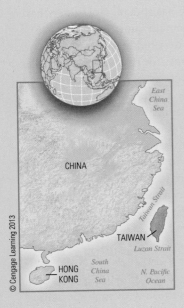

As Mahayana Buddhists, Taiwanese Chan (Zen) monastics believe that all humans are able to reach enlightenment and be released from reincarnation. But they believe it is easier for some because of the situation into which they are born—for example, if one is born in a country where Buddhism is practiced, in a family that teaches proper behavior, or with exceptional mental or physical gifts.

Chan monastics view contrasting human circumstances as the result of the karma accrued in previous lives. They believe certain behavior—such as diligently practicing Buddhism—improves karma and the chances of attaining spiritual goals in this lifetime or coming back in a better birth. Other behavior—such as killing a living being, eating meat, desiring or becoming attached to things or people—accrues bad karma.

One way karma manifests itself is in one's sex. Taiwanese Buddhists believe that being born female makes it harder to attain spiritual goals. This idea comes, in part, from the inferior status of women in Taiwan and the belief that their "complicated bodies" and monthly menstruation cycles can distract them. Moreover, they believe, women are more enmeshed in their families than men, and their emotional ties keep them focused on worldly rather than spiritual tasks.

Taiwanese Buddhists who decide to become monks and nuns must break from their families to enter a monastery. Since women are thought to be more attached to their families than are men, leaving home is seen as a particularly big step for nuns and a sign that they are more like men than most women. In fact, a nun's character is considered masculine, unlike the frightened, indecisive, and emotional traits usually associated with women in Taiwan. When they leave home nuns even stop referring to themselves as women and call one another *shixiong* ("dharma brother"). They use this linguistic change to signal that they identify themselves as men

and to remind one another to behave like men, particularly like the monks at the temple.

Monastics also reduce their attachments to worldly things like music and food. Nuns usually emphasize forsaking food and eat as little as possible. Their appearance, already quite masculine because they shave their heads and wear loose, gray clothing, becomes even more so when they lose weight—particularly in their hips, breasts, and thighs. Also, after becoming monastics, they often experience a slowing or stopping of their menses. Although these physical changes can be attributed to change in diet and lifestyle, the nuns point to them as signs they are becoming men, making progress toward their spiritual goals, and improving their karma. ∎

Biocultural Question

The Zen Buddhist ideal of enlightenment, realized when the soul is released from reincarnation, prescribes an extreme ascetic lifestyle for nuns that makes them physically incapable of biological reproduction. Do you think that their infertility allows these female monastics to emotionally adapt to a way of life that denies them motherhood?

For a more detailed treatment of this topic, see Crane, H. (2001). *Men in spirit: The masculinization of Taiwanese Buddhist nuns*. Doctoral dissertation, Brown University.

---

term *shaman* has also been applied to a variety of part-time spiritual leaders and traditional healers ("medicine men") active in North and South American indigenous communities and beyond.

As defined by U.S. anthropologist Michael Harner, famous for his participant observation among Shuar (or Jivaro) Indian shamans in the Amazon rainforest, a **shaman** is "a man or woman who enters an altered state of consciousness—at will—to contact and utilize an ordinarily hidden reality in order to acquire knowledge, power, and to help other persons. The shaman has at least one, and usually more, 'spirits' in his or her personal service."[5]

[5]Harner, M. (1980). *The way of the shaman: A guide to power and healing* (p. 20). San Francisco: Harper & Row.

The term *shaman* has been popularized in recent decades, so much so that any non-Western local priest, healer, or diviner is often referred to as one.[6] In addition to so-called new age enthusiasts, among whom shamanism is particularly popular, faith healers and other evangelists among fundamentalist Christians share many of the characteristics of shamanism.

Typically, one becomes a shaman by passing through stages of learning and practical experience, often involving psychological and emotional ordeals brought about by isolation, fasting, physical torture, sensory deprivation, and/or hallucinations. These hallucinations (derived from the Latin word for "mental wandering") occur when the shaman is in a trance, which may occur spontaneously but can also be induced by drumming or consuming mind-altering drugs such as psychoactive vines or mushrooms.

Because shamanism is rooted in altered states of consciousness (and the human nervous system universally produces these trance states), individuals involved in shamanism experience similarly structured visual, auditory, somatic (touch), olfactory (smell), and gustatory (taste) hallucinations. The widespread occurrence of shamanism and the remarkable similarities among shamanic traditions everywhere are consequences of this universal neurological inheritance. At the same time, the meanings ascribed to sensations experienced in altered states and made of their content are culturally determined; hence, despite their overall similarities, local traditions always vary in their details.

The shaman is essentially a religious go-between who acts on behalf of a human client, often to bring about healing or to foretell some future event. To do so, the shaman intervenes to influence or impose his or her will on supernatural powers. The shaman can be contrasted with the priest or priestess, whose "clients" are the deities. Priests and priestesses frequently tell the faithful followers what to do, while the shaman challenges or negotiates with the spirits. In return for services rendered, the shaman may collect a fee—fresh meat, yams, money, or a favorite possession. In some cases, the added prestige, authority, and social power attached to the shaman's status are reward enough.

When acting on behalf of a client, the shaman may put on something of a dramatic performance that heightens the psychological and emotional impact. Typically, he or she enters a trance state and experiences a sensation of traveling to the alternate world and seeing and interacting with spirit beings. The shaman tries to impose his or her will upon these spirits, an inherently dangerous contest, considering the superhuman powers spirits usually are thought to possess.

An example of this can be seen in the trance dances of the Ju/'hoansi Bushmen of Africa's Kalahari Desert. Among the Ju/'hoansi, shamans constitute, on average, about half the men and a third of the older women in any group. Their most common reasons for going into trance are to bring rain, control animals, and to heal the sick. Healing is an important activity of shamans across cultures, as illustrated in this chapter's Original Study about Ju/'hoansi healers on page 326.

In many human societies, sleight-of-hand and ventriloquism occur at the same time as trancing. Among Arctic peoples, for example, a shaman may summon spirits in the dark and produce flapping noises and strange voices to impress the audience. Some Western observers regard this kind of trickery as evidence of the fraudulent nature of shamanism. However, those who have studied shamanic practices agree that even though shamans know perfectly well that they are manipulating people with their illusions, they really believe in their power to deal with supernatural beings and spiritual forces. Their power, verified by the trance experience, gives them the right as well as the ability to manipulate people in minor technical matters. In short, the shaman regards his or her ability to perform extraordinary tricks such as sleight-of-hand and other illusions as further proof of superior powers.

The importance of shamanism in a society should not be underestimated. It promotes, through the drama of performance, a release of tension. And it provides psychological assurance that prevailing upon supernatural powers and spirits otherwise beyond human control can bring about invulnerability from attack, success at love, or the return of health. In fact, a frequent reason for a shamanic performance is poor health—a concept that is difficult to define effectively in cross-cultural terms. Not only do people in diverse cultures recognize and experience different types of illnesses, they may also view and explain them in different terms. The culturally defined diagnosis of an illness in turn determines how the patient

▲▲

shaman A person who enters an altered state of consciousness, at will, to contact and utilize an ordinarily hidden reality in order to acquire knowledge, power, and to help others.

▼▼

[6]Kehoe, A. (2000). *Shamans and religion: An anthropological exploration in critical thinking.* Prospect Heights, IL: Waveland Press.

ORIGINAL STUDY

Healing among the Ju/'hoansi of the Kalahari

By Marjorie Shostak

One way the spirits affect humans is by shooting them with invisible arrows carrying disease, death, or misfortune. If the arrows can be warded off, illness will not take hold. If illness has already penetrated, the arrows must be removed to enable the sick person to recover. An ancestral spirit may exercise this power against the living if a person is not being treated well by others. If people argue with her frequently, if her husband shows how little he values her by carrying on blatant affairs, or if people refuse to co-operate or share with her, the spirit may conclude that no one cares whether or not she remains alive and may "take her into the sky."

© Iven DeVore/Anthro-Photo

▲▲▲ When entering trance, Ju/'hoansi healers are assisted by others among the trance dancers.

Interceding with the spirits and drawing out their invisible arrows is the task of [Ju/'hoansi] healers, men and women who possess the powerful healing force called *n/um* [the Ju/'hoansi equivalent of *mana*]. *N/um* generally remains dormant in a healer until an effort is made to activate it. Although an occasional healer can accomplish this through solo singing or instrumental playing, the usual way of activating *n/um* is through the medicinal curing ceremony or trance dance. To the sound of undulating melodies sung by women, healers dance around and around the fire, sometimes for hours. The music, the strenuous dancing, the smoke, the heat of the fire, and the healers' intense concentration cause their *n/um* to heat up. When it comes to a boil, trance is achieved.

At this moment the *n/um* becomes available as a powerful healing force, to serve the entire community. In trance, a healer lays hands on and ritually cures everyone sitting around the fire. His hands flutter lightly beside each person's head or chest or wherever illness is evident; his body trembles; his breathing becomes deep and coarse; and he becomes coated with a thick sweat—also considered to be imbued with power. Whatever "badness" is discovered in the person is drawn into the healer's own body and met by the *n/um* coursing up his spinal column. The healer gives a mounting cry that culminates in a soul-wrenching shriek as the illness is catapulted out of his body and into the air.

While in trance, many healers see various gods and spirits sitting just outside the circle of firelight, enjoying the spectacle of the dance. Sometimes the spirits are recognizable—departed relatives and friends—at other times they are "just people." Whoever these beings are, healers in trance usually blame them for whatever misfortune is being experienced by the community. They are

barraged by hurled objects, shouted at, and aggressively warned not to take any of the living back with them to the village of the spirits.

To cure a very serious illness, the most experienced healers may be called upon, for only they have enough knowledge to undertake the dangerous spiritual exploration that may be necessary to effect a cure. When they are in a trance, their souls or vital spirits are said to leave their bodies and to travel to the spirit world to discover the cause of the illness or the problem. An ancestral spirit or a god is usually found responsible and asked to reconsider. If the healer is persuasive and the spirit agrees, the sick person recovers. If the spirit is elusive or unsympathetic, a cure is not achieved. The healer may go to the principal god, but even this does not always work. As one healer put it, "Sometimes, when you speak with God, he says, 'I want this person to die and won't help you make him better.' At other times, God helps; the next morning, someone who has been lying on the ground, seriously ill, gets up and walks again."

These journeys are considered dangerous because while the healer's soul is absent his body is in half-death. Akin to loss of consciousness, this state has been observed and verified by medical and scientific investigators. The power of other healers' *n/um* is all that is thought to protect the healer in this state from actual death. He receives lavish attention and care—his body is vigorously massaged, his skin is rubbed with sweat, and hands are laid on him. Only when consciousness returns—the signal that his soul has been reunited with his body—do the other healers cease their efforts. ■

From Shostak, M. (1981). A healing ritual. In *Nisa: The life and words of a !Kung woman* (pp. 291–293). Cambridge, Mass: Harvard University Press. Reprinted by permission of the publisher.

will be treated according to the beliefs of the culture, in order to achieve healing.

Although the psychological effects of the shamanic treatment are not known, the connection between mind and body may contribute to the patient's recovery. From an anthropological perspective, shamanic healings can be understood by means of a three-cornered model: the *shamanic complex* (▶ **Figure 15.3**). This triangle is created by the relationships among the shaman and the patient and the community to which both belong.

For healing to occur, the shaman needs to be convinced of the effectiveness of his or her spiritual powers and techniques. Likewise, the patient must see the shaman as a genuine healing master using appropriate techniques. Finally, to close the triangle's "magic field," the community within which the shaman operates on the patient must view the healing ceremony and its practitioner as potentially effective and beneficial.

Such dynamics are not unique to shamanic healing ceremonies, for similar social psychological processes are involved in Western medical treatments. Consider, for example, the *placebo effect*—the beneficial result a patient experiences after a particular treatment, due to his or her expectations concerning the treatment rather than from the treatment itself. Notably, some physicians involved in modern medicine work collaboratively with practitioners of traditional belief systems toward the healing of various illnesses.

Sacred Performances: Rituals and Ceremonies

Rituals are acts or procedures established by custom or prescribed by authority as proper to a certain formal occasion. Religious ritual is the means through which people relate to the supernatural; it is religion in action. Ritual serves to relieve social tensions and reinforce a group's collective bonds. More than this, it provides a means of marking many important events and lessening the social disruption and individual suffering of crises, such as death. Ceremonial acts are not all religious in nature (consider, for example, college graduation ceremonies in North America), but those that are play a crucial role in religious activity. Anthropologists have classified several different types of ritual, including rites of passage and rites of intensification.

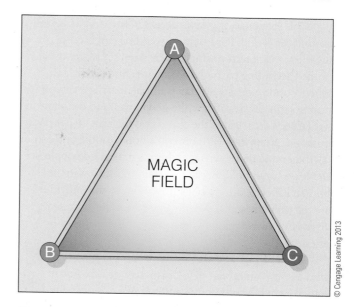

Figure 15.3 The Shamanic Complex Shamanic healing takes place within a "magic field" created when the shaman (A) and patient (B), as well as their community (C), are all convinced that the shaman is a genuine healing master using appropriate techniques that are effective and beneficial. Similar psychological processes are involved in Western medical treatments.

© Cengage Learning 2013

Rites of Passage

Rites of passage are rituals that mark important ceremonial moments when members of a society move from one distinctive social stage in life to another. When crossing the boundary between such stages, people briefly cease to be part of the stage left behind and have not yet become integrated into the next. Like travelers passing through a border area between two countries not controlled by either of them, they are neither here nor there. Guiding people through such uncertain transit zones, rituals associated with changing social status unfold in three phases: *separation*, *transition*, and *incorporation*; the first being ceremonial removal of the individual from everyday society, followed by a period of ritual isolation, and, finally, formal return and readmission back into society in his or her new status.[7]

▲▲

ritual An act or procedure established by custom or prescribed by authority as proper to a certain formal occasion.

rite of passage A three-phased ritual that marks an important ceremonial moment when members of a society move from one distinctive social stage in life to another.

▼▼

[7]See van Gennep, A. (1960). *The rites of passage.* Translated by M. Vizedom & G. L. Caffee. Chicago: University of Chicago Press. (orig. 1909)

This sequence of phases occurs in rites of passage all around the world. For instance, wedding ceremonies marking the transition from single to married status are usually phased according to this basic scheme. Such is the case when a bride enters a Roman Catholic marriage ceremony traditionally dressed in a white gown, walks to the altar on her father's arm, leaves the church on the arm of her new husband, disappears with him on a honeymoon, and some days later quietly returns with him as a married couple sharing a household. Because certain transitions in the human life cycle are crucially important to the individual as well as to the social order of the community, these rituals may involve a religious specialist, such as a priest or priestess.

Rites of passage also occur when people are initiated as new members of a distinctive group. For instance, when Maasai boys in East Africa's grasslands move into the warrior age set, they are ritually removed from their families and circumcised, returning weeks later as armed young men with a distinctive hairstyle and dress. Likewise, when a young U.S. male is recruited into the army and becomes a soldier, he submits to a ritual head shaving, dresses in uniform, and enters boot camp for a few weeks of basic training. Ritual head shaving also takes place when a Buddhist boy in Nepal leaves home and enters a monastery to become a monk.

MALE INITIATION RITES AMONG THE AUSTRALIAN ABORIGINES

The Australian Aborigines provide a distinctive example of an initiation rite into manhood. When the clan elders decide it is time for this ceremony, all the boys of a certain age group are taken away from the encampment where their families reside (separation). As the boys depart, the women cry and make a ritual show of resistance. At a place distant from the encampment, groups of men from several districts gather with the boys. The male elders sing and dance, while the initiates act as though they are dead. The climax of this part of the ritual is a bodily operation, such as circumcision or the knocking out of a tooth. Australian anthropologist A. P. Elkin comments:

> This is partly a continuation of the drama of death. The tooth-knocking, circumcision, or other symbolical act "killed" the novice; after this he does not return to the general camp and normally may not be seen by any woman. He is dead to the ordinary life of the tribe.[8]

In this transitional stage, the novice may be shown secret ceremonies and receive some instruction, but the most significant element is his complete removal from society. In the course of these Australian puberty rites, the initiate must learn the lore that all adult men are expected to know; in effect, he is given a cram course in manhood. The trauma of the occasion is a pedagogical technique that ensures he will learn and remember everything. He has been prepared for adulthood in a society where courage and endurance are considered important male virtues.

On his return to society (incorporation), the novice is welcomed with ceremonies, as though he had returned from the dead. This alerts the society at large to the individual's new status; people can expect him to act in certain ways, and in return they must act in the appropriate ways toward him. Through this ritual, the individual's new rights and duties are thus clearly defined.

FEMALE INITIATION RITES AMONG THE WEST AFRICAN MENDE

In a similar way to the male initiation rite described above, female initiation rites help prepare Mende girls in West Africa for womanhood. After they have begun to menstruate, marking the biological change toward sexual maturity, they are removed from society to spend weeks or even months in seclusion. There they discard the clothes of childhood, smear their bodies with white clay, and dress in short skirts and many strands of beads.

Shortly after entering this transitional stage, the girls undergo clitoridectomy, a removal of the clitoris. The girls (and Mende in general) believe this form of female circumcision enhances their reproductive potential. While the girls are secluded, experienced women train them in the moral and practical responsibilities of potential child bearers. With the training comes a good deal of singing, dancing, storytelling, and food—and a strong sense of sisterhood.

The pain and danger of the surgery, endured in the context of intense social support from other women, serve as a metaphor for childbirth, which may well take place in the same place of seclusion, again with the support of experienced women. They emerge from their initiation as women in knowledgeable control of their sexuality, eligible for marriage and childbearing. Having gone through this ritual, a traditional Mende woman knows she is "all woman."[9]

---

[8]Elkin, A. P. (1964). *The Australian Aborigines*. Garden City, NY: Doubleday/Anchor Books.

[9]MacCormack, C. P. (1977). Biological events and cultural control. *Signs 3*, 98.

In recent decades, various activist groups in North America and western Europe, in particular, have identified clitoridectomy as one of several forms of female genital mutilation (FGM). Practiced in Africa and Asia especially, FGM has been condemned as a human rights violation, and committees to end the practice have been organized in many countries across the African continent.[10] Notably, women's breast implant surgery has been compared to FGM as Western industrialized society's version of what it takes to be "all woman."

Rites of Intensification

Rites of intensification are rituals that take place during a crisis in the life of the group and serve to bind individuals together. Whatever the precise nature of the crisis—a drought that threatens crops, the sudden appearance of an enemy war party, the onset of an epidemic—mass ceremonies are performed to ease the sense of danger. This unites people in a common effort so that fear and confusion yield to collective action and a degree of optimism. The balance in the relations of all concerned is restored to normal, and the community's values are celebrated and affirmed.

While an individual's death might be regarded as the ultimate crisis, or point of separation, in that person's life, it is, as well, a point of separation for the entire group, particularly if the group is small. A member of the community has been removed, so its composition has been seriously altered. The survivors therefore must readjust and restore balance. They also need to reconcile themselves to the loss of someone to whom they were emotionally tied. As such, funerary ceremonies can be seen as rites of intensification that permit the living to express in nondisruptive ways their emotional upset over the death while providing for social readjustment.

Rites of intensification do not have to be limited to times of overt crisis. In regions with marked differences in seasons where human activities must change accordingly, these rites will take the form of annual ceremonies. These are particularly common among horticultural and agricultural peoples, with their planting and harvest ceremonies. Because these are critical times for such cultures, the ceremonies express reverence toward nature's generation and fertility upon which people's very existence depends.

Participation in rituals of reverence and celebration during planting and harvest seasons reinforces group in-

© Luca Tettoni

▲▲▲ A remarkable cultural example of a rite of intensification is the Hindu cremation ceremony on the island of Bali, Indonesia, shown here. The Balinese deal with death by turning what could be a painful emotional experience of grief and loss into a joyous celebration of life's progressive continuity by being reborn in a future existence. At the same time, as a social reminder of Hindu caste differences, the family of a deceased relative uses this elaborate public ceremony to display its wealth and social rank. Everyone can see that some funeral pyres, such as those built for members of a noble or royal family on the island, are bigger and more beautiful than others.

volvement. It also serves as a kind of dress rehearsal for crisis situations by promoting the custom of relying on supernatural forces—a practice that may make a crucial difference under stressful circumstances when it is important not to give way to fear and despair.

Magic

Among the most fascinating of ritual practices is the belief that supernatural powers can be compelled to act in certain ways for good or evil purposes by recourse to specified formulas. This is a classical anthropological notion of **magic**. Many societies have magical rituals to ensure good

▲▲▲

rite of intensification A ritual that takes place during a crisis in the life of the group and serves to bind individuals together.

magic The belief that supernatural powers can be compelled to act in certain ways for good or evil purposes by recourse to specified formulas.

▼▼

[10]World Health Organization. (2010, February). Female genital mutilation. Fact sheet no. 241. http://www.who.int/mediacentre/factsheets/fs241/en/ (retrieved September 16, 2011); Dirie, W., & Miller, C. (1998). *Desert flower: The extraordinary journey of a desert nomad* (pp. 218, 219). New York: William Morrow.

▲▲▲ This hundred-year-old carving from Congo in Central Africa is a fetish, an object believed to possess magical powers. Called a *nkondi*, the wooden carving's power comes in part from magic herbs hidden inside.

crops, the replenishment of game, the fertility of domestic animals, and the avoidance or healing of illness.

Although many Western peoples today—seeking to objectify and demythologize their world—have tried to suppress magic mysteries in their own consciousness, they continue to be fascinated by them. Not only are books and films about demonic possession and witchcraft avidly devoured and discussed, but horoscope columns are a regular feature of daily newspapers in the United States. And magical rituals are still commonly practiced by many Westerners seeking some luck where the outcome is in doubt or beyond factual influence—from lighting a votive candle for someone going through a hard time, to wearing lucky boxers on a hot date, to the curious gesturing baseball pitchers perform before each throw. Anthropologists distinguish between two fundamental principles of magic. The first principle, that like produces like, is identified as **imitative magic** or *sympathetic magic*. In Myanmar (Burma) in Southeast Asia, for example, a rejected lover might engage a sorcerer to make an image of his would-be love. If this image were tossed

into water, to the accompaniment of certain charms, it was expected that the hapless girl would go mad. Thus the girl would suffer a fate similar to that of her image.

The second principle is that of **contagious magic**—the idea that things or persons once in contact can influence each other after the contact is broken. The most common example of contagious magic is the permanent relationship between an individual and any part of his or her body, such as hair, fingernails, or teeth. For instance, the Basutos of Lesotho in southern Africa were careful to conceal their extracted teeth, because these might fall into the hands of certain mythical beings who could harm the owners of the teeth by working magic on them. Related to this is the custom, in Western societies, of treasuring things that have been touched by special people. Such items range from a saint's relics to possessions of other admired or idolized individuals, from rock stars to sport heroes to spiritual gurus.

Witchcraft

In 1692, English colonists in Salem, Massachusetts, blamed their misfortunes—crop failures, enemy raids, infant deaths, and other miseries—on Satan, the devil. Some 200 fellow settlers were accused of being witches, Satan's servants. Of these, thirteen women and six men were hanged, and one 80-year-old farmer was tortured to death. **Witchcraft** is an explanation of events based on the belief that certain individuals possess an innate psychic power capable of causing harm, including sickness and death. It involves **divination**, a magical procedure or spiritual ritual designed to learn what is not knowable by ordinary means, such as foretelling the future by interpreting omens.

Although many North Americans suppose it to be something that belongs to a more superstitious past, witchcraft is alive and well in the United States today. We see this in the emergence of the "witch cult" known as Wicca, mentioned earlier in this chapter. It began to flourish in the 1960s, including among highly educated segments of U.S. society. Inspired by various pre-Christian western European beliefs, in particular the idea of a sacred Mother Earth, Wicca is a nature-centered religion. Contrary to widespread rumor, its self-styled witches do not worship Satan and are not concerned with working evil. In fact, Wicca's core ethical statement, known as the Wiccan Rede, states "An Ye Harm None, Do What Ye Will."[11]

Ibibio Witchcraft

North Americans are by no means alone in having a contemporary interest in witchcraft. For example, as the

Ibibio of Nigeria have become increasingly exposed to modern education and scientific training, their reliance on witchcraft as an explanation for misfortune has increased.[12] Furthermore, it is often the younger, more educated members of Ibibio society who accuse others of bewitching them. The accused are often older, more traditional members of society. Thus we see an expression of the intergenerational hostility that often exists in fast-changing traditional societies.

Ibibio witchcraft beliefs are highly developed and longstanding—as they are among most traditional peoples of sub-Saharan Africa. A rat that eats a person's crops is not really a rat but a witch that changed into one. If a young and enterprising man cannot get a job or fails an exam, he has been bewitched. If someone's money is wasted or if the person becomes sick, is bitten by a snake, or is struck by lightning, the reason is always the same—witchcraft.

Indeed, traditional Ibibio attribute virtually all misfortune, illness, or death to the malevolent activity of witches. The modern Ibibio's knowledge about the role of microorganisms in disease has little impact on this; after all, scientific explanations say nothing about why these were sent to the afflicted individual. Although Ibibio religious beliefs provide alternative reasons for misfortune, those more conventional accounts do not elicit nearly as much sympathy from others. If evil befalls a person, witchcraft is a far more satisfying explanation than, for example, offspring disobedience or violation of a taboo.

Ibibio witches are thought to be men or women who have within them a special substance acquired from another established witch. From swallowing this substance—made up of needles, colored threads, and other ingredients—one is believed to become endowed with an extraordinary power that causes injury, even death, to others regardless of whether or not its possessor intends harm. The power is purely psychic, and witches do not perform rites or make use of "bad medicine." Their powers are believed to give them the ability to transform into animals and travel any distance at incredible speed to get at their unsuspecting victims, whom they may torture or kill by transferring the victim's soul or vital spirit into an animal, which is then eaten.

To identify a witch, an Ibibio looks for any person living in the region whose behavior is considered odd, out of the ordinary, immoral, or antisocial. Witches are apt to look and act mean and to be socially disruptive people in the sense that their behavior exceeds the range of variance considered acceptable.

The Ibibio make a distinction between *sorcerers,* whose acts are especially diabolical and destructive, and *witches,* whose witchcraft is relatively harmless, even though their powers are thought to be greater than those of their malevolent counterparts. Sorcerers are the very embodiment of a society's conception of evil—beings that flout the rules of sexual behavior and disregard every other standard of decency. Witches are often the community's nonconformists. Typically, they are morose, arrogant, and unfriendly people who keep to themselves but otherwise cause little disturbance. Such witches are thought to be dangerous when offended—likely to retaliate by causing sickness, death, crop failure, cattle disease, or any number of lesser ills. Not surprisingly, people viewed as witches are usually treated with considerable caution, respect, and even fear.[13]

Functions of Witchcraft

Why witchcraft? We might better ask, why not? In a world where there are few proven techniques for dealing with everyday crises, especially sickness, a belief in witches is not foolish; it is indispensable.[14] No one wants to resign oneself to illness, and if the malady is caused by a witch's curse, then magical countermeasures should cure it.

Not only does the idea of personalized evil answer the problem of unmerited suffering, but it also provides an explanation for many happenings for which no cause can be discovered. Witchcraft, then, cannot be refuted. Even if we could convince a person that his or her illness was due to natural causes, the victim would still ask, as the Ibibio do, Why me? Why now? Such a view leaves no room for pure

▲▲

imitative magic Magic based on the principle that like produces like; sometimes called *sympathetic magic.*

contagious magic Magic based on the principle that things or persons once in contact can influence each other after the contact is broken.

witchcraft An explanation of events based on the belief that certain individuals possess an innate psychic power capable of causing harm, including sickness and death.

divination A magical procedure or spiritual ritual designed to learn what is not knowable by ordinary means, such as foretelling the future by interpreting omens.

▼▼

---

[12]Offiong, D. (1985). Witchcraft among the Ibibio of Nigeria. In A. C. Lehmann & J. E. Myers (Eds.), *Magic, witchcraft, and religion* (pp. 152–165). Palo Alto, CA: Mayfield.

[13]See Mair, L. (1969). *Witchcraft* (p. 37). New York: McGraw-Hill.

[14]Ibid.

chance; everything must be assigned a cause or a meaning. Witchcraft offers an explanation and, in so doing, also provides both the basis and the means for taking counteraction.

Nor is witchcraft always entirely harmful. Its positive functions are noted in many African societies where people traditionally believe witches may cause sickness, death, or other harm. If people in the community agree that evildoing magic is in play, the ensuing search for the perpetrator of the misfortune becomes, in effect, a communal probe into dysfunctional social behavior. A witch-hunt is, in fact, a systematic investigation, through a public hearing, into all social relationships involving the victim of the sickness or death. Was a husband or wife unfaithful or a son lacking in the performance of his duties? Were an individual's friends uncooperative, or was the victim guilty of any of these wrongs? Accusations are reciprocal, and before long just about every unsocial or hostile act that has occurred in that society since the last outbreak of witchcraft (as manifested in sickness, death, or some other misfortune) is brought into the open.[15]

Through such periodic public scrutiny of behavior, people are reminded of what their society regards as both strengths and weaknesses of character. This encourages individuals to suppress as best they can those personality traits that are looked upon with disapproval, for if they do not, they at some time may be accused of being a witch. A belief in witchcraft thus serves as a broad control on antisocial behavior.

Consequences of Witchcraft

Anthropological research suggests that witchcraft, despite its often-negative image, frequently functions in a very positive way to manage tensions within a society. Nonetheless, events may get out of hand, particularly in crisis situations, when widespread accusations may cause great suffering. This certainly was the case in the Salem witch trials, but those pale in comparison to the half a million individuals executed as witches in Europe from the 15th through the 17th centuries. This was a time of profound change in European societies, marked by a good deal of political and religious conflict. At such times, it is all too easy to search out scapegoats to blame for what people believe are undesirable changes.

Religion in Cultural Change: Revitalization Movements

No anthropological consideration of religion is complete without some mention of revitalization movements. As noted in Chapter 14, these are movements for radical cultural reform in response to widespread social disruption and collective feelings of great stress and despair.

Many such movements developed in indigenous societies where European colonial exploitation caused enormous upheaval.

Among the various types of revitalization movements is the **cargo cult**—a spiritual movement (especially noted in Melanesia) in reaction to disruptive contact with Western capitalism, promising resurrection of deceased relatives, destruction or enslavement of white foreigners, and the magical arrival of utopian riches. Indigenous Melanesians referred to the white man's wealth as "cargo" (English for trade goods transported by ships or airplanes). In times of great social stress, native prophets emerged, predicting that the time of suffering would come to an end, and a new paradise on earth would soon arrive. Their deceased ancestors would return to life, and the rich white man would magically disappear—swallowed by an earthquake or swept away by a huge wave. However, their cargo would be left for the prophets and their cult followers who performed rituals to hasten this supernatural redistribution of wealth.[16]

One of many cargo cults arose in 1931 at Buka, in the Solomon Islands (in the Pacific Ocean). A native religious movement suddenly emerged there when prophets predicted that a deluge would soon engulf all whites, and a ship would then arrive filled with Western industrial commodities. The prophets told their followers to construct a storehouse for the goods and to prepare themselves to chase away the colonial police. They also spread word that the ship would come only after the natives had used up all their own supplies, and as a result believers ceased working in the fields. Although the leaders of the movement were arrested, the cult continued for some years.

As deliberate efforts to construct a more satisfying culture, revitalization movements aim to reform not just the religious sphere of activity but an entire cultural system. Such drastic measures are taken when a group's anxiety and frustration have become so intense that the only way to reduce the stress is to overturn the entire social system and replace it with a new one. Extreme and sometimes violent religious reactions to foreign domination are so common that anthropologists have sought to formulate their underlying causes and general characteristics.

Revitalization movements are by no means restricted to indigenous peoples historically dominated by colonial powers. In the United States alone hundreds of them have sprung up in various parts of the country, ranging from Mormonism, which began in the 19th century, to the more recent Unification Church led by Reverend Sun

---

[15]Turnbull, C. M. (1983). *The human cycle* (p. 181). New York: Simon & Schuster.

[16]For more on cargo cults, see Lindstrom, L. (1993). *Cargo cult: Strange stories of desire from Melanesia and beyond.* Honolulu: University of Hawaii Press; and Worsley, P. (1957). *The trumpet shall sound: A study of "cargo" cults in Melanesia.* London: Macgibbon & Kee.

◀
◀ In 2010, the ancient tradition of Druidry was officially recognized as a religion in Great Britain. Stonehenge, the 4,500-year-old Neolithic site pictured here, is one of its sacred centers. With some 10,000 followers, modern Druidry is rooted in the pre-Christian tradition of the Celtic peoples indigenous to the British Isles and other parts of Europe.

Myung Moon, and the Black Muslims led by Prophet Elijah Muhammad. Recent North American revitalization movements also include the American Indian revival of the spectacular Sun Dance ceremony, now held each summer at various reservations in the Great Plains, and sweat lodge rituals.

Such spiritual neo-traditions[17] are also on the rise in Europe. In Great Britain, for example, growing numbers of people are attracted to an indigenous form of "eco-spiritualism"[18] and follow the ancient tradition of Druidry. They worship natural forces such as thunder and the sun, as well as spirits they believe arise from places such as mountains and rivers. They do not worship a single god or creator but seek to cultivate a sacred relationship with the natural world.

A similar revival has occurred in Scandinavia, of an indigenous religion known as Asatru, a name based on a family of gods (*Æsir*) in Germanic (Nordic) mythology and faith (*trú*). The weekday names Wednesday, Thursday, and Friday are named after the supreme god Woden (Odin), his son Thor, and his wife Freyja (Frigg).

In Africa, during and following the period of foreign colonization and religious conversion, indigenous groups resisted or creatively revised Christian teachings and formed culturally appropriate religious movements. Since the 1970s thousands of indigenous Christian churches have been founded, often born of alternative theological interpretations, divinely inspired revelations, or cultural disagreements between African Christians and European or North American missionaries over the extent to which traditional African practices (such as animism, ancestor worship, and polygamy) were permissible. Today the African continent is as religiously diverse as ever. Although at least 40 percent of the population is Christian and more than another 40 percent is Muslim, African indigenous religions persist and are often merged with Christianity and Islam. This is an example of *syncretism*, defined in Chapter 14 as the creative blending of indigenous and foreign beliefs and practices into new cultural forms.

Persistence of Spirituality and Religion

Interestingly, millions of people caught up in the radical upheaval of globalization are turning to religious rules of moral conduct to quiet the anxiety of a world fraught with dangers and uncertainties. The need to find deeper meaning in life and to make sense of an increasingly complex, uncharted, confusing, and even frightening world drives humans to continue their explorations—religious and spiritual, as well as scientific.

As chronicled in this chapter, the quest for metaphysical explanations and revelations occurs all around the globe in countless ways—from massive religious gatherings to the recurrent rise of new spiritual leaders and religious movements, growing participation in pilgrimages and spiritual healing ceremonies, and persistent efforts to safeguard certain buildings and natural places that people have designated as sacred sites. ✳

---

[17]Prins, H. E. L. (1994). Neo-traditions in Native communities: Sweat lodge and Sun Dance among the Micmac today. In W. Cowan (Ed.), *Proceedings of the 25th Algonquian conference* (pp. 383–394). Ottawa: Carleton University Press.

[18]This term is used in Prins, H. E. L. (1996). *The Mi'kmaq: Resistance, accommodation, and cultural survival* (p. 206). New York: Harcourt Brace.

▲▲▲▲▲▲▲▲▲▲▲▲▲▲▲▲▲▲▲▲▲▲▲▲▲▲▲▲▲▲▲▲▲▲▲▲▲▲

cargo cult A spiritual movement (especially noted in Melanesia) in reaction to disruptive contact with Western capitalism, promising resurrection of deceased relatives, destruction or enslavement of white foreigners, and the magical arrival of utopian riches.

▼▼▼▼▼▼▼▼▼▼▼▼▼▼▼▼▼▼▼▼▼▼▼▼▼▼▼▼▼▼▼▼▼▼▼▼▼▼

Chapter Checklist

What are religion and spirituality, and what role do they play in a cultural system?

✔ Religion, an organized system of ideas about the spiritual sphere or the supernatural, is a key part of every culture's worldview. It consists of beliefs and practices by which people try to interpret and/or influence aspects of the universe otherwise beyond their control. Like religion, spirituality is concerned with sacred matters, but it is often individual rather than collective and does not require a distinctive format or traditional organization.

✔ Among food-foraging peoples, religion is intertwined in everyday life. As societies become more complex, religion may be restricted to particular occasions.

✔ Spiritual and religious beliefs and practices fulfill numerous social and psychological needs, such as reducing anxiety by providing an orderly view of the universe and answering existential questions, including those concerning suffering and death.

✔ A traditional religion reinforces group norms, provides moral sanctions for individual conduct, and furnishes the ideology of common purpose and values that support social solidarity and the well-being of the community. People often turn to religion or spirituality in the hope of reaching a specific goal, such as the healing of physical, emotional, or social ills.

What types of supernatural beings and forces are included in the worldview of humans?

✔ Religion is characterized by a belief in supernatural beings and forces, which can be appealed to for aid through prayer, sacrifice, and other rituals. Supernatural beings may be grouped into three categories: major deities (gods and goddesses), ancestral spirits, and other sorts of spirit beings.

✔ Gods and goddesses are great but remote beings that control the universe. Whether people recognize gods, goddesses, or both has to do with how men and women relate to each other in everyday life. Belief in ancestral spirits is based on the idea that human beings are made up of a body and a soul or vital spirit. Freed from the body at death, the spirit continues to participate in human affairs. This belief is characteristic of descent-based groups with their associated ancestor orientation.

✔ Animism, the belief that nature is animated or energized by distinct personalized spirit beings separable from bodies, is common among peoples who see themselves as part of nature rather than superior to it. Animatism, sometimes found alongside animism, is a belief that nature is enlivened or energized by an impersonal spiritual force or supernatural energy, which may make itself manifest in any special place, thing, or living creature.

✔ Myths are sacred narratives that explain the fundamentals of human existence (where we and everything in our world came from, why we are here, and where we are going) and set cultural standards for "right" behavior. Among the oldest examples are the sacred texts of Hinduism, known as Vedas, recorded some 3,500 years ago.

What are religious specialists and rituals?

✔ All human societies have specialists—priests and priestesses and/or shamans—to guide religious practices and to intervene with the supernatural world.

✔ Priests and priestesses are the socially initiated, ceremonially inducted members of a recognized religious organization, with a rank and function that belong to them as holders of a position others have held before.

✔ Shamans are individuals skilled at entering an altered state of consciousness to contact and utilize an ordinarily hidden reality in order to acquire knowledge and supernatural power to help other people. Their special powers have come to them through some personal experience.

✔ Religious ritual is the means through which people relate to the supernatural; it is religion in action. Ritual serves to relieve social tensions and reinforce a group's collective bonds. It provides a means of marking many important events and lessening the social disruption and individual suffering of crises, such as death.

✔ Rites of passage are rituals that mark important ceremonial moments when members of a society move from one distinctive social stage in life to another in a three-phase journey: separation, transition, and incorporation.

✔ Rites of intensification are rituals that ease anxiety and bind people together when they face a collective crisis or change—from drought, death, epidemic, or attack to seasonal shifts of crucial subsistence activities such as planting and harvesting.

What are magic and witchcraft?

✔ People in many cultures believe in magic, the idea that supernatural powers can be compelled to act in certain ways for good or evil purposes through specified formulas. Many societies have magical rituals to ensure good fortune. Magic is considered to be both imitative (like produces like) and contagious.

✔ Witchcraft is an explanation of events based on the belief that certain individuals possess an innate psychic power capable of causing harm, including sickness and death. It involves divination, a magical procedure or spiritual ritual designed to learn what is not knowable by ordinary means. Witchcraft beliefs among the Ibibio people of Nigeria in sub-Saharan Africa provide a fascinating example.

✔ The idea of personalized evil offered by witchcraft answers the problem of unmerited suffering and provides an explanation for many happenings for which no cause can be discovered.

✔ Witchcraft may function in the realm of social control. If people in the community agree that evildoing magic is in play, the ensuing search for the perpetrator of the misfortune becomes, in effect, a communal probe into dysfunctional social behavior.

What are revitalization movements, and how are they connected to social upheaval?

✔ Revitalization movements, which can happen in any culture, arise when people seek radical cultural reform in response to widespread social disruption and collective feelings of anxiety and despair. The cargo cult is an example—a spiritual movement (especially in Melanesia) in reaction to disruptive contact with Western capitalism, promising resurrection of deceased relatives and the destruction or enslavement of white foreigners whose cargo (trade goods) would be redistributed in a new utopian society.

✔ Revitalization movements are not restricted to indigenous peoples historically dominated by colonial powers. In the United States alone, hundreds have sprung up in various parts of the country, ranging from Mormonism, which began in the 19th century, to the more recent Unification Church and the Black Muslims.

Questions for Reflection

1. How does your culture, including your religious or spiritual beliefs, offer you guidance in finding meaningful answers to big questions, such as the origin of our species, when human life begins, where your personal soul or spirit comes from, and what happens to that soul after your material remains are buried or cremated?

2. Can you think of some similarities and differences among the shaman, priest (or any other preacher), and medical doctor as healers?

3. Graduation is a rite of passage, also known as commencement or convocation, when a high-ranking university official presents students who have completed their studies an academic degree. Can you identify the three phases in this ceremony?

4. Revitalization movements occur in reaction to the upheavals caused by rapid colonization and modernization. Do you think that the rise of Christian fundamentalism in the North American Bible Belt today is a response to such upheavals?

5. In postindustrial societies such as western Europe, the United States, and Canada, there is growing interest in shamanism and alternative healing techniques. Is there any relationship between globalization and this phenomenon?

Key Terms

worldview
religion
spirituality
myth
polytheism
pantheon
animism

animatism
priest or priestess
shaman
ritual
rite of passage
rite of intensification
magic

imitative magic
contagious magic
witchcraft
divination
cargo cult

Online Study Resources

Login to **www.cengagebrain.com** to access the resources your instructor has assigned and to purchase materials. For this book, you can access:

CourseMate
Access chapter-specific learning tools including flashcards, glossaries, practice quizzes, videos, and more in your Anthropology CourseMate.

VISUAL ESSENCE

For at least 10,000 years humans have survived not only by adapting to their natural environment but by transforming it to fit their needs. They have turned deserts, forests, swamps, and mountainsides into pastures, farmlands, and industrial centers, creating new survival opportunities (and often some unanticipated challenges) for an ever-growing population. Since the beginning of the industrial revolution about two centuries ago, modern technology has radically increased production, transportation, and communication throughout the world. During this period, the human population grew from 1 billion to more than 7 billion, and a worldwide web of interconnectivity emerged. Since the launching of the first communication satellites in the mid-20th century and the commercialization of the World Wide Web over the past two decades, humans have participated in the development of a very large and exceedingly complex global village. With access to computers and an ever-growing range of other digital tools serving as electronic extensions of our brains, most of us enter this cyberspace on a daily basis, using the Internet for a multitude of reasons with a multiplicity of social media. In China, cyber cafes known as 网吧 (*wangba*) can be found in most cities. This one is in the capital city, Beijing.

16 Global Changes and the Role of Anthropology

people who know little about it may superficially describe anthropology as an exotic discipline interested mainly in what happened long ago and far away. The most popular stereotype is that anthropologists devote all of their attention to digging up the past and describing the last surviving tribal communities with traditional ways of life. Yet, as noted throughout this book, anthropologists also investigate the ways and workings of industrial and postindustrial societies. Indeed, anthropologists are interested in the entire range of human cultures past and present—in their similarities and differences and in the multiple ways they influence one another.

In this era marked by rapid and radical change all around the world, many anthropologists wonder what today's globalizing processes will create and what will be transformed, disrupted, or damaged beyond repair. When traditional communities are exposed to intense contact with technologically empowered groups, their cultures typically change with unprecedented speed, often for the worse, disintegrating and losing support systems. Because globalization seems unstoppable, we are compelled to ask: How can the thousands of different societies having existed for centuries, if not millennia, maintain their distinctive cultural identities and deal successfully with the multiple challenges hurled at them?

In this chapter you will learn to:

- **Explain why anthropological insights on cultural change are key to a deeper understanding of today's complex world.**

- **Analyze the fundamental role of power in structuring societies and their cultures.**

- **Distinguish between hard and soft power.**

- **Define and give examples of structural violence.**

- **Describe how globalization disrupts and reorganizes cultures all across the globe, with both positive and negative consequences.**

Modernization in the Age of Globalization

One of the most frequently used terms to describe social and cultural changes as they are occurring today is **modernization.** This is most clearly defined as an all-encompassing process of economic change, whereby developing societies acquire some of the social and political characteristics common to Western industrial societies.

The dominant idea behind this concept is that "becoming modern" is becoming like European, North American, and other wealthy industrial or postindustrial societies, with the implication that not to do so is to be stuck in the past—backward, inferior, and needing to be improved. It is unfortunate that the term **modernization** continues to be so widely used. The best we can do here is to recognize its culture-bound bias, even as we continue to use it.

The process of modernization in societies all across the globe may be best understood as consisting of five subprocesses, all interrelated and with no fixed order of appearance:

- *Technological development:* In the course of modernization, traditional knowledge and techniques give way to the application of scientific knowledge and techniques borrowed mainly from the industrialized West.

- *Agricultural development:* This is represented by a shift in emphasis from subsistence farming to commercial farming. Instead of raising crops and livestock for their own use, people turn with growing frequency to the production of cash crops, with increased reliance on a cash economy and on global markets for selling farm products and purchasing goods.

- *Urbanization:* This subprocess is marked particularly by population movements from rural settlements into cities.

- *Industrialization:* Here human and animal power become less important, and greater emphasis is placed on material forms of energy—especially fossil fuels—to drive machines.

- *Telecommunication:* The fifth and most recent subprocess involves electronic and digital media processing and sharing of news, commodity prices, fashions, and entertainment, as well as political and religious opinions. Information is widely dispersed to a mass audience, far across national borders.

Throughout the so-called underdeveloped world, in Africa, Asia, Latin America, and elsewhere, whole countries are in the throes of extreme political and economic change and overall cultural transformation. In fact, inventions and major advances in industrial production, mass transportation, and communication and information technologies are transforming societies in Europe and North America as well. As discussed in Chapter 1, this worldwide process of accelerated modernization in which all parts of the earth are becoming interconnected in one vast interrelated and all-encompassing system is known as *globalization*, evidenced in global movements of natural resources, trade goods, human labor, finance capital, information, and infectious diseases.

In many societies, this modernization process is now happening very fast, often without the time needed to adjust gradually. Changes that took generations to accomplish in Europe and North America are attempted within the span of a single generation in developing countries. In the process, cultures frequently face unforeseen disruptions and a rapid erosion of dearly held values

they had no intention of giving up. Anthropologists doing fieldwork in distant communities throughout the world witness how these traditional cultures have been impacted, and often destroyed, by powerful global forces.

A Global Culture?

Despite vast geographic distance, human populations have always interacted. The interaction intensified about 500 years ago, when the first sailing ship successfully circumnavigated the entire globe—an almost three-year journey that was completed in 1522, but at great cost. Four of the five Spanish ships perished, as did most of the crew, as well as the seafarer Ferdinand Magellan who led this epic voyage of discovery.

Since then, peoples inhabiting every far-flung corner of the world have come in contact with one another, directly or indirectly. Many benefited from the new opportunities and prospered, enjoying new commodities, such as sugar, spices, tobacco, silk, and other exotic luxuries. And regional crops such as potatoes, wheat, rice, and corn were transported across every ocean and became staple foods worldwide. However, these trade networks also spread diseases, and huge numbers died in terrible epidemics. Moreover, many millions were forced into slave labor or lost their independence and self-determination under repressive colonial rule.

About two centuries ago, the invention of steam engines and other machinery brought about the industrial revolution, with large-scale factory production and an expanding transportation network of steam-powered trains and ships. Modern mass transportation and recent revolutions in telecommunications technology—from print media to telegraph and telephone to radio, television, satellites, and the Internet—make it possible to exchange more information with more people faster and over greater distances. Obviously, this global flow of humans, their products, and their ideas plays a major role in cultural change.

A popular belief since the mid-1900s has been that in the future, all humanity will share a single homogeneous global culture. This idea is based largely on the observation that developments in technology, communication, transportation, and trade are causing peoples of the world to increasingly enjoy the same entertainment, watch the same world news, eat the same foods, wear the same types of clothing, play the same sports, dance to the same music, and communicate in the same languages via satellite and the Internet. The continuation of such trends, so this thinking goes, would mean that North Americans who travel a hundred years from now to Botswana, Colombia, or Denmark would find local inhabitants living in a manner identical or similar to theirs.

Certainly it is striking—the extent to which items such as Western-style fast food, soft drinks, clothing, music, and movies have spread to virtually all parts of the world. For example, the U.S.-based global corporation McDonald's operates the world's largest fast-food chain, daily serving about 60 million customers in some 33,000 restaurants in almost 120 countries.[1] Famous for its Big Mac hamburger, it has become emblematic of the homogenizing of the world's different cultures in the age of globalization, sometimes referred to as the "McDonaldization" of societies.[2] Indeed, well beyond the realm of food, many countries—such as Japan and Costa Rica—already appear to have gone a long way toward becoming Westernized.

Yet, as we look at reactionary movements—including the rise of religious fundamentalism, nationalism, and ethnic identity politics around the world—this forecast seems unlikely. In fact, drawing on comparative historical and cross-cultural research, anthropologists call attention to something that all large states throughout time have had in common: a tendency to come apart. Not only have the great empires of the past, without exception, broken up into numbers of smaller independent units, but states in virtually all parts of the world today show this same tendency to fragment, usually along major geographic and ethnic divisions.

The threat of political collapse is ever-present in multi-ethnic states, especially when these countries are large, are difficult to travel in, and lack major unifying cultural forces such as a common national language. Such has been the case, for instance, with Afghanistan. This vast, mountainous country is inhabited by several major ethnic groups, including Pashtun (who live mainly in the south) and Tajik, Uzbek, Hazara, and Turkmen (who live mainly in the north). Although the Pashtun are greatest in number and have been most dominant during the last 200 years, they were never able to successfully impose their political will on the other ethnic groups, who maintain a great deal of independence. Nor did they succeed in making their own native tongue, Pashto, the country's national language.

The tendency of multi-ethnic states to break apart has been especially noteworthy since the end of the Cold War between the United States and the former Soviet Union around 1990. For example, 1991 saw the dramatic breakup of the Soviet Union into about a dozen independent republics—Russia, Armenia, Belarus, Estonia, Ukraine, and Georgia, among others. In 2008, seventeen years after Georgia gained its own independence as an internationally recognized state, this multi-ethnic republic diminished in size when two of its ethnically distinct regions, South Ossetia and Abkhazia, officially split after

▲▲▲ A U.S.-based company founded in 1955, McDonald's is the leading global food service retailer with more than 33,000 restaurants in 118 countries. Its Golden Arches have become an internationally recognized symbol for fast-service fries, chicken, hamburgers, salads, and milkshakes. Most of these restaurants are franchises owned and operated by local businesspeople who are members of the same society as most of their customers. Success depends not only on quality fast food and quick service, but also on respecting cultural food taboos. In India, home to nearly a billion Hindus who follow a beef taboo, the Big Mac is made with lamb or chicken and is known as a Maharaja Mac. Beef burgers are not a problem in Saudi Arabia, where the first McDonald's franchise opened in 1993. Operated by Arab Muslims, there are now 100 McDonald's there, including this one in the capital city of Riyadh, where men and women are gender segregated in different lines and dining areas.

Patrick Baz/AFP/Getty Images

[1] The latest from McDonald's. (2011). *About McDonald's Media Center.* http://www.aboutmcdonalds.com/mcd/media_center.html (retrieved September 18, 2011).

[2] Referring to the "process by which institutions in society become standardized and focused on efficiency and predictability," this term was first coined by George Ritzer in his 1983 article "The McDonaldization of Society," *Journal of American Culture 6* (1), 100–107. Since the 1990s, this term has also been used by antiglobalization activists seeking to safeguard their traditional cultures against the onslaught of modernization.

▲▲▲▲▲▲▲▲▲▲▲▲▲▲▲▲▲▲▲▲▲▲▲▲▲▲▲▲▲▲▲▲▲▲▲▲▲▲

modernization The process of economic change, whereby developing societies acquire some of the social and political characteristics of Western industrial societies; five subprocesses are involved: technological development, agricultural development, urbanization, industrialization, and telecommunication.

▼▼▼▼▼▼▼▼▼▼▼▼▼▼▼▼▼▼▼▼▼▼▼▼▼▼▼▼▼▼▼▼▼▼▼▼▼▼

years of separatist pressure. Most recently, in July 2011 Sudan in northeastern Africa officially split along an ethnic, religious, and geographic fault line, producing international recognition of the Republic of South Sudan as the 193rd United Nations member state.

The splintering tendency of multi-ethnic states can also be seen in separatist movements such as that of French-speaking peoples in Canada, Basques in Spain, Karen in Myanmar (Burma), Kurds in Turkey and Iraq, and so on—this list is far from exhaustive. Nor is the United States immune, as can be seen in Native American nations seeking to secure greater political self-determination on their reservations.

Despite these examples, there are also a few instances of reunification. Best known among these is the 1990 reunification of Germany, divided since the end of World War II as East and West Germany, into one large federal republic. Another notable exception is the integration of twenty-seven European countries into the European Union—despite the hindrances of linguistic differences, distinctive cultural traditions, and bureaucratic red tape.

Many global integrative mechanisms operate to counter the divergent forces at work. These include international sporting events from Wimbledon to the Olympics, plus organizations ranging from UNESCO to Rotary Clubs, Boy Scouts, and Girl Guides, as well as

humanitarian aid organizations such as Doctors Without Borders and Save the Children. Notably, while such mechanisms connect people all around the world, they do not represent a global culture.

Doubts about a Global Cultural Unification

The idea of a global culture shared by most, if not all, peoples of the world today may have popular appeal in certain circles. A common language, for instance, would greatly facilitate international exchange, and a shared ideology (with everyone having a similar worldview and ideals) might lessen cross-cultural misunderstandings and conflicting viewpoints that have led so often to violence over the past several hundred years.

However, anthropologists greet this prognosis with skepticism, suspecting that distinctive worldviews will persist, even in the face of massive changes. Moreover, new ideologies are emerging, and those that are changing are not necessarily changing in the same fashion. In fact, not all peoples react the same way to the forces of globalization. Those who are willing and able to make the required adjustments may actually benefit from the transformation in their cultures, whereas others less well positioned for the changes may resist and/or have a deeply troubling experience. In short, globalization is a complex and dynamic process with a vast range of national, regional, and even local cultural reactions and adjustments.

Some have argued that perhaps a global culture would be desirable in the future, because some traditional cultures may be too specialized to adjust to a changed environment. For instance, when Amazonian Indians pursuing traditional ways of life that are well adapted to South America's tropical rainforest are confronted with sudden, radical changes brought on by foreign invaders, their long-established cultures often collapse. The reason for this, it is argued, is that the forest-dwellers' traditions and political and social organizations are not adapted to modern ways and that they are naturally destined to give way to the new. The flaw with this argument is that, far from being unable to adapt, such traditional peoples have been robbed repeatedly of the opportunity to work out their own

© Paul Gilham/Getty Images

▲▲▲ **The Olympics are unique among the many strands in today's global web. Inspired by the ancient Greek sporting event held at Olympia more than 2,000 years ago, the games have become a global spectacle, with thousands of athletes from all around the world competing in a different country every four years. In today's world—where powerful states have conquered and destroyed many smaller nations and tens of millions have been killed in warfare worldwide—this global sports gathering is a crucial ritual, celebrating international peace in a friendly rivalry for medals and prestige. Pictured here is the opening ceremony of the 2008 Olympics in China.**

adaptations according to their own priorities. Their demise is caused not by laws of nature but rather by the political and economic choices of powerful outside forces.

Pluralistic Societies and Multiculturalism

If a single homogenous global culture is not necessarily the wave of the future, what is? Some predict a world in which ethnic groups will become more nationalistic in response to globalization, each group stressing its unique cultural heritage and emphasizing differences with neighboring groups. But not all ethnic groups organize themselves politically as distinctive nations with their own state. In fact, it has been common for two or more neighboring ethnic groups or nations to draw together in a loose political union while maintaining their particular cultural identities.

Because such *pluralistic societies* lack a common cultural identity and heritage, and often do not share the same language or religion, political relationships between ethnic groups can be tense. When feelings of ethnonationalism are not far from the surface, political pressure may build up and result in separation and independence.

One way of curbing divisive pressures in pluralistic or multi-ethnic societies is the adoption of a public policy based on mutual respect and tolerance for cultural differences. Known as **multiculturalism,** such an official policy or doctrine asserts the value of different cultures coexisting within a country and stresses the reciprocal responsibility of all citizens to accept the rights of others to freely express their views and values. In contrast to state policies in which a dominant ethnic group uses its power to impose its own culture as the national standard, forcing other groups within the same state to assimilate, multiculturalism involves a public policy for managing a society's cultural diversity. Examples of long-established multiculturalism may be seen in states such as Switzerland (where German-, French-, Italian-, and Romansh-speaking peoples coexist under the same government) and Canada (where French- and English-speaking Canadians as well as dozens of indigenous nations live side by side).

Although cultural pluralism is still more common than multiculturalism, several multi-ethnic countries have recently changed their official melting pot ideology and associated policies of assimilation. One example of a country moving toward multiculturalism is the United States, which now has over 120 different ethnic groups within its borders, in addition to hundreds of federally recognized American Indian groups. Another is Australia, now counting over a hundred ethnic groups and with eighty languages spoken within its territorial boundaries. Similar changes are also underway in many European countries where millions of foreign immigrants have settled during the past few decades. Such changes are not easy; they may engender protests or violent reactions and have resulted in official policy reversals along the way.

We cannot ignore the fact that historically what has been called "nation building" in all parts of the world almost always involves attempts to subordinate or even destroy the cultures of peoples whose nationalities differ from those in control of the government.[3] During the last two decades of the 20th century, states were borrowing more money to fight peoples within their own boundaries than for all their other programs combined. Nearly all state debt in Africa and nearly half of all other debt in "underdeveloped" countries come from the cost of weapons purchased by states to fight their own citizens.[4] The more divergent cultural traditions are, the more difficult it is to make pluralism work.

Pluralistic Societies and Ethnocentrism

A major obstacle to the successful functioning of a pluralistic society is each ethnic group's loyalty toward its distinctive language and unique cultural traditions, from which its members derive psychological support and a firm social bond to their community. Such ethnic pride is often tied to the belief that the ways of one's own culture are the only proper ones. To overcome this kind of cultural superiority complex or ethnocentrism, a pluralistic society may have to develop a common superstructure with an ideological force that binds different peoples together with a collective sense of shared identity and destiny.

As illustrated again and again in this book, it is all too easy to turn ethnic pride and loyalty into a charter for denigrating people with different cultural practices and exploiting them for the benefit of one's own group. Although this is not an inevitable result, when it does occur, unrest, hostility, and violence commonly ensue.[5]

---

[3]Van den Berghe, P. (1992). The modern state: Nation builder or nation killer? *International Journal of Group Tensions* 22 (3), 191–208.

[4]*Cultural Survival Quarterly.* (1991). *15* (4), 38.

[5]Nieftagodien, N. (2008, June 16). Incoherent response to crisis: If the government does not address unemployment and housing demands, the worst is still to come. *The Star*, Johannesburg. South Africa. http://www.highbeam.com/doc/1G1-180098871.html (retrieved September 18, 2011).

▲▲

multiculturalism The public policy for managing cultural diversity in a multi-ethnic society, officially stressing mutual respect and tolerance for cultural differences within a country's borders.

▼▼

▲▲▲ Although South Africa's apartheid regime was abolished in 1992 and a white minority no longer politically dominates the pluralistic country, social tensions between different ethnic groups remain. With few opportunities to earn money, many of the 8 million people living in Johannesburg's squalid townships and squatter camps are unemployed and impoverished and blame foreign immigrants for the misery. This *xenophobia* ("fear of strangers") has frequently turned violent, resulting in bloody assaults against foreigners, many of whom are from poor neighboring countries such as Zimbabwe and Mozambique. Dozens have been killed, hundreds cruelly beaten, and thousands forced to flee. But, there is a counter voice: Here we see a demonstration of South Africans and immigrants protesting the brutal murder of forty foreign laborers in Johannesburg in 2008.

the entire globe. Doing this, of course, requires a great deal of power.

As discussed in Chapter 14, power refers to the ability of individuals or groups to impose their will on others and make them do things even against their own wants or wishes. Power plays a major role in coordinating and regulating collective behavior toward imposing or maintaining law and order within—and beyond—a particular community or society.

There are different levels of power within societies, as well as among societies. U.S. anthropologist Eric Wolf has pointed out the importance of understanding a macro level of power that he refers to as **structural power**—power that organizes and orchestrates the systemic interaction within and among societies, directing economic and political forces on the one hand and ideological forces that shape public ideas, values, and beliefs on the other.[6] The concept of structural power applies not only to regional political organizations such as chiefdoms or states, but also captures the complex new cultural formations currently restructuring and transfiguring societies and environments everywhere on earth.

Joseph Nye—a Harvard University political scientist and former assistant secretary of defense in the U.S. government—refers to these two major interacting forces in the worldwide arena as "hard power" and "soft power."[7] **Hard power** is the kind of coercive power that is backed up by economic or military force. **Soft power** co-opts rather than coerces, pressing others through attraction and persuasion to change their ideas, beliefs, values, and behaviors. Although propaganda is a form of soft power, the exercise of ideological influence (the global struggle for hearts and minds) also operates through more subtle means, such as foreign aid, international diplomacy, news media, sports, entertainment, museum exhibits, and academic exchanges.

In the world today, powerful governments frequently operate on the basis of the political idea that no group has the right to stand in the way of "the greater good for the greater number." This concept is commonly used to justify the expropriation of natural resources in regions traditionally occupied by subsistence farmers, pastoral nomads, or food foragers—without respect for the rights, concerns, or wishes of these peoples. But is it truly the greater good for the greater number?

Structural Power in the Age of Globalization

A new form of expansive international capitalism has emerged since the mid-1900s. Operating under the banner of globalization, it builds on earlier cultural structures of worldwide trade networks, and it is the successor to a system of colonialism in which a handful of powerful, mainly European capitalist states ruled and exploited foreign nations inhabiting distant territories.

Enormously complex and turbulent, globalization is a dynamically structured process in which individuals, business corporations, and political institutions actively rearrange and restructure the political field to their own competitive advantage, vying for increasingly scarce natural resources, cheap labor, new commercial markets, and ever-larger profits. In the age of globalization, this restructuring occurs in a vast arena spanning

[6]Wolf, E. (1999). *Envisioning power: Ideologies of dominance and crisis* (p. 5). Berkeley: University of California Press.

[7]Nye, J. (2002). *The paradox of American power: Why the world's only superpower can't go it alone.* New York: Oxford University Press.

Percentage of Global Military Spending by Country

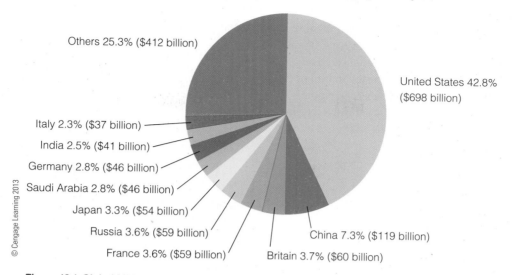

© Cengage Learning 2013

Figure 16.1 Global Military Spending by Country In 2010, world military spending reached $1.63 trillion, with the United States accounting for nearly 43 percent of the total. (Expenditures are rounded to the nearest billion.)

Source: Stockholm International Peace Research Institute.

Military Hard Power

Today the United States has more hard power at its disposal than any of its allies or rivals worldwide. It is the global leader in military expenditure, spending nearly $698 billion in 2010, followed by China ($119 billion). In fact, as the world's still dominant superpower, the United States is responsible for nearly 43 percent of the $1.63 trillion spent on arms worldwide (▶ **Figure 16.1**).[8]

Moreover, although there are seven other nuclear weapons states (Britain, France, and China, as well as Israel, India, Pakistan, and North Korea, collectively possessing nearly 1,000 active nuclear warheads), Russia and the United States have by far the largest nuclear arsenals at their disposal. Russia has 4,400 operational warheads, plus a stockpile of 7,000 intact but nonoperational warheads. The United States possesses just under 2,500 warheads, plus about 2,600 that are inactive and 3,500 that are "retired and awaiting dismantlement."[9]

In addition to military might, hard power involves using economic strength as a political instrument of coercion or intimidation in the global structuring process. Among other things, this means that economic size and productivity, technological capability, and finance capital may be brought to bear on the global market, forcing less

powerful states to weaken the systems protecting their workers, natural resources, and local markets.

As the world's largest economy and leading exporter, the United States has long pushed for free trade for its corporations doing business on a global scale. Sometimes it uses military power to impose changes on a foreign political landscape by means of armed interventions or full-scale invasions. Throughout its history, the United States (like several other powerful countries, including Russia, Britain, and France) has engaged in such military interventions around the world. Because of this, many see the United States as an ever-present threat, apt to use overwhelming military force in order to benefit its corporate interests from fruit to fuel, from microchips to automobiles. The corporations, in turn, wield enormous political and financial power over governments and international organizations, including the World Trade Organization, headquartered in Geneva, and global banking institutions such as the International Monetary Fund (IMF) and World Bank, both based in Washington, DC.

▲▲▲

structural power Power that organizes and orchestrates the systemic interaction within and among societies, directing economic and political forces on the one hand and ideological forces that shape public ideas, values, and beliefs on the other.

hard power Power that coerces others and that is backed up by economic or military force.

soft power Power that co-opts rather than coerces, pressing others through attraction and persuasion to change their ideas, beliefs, values, and behaviors.

▼▼

---

[8]World military spending reached $1.6 trillion in 2010. (2011, April 11). Press release, Stockholm International Peace Research Institute. http://www.sipri.org/media/pressreleases/milex (retrieved September 18, 2011).

[9]Arms Control Association. (2011). Nuclear weapons: Who has what at a glance. http://www.armscontrol.org/factsheets/Nuclearweaponswhohaswhat (retrieved September 18, 2011).

Home to more global corporations than any other country, the United States is endeavoring to protect its interests by investing in what it refers to as a "global security environment." Numerous other countries, unable to afford expensive weapons systems or blocked from developing or acquiring them, have invested in biological or chemical warfare technology. Still others, including relatively powerless political groups, have resorted to insurgencies, guerrilla tactics, or even terrorism.

Economic Hard Power

Global corporations, rare before the latter half of the 20th century, now are a far-reaching economic and political force in the world. Modern-day business giants such as General Electric, Shell, and Toyota are actually clusters of several corporations joined by ties of common ownership and responsive to a related management strategy. Usually tightly controlled by a head office in one country, megacorporations organize and integrate production across the international boundaries of different countries for interests formulated in corporate boardrooms, irrespective of whether these are consistent with the interests of people in the countries where they operate. These megacorporations are the products of the technological revolution, for without fast mass transportation, sophisticated data-processing equipment, and telecommunication, they could not conduct or manage their transnational capitalist operations.

Though typically thought of as responding impersonally to outside market forces, megacorporations are in fact controlled by a shrinking number of wealthy capitalists who benefit directly from their operations. Yet, unlike political leaders, the world's largest individual stockholders and most powerful directors are virtually unknown to the general public. For that matter, most people cannot even name the world's ten leading global corporations, which include Walmart, Shell, and Toyota (▶ **Figure 16.2**). In 2010, each of the top ten business giants generated annual revenues at or above $200 billion, and four of them topped the $300 billion mark.[10]

So great is the power of large businesses operating all across the globe that they increasingly thwart the wishes of national governments or international organizations such as the United Nations, the Red Cross, and the International Court of Justice. Because megacorporations restrict information about their operations, it can be difficult for governments to make informed policy decisions. It took years for the U.S. Congress to extract information from tobacco companies to decide what to do about tobacco legislation, and it is nearly as slow-going today to get energy and media companies to provide data needed for regulatory purposes.

Beyond this, global corporations have repeatedly shown they can overrule foreign policy decisions. This raises the unsettling issue of whether or not the global arena should be controlled by immense powerful private corporations interested primarily in financial profits. According to one market research organization,

> Today, the top 100 companies control 33 percent of the world's assets, but employ only one percent of the world's workforce. . . . Wal-Mart is bigger than South Africa. The mega-corporations roam freely around the globe, lobbying legislators, bankrolling elections and playing governments off against each other to get the best deals. Their private hands control the bulk of the world's news and information flows.[11]

Global corporations are changing the shape of the world and the lives of individuals from every walk of life, including those they employ. In the never-ending search for cheap labor, megacorporations have returned to a practice once common in the textile mills of 19th-century Britain and New England, but now on a much larger scale. More than ever before, they have come to favor women for low-skilled assembly jobs. In so-called underdeveloped countries, as subsistence farming gives way to mechanized agriculture for the production of export crops, women are less able to contribute to their families' survival. Together with the devaluation of domestic work, this places pressure on women to seek jobs outside the household to contribute to its support. Since most women in these countries do not have the time or resources to get an education or to develop special job skills, only low-paying jobs are open to them.

Faceless relations between producers and consumers, among whom there is a grossly unequal distribution of power, have exacted a high cost: a terrible sense of indifference, apathy, even a loss of faith in the dehumanized system itself. When workers do not trust their bosses, and bosses do not trust one another, production and trade relations on every level are damaged or ruined. This alienation may ultimately lead to a systemic breakdown.[12] With production, trading, and banking operations on a global scale, the breakdown in one part of the system may trigger a worldwide chain reaction of failures. Such was the global crisis triggered by the bankruptcy of a handful of mismanaged Wall Street firms in 2008.[13]

---

[10]Global 500. (2011). *CNN Money.* http://money.cnn.com/magazines/fortune/global500/2011/ (retrieved September 18, 2011).

[11]Lasn, K., & Liacas, T. (2000, August/September). Birth of the corporate "I." *Adbusters* (31). http://www.nancho.net/corperson/adbcorpI.html (retrieved September 18, 2011); see also Hertz, N. (2001). *The silent takeover: Global capitalism and the death of democracy* (p. 43). New York: Arrow Books.

[12]Nader, L. (Ed.). (1981). *No access to law: Alternatives to the American judicial system.* New York: Academic Press.

[13]Notably, as Brazilian anthropologist Gustavo Lins Ribeiro points out, today even informal economies, burgeoning in Latin America and elsewhere, are globalized. See Ribeiro, G. L. (2009). Nonhegemonic globalizations: Alternative transnational processes and agents. *Anthropological Theory* 9 (3), 297–329.

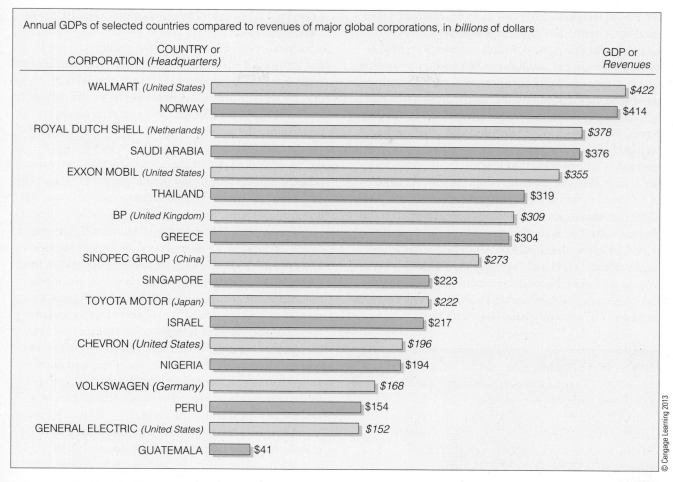

Annual GDPs of selected countries compared to revenues of major global corporations, in *billions* of dollars

COUNTRY or CORPORATION (*Headquarters*)	GDP or Revenues
WALMART (*United States*)	*$422*
NORWAY	$414
ROYAL DUTCH SHELL (*Netherlands*)	*$378*
SAUDI ARABIA	$376
EXXON MOBIL (*United States*)	*$355*
THAILAND	$319
BP (*United Kingdom*)	*$309*
GREECE	$304
SINOPEC GROUP (*China*)	*$273*
SINGAPORE	$223
TOYOTA MOTOR (*Japan*)	*$222*
ISRAEL	$217
CHEVRON (*United States*)	*$196*
NIGERIA	$194
VOLKSWAGEN (*Germany*)	*$168*
PERU	$154
GENERAL ELECTRIC (*United States*)	*$152*
GUATEMALA	$41

© Cengage Learning 2013

Figure 16.2 GDPs of Selected Countries and Revenues of Global Corporations In today's consumer-driven world, it is not uncommon for the yearly revenues of large multinational corporations to equal and even exceed the total value of all goods and services produced within many countries per year, known as a country's gross domestic product (GDP). This graph shows the annual GDPs of selected countries alongside the annual revenues of leading global corporations. Notably, Walmart revenues exceeded the GDPs of 173 of the world's 195 countries. Not shown here are the countries with the highest and lowest GDPs. Nearly half have GDPs under $20 billion, and twenty fall below $1 billion. Only fourteen countries surpass $1 trillion, including the United States at nearly $15 trillion, with China in second place at nearly $6 trillion. Note that GDP says nothing about the unequal distribution of wealth within a country.

Source: Based on the Global 500 list of corporate revenues for 2010 at http://money.cnn.com/magazines/fortune/global500/2011/ and the 2010 GDP figures provided by World Bank at http://siteresources.worldbank.org/DATASTATISTICS/Resources/GDP.pdf (retrieved September 30, 2011).

Soft Power: A Global Media Environment

In addition to reliance on military and economic hard power in the global quest for dominance and profit, competing states and corporations utilize the ideological persuasion of soft power as transmitted through electronic and digital media, communication satellites, and other information technology. One of the major tasks of soft power is to sell the general idea of globalization as something positive and progressive (as "freedom," "free" trade, "free" market) and to frame or brand anything that opposes capitalism in negative terms.

Global mass media corporations like Cable News Network (CNN) possess enormous soft power. This U.S.-based private company produces and distributes news

and other information through transnational cable and satellite networks, as well as websites. With bureaus in over thirty countries, its 24-hour news coverage is available to more than 1.5 billion people all over the world. Like other media giants, such as Al Jazeera, CNN not only reports news but also selects the visual imagery and determines what to stress or repress. By means of their awesome soft power, these corporations influence public perception and action ("hearts and minds").

The far-reaching capabilities of modern electronic and digital technologies have led to the creation of a new global media environment that plays a major role in how individuals and even societies view themselves and their place in the world. The global flow of information made possible by fiber optic cables, cell towers, and communication satellites orbiting the earth is almost entirely digital-electronic, taking place in a new, boundless cultural space termed a "global mediascape."[14]

In recent years, the power of corporations has become all the greater through media expansion. Over the past two decades, a global commercial media system has developed, dominated by a few megacorporations (such as General Electric and Disney), most based in the United States. Having control of television and other media, as well as the advertising industry, gives global corporations enormous influence on the ideas and behavior of hundreds of millions of ordinary people across the world.

Consider, for example, the powerful marketing messages that shape cultural standards concerning the ideal human body. The widespread nature of this concern is evident in the abundance of TV infomercials selling workout equipment and "age-defying" cosmetic products, as well as highly popular plastic surgery reality shows such as E! Entertainment's long-running *Dr. 90210* and Logo TV's recently launched *Pretty Hurts*.

© Harald E. L. Prins

▲▲▲ The poorest people in the world, such as this Maka Indian woman in Paraguay, often wear clothing discarded by those who are better off—and people from all walks of life can be found wearing clothes with corporate logos. The power that big business (such as the Disney media corporation) has over individuals is illustrated by the fact that corporations influence consumers to pay for goods that advertise corporate products.

Problems of Structural Violence

Structural power and its associated concepts of hard and soft power enable us to better understand the global arena in which local communities are compelled to operate and the unequal distribution of wealth, health, and power in today's world. When structural power undermines the well-being of others, we may speak of **structural violence**—physical and/or psychological harm—including repression, environmental destruction, poverty, hunger, illness, and premature death—caused by impersonal, exploitative, and unjust social, political, and economic systems.[15]

The Universal Declaration of Human Rights, officially adopted by all members of the United Nations in 1948, provides a useful baseline for identifying structural violence. Anthropologists played a key role in drafting this important document, which begins with the statement that "recognition of the inherent dignity and of the equal and inalienable rights of all members of the human family is the foundation of freedom, justice and peace in the world."[16] Generally speaking, structural violence concerns the impersonal systemic violation of the human rights of individuals and communities to a healthy, peaceful, and dignified life.

Although human rights abuses are nothing new, globalization has enormously expanded and intensified structural violence. For instance, it is leading to an ever-widening gap between the wealthiest and poorest peoples, the powerful and powerless. In 1960 the average income for the twenty wealthiest countries in the world was fifteen times that of the twenty poorest. Today it is thirty times higher.[17]

Notably, these figures fail to indicate that some of the poorest countries in the world have a small number of very rich citizens, and that very wealthy countries include many poor inhabitants. In fact, the income disparity between rich and poor within many countries has been widening in recent years—as evident in the Income Inequality Index annually posted by the United Nations. The index ranges from 0 to 100, with 0 corresponding to perfect equality (where everyone has the same income) and 100 corresponding to perfect inequality (where one person has all the income and everyone else has zero income).

---

[14]Appadurai, A. (1990). Disjuncture and difference in the global cultural economy. *Public Culture 2*, 1–24.

[15]See Farmer, P. (1996). On suffering and structural violence: A view from below. *Daedelus 125* (1), 261–283.

[16]Universal Declaration of Human Rights. www.ccnmtl.columbia.edu/projects/mmt/udhr (retrieved September 19, 2011).

[17]World Bank poverty statistics. (n.d.). http://web.worldbank.org/WBSITE/EXTERNAL/TOPICS/EXTPOVERTY/0,,menuPK:336998~pagePK:149018~piPK:149093~theSitePK:336992,00.html (retrieved September 30, 2011).

Measuring the gap between the richest and poorest 10 percent of the population in China, for example, the Income Inequality Index shows that the world's largest communist country is even more unequal (21.5) than the United States, the world's largest capitalist country (15.9). By comparison, other wealthy industrialized countries have a much more equal income distribution, including Germany (6.9) and Japan (4.5).

On the other hand, the greatest income disparities between the richest and poorest 10 percent can be found in some of the poorest countries, including Paraguay (65.4), the Central African Republic (69.2), and Haiti (71.7).[18] However, the United States now has the highest income inequality in the wealthy industrialized world, and the big gap between rich and poor is widening.

Measured on a global scale, the wealth of the ultra-rich has reached stratospheric proportions. A dozen years ago, the annual United Nations Human Development Report presented its findings in a way that captured widespread attention, noting that the world's 225 richest individuals had a combined wealth equal to the annual income of the poorest 47 percent of the entire world population. In broader terms, it reported that, the richest 20 percent of the human population consumed 86 percent of all the world's goods and services and that the other 80 percent of humanity had the benefit of only 14 percent. The poorest 20 percent had a mere 1.3 percent of those goods and services.[19] The disparity between the have-lots and the have-nots continues. Today, the 12 percent of the world's population that lives in North America and western Europe accounts for 60 percent of private consumption spending, while the third living in South Asia and sub-Saharan Africa accounts for only 3.2 percent. As many as 2.8 billion people on the planet struggle to survive on less than $2 a day.[20]

Structural violence has countless manifestations in addition to widespread poverty. These range from the cultural destruction already indicated to hunger and obesity, and environmental degradation, all discussed in the remaining pages of this chapter.

Overpopulation and Poverty

In 1750, 1 billion people lived on earth. Over the next two centuries our numbers climbed to nearly 2.5 billion. And between 1950 and 2000 the world population soared above 6 billion. Today, the world's population is about 7 billion, with India and China each having more than 1 billion inhabitants. Such increases are highly significant because population growth increases the scale of hunger and pollution—and the many troubles tied to them. Although controlling population growth does not eliminate the other difficulties, we are unlikely to be able to solve these two big issues unless population growth is stopped or even reversed.

Despite progress in population control, the number of humans on earth continues to grow overall. Projections are extremely tricky, given variables such war, famine, and infectious diseases, but current projections suggest that global population will surge beyond 10 billion by the end of this century.[21] The severity of the situation becomes clear with the realization that the present world population can be sustained only by using up non-renewable resources such as oil.

Hunger and Obesity

As frequently dramatized in media reports, hundreds of millions of people face hunger on a regular basis, leading to a variety of health problems, premature death, and other forms of suffering. Today, over a quarter of the world's countries do not produce enough food to feed their populations, and they cannot afford to import what is needed.

Hunger is caused not only by shortages due to environmental factors such as drought and pests, but also by human actions. In fact, during the 20th century, 44 million people died as a result of human-made famine.[22] For example, in several sub-Saharan African countries plagued by decades of civil strife, it has been almost impossible to grow and harvest crops because roaming militias, underpaid soldiers, and hordes of hungry refugees constantly raid fields.

[18]List of countries by income equality. http://en.wikipedia.org/wiki/List_of_countries_by_income_equality (retrieved September 19, 2011). This site features a list of countries organized by income inequality metrics. It draws wealth figures from various sources, including the United Nations and the U.S. Central Intelligence Agency. See also: Davies, J. B., et al. (2007). *The worl distribution of household wealth*. Santa Cruz, CA: University of California, Mapping Global Inequalities, Center for Global, International, and Regional Studies.

[19]Crossette, B. (1998, September 27). Kofi Annan's astonishing facts! *New York Times*, D16.

[20]The State of Consumption Today. Worldwatch Institute. Washington, DC: Worldwatch Institute. http://www.worldwatch.org/node/810 (retrieved October 3, 2011).

[21]Kaiser, J. (2011, May 4). 10 billion plus: Why world population projections were too low. *Science Insider*. http://news.sciencemag.org/scienceinsider/2011/05/10-billion-plus-why-world-population.html (retrieved October 3, 2011).

[22]The Hunger Project. (2011). www.thp.org; White, M. (2001). *Historical atlas of the twentieth century*. http://users.erols.com/mwhite28/20centry.htm (retrieved September 19, 2011).

▲▲▲

structural violence Physical and/or psychological harm (including repression, environmental destruction, poverty, hunger, illness, and premature death) caused by impersonal, exploitative, and unjust social, political, and economic systems.

▼▼▼

Beyond violent political, ethnic, or religious conflicts that uproot families from their traditional food sources, famine is fueled by a global food production and distribution system geared to satisfy the demands of the world's most powerful countries. For example, in Africa, Asia, and Latin America, millions of acres once devoted to subsistence farming have been given over to the raising of cash crops for export. This has enriched members of elite social classes in these parts of the world, while satisfying the appetites of people in developed countries for coffee, tea, chocolate, bananas, and beef. Small-scale farmers who used to till the land for their own food needs have been relocated—either to urban areas, where all too often there is no employment for them, or to areas ecologically unsuited for farming.

Also of note, governments of the wealthiest capitalist states in North America and western Europe spend between $100 billion and $300 billion annually on agricultural subsidies given primarily to large farmers and agricultural corporations. Small farmers in poor countries cannot compete with subsidized agribusinesses that are selling mass-produced and often genetically engineered crops. Many small farmers have been forced to quit farming, leave their villages, and seek work in cities or as migrant workers abroad.

Today, about 1 billion people in the world experience chronic hunger. A majority (almost 650 million) of these people live in Asia and the Pacific islands. Next comes sub-Saharan Africa with about 265 million, followed by the Middle East and North Africa with 53 million, and another 15 million in the world's wealthy countries.[23] Of particular note, every year, famine claims the lives of some 6 million children ages 5 and under, and those who survive it often suffer physical and mental impairment.[24]

Most of the world's hungry are victims of structural violence. This is because the increasing rate of starvation is due not only to environmental calamities, but to human actions ranging from warfare to massive job cuts, growing poverty rates, and the collapse of local markets caused by foreign imports.

Ironically, while many millions of people are starving, many millions of others are overeating—literally eating themselves to death. In fact, the number of overfed people now exceeds those who are underfed. According to the Worldwatch Institute in Washington, DC, more than 1.1 billion people worldwide are now overweight. And over 350 million of these are obese but still often malnourished in that their diets lack certain nutrients.

Seriously concerned about the sharp rise in associated health problems (including stroke, diabetes, cancer, and heart disease), the World Health Organization classifies obesity as a global epidemic. Overeating is particularly unhealthy for individuals living in societies where machines have eased the physical burdens of work and other human activities, which helps explain why more

© Oli Scarff/Getty Images

▲▲▲ In Somalia, Africa, extended drought and years of civil war have caused a great famine. In the summer of 2011, the United Nations estimated that a third of Somali citizens were undernourished. So many died that officials stopped counting. Pictured here are Somali people lined up for food at a refugee camp in Dadaab, Kenya, near the Somalia border.

than half of the people in some industrial and post-industrial countries are overweight.

However, the obesity epidemic is not due solely to excessive eating and lack of physical activity. A key ingredient is the high sugar and fat content of mass-marketed foods. Thus in Japan, where food habits differ significantly from those in the United States, obesity plagues just over 3 percent of the population, compared to the U.S. rate of 32 percent. In fact, U.S. obesity figures have doubled over the past three decades, placing it at the top of the obesity chart among wealthy industrialized countries. Obesity rates differ between men and women,

---

[23]Food and Agriculture Organization of the United Nations. (2009, June 19). 1.02 billion people hungry: One sixth of humanity undernourished—more than ever before. http://www.fao.org/news/story/en/item/20568/icode/ (retrieved September 19, 2011).

[24]The Hunger Project; see also Swaminathan, M. S. (2000). Science in response to basic human needs. *Science 287,* 425.

higher and lower income groups, and among various ethnic groups. The highest U.S. rate is among African American women, half of whom suffer from obesity.[25]

The problem has become a serious concern even in some developing countries, especially where people have switched to a diet based on processed or canned fast food. The highest rates of obesity in the world can now be found among island nations in the Pacific Ocean, such as Fiji, Samoa, and Tonga. Topping the world's obesity prevalence list is the island of Nauru, formerly known as Pleasant Island.

Traditionally, Nauruans valued food as a symbol of well-being and social pride, considered fat to be a sign of beauty, and associated large body size with strength and prosperity.[26] In the days when Nauruans still depended largely on fishing and gathering for most of their food, obesity was not a medical problem. However, when royalties from phosphate mining provided each family with large amounts of cash, the Nauruan diet and lifestyle changed radically for the worse. Today, phosphate wealth has disappeared, but the junk food diet remains, and 80 percent of the indigenous population of this small island republic in Micronesia has become obese; about 30 percent of them now have diabetes.[27]

Pollution and Global Warming

Pollution is another key aspect of structural violence brought on by the world's most powerful countries, which are also the greatest producers and consumers of energy. During the past 200 years, global cultural development has relied on burning increasing quantities of fossil fuels (coal, oil, and gas), with dire results: Massive deforestation and desertification, along with severe air, water, and soil pollution, now threaten all life on earth.

In addition, fossil fuel use has dramatically increased carbon dioxide levels, trapping more heat in the earth's atmosphere. Most atmospheric scientists believe that the efficiency of the atmosphere in retaining heat—

the greenhouse effect—is being enhanced by increased carbon dioxide, methane, and other gases produced by industrial and agricultural activities. The result, a period of global warming, threatens to dramatically alter climates in all parts of the world.

Rising temperatures are causing more and greater storms, droughts, and heat waves, devastating populations in vulnerable areas. And if the massive meltdown of Arctic ice now underway continues, rising sea levels will inundate low coastal areas worldwide. Entire islands may soon disappear, including thousands of villages and even large cities.

Experts also predict that global warming will lead to an expansion of the geographic ranges of tropical diseases and increase the incidence of respiratory diseases due to additional smog caused by warmer temperatures. Also, they expect an increase in deaths due to heat waves, as witnessed in the 52,000 deaths attributed to the 2003 heat wave in Europe.[28]

Especially since the industrial revolution about two centuries ago, societies have experienced the negative effects of environmental degradation. Much of this degradation is caused by ever-increasing amounts of non-biodegradable waste and toxic emissions into the soil, water, and air. Until very recently, much of this pollution was officially tolerated for the sake of maximizing profits that primarily benefit select individuals, groups, and societies. Today industries in many parts of the world are producing highly toxic waste at unprecedented rates. Pollutants such as various oxides of nitrogen or sulfur cause the development of acid precipitation, which damages soil, vegetation, and wildlife. Air pollution in the form of smog is often dangerous for human health.

Moreover, poisonous smokestack gases are clearly implicated in acid rain, which is damaging lakes and forests all over northeastern North America. Air containing water vapor with a high acid content is, of course, harmful to the lungs, but there is a greater health hazard involved. As groundwater and surface water become more acidic, the solubility of lead, cadmium, mercury, and aluminum, all of them toxic, rises sharply. For instance, for 17 percent of the world's farmland, the aluminum contamination is high enough to be toxic to plants—and has been linked to senile dementia, Alzheimer's, and Parkinson's disease, three major health problems in industrial countries.

Finding their way into the world's oceans, toxic substances also create hazards for seafood consumers. For instance, Canadian Inuit face health problems related to eating fish and sea mammals that feed in waters contaminated by industrial chemical waste such as polychlorinated biphenyls (PCBs) (see the Biocultural Connection, page 350). Environmental poisoning affects peoples all across the globe (▶ **Figure 16.3**). Also of great concern are harmful chemicals in plastics used for water bottles, baby bottles, and can linings, as discussed in Chapter 7.

---

[25]Centers for Disease Control and Prevention. (2009). Differences in prevalence of obesity among black, white, and Hispanic adults—United States, 2006–2008. *Morbidity and Mortality Weekly Report 58* (27), 740–744; Drewnowski, A., & Specter, S. E. (2004). Poverty and obesity: The role of energy density and energy costs. *American Journal of Clinical Nutrition 79* (1), 6–16.

[26]Pollock, N. J. (1995). Social fattening patterns in the Pacific—the positive side of obesity. A Nauru case study. In I. DeGarine & N. J. Pollock (Eds.), *Social aspects of obesity* (pp. 87–109). London: Routledge.

[27]That said, not all people who are overweight or obese are so because they eat too much junk food and do too little exercise. In addition to cultural factors, being overweight or obese can also have genetic or other biological causes.

[28]Larsen, J. (2006, July 28). *Setting the record straight: More than 52,000 Europeans died from heat in summer 2003. Earth Policy Institute.* http://www.earth-policy.org/plan_b_updates/2006/update56 (retrieved September 19, 2011).

BIOCULTURAL CONNECTION

Toxic Breast Milk Threatens Arctic Culture

© Bryan & Cherry Alexander/Arctic Photos

Asked to picture the Inuit people inhabiting the Arctic coasts of Canada, Greenland, and Labrador, you are likely to envision them dressed in fur parkas and moving across a pristine, snow-covered landscape on dogsleds—perhaps coming home from hunting seal, walrus, or whale.

Such imaginings are still true—except for the pristine part. Although Inuit live nearer to the North Pole than to any city, factory, or farm, they are not isolated from the pollutants of modern society. Chemicals originating in the cities and farms of North America, Europe, and Asia travel thousands of miles to Inuit territories via winds, rivers, and ocean currents. These toxins have a long life in the Arctic, breaking down very slowly due to icy temperatures and low sunlight. Ingested by zooplankton, the chemicals spread through the seafood chain as one species consumes another. The result is alarming levels of pesticides, mercury, and industrial chemicals in Arctic animals—and in the Inuit people who rely on fishing and hunting for food.

Of particular note are toxic chemicals known as PCBs (polychlorinated biphenyls), used widely over several decades

for numerous purposes, such as industrial lubricants, insulating materials, and paint stabilizers. Research shows a widespread presence of PCBs in the breast milk of women around the globe. But nowhere on earth is the concentration higher than among the Inuit—on average seven times that of nursing mothers in Canada's biggest cities.[a]

PCBs have been linked to a wide range of health problems, from liver damage to weakened immune systems to cancer. Studies of children exposed to PCBs in the womb and through breast milk show impaired learning and memory functions. Beyond having a destructive impact on the health of humans (and other animal species), PCBs are impacting the economy, social organization, and psychological well-being of Arctic peoples. Nowhere is this more true than among the 450 Inuit living on Broughton Island, near Canada's Baffin Island. Here, word of skyrocketing PCB levels cost the community its valuable market for Arctic char fish. Inuit in other locations refer to them as "PCB people," and it is said that Inuit men now avoid marrying women from the island.[b]

The Inuit people soundly reject the suggestion that the answer to these problems is a change of diet; they have no real alternatives for affordable food. Abandoning the consumption of traditional seafood would destroy a 4,000-year-old culture based on hunting and fishing. Countless aspects of traditional Inuit culture—from worldview and social arrangements to vocabularies and myths—are linked to Arctic animals and the skills it takes to rely on them for food and many other resources. As one Inuit put it: "Our foods do more than nourish our bodies. They feed our souls. When I eat Inuit foods, I know who I am."[c]

The manufacture of PCBs is now banned in many Western countries (including the United States), and PCB

levels are gradually declining worldwide. However, because of their persistence (and widespread presence in remnant industrial goods such as fluorescent lighting fixtures and electrical appliances), they are still the highest-concentration toxins in breast milk, even among mothers born after the ban.

While PCB contamination declines, other commercial chemicals are finding their way northward. To date, about 200 hazardous compounds originating in industrialized regions have been detected in the bodies of Arctic peoples.[d] Global warming is fueling the problem, because as glaciers and snow melt, long-stored toxins are released. ■

Biocultural Question

Because corporations are able to profit from large-scale and far-reaching commercial activities, we should not be surprised that their operations may also cause serious damage to fellow humans in remote natural environments. What do you think of the profiteering of structural violence?

[a]Colborn, T., et al. (1997). *Our stolen future* (pp. 107–108). New York: Plume/Penguin Books.

[b]Arctic Monitoring Assessment Project. (2003). *AMAP assessment 2002: Human health in the Arctic* (pp. xii–xiii, 22–23). Oslo: AMAP.

[c]Ingmar Egede, quoted in Cone, M. (2005). *Silent snow: The slow poisoning of the Arctic* (p. 1). New York: Grove Press.

[d]Additional sources: Johansen, B. E. (2002). The Inuit's struggle with dioxins and other organic pollutants. *American Indian Quarterly* 26 (3), 479–490; Natural Resources Defense Council. (2005, March 25). *Healthy milk, healthy baby: Chemical pollution and mother's milk.* http://www.nrdc.org/breastmilk/ (retrieved September 19, 2011); Williams, F. (2005, January 9). Toxic breast milk? *New York Times.*

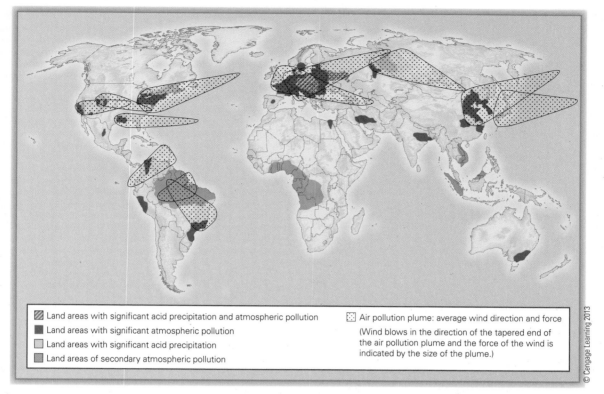

Land areas with significant acid precipitation and atmospheric pollution

Land areas with significant atmospheric pollution

Land areas with significant acid precipitation

Land areas of secondary atmospheric pollution

Air pollution plume: average wind direction and force

(Wind blows in the direction of the tapered end of the air pollution plume and the force of the wind is indicated by the size of the plume.)

© Cengage Learning 2013

Figure 16.3 Global Pollution Almost all processes of physical geography begin and end with flows of energy and matter among land, sea, and air. Because of the primacy of the atmosphere in this exchange system, air pollution is potentially one of the most dangerous human modifications in environmental systems. Pollutants such as various oxides of nitrogen or sulfur cause the development of acid precipitation, which damages soil, vegetation, and wildlife. Air pollution in the form of smog is often dangerous for human health. And most atmospheric scientists believe that the efficiency of the atmosphere in retaining heat—the greenhouse effect—is being enhanced by increased carbon dioxide, methane, and other gases produced by industrial and agricultural activities. The result, global warming, threatens to dramatically alter climates in all parts of the world.

Source: Allen, J. L., & Shalinsky, A. C. (2004). *Student atlas of anthropology* (p. 123). Copyright © 2004 by The McGraw-Hill Companies. Reproduced by permission of McGraw-Hill Contemporary Learning Series.

Structural violence also manifests itself in the shifting of manufacturing and hazardous waste disposal from developed to developing countries. In the late 1980s, a tightening of environmental regulations in industrialized countries led to a dramatic rise in the cost of hazardous waste disposal. Seeking cheaper ways to get rid of the wastes, "toxic traders" began shipping hazardous waste to eastern Europe and especially to poor and underdeveloped countries in western Africa—thereby passing on the health risks of poison cargo to the world's poorest people.

When news of this became public, international outrage about the poisoning of soil, air, and water in these poor countries led to the Basel Convention, an international agreement to prohibit the export of hazardous wastes and minimize their generation. Today the scope of the convention is severely limited by the fact that the United States, the largest toxic residue producer in the world, has not ratified the agreement.[29] Moreover, unscrupulous entrepreneurs and corrupt government officials in these destitute countries have found ways to circumvent the treaty obligations.

Whereas a small number of wealthy countries—primarily in western Europe and North America—have reaped many economic benefits of early industrialization and global trade, they are also responsible for an estimated two-thirds of the atmospheric buildup of heat-trapping carbon dioxide (CO_2). By contrast, all of Africa, a huge continent three times larger than Europe, is responsible for less than 3 percent of the global CO_2 emissions in the past hundred years. Measuring the inequality in human terms, each person in North America adds, on average, 20 tons of carbon dioxide (a greenhouse gas) a year to the atmosphere. In underdeveloped countries, less than 3 tons per person are emitted.[30] One North American consumes hundreds of times the resources of a single African, with all that implies with respect to waste disposal and environmental degradation

[29]Hazardous waste trafficking. (2011). http://www.choike.org/2009/eng/informes/1157.html (retrieved September 19, 2011).

[30]Broecker, W. S. (1992, April). Global warming on trial. *Natural History,* 14.

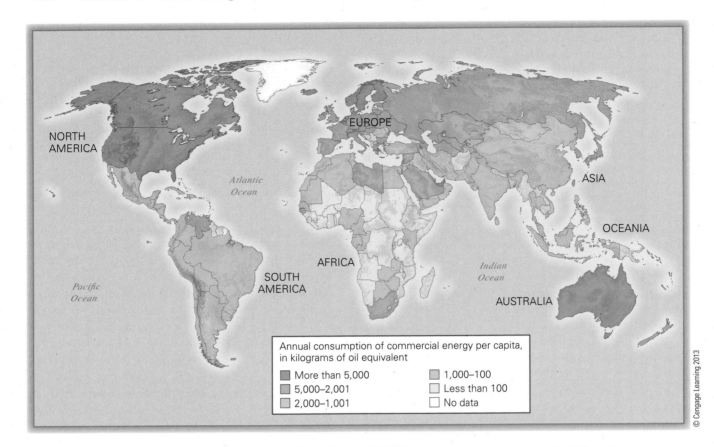

© Cengage Learning 2013

Figure 16.4 Global Energy Consumption Most of the world's highest energy consumers are in North America and western Europe where at least 100 gigajoules of commercial energy per year are consumed by each person. (A gigajoule is the equivalent of about 3.5 metric tons of coal.) In some of these countries, such as the United States and Canada, the consumption rates are in the 300-gigajoule range. At the other end of the scale are low-income countries, with consumption rates often less than 1 percent of those in the United States. (These figures do not include the consumption of noncommercial energy—the traditional fuels of firewood, animal dung, and other organic matter widely used in the less developed parts of the world.)

Source: Allen, J. L., & Shalinsky, A. C. (2004). *Student atlas of anthropology* (p. 98). Copyright © 2004 by The McGraw-Hill Companies. Reproduced by permission of McGraw-Hill Contemporary Learning Series.

(▶ **Figure 16.4**). According to U.S. botanist Peter Raven, "if everyone lived like Americans, you'd need three planet earths . . . to sustain that level of consumption."[31]

Reactions to Globalization

No matter how effectively a dominant state or corporation combines its hard and soft power, globalization does run into opposition. Pockets of resistance exist within the wealthy industrial and postindustrial states as well as elsewhere in the world. This resistance may be manifested in the rise of traditionalism and revitalization movements—efforts to return to life as it was (or how people think it was) before the familiar order became unhinged and people became unsettled. Some of these reactionary movements may take the form of resurgent ethnonationalism or religious fundamentalist movements. Others may find expression in alternative grassroots movements—from radical environmental groups to peace groups to the more recently formed ecotarian movement

that focuses on selecting food based on the ecological impact of its production and transportation.

While it is true that states and big corporations have expanded their power and influence through electronic communication technologies, it is also true that these same technologies present opportunities to individuals and groups that have traditionally been powerless. They provide a means of distributing information and promoting activities that are distinct from or in opposition to those of dominant society.

One striking case of a cultural reaction to globalization is the Taliban, a group of Muslim religious fundamentalists in Afghanistan. The Taliban (the Pashto word for "students," specifically of Islam) helped to force the Russian army out of their country and end the subsequent civil war; then they rose to power in the 1990s and imposed a radical version of traditional Islamic law (Shariah) in an effort to create an Islamic republic based on strict religious values.

---

[31]Quoted in Becker, J. (2004, March). *National Geographic*, 90.

In the United States, there has been a similar, though less radical, reaction against modernity. "Born again" and other fundamentalist citizens seek to shape or transform not only their towns but also states and even the entire country by electing politicians committed to forging a national culture based on what they see as American patriotism, English-only legislation, and traditional Christian values.[32]

Ethnic Minorities and Indigenous Peoples: Struggles for Human Rights

Throughout this book, we have discussed a wide range of cultures all across the globe. Many of our examples involve peoples who see themselves as members of distinct nations by virtue of their birth and their cultural and territorial heritage—nations over whom peoples of some other ethnic background have tried to assert political control. An estimated 5,000 such national groups exist in the world today, as opposed to the 193 states formally admitted as members of the United Nations (nearly four times the original 51 members at its founding in 1945).[33] Although some of these national or ethnic groups are small in population and area—100 or so people living on a few acres—many others are quite large. The Karen people inhabiting southern and southeastern Myanmar (Burma), for example, number some 4.5 to 5 million, exceeding the population of nearly half of the countries in the world. And Kurds, living in Turkey, Iran, and Iraq, number about 30 million.

Groups react differently to forced annexation and domination by state regimes controlled by people of other nations—ranging from the nonviolence of the Saami in Scandinavia, Inuit of Nunavut in northern Canada, or Maori of New Zealand to bloody battles for national independence by Basque separatists in Spain, Karen in Myanmar (Burma), Chechens in southern Russia, or Palestinians in the Middle East. In pursuit of self-determination, national autonomy, independence, or another political objective, many struggles have been going on for years or even decades.

Since the mid-1900s, global institutions such as the United Nations have tried to address the problem of discrimination, repression, and crimes against humanity—in particular, genocide. For example, even though it often fails to act on it, the General Assembly's 1966 Covenant of Human Rights states unequivocally:

> In those states in which ethnic, religious or linguistic minorities exist, persons belonging to such minorities shall not be denied the rights, in community with the other members of their group, to enjoy their own culture, to profess and practice their own religion or to use their own language.[34]

This covenant applies not only to minority groups, but also to indigenous peoples, who comprise about 5 percent of the world's population. Nearly all indigenous groups are relatively small nations. Typically, they have suffered repression or discrimination by ethnically different, more powerful, and almost always more heavily populated groups that have gained control over their ancestral homelands. In the early 1970s indigenous peoples began to organize self-determination movements, resisting acculturation and challenging violations of their human rights. Joining forces across international borders, they established the World Council of Indigenous Peoples in 1975.

In 2007, after many years of popular media campaigns, political lobbying, and diplomatic pressure by hundreds of indigenous leaders and other activists all around the globe, the U.N. General Assembly finally adopted the Declaration of the Rights of Indigenous Peoples. A foundational document in the global human rights struggle, it contains some 150 articles urging respect for indigenous cultural heritage, calling for official recognition of indigenous land titles and rights of self-determination, and demanding an end to all forms of oppression and discrimination as a principle of international law.

Global Migrations: Refugees, Migrants, and Diasporic Communities

Structural power and structural violence may both be involved in human migration. Throughout human history, individuals, families, and sometimes entire communities have migrated in pursuit of food, safety, and opportunity. Migration has always had a significant effect on world social geography, contributing to cultural change and development, to the diffusion of ideas and innovations, and to the complex mixture of peoples and cultures found in the world today.

Internal migration occurs within the boundaries of a country. Often unable to sustain themselves in the rural backlands, people all over the world continue to

---

[32]Marsella, A. J. (1982). Pulling it together: Discussion and comments. In S. Pastner & W. A. Haviland (Eds.), *Confronting the creationists* (pp. 79–80). *Northeaster Anthropological Association, Occasional Proceedings*, 1.

[33]*Cultural Survival Quarterly*. (1991). 15 (4), 38.

[34]Quoted in Bodley, J. H. (1990). *Victims of progress* (3rd ed., p. 99). Mountain View, CA: Mayfield.

internal migration The movement of people within the boundaries of a country.

© EPA/Laurent Gilleron/Corbis

▲▲▲ In 1982 the United Nations Sub-Commission on the Promotion and Protection of Human Rights established a Working Group on Indigenous Populations (WGIP). Eleven years later WGIP completed a draft of the Declaration of the Rights of Indigenous Peoples, ratified in 2007.

move to large urban areas, hoping to find a better life. All too often they live out their days in poor, congested, and diseased slums while attempting to achieve what is usually beyond their reach. **External migration** is movement from one country to another. Such migration may be voluntary—people seeking better conditions and opportunities—but it may also be forced or imposed—people who have been taken as slaves or prisoners, or driven from their homelands by war, political unrest, religious persecution, or environment disasters. ▶ **Figure 16.5** shows the patterns of worldwide migration.

Today, nearly 45 million people in almost half of the world's countries are either internally displaced or have crossed international borders as refugees. Some 15 million of these people have been forced outside their countries, most of them suffering in makeshift camps where they cannot make a living.[35] In some cases, large numbers of an ethnic group are forced to abandon their homes and flee for their lives. For instance, some 15 million Africans are currently uprooted. In war-torn Sudan alone, more than 4.5 million people have been driven from their homes.[36]

In addition to such forced displacements, tens of thousands of people migrate to wealthy countries every year in search of wage labor and a better future for themselves and their offspring. While most cross international borders as legal immigrants, seeking work permits and ultimately citizenship in their new homeland, untold numbers are illegal and do not enjoy many important rights and benefits. Although migrants may experience hardship, disappointment, and sometimes failure in their new countries, those who remain trapped in their troubled homelands often face worse challenges: malnutrition, hunger, chronic disease, and violence, resulting in a low life expectancy for many.

Legal or not, many of these immigrants face great challenges as poor newcomers in these societies—all the more so because they may encounter racism and discrimination. As a consequence, many newcomers form or join communities with those who have come from the same part of the world. Modern transportation and telecommunication technology make it possible for these *diasporic communities*, which exist all across the globe, to remain in contact with relatives and friends who have settled elsewhere, as well as with their country of origin. Indicative of this aspect of globalization is that today about 200 million people (almost 3 percent of the world's population) live outside their countries of birth—not as refugees or immigrants but as transnationals who earn their living in one country while remaining citizens of another.

Over the past few decades, mass migration across international borders has dramatically changed the ethnic composition of affluent societies in North America and western Europe. The 13 million Mexicans now residing in the United States represent about one-fourth of all foreign-born newcomers. As the largest and fastest-growing group of immigrants in the United States, they are settled primarily in California and Texas where many form Spanish-speaking ethnic enclaves. In addition there are over 25 million other immigrants from Asian countries, such as China and India, and African countries, such as Nigeria and Ethiopia. Today, almost 2 million African immigrants live in the United States, a 55-fold increase since the 1960s, with large clusters of different nationalities from that continent concentrated in Washington, DC, New York City, Atlanta, and other major metropolitan areas.

On the other side of the Atlantic, about 1.5 million Africans and another 2 million people from other parts of the world, mainly from former colonial territories, now live in France. England is now home to over 1.5 million South Asians, plus another 1.3 million people of African descent, also primarily hailing from the former British colonies. And almost 2.5 million people of

[35]UN Refugee Agency. (2011, June 20). World Refugee Day: UNHCR report finds 80 per cent of world's refugees in developing countries. www.unhcr.org/4dfb66ef9.html (retrieved October 4, 2011).

[36]Essoungou, A-M. (2010, April). Africa's displaced people: Out of the shadows. *Africa Renewal*, 6.

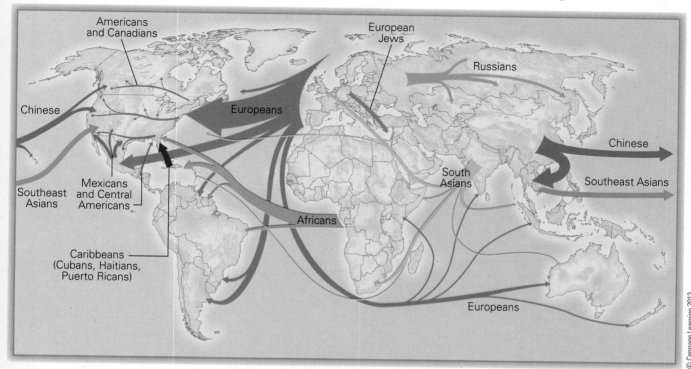

Figure 16.5 Worldwide Migration Migration continues to have a significant effect on world social geography, contributing to cultural change and development, to the diffusion of ideas and innovations, and to the complex mixture of people and cultures found in the world today. Internal migration occurs within the boundaries of a country; external migration is movement from one country or region to another. Not shown here are recent migration waves from Africa and Turkey to Europe.

Source: Allen, J. L., & Shalinsky, A. C. (2004). *Student atlas of anthropology* (p. 73). Copyright © 2004 by The McGraw-Hill Companies. Reproduced by permission of McGraw-Hill Contemporary Learning Series.

Turkish origin now reside in western Germany. Initially needed as cheap unskilled laborers, Turks were hired as "guest workers" in highly industrialized urban areas. Because most of them remained, the authorities instituted a family reunification policy, which resulted in hundreds of thousands of Turkish relatives entering the country. Even after several decades in Germany, most German Turks do not possess citizenship and have not become culturally integrated into German society. Turkish, spoken by Germany's largest ethnic minority, has become that country's second language.

One fascinating aspect of this global movement is the electronic transfer of money to relatives and friends still living in ancestral cities or villages abroad. For example, Mexicans working in the United States send an estimated $26 billion of their yearly U.S. earnings by means of money transfers (remittances) to relatives left behind in their home regions. Without these payments, many local communities throughout Mexico would face major economic problems. Worldwide, electronic transfers total some $330 billion per year.[37]

Concluding Remarks

As discussed in Chapter 1, anthropology is the comparative study of humankind everywhere and throughout time. It seeks to produce reliable knowledge about different peoples and cultures, their ideas and behaviors. Since the beginning of the discipline in the mid-1800s, generations of anthropologists have studied our species in all its cultural and biological variation. In the process, they have described in great detail an enormous number and range of different cultures and biological variations.

Today, many of the cultures studied by the earliest anthropologists more than a century ago have changed profoundly in response to powerful outside influences and internal dynamics. Others have disappeared as a

▲▲▲

external migration The movement of people from one country to another. Moves can be voluntary (people seeking better conditions and opportunities), involuntary (people being taken as slaves or prisoners, or driven from their homelands by war, political unrest, religious persecution, or environment disasters), or imposed (people who though not entirely forced to move are advised to move by the circumstances).

▼▼▼

[37]Migration and remittances. (2011). *World Bank*. www.world-bank.org/prospects/migrationandremittances (retrieved October 4, 2011).

ANTHROPOLOGY APPLIED

Paul Farmer: Anthropology and Local Health Care Worldwide

Mark Rosenberg 8-2001

Medical anthropologist Paul Farmer —doctor, Harvard professor, world-renowned infectious disease specialist, and recipient of a MacArthur "genius" grant—grew up in a trailer park in Florida without running water.[a] Admitted to Duke University on scholarship, he majored in anthropology and labored alongside poor Haitian farmworkers in North Carolina's tobacco fields. After getting his bachelor's degree in 1982, he spent a year in Haiti and found his life's calling: to diagnose and cure infectious diseases and transform health care on a global scale by focusing on the world's poorest communities. Returning to the United States, Farmer earned both a medical degree and a doctorate in anthropology from Harvard in 1990.

While still a graduate student, Farmer returned frequently to Haiti. Increasingly involved in health issues

result of deadly epidemics, violent conflicts, acculturation, ethnocide, or genocide. All too often, the only detailed records we now possess of these altered and vanished cultures are those that some visiting anthropologist was able to document before it was too late.

But, anthropologists do much more than try to preserve precious information about distinctive peoples and cultures. As chronicled in the pages of this book, they also try to explain why our bodies and cultures are similar or different, why and how they did or did not change. Moreover, they try to identify the particular knowledge and insights that each culture holds concerning the human condition—including contrasting views about the place of human beings in the world, how natural resources are used and treated, and how one relates to fellow humans and other species.

Anthropologists are trained to understand and explain economic, social, political, ideological, biological, and environmental features and processes as parts of interrelated dynamic systems. Theoretical concepts, such as structural power and structural violence, indicate how remote and seemingly unrelated factors and processes are connected in complex and significant ways.

A holistic and integrative perspective, as developed and tested by several generations of anthropologists in the course of more than a century of cross-cultural research in all parts of the world, has become essential to our understanding of such troubling problems as overpopulation, poverty, food shortages, environmental destruction, and disease in the age of globalization. The value of this perspective has been confirmed

in the area of Cange, a remote village in Haiti's destitute Central Plateau region, he (with a trio of fellow activists) formed a group called Zanmi Lasante (Haitian Kreyol for "Partners in Health"). In 1985, Zanmi Lasante established a clinic with financial support from a Boston philanthropist. Two years later they founded the Boston-based Partners in Health (PIH) foundation to support their growing endeavor to help the poorest of the poor deal with infectious diseases, especially AIDS and tuberculosis. The endeavor includes research (ethnographic as well as medical) needed to carry the work forward with a clear vision.

As an applied anthropologist aiming to ease human suffering, Farmer bases his activism on holistic and interpretive ethnographic analysis that, in his words, includes "a historical understanding of the large-scale social and economic structures in which affliction is embedded."[b] Issues of structural violence are fundamental in his research and practice. Noting that social and economic inequalities "have powerfully sculpted not only the [demographic] distribution of infectious diseases but also the course of health outcomes among the afflicted," he concludes, "Inequality itself constitutes our modern plague."

Since its founding, Zanmi Lasante has expanded its one-room clinic to a multiservice health complex that includes a primary school, an infirmary, a surgery wing, a training program for health outreach workers, a 104-bed hospital, a women's clinic, and a pediatric care facility. Moreover, it has pioneered the treatment of multidrug-resistant tuberculosis and HIV in Haiti. And Partners in Health, now funded by a wide range of organizations, has expanded its reach to include Lesotho, Malawi, and Rwanda in Africa, as well as Peru, Mexico, Russia, and the United States. The foundation's influence continues to grow, fueled by Farmer's passionate conviction that "health is a human right."

In concert with his active and extensive work with PIH around the globe, Farmer is a professor of medical anthropology in Harvard's Department of Social Medicine, maintains an active practice in infectious diseases, and is chief of the Division of Social Medicine and Health Inequalities at Brigham and Women's Hospital in Boston. Among numerous honors, he has received the Margaret Mead Award from the American Anthropological Association and is the subject of a Pulitzer Prize–winning book by Tracy Kidder. ◼

[a] This profile draws from numerous sources, including: Kidder, T. (2003). *Mountains beyond mountains: The quest of Dr. Paul Farmer, a man who would cure the world.* New York: Random House; Farmer, P. (2004, June). An anthropology of structural violence. *Current Anthropology 45*, 3; Farmer, P. (1996). On suffering and structural violence: A view from below. *Daedelus 125* (1), 261–283.
[b] Farmer, P. (2001). *Infections and inequalities: The modern plagues.* Berkeley: University of California Press.

by international organizations that now employ anthropologists for their professional insights. For example, after a series of ill-conceived and mismanaged development projects that harmed more than helped local populations, the World Bank contracted dozens of anthropologists for projects all around the world. The same is true for other international organizations, as well as some global corporations and state government agencies.

There have always been anthropologists who reach beyond studying different cultures to assist besieged groups struggling to survive in today's rapidly changing world. In so doing, they put into practice their own knowledge about humankind—knowledge deepened through the comparative perspective of anthropology, which is cross-culturally, historically, and biologically informed. Counted among these applied anthropologists is Paul Farmer, a world-renowned medical doctor, anthropologist, and human rights activist (see the Anthropology Applied feature).

Because anthropological research involves a distinct holistic approach, it has successfully contributed to the solving of practical problems on local and global levels. For this and many other reasons, the discipline has always drawn a unique group of people to it. Many of them are inspired by the old but still valid idea that anthropology must aim to live up to its longstanding ideal as the most liberating of the sciences. As stated by the famous anthropologist Margaret Mead, "Never doubt that a small group of committed people can change the world; indeed it is the only thing that ever has."

Chapter Checklist

Why are anthropological insights on cultural change key to a deeper understanding of today's complex world?

✔ Anthropology's investigation of the entire range of human cultures past and present includes observing and analyzing how cultures are impacted by modernization.

✔ Modernization—the all-encompassing and global process of political and socioeconomic change, whereby developing societies acquire cultural characteristics common to Western industrial societies—has five subprocesses: technological development, agricultural development, urbanization, industrialization, and telecommunication. Today we see a worldwide process of accelerated modernization known as globalization.

✔ Some people believe that rapid developments in communication, transportation, and world trade are leading toward a single world culture that could lessen chances for conflict. Most anthropologists are skeptical of this belief because comparative historical and cross-cultural research shows the persistence of distinctive worldviews and the tendency of large multi-ethnic states to come apart.

✔ Ethnic tension, common in pluralistic societies, sometimes turns violent, leading to formal separation. To manage cultural diversity within such societies, some countries have adopted multiculturalism, an official public policy of mutual respect and tolerance for cultural differences.

✔ To overcome the ethnocentrism common in every ethnic group, a pluralistic society may have to develop a common superstructure with an ideological force that binds different people together with a shared sense of identity and destiny.

What is structural power?

✔ Structural power refers to the global forces that direct economic and political institutions and shape public ideas and values. It comes in two forms: hard power, which is coercive and is backed up by economic and military force, and soft power, which co-opts through ideological persuasion.

✔ The most powerful country in the world today remains the United States, home to more global corporations than any other country. Responsible for 43 percent of the world's $1.6 trillion military expenditures, it engages in military interventions around the world to defend or benefit its corporate interests.

✔ Cutting across international boundaries, global corporations are a powerful force for worldwide integration despite the political, linguistic, religious, and other cultural differences that separate people. Their power and wealth often exceeds that of national governments.

✔ Major players in the globalization process, these megacorporations have huge influence on the ideas and behavior of people worldwide. In pursuit of wealth and power, states and corporations now compete for increasingly scarce natural resources, cheap labor, new commercial markets, and ever-larger profits in a huge political arena spanning the entire globe.

✔ Competing states and corporations utilize the ideological persuasion of soft power (as transmitted through electronic and digital media, communication satellites, and other information technology) to sell the general idea of globalization as something positive and to frame or brand anything that opposes capitalism in negative terms.

✔ The far-reaching capabilities of modern communication technologies have led to the creation of a new global media environment that plays a major role in how individuals and even societies view themselves and their place in the world.

✔ While providing megaprofits for large corporations, globalization often wreaks havoc in many traditional cultures and disrupts long-established social organization. This engenders worldwide resistance against superpower domination—and with that an emerging world system that is inherently unstable, vulnerable, and unpredictable.

How has the globalization of structural power led to an increase in structural violence?

✔ One result of globalization is the expansion and intensification of structural violence—physical and/or psychological harm (including repression, cultural and environmental destruction, poverty, hunger and obesity, illness, and premature death) caused by impersonal, exploitative, and unjust social, political, and economic systems. In short, it is a systemic violation of the human rights of individuals and communities to a healthy, peaceful, and dignified life as defined by the Universal Declaration of Human Rights adopted by members of the United Nations in 1948.

✔ Reactions against the structural violence of globalization include the rise of traditionalism and revitalization movements—efforts to return to life as it was (or how people think it was) before the familiar order became unhinged and people became unsettled. These may take the form of resurgent ethnonationalism or religious fundamentalist movements.

✔ Structural power and structural violence can both play a role in human migration. Internal migration occurs within the boundaries of a country. Often unable to sustain themselves in the rural backlands, people move to the large urban areas, hoping to find a better life. External migration is movement from one country to another; it can be voluntary, involuntary, or imposed.

How might anthropological know-how help counter structural violence?

✔ Some dramatic changes in cultural values and motivations, as well as in social institutions and the types of technologies we employ, are required if humans are going to realize a sustainable future for generations to come. The shortsighted emphasis on consumerism and individual self-interest so characteristic of the world's affluent countries needs to be abandoned in favor of a more balanced social and environmental ethic.

✔ Anthropologists have a contribution to make in bringing about this shift.

They are well versed in the dangers of culture-bound thinking, and they bring a holistic biocultural and comparative historical perspective to the challenge of understanding and balancing the needs and desires of local communities in the age of globalization.

✔ Inspired by human rights ideals, there have always been "applied" anthropologists who reach beyond studying different cultures to assist besieged groups struggling to survive in today's rapidly changing world.

Questions for Reflection

1. When societies become involved in the modernizing process, all levels of their cultural systems are affected by these changes. Do you think that people are fully aware of the long-term consequences of the changes they themselves may have welcomed? Can you come up with any examples of unforeseen changes in your own community or neighborhood?

2. Considering the relationship between structural power and structural violence, does your own lifestyle—in terms of buying clothes and food, driving cars, and so on—reflect or have an effect on the globalization process?

3. In the global mediascape, television viewers and Internet users are not only consumers of news and entertainment but are also exposed to soft power. Can you think of an example of soft power in your daily life? And at which point does such influence turn into propaganda or manipulation?

4. When you hear or read about Muslim religious fundamentalists in western Asia or northern Africa strongly defending their traditional beliefs and practices, or even aggressively rejecting modern changes imported from the United States or Europe, do you recognize similar reactionary move-

ments in your own country? What fuels such reactions?

5. The World Health Organization, UNESCO, Oxfam, and Amnesty International are global institutions concerned with checking structural violence and human rights violations. Confronted with genocidal conflicts, famines, epidemics, and torture of political prisoners, activists in these organizations try to improve the human condition. Why do you think that an anthropological perspective on such worldwide problems might be of practical use? Can you think of an example?

Key Terms

modernization
multiculturalism
structural power

hard power
soft power
structural violence

internal migration
external migration

Online Study Resources

Login to **www.cengagebrain.com** to access the resources your instructor has assigned and to purchase materials. For this book, you can access:

CourseMate
Access chapter-specific learning tools including flashcards, glossaries, practice quizzes, videos, and more in your Anthropology CourseMate.

Glossary

absolute dating In archaeology and paleoanthropology, dating archaeological or fossil materials in units of absolute time using scientific properties such as rates of decay of radioactive elements; also known as *chronometric dating*.

acculturation The massive cultural change that occurs in a society when it experiences intensive firsthand contact with a more powerful society.

action theory The theory that self-serving actions by forceful leaders play a role in civilization's emergence.

adaptation A series of beneficial adjustments to the environment.

adjudication A mediation with an unbiased third party making the ultimate decision.

age grade An organized category of people based on age; every individual passes through a series of such categories over his or her lifetime.

age set A formally established group of people born during a certain time span who move together through the series of age-grade categories.

agriculture Intensive crop cultivation, employing plows, fertilizers, and/or irrigation.

alleles Alternate forms of a single gene.

alphabet A series of symbols representing the sounds of a language arranged in a traditional order.

anagenesis A sustained directional shift in a population's average characteristics.

analogies In biology, structures possessed by different organisms that are superficially similar due to similar function but that do not share a common developmental pathway or structure.

animatism The belief that nature is enlivened or energized by an impersonal spiritual force or supernatural energy, which may make itself manifest in any special place, thing, or living creature.

animism The belief that nature is enlivened or energized by distinct personalized spirit beings separable from bodies.

anthropoids A subdivision within the primate order based on shared anatomical characteristics; includes New World monkeys,

Old World monkeys, and apes (including humans).

anthropology The study of humankind in all times and places.

applied anthropology The use of anthropological knowledge and methods to solve practical problems, often for a specific client.

arboreal Living in the trees.

archaeology The study of cultures through the recovery and analysis of material remains and environmental data.

Archaic cultures The term used to refer to Mesolithic cultures in the Americas.

Ardipithecus One of the earliest genera of bipeds that lived in eastern Africa. *Ardipithecus* is actually divided into two species, the older of which dates to between 5.2 and 5.8 million years ago, and the younger, *A. ramidus,* dated to around 4.4 million years ago.

artifact Any object fashioned or altered by humans.

Australopithecus The genus including several species of early bipeds from southern and eastern Africa living between about 1.1 and 4.3 million years ago, one of whom was directly ancestral to humans.

balanced reciprocity A mode of exchange in which the giving and the receiving are specific as to the value of the goods or services and the time of their delivery.

band A relatively small and loosely organized kin-ordered group that inhabits a specific territory and that may split periodically into smaller extended family groups that are politically independent.

binocular vision Vision with increased depth perception from two eyes set next to each other allowing their visual fields to overlap.

bioarchaeology The archaeological study of human remains emphasizing the preservation of cultural and social processes in the skeleton.

biocultural An approach that focuses on the interaction of biology and culture.

biological anthropology The systematic study of humans as biological organisms; also known as *physical anthropology.*

bipedalism A special form of locomotion on two feet found in humans and their ancestors.

brachiation Moving from branch to branch using the arms, with the body hanging suspended below.

bride-price The money or valuable goods paid by the groom or his family to the bride's family upon marriage; also called *bridewealth.*

bride service A designated period of time when the groom works for the bride's family.

bridewealth The money or valuable goods paid by the groom or his family to the bride's family upon marriage; also called bride-price.

Bronze Age In the Old World, the period marked by the production of tools and ornaments of bronze; began about 5,000 years ago in China and Southwest Asia and about 500 years earlier in Southeast Asia.

cargo cult A spiritual movement (especially noted in Melanesia) in reaction to disruptive contact with Western capitalism, promising resurrection of deceased relatives, destruction or enslavement of white foreigners, and the magical arrival of utopian riches.

carrying capacity The number of people that the available resources can support at a given level of food-getting techniques.

caste A closed social class in which membership is determined by birth and fixed for life.

chiefdom A politically organized society in which several neighboring communities inhabiting a territory are united under a single ruler.

chromatid One half of the X shape of chromosomes visible once replication is complete. Sister chromatids are exact copies of each other.

chromosomes In the cell nucleus, the structures visible during cellular division containing long strands of DNA combined with a protein.

chronometric dating In archaeology and paleoanthropology, dating archaeological or fossil materials in units of absolute time using scientific properties such as rates of decay of radioactive elements; also known as *absolute dating.*

civil disobedience Refusal to obey civil laws in an effort to induce change in governmental policy or legislation, characterized by the use of passive resistance or other nonviolent means.

civilization In anthropology, societies in which large numbers of people live in cities, are socially stratified, and are governed by a ruling elite working through centrally organized political systems called states.

cladogenesis Speciation through a branching mechanism whereby an ancestral population gives rise to two or more descendant populations.

clan An extended unilineal kin-group, often consisting of several lineages, whose members claim common descent from a remote ancestor, usually legendary or mythological.

clines The gradual changes in the frequency of an allele or trait over space.

code switching The practice of changing from one mode of speech to another as the situation demands, whether from one language to another or from one dialect of a language to another.

co-marriage A marriage form in which several men and women have sexual access to one another; also called *group marriage*.

common-interest association An association that results from the act of joining, based on sharing particular activities, objectives, values, or beliefs.

community A unit of primate social organization composed of fifty or more individuals who together inhabit a large geographic area.

conjugal family A family established through marriage.

consanguineal family A family of blood relatives, consisting of related women, their brothers, and the women's offspring.

conspicuous consumption A showy display of wealth for social prestige.

contagious magic Magic based on the principle that things or persons once in contact can influence each other after the contact is broken.

continental drift In the theory of plate tectonics, the movement of continents embedded in underlying plates on the earth's surface in relation to one another over the history of life on earth.

convergent evolution In cultural evolution, the development of similar cultural adaptations to similar environmental conditions by different peoples with different ancestral cultures.

core values Those values especially promoted by a particular culture.

cross cousin The child of a mother's brother or a father's sister.

cultural adaptation A complex of ideas, activities, and technologies that enable people to survive and even thrive in their environment.

cultural anthropology The study of customary patterns in human behavior, thought, and feelings. It focuses on humans as culture-producing and culture-reproducing creatures. Also known as *social* or *sociocultural anthropology*.

cultural control Control through beliefs and values deeply internalized in the minds of individuals.

cultural evolution Cultural change over time—not to be confused with progress.

cultural relativism The idea that one must suspend judgment of other people's practices in order to understand them in their own cultural terms.

cultural resource management A branch of archaeology concerned with survey and/or excavation of archaeological and historical remains that might be threatened by construction or development; also involved with policy surrounding protection of cultural resources.

culture A society's shared and socially transmitted ideas, values, and perceptions, which are used to make sense of experience and generate behavior and are reflected in that behavior.

culture-bound syndrome A mental disorder specific to a particular ethnic group; also known as *ethnic psychosis*.

culture-bound theories Theories about the world and reality based on the assumptions and values of one's own culture.

datum point The starting point or reference for a grid system.

dependence training Childrearing practices that foster compliance in the performance of assigned tasks and dependence on the domestic group, rather than reliance on oneself.

descent group Any kin-group whose members share a direct line of descent from a real (historical) or fictional common ancestor.

dialects The varying forms of a language that reflect particular regions, occupations, or social classes and that are similar enough to be mutually intelligible.

diffusion The spread of certain ideas, customs, or practices from one culture to another.

discourse An extended communication on a particular subject.

displacement A term referring to things and events removed in time and space.

diurnal Active during the day and at rest at night.

divination A magical procedure or spiritual ritual designed to discern what is not knowable by ordinary means, such as foretelling the future by interpreting omens.

DNA (deoxyribonucleic acid) The genetic material consisting of a complex molecule whose base structure directs the synthesis of proteins.

doctrine An assertion of opinion or belief formally handed down by an authority as true and indisputable.

domestication An evolutionary process whereby humans modify, intentionally or unintentionally, the genetic makeup of a population of plants or animals, sometimes to the extent that members of the population are unable to survive and/or reproduce without human assistance.

dominant In genetics, a term to describe the ability of an allele for a trait to mask the presence of another allele.

dominance hierarchy An observed ranking system in animal groups ordering individuals from high (alpha) to low standing corresponding to predictable behavioral interactions including domination.

dowry A payment at the time of a woman's marriage that comes from her inheritance, made to either her or her husband.

economic system An organized arrangement for producing, distributing, and consuming goods.

ecosystem A system, or a functioning whole, composed of both the natural environment and all the organisms living within it.

egalitarian societies Societies in which everyone has about the same rank and power and about the same access to basic resources.

EGO In kinship studies, the central person from whom the degree of each kinship relationship is traced.

eliciting devices Activities and objects used to draw out individuals and encourage them to recall and share information.

empirical Research based on observations of the world rather than on intuition or faith.

enculturation The process by which a society's culture is passed on from one generation to the next and individuals become members of their society.

endogamy Marriage within a particular group or category of individuals.

Eskimo system Kinship reckoning in which the nuclear family is emphasized by specifically identifying the mother, father, brother, and sister, while lumping together all other relatives into broad categories such as uncle, aunt, and cousin.

ethnic group People who collectively and publicly identify themselves as a distinct group based on shared cultural features such as common origin, language, customs, and traditional beliefs.

ethnicity This term, rooted in the Greek word *ethnikos* (*"nation"*) and related to *ethnos* (*"custom"*), is the expression of the set of cultural ideas held by an ethnic group.

ethnic psychosis A mental disorder specific to a particular ethnic group; also known as *culture-bound syndrome.*

ethnocentrism The belief that the ways of one's own culture are the only proper ones.

ethnocide The violent eradication of an ethnic group's collective cultural identity as a distinctive people; occurs when a dominant society deliberately sets out to destroy another society's cultural heritage.

ethnography A detailed description of a particular culture primarily based on fieldwork.

ethnolinguistics A branch of linguistics that studies the relationships between language and culture and how they mutually influence and inform each other.

ethnology The study and analysis of different cultures from a comparative or historical point of view, utilizing ethnographic accounts and developing anthropological theories that help explain why certain important differences or similarities occur among groups.

Eve hypothesis The hypothesis that modern humans are all derived from one single population of archaic *Homo Sapiens* who migrated out of Africa after 100,000 years ago, replacing all other archaic forms due to their superior cultural capabilities; also known as the *recent African origins hypothesis* or the *out of Africa hypothesis.*

evolution The changes in allele frequencies in populations; also known as *microevolution.*

exogamy Marriage outside the group.

extended family Two or more closely related nuclear families clustered together into a large domestic group.

external migration The voluntary or involuntary movement of people from one country to another.

family Two or more people related by blood, marriage, or adoption. The family may take many forms, ranging from a single parent with one or more children, to a married couple or polygamous spouses with or without offspring, to several generations of parents and their children.

fieldwork The term anthropologists use for on-location research.

fission In kinship studies, the splitting of a descent group into two or more new descent groups.

food foraging A mode of subsistence involving some combination of hunting, fishing, and gathering of wild plant foods.

forensic anthropology The analysis of human skeletal remains for identification or legal purposes.

formal interview A structured question–answer session, carefully notated as it occurs and based on prepared questions.

fossil The preserved remains of past life forms.

founder effects A particular form of genetic drift deriving from a small founding population not possessing all the alleles present in the original population.

gender The cultural elaborations and meanings assigned to the biological differentiation between the sexes.

gendered speech Distinct male and female speech patterns that vary across social and cultural settings.

gene flow The introduction of alleles from the gene pool of one population into that of another.

gene pool All the genetic variants possessed by members of a population.

generalized reciprocity A mode of exchange in which the value of the gift is not calculated, nor is the time of repayment specified.

genes The portions of DNA molecules that direct the synthesis of specific proteins.

genetic drift The chance fluctuations of allele frequencies in the gene pool of a population.

genocide The physical extermination of one people by another, either as a deliberate act or as the accidental outcome of activities carried out by one people with little regard for their impact on others.

genome The complete structure sequence of DNA for a species.

genotype The alleles possessed for a particular trait.

genus, genera In the system of plant and animal classification, a group of like species.

gestures Facial expressions and bodily postures and motions that convey intended as well as subconscious messages.

globalization Worldwide interconnectedness, evidenced in fast-moving global movements of natural resources, trade goods, human labor, finance capital, information, and infectious diseases.

gracile australopithecines Members of the genus *Australopithecus* possessing a more lightly built chewing apparatus; likely had a diet that included more meat than that of the robust australopithecines.

grammar The entire formal structure of a language, including morphology and syntax.

grave goods Items such as utensils, figurines, and personal possessions, symbolically placed in the grave for the deceased person's use in the afterlife.

grid system A system for recording data from an archaeological excavation into three dimensions.

grooming The ritual cleaning of another animal's coat to remove parasites and other matter.

group marriage A marriage form in which several men and women have sexual access to one another; also called *co-marriage.*

haplorhines A subdivision within the primate order based on shared genetic characteristics; includes tarsiers, New World monkeys, Old World monkeys, and apes (including humans).

hard power Power that coerces others and that is backed up by economic or military force.

Hawaiian system Kinship reckoning in which all relatives of the same sex and generation are referred to by the same term; also known as the *generational system*.

hemoglobin The protein that carries oxygen in the red blood cells.

heterozygous A term to describe a chromosome pair that bears different alleles for a single gene.

historical archaeology The archaeological study of places for which written records exist.

holistic perspective A fundamental principle of anthropology: The various parts of human culture and biology must be viewed in the broadest possible context in order to understand their interconnections and interdependence.

Homo erectus "Upright human." A species within the genus *Homo* first appearing just after 2 million years ago in Africa and ultimately spreading throughout the Old World.

Homo habilis "Handy human." The first fossil members of the genus *Homo* appearing 2.5 million years ago, with larger brains and smaller faces than australopithecines.

homologies In biology, structures possessed by two different organisms that arise in similar fashion and pass through similar stages during embryonic development, although they may have different functions.

homozygous A term to describe a chromosome pair that bears identical alleles for a single gene.

horticulture The cultivation of crops in food gardens, carried out with simple hand tools such as digging sticks and hoes.

household A domestic unit of one or more persons living in the same residence. Other than family members, a household may include nonrelatives, such as servants.

Human Relations Area Files (HRAF) A vast collection of cross-indexed ethnographic, biocultural, and archaeological data catalogued by cultural characteristics and geographic location.

hydraulic theory The theory that explains civilization's emergence as the result of the construction of elaborate irrigation systems, the functioning of which required full-time managers whose control blossomed into the first governing body and elite social class; also known as *irrigation theory*.

hypothesis A tentative explanation of the relation between certain phenomena.

imitative magic Magic based on the principle that like produces like; sometimes called *sympathetic magic*.

incest taboo The prohibition of sexual relations between closely related individuals.

incorporation In a rite of passage, reincorporation of a temporarily removed individual into society in his or her new status.

independence training Childrearing practices that promote independence, self-reliance, and personal achievement.

industrial food production Large-scale businesses involved in mass food production, processing, and marketing, which primarily rely on labor-saving machines.

industrial society A society in which human labor, hand tools, and animal power are largely replaced by machines, with an economy primarily based on big factories.

informal economy A network of producing and circulating marketable commodities, labor, and services that for various reasons escape government control.

informal interview An unstructured, open-ended conversation in everyday life.

informed consent A formal recorded agreement between the subject and the researcher to participate in the research.

infrastructure The economic foundation of a society, including its subsistence practices and the tools and other material equipment used to make a living.

innovation Any new idea, method, or device that gains widespread acceptance in society.

internal migration The movement of people within the boundaries of a country.

intersexuals People born with reproductive organs, genitalia, and/or sex chromosomes that are not exclusively male or female.

irrigation theory The theory that explains civilization's emergence as the result of the construction of elaborate irrigation systems, the functioning of which required full-time managers whose control blossomed into the first governing body and elite social class; also known as *hydraulic theory*.

Iroquois system Kinship reckoning in which a father and a father's brother are referred to by a single term, as are a mother and a mother's sister, but a father's sister and mother's brother are given separate terms. Parallel cousins are classified with brothers and sisters, while cross cousins are classified separately but not equated with relatives of some other generation.

key consultants Members of the society being studied who provide information that helps the researchers understand the meaning of what they observe. Early anthropologists referred to such individuals as *informants*.

kindred An individual's genetically close blood relatives on the maternal and paternal sides of his or her family.

kinesics The study of nonverbal signals in body language including facial expressions and bodily postures and motions.

kinship A network of relatives within which individuals possess certain mutual rights and obligations.

Kula ring A form of balanced reciprocity that reinforces trade and social relations among the seafaring Melanesians who inhabit a large ring of islands in the southwestern Pacific Ocean.

lactase An enzyme in the small intestine that enables humans to assimilate lactose.

lactose A sugar that is the primary constituent of fresh milk.

language a system of communication using symbolic sounds, gestures, or marks that are put together according to certain rules, resulting in meanings that are intelligible to all who share that language.

language family A group of languages descended from a single ancestral language.

law Formal rules of conduct that, when violated, effectuate negative sanctions.

law of independent assortment The Mendelian principle that genes controlling different traits are inherited independently of one another.

law of segregation The Mendelian principle that variants of genes for a particular trait retain their separate identities through the generations.

legitimacy In politics, the right of political leaders to govern—to hold, use, and allocate power—based on the values a particular society embraces.

leveling mechanism A cultural obligation compelling prosperous members of a community to give away goods, host public feasts, provide free service, or otherwise demonstrate generosity so that no one permanently accumulates significantly more wealth than anyone else.

lineage A unilineal kin-group descended from a common ancestor or founder who lived four to six generations ago and in which relationships among members can be exactly stated in genealogical terms.

linguistic anthropology The study of human languages.

linguistic divergence The development of different languages from a single ancestral language.

linguistic nationalism The attempt by ethnic minorities and even countries to proclaim independence by purging their language of foreign terms.

linguistic relativity The idea that language to some extent shapes the way in which people perceive and think about the world.

linguistics The modern scientific study of all aspects of language.

Lower Paleolithic A period of time beginning with the earliest Oldowan tools, spanning from about 200,000 to 2.6 million years ago; also known as *Old Stone Age*.

macroevolution Evolution above the species level or leading to the formation of new species.

magic The belief that supernatural powers can be compelled to act in certain ways for good or evil purposes by recourse to specified formulas.

mammals The class of vertebrate animals distinguished by bodies covered with hair or fur who suckle or nurse their young.

market exchange The buying and selling of goods and services, with prices set by rules of supply and demand.

marriage A culturally sanctioned union between two or more people that establishes certain rights and obligations between the people, between them and their children, and between them and their in-laws. Such marriage rights and obligations most often include, but are not limited to, sex, labor, property, childrearing, exchange, and status.

material culture The durable aspects of culture such as tools, structures, and art.

matrilineal descent Descent traced exclusively through the female line of ancestry to establish group membership.

matrilocal residence A residence pattern in which a married couple lives in the wife's mother's place of residence.

mediation The settlement of a dispute through negotiation assisted by an unbiased third party.

medical anthropology The specialization in anthropology that brings theoretical and applied approaches from cultural and biological anthropology to the study of human sickness and health.

meiosis A kind of cell division that produces the sex cells, each of which has half the number of chromosomes found in other cells of the organism.

melanin A dark pigment produced in the outer layer of the skin that protects against damaging ultraviolet solar radiation.

Mesoamerica The region extending from central Mexico to northern Central America.

Mesolithic The Middle Stone Age of Europe, Asia, and Africa beginning about 12,000 years ago.

microevolution The changes in allele frequencies in populations; also known as *evolution*.

microlith A small blade of flint or similar stone, several of which were hafted together in wooden handles to make tools; widespread in the Mesolithic.

middens A refuse or garbage disposal area in an archaeological site.

mitosis A kind of cell division that produces new cells having exactly the same number of chromosome pairs, and hence copies of genes, as the parent cell.

modal personality Those character traits that occur with the highest frequency in a social group and are therefore the most representative of its culture.

modernization The process of economic change, whereby developing societies acquire some of the social and political characteristics of Western industrial societies; five key subprocesses are involved: technological development, agricultural development, urbanization, industrialization, and telecommunication.

moiety Each group, usually consisting of several clans, that results from a division of a society into two halves on the basis of descent.

molecular anthropology The anthropological study of genes and genetic relationships, which contributes significantly to our understanding of human evolution, adaptation, and diversity.

money A means of exchange used to make payments for other goods and services as well as to measure their value.

monogamy A marriage form in which both partners have just one spouse.

morphemes The smallest units of sound that carry a meaning in language. They are distinct from phonemes, which can alter meaning but have no meaning by themselves.

morphology The study of the patterns or rules of word formation in a language, including the guidelines for verb tense, pluralization, and compound words.

Mousterian tool tradition The tool industry of the Neandertals and their contemporaries of Europe, Southwest Asia, and North Africa from 40,000 to 125,000 years ago.

multiculturalism The public policy for managing cultural diversity in a multi-ethnic society, officially stressing mutual respect and tolerance for cultural differences within a country's borders.

multiregional hypothesis The hypothesis that modern humans originated through a process of simultaneous local transition from *Homo erectus to Homo sapiens* throughout the inhabited world.

mutation The chance alteration of genetic material that produces new variation.

myth A sacred narrative that explains the fundamentals of human existence—where we and everything in our world came from, why we are here, and where we are going.

naming ceremony A special event or ritual to mark the naming of a child.

nation A people who share a collective identity based on a common culture, language, territorial base, and history.

Natufian culture A Mesolithic culture from the lands that are now Israel, Lebanon, and western Syria, between about 10,200 and 12,500 years ago.

natural selection The evolutionary process through which factors in the environment exert pressure, favoring some individuals over others to produce the next generation.

Neandertals A distinct group within the genus *Homo* inhabiting Europe and Southwest Asia from approximately 30,000 to 125,000 years ago.

negative reciprocity A mode of exchange in which the aim is to get something for as little as possible. Neither fair nor balanced, it may involve hard bargaining, manipulation, outright cheating, or theft.

negotiation The use of direct argument and compromise by the parties to a dispute to arrive voluntarily at a mutually satisfactory agreement.

Neolithic The New Stone Age; a prehistoric period beginning about 10,000 years ago in which peoples possessed stone-based technologies and depended on domesticated crops and/or animals for subsistence.

Neolithic revolution The domestication of plants and animals by peoples with stone-based technologies, beginning about 10,000 years ago and leading to radical transformations in cultural systems; sometimes referred to as the *Neolithic transition*.

neolocal residence A residence pattern in which a married couple establishes its household in a location apart from either the husband's or the wife's relatives.

new reproductive technologies (NRTs) Alternative means of reproduction such as surrogate motherhood and in vitro fertilization.

nocturnal Active at night and at rest during the day.

nuclear family A group consisting of one or more parents and dependent offspring, which may include a stepparent, stepsiblings, and adopted children. Until recently this term referred only to the father, mother, and child(ren) unit.

Oldowan tool tradition The first stone tool industry, beginning between 2.5 and 2.6 million years ago.

Old Stone Age A period of time beginning with the earliest Oldowan tools, spanning from about 200,000 to 2.6 million years ago; also known as the *Lower Paleolithic*.

opposable The ability to bring the thumb or big toe in contact with the tips of the other digits on the same hand or foot in order to grasp objects.

out of Africa hypothesis The hypothesis that modern humans are all derived from one single population of archaic *Homo Sapiens* who migrated out of Africa after 100,000 years ago, replacing all other archaic forms due to their superior cultural capabilities; also known as the *recent African origins hypothesis* or the *Eve hypothesis*.

ovulation The moment when an egg released from an ovary into the womb is receptive for fertilization.

paleoanthropology The anthropological study of biological changes through time (evolution) to understand the origins and predecessors of the present human species.

pantheon All the gods and goddesses of a people.

paralanguage Voice effects that accompany language and convey meaning. These include vocalizations such as giggling, groaning, or sighing, as well as voice qualities such as pitch and tempo.

parallel cousin The child of a father's brother or a mother's sister.

parallel evolution In cultural evolution, the development of similar cultural adaptations to similar environmental conditions by peoples whose ancestral cultures are already somewhat alike.

participant observation In ethnography, the technique of learning a people's culture through social participation and personal observation within the community being studied, as well as interviews and discussion with individual members of the group over an extended period of time.

pastoralism The breeding and managing of migratory herds of domesticated grazing animals, such as goats, sheep, cattle, llamas, and camels.

patrilineal descent Descent traced exclusively through the male line of ancestry to establish group membership.

patrilocal residence A residence pattern in which a married couple lives in the husband's father's place of residence.

peasant A small-scale producer of crops or livestock living on land self-owned or rented in exchange for labor, crops, or money and exploited by more powerful groups in a complex society.

personality The distinctive way a person thinks, feels, and behaves.

phenotype The observable or testable appearance of an organism that may or may not reflect a particular genotype due to the variable expression of dominant and recessive alleles.

phonemes The smallest units of sound that make a difference in meaning in a language.

phonetics The systematic identification and description of distinctive speech sounds in a language.

phonology The study of language sounds.

phratry A unilineal descent group composed of at least two clans that supposedly share a common ancestry, whether or not they really do.

physical anthropology The systematic study of humans as biological organisms; also known as *biological anthropology*.

pluralistic society A society in which two or more ethnic groups or nationalities are politically organized into one territorial state but maintain their cultural differences.

political organization The way power, as the capacity to do something, is accumulated, arranged, executed, and structurally embedded in society; the means through which a society creates and maintains social order and reduces social disorder.

polyandry A marriage form in which a woman is married to two or more men at one time; a form of polygamy.

polygamy A marriage form in which one individual has multiple spouses at the same time; from the Greek words *poly* ("many") and *gamos* ("marriage").

polygenetic inheritance Two or more genes contributing to the phenotypic expression of a single characteristic.

polygyny A marriage form in which a man is married to two or more women at the same time; a form of polygamy.

polytheism The belief in multiple gods and/or goddesses, as contrasted with monotheism—the belief in one god or goddess.

population In biology, a group of similar individuals that can and do interbreed.

postindustrial society A society with an economy based on research and development of new knowledge and technologies, as well as providing information, services, and finance capital on a global scale.

potlatch On the northwestern coast of North America, an indigenous ceremonial event in which a village chief publicly gives away stockpiled food and other goods that signify wealth.

power The ability of individuals or groups to impose their will upon others and make them do things even against their own wants or wishes.

prehensile The ability to grasp.

prehistory A conventional term used to refer to the period of time before the appearance of written records; does not deny the existence of history, merely of *written* history.

prestige economy The creation of a surplus for the express purpose of displaying wealth and giving it away to raise one's status.

priest or priestess A full-time religious specialist formally recognized for his or her role in guiding the religious practices of others and for contacting and influencing supernatural powers.

primary innovation The creation, invention, or chance discovery of a completely new idea, method, or device.

primates The group of mammals that includes lemurs, lorises, tarsiers, monkeys, apes, and humans.

primatology The study of living and fossil primates.

progress The ethnocentric notion that humans are moving forward to a higher, more advanced stage in their development toward perfection.

prosimians A subdivision within the primate order; includes lemurs, lorises, and tarsiers.

proxemics The cross-cultural study of people's perception and use of space.

punctuated equilibria A model of macroevolutionary change that suggests evolution occurs via long periods of stability or stasis punctuated by periods of rapid change.

race In biology, the taxonomic category of subspecies that is not applicable to humans because the division of humans into discrete types does not represent the true nature of human biological variation. In some societies race is an important social category.

racism A doctrine of superiority by which one group justifies the dehumanization of others based on their distinctive physical characteristics.

rebellion Organized armed resistance to an established government or authority in power.

recent African origins hypothesis The hypothesis that modern humans are all derived from one single population of archaic *Homo Sapiens* who migrated out of Africa after 100,000 years ago, replacing all other archaic forms due to their superior cultural capabilities; also known as the *Eve hypothesis* or the *out of Africa hypothesis*.

recessive A term to describe an allele for a trait whose expression is masked by the presence of a dominant allele.

reciprocity The exchange of goods and services, of approximately equal value, between two parties.

redistribution A mode of exchange in which goods flow into a central place, where they are sorted, counted, and reallocated.

relative dating In archaeology and paleoanthropology, designating an event, object, or fossil as being older or younger than another by noting the position in the earth, by measuring the amount of chemicals contained in fossil bones and artifacts, or through association with other plant, animal, or cultural remains.

religion An organized system of ideas about the spiritual sphere or the supernatural, along with associated ceremonial practices by which people try to interpret and/or influence aspects of the universe otherwise beyond their control.

revitalization movements Social movements for radical cultural reform in response to widespread social disruption and collective feelings of great stress and despair.

revolution Radical change in a society or culture. In the political arena, it involves the forced overthrow of an old government and establishment of a completely new one.

rite of intensification A ritual that takes place during a crisis in the life of the group and serves to bind individuals together.

rite of passage A three-phased ritual that marks an important ceremonial moment when members of a society move from one distinctive social stage in life to another.

ritual An act or procedure established by custom or prescribed by authority as proper to a certain formal occasion.

robust australopithecines Several species within the genus *Australopithecus,* who lived from 1.1 to 2.5 million years ago in eastern and southern Africa; known for the rugged nature of their chewing apparatus (large back teeth, large chewing muscles, and a bony ridge on their skull tops to allow for these large muscles).

sanction An externalized social control designed to encourage conformity to social norms.

secondary innovation The deliberate application or modification of an existing idea, method, or device.

self-awareness The ability to identify oneself as an individual, to reflect on oneself, and to evaluate oneself.

separation In a rite of passage, the temporary ritual removal of the individual from society.

serial monogamy A marriage form in which a man or a woman marries or lives with a series of partners in succession.

shaman A person who enters an altered state of consciousness to contact and utilize an ordinarily hidden reality in order to acquire knowledge, power, and to help others.

sickle-cell anemia An inherited form of anemia caused by a mutation in the hemoglobin protein that causes the red blood cells to assume a sickle shape.

signals Instinctive sounds and gestures that have a natural or self-evident meaning.

slash-and-burn cultivation An extensive form of horticulture in which the natural vegetation is cut, the slash is subsequently burned, and crops are then planted among the ashes; also known as *swidden farming.*

social class A category of individuals who enjoy equal or nearly equal prestige according to the hierarchical system of evaluation.

social control External control through open coercion.

social mobility An upward or downward change in one's social class position in a stratified society.

social structure The rule-governed relationships—with all their rights and obligations—that hold members of a society together. This includes households, families, associations, and power relations, including politics.

society An organized group or groups of interdependent people who generally share a common territory, language, and culture and who act together for collective survival and well-being.

sociolinguistics The study of the relationship between language and society through examining how social categories—such as age, gender, ethnicity, religion, occupation, and class—influence the use and significance of distinctive styles of speech.

soft power Power that co-opts rather than coerces, pressing others through attraction and persuasion to change their ideas, beliefs, values, and behaviors.

soil marks The stains that show up on the surface of recently plowed fields that reveal an archaeological site.

speciation The process of forming new species.

species The smallest working units in biological classificatory systems; reproductively isolated populations or groups of populations capable of interbreeding to produce fertile offspring.

spirituality Concern with the sacred, as distinguished from material matters. In contrast to religion, spirituality is often individual rather than collective and does not require a distinctive format or traditional organization.

state A political institution established to manage and defend a complex, socially stratified society occupying a defined territory.

stereoscopic vision Complete three-dimensional vision, or depth perception, from binocular vision and nerve connections that run from each eye to both sides of the brain allowing nerve cells to integrate the images derived from each eye.

stratified In archaeology, a term describing sites where the remains lie in layers, one upon another.

stratified societies Societies in which people are hierarchically divided and ranked into social strata, or layers, and do not share equally in basic resources that support income, status, and power.

strepsirhines A subdivision within the primate order based on shared genetic characteristics; includes lemurs and lorises.

structural power Power that organizes and orchestrates the systemic interaction within and among societies, directing economic and political forces on the one hand and ideological forces that shape public ideas, values, and beliefs on the other.

structural violence Physical and/or psychological harm caused by impersonal, exploitative, and unjust social, political, and economic systems.

subculture A distinctive set of ideas, values, and behavior patterns by which a group within a larger society operates, while still sharing common standards with that larger society.

superstructure The collective body of ideas, beliefs, and values by which a group of people makes sense of the world—its shape, challenges, and opportunities—and their place in it.

swidden farming An extensive form of horticulture in which the natural vegetation is cut, the slash is subsequently burned, and crops are then planted among the ashes; also known as *slash-and-burn cultivation.*

symbol A sound, gesture, mark, or other sign that is arbitrarily linked to something else and represents it in a meaningful way.

sympathetic magic Magic based on the principle that like produces like; also known as *imitative magic.*

syncretism The creative blending of indigenous and foreign beliefs and practices into new cultural forms.

syntax The patterns or rules by which words are arranged into phrases and sentences.

taxonomy The science of classification.

technology Tools and other material equipment, together with the knowledge of how to make and use them.

theory In science, an explanation of natural phenomena, supported by a reliable body of data.

thrifty genotype Human genotype that permits efficient storage of fat to draw on in times of food shortage and conservation of glucose and nitrogen.

tonal language A language in which the sound pitch of a spoken word is an essential part of its pronunciation and meaning.

tool An object used to facilitate some task or activity.

totemism The belief that people are related to particular animals, plants, or natural objects by virtue of descent from common ancestral spirits.

tradition Customary ideas and practices passed on from generation to generation, which in a modernizing society may form an obstacle to new ways of doing things.

transgenders People who cross over or occupy a culturally accepted intermediate position in the binary male–female gender construction; also identified as third gender people or by various culturally specific names such as "two spirits," used in many Native American groups.

transition In a rite of passage, temporary isolation of the individual following separation and prior to incorporation into society.

tribe In anthropology, the term for a range of kin-ordered groups that are politically integrated by some unifying factor and whose members share a common ancestry, identity, culture, language, and territory.

unilineal descent Descent traced exclusively through either the male or the female line of ancestry to establish group membership.

Upper Paleolithic A period of time from about 40,000 until about 10,000 years ago that marks the beginning of behavioral modernity. The tool industries of this time are characterized by long, slim blades that produced an explosion of creative symbolic forms.

vegeculture The cultivation of domesticated root crops, such as yams and taro.

whistled speech An exchange of whistled words using a phonetic emulation of the sounds produced in spoken voice.

witchcraft An explanation of events based on the belief that certain individuals possess an innate psychic power capable of causing harm, including sickness and death.

worldview The collective body of ideas that members of a culture generally share concerning the ultimate shape and substance of their reality.

writing system A set of visible or tactile signs used to represent units of language in a systematic way.

Bibliography

Abbot, E. (2001). *A history of celibacy.* Cambridge, MA: Da Capo Press.

Abu-Lughod, L. (1986). *Veiled sentiments: Honor and poetry in a Bedouin society.* Berkeley: University of California Press.

Adams, R. E. W. (1977). *Prehistoric Mesoamerica.* Boston: Little, Brown.

Adams, R. M. (1966). *The evolution of urban society.* Chicago: Aldine.

Adams, R. M. (2001). Scale and complexity in archaic states. *Latin American Antiquity 11,* 188.

Adbusters. www.adbusters.org (retrieved October 2, 2011).

Allen, J. L., & Shalinsky, A. C. (2003). *Student atlas of anthropology.* New York: McGraw-Hill.

Allen, J. S., & Cheer, S. M. (1996). The non-thrifty genotype. *Current Anthropology 37,* 831–842.

Alvard, M. S., & Kuznar, L. (2001). Deferred harvest: The transition from hunting to animal husbandry. *American Anthropologist 103* (2), 295–311.

Ambrose, S. H. (2001). Paleolithic technology and human evolution. *Science 291,* 1748–1753.

American Anthropological Association. (1998). Statement on "race." http://www.aaanet.org/stmts/racepp.htm (retrieved August 29, 2011).

Amiran, R. (1965). The beginnings of pottery-making in the Near East. In F. R. Matson (Ed.), *Ceramics and man* (pp. 240–247). Viking Fund Publications in Anthropology, no. 41.

Anderson, S. (2010, February). The polygamists. *National Geographic, 36,* 39. http://ngm.nationalgeographic.com/2010/02/polygamists/anderson-text (retrieved September 6, 2011).

Andrews, L. B., & Nelkin, D. (1996). The bell curve: A statement. *Science 271,* 13.

Appadurai, A. (1990). Disjuncture and difference in the global cultural economy. *Public Culture 2,* 1–24.

Appadurai, A. (1996). *Modernity at large: Cultural dimensions of globalization.* Minneapolis: University of Minnesota Press.

Appenzeller, T. (1998). Art: Evolution or revolution? *Science 282,* 1451–1454.

Arctic Monitoring Assessment Project. (2003). *AMAP assessment 2002: Human health in the Arctic* (pp. xii–xiii, 22–23). Oslo: AMAP.

Arms Control Association. (2011). Nuclear weapons: Who has what at a glance. http://www.armscontrol.org/factsheets/Nuclearweaponswhohaswhat (retrieved September 18, 2011).

Armstrong, D. F., Stokoe, W. C., & Wilcox, S. E. (1993). Signs of the origin of syntax. *Current Anthropology 34,* 349–368.

Ashmore, W. (Ed.). (1981). *Lowland Maya settlement patterns.* Albuquerque: University of New Mexico Press.

Aureli, F., & de Waal, F. B. M. (2000). *Natural conflict resolution.* Berkeley: University of California Press.

Avedon, J. F. (1997). *In exile from the land of snows: The definitive account of the Dalai Lama and Tibet since the Chinese conquest.* New York: Harper.

Axel-Lute, P. (2002, September). Same-sex marriage: A selective bibliography of the legal literature. http://law-library.rutgers.edu/SSM.html (retrieved August 23, 2011).

Babiker, M. A., et al. (1996). Unnecessary deprivation of common food items in glucose-6-phosphate dehydrogenase deficiency. *Annals of Saudi Arabia 16* (4), 462–463.

Baker, P. (Ed.). (1978). *The biology of high altitude peoples.* London: Cambridge University Press.

Balandier, G. (1971). *Political anthropology.* New York: Pantheon.

Balikci, A. (1970). *The Netsilik Eskimo.* Garden City, NY: Natural History Press.

Balter, M. (1998). Why settle down? The mystery of communities. *Science 282,* 1442–1444.

Balter, M. (1999). A long season puts Çatalhöyük in context. *Science 286,* 890–891.

Balter, M. (2001). Did plaster hold Neolithic society together? *Science 294,* 2278–2281.

Balter, M. (2001). In search of the first Europeans. *Science 291,* 1724.

Banton, M. (1968). Voluntary association: Anthropological aspects. In *International encyclopedia of the social sciences* (vol. 16, pp. 357–362). New York: Macmillan.

Barham, L. S. (1998). Possible early pigment use in South-Central Africa. *Current Anthropology 39,* 703–710.

Barnard, A. (1995). Monboddo's *Orang Outang* and the definition of man. In R. Corbey & B. Theunissen (Eds.), *Ape, man, apeman: Changing views since 1600* (pp. 71–85). Leiden: Department of Prehistory, Leiden University.

Barnouw, V. (1985). *Culture and personality* (4th ed.). Homewood, IL: Dorsey Press.

Barr, R. G. (1997, October). The crying game. *Natural History,* 47.

Barth, F. (1961). *Nomads of south Persia: The Basseri tribe of the Khamseh confederacy.* Boston: Little, Brown.

Barth, F. (1962). Nomadism in the mountain and plateau areas of South West Asia. *The problems of the arid zone* (pp. 341–355). Paris: UNESCO.

Bar-Yosef, O. (1986). The walls of Jericho: An alternative interpretation. *Current Anthropology 27,* 160.

Bar-Yosef, O., Vandermeesch, B., Arensburg, B., Belfer-Cohen, A., Goldberg, P., Laville, H., Meignen, L., Rak, Y., Speth, J. D., Tchernov, E., Tillier, A-M., & Weiner, S. (1992). The excavations in Kebara Cave, Mt. Carmel. *Current Anthropology 33,* 497–550.

Bascom, W. (1969). *The Yoruba of southwestern Nigeria.* New York: Holt, Rinehart & Winston.

Bayer, R. (1987). Homosexuality and American psychiatry: The politics of diagnosis. Princeton, NJ: Princeton University Press.

Becker, J. (2004, March). China's growing pains. *National Geographic,* 68–95.

Bednarik, R. G. (1995). Concept-mediated marking in the Lower Paleolithic. *Current Anthropology 36,* 606.

Beeman, W. O. (2000). Introduction: Margaret Mead, cultural studies, and international understanding. In M. Mead & R. Métraux (Eds.), *The study of culture at a distance* (pp. xiv–xxxi). New York and Oxford, UK: Berghahn Books.

Behrensmeyer, A. K., Todd, N. E., Potts, R., & McBrinn, G. E. (1997). Late Pliocene faunal turnover in the Turkana basin, Kenya, and Ethiopia. *Science 278,* 1589–1594.

Bekoff, M., et al. (Eds.). (2002). *The cognitive animal: Empirical and theoretical perspectives on animal cognition.* Cambridge, MA: MIT Press.

Bell, D. (1997). Defining marriage and legitimacy. *Current Anthropology 38,* 241.

Belshaw, C. S. (1958). The significance of modern cults in Melanesian development. In W. Lessa & E. Z. Vogt (Eds.), *Reader in comparative religion: An anthropological approach.* New York: Harper & Row.

Benedict, R. (1959). *Patterns of culture.* New York: New American Library.

Bennett, R. L., et al. (2002, April). Genetic counseling and screening of consanguineous couples and their offspring: Recommendations of the National Society of Genetic Counselors. *Journal of Genetic Counseling 11* (2), 97–119.

Berdan, F. F. (1982). *The Aztecs of Central Mexico.* New York: Holt, Rinehart & Winston.

Bermúdez de Castro, J. M., Arsuaga, J. L., Carbonell, E., Rosas, A., Martinez, I., & Mosquera, M. (1997). A hominid from the lower Pleistocene of Atapuerca, Spain: Possible ancestor to Neandertals and modern humans. *Science 276,* 1392–1395.

Bernal, I. (1969). *The Olmec world.* Berkeley: University of California Press.

Bernard, H. R. (2002). *Research methods in anthropology: Qualitative and quantitative approaches* (3rd ed.). Walnut Creek, CA: Altamira Press.

Berra, T. M. (1990). *Evolution and the myth of creationism.* Stanford, CA: Stanford University Press.

Berreman, G. D. (1968). Caste: The concept of caste. *International encyclopedia of the social sciences* (vol. 2, pp. 333–338). New York: Macmillan.

Betzig, L. (1989). Causes of conjugal dissolution: A cross-cultural study. *Current Anthropology 30,* 654–676.

Bicchieri, M. G. (Ed.). (1972). *Hunters and gatherers today: A socioeconomic study of eleven such cultures in the twentieth century.* New York: Holt, Rinehart & Winston.

Binford, L. R. (1972). *An archaeological perspective.* New York: Seminar Press.

Binford, L. R., & Chuan, K. H. (1985). Taphonomy at a distance: Zhoukoudian, the cave home of Beijing man? *Current Anthropology 26,* 413–442.

Birdsell, J. H. (1977). The recalibration of a paradigm for the first peopling of Greater Australia. In J. Allen, J. Golson, & R. Jones (Eds.), *Sunda and Sahul: Prehistoric studies in Southeast Asia, Melanesia, and Australia* (pp. 113–167). New York: Academic Press.

Blackless, M., et al. (2000). How sexually dimorphic are we? Review and synthesis. *American Journal of Human Biology 12,* 151–166.

Blakey, M. (2003, October 29). Personal communication. *African Burial Ground Project.* Department of Anthropology, College of William & Mary.

Blok, A. (1974). *The mafia of a Sicilian village 1860–1960.* New York: Harper & Row.

Blumer, M. A., & Byrne, R. (1991). The ecological genetics and domestication and the origins of agriculture. *Current Anthropology 32,* 30.

Boas, F. (1909, May 28). Race problems in America. *Science 29* (752), 839–849.

Boas, F. (1962). *Primitive art.* Gloucester, MA: Peter Smith.

Boas, F. (1966). *Race, language and culture.* New York: Free Press.

Bodley, J. H. (1998). *Victims of progress* (4th ed.). San Francisco: McGraw-Hill.

Bodley, J. H. (2000). *Anthropology and contemporary human problems* (4th ed.). Palo Alto, CA: Mayfield.

Boehm, C. (2000). The evolution of moral communities. *School of American Research, 2000 Annual Report,* 7.

Bohannan, P. (Ed.). (1967). *Law and warfare: Studies in the anthropology of conflict.* Garden City, NY: Natural History Press.

Bohannan, P., & Dalton, G. (Eds.). (1962). *Markets in Africa.* Evanston, IL: Northwestern University Press.

Bohannan, P., & Middleton, J. (Eds.). (1968). *Kinship and social organization.* Garden City, NY: Natural History Press.

Bohannan, P., & Middleton, J. (Eds.). (1968). *Marriage, family, and residence.* Garden City, NY: Natural History Press.

Bolinger, D. (1968). *Aspects of language.* New York: Harcourt.

Bongaarts, J. (1998). Demographic consequences of declining fertility. *Science 182,* 419.

Bonvillain, N. (2000). *Language, culture, and communication: The meaning of messages* (3rd ed.). Upper Saddle River, NJ: Prentice-Hall.

Bordes, F. (1972). *A tale of two caves.* New York: Harper & Row.

Bornstein, M. H. (1975). The influence of visual perception on culture. *American Anthropologist 77* (4), 774–798.

Boshara, R. (2003, January/February). Wealth inequality: The $6,000 solution. *Atlantic Monthly.*

Brace, C. L. (1981). Tales of the phylogenetic woods: The evolution and significance of phylogenetic trees. *American Journal of Physical Anthropology 56,* 411–429.

Brace, C. L. (2000). *Evolution in an anthropological view.* Walnut Creek, CA: Altamira Press.

Brace, C. L., Nelson, H., & Korn, N. (1979). *Atlas of human evolution* (2nd ed.). New York: Holt, Rinehart & Winston.

Bradford, P. V., & Blume, H. (1992). *Ota Benga: The Pygmy in the zoo.* New York: St. Martin's Press.

Braidwood, R. J. (1960). The agricultural revolution. *Scientific American 203,* 130–141.

Braidwood, R. J. (1975). *Prehistoric men* (8th ed.). Glenview, IL: Scott, Foresman.

Brain, C. K. (1968). Who killed the Swartkrans ape-men? *South African Museums Association Bulletin 9,* 127–139.

Brain, C. K. (1969). The contribution of Namib Desert Hottentots to an understanding of australopithecine bone accumulations. *Scientific Papers of the Namib Desert Research Station,* 13.

Branda, R. F., & Eatoil, J. W. (1978). Skin color and photolysis: An evolutionary hypothesis. *Science 201,* 625–626.

Brettell, C. B., & Sargent, C. F. (Eds.). (2000). *Gender in cross-cultural perspective* (3rd ed.). Upper Saddle River, NJ: Prentice-Hall.

Brew, J. O. (1968). *One hundred years of anthropology.* Cambridge, MA: Harvard University Press.

Broecker, W. S. (1992, April). Global warming on trial. *Natural History,* 14.

Brothwell, D. R., & Higgs, E. (Eds.). (1969). *Science in archaeology* (rev. ed.). London: Thames & Hudson.

Brown, B., Walker, A., Ward, C. V., & Leakey, R. E. (1993). New *Australopithecus boisei* calvaria from East Lake Turkana, Kenya. *American Journal of Physical Anthropology 91,* 137–159.

Brown, D. E. (1991). *Human universals.* New York: McGraw-Hill.

Brown, P., et al. (2004). A new small-bodied hominin from the Late Pleistocene of Flores, Indonesia. *Nature 431,* 1055–1061.

Brunet, M., et al. (2002). A new hominid from the Upper Miocene of Chad, Central Africa. *Nature 418,* 145–151.

Buck, P. H. (1938). *Vikings of the Pacific.* Chicago: University Press of Chicago.

Burling, R. (1970). *Man's many voices: Language in its cultural context.* New York: Holt, Rinehart & Winston.

Burling, R. (1993). Primate calls, human language, and nonverbal communication. *Current Anthropology 34,* 25–53.

Byers, D. S. (Ed.). (1967). *The prehistory of the Tehuacan Valley: Environment and subsistence* (vol. 1). Austin: University of Texas Press.

Cachel, S. (1997). Dietary shifts and the European Upper Paleolithic transition. *Current Anthropology 38,* 590.

Callaway, E. (2007, December 3). Chimp beats students at computer game. Published online: *Nature,* doi:10.1038/news.2007.317.

Canton Fair ends with trade volume growth. (2011, May 6). Xinhua News Agency. http://english.peopledaily.com.cn/90001/90778/90861/7371496.html (retrieved September 4, 2011).

Carneiro, R. L. (1970). A theory of the origin of the state. *Science 169,* 733–738.

Caroulis, J. (1996). Food for thought. *Pennsylvania Gazette 95* (3), 16.

Carroll, J. B. (Ed.). (1956). *Language, thought and reality: Selected writings of Benjamin Lee Whorf.* Cambridge, MA: MIT Press.

Cartmill, M. (1998). The gift of gab. *Discover 19* (11), 64.

Cashdan, E. (1989). Hunters and gatherers: Economic behavior in bands. In S. Plattner (Ed.), *Economic anthropology* (pp. 21–48). Stanford, CA: Stanford University Press.

Catford, J. C. (1988). *A practical introduction to phonetics.* Oxford, UK: Clarendon Press.

Cavalli-Sforza, L. L. (1977). *Elements of human genetics.* Menlo Park, CA: W. A. Benjamin.

Centers for Disease Control and Prevention. (2009). Differences in prevalence of obesity among black, white, and Hispanic adults— United States, 2006–2008. *Morbidity and Mortality Weekly Report 58* (27), 740–744.

Chagnon, N. A. (1988). *Yanomamo: The fierce people* (3rd ed.). New York: Holt, Rinehart & Winston.

Chagnon, N. A. (1990). On Yanomamo violence: Reply to Albert. *Current Anthropology 31* (2), 49–53.

Chagnon, N. A., & Irons, W. (Eds.). (1979). *Evolutionary biology and human social behavior.* North Scituate, MA: Duxbury Press.

Chan, J. W. C., & Vernon, P. E. (1988). Individual differences among the peoples of China. In J. W. Berry (Ed.), *Human abilities in cultural context* (pp. 340–357). Cambridge, UK: Cambridge University Press.

Chance, N. A. (1990). *The Iñupiat and Arctic Alaska: An ethnography of development.* New York: Harcourt.

Chang, K. C. (Ed.). (1968). *Settlement archaeology.* Palo Alto, CA: National Press.

Chang, L. (2005, June 9). A migrant worker sees rural home in new light. *Wall Street Journal.*

Chase, C. (1998). Hermaphrodites with attitude. *Gay and Lesbian Quarterly 4* (2), 189–211.

Chicurel, M. (2001). Can organisms speed their own evolution? *Science 292,* 1824–1827.

Childe, V. G. (1951). *Man makes himself.* New York: New American Library. (orig. 1936)

Childe, V. G. (1954). *What happened in history.* Baltimore: Penguin Books.

Cigno, A. (1994). *Economics of the family.* New York: Oxford University Press.

Ciochon, R. L., & Fleagle, J. G. (Eds.). (1987). *Primate evolution and human origins.* Hawthorne, NY: Aldine.

Ciochon, R. L., & Fleagle, J. G. (1993). *The human evolution source book.* Englewood Cliffs, NJ: Prentice-Hall.

Clark, E. E. (1966). *Indian legends of the Pacific Northwest.* Berkeley: University of California Press.

Clark, G. (1967). *The Stone Age hunters.* New York: McGraw-Hill.

Clark, G. (1972). *Starr Carr: A case study in bioarchaeology.* Reading, MA: Addison-Wesley.

Clark, G. A. (1997). Neandertal genetics. *Science 277,* 1024.

Clark, G. A. (2002). Neandertal archaeology: Implications for our origins. *American Anthropologist 104* (1), 50–67.

Clark, J. G. D. (1962). *Prehistoric Europe: The economic basis.* Stanford, CA: Stanford University Press.

Clark, W. E. L. (1960). *The antecedents of man.* Chicago: Quadrangle Books.

Clark, W. E. L. (1966). *History of the primates* (5th ed.). Chicago: University of Chicago Press.

Clark, W. E. L. (1967). *Man-apes or ape-men? The story of discoveries in Africa.* New York: Holt, Rinehart & Winston.

Clarke, R. J. (1998). First ever discovery of a well preserved skull and associated skeleton of *Australopithecus. South African Journal of Science 94,* 460–464.

Clarke, R. J., & Tobias, P. V. (1995). Sterkfontein member 2 foot bones of the oldest South African hominid. *Science 269,* 521–524.

Clay, J. W. (1996). What's a nation? In W. A. Haviland & R. J. Gordon (Eds.), *Talking about people* (2nd ed., pp. 188–189). Mountain View, CA: Mayfield.

Clough, S. B., & Cole, C. W. (1952). *Economic history of Europe* (3rd ed.). Lexington, MA: Heath.

Coe, S. D. (1994). *America's first cuisines.* Austin: University of Texas Press.

Coe, W. R. (1967). *Tikal: A handbook of the ancient Maya ruins.* Philadelphia: University of Pennsylvania Museum.

Coe, W. R., & Haviland, W. A. (1982). *Introduction to the archaeology of Tikal.* Philadelphia: University Museum.

Cohen, M. N. (1977). *The food crisis in prehistory.* New Haven, CT: Yale University Press.

Cohen, M. N. (1995). Anthropology and race: The bell curve phenomenon. *General Anthropology 2* (1), 1–4.

Cohen, M. N., & Armelagos, G. J. (1984). *Paleopathology at the origins of agriculture.* Orlando: Academic Press.

Cohen, M. N., & Armelagos, G. J. (1984). Paleopathology at the origins of agriculture: Editors' summation. In *Paleopathology at the origins of agriculture* (p. 594). Orlando: Academic Press.

Colburn, T., Dumanoski, D., & Myers, J. P. (1996). Hormonal sabotage. *Natural History 3,* 45–46.

Colburn, T., et al. (1997). *Our stolen future.* New York: Plume/Penguin Books.

Cole, J. W., & Wolf, E. R. (1999). *The hidden frontier: Ecology and ethnicity in an alpine valley* (with a new introduction). Berkeley: University of California Press.

Collier, J., & Collier, M. (1986). *Visual anthropology: Photography as a research method.* Albuquerque: University of New Mexico Press.

Collier, J., Rosaldo, M. Z., & Yanagisako, S. (1982). Is there a family? New anthropological views. In B. Thorne & M. Yalom (Eds.), *Rethinking the family: Some feminist questions* (pp. 25–39). New York: Longman.

Collier, J. F., & Yanagisako, S. J. (Eds.). (1987). *Gender and kinship: Essays toward a unified analysis.* Stanford, CA: Stanford University Press.

Cone, M. (2005). *Silent snow: The slow poisoning of the Arctic.* New York: Grove Press.

Conner, M. (1996). The archaeology of contemporary mass graves. *SAA Bulletin 14* (4), 6, 31.

Conroy, G. C. (1997). *Reconstructing human origins: A modern synthesis.* New York: Norton.

Coon, C. S., Garn, S. N., & Birdsell, J. (1950). *Races: A study of the problems of race formation in man.* Springfield, IL: Thomas.

Cooper, A., Poinar, H. N., Pääbo, S., Radovci, C. J., Debénath, A., Caparros, M., Barroso-Ruiz, C., Bertranpetit, J., Nielsen-March, C., Hedges, R. E. M., & Sykes, B. (1997). Neanderthal genetics. *Science 277,* 1021–1024.

Coppa, A., et al. (2006). Early Neolithic tradition of dentistry. *Nature 440,* 755–756.

Coppens, Y., Howell, F. C., Isaac, G. L., & Leakey, R. E. F. (Eds.). (1976). *Earliest man and environments in the Lake Rudolf Basin: Stratigraphy, paleoecology, and evolution.* Chicago: University of Chicago Press.

Corbey, R. (1995). Introduction: Missing links, or the ape's place in nature. In R. Corbey & B. Theunissen (Eds.), *Ape, man, apeman: Changing views since 1600* (p. 1). Leiden: Department of Prehistory, Leiden University.

Cornwell, T. (1995, November 10). Skeleton staff. *Times Higher Education,* 20.

Corruccini, R. S. (1992). Metrical reconsideration of the Skhul IV and IX and Border Cave I crania in the context of modern human origins. *American Journal of Physical Anthropology 87,* 433–445.

Cottrell, L. (1963). *The lost pharaohs.* New York: Grosset & Dunlap.

Courlander, H. (1971). *The fourth world of the Hopis.* New York: Crown.

Cowgill, G. L. (1997). State and society at Teotihuacan, Mexico. *Annual Review of Anthropology 26,* 129–161.

Crane, H. (2001). *Men in spirit: The masculinization of Taiwanese Buddhist nuns.* Doctoral dissertation, Brown University.

Cretney, S. (2003). *Family law in the twentieth century: A history*. New York: Oxford University Press.

Criminal Code of Canada, § 718.2(e).

Crocker, W. A., & Crocker, J. (1994). *The Canela: Bonding through kinship, ritual, and sex*. Fort Worth: Harcourt Brace.

Crossette, B. (1998, September 27). Kofi Annan's astonishing facts! *New York Times*, D16.

Crystal, D. (2002). *Language death*. Cambridge, UK: Cambridge University Press.

Culbert, T. P. (Ed.). (1973). *The Classic Maya collapse*. Albuquerque: University of New Mexico Press.

Culotta, E. (1995). New hominid crowds the field. *Science 269*, 918.

Culotta, E., & Koshland, D. E., Jr. (1994). DNA repair works its way to the top. *Science 266*, 1926.

Dalton, G. (Ed.). (1967). *Tribal and peasant economics: Readings in economic Anthropology*. Garden City, NY: Natural History Press.

Dalton, G. (1971). *Traditional tribal and peasant economics: An introductory survey of economic anthropology*. Reading, MA: Addison-Wesley.

Daniel, G. (1970). *The first civilizations: The archaeology of their origins*. New York: Apollo Editions.

Daniel, G. (1975). *A hundred and fifty years of archaeology* (2nd ed.). London: Duckworth.

Darwin, C. (1887). *Autobiography*. Reprinted in *The life and letters of Charles Darwin* (1902). F. Darwin (Ed.), London: John Murray.

Darwin, C. (1936). *The descent of man and selection in relation to sex*. New York: Random House (Modern Library). (orig. 1871)

Darwin, C. (1967). *On the origin of species*. New York: Atheneum. (orig. 1859)

Davenport, W. (1959). Linear descent and descent groups. *American Anthropologist 61*, 557–573.

Davies, G. (2005). *A history of money from the earliest times to present day* (3rd ed.). Cardiff, UK: University of Wales Press.

Davies, J. B., et al. (2007). *The world distribution of household wealth*. Santa Cruz: University of California, Mapping Global Inequalities, Center for Global, International, and Regional Studies.

Davies, S. G. (2007). *Challenging gender norms: Five genders among the Bugis in Indonesia*. Belmont, CA: Thomson Wadsworth.

A decade of CSQ. (1991, Winter). *Cultural Survival Quarterly 15*(4), entire issue.

Deetz, J. (1967). *Invitation to archaeology*. New York: Doubleday.

Deetz, J. (1977). *In small things forgotten: The archaeology of early American life*. Garden City, NY: Anchor Press/Doubleday.

del Carmen Rodríguez Martínez, M., et al. (2006). Oldest writing in the New World. *Science 313* (5793), 1610–1614.

d'Errico, F., Zilhão, J., Julien, M., Baffier, D., & Pelegrin, J. (1998). Neandertal acculturation in Western Europe? *Current Anthropology 39*, 521.

Dettwyler, K. A. (1994). *Dancing skeletons: Life and death in West Africa*. Prospect Heights, IL: Waveland Press.

Dettwyler, K. A. (1997, October). When to wean. *Natural History*, 49.

DeVore, I. (Ed.). (1965). *Primate behavior: Field studies of monkeys and apes*. New York: Holt, Rinehart & Winston.

de Waal, F. (1996). *Good natured: The origins of right and wrong in humans and other animals*. Cambridge, MA: Harvard University Press.

de Waal, F., Kano, T., & Parish, A. R. (1998). Comments. *Current Anthropology 39*, 408, 410, 413.

de Waal, F. B. M. (2000). Primates—A natural heritage of conflict resolution. *Science 28*, 586–590.

de Waal, F. B. M. (2001). *The ape and the sushi master*. New York: Basic Books.

de Waal, F. B. M. (2001). Sing the song of evolution. *Natural History 110* (8), 77.

de Waal, F. B. M., & Johanowicz, D. L. (1993). Modification of reconciliation behavior through social experience: An experiment with two macaque species. *Child Development 64*, 897–908.

Diamond, J. (1994). How Africa became black. *Discover 15* (2), 72–81.

Diamond, J. (1994). Race without color. *Discover 15* (11), 83–89.

Diamond, J. (1997). *Guns, germs, and steel*. New York: Norton.

Diamond, J. (1998). Ants, crops, and history. *Science 281*, 1974–1975.

Diamond, J. (2005). *Collapse: How societies choose to fail or succeed*. New York: Viking/Penguin Books.

Dirie, W., & Miller, C. (1998). *Desert flower: The extraordinary journey of a desert nomad*. New York: William Morrow.

Dixon, J. E., Cann, J. R., & Renfrew, C. (1968). Obsidian and the origins of trade. *Scientific American 218*, 38–46.

Dobyns, H. F., Doughty, P. L., & Lasswell, H. D. (Eds.). (1971). *Peasants, power, and applied social change*. London: Sage.

Dobzhansky, T. (1962). *Mankind evolving*. New Haven, CT: Yale University Press.

Dozier, E. (1970). *The Pueblo Indians of North America*. New York: Holt, Rinehart & Winston.

Draper, P. (1975). !Kung women: Contrasts in sexual egalitarianism in foraging and sedentary contexts. In R. Reiter (Ed.), *Toward an anthropology of women* (pp. 77–109). New York: Monthly Review Press.

Drewnowski, A., & Specter, S. E. (2004). Poverty and obesity: The role of energy density and energy costs. *American Journal of Clinical Nutrition 79* (1), 6–16.

Driver, H. (1964). *Indians of North America*. Chicago: University of Chicago Press.

Dubois, C. (1944). *The people of Alor*. Minneapolis: University of Minnesota Press.

Dubos, R. (1968). *So human an animal*. New York: Scribner.

Dumurat-Dreger, A. (1998, May/June). "Ambiguous sex" or ambivalent medicine? *The Hastings Center Report 28* (3), 2435 (posted on the Intersex Society of North America website: www.isna.org).

Dunbar, P. (2008, January 19). The pink vigilantes: The Indian women fighting for women's rights. *Mail Online*. http://www.dailymail.co.uk/news/article-509318/The-pink-vigilantes-The-Indian-women-fighting-womens-rights.html (retrieved September 15, 2011).

Dundes, A. (1980). *Interpreting folklore*. Bloomington: Indiana University Press.

Dunham, S. A. (2009). *Surviving against the odds: Village industry in Indonesia*. Durham, NC: Duke University Press.

Durant, J. C. (2000, April 23). Everybody into the gene pool. *New York Times Book Review*, 11.

Duranti, A. (2001). Linguistic anthropology: History, ideas, and issues. In A. Duranti (Ed.), *Linguistic anthropology: A reader* (pp. 1–38). Oxford UK: Blackwell Press.

Durkheim, E. (1964). *The division of labor in society*. New York: Free Press.

Durkheim, E. (1965). *The elementary forms of the religious life*. New York: Free Press.

Du Toit, B. M. (1991). *Human sexuality: Cross cultural readings*. New York: McGraw-Hill.

Eastman, C. M. (1990). *Aspects of language and culture* (2nd ed.). Novato, CA: Chandler & Sharp.

Eating disorders (most recent) by country. *Nationmaster.com*. http://www.nationmaster.com/graph/mor_eat_dis-mortality-eating-disorders (retrieved September 19, 2011).

Eaton, S. B., Konner, M., & Shostak, M. (1988). Stone-agers in the fast lane: Chronic degenerative diseases in evolutionary perspective. *American Journal of Medicine 84* (4), 739–749.

Edey, M. A., & Johannson, D. (1989). *Blueprints: Solving the mystery of evolution*. Boston: Little, Brown.

Edwards, J. (Ed.). (1999). *Technologies of procreation: Kinship in the age of assisted conception.* New York: Routledge.

Edwards, S. W. (1978). Nonutilitarian activities on the Lower Paleolithic: A look at the two kinds of evidence. *Current Anthropology 19* (1), 135–137.

Egan, T. (1999, February 28). The persistence of polygamy. *New York Times Magazine, 52.*

Egede, I. Quoted in Cone, M. (2005). *Silent snow: The slow poisoning of the Arctic.* New York: Grove Press.

Eggan, F. (1954). Social anthropology and the method of controlled comparison. *American Anthropologist 56,* 743–763.

Eiseley, L. (1958). *Darwin's century: Evolution and the men who discovered it.* New York: Doubleday.

Eisenstadt, S. N. (1956). *From generation to generation: Age groups and social structure.* New York: Free Press.

el Guindi, F. (2004). *Visual anthropology: Essential method and theory.* Walnut Creek, CA: Altamira Press.

Elkin, A. P. (1964). *The Australian Aborigines.* Garden City, NY: Doubleday/Anchor Books.

Ellis, C. (2006). *A dancing people: Powwow culture on the southern plains.* Lawrence: University Press of Kansas.

Ember, C. R., & Ember, M. (1996). What have we learned from cross-cultural research? *General Anthropology 2* (2), 5.

Enard, W., et al. (2002). Molecular evolution of FOXP2, a gene involved in speech and language. *Nature 418,* 869–872.

Erickson, P. A., & Murphy, L. D. (2003). *A history of anthropological theory* (2nd ed.). Peterborough, Ontario: Broadview Press.

Errington, F. K., & Gewertz, D. B. (2001). *Cultural alternatives and a feminist anthropology: An analysis of culturally constructed gender interests in Papua New Guinea.* Cambridge, UK, and New York: Cambridge University Press.

Ervin-Tripp, S. (1973). *Language acquisition and communicative choice.* Stanford, CA: Stanford University Press.

Esber, G. S., Jr. (1987). Designing Apache houses with Apaches. In R. M. Wulff & S. J. Fiske (Eds.), *Anthropological praxis: Translating knowledge into action* (pp. 187–196). Boulder, CO: Westview Press.

Essoungou, A-M. (2010, April). Africa's displaced people: Out of the shadows. *Africa Renewal, 6.*

Evans, W. (1968). *Communication in the animal world.* New York: Crowell.

Evans-Pritchard, E. E. (1968). *The Nuer: A description of the modes of livelihood and political institutions of a Nilotic people.* London: Oxford University Press.

Fagan, B. M. (1995). *People of the earth* (8th ed.). New York: HarperCollins.

Fagan, B. M. (1995). The quest for the past. In L. L. Hasten (Ed.), *Annual editions 95/96: Archaeology* (p. 10). Guilford, CT: Dushkin.

Fagan, B. M. (1999). *Archaeology: A brief introduction* (7th ed.). New York: Longman.

Fagan, B. M. (2000). *Ancient lives: An introduction to archaeology.* Englewood Cliffs, NJ: Prentice-Hall.

Falk, D. (1975). Comparative anatomy of the larynx in man and the chimpanzee: Implications for language in Neanderthal. *American Journal of Physical Anthropology 43* (1), 123–132.

Falk, D. (1989). Ape-like endocast of "Ape Man Taung." *American Journal of Physical Anthropology 80,* 335–339.

Falk, D. (1993). A good brain is hard to cool. *Natural History 102* (8), 65.

Falk, D. (1993). Hominid paleoneurology. In R. L. Ciochon & J. G. Fleagle (Eds.), *The human evolution source book.* Englewood Cliffs, NJ: Prentice-Hall.

Falk, D., et al. (2005). The brain of LB1, *Homo floresiensis. Science 308,* 242–245.

Farmer, P. (1992). *AIDS and accusation: Haiti and the geography of blame.* Berkeley: University of California Press.

Farmer, P. (1996). On suffering and structural violence: A view from below. *Daedalus 125* (1), 261–283.

Farmer, P. (2001). *Infections and inequalities: The modern plagues.* Berkeley: University of California Press.

Farmer, P. (2004, June). An anthropology of structural violence. *Current Anthropology 45,* 3.

Fausto-Sterling, A. (1993, March/April). The five sexes: Why male and female are not enough. *The Sciences 33* (2), 20–24.

Fausto-Sterling, A. (2000, July/August). The five sexes revisited. *The Sciences 40* (4), 19–24.

Fausto-Sterling, A. (2003, August 2). Personal e-mail communication.

Fedigan, L. M. (1986). The changing role of women in models of human evolution. *Annual Review of Anthropology 15,* 25–56.

Ferrie, H. (1997). An interview with C. Loring Brace. *Current Anthropology 38,* 851–869.

Finkler, K. (2000). *Experiencing the new genetics: Family and kinship on the medical frontier.* Philadelphia: University of Pennsylvania Press.

Firth, R. (1952). *Elements of social organization.* London: Watts.

Firth, R. (1957). *Man and culture: An evaluation of Bronislaw Malinowski.* London: Routledge.

Firth, R. (Ed.). (1967). *Themes in economic anthropology.* London: Tavistock.

Fisher, R., & Ury, W. L. (1991). *Getting to yes: Negotiating agreement without giving in* (2nd ed.). Boston: Houghton Mifflin.

Flannery, K. V. (1973). The origins of agriculture. In B. J. Siegel, A. R. Beals, & S. A. Tyler (Eds.), *Annual review of anthropology* (vol. 2, pp. 271–310). Palo Alto, CA: Annual Reviews.

Flannery, K. V. (Ed.). (1976). *The Mesoamerican village.* New York: Seminar Press.

Fogel, R., & Riquelme, M. A. (2005). *Enclave sojero. Merma de soberania y pobreza.* Asuncion: Centro de Estudios Rurales Interdisciplinarias.

Folger, T. (1993). The naked and the bipedal. *Discover 14* (11), 34–35.

Food and Agriculture Organization of the United Nations. (2009, June 19). *1.02 billion people hungry: One sixth of humanity undernourished—more than ever before.* http://www.fao.org/news/story/en/item/20568/icode/ (retrieved September 19, 2011).

Forbes, J. D. (1964). *The Indian in America's past.* Englewood Cliffs, NJ: Prentice-Hall.

Forde, C. D. (1955). The Nupe. In D. Forde (Ed.), *Peoples of the Niger-Benue confluence.* London: International African Institute (Ethnographic Survey of Africa. Western Africa, part 10).

Forde, C. D. (1968). Double descent among the Yakö. In P. Bohannan & J. Middleton (Eds.), *Kinship and social organization* (pp. 179–191). Garden City, NY: Natural History Press.

Forste, R. (2008). *Prelude to marriage, or alternative to marriage? A social demographic look at cohabitation in the U.S.* Working paper. Social Science Electronic Publishing. http://papers.ssrn.com/sol3/papers.cfm?abstract_id=269172 (retrieved September 7, 2011).

Fortes, M. (1950). Kinship and marriage among the Ashanti. In A. R. Radcliffe-Brown & C. D. Forde (Eds.), *African systems of kinship and marriage.* London: Oxford University Press.

Fortes, M. (1969). *Kinship and the social order: The legacy of Lewis Henry Morgan.* Chicago: Aldine.

Fortes, M., & Evans-Prichard, E. E. (Eds.). (1962). *African political systems.* London: Oxford University Press. (orig. 1940)

Fossey, D. (1983). *Gorillas in the mist.* Burlington, MA: Houghton Mifflin.

Foster, G. M. (1955). Peasant society and the image of the limited good. *American Anthropologist 67,* 293–315.

Fouts, R. S., & Waters, G. (2001). Chimpanzee sign language and Darwinian continuity: Evidence for a neurology continuity of language. *Neurological Research 23,* 787–794.

Fox, R. (1967). *Kinship and marriage in an anthropological perspective.* Baltimore: Penguin Books.

Fox, R. (1968). *Encounter with anthropology.* New York: Dell.

Fox, R. (1981, December 3). [Interview]. Coast Telecourses, Inc., Los Angeles.

Frake, C. O. (1992). Lessons of the Mayan sky. In A. F. Aveni (Ed.), *The sky in Mayan literature* (pp. 274–291). New York: Oxford University Press.

Frankfort, H. (1968). *The birth of civilization in the Near East.* New York: Barnes & Noble.

Fraser, D. (1962). *Primitive art.* New York: Doubleday.

Fraser, D. (Ed.). (1966). *The many faces of primitive art: A critical anthology.* Englewood Cliffs, NJ: Prentice-Hall.

Frayer, D. W. (1981). Body size, weapon use, and natural selection in the European Upper Paleolithic and Mesolithic. *American Anthropologist 83,* 57–73.

Frazer, J. G. (1961, reissue). *The new golden bough.* New York: Doubleday, Anchor Books.

Freeman, J. D. (1960). The Iban of western Borneo. In G. P. Murdock (Ed.), *Social structure in Southeast Asia.* Chicago: Quadrangle Books.

Freeman, L. G. (1992). *Ambrona and Torralba: New evidence and interpretation.* Paper presented at the 91st Annual Meeting, American Anthropological Association.

Fried, M. (1967). *The evolution of political society: An essay in political anthropology.* New York: Random House.

Fried, M. (1972). *The study of anthropology.* New York: Crowell.

Fried, M., Harris, M., & Murphy, R. (1968). *War: The anthropology of armed conflict and aggression.* Garden City, NY: Natural History Press.

Friedl, E. (1975). *Women and men: An anthropologist's view.* New York: Holt, Rinehart & Winston.

Friedman, J. (Ed.). (2003). *Globalization, the state, and violence.* Walnut Creek, CA: Altamira Press.

Frye, D. P. (2000). Conflict management in cross-cultural perspective. In F. Aureli & F. B. M. de Waal, *Natural conflict resolution* (pp. 334–351). Berkeley: University of California Press.

Frye, M. (1983). *Sexism.* In *The politics of reality* (pp. 17–40). New York: Crossing Press.

Gamble, C. (1986). *The Paleolithic settlement of Europe.* Cambridge, UK: Cambridge University Press.

Garn, S. M. (1970). *Human races* (3rd ed.). Springfield, IL: Thomas.

Geertz, C. (1963). *Agricultural involution: The process of ecological change in Indonesia.* Berkeley: University of California Press.

Geertz, C. (1984). Distinguished lecture: Antirelativism. *American Anthropologist 86,* 263–278.

Gene study suggests Polynesians came from Taiwan. (2005, July 4). Reuters.

Gettleman, J. (2011, July 9). South Sudan, the newest nation, is full of hope and problems. *New York Times.* http://www.post-gazette.com/pg/11190/1159402-82-0.stm (retrieved August 22, 2011).

Gibbons, A. (1997). Ideas on human origins evolve at anthropology gathering. *Science 276,* 535–536.

Gibbs, J. L., Jr. (1965). The Kpelle of Liberia. In J. L. Gibbs Jr. (Ed.), *Peoples of Africa* (pp. 216–218). New York: Holt, Rinehart & Winston.

Gierstorfer, C. (2007). Peaceful primates, violent acts. *Nature 447,* 7.

Gilley, B. J. (2007). *Becoming two-spirit: Gay identity and social acceptance in Indian Country.* Lincoln: University of Nebraska Press.

Ginsburg, F. D., Abu-Lughod, L., & Larkin, B. (Eds.). (2002). *Media worlds: Anthropology on new terrain.* Berkeley: University of California Press.

Gleason, H. A., Jr. (1966). *An introduction to descriptive linguistics* (rev. ed.). New York: Holt, Rinehart & Winston.

Gledhill, J. (2000). *Power and its disguises: Anthropological perspectives on politics* (2nd ed.). Boulder, CO: Pluto Press.

Global 500: Our annual ranking of the world's largest corporations. (2011). *CNN Money.* http://money.cnn.com/magazines/fortune/global500/2011/ (retrieved September 18, 2011).

Godfrey, T. (2000, December 27). Biotech threatening biodiversity. *Burlington Free Press,* 10A.

Gonzalez, J. (2002, January 11). Tracking Africa's fast-growing indigenous churches on DVD. *UA News.* http://uanews.org/node/5799 (retrieved September 16, 2011).

Goodall, J. (1986). *The chimpanzees of Gombe: Patterns of behavior.* Cambridge, MA: Belknap Press.

Goodall, J. (1990). *Through a window: My thirty years with the chimpanzees of Gombe.* Boston: Houghton Mifflin.

Goodall, J. (2000). *Reason for hope: A spiritual journey.* New York: Warner Books.

Goode, W. (1963). *World revolution and family patterns.* New York: Free Press.

Goodenough, W. (Ed.). (1964). *Explorations in cultural anthropology: Essays in honor of George Murdock.* New York: McGraw-Hill.

Goodenough, W. (1965). Rethinking status and role: Toward a general model of the cultural organization of social relationships. In M. Benton (Ed.), *The relevance of models for social anthropology.* New York: Praeger.

Goodenough, W. H. (1990). Evolution of the human capacity for beliefs. *American Anthropologist 92,* 601.

Goodman, A., & Armelagos, G. J. (1985). Death and disease at Dr. Dickson's mounds. *Natural History 94* (9), 12–18.

Goodwin, R. (1999). *Personal relationships across cultures.* New York: Routledge.

Goody, J. (1969). *Comparative studies in kinship.* Stanford, CA: Stanford University Press.

Goody, J. (Ed.). (1972). *Developmental cycle in domestic groups.* New York: Cambridge University Press.

Goody, J. (1976). *Production and reproduction: A comparative study of the domestic domain.* Cambridge, UK: Cambridge University Press.

Goody, J. (1983). *The development of the family and marriage in Europe.* Cambridge, MA: Cambridge University Press.

Gordon, R. J. (1992). *The Bushman myth: The making of a Namibian underclass.* Boulder, CO: Westview Press.

Gordon, R. J., & Megitt, M. J. (1985). *Law and order in the New Guinea highlands.* Hanover, NH: University Press of New England.

Gottlieb, A. (2003). *The afterlife is where we come from: The culture of infancy in West Africa.* Chicago: University of Chicago Press.

Gottlieb, A. (2004). Babies as ancestors, babies as spirits: The culture of infancy in West Africa. *Expedition 46* (3), 13–21.

Gottlieb, A. (2005). Non-Western approaches to spiritual development among infants and young children: A case study from West Africa. In P. L. Benson et al. (Eds.), *The handbook of spiritual development in childhood and adolescence* (pp. 150–162). Thousand Oaks, CA: Sage.

Gould, S. J. (1983). *Hen's teeth and horses' toes.* New York: Norton.

Gould, S. J. (1989). *Wonderful life.* New York: Norton.

Gould, S. J. (1991). *Bully for brontosaurus.* New York: Norton.

Gould, S. J. (1991). *The flamingo's smile: Reflections in natural history.* New York: Norton.

Gould, S. J. (1994). The geometer of race. *Discover 15* (11), 65–69.

Gould, S. J. (1996). *Full house: The spread of excellence from Plato to Darwin.* New York: Harmony Books.

Gould, S. J. (1996). *The mismeasure of man* (rev. ed.). New York: Norton.

Gould, S. J. (1997). *Questioning the millennium.* New York: Crown.

Gould, S. J. (2000). What does the dreaded "E" word mean anyway? *Natural History 109* (1), 34–36.

Gray, P. B. (2004, May). HIV and Islam: Is HIV prevalence lower among Muslims? *Social Science & Medicine 58* (9), 1751–1756.

Green, R. E., et al. (2010, May 7). A draft sequence of the Neandertal genome. *Science 328,* 710–722.

Greenberg, J. H. (1968). *Anthropological linguistics: An introduction.* New York: Random House.

Greymorning, S. N. (2001). Reflections on the Arapaho Language Project or, when Bambi spoke Arapaho and other tales of Arapaho language revitalization efforts. In K. Hale & L. Hinton, *The green book of language revitalization in practice* (pp. 287–297). New York: Academic Press.

Grine, F. E. (1993). Australopithecine taxonomy and phylogeny: Historical background and recent interpretation. In R. L. Ciochon & J. G. Fleagle (Eds.), *The human evolution source book.* Englewood Cliffs, NJ: Prentice-Hall.

Grossman, J. (2002, April 8). Should the law be kinder to kissin' cousins? A genetic report should cause a rethinking of incest laws. *Find Law.* http://writ.news.findlaw.com/grossman/20020408.html (retrieved September 5, 2011).

Grün, R., & Thorne, A. (1997). Dating the Ngandong humans. *Science 276,* 1575.

Guillette, E. A., et al. (1998, June). An anthropological approach to the evaluation of preschool children exposed to pesticides in Mexico. *Environmental Health Perspectives 106,* 347.

Guthrie, S. (1993). *Faces in the clouds: A new theory of religions.* New York: Oxford University Press.

Gutin, J. A. (1995). Do Kenya tools root birth of modern thought in Africa? *Science 270,* 1118–1119.

Hafkin, N., & Bay, E. (Eds.). (1976). *Women in Africa.* Stanford, CA: Stanford University Press.

Hager, L. (1989). *The evolution of sex differences in the hominid bony pelvis.* Doctoral dissertation. University of California, Berkeley.

Hahn, R. A. (1992). The state of federal health statistics on racial and ethnic groups. *Journal of the American Medical Association 267* (2), 268–271.

Hall, E. T. (1959). *The silent language.* Garden City, NY: Anchor Press/Doubleday.

Hall, E. T. (1963). A system for the notation of proxemic behavior. *American Anthropologist 65,* 1003–1026.

Hall, E. T. (1990). *The hidden dimension.* New York: Anchor Books.

Hamblin, D. J., & the Editors of Time-Life. (1973). *The first cities.* New York: Time-Life.

Hamburg, D. A., & McGown, E. R. (Eds.). (1979). *The great apes.* Menlo Park, CA: Cummings.

Hammond, D. (1972). *Associations.* Reading, MA: Addison-Wesley.

Hanson, A. (1989). The making of the Maori: Culture invention and its logic. *American Anthropologist 91* (4), 890–902.

Harlow, H. F. (1962). Social deprivation in monkeys. *Scientific American 206,* 1–10.

Harner, M. (1980). *The way of the shaman: A guide to power and healing.* San Francisco: Harper & Row.

Harpending, H., & Cochran, G. (2002). In our genes. *Proceedings of the National Academy of Sciences, USA 99* (1), 10–12.

Harpending, J. H., & Harpending, H. C. (1995). Ancient differences in population can mimic a recent African origin of modern humans. *Current Anthropology 36,* 667–674.

Harris, M. (1968). *The rise of anthropological theory: A history of theories of culture.* New York: Crowell.

Harris, M. (1989). *Cows, pigs, wars, and witches: The riddles of culture.* New York: Vintage/Random House.

Harrison, G. G. (1975). Primary adult lactase deficiency: A problem in anthropological genetics. *American Anthropologist 77,* 815–819.

Hart, C. W., Pilling, A. R., & Goodale, J. (1988). *Tiwi of north Australia* (3rd ed.). New York: Holt, Rinehart & Winston.

Hart, D., & Sussman, R. W. (2005). *Man the hunted: Primates, predators, and human evolution.* Boulder, CO: Westview Press.

Hartwig, W. C., & Doneski, K. (1998). Evolution of the Hominid hand and toolmaking behavior. *American Journal of Physical Anthropology 106,* 401–402.

Hasnain, M. (2005, October 27). Cultural approach to HIV/AIDS harm reduction in Muslim countries. *Harm Reduction Journal 2,* 23.

Hatcher, E. P. (1985). *Art as culture, an introduction to the anthropology of art.* New York: University Press of America.

Haviland, W. (1967). Stature at Tikal, Guatemala: Implications for ancient Maya, demography, and social organization. *American Antiquity 32,* 316–325.

Haviland, W. (1970). Tikal, Guatemala and Mesoamerican urbanism. *World Archaeology 2,* 186–198.

Haviland, W. A. (1972). A new look at Classic Maya social organization at Tikal. *Ceramica de Cultura Maya 8,* 1–16.

Haviland, W. A. (1974). Farming, seafaring and bilocal residence on the coast of Maine. *Man in the Northeast 6,* 31–44.

Haviland, W. A. (1975). The ancient Maya and the evolution of urban society. *University of Northern Colorado Museum of Anthropology,* Miscellaneous Series, 37.

Haviland, W. A. (1997). The rise and fall of sexual inequality: Death and gender at Tikal, Guatemala. *Ancient Mesoamerica 8,* 1–12.

Haviland, W. A. (2002). Settlement, society and demography at Tikal. In J. Sabloff (Ed.), *Tikal.* Santa Fe: School of American Research.

Haviland, W. A. (2003). *Tikal, Guatemala: A Maya way to urbanism.* Paper prepared for Third INAH/Penn State Conference on Mesoamerican Urbanism.

Haviland, W. A., & Moholy-Nagy, H. (1992). Distinguishing the high and mighty from the hoi polloi at Tikal, Guatemala. In A. F. Chase & D. Z. Chase (Eds.), *Mesoamerican elites: An archaeological assessment.* Norman: Oklahoma University Press.

Haviland, W. A., & Power, M. W. (1994). *The original Vermonters: Native inhabitants, past and present* (2nd ed.). Hanover, NH: University Press of New England.

Haviland, W. A., et al. (1985). *Excavations in small residential groups of Tikal: Groups 4F-1 and 4F-2.* Philadelphia: University Museum.

Hays, H. R. (1965). *From ape to angel: An informal history of social anthropology.* New York: Knopf.

Hazardous waste trafficking. (2011). http://www.choike.org/2009/eng/informes/informes/1157.html (retrieved September 19, 2011).

Heilbroner, R. L. (1972). *The making of economic society* (4th ed.). Englewood Cliffs, NJ: Prentice-Hall.

Heilbroner, R. L., & Thurow, L. C. (1981). *The economic problem* (6th ed.). Englewood Cliffs, NJ: Prentice-Hall.

Heitzman, J., & Wordem, R. L. (Eds.). (2006). *India: A country study* (sect. 2, 5th ed.). Washington, DC: Federal Research Division, Library of Congress.

Helm, J. (1962). The ecological approach in anthropology. *American Journal of Sociology 67,* 630–649.

Henry, D. O., et al. (2004). Human behavioral organization in the Middle Paleolithic: Were Neandertals different? *American Anthropologist 107* (1), 17–31.

Henry, J. (1965). *Culture against man.* New York: Vintage.

Herdt, G. (Ed.). (1996). *Third sex, third gender: Beyond sexual dimorphism in culture and history.* New York: Zone.

Herdt, G. H. (1993). Semen transactions in Sambia culture. In D. N. Suggs & A. W. Mirade (Eds.), *Culture and human sexuality* (pp. 298–327). Pacific Grove, CA: Brooks/Cole.

Herskovits, M. J. (1952). *Economic anthropology: A study in comparative economics* (2nd ed.). New York: Knopf.

Herskovits, M. J. (1964). *Cultural dynamics.* New York: Knopf.

Hertz, N. (2001). *The silent takeover: Global capitalism and the death of democracy.* New York: Arrow Books.

Hewes, G. W. (1973). Primate communication and the gestural origin of language. *Current Anthropology 14*, 5–24.

Hobaiter, C., & Byrne, R. W. (2011, July). The gestural repertoire of the wild chimpanzee. *Animal Cognition 14* (4).

Hodgen, M. (1964). *Early anthropology in the sixteenth and seventeenth centuries.* Philadelphia: University of Pennsylvania Press.

Hoebel, E. A. (1958). *Man in the primitive world: An introduction to anthropology.* New York: McGraw-Hill.

Hoebel, E. A. (1960). *The Cheyennes: Indians of the Great Plains.* New York: Holt, Rinehart & Winston.

Hoebel, E. A. (1972). *Anthropology: The study of man* (4th ed.). New York: McGraw-Hill.

Holden, C. (1999). Ancient child burial uncovered in Portugal. *Science 283*, 169.

Hole, F. (1966). Investigating the origins of Mesopotamian civilization. *Science 153*, 605–611.

Hole, F., & Heizer, R. F. (1969). *An introduction to prehistoric archeology.* New York: Holt, Rinehart & Winston.

Holloway, R. L. (1980). The O. H. 7 (Olduvai Gorge, Tanzania) hominid partial brain endocast revisited. *American Journal of Physical Anthropology 53*, 267–274.

Holloway, R. L. (1981). The Indonesian Homo erectus brain endocast revisited. *American Journal of Physical Anthropology 55*, 503–521.

Holloway, R. L. (1981). Volumetric and asymmetry determinations on recent hominid endocasts: Spy I and II, Djebel Jhroud 1, and the Salb *Homo erectus* specimens, with some notes on Neanderthal brain size. *American Journal of Physical Anthropology 55*, 385–393.

Holloway, R. L., & de LaCoste-Lareymondie, M. C. (1982). Brain endocast asymmetry in pongids and hominids: Some preliminary findings on the paleontology of cerebral dominance. *American Journal of Physical Anthropology 58*, 101–110.

Holmes, L. D. (2000). "Paradise Bent" (film review). *American Anthropologist 102* (3), 604–605.

Hopkin, M. (2007, February 22). Chimps make spears to catch dinner. Published online: *Nature*, doi:10.1038/news070219–11.

Horst, H., & Miller, D. (2006). *The cell phone: An anthropology of communication.* New York: Berg.

Hostetler, J., & Huntington, G. (1971). *Children in Amish society.* New York: Holt, Rinehart & Winston.

Houle, A. (1999). The origin of platyrrhines: An evaluation of the Antarctic scenario and the floating island model. *American Journal of Physical Anthropology 109*, 554–556.

Howell, F. C. (1970). *Early man.* New York: Time-Life.

Hsu, F. L. (1961). *Psychological anthropology: Approaches to culture and personality.* Homewood, IL: Dorsey Press.

Hsu, F. L. K. (1979). The cultural problems of the cultural anthropologist. *American Anthropologist 81*, 517–532.

Hubert, H., & Mauss, M. (1964). *Sacrifice.* Chicago: University of Chicago Press.

Human Development Report. (2002). *Deepening democracy in a fragmented world.* United Nations Development Program.

Human Rights Watch and the Center for Human Rights and Global Justice. (2007). Hidden apartheid: Caste discrimination against India's "Untouchables." http://www.chrgj.org/docs/IndiaCERDShadowReport.pdf (retrieved September 15, 2011).

The Hunger Project. www.thp.org

Hymes, D. (1964). *Language in culture and society: A reader in linguistics and anthropology.* New York: Harper & Row.

Hymes, D. (Ed.). (1972). *Reinventing anthropology.* New York: Pantheon.

Hymes, D. (1974). *Foundations in sociolinguistics: An ethnographic approach.* Philadelphia: University of Pennsylvania Press.

Inda, J. X., & Rosaldo, R. (Eds.) (2001). *The anthropology of globalization: A reader.* Malden, MA, and Oxford, UK: Blackwell Press.

Ingmanson, E. J. (1998). Comment. *Current Anthropology 39*, 409.

Inkeles, A., & Levinson, D. J. (1954). National character: The study of modal personality and socio-cultural systems. In G. Lindzey (Ed.), *Handbook of social psychology.* Reading, MA: Addison-Wesley.

Inoue, S., & Matsuzawa, T. (2007). Working memory of numerals in chimpanzees. *Current Biology 17*, 23, 1004–1005.

International Lesbian, Gay, Bisexual, Trans, and Intersex Association (ILGA). (2009). *The 2009 report on state-sponsored homophobia.*

Iraq Coalition Casualty Count. icasualties.org

Irvine, M. (1999, November 24). Mom-and-pop houses grow rare. *Burlington Free Press.*

Italy–Germany verbal war hots up. (2003, July 9). *Deccan Herald.* (Bangalore, India).

It's the law: Child labor protection. (1997, November/December). *Peace and Justice News*, 11.

Jacobs, S. E. (1994). Native American two-spirits. *Anthropology Newsletter 35* (8), 7.

Jacoby, R., & Glauberman, N. (Eds.). (1995). *The Bell Curve debate.* New York: Random House.

Jane Goodall Institute. www.janegoodall.org/janes-story (retrieved August 6, 2011).

Jennings, F. (1976). *The invasion of America.* New York: Norton.

Jennings, J. D. (1974). *Prehistory of North America* (2nd ed.). New York: McGraw-Hill.

Johansen, B. E. (2002). The Inuit's struggle with dioxins and other organic pollutants. *American Indian Quarterly 26* (3), 479–490.

Johanson, D., & Shreeve, J. (1989). *Lucy's child: The discovery of a human ancestor.* New York: Avon.

Johanson, D. C., & Edey, M. (1981). *Lucy, the beginnings of humankind.* New York: Simon & Schuster.

Johanson, D. C., & White, T. D. (1979). A systematic assessment of early African hominids. *Science 203*, 321–330.

John, V. (1971). Whose is the failure? In C. L. Brace, G. R. Gamble, & J. T. Bond (Eds.), *Race and intelligence.* Washington, DC: American Anthropological Association.

Johnson, D. (1991, April 9). Polygamists emerge from secrecy, seeking not just peace but respect. *New York Times*, A22.

Jolly, A. (1985). *The evolution of primate behavior* (2nd ed.). New York: Macmillan.

Jolly, A. (1991). Thinking like a vervet. *Science 251*, 574.

Jolly, C. J. (1970). The seed eaters: A new model of hominid differentiation based on a baboon analogy. *Man 5*, 5–26.

Jolly, C. J., & Plog, F. (1986). *Physical anthropology and archaeology* (4th ed.). New York: Knopf.

Jones, S. (2005). Transhumance re-examined. *Journal of the Royal Anthropological Institute 11* (4), 841–842.

Jones, S., Martin, R., & Pilbeam, D. (1992). *Cambridge encyclopedia of human evolution.* New York: Cambridge University Press.

Joukowsky, M. A. (1980). *A complete field manual of archeology: Tools and techniques of field work for archaeologists.* Englewood Cliffs, NJ: Prentice-Hall.

Joyce, C. (1991). *Witnesses from the grave: The stories bones tell.* Boston: Little, Brown.

Kahn, H., & Wiener, A. J. (1967). *The year 2000.* New York: Macmillan.

Kaiser, J. (1994). A new theory of insect wing origins takes off. *Science 266*, 363.

Kaiser, J. (2011, May 4). 10 billion plus: Why world population projections were too low. *Science Insider.* http://news.sciencemag.org/scienceinsider/2011/05/10-billion-plus-why-world-population.html (retrieved October 3, 2011).

Kalwet, H. (1988). *Dreamtime and inner space: The world of the shaman.* New York: Random House.

Kaplan, D. (1972). *Culture theory.* Englewood Cliffs, NJ: Prentice-Hall.

Kaplan, D. (2000). The darker side of the original affluent society. *Journal of Anthropological Research 53* (3), 301–324.

Kaplan, M. (2007, May 31). Upright orangutans point way to walking. Published online: *Nature,* doi:10.1038/news070528–8.

Kaplan, M. (2008, August 5). Almost half of primate species face extinction. Published online: *Nature,* doi:10.1038/news.2008.1013.

Karavani, I., & Smith, F. H. (2000). More on the Neanderthal problem: The Vindija case. *Current Anthropology 41,* 839.

Kardiner, A. (1939). *The individual and his society: The psycho-dynamics of primitive social organization.* New York: Columbia University Press.

Kardiner, A., & Preble, E. (1961). *They studied men.* New York: Mentor.

Kay, R. F., Fleagle, J. G., & Simons, E. L. (1981). A revision of the Oligocene apes of the Fayum Province, Egypt. *American Journal of Physical Anthropology 55,* 293–322.

Kay, R. F., Ross, C., & Williams, B. A. (1997). Anthropoid origins. *Science 275,* 797–804.

Keen, B. (1971). *The Aztec image in western thought.* New Brunswick, NJ: Rutgers University Press.

Kehoe, A. (2000). *Shamans and religion: An anthropological exploration in critical thinking.* Prospect Heights, IL: Waveland Press.

Kelly, T. L. (2006). *Sadhus, the great renouncers.* Photography exhibit, Indigo Gallery, Naxal, Kathmandu, Nepal. http://www.asianart.com/exhibitions/sadhus/index.html (retrieved September 2, 2011).

Kennickell, A. B. (2003, November). *A rolling tide: Changes in the distribution of wealth in the U.S. 1989–2001.* Washington, DC: Federal Reserve Board/Levy Economics Institute.

Kenyon, K. (1957). *Digging up Jericho.* London: Ben.

Key, M. R. (1975). *Paralanguage and kinesics: Nonverbal communication.* Metuchen, NJ: Scarecrow Press.

Kidder, T. (2003). *Mountains beyond mountains: The quest of Dr. Paul Farmer, a man who would cure the world.* New York: Random House.

King, J. (2010. July 28). Reducing the crack and powder cocaine sentencing disparity should also reduce racial disparities in sentences and prisons. *NACDL news release.* http://www.nacdl.org/public.nsf/NewsReleases/2010mn23?OpenDocument (retrieved September 9, 2011).

Kirkpatrick, R. C. (2000). The evolution of human homosexual behavior. *Current Anthropology 41,* 384.

Kleinman, A. (1976). Concepts and a model for the comparison of medical systems as cultural systems. *Social Science and Medicine 12* (2B), 85–95.

Kluckhohn, C. (1970). *Mirror for man.* Greenwich, CT: Fawcett.

Kluckhohn, C. (1994). Navajo witchcraft. *Papers of the Peabody Museum of American Archaeology and Ethnology 22* (2).

Knauft, B. (1991). Violence and sociality in human evolution. *Current Anthropology 32,* 391–409.

Knight, C., Studdert-Kennedy, M., & Hurford, J. (Eds.). (2000). *The evolutionary emergence of language: Social function and the origins of linguistic form.* Cambridge, UK: Cambridge University Press.

Koch, G. (1997). Songs, land rights, and archives in Australia. *Cultural Survival Quarterly 20* (4).

Konner, M., & Worthman, C. (1980). Nursing frequency, gonadal function, and birth spacing among !Kung hunter-gatherers. *Science 207,* 788–791.

Koufos, G. (1993). Mandible of *Ouranopithecus macedoniensis* (hominidae: primates) from a new late Miocene locality in Macedonia (Greece). *American Journal of Physical Anthropology 91,* 225–234.

Krader, L. (1968). *Formation of the state.* Englewood Cliffs, NJ: Prentice-Hall.

Krajick, K. (1998). Greenfarming by the Incas? *Science 281,* 323.

Kramer, P. A. (1998). The costs of human locomotion: Maternal investment in child transport. *American Journal of Physical Anthropology 107,* 71–85.

Kraybill, D. B. (2001). *The riddle of Amish culture.* Baltimore: Johns Hopkins University Press.

Kroeber, A. (1958). Totem and taboo: An ethnologic psycho-analysis. In W. Lessa & E. Z. Vogt (Eds.), *Reader in comparative religion: An anthropological approach.* New York: Harper & Row.

Kroeber, A. L. (1939). Cultural and natural areas of native North America. In *American archaeology and ethnology* (vol. 38). Berkeley: University of California Press.

Kroeber, A. L. (1963). *Anthropology: Cultural processes and patterns.* New York: Harcourt.

Kroeber, A. L., & Kluckhohn, C. (1952). *Culture: A critical review of concepts and definitions.* Cambridge, MA: Harvard University Press.

Kruger, J., et al. (2005, December). Egocentrism over e-mail: Can people communicate as well as they think? *Journal of Personality and Social Psychology 89* (6), 925–936.

Kuefler, M. (2007). The marriage revolution in late antiquity: The Theodosian Code and later Roman marriage law. *Journal of Family History 32* (4), 343–370.

Kuhn, T. (1968). *The structure of scientific revolutions.* Chicago: University of Chicago Press.

Kummer, H. (1971). *Primate societies: Group techniques of ecological adaptation.* Chicago: Aldine.

Kunzig, R. (1999). A tale of two obsessed archaeologists, one ancient city and nagging doubts about whether science can ever hope to reveal the past. *Discover 20* (5), 84–92.

Kuper, H. (1965). The Swazi of Swaziland. In J. L. Gibbs (Ed.), *Peoples of Africa* (pp. 479–511). New York: Holt, Rinehart & Winston.

Kurtz, D. V. (2001). *Political anthropology: Paradigms and power.* Boulder, CO: Westview Press.

Kushner, G. (1969). *Anthropology of complex societies.* Stanford, CA: Stanford University Press.

La Barre, W. (1945). Some observations of character structure in the Orient: The Japanese. *Psychiatry,* 8.

LaFont, S. (Ed.). (2003). *Constructing sexualities: Readings in sexuality, gender, and culture.* Upper Saddle River, NJ: Prentice-Hall.

Lai, C. S. L., et al. (2001). A forkhead-domain gene is mutated in severe speech and language disorder. *Nature 413,* 519–523.

Lakoff, R. T. (2004). *Language and woman's place.* M. Bucholtz (Ed.). New York: Oxford University Press.

Lampl, M., Velhuis, J. D., & Johnson, M. L. (1992). Saltation and stasis: A model of human growth. *Science 258* (5083), 801–803.

Lancaster, J. B. (1975). *Primate behavior and the emergence of human culture.* New York: Holt, Rinehart & Winston.

Landau, M. (1991). *Narratives of human evolution.* New Haven, CT, and London: Yale University Press.

Landes, R. (1982). Comment. *Current Anthropology 23,* 401.

Lang, I. A., et al. (2008). Association of urinary bisphenol A concentration with medical disorders and laboratory abnormalities in adults. *Journal of the American Medical Association 300* (11), 1303–1310.

Langan, P., & Harlow, C. (1994). *Child rape victims, 1992.* Washington, DC: Bureau of Justice Statistics, U.S. Department of Justice.

Lanning, E. P. (1967). *Peru before the Incas.* Englewood Cliffs, NJ: Prentice-Hall.

Lanternari, V. (1963). *The religions of the oppressed.* New York: Mentor.

Larsen, J. (2006, July 28). Setting the record straight: More than 52,000 Europeans died from heat in summer 2003. *Earth Policy Institute.* http://www.earth-policy.org/plan_b_updates/2006/update56 (retrieved September 19, 2011).

Lasn, K., & Liacas, T. (2000, August/September). Birth of the corporate "I." *Adbusters* (31). http://www.nancho.net/corperson/adbcorpI.html (retrieved September 18, 2011).

The latest from McDonald's. (2011). *About McDonald's Media Center.* http://www.aboutmcdonalds.com/mcd/media_center.html (retrieved September 18, 2011).

Laurel, K. (1990). In the company of witches. *Natural History, 92.*

Lawler, A. (2001). Writing gets a rewrite. *Science 292,* 2419.

Layton, R. (1991). *The anthropology of art* (2nd ed.). Cambridge, UK: Cambridge University Press.

Leach, E. (1961). *Rethinking anthropology.* London: Athione Press.

Leach, E. (1962). The determinants of differential cross-cousin marriage. *Man 62,* 238.

Leach, E. (1962). On certain unconsidered aspects of double descent systems. *Man 214,* 13–34.

Leach, E. (1965). *Political systems of highland Burma.* Boston: Beacon Press.

Leach, E. (1982). *Social anthropology.* Glasgow: Fontana Paperbacks.

Leacock, E. (1981). *Myths of male dominance: Collected articles on women cross culturally.* New York: Monthly Review Press.

Leacock, E. (1981). Women's status in egalitarian society: Implications for social evolution. In *Myths of male dominance: Collected articles on women cross culturally.* New York: Monthly Review Press.

Leakey, L. S. B. (1965). *Olduvai Gorge, 1951–1961* (vol. 1). London: Cambridge University Press.

Leakey, L. S. B. (1967). Development of aggression as a factor in early man and prehuman evolution. In C. Clements & D. Lundsley (Eds.), *Aggression and defense.* Los Angeles: University of California Press.

Leakey, L. S. B., Tobias, P. B., & Napier, J. R. (1964). A new species of the genus *Homo* from Olduvai Gorge. *Nature 202,* 7–9.

Leakey, M. D. (1971). *Olduvai Gorge: Excavations in Beds I and II. 1960–1963.* London and New York: Cambridge University Press.

Leakey, M. G., Spoor, F., Brown, F. H., Gathogo, P. N., Kiare, C., Leakey, L. N., & McDougal, I. (2001). New hominin genus from eastern Africa shows diverse middle Pliocene lineages. *Nature 410,* 433–440.

Leap, W. L. (1987). Tribally controlled culture change: The Northern Ute language revival project. In R. M. Wulff & S. J. Fiske (Eds.), *Anthropological praxis: Translating knowledge into action* (pp. 197–211). Boulder, CO: Westview Press.

Leave none to tell the story: Genocide in Rwanda. (1999, March). http://www.hrw.org/legacy/reports/1999/rwanda/ (retrieved September 16, 2011).

Leavitt, G. C. (1990). Sociobiological explanations of incest avoidance: A critical review of evidential claims. *American Anthropologist 92,* 982.

Leclerc-Madlala, S. (2002). Bodies and politics: Healing rituals in the democratic South Africa. In V. Faure (Ed.), *Les cahiers de l'IFAS,* no. 2. Johannesburg: The French Institute.

Lee, A. (2011, June 13). Facebook users DROP in U.S.: Millions left the social network in May 2011. *Huffington Post.* http://www.huffingtonpost.com/2011/06/13/facebook-users-members-us-growth-drops-may-2011_n_875810.html (retrieved September 14, 2011).

Lee, R. B. (1993). *The Dobe Ju/'hoansi.* Fort Worth: Harcourt Brace.

Lee, R. B., & Daly, R. H. (1999). *The Cambridge encyclopedia of hunters and gatherers.* New York: Cambridge University Press.

Lee, R. B., & DeVore, I. (Eds.). (1968). *Man the hunter.* Chicago: Aldine.

Leeds, A., & Vayda, A. P. (Eds.). (1965). *Man, culture and animals: The role of animals in human ecological adjustments.* Washington, DC: American Association for the Advancement of Science.

Lees, R. (1953). The basis of glottochronology. *Language 29,* 113–127.

Lehman, E. C., Jr. (2002, Fall). Women's path into the ministry. *Pulpit & Pew Research Reports 1,* 4.

Lehmann, A. C., & Myers, J. E. (Eds.). (1993). *Magic, witchcraft and religion: An anthropological study of the supernatural* (3rd ed.). Mountain View, CA: Mayfield.

Lehmann, W. P. (1973). *Historical linguistics: An introduction* (2nd ed.). New York: Holt, Rinehart & Winston.

Leigh, S. R., & Park, P. B. (1998). Evolution of human growth prolongation. *American Journal of Physical Anthropology 107,* 331–350.

Leinhardt, G. (1964). *Social anthropology.* London: Oxford University Press.

LeMay, M. (1975). The language capability of Neanderthal man. *American Journal of Physical Anthropology 43* (1), 9–14.

Lenski, G. (1966). *Power and privilege: A theory of social stratification.* New York: McGraw-Hill.

Leroi-Gourhan, A. (1968). The evolution of Paleolithic art. *Scientific American 218,* 58ff.

Lestel, D. (1998). How chimpanzees have domesticated humans. *Anthropology Today 12* (3).

Lett, J. (1987). *The human enterprise: A critical introduction to anthropological theory.* Boulder, CO: Westview Press.

Levine, N. E., & Silk, J. B. (1997). Why polyandry fails. *Current Anthropology 38,* 375–398.

Levine, R. (1973). *Culture, behavior and personality.* Chicago: Aldine.

Lévi-Strauss, C. (1963). The sorcerer and his magic. In *Structural anthropology.* New York: Basic Books.

Lewellen, T. C. (2002). *The anthropology of globalization: Cultural anthropology enters the 21st century.* Westport, CT: Greenwood Publishing Group/Bergin & Garvey.

Lewin, R. (1983). Is the orangutan a living fossil? *Science 222,* 1223.

Lewin, R. (1985). Tooth enamel tells a complex story. *Science 228,* 707.

Lewin, R. (1986). New fossil upsets human family" *Science 233,* 720–721.

Lewin, R. (1987). Debate over emergence of human tooth pattern. *Science 235,* 749.

Lewin, R. (1987). The earliest "humans" were more like apes. *Science 236,* 1062–1063.

Lewin, R. (1987). Four legs bad, two legs good. *Science 235,* 969.

Lewin, R. (1987). Why is ape tool use so confusing? *Science 236,* 776–777.

Lewin, R. (1988). Molecular clocks turn a quarter century. *Science 235,* 969–971.

Lewin, R. (1993). Paleolithic paint job. *Discover 14* (7), 64–70.

Lewis, I. M. (1965). Problems in the comparative study of unilineal descent. In M. Banton (Ed.), *The relevance of models for social organization.* London: Tavistock.

Lewis, I. M. (1976). *Social anthropology in perspective.* Harmondsworth, UK: Penguin Books.

Lewis-Williams, J. D. (1990). *Discovering southern African rock art.* Cape Town and Johannesburg: David Philip.

Lewis-Williams, J. D., & Dowson, T. A. (1988). Signs of all times: Entoptic phenomena in Upper Paleolithic art. *Current Anthropology 29,* 201–245.

Lewis-Williams, J. D., & Dowson, T. A. (1993). On vision and power in the Neolithic: Evidence from the decorated monuments. *Current Anthropology 34,* 55–65.

Lewis-Williams, J. D., Dowson, T. A., & Deacon, J. (1993). Rock art and changing perceptions of Southern Africa's past: Ezeljagdspoort reviewed. *Antiquity 67,* 273–291.

Lewontin, R. C. (1972). The apportionment of human diversity. In T. Dobzhansky et al. (Eds.), *Evolutionary biology* (pp. 381–398). New York: Plenum Press.

Lewontin, R. C., Rose, S., & Kamin, L. J. (1984). *Not in our genes.* New York: Pantheon.

Li, X., Harbottle, G., Zhang, J., & Wang, C. (2003). The earliest writing? Sign use in the seventh millennium BC at Jiahu, Henan Province, China. *Antiquity 77*, 31–44.

Lieberman, P. (2006). *Toward an evolutionary biology of language.* Cambridge, MA: Belknap Press.

Lindenbaum, S. (1978). *Kuru sorcery: Disease and danger in the New Guinea highlands.* New York: McGraw-Hill.

Lindstrom, L. (1993). *Cargo cult: Strange stories of desire from Melanesia and beyond.* Honolulu: University of Hawaii Press.

List of countries by income equality. *Wikipedia.* http://en.wikipedia.org/wiki/List_of_countries_by_income_equality (retrieved September 19, 2011).

Little, K. (1964). The role of voluntary associations in West African urbanization. In P. van den Berghe (Ed.), *Africa: social problems of change and conflict.* San Francisco: Chandler.

Littlewood, R. (2004). Commentary: Globalization, culture, body image, and eating disorders. *Culture, Medicine, and Psychiatry 28* (4), 597–602.

Livingstone, F. B. (1973). The distribution of abnormal hemoglobin genes and their significance for human evolution. In C. Loring Brace & J. Metress (Eds.), *Man in evolutionary perspective.* New York: Wiley.

Lloyd, C. B. (Ed.). (2005). *Growing up global: The changing transitions to adulthood in developing countries.* Washington, DC: National Academies Press.

Lochhead, C. (2004, February 5). Court says same-sex marriage is a right. *San Francisco Chronicle.*

Lock, M. (2001). *Twice dead: Organ transplants and the reinvention of death.* Berkeley: University of California Press.

Lorenzo, C., Carretero, J. M., Arsuaga, J. L., Gracia, A., & Martinez, I. (1998). Intrapopulational body size variation and cranial capacity variation in middle Pleistocene humans: The Sima de los Huesos sample (Sierra de Atapuerca, Spain). *American Journal of Physical Anthropology 106*, 19–33.

Lovejoy, C. O. (1981). Origin of man. *Science 211* (4480), 341–350.

Lowie, R. H. (1948). *Social organization.* New York: Holt, Rinehart & Winston.

Lowie, R. H. (1956). *Crow Indians.* New York: Holt, Rinehart & Winston. (orig. 1935)

Lowie, R. H. (1966). *Culture and ethnology.* New York: Basic Books.

Lucy, J. A. (1997). Linguistic relativity. *Annual Review of Anthropology 26*, 291–312.

Luhrmann, T. M. (2001). *Of two minds: An anthropologist looks at American psychiatry.* New York: Vintage.

Lustig-Arecco, V. (1975). *Technology strategies for survival.* New York: Holt, Rinehart & Winston.

MacCormack, C. P. (1977). Biological events and cultural control. *Signs 3*, 93–100.

MacLarnon, A. M., & Hewitt, G. P. (1999). The evolution of human speech: The role of enhanced breathing control. *American Journal of Physical Anthropology 109*, 341–363.

MacNeish, R. S. (1992). *The origins of agriculture and settled life.* Norman: University of Oklahoma Press.

Madison Avenue relevance. (1999). *Anthropology Newsletter 40* (4), 32.

Mair, L. (1969). *Witchcraft.* New York: McGraw-Hill.

Mair, L. (1971). *Marriage.* Baltimore: Penguin Books.

Malefijt, A. D. W. (1969). *Religion and culture: An introduction to anthropology of religion.* London: Macmillan.

Malefijt, A. D. W. (1974). *Images of man.* New York: Knopf.

Malinowski, B. (1922). *Argonauts of the western Pacific.* London: Routledge & Kegan Paul.

Malinowski, B. (1945). *The dynamics of culture change.* New Haven, CT: Yale University Press.

Mann, A., Lampl, M., & Monge, J. (1990). Patterns of ontogeny in human evolution: Evidence from dental development. *Yearbook of Physical Anthropology 33*, 111–150.

Mann, C. C. (2002). The real dirt on rainforest fertility. *Science 297*, 920–923.

Mann, C. C. (2005). *1491: New revelations of the Americas before Columbus.* New York: Knopf.

Marcus, J., & Flannery, K. V. (1996). *Zapotec civilization: How urban society evolved in Mexico's Oaxaca Valley.* New York: Thames & Hudson.

Marks, J. (1995). *Human biodiversity: Genes, race, and history.* Hawthorne, NY: Aldine.

Marks, J. (2000, April 8). A feckless quest for the basketball gene. *New York Times.*

Marks, J. (2000, May 12). 98% alike (what our similarity to apes tells us about our understanding of genetics). *Chronicle of Higher Education*, B7.

Marks, J. (2002). *What it means to be 98 percent chimpanzee: Apes, people, and their genes.* Berkeley: University of California Press.

Marsella, A. J., & White, G. (1982). *Cultural conceptions of mental health and therapy.* New York: Springer.

Marsella, J. (1982). Pulling it together: Discussion and comments. In S. Pastner & W. A. Haviland (Eds.), *Confronting the creationists* (pp. 79–80). *Northeastern Anthropological Association, Occasional Proceedings*, 1.

Marshack, A. (1972). *The roots of civilization: A study in prehistoric cognition: The origins of art, symbol and notation.* New York: McGraw-Hill.

Marshack, A. (1976). Some implications of the Paleolithic symbolic evidence for the origin of language. *Current Anthropology 17* (2), 274–282.

Marshack, A. (1989). Evolution of the human capacity: The symbolic evidence. *Yearbook of physical anthropology* (vol. 32, pp. 1–34). New York: Alan R. Liss.

Marshall, L. (1961). Sharing, talking and giving: Relief of social tensions among !Kung Bushmen. *Africa 31*, 231–249.

Marshall, M. (1990). Two tales from the Trukese taproom. In P. R. DeVita (Ed.), *The humbled anthropologist* (pp. 12–17). Belmont, CA: Wadsworth.

Martin, E. (1994). *Flexible bodies: Tracking immunity in American culture from the days of polio to the age of AIDS.* Boston: Beacon Press.

Martin, E. (1999). Flexible survivors. *Anthropology News 40* (6), 5–7.

Martin, E. (2009). *Bipolar expeditions: Mania and depression in American culture.* Princeton, NJ: Princeton University Press.

Martorell, R. (1988). Body size, adaptation, and function. *GDP*, 335–347.

Mascia-Lees, F. E., & Black, N. J. (2000). *Gender and anthropology.* Prospect Heights, IL: Waveland Press.

Mason, J. A. (1957). *The ancient civilizations of Peru.* Baltimore: Penguin Books.

Matson, F. R. (Ed.). (1965). *Ceramics and man.* New York: Viking Fund Publications in Anthropology, no. 41.

Maybury-Lewis, D. (1960). Parallel descent and the Apinaye anomaly. *Southwestern Journal of Anthropology 16*, 191–216.

Maybury-Lewis, D. (1984). The prospects for plural societies. *1982 Proceedings of the American Ethnological Society.*

Maybury-Lewis, D. (1993, Fall). A new world dilemma: The Indian question in the Americas. *Symbols*, 17–23.

Maybury-Lewis, D. (1993). A special sort of pleading. In W. A. Haviland & R. J. Gordon (Eds.), *Talking about people* (2nd ed.). Mountain View, CA: Mayfield.

Maybury-Lewis, D. (2001). *Indigenous peoples, ethnic groups, and the state* (2nd ed.). Boston: Allyn & Bacon.

McCorriston, J., & Hole, F. (1991). The ecology of seasonal stress and the origins of agriculture in the Near East. *American Anthropologist 93*, 46–69.

McDermott, L. (1996). Self-representation in Upper Paleolithic female figurines. *Current Anthropology 37*, 227–276.

McGrew, W. C. (2000). Dental care in chimps. *Science 288*, 1747.

McHenry, H. (1975). Fossils and the mosaic nature of human evolution. *Science 190*, 425–431.

McHenry, H. M. (1992). Body size and proportions in early hominids. *American Journal of Physical Anthropology 87*, 407–431.

McKenna, J. (1999). Co-sleeping and SIDS. In W. Trevathan, E. O. Smith, & J. J. McKenna (Eds.), *Evolutionary medicine*. London: Oxford University Press.

McKenna, J. J. (2002, September–October). Breastfeeding and bedsharing. *Mothering, 28–37*.

McKenna, J. J., & McDade, T. (2005, June). Why babies should never sleep alone: A review of the co-sleeping controversy in relation to SIDS, bedsharing, and breastfeeding. *Pediatric Respiratory Reviews 6* (2), 134–152.

Mead, A. T. P. (1996). Genealogy, sacredness, and the commodities market. *Cultural Survival Quarterly 20* (2).

Mead, M. (1928). *Coming of age in Samoa*. New York: Morrow.

Mead, M. (1950). *Sex and temperament in three primitive societies*. New York: New American Library. (orig. 1935)

Mead, M. (1963). *Sex and temperament in three primitive societies* (3rd ed). New York: Morrow. (orig. 1935)

Mead, M. (1970). *Culture and commitment*. Garden City, NY: Natural History Press, Universe Books.

Medicine, B. (1994). Gender. In M. B. Davis (Ed.), *Native America in the twentieth century*. New York: Garland.

Melaart, J. (1967). *Catal Hüyük: A Neolithic town in Anatolia*. London: Thames & Hudson.

Mellars, P. (1989). Major issues in the emergence of modern humans. *Current Anthropology 30*, 356–357.

Meltzer, D., Fowler, D., & Sabloff, J. (Eds.). (1986). *American archaeology: Past & future*. Washington, DC: Smithsonian Institution Press.

Merin, Y. (2002). *Equality for same-sex couples: The legal recognition of gay partnerships in Europe and the United States*. Chicago: University of Chicago Press.

Merrell, D. J. (1962). *Evolution and genetics: The modern theory of genetics*. New York: Holt, Rinehart & Winston.

Merriam, A. P. (1964). *The anthropology of music*. Chicago: Northwestern University Press.

Merzenich, H., Zeeb, H., & Blettner, M. (2010). Decreasing sperm quality: A global problem? Published online, *BMC Public Health*, doi:10.1186/1471-2458-10-24 (retrieved September 11, 2011).

Mesghinna, H. M. (1966). Salt mining in Enderta. *Journal of Ethiopian Studies 4* (2).

Meyer, J. (2008). Typology and acoustic strategies of whistled languages: Phonetic comparison and perceptual cues of whistled vowels. *Journal of the International Phonetic Association 38*, 69–94.

Meyer, J., & Gautheron, B. (2006). Whistled speech and whistled languages. In K. Brown (Ed.), *Encyclopedia of language & linguistics* (2nd ed., vol. 13, pp. 573–576). Oxford, UK: Elsevier.

Michaels, J. W. (1973). *Dating methods in archaeology*. New York: Seminar Press.

Migration and remittances. (2011). World Bank. www.worldbank.org/prospects/migrationandremittances (retrieved September 19, 2011).

Miles, H. L. W. (1993). Language and the orangutan: The "old person" of the forest. In P. Cavalieri & P. Singer (Eds.), *The great ape project* (pp. 45–50). New York: St. Martin's Press.

Millon, R. (1973). *Urbanization of Teotihuacán, Mexico: The Teotihuacán map* (vol. 1, part 1). Austin: University of Texas Press.

Mintz, S. (1996). A taste of history. In W. A. Haviland & R. J. Gordon (Eds.), *Talking about people* (2nd ed., pp. 81–82). Mountain View, CA: Mayfield.

Mitchell, W. E. (1978). *Mishpokhe: A study of New York City Jewish family clubs*. The Hague: Mouton.

Molnar, S. (1992). *Human variation: Races, types and ethnic groups* (3rd ed.). Englewood Cliffs, NJ: Prentice-Hall.

Monaghan, L., Hinton, L., & Kephart, R. (1997). Can't teach a dog to be a cat? The dialogue on ebonics. *Anthropology Newsletter 38* (3), 1, 8, 9.

Montagu, A. (1964). *The concept of race*. London: Macmillan.

Montagu, A. (1975). *Race and IQ*. New York: Oxford University Press.

Montagu, A. (1998). *Man's most dangerous myth: The fallacy of race* (6th ed.). Lanham, MD: Rowman & Littlefield.

Morello, C. (2011, May 18). Number of long-lasting marriages in U.S. has risen, Census Bureau reports. *Washington Post*.

Morgan, L. H. (1877). *Ancient society*. New York: World Publishing.

Moscati, S. (1962). *The face of the ancient orient*. New York: Doubleday.

Murdock, G. P. (1965). *Social structure*. New York: Free Press.

Murdock, G. P. (1971). How culture changes. In H. L. Shapiro (Ed.), *Man, culture and society* (2nd ed.). New York: Oxford University Press.

Murphy, R., & Kasdan, L. (1959). The structure of parallel cousin marriage. *American Anthropologist 61*, 17–29.

Must, B., & Ludewig, K. (2010). Mobile money: Cell phone banking in developing countries. *Policy Matters Journal 7* (2), 26–33.

Mydens, S. (2001, August 12). He's not hairy, he's my brother. *New York Times*. www.nytimes.com/2001/08/12/weekinreview/ideas-trends-he-s-not-hairy-he-s-my-brother.html (retrieved August 8, 2011).

Nabhan, G. P. (2004). *Why some like it hot: Food, genes, and cultural diversity*. Washington, DC: Island Books.

Nader, L. (Ed.). (1969). *Law in culture and society*. Chicago: Aldine.

Nader, L. (Ed.). (1981). *No access to law: Alternatives to the American judicial system*. New York: Academic Press.

Nader, L. (Ed.). (1996). *Naked science: Anthropological inquiry into boundaries, power, and knowledge*. New York: Routledge.

Nader, L. (1997). Controlling processes: Tracing the dynamics of power. *Current Anthropology 38*, 715–717.

Nanda, S. (1990). *Neither man nor woman: The hijras of India*. Belmont, CA: Wadsworth.

Nanda, S. (1992). Arranging a marriage in India. In P. R. DeVita (Ed.), *The naked anthropologist* (pp. 139–143). Belmont, CA: Wadsworth.

Natadecha-Sponsal, P. (1993). The young, the rich and the famous: Individualism as an American cultural value. In P. R. DeVita & J. D. Armstrong (Eds.), *Distant mirrors: America as a foreign culture* (pp. 46–53). Belmont, CA: Wadsworth.

Natural Resources Defense Council. (2005, March 25). *Healthy milk, healthy baby: Chemical pollution and mother's milk*. http://www.nrdc.org/breastmilk/ (retrieved September 19, 2011).

Neer, R. M. (1975). The evolutionary significance of vitamin D, skin pigment, and ultraviolet light. *American Journal of Physical Anthropology 43*, 409–416.

Nesbitt, L. M. (1935). *Hell-hole of creation*. New York: Knopf.

Nettl, B. (1956). *Music in primitive culture*. Cambridge, MA: Harvard University Press.

Newman, P. L. (1965). *Knowing the Gururumba*. New York: Holt, Rinehart & Winston.

Nieftagodien, N. (2008, June 16). Incoherent response to crisis: If the government does not address unemployment and housing demands, the worst is still to come. *The Star*, Johannesburg. South Africa. http://www.highbeam.com/doc/1G1-180098871.html (retrieved September 18, 2011).

Nietschmann, B. (1987). The third world war. *Cultural Survival Quarterly 11* (3), 1–16.

Noack, T. (2001). Cohabitation in Norway: An accepted and gradually more regulated way of living. *International Journal of Law, Policy, and the Family 15* (1), 102–117.

Norbeck, E., Price-Williams, D., & McCord, W. (Eds.). (1968). *The study of personality: An interdisciplinary appraisal.* New York: Holt, Rinehart & Winston.

Normile, D. (1998). Habitat seen as playing larger role in shaping behavior. *Science 279,* 1454.

Norris, R. S., & Kristensen, H. M. (2006, July/August). Global nuclear stockpiles, 1945–2006. *Bulletin of the Atomic Scientists 62* (4), 64–66.

Nye, J. (2002). *The paradox of American power: Why the world's only superpower can't go it alone.* New York: Oxford University Press.

Oakley, K. P. (1964). *Man the tool-maker.* Chicago: University of Chicago Press.

O'Barr, W. M., & Conley, J. M. (1993). When a juror watches a lawyer. In W. A. Haviland & R. J. Gordon (Eds.), *Talking about people* (2nd. ed., pp. 42–45). Mountain View, CA: Mayfield.

Oboler, R. S. (1980). Is the female husband a man? Woman/woman marriage among the Nandi of Kenya. *Ethnology 19,* 69–88.

O'Carroll, E. (2008, June 27). Spain to grant some human rights to apes. *Christian Science Monitor.*

Office of the United Nations Higher Commissioner for Human Rights, Committee on the Elimination of Racial Discrimination, India. (2007, March). *Consideration of state reports.* www2.ohchr.org/english/bodies/cerd/cerds70.htm (retrieved September 15, 2011).

Offiong, D. (1985). Witchcraft among the Ibibio of Nigeria. In A. C. Lehmann & J. E. Myers (Eds.), *Magic, witchcraft, and religion* (pp. 152–165). Palo Alto, CA: Mayfield.

Okonjo, K. (1976). The dual-sex political system in operation: Igbo women and community politics in midwestern Nigeria. In N. Hafkin & E. Bay (Eds.), *Women in Africa.* Stanford, CA: Stanford University Press.

Olszewski, D. I. (1991). Comment. *Current Anthropology 32,* 43.

O'Mahoney, K. (1970). The salt trade. *Journal of Ethiopian Studies 8* (2).

The 109th Canton Fair—New services and products lead to increased trade. (2011, May 5). *PR Newswire.* http://www.prnewswire.com/news-releases/the-109th-canton-fair---new-services-and-products-lead-to-increased-trade-122821239.html (retrieved September 4, 2011).

Ong, A. (1999). *Flexible citizenship: The cultural logics of transnationality.* Durham, NC: Duke University Press.

Ortiz, A. (1969). *The Tewa world.* Chicago: University of Chicago Press.

Oswalt, W. H. (1972). *Habitat and technology.* New York: Holt, Rinehart & Winston.

Oswalt, W. H. (1972). *Other peoples other customs: World ethnography and its history.* New York: Holt, Rinehart & Winston.

Otten, C. M. (1971). *Anthropology and art: Readings in cross-cultural aesthetics.* Garden City, NY: Natural History Press.

Ottenheimer, M. (1996). *Forbidden relatives: The American myth of cousin marriage.* Champaign: University of Illinois Press.

Parker, S., & Parker, H. (1979). The myth of male superiority: Rise and demise. *American Anthropologist 81* (2), 289–309.

Parkin, R. (1997). *Kinship: An introduction to basic concepts.* Cambridge, MA: Blackwell Press.

Partridge, W. (Ed.). (1984). *Training manual in development anthropology.* Washington, DC: American Anthropological Association.

Patterson, F., & Linden, E. (1981). *The education of Koko.* New York: Holt, Rinehart & Winston.

Patterson, F. G. P., & Gordon, W. (2002). Twenty-seven years of Project Koko and Michael. In B. Galdikas et al. (Eds.), *All apes great and small: Chimpanzees, bonobos, and gorillas* (vol. 1, pp. 165–176). New York: Kluwer Academic.

Patterson, T. C. (1981). *Archeology: The evolution of ancient societies.* Englewood Cliffs, NJ: Prentice-Hall.

Pease, T. (2000, Spring). Taking the third side. *Andover Bulletin.*

Pelto, G. H., Goodman, A. H., & Dufour, D. L. (Eds.). (2000). *Nutritional anthropology: Biocultural perspectives on food and nutrition.* Mountain View, CA: Mayfield.

Penniman, T. K. (1965). *A hundred years of anthropology.* London: Duckworth.

Pennisi, E. (1999). Genetic study shakes up out of Africa theory. *Science 283,* 1828.

Peters, C. R. (1979). Toward an ecological model of African Plio-Pleistocene hominid adaptations. *American Anthropologist 81* (2), 261–278.

Petersen, J. B., Neuves, E., & Heckenberger, M. J. (2001). Gift from the past: *Terra preta* and prehistoric American occupation in Amazonia. In C. McEwan & C. Barreo (Eds.), *Unknown Amazon* (pp. 86–105). London: British Museum Press.

Peterson, F. L. (1962). *Ancient Mexico: An introduction to the pre-Hispanic cultures.* New York: Capricorn Books.

Pew Forum on Religion and Public Life. (2008). *U.S. religious landscape survey.* Washington, DC: Pew Research Center.

Pew Research Center. (2007). *Global attitudes survey.* Washington, DC: Pew Research Center.

Pfeiffer, J. E. (1977). *The emergence of society.* New York: McGraw-Hill.

Pfeiffer, J. E. (1978). *The emergence of man.* New York: Harper & Row.

Pfeiffer, J. E. (1985). *The creative explosion.* Ithaca, NY: Cornell University Press.

Piddocke, S. (1965). The potlatch system of the southern Kwakiutl: A new perspective. *Southwestern Journal of Anthropology 21,* 244–264.

Piggott, S. (1965). *Ancient Europe.* Chicago: Aldine.

Pilbeam, D. (1987). Rethinking human origins. In *Primate evolution and human origins.* Hawthorne, NY: Aldine.

Pilbeam, D., & Gould, S. J. (1974). Size and scaling in human evolution. *Science 186,* 892–901.

Pinker, S. (1994). *The language instinct: How the mind creates language.* New York: William Morrow.

Piperno, D. R., & Fritz, G. J. (1994). On the emergence of agriculture in the new world. *Current Anthropology 35,* 637–643.

Plattner, S. (1989). Markets and market places. In S. Plattner (Ed.), *Economic anthropology.* Stanford, CA: Stanford University Press.

Pohl, M. E. D., Pope, K. O., & von Nagy, C. (2002). Olmec origins of Mesoamerican writing. *Science 298,* 1984–1987.

Polanyi, K. (1968). The economy as instituted process. In E. E. LeClair Jr. & H. K. Schneider (Eds.), *Economic anthropology: Readings in theory and analysis* (pp. 127–138). New York: Holt, Rinehart & Winston.

Pollan, M. (2001). *The botany of desire: A plant's-eye view of the world.* New York: Random House.

Pollock, N. J. (1995). Social fattening patterns in the Pacific—the positive side of obesity. A Nauru case study. In I. DeGarine & N. J. Pollock (Eds.), *Social aspects of obesity* (pp. 87–109). London: Routledge.

Pospisil, L. (1963). *The Kapauku Papuans of West New Guinea.* New York: Holt, Rinehart & Winston.

Pospisil, L. (1971). *Anthropology of law: A comparative theory.* New York: Harper & Row.

Premack, A. J., & Premack, D. (1972). Teaching language to an ape. *Scientific American 277* (4), 92–99.

Price, T. D., & Feinman, G. M. (Eds.). (1995). *Foundations of social inequality.* New York: Plenum Press.

Pringle, H. (1997). Ice Age communities may be earliest known net hunters. *Science 277,* 1203–1204.

Pringle, H. (1998). The slow birth of agriculture. *Science 282,* 1446–1449.

Prins, H. E. L. (1994). Neo-traditions in Native communities: Sweat lodge and Sun Dance among the Micmac today, In W. Cowan (Ed.), *Proceedings of the 25th Algonquian conference* (pp. 383–394). Ottawa: Carleton University Press.

Prins, H. E. L. (1996). *The Mi'kmaq: Resistance, accommodation, and cultural survival.* New York: Harcourt Brace.

Puleston, D. E. (1983). *The settlement survey of Tikal.* Philadelphia: University Museum.

Radcliffe-Brown, A. R. (1931). Social organization of Australian tribes. *Oceana Monographs 1,* 29.

Radcliffe-Brown, A. R., & Forde, C. D. (Eds.). (1950). *African systems of kinship and marriage.* London: Oxford University Press.

Radin, P. (1923). The Winnebago tribe. In *37th annual report of the Bureau of American Ethnology, 1915–1916* (pp. 33–550). Washington, DC: U.S. Government Printing Office.

Ramos, A. R. (1987). Reflecting on the Yanomami: Ethnographic images and the pursuit of the exotic. *Current Anthropology 2* (3), 284–304.

Rapp, R. (1999). *Testing women, testing the fetus: The social impact of amniocentesis in America (The Anthropology of Everyday Life).* New York: Routledge.

Rappaport, R. A. (1969). Ritual regulation of environmental relations among a New Guinea people. In A. P. Vayda (Ed.), *Environment and cultural behavior* (pp. 181–201). Garden City, NY: Natural History Press.

Rappaport, R. A. (1984). *Pigs for the ancestors* (enl. ed.). New Haven, CT: Yale University Press.

Rappaport, R. A. (1999). *Holiness and humanity: Ritual in the making of religious life.* New York: Cambridge University Press.

Rathje, W., & Murphy, C. (2001). *Rubbish! The archaeology of garbage.* Tucson: University of Arizona Press.

Rathje, W. L. (1974). The garbage project: A new way of looking at the problems of archaeology. *Archaeology 27,* 236–241.

Rathje, W. L. (1993). Rubbish! In W. A. Haviland & R. J. Gordon (Eds.), *Talking about people: Readings in contemporary cultural anthropology.* Mountain View, CA: Mayfield.

Raven, P. Quoted in Becker, J. (2004, March). *National Geographic,* 90.

Read, C. E. (1973). *The role of faunal analysis in reconstructing human behavior: A Mousterian example.* Paper presented at the meetings of the California Academy of Sciences, Long Beach.

Read-Martin, C. E., & Read, D. W. (1975). Australopithecine scavenging and human evolution: An approach from faunal analysis. *Current Anthropology 16* (3), 359–368.

Recer, P. (1998, February 16). Apes shown to communicate in the wild. *Burlington Free Press,* 12A.

Redman, C. L. (1978). *The rise of civilization: From early farmers to urban society in the ancient Near East.* San Francisco: Freeman.

Reid, J. J., Schiffer, M. B., & Rathje, W. L. (1975). Behavioral archaeology: Four strategies. *American Anthropologist 77,* 864–869.

Reina, R. E. (1966). *The law of the saints.* Indianapolis: Bobbs-Merrill.

Reiter, R. (Ed.). (1975). *Toward an anthropology of women.* New York: Monthly Review Press.

Relethford, J. H. (2001). Absence of regional affinities of Neandertal DNA with living humans does not reject multiregional evolution. *American Journal of Physical Anthropology 115,* 95–98.

Relethford, J. H., & Harpending, H. C. (1994). Craniometric variation, genetic theory, and modern human origins. *American Journal of Physical Anthropology 95,* 249–270.

Renfrew, C. (1973). *Before civilization: The radiocarbon revolution and prehistoric Europe.* London: Jonathan Cape.

Reynolds, V. (1994). Primates in the field, primates in the lab. *Anthropology Today 10* (2), 4.

Ribeiro, G. L. (2009). Non-hegemonic globalizations: Alternative transnational processes and agents. *Anthropological Theory 9* (3), 297–329.

Rice, D. S., & Prudence, M. (1984). Lessons from the Maya. *Latin American Research Review 19* (3), 7–34.

Rice, P. (2000). Paleoanthropology 2000—part 1. *General Anthropology 7* (1), 11.

Richmond, B. G., Fleagle, J. K., & Swisher III, C. C. (1998). First hominoid elbow from the Miocene of Ethiopia and the evolution of the Catarrhine elbow. *American Journal of Physical Anthropology 105,* 257–277.

Richter, C. A., et al. (2007). In vivo effects of bisphenol A in laboratory rodent studies. *Reproductive Toxicology 24* (2), 199–224.

Rideout, V. J., Foehr, U. G., & Roberts, D. F. (2010, January). *Generation M²: Media in the lives of 8- to18-year-olds.* A Kaiser Family Foundation Study. Menlo Park, CA: Henry J. Kaiser Family Foundation. http://www.kff.org/entmedia/upload/8010.pdf (retrieved September 15, 2011).

Ridley, M. (1999). *Genome: The autobiography of a species in 23 chapters.* New York: HarperCollins.

Rightmire, G. P. (1990). *The evolution of Homo erectus: Comparative anatomical studies of an extinct human species.* Cambridge, UK: Cambridge University Press.

Rightmire, G. P. (1998). Evidence from facial morphology for similarity of Asian and African representatives of Homo erectus. *American Journal of Physical Anthropology 106,* 61–85.

Rindos, D. (1984). *The origins of agriculture: An evolutionary perspective.* Orlando: Academic Press.

Ritzer, G. (1983). The McDonaldization of society, *Journal of American Culture 6* (1), 100–107.

Ritzer, G. (2007). *The coming of post-industrial society* (2nd ed.). New York: McGraw-Hill.

Rochat, P. (2001). Origins of self-concept. In G. Bremner & A. Fogel (Eds.), *Blackwell handbook of infant development* (pp. 191–212). Malden, MA: Blackwell Press.

Rogers, J. (1994). Levels of the genealogical hierarchy and the problem of hominoid phylogeny. *American Journal of Physical Anthropology 94,* 81–88.

Romer, A. S. (1945). *Vertebrate paleontology.* Chicago: University of Chicago Press.

Rosas, A., & Bermúdez de Castro, J. M. (1998). On the taxonomic affinities of the Dmanisi mandible (Georgia). *American Journal of Physical Anthropology 107,* 145–162.

Roscoe, P. B. (1995). The perils of "positivism" in cultural anthropology. *American Anthropologist 97,* 497.

Roscoe, W. (1991). *Zuni man-woman.* Albuquerque: University of New Mexico Press.

Rowe, T. (1988). New issues for phylogenetics. *Science 239,* 1183–1184.

Ruhlen, M. (1994). *The origin of language: Tracing the evolution of the mother tongue.* New York: Wiley.

Rupert, J. L., & Hochachka, P. W. (2001). The evidence for hereditary factors contributing to high altitude adaptation in Andean natives: A review. *High Altitude Medicine & Biology 2* (2), 235–256.

Ruvolo, M. (1994). Molecular evolutionary processes and conflicting gene trees: The hominoid case. *American Journal of Physical Anthropology 94,* 89–113.

Rymer, R. (1994). *Genie: A scientific tragedy.* New York: HarperCollins.

Sabloff, J. A. (1989). *The cities of ancient Mexico.* New York: Thames & Hudson.

Sabloff, J. A., & Lambert-Karlovsky, C. C. (1973). *Ancient civilization and trade.* Albuquerque: University of New Mexico Press.

Sabloff, J. A., & Lambert-Karlovsky, C. C. (Eds.). (1974). *The rise and fall of civilizations, modern archaeological approaches to ancient cultures.* Menlo Park, CA: Cummings.

Sachs, E., Rosenfeld, B., Lhewa, D., Rasmussen, A., & Keller, A. (2008). Entering exile: Trauma, mental health, and coping among Tibetan refugees arriving in Dharamsala, India. *Journal of Traumatic Stress 21* (2), 199–208.

Sacks, O. (1998). *Island of the colorblind.* New York: Knopf.

Sahlins, M. (1961). The segmentary lineage: An organization of predatory expansion. *American Anthropologist 63*, 322–343.

Sahlins, M. (1968*). Tribesmen.* Englewood Cliffs, NJ: Prentice-Hall.

Sahlins, M. (1972). *Stone Age economics.* Chicago: Aldine.

Sakineh Mohammadi Ashtiani. (2011, January 18). *New York Times.* http://topics.nytimes.com/top/reference/timestopics/people/a/sakineh_mohammadi_ashtiani/index.html (retrieved September 5, 2011).

Sanday, P. R. (1975). On the causes of IQ differences between groups and implications for social policy. In M. F. A. Montagu (Ed.), *Race and IQ* (pp. 232–238). New York: Oxford University Press.

Sanday, P. R. (1981). *Female power and male dominance: On the origins of sexual inequality.* Cambridge, UK: Cambridge University Press.

Sanday, P. R. (2002). *Women at the center: Life in a modern matriarchy.* Ithaca, NY: Cornell University Press.

Sangree, W. H. (1965). The Bantu Tiriki of western Kenya. In J. L. Gibbs Jr. (Ed.), *Peoples of Africa* (pp. 69–72). New York: Holt, Rinehart & Winston.

Sanjek, R. (1990). On ethnographic validity. In R. Sanjek (Ed.), *Field notes.* Ithaca, NY: Cornell University Press.

Sapir, E. (1921*). Language.* New York: Harcourt.

Sawert, H. (2002, October 11–12). *TB and poverty in the context of global TB control.* World Health Organization. Satellite Symposium on TB & Poverty.

Scarr-Salapatek, S. (1971). Unknowns in the IQ equation. *Science 174,* 1223–1228.

Schaeffer, S. B., & Furst, P. T. (Eds.). (1996). *People of the peyote: Huichol Indian history, religion, and survival.* Albuquerque: University of New Mexico Press.

Schaller, G. B. (1971). *The year of the gorilla.* New York: Ballantine.

Scheflen, A. E. (1972). *Body language and the social order.* Englewood Cliffs, NJ: Prentice-Hall.

Schepartz, L. A. (1993). Language and human origins. *Yearbook of Physical Anthropology 36,* 91–126.

Scheper-Hughes, N. (1979). *Saints, scholars and schizophrenics.* Berkeley: University of California Press.

Scheper-Hughes, N. (2003, May 10). Keeping an eye on the global traffic in human organs. *Lancet 361* (9369), 1645–1648.

Schrire, C. (Ed.). (1984). *Past and present in hunter-gatherer studies.* Orlando: Academic Press.

Schusky, E. L. (1975). *Variation in kinship.* New York: Holt, Rinehart & Winston.

Schusky, E. L. (1983). *Manual for kinship analysis* (2nd ed.). Lanham, MD: University Press of America.

Schuster, C., & Carpenter, E. (1996). *Patterns that connect: Social symbolism in ancient and tribal art.* New York: Abrams.

Schwartz, J. H. (1984). Hominoid evolution: A review and a reassessment. *Current Anthropology 25* (5), 655–672.

Scupin, R. (Ed.). (2000). *Religion and culture: An anthropological focus.* Upper Saddle River, NJ: Prentice-Hall.

Sellen, D. W., & Mace, R. (1997). Fertility and mode of subsistence: A phylogenetic analysis. *Current Anthropology 38,* 886.

Semenov, S. A. (1964). *Prehistoric technology.* New York: Barnes & Noble.

Sen, G., & Grown, C. (1987). *Development, crisis, and alternative visions: Third World women's perspectives.* New York: Monthly Review Press.

Senut, B., et al. (2001). First hominid from the Miocene (Lukeino formation, Kenya). *C. R. Academy of Science, Paris 332,* 137–144.

Seyfarth, R.M., et al. (1980). Monkey responses to three different alarm calls: Evidence for predator classification and semantic communication. *Science 210,* 801–803.

Shapiro, H. (Ed.). (1971). *Man, culture and society* (2nd. ed.). New York: Oxford University Press.

Sharer, R. J., & Ashmore, W. (1993). *Archaeology: Discovering our past* (2nd ed.). Palo Alto, CA: Mayfield.

Sheets, P. D. (1993). Dawn of a new Stone Age in eye surgery. In R. J. Sharer & W. Ashmore, *Archaeology: Discovering our past* (2nd ed.). Palo Alto, CA: Mayfield.

Shinnie, M. (1970). *Ancient African kingdoms.* New York: New American Library.

Shipman, P. (1981). *Life history of a fossil: An introduction to taphonomy and paleoecology.* Cambridge, MA: Harvard University Press.

Shook, J. R., et al. (Eds.). (2004). *Dictionary of modern American philosophers, 1860–1960.* Bristol, UK: Thoemmes Press.

Shore, B. (1996). *Culture in mind: Meaning, construction, and cultural cognition.* New York: Oxford University Press.

Shostak, M. (1983). *Nisa: The life and words of a !Kung woman.* New York: Random House.

Shreeve, J. (1994). Terms of estrangement. *Discover 15* (11), 60.

Shreeve, J. (1995). *The Neandertal enigma: Solving the mystery of modern human origins.* New York: William Morrow.

Shuey, A. M. (1966). *The testing of Negro intelligence.* New York: Social Science Press.

Simons, E. L. (1972). *Primate evolution.* New York: Macmillan.

Simons, R. C., & Hughes, C. C. (Eds.). (1985). *The culture-bound syndromes: Folk illnesses of psychiatric and anthropological interest.* New York: Springer.

Simpson, G. G. (1949). *The meaning of evolution.* New Haven, CT: Yale University Press.

Simpson, S. (1995, April). Whispers from the ice. *Alaska,* 23–28.

Sjoberg, G. (1960). *The preindustrial city.* New York: Free Press.

Skelton, R. R., McHenry, H. M., & Drawhorn, G. M. (1986). Phylogenetic analysis of early hominids. *Current Anthropology 27,* 21–43.

Skolnick, A., & Skolnick, J. (Eds.). (2001). *Family in transition* (11th ed.). Boston: Allyn & Bacon.

Slobin, D. I. (1971). *Psycholinguistics.* Glenview, IL: Scott Foresman.

Small, M. F. (1997). Making connections. *American Scientist 85,* 503.

Small, M. F. *(2008, August 15). Why red is such a potent color. Live Science.* www.livescience.com/5043-red-potent-color.html (retrieved August 8, 2011).

Smedley, A. (1998). *Race in North America: Origin and evolution of a worldview.* Boulder, CO: Westview Press.

Smith, B. D. (1977). Archaeological inference and inductive confirmation. *American Anthropologist 79* (3), 598–617.

Smith, B. H. (1994). Patterns of dental development in *Homo, Australopithecus, Pan,* and *gorilla. American Journal of Physical Anthropology 94,* 307–325.

Smith, M. D. (2008, September 16). Indian child labor exploited in production of soccer balls. *Huffington Post.* http://www.aolnews.com/2008/09/16/indian-child-labor-exploited-in-production-of-soccer-balls/ (retrieved October 4, 2011).

Smith, P. E. L. (1976). *Food production and its consequences* (2nd ed.). Menlo Park, CA: Cummings.

Smith, R. (1970). Social stratification in the Caribbean. In L. Plotnicov & A. Tudin (Eds.), *Essays in comparative social stratification.* Pittsburgh: University of Pittsburgh Press.

Smuts, B. (1987). What are friends for? *Natural History 96* (2), 36–44.

Snowden, C. T. (1990). Language capabilities of nonhuman animals. *Yearbook of Physical Anthropology 33,* 215–243.

Spencer, R. F. (1984). North Alaska Coast Eskimo. In D. Damas (Ed.), *Arctic: Handbook of North American Indians* (vol. 5, pp. 320–337). Washington, DC: Smithsonian Institution Press.

Spradley, J. P. (1979). *The ethnographic interview.* New York: Holt, Rinehart & Winston.

Spradley, J. P. (1980). *Participant observation.* New York: Holt, Rinehart & Winston.

Stacey, J. (1990). *Brave new families.* New York: Basic Books.

Stahl, A. B. (1984). Hominid dietary selection before fire. *Current Anthropology 25,* 151–168.

Stanford, C. B. (1998). The social behavior of chimpanzees and bonobos: Empirical evidence and shifting assumptions. *Current Anthropology 39,* 399–420.

Stanford, C. B. (2001). *Chimpanzee and red colobus: The ecology of predator and prey.* Cambridge, MA: Harvard University Press.

Stanley, S. M. (1979). *Macroevolution.* San Francisco: Freeman.

Stannard, D. E. (1992). *American holocaust.* Oxford, UK: Oxford University Press.

The State of Consumption Today. Worldwatch Institute. Washington, DC: Worldwatch Institute. http://www.worldwatch.org/node/810 (retrieved October 3, 2011).

Stedman, H. H., et al. (2004). Myosin gene mutation correlates with anatomical changes in the human lineage. *Nature 428,* 415–418.

Stein, R., & St. George, D. (2009, May 13). Babies increasingly born to unwed mothers. *Washington Post.*

Steward, J. H. (1972). *Theory of culture change: The methodology of multilinear evolution.* Urbana: University of Illinois Press.

Stiglitz, J. E. (2003). *Globalization and its discontents.* New York: Norton.

Stiles, D. (1979). Early Acheulean and developed Oldowan. *Current Anthropology 20* (1), 126–129.

Stiles, D. (1992). The hunter-gatherer "revisionist" debate. *Anthropology Today 8* (2), 13–17.

Stirton, R. A. (1967). *Time, life, and man.* New York: Wiley.

Stocking, G. W., Jr. (1968). *Race, culture and evolution: Essays in the history of anthropology.* New York: Free Press.

Stone, L. (1998). *Kinship and gender: An introduction.* Boulder, CO: Westview Press.

Stringer, C. B., & McKie, R. (1996). *African exodus: The origins of modern humanity.* London: Jonathan Cape.

Stuart-MacAdam, P., & Dettwyler, K. A. (Eds.). (1995). *Breastfeeding: Biocultural perspectives.* New York: Aldine.

Study estimates 250,000 active child soldiers. (2006, July 26). Associated Press.

Suarez-Orozoco, M. M., Spindler, G., & Spindler, L. (1994). *The making of psychological anthropology, II.* Fort Worth: Harcourt Brace.

Suwa, G., Kono, R. T., Katoh, S., Asfaw, B., & Beyene, Y. (2007, August 23). A new species of great ape from the late Miocene epoch in Ethiopia. *Nature 448,* 921–924. Published online: doi:10.1038/nature06113.

Swadesh, M. (1959). Linguistics as an instrument of prehistory. *Southwestern Journal of Anthropology 15,* 20–35.

Swaminathan, M. S. (2000). Science in response to basic human needs. *Science 287,* 425.

Swartz, M. J., Turner, V. W., & Tuden, A. (1966). *Political anthropology.* Chicago: Aldine.

Swisher III, C. C., Curtis, G. H., Jacob, T., Getty, A. G., & Widiasmoro, A. S. (1994). Age of the earliest known hominids in Java, Indonesia. *Science 263,* 1118–1121.

Tannen, D. (1990). *You just don't understand: Women and men in conversation.* New York: Morrow.

Tapper, M. (1999). *In the blood: Sickle-cell anemia and the politics of race.* Philadelphia: University of Pennsylvania Press.

Tax, S. (Ed.). (1962). *Anthropology today: Selections.* Chicago: University of Chicago Press.

Tax, S., Stanley, S., et al. (1975). In honor of Sol Tax. *Current Anthropology 16,* 507–540.

Taxation statistics. (2011). *NationMaster.com.* http://www.nationmaster.com/graph/tax_hig_mar_tax_rat_ind_rat-highest-marginal-tax-rate-individual (retrieved September 20, 2011).

Tax rates around the world. (2011). *Wikipedia.* http://en.wikipedia.org/wiki/Tax_rates_around_the_world (retrieved September 20, 2011).

Taylor, G. (2000). *Castration: Abbreviated history of western manhood.* New York: Routledge.

Templeton, A. R. (1994). Eve: Hypothesis compatibility versus hypothesis testing. *American Anthropologist 96* (1), 141–147.

Templeton, A. R. (1995). The "Eve" hypothesis: A genetic critique and reanalysis. *American Anthropologist 95* (1), 51–72.

Templeton, A. R. (1996). Gene lineages and human evolution. *Science 272,* 1363–1364.

Thomas, E. M. (1994). *The tribe of the tiger: Cats and their culture.* New York: Simon & Schuster.

Thorne, A. G., & Wolpoff, M. D. H. (1981). Regional continuity in Australasian Pleistocene hominid evolution. *American Journal of Physical Anthropology 55,* 337–349.

Thornhill, N. Quoted in Haviland, W. A., & Gordon, R. J. (Eds.). (1993). *Talking about people* (p. 127). Mountain View, CA: Mayfield.

Thorpe, S. K. S., Holder, R. L., & Crompton, R. H. (2007). Origin of human bipedalism as an adaptation for locomotion on flexible branches. *Science 316,* 1328–1331.

Timmons, H., & Kumar, H. (2009, July 3). Indian court overturns gay sex ban. *New York Times.*

Tobias, P. V., & von Konigswald, G. H. R. (1964). A comparison between the Olduvai hominines and those of Java and some implications for hominid phylogeny. *Nature 204,* 515–518.

Trevor-Roper, H. (1992). Invention of tradition: The highland tradition of Scotland. In E. Hobsbawm & T. Ranger (Eds.), *The invention of tradition* (ch. 2). Cambridge, UK: Cambridge University Press.

Trinkaus, E. (1986). The Neanderthals and modern human origins. *Annual Review of Anthropology 15,* 197.

Trinkaus, E., & Shipman, P. (1992). *The Neandertals: Changing the image of mankind.* New York: Knopf.

Trouillot, M. R. (1996). Culture, color, and politics in Haiti. In S. Gregory & R. Sanjek (Eds.), *Race.* New Brunswick, NJ: Rutgers University Press.

Trouillot, M. R. (2003). *Global transformations: Anthropology and the modern world.* New York: Palgrave Macmillan.

Tumin, M. M. (1967). *Social stratification: The forms and functions of inequality.* Englewood Cliffs, NJ: Prentice-Hall.

Turnbull, C. (1983). *Mbuti Pygmies: Change and adaptation.* New York: Holt, Rinehart & Winston.

Turnbull, C. M. (1961). *The forest people.* New York: Simon & Schuster.

Turnbull, C. M. (1983). *The human cycle.* New York: Simon & Schuster.

Turner, T. (1991). Major shift in Brazilian Yanomami policy. *Anthropology Newsletter 32* (5), 1, 46.

Turner, V. W. (1957). *Schism and continuity in an African society.* Manchester, UK: University Press.

Turner, V. W. (1969). *The ritual process.* Chicago: Aldine.

Tylor, E. B. (1871). *Primitive culture: Researches into the development of mythology, philosophy, religion, language, art and customs.* London: Murray.

Tylor, E. B. (1931). Animism. In V. F. Calverton (Ed.), *The making of man: An outline of anthropology.* New York: Modern Library.

Ucko, P. J., & Rosenfeld, A. (1967). *Paleolithic cave art.* New York: McGraw-Hill.

Ucko, P. J., Tringham, R., & Dimbleby, G. W. (Eds.). (1972). *Man, settlement, and urbanism.* London: Duckworth.

UNAIDS. (2009). *2009 AIDS epidemic update.* http://www.unaids.org/en/dataanalysis/epidemiology/2009aidsepidemicupdate/ (retrieved September 5, 2011).

UNESCO Institute for Statistics. http://www.uis.unesco.org/Literacy/Pages/default.aspx (retrieved September 1, 2011).

UNICEF. (2011, February 23). *Child protection from violence, exploitation, and abuse.* www.unicef.org/protection/index_childlabour.html (retrieved September 15, 2011).

United Nations Literacy Decade (2003–2012). UNESCO. http://www.unesco.org/new/en/education/themes/education-building-blocks/literacy/un-literacy-decade/ (retrieved September 19, 2011).

Universal Declaration of Human Rights. www.ccnmtl.columbia.edu/projects/mmt/udhr (retrieved September 19, 2011).

UN Refugee Agency. (2011, June 20). *World Refugee Day: UNHCR report finds 80 per cent of world's refugees in developing countries.* www.unhcr.org/4dfb66ef9.html (retrieved October 4, 2011).

Ury, W. L. (1993). *Getting past no: Negotiating your way from confrontation.* New York: Bantam Books.

Ury, W. L. (1999). *Getting to peace: Transforming conflict at home, at work, and in the world.* New York: Viking.

Ury, W. (2002, Winter). A global immune system. *Andover Bulletin.*

Ury, W. L. (Ed.). (2002). *Must we fight? From the battlefield to the schoolyard—A new perspective on violent conflict and its prevention.* Hoboken, NJ: Jossey-Bass.

U.S. Census Bureau. (2008). *American community survey, 2006–2008.*

U.S. Census Bureau. (2010).

U.S. Department of Health and Human Services, Administration on Children, Youth, and Families. (2005). *Child maltreatment 2003.* Washington, DC: U.S. Government Printing Office.

Valentine, C. A. (1968). *Culture and poverty.* Chicago: University of Chicago Press.

Van Allen, J. (1997). Sitting on a man: Colonialism and the lost political institutions of Igbo women. In R. Grinker & C. Steiner (Eds.), *Perspectives on Africa* (p. 450). Boston: Blackwell Press.

Van den Berghe, P. (1992). The modern state: Nation builder or nation killer? *International Journal of Group Tensions 22* (3), 191–208.

Van Gennep, A. (1960). *The rites of passage.* Translated by M. Vizedom & G. L. Caffee. Chicago: University of Chicago Press. (orig. 1909)

Van Willigen, J. (1986). *Applied anthropology.* South Hadley, MA: Bergin & Garvey.

Vincent, J. (1979). On the special division of labor, population, and the origins of agriculture. *Current Anthropology 20* (2), 422–425.

Voget, F. W. (1975). *A history of ethnology.* New York, Holt, Rinehart & Winston.

Vogt, E. Z. (1990). *The Zinacantecos of Mexico: A modern Maya way of life* (2nd ed.). Fort Worth: Holt, Rinehart & Winston.

vom Saal, F. S., & Myers, J. P. (2008). Bisphenol A and risk of metabolic disorders. *Journal of the American Medical Association 300* (11), 1353–1355.

Wagner, P. L. (1960). *A history of ethnology.* New York: Holt, Rinehart & Winston.

Wallace, A. F. C. (1956). Revitalization movements. *American Anthropologist 58,* 264–281.

Wallace, A. F. C. (1966). *Religion: An anthropological view.* New York: Random House.

Wallace, A. F. C. (1970). *Culture and personality* (2nd ed.). New York: Random House.

Wallace, E., & Hoebel, E. A. (1952). *The Comanches.* Norman: University of Oklahoma Press.

Walrath, D. (2006). Gender, genes, and the evolution of human birth. In P. L. Geller & M. K. Stockett (Eds.), *Feminist anthropology: Past, present, and future.* Philadelphia: University of Pennsylvania Press.

Wardhaugh, R. (1972). *Introduction to linguistics.* New York: McGraw-Hill.

Washburn, S. L., & Moore, R. (1980). *Ape into human: A study of human evolution* (2nd ed.). Boston: Little, Brown.

Weatherford, J. (1988). *Indian givers: How the Indians of the Americas transformed the world.* New York: Ballantine.

Weaver, M. P. (1972). *The Aztecs, Maya and their predecessors.* New York: Seminar Press.

Weiner, A. B. (1977). Review of Trobriand cricket: An ingenious response to colonialism. *American Anthropologist 79,* 506.

Weiner, A. B. (1988). *The Trobrianders of Papua New Guinea.* New York: Holt, Rinehart & Winston.

Weiner, J. S. (1955). *The Piltdown forgery.* Oxford, UK: Oxford University Press.

Weiner, M. (1966). *Modernization: The dynamics of growth.* New York: Basic Books.

Weiss, M. L., & Mann, A. E. (1990). *Human biology and behavior* (5th ed.). Boston: Little, Brown.

Weitzman, L. J. (1985). *The divorce revolution: The unexpected social and economic consequences for women and children in America.* New York: Free Press.

Werner, D. (1990). *Amazon journey.* Englewood Cliffs, NJ: Prentice-Hall.

Wernick, R., & the Editors of Time-Life. (1973). *The monument builders.* New York: Time-Life.

Wheeler, P. (1993). Human ancestors walked tall, stayed cool. *Natural History 102* (8), 65–66.

Whelehan, P. (1985). Review of incest, a biosocial view. *American Anthropologist 87,* 678.

White, D. R. (1988). Rethinking polygyny: Co-wives, codes, and cultural systems. *Current Anthropology 29,* 529–572.

White, L. (1949). *The science of culture: A study of man and civilization.* New York: Farrar, Strauss.

White, L. (1959). *The evolution of culture: The development of civilization to the fall of Rome.* New York: McGraw-Hill.

White, M. (2001). *Historical atlas of the twentieth century.* http://users.erols.com/mwhite28/20centry.htm (retrieved September 16, 2011).

White, P. (1976). *The past is human* (2nd ed.). New York: Maplinger.

White, R. (1992). The earliest images: Ice Age "art" in Europe. *Expedition 34* (3), 37–51.

White, T., Asfaw, B., Degusta, D., Gilbert, H., Richards, G., Suwa, G., & Howell, F. C. (2003). Pleistocene *Homo sapiens* from the Middle Awash, Ethiopia. *Nature 423,* 742–747.

White, T. D. (1979). Evolutionary implications of Pliocene hominid footprints. *Science 208,* 175–176.

White, T. D. (2003). Early hominids—diversity or distortion? *Science 299,* 1994–1997.

White, T. D., & Toth, N. (2000). Cutmarks on a Plio-Pleistocene hominid from Sterkfontein, South Africa. *American Journal of Physical Anthropology 111,* 579–584.

Whitehead, N. L., & Ferguson, R. B. (1993, November). Deceptive stereotypes about tribal warfare. *Chronicle of Higher Education,* A48.

Whiting, B. B. (Ed.). (1963). *Six cultures: Studies of child rearing.* New York: Wiley.

Whiting, J. W. M., & Child, I. L. (1953). *Child training and personality: A cross-cultural study.* New Haven, CT: Yale University Press.

Whorf, B. (1946). The Hopi language, Toreva dialect. In *Linguistic structures of Native America.* New York: Viking Fund.

Whyte, A. L. H. (2005). Human evolution in Polynesia. *Human Biology 77* (2), 157–177.

The Wiccan Rede. *The Celtic Connection.* http://www.wicca.com/celtic/wicca/rede.htm

Willey, G. R. (1966). *An introduction to American archaeology: North America* (vol. 1). Englewood Cliffs, NJ: Prentice-Hall.

Willey, G. R. (1971). *An introduction to American archaeology: South America* (vol. 2). Englewood Cliffs, NJ: Prentice-Hall.

Williams, F. (2005, January 9). Toxic breast milk? *New York Times Magazine.*

Williamson, R. K. (1995). The blessed curse: Spirituality and sexual difference as viewed by

Euro-American and Native American cultures. *The College News 18* (4).

Wills, C. (1994). The skin we're in. *Discover 15* (11), 79.

Wilson, A. K., & Sarich, V. M. (1969). A molecular time scale for human evolution. *Proceedings of the National Academy of Science 63,* 1089–1093.

Wingert, P. (1965). *Primitive art: Its tradition and styles.* New York: World.

Winick, C. (Ed.). (1970). *Dictionary of anthropology.* Totowa, NJ: Littlefield, Adams.

Wirsing, R. L. (1985). The health of traditional societies and the effects of acculturation. *Current Anthropology 26* (3), 303–322.

Wittfogel, K. A. (1957). *Oriental despotism, a comparative study of total power.* New Haven, CT: Yale University Press.

Wolf, E. R. (1966). *Peasants.* Englewood Cliffs, NJ: Prentice-Hall.

Wolf, E. R. (1982). *Europe and the people without history.* Berkeley: University of California Press.

Wolf, E. R. (1999). *Envisioning power: Ideologies of dominance and crisis.* Berkeley: University of California Press.

Wolf, M. (1972). *Women and the family in rural Taiwan.* Stanford, CA: Stanford University Press.

Wolf, M. (1985). *Revolution postponed: Women in contemporary China.* Stanford, CA: Stanford University Press.

Wolfson, H. (2000, January 22). Polygamists make the Christian connection. *Burlington Free Press,* 2c.

Wolpoff, M. H. (1977). Review of earliest man in the Lake Rudolf Basin. *American Anthropologist 79,* 708–711.

Wolpoff, M. H. (1982). *Ramapithecus and hominid origins. Current Anthropology 23,* 501–522.

Wolpoff, M. H. (1993). Evolution in *Homo erectus:* The question of stasis. In R. L. Ciochon & J. G. Fleagle (Eds.), *The human evolution source book.* Englewood Cliffs, NJ: Prentice-Hall.

Wolpoff, M. H. (1993). Multiregional evolution: The fossil alternative to Eden. In R. L. Ciochon & J. G. Fleagle (Eds.), *The human evolution source book.* Englewood Cliffs, NJ: Prentice-Hall.

Wolpoff, M. (1996). *Australopithecus:* A new look at an old ancestor. *General Anthropology 3* (1), 2.

Wolpoff, M., & Caspari, R. (1997). *Race and human evolution.* New York: Simon & Schuster.

Wolpoff, M. H., Wu, X. Z., & Thorne, A. G. (1984). Modern *Homo sapiens* origins: A general theory of hominid evolution involving fossil evidence from east Asia. In F. H. Smith & F. Spencer (Eds.), *The origins of modern humans* (pp. 411–483). New York: Alan R. Liss.

Wong, E. (2011, January 17). Tibetan who set himself afire dies. *New York Times.*

Wood, B., & Aiello, L. C. (1998). Taxonomic and functional implications of mandibular scaling in early hominines. *American Journal of Physical Anthropology 105,* 523–538.

Wood, B., Wood, C., & Konigsberg, L. (1994). *Paranthropus boisei:* An example of evolutionary stasis? *American Journal of Physical Anthropology 95,* 117–136.

Woodward, V. (1992). *Human heredity and society.* St. Paul, MN: West.

Woolfson, P. (1972). Language, thought, and culture. In V. P. Clark, P. A. Escholz, & A. F. Rosa (Eds.), *Language.* New York: St. Martin's Press.

World Bank. (1982). *Tribal peoples and economic development.* Washington, DC: World Bank.

World Bank Poverty Statistics. *How is poverty measured?* http://web.worldbank.org/WBSITE/EXTERNAL/TOPICS/EXTPOVERTY/0,,menuPK:336998~pagePK:149018~piPK:149093~theSitePK:336992,00.html (retrieved September 30, 2011).

World Health Organization. (2003). *Global strategy on infant and young child feeding.* Geneva: WHO.

World Health Organization. (2004). *Statistical information system.* http://www.who.int/whosis/en/ (retrieved September 2, 2011).

World Health Organization. (2010, February). *Female genital mutilation.* Fact sheet no. 241. http://www.who.int/mediacentre/factsheets/fs241/en/ (retrieved September 16, 2011).

World military spending reached $1.6 trillion in 2010. (2011, April 11). Press release, Stockholm International Peace Institute. http://www.sipri.org/media/pressreleases/milex (retrieved September 18, 2011).

Worsley, P. (1957). *The trumpet shall sound: A study of "cargo" cults in Melanesia.* London: Macgibbon & Kee.

Worsley, P. (1959, May). Cargo cults. *Scientific American 200,* 117–128.

Wrangham, R., & Peterson, D. (1996). *Demonic males.* Boston: Houghton Mifflin.

Wright, R. (1984). Towards a new Indian policy in Brazil. *Cultural Survival Quarterly 8* (1).

Wright, R. M. (1997). Violence on Indian day in Brazil 1997: Symbol of the past and future. *Cultural Survival Quarterly 21* (2), 47–49.

Wulff, R. M., & Fiske, S. J. (1987). *Anthropological praxis: Translating knowledge into action.* Boulder, CO: Westview Press.

Yip, M. (2002). *Tone.* New York: Cambridge University Press.

Young, A. (1981). The creation of medical knowledge: Some problems in interpretation. *Social Science and Medicine 17,* 1205–1211.

Young, W. (Ed.). (2000). Kimball award winner. *Anthropology News 41* (8), 29.

Zeder, M. A., & Hesse, B. (2000). The initial domestication of goats (*Capra hircus*) in the Zagros Mountains 10,000 years ago. *Science 287,* 2254–2257.

Zilhão, J. (2000). Fate of the Neandertals. *Archaeology 53* (4), 30.

Zimmer, C. (1999). New date for the dawn of dream time. *Science 284,* 1243.

Zohary, D., & Hopf, M. (1993). *Domestication of plants in the Old World* (2nd ed.). Oxford, UK: Clarendon Press.

Index

H

habitat destruction and restoration (primate habitats), 71–72, *71*

Haiti
- Partners in Health foundation (Farmer), 356–357
- the "color question", 145

Hall, Edward, 188

Hallowell, Irving, 213

hallucinations of shamans, *325*

Hammurabi, 130

Han (Chinese), *273*

handedness and language abilities, 88, 191

haplorhines, **60**, **61**
- *See also* apes; humans; monkeys; tarsiers

hard power, **342–345**

Harner, Michael, 324

Harris, Marvin, 160–161

Hawaiian kinship system, **278**, *278*, **279**

hazardous waste disposal, 351

healing ceremonies, shamanic, 325–327

health problems
- in civilizations, 135
- congenital defects risk from cousin marriages, 250
- food production and, 115
- from high-starch/Western diets, 98, 115, 151
- from hormone-disrupting chemicals, 152–154
- hunger as structural violence, 347–348
- the Neolithic revolution and, 110, 114–116, *116*
- obesity as structural violence, 348–349
- from PCBs, 350
- from plastics, 154
- *See also* disease(s)

hemoglobin, **40**

hemoglobin abnormalities: malaria and, 45

hemolytic crisis, 153

herd animals
- disappearances in the Mesolithic, 100
- domestication of, 102

heredity, 35–40
- cell division, 38–40
- dominant and recessive alleles/traits, **40**
- gene transmission, 35–36, 38–40, 147
- *See also* genes; inheritance

hermaphrodites, 209

Herodotus, 129

Herrnstein, Richard, 147

heterozygous chromosomes, *39*, 40

heterozygous individuals, 40, 45, *45*

hierarchical approach to human classification, 141, 142–143, 147, 166
- criticism of, 143–144, 147–148

hieroglyphic systems
- Egyptian, 193
- Maya, 129

high altitude: human adaptation to, 30, 150, 222

high-starch diets (Western diet): health problems from, 98, 115

Hindu caste system, 283–284, *283*
- social mobility within, 286–287

Hindu creation story, 31–32

Hindu sadhu practices, 212, *213*

historical archaeology, **10**, *11*

historical linguistics, 9, 180–183

hit-and-run archaeology, 19

HIV/AIDS
- cultural challenge, 247
- religious prohibitions on sexual behavior and, 247

holistic perspective of anthropology/anthropologists, 2, 3–**5**, 26, 174, 356–357

Holmes, Lowell, 211

the Holocaust, 145–146, 308

homeobox genes, 47, 48

hominids/hominins, 33t
- adaptations, 83–84
- protein requirements, 82
- scavenging by, 82, 83
- *See also* human ancestors; humans

hominoids, 33t, 55, 62, 77
- first hominoids, 77
- *See also* apes

Homo erectus, 85–88
- skull, *89*
- spread throughout the world, 85–86, *85*
- timeline, *91*

Homo floresiensis, 90

Homo genus: evolution from australopithecines, 84

Homo habilis, 82–**83**, 85
- skull, *89*
- timeline, *91*

Homo sapiens, 33t
- *See also* archaic *Homo sapiens* variants; humans

Homo sapiens idaltu fossils, 94

homogenization of different cultures, 339, *339*

homologies (anatomical features), 33–34, *34*

homophobic laws, 211–212

homosexual behavior
- cultural standards, 211–212
- decriminalization of in England, 212
- in humans vs. animals, 27
- male-to-male sexual initiation rituals, 246

homosexuality
- as not considered to be a mental disorder, 212
- social acceptance/condemnation of, 246

homosexuals
- marriages between, 27, *248*, 256–257
- transgenders as not, 211

homozygous chromosomes, *39*, 40

homozygous individuals, 40, 44, 45, *45*

Hopi Indians
- divorce custom, 258
- farming practices, 117
- language, 8, 186–187
- matrilocal residence, 263
- totemism, 275

Horeb, Mount, 322

hormone-disrupting chemicals, 152–154

horticultural peoples/societies, 108, 117, 225
- descent system, 274
- division of labor, 231, 232
- gender grouping, 231, 279
- matrilocal residence in, 263
- tool use customs, 230

horticulture, **101**, 108, **225–226**
- *See also* farming

hot climates: developmental adaptation to, 46

households, **259**
- cohabitation households, 261–262
- extended family households, *261*
- functions, 233
- married couple residence patterns: newlyweds, 262–263; separate households for men and women, 259, 260, *273*
- nonfamily households, 260
- NRTs and household diversity, 264
- nuclear family households, 260
- polygamous households, *251*

single-parent households, 262

telecommunication and, 263

types in the U.S., *262*

housing (dwellings)
- Apache house design, 168
- in the Mesolithic, 100
- in Neolithic vs. food-forager culture, 113
- in Pueblo cultures, *134*

HRAFs (Human Relations Area Files), **25**

Hsu, Francis, 207

Hudson, Charles, 136

human adaptation, 13, 221
- developmental adaptation, 13, 46
- to diseases, 44–46, 135
- to high altitude, 30, 150, 222
- studies, 13
- in the Upper Paleolithic, 91–93
- *See also* bipedalism; human evolution

human ancestors
- in eastern Africa, 77–78, 78–79, 80, 81, 82–83
- skulls, *89*, 90; robust australopithecine skull, 81, *82*; Toumai, *78*, *91*
- in southern Africa, 81, 86
- *See also* archaic *Homo sapiens* variants; *Ardipithecus ramidus*; australopithecines; *Homo erectus*; *Homo habilis*; Neandertals

human classification
- fingerprint patterns, *144*
- taxonomic categories, 33t
- *See also* hierarchical approach to human classification

human diversity, 30, 140–156
- *See also* human variation

human evolution, 75–97
- brain expansion, 84
- brain expansion from jaw muscle reduction, 84
- cultural evolution, 223–224
- primates and, 12
- study of. *See* paleoanthropology
- timeline, *91*
- *See also* bipedalism; human ancestors

human genome, 36–37

human growth studies, 12–13

Human Relations Area Files (HRAFs), **25**

human remains
- dating methods, 22, 23t
- Kennewick Man, 11, *12*, 26, 46
- "Lucy's baby", *22*
- Native American remains preservation, 11
- ownership ethics, 26
- Ukkuqsi excavation, 18–19
- *See also* bioarchaeology; forensic anthropology; forensic archaeology

human rights
- for apes, 163
- Covenant of Human Rights, 353
- Declaration of the Rights of Indigenous Peoples, 353
- indigenous peoples' struggles, 353
- Universal Declaration on Human Rights, 346

human rights abuses
- crimes against humanity, 307
- ethnocide, *308*, **309**
- female genital mutilation, 329
- forensic anthropology and, 14–15, 285
- genocide, 145–146, **308**–309
- traditional practices as, 25; female genital mutilation, 329

human variation, 13
- biological, 141; in gender, *164*
- climate and, 46